Early Neo-Classicism in France

FABER MONOGRAPHS ON FURNITURE

General Editor: Peter Thornton

REGENCY FURNITURE
Clifford Musgrave

SHERATON FURNITURE
Ralph Fastnedge

NINETEENTH-CENTURY ENGLISH FURNITURE
Elizabeth Aslin

ADAM AND HEPPLEWHITE AND OTHER NEO-CLASSICAL FURNITURE
Clifford Musgrave

EMPIRE FURNITURE 1800–1825
Serge Grandjean

CHIPPENDALE FURNITURE
Anthony Coleridge

SPANISH LEATHER
John W. Waterer

BIEDERMEIER FURNITURE
Georg Himmelheber

First published in 1974
by Faber and Faber Limited
3 Queen Square London WC1
Printed in Great Britain by
W & J Mackay Limited, Chatham

ISBN 0 571 08717 5

EARLY NEO-CLASSICISM IN FRANCE

The creation of the Louis Seize style in architectural decoration, furniture and ormolu, gold and silver, and Sèvres porcelain in the mid-eighteenth century

by

SVEND ERIKSEN

translated from the Danish and edited by

PETER THORNTON

Keeper, Department of Furniture and Woodwork
Victoria and Albert Museum

FABER AND FABER LIMITED

3 Queen Square London

A. Le Lorrain. Furniture made for Lalive de Jully, about 1757

EDITOR AND TRANSLATOR'S FOREWORD

Fiske Kimball's *Creation of the Rococo* was published in 1943. Although its impact was hardly felt until some time after the War, this important book laid extensive foundations for a new and better understanding of the Rococo style and there can be few scholars working in the field today who do not recognize their great debt to this American art-historian for his painstaking survey of that absorbing subject. Before the appearance of Kimball's book, much uncertainty must have reigned, and confusion over what actually constituted Rococo and how it originated must have been widespread. As I write this Foreword, in 1972, with the present book about to appear, I can at any rate say that such a situation still prevails with regard to the early stages of Neo-Classicism. This, too, is a perplexing phase of art history to which we have long needed the key. Svend Eriksen is altogether too modest when he claims in his Preface that he has merely put a few more pieces of the jig-saw puzzle together, for his book provides us with so many fresh facts and marshals the previously known facts in such a methodical manner that we are carried forward with an immense bound to a point where we can see the whole territory quite clearly. Certainly, there are many areas about which we lack information, but we can no longer say that the outline is indistinct; nor is the development uncharted.

As one reads this book the intricate network of relationships between the principal characters concerned in the evolution of Neo-Classicism becomes apparent (any uncertainty the reader may have about an individual can usually be resolved by a glance at the well-documented biographies provided at the end), and we find the names of the same people cropping up time and time again, in different combinations. Many of these people made their mark in several fields, and it is fascinating to follow the results of their intervention, as the story unfolds, first in architecture and then in the decorative arts.

To survey in depth in a single volume the developments in the various branches of the decorative arts—in furniture, in porcelain, in precious metals, and in the field of ornamental bronzes—is a new departure which few readers will fail to find rewarding, and I think no apology is needed to students of furniture history for including, in a book that is ostensibly one of a series of monographs on furniture, material that throws so much light on the evolution of the new style as a whole. It has never been possible to limit serious scholarship within the narrow confines thrown up round a single class of objects—be it furniture, or porcelain, or snuff-boxes—but the present volume is a particularly good example of how enriching the wider approach can be.

I hope that it will one day be possible to match Svend Eriksen's work on early Neo-Classicism in France with an equivalent survey of the developments in England. Excellent work has, of course, already been done, but an 'all-embracing monograph' is still required. What does transpire from Eriksen's survey, however, is that the developments in the two countries ran roughly parallel and that exchanges of ideas and designs are likely to have been more frequent than has generally been supposed. As John Harris has pointed out, Sir William Chambers knew several of the principal French characters in the story very well and no doubt it will gradually become clear that there were other close personal contacts between the English and the French artists involved. Perhaps the most surprising revelation Eriksen makes is that, while the initial leap into Neo-Classicism by a handful of French artists and connoisseurs was sudden, the style took a long time to become accepted generally—even in fashionable circles. Neo-Classicism did not triumph over the whole field until well into the 1770s. The same happened in England. There, too, initial attempts were made in the 1750s to introduce a new style based on Classical principles. It took many years before the Rococo finally yielded—even in this country, where the Rococo never settled very happily and the Neo-Palladian concept of Classicism was no mere distant memory but part of a potent tradition still affecting the work of numerous artists and craftsmen, a tradition of which evidence was to be seen in every direction.

Danish is a Germanic language and although modern Danes speak and write in a straightforward manner, learned writing is still often couched in the convoluted style that was general fifty years ago. Moreover, this style may nowadays be used to achieve a somewhat humorous effect. The present author, who wears his scholarship lightly and studiously avoids the pompous, writes in an entertaining and deftly blended mixture of the traditional academic style and colloquial Danish. The result is refreshing and stimulating. But I confess that I have not always found it easy to convey in English the subtler nuances of this often fairly breezy style. I am, however, entirely responsible for the translation, and I hope the author will forgive me if I have failed to convey the spirit of his text at every stage.

In his Preface, he suggests that I must have found the translation of this work tedious. Certainly, it took me quite a while because the work had to be accomplished in my spare time, but the book is so packed with fascinating information that working through it slowly has been an extremely rewarding task. What is more, I regard it as a considerable privilege to have been to some extent instrumental in bringing about the publication of so important a book.

London 1972

PETER THORNTON
Editor and Translator

CONTENTS

APPENDICES

ILLUSTRATIONS

COLOUR PLATES

MONOCHROME PLATES

(*at end of book*)

EDITOR'S NOTE ON FRENCH TRANSLATIONS

The translation of the modern Danish text was comparatively straightforward and the translator was of course able to consult the author, whose English is extremely good, on any points that were in doubt. The publishers requested that the numerous quotations from eighteenth century French sources should also be translated for the benefit of those readers who may find their French inadequate and their understanding of the author's text thus diminished. I would like to stress that, in my translations from the French, I have aimed at giving the general sense of the quotation only, and scholars will presumably rely on the original French texts in all serious discussions of the questions raised in this book.

The various texts comprising the appendices to this volume are literary essays that seemed to deserve more subtle treatment than I felt able to give them, and I therefore invited my colleague, Mr. Ronald Lightbown, to render them into English prose that reflects something of the quality of the original French. I am exceedingly grateful to him for doing this with his customary skill and sensitivity.

PETER THORNTON

ABBREVIATIONS

AAA—Affiches, annonces et avis divers

AAF—Archives de l'art français

Arch. Nat.—Archives Nationales, Paris

Arch. Seine—Archives du Département de la Seine et de la Ville de Paris, Paris

Bapst, *Les Germain*—Germain Bapst, *Etudes sur l'orfèvrerie française au XVIIIe siècle, les Germain, orfèvres-sculpteurs du Roy*, Paris, 1887

B.N.Est.Inv.—Bibliothèque Nationale, Département des Estampes, *Inventaire du fonds français, graveurs du dix-huitième siècle*, par Marcel Roux, vol. Iff., Paris, 1931

BSHAF—Bulletin de la Société de l'Histoire de l'Art Français

Cochin, *Mémoires*—Charles-Nicolas Cochin, *Mémoires inédits sur le comte de Caylus, Bouchardon, les Slodtz*, publiés . . . par M. Charles Henry, Paris, 1880

Cochin, *Oeuvres*—Charles-Nicolas Cochin, *Oeuvres diverses*, 3 vols., Paris, 1757

Corr. des Dir.—Correspondance des directeurs de l'Académie de France à Rome . . ., Paris, 1887

Dez. d'Argenville, *Paris*—Antoine-Nicolas Dezallier d'Argenville, *Voyage pittoresque de Paris . . .*, Paris, 1749, and later editions

Fels, *Gabriel*—Comte de Fels, *Ange-Jacques Gabriel, Premier Architecte du Roi*, Paris, 1924

Gallet, *Demeures*—Michel Gallet, *Demeures parisiennes, l'époque de Louis XVI*, Paris, 1964

Gaz.d.B-A.—Gazette des Beaux-Arts

Granges de Surgères, *Artistes français*—Le Marquis de Granges de Surgères, *Artistes français des XVIIe et XVIIIe siècles (1681–1787), extraits des comptes des Etats de Bretagne*, Paris, 1893

Guiffrey, *Académie de Saint-Luc*—Jules Guiffrey, *Histoire de l'Académie de Saint-Luc*, in *Archives de l'Art Français*, Nouvelle Période, vol. IX, Paris, 1915

Guiffrey, *Les Caffieri*—Jules Guiffrey, *Les Caffieri, sculpteurs et fondeurs-ciseleurs; étude sur la statuaire et sur l'art de bronze en France au XVIIe et au XVIIIe siècles*, Paris, 1877

Guiffrey, *Scellés*—Jules Guiffrey, *Scellés et inventaires d'artistes français*, 3 vols., Paris, 1883–85

Hautecoeur, *Histoire, première moitié*—Louis Hautecoeur, *Histoire de l'architecture classique en France*, vol. III, *Première moitié du XVIIIe siècle, le style Louis XV*, Paris, 1950

Hautecoeur, *Histoire, seconde moitié*—Louis Hautecoeur, *Histoire de l'architecture classique en France*, vol. IV, *seconde moitié du XVIIIe siècle, le style Louis XVI, 1750–1792*, Paris, 1952

Hautecoeur, *Rome*—Louis Hautecoeur, *Rome et la renaissance de l'antiquité à la fin du XVIIIe siècle*, Paris, 1912

Herluison, *Actes*—H. Herluison, *Actes d'Etat-civil d'artistes français, peintres, graveurs, sculpteurs, architectes, extraits des registres de l'Hôtel de Ville de Paris, détruits dans l'incendie du 24 mai 1871*, Paris, 1873

Jal, *Dictionnaire*—Auguste Jal, *Dictionnaire critique de biographie et d'histoire*, Paris, 1872

Kimball, *Creation*—Fiske Kimball, *The Creation of the Rococo*, Philadelphia, 1943

Lazare Duvaux, *Livre-Journal*—*Livre-Journal de Lazare Duvaux marchand-bijoutier ordinaire du Roy 1748–1758* . . ., vol. II, Paris, 1873

Min. Central—Minutier central des notaires parisiens, Archives Nationales, Paris

NAAF—*Nouvelles Archives de l'Art Français*

Rapports d'Experts—*Rapports d'experts 1712–1791, procès-verbaux d'expertises d'oeuvres d'art extraits du fonds du Châtelet, aux Archives Nationales*, Georges Wildenstein, Paris, 1921

Salverte, *Ébénistes*—Comte François de Salverte, *Les ébénistes du XVIIIe siècle, leurs oeuvres et leurs marques*, Paris–Brussels, 1923

Verlet, *French Royal Furniture*—Pierre Verlet, *French Royal Furniture: an historical survey followed by a study of forty pieces preserved in Great Britain and the United States*, London, 1963

Verlet, *La Maison*—Pierre Verlet, *La maison du XVIIIe siècle en France, société, décoration, mobilier*, Fribourg, 1966

Verlet, *Marchands-merciers*—Pierre Verlet, 'Le commerce des objets d'art et les marchands-merciers à Paris au XVIIIe siècle', in *Annales*, quarterly review, 13th year, No. 1, January–March 1958, pp. 10–29.

Verlet, *Mobilier royal I*—Pierre Verlet, *Le mobilier royal français, meubles de la Couronne conservés en France*, Paris, 1945

Verlet, *Mobilier royal II*—Pierre Verlet, *Le mobilier royal français, meubles de la Couronne conservés en France; avec une étude sur le Garde-Meuble de la Couronne*, Paris, 1955

Vial, Marcel and Girodie—Henri Vial, Adrien Marcel and André Girodie, *Les artistes décorateurs du bois*, 2 vols., Paris, 1912–22

Vieux hôtels de Paris—J. Vacquier, P. Jarry and H. Soulange-Bodin, *Les vieux hôtels de Paris*, 24 vols., Paris, 1914

Watson, *Louis XVI Furniture*—F. J. B. Watson, *Louis XVI Furniture*, London, 1960

Watson, *Wallace Collection Furniture*—F. J. B. Watson, *Wallace Collection Catalogues: Furniture*, Text with Historical Notes and Illustrations, London, 1956

Watson, *Wrightsman Collection*—F. J. B. Watson, *The Wrightsman Collection*, 2 vols., New York, 1966

PREFACE

I feel obliged to admit straight away that I cannot truly honour the promise implied by the title of this book! I do not feel qualified to give a true picture of exactly how, when and by whom Neo-Classicism—the *Style Louis Seize*, as the French call it—was created in the field of room-decoration, furniture and the other decorative arts in France. I well realise that our knowledge is still far too limited and too patchy to enable us to do so. On the other hand, the book's title succinctly defines the field about which I would like to know more.

The book springs from the fact that, in the course of some years' search in museums and private collections, I have come across a variety of objects which would seem to stand stylistically somewhere between the Rococo and the Neo-Classical phases—between *Louis Quinze* and *Louis Seize*—and I have tried to assemble information that might increase our understanding of the artistic developments at that stage. In many instances I have not succeeded in discovering data which could be linked directly with the surviving objects and these must therefore remain undocumented for the time being. I have, furthermore, searched extensively in archives for documentary evidence reflecting on the general problems concerned, irrespective of whether the documents threw light on works of art that survive. It had of course been hoped that it might be possible to link the surviving objects with the surviving documentary evidence, and it would have been ideal if one could have illustrated only those items which were backed by a substantial body of facts, and if each quotation could have been supported by a surviving example. But then this would have been an exceedingly slim volume! So, in the hope that future students will have better luck, a number of undocumented works of art have been included in the survey, while some of the documentary material quoted may seem to be largely of an academic nature, although it will perhaps one day prove to have some practical application.

Many readers, especially in England, will probably wonder why the evidence is so uneven. As far as furniture is concerned, it is because in France one hardly ever knows where a piece has come from and does not therefore know in which set of family archives to search for the relevant information. In England, by contrast, a great deal of furniture remains in the very houses for which it was produced. The biographies of artists and craftsmen, for their part, are often somewhat meagre because French archives are so extensive in certain directions that it would take far more than a lifetime to work through them; in other aspects the very same collections are hopelessly poor. The latter is particularly the case with such basic sources as church registers, whence the elementary biographical facts are normally culled, for all those from the city of Paris for the years before 1800 no longer exist; they were all burnt in the *communard* riots of 1871.

What has been said serves to explain—and, it is hoped, excuse—the fact that the book has taken the form it has. The reader will not find new theories set forward, nor will he find an analysis of the stylistic developments differing greatly from what writers like Blondel, Patte, Dumonthier, de Ricci, Dacier, Hautecoeur, Verlet, Watson and Gallet have already given. Indeed, it hardly pretends to be more than a kind of picture-book with an accompanying commentary and a listing of the relevant facts. To put it another way, the book is intended as an aid to the piecing together of a vast jig-saw puzzle which fell on the floor some two hundred years ago, and which a number of people have already tried to put together again. Unfortunately many of the pieces seem to have disappeared completely and many others are so defaced that we can scarcely judge which way up they should go or, indeed, whether they belong to the puzzle at all! Yet no game is worth playing if it is too easy and, as far as a jig-saw puzzle is concerned, one can derive much pleasure from just piecing bits of it together even if one has to leave it full of enormous holes. One is satisfied if one can set out enough pieces in their proper places so that it is clear to oneself and others that the picture has become slightly larger. At any rate, the present writer has enjoyed himself, and not least because his wife—between the chores of running the house and caring for the family—has shared the fun with him.

Hardly any Danish scholars for the past three generations or so can have failed to find themselves indebted sooner or later to the Fund set up by the Jacobsens, the men who had founded the world-famous Carlsberg Breweries during the last century. The Fund supports studies in many fields, but Danish art-historians have at least as good reason to be grateful to the Fund as their colleagues in other branches of research. The generosity extended over many years to me by the Ny Carlsbergfond, which has enabled me to make frequent journeys abroad and to order a large number of often rather expensive photographs, has been of a very high order and I wish to record my gratitude for this support and encouragement most emphatically.

I also have a deep sense of gratitude towards the institution I serve—the Danish Museum of Decorative Arts or Kunstindustrimuseet. The Museum Library where I function has been my veritable workshop, and I am fully conscious of how great has been the forebearance and understanding shown to me by the former Director, the late Erik Zahle, and his successor, Erik Lassen, as I have juggled with the difficulties of keeping my private studies divorced from my official duties. In the same way I have been privileged to spend two years at Waddesdon Manor in Buckinghamshire and enjoyed the considerable benefits which are to be gained from being surrounded by so large and so distinguished a collection of eighteenth-century French furniture and other works of art.

Clearly I am especially indebted to those of my colleagues and friends who are engaged in studies related to the subject of this book. Over many years I have drawn so greatly on their knowledge and their friendship—both by letter and in conversation—that I no longer know to whom I owe the most! So I thank them all but must mention in particular Geoffrey de Bellaigue, Michel Gallet, John and Eileen Harris, Pierre Verlet and Francis Watson—all of whose names will be familiar to the reader with even the slightest knowledge of this field.

I would also make special mention of Peter Thornton, the editor of this series of monographs, who undertook the burden of translating into English the original Danish text. No one could have been better suited to carry out this tedious task, for not only is he bilingual but he is also himself deeply engaged in eighteenth-century studies and was thus in a position to make numerous corrections and additions, all of which were exceedingly welcome.

I have had to trouble the staff of many public institutions during my studies and would like to record my gratitude for the help I have been given at so many levels. I extend especial thanks to the helpful staff of the Archives Nationales, and particularly to Madame Madeleine Jurgens Connat of the Minutier Central des Notaires. I also want to thank Madame Nicole Felkay of the Archives du Département de la Seine et de la Ville de Paris which has been renamed the Archives de Paris, Mademoiselle Else Dahl of the Bibliothèque Nationale, Daniel Alcouffe and Serge Grandjean of the Musée du Louvre, Gunnar W. Lundberg of the Institut Tessin, Robert de Micheaux of the Musée des Arts Décoratifs, Lyons, and Miss Rosamund Griffin at Waddesdon Manor. My debt is no less to colleagues further afield—to James Parker at the Metropolitan Museum of Art and Robert Wark at the Huntington Collection in California, Madame Teresa Sulerzyska in the Print Room of the University Library in Warsaw and Stanislas Lorenz and Marek Kwiatkowski in the Warsaw Museum Narodwe. Dr. Tove Clemmensen of the National Museum in Copenhagen, a colleague much closer to home, has also earned my special gratitude. I should like to thank Mrs Clive Wainwright for preparing the index.

To all those numerous and private owners who have allowed me to study the works of art in their collections and who have allowed me to illustrate many of their objects in this work, I also wish to record my indebtedness. Unless they have asked to remain anonymous, I have recorded their names in the respective notes to the illustrations. In the case of the engravings reproduced here, most of which are illustrations to works in the Danish Royal Print Room and in the Museum of Decorative Arts in Copenhagen, I have only mentioned their whereabouts when the plate concerned has been unique or extremely rare.

The illustrations are reproduced from photographs supplied by the institutions mentioned in the relevant notes or taken by the following: Claude Basnier, Paris; J. E. Bulloz, Paris; Christie, Manson and Woods, London; Connaissance des Arts, Paris; A. C. Cooper, London; Giraudon, Paris; Helga Photo Studio, New York; Jacek Noyszewski, Warsaw; Sotheby & Co., London; Taylor & Dull, New York; Institut Tessin, Paris; Roger Guillemot, Paris; Ole Woldbye, Copenhagen; Lauros, Paris.

Throughout the book the reader will find numerous quotations from eighteenth century French sources—in printed and manuscript form—in which spellings, punctuation and the use of accents often differ from modern usage. In the manuscript sources, and particularly those originating from artists and craftsmen, there is in addition an abundance of downright misspellings. I have considered it historically correct not to standardize or 'modernize' such quotations, however tempting this has been on occasion.

Copenhagen 1970 SVEND ERIKSEN

INTRODUCTION

There was one man already in the eighteenth century whose qualifications enabled him to give a clear and balanced commentary on the stylistic development in the field of French interior decoration from the time of Louis XIV to that of Louis XVI—that is, from what we call the Baroque, through the Rococo, into Neo-Classicism. His statements are of great value because he was born in 1723 and therefore was himself witness to many of these developments, and because he was interested in these matters and is therefore likely to have been at the very least as well-informed as most of his contemporaries. His name was Pierre Patte. He was an architect, draughtsman, and writer who is indeed still best remembered for his essays on architecture and interior decoration.

Patte's survey of these developments is included in the fifth volume of *Cours d'Architecture* which was published in 1777 as a continuation of J.-F. Blondel's work of the same title. What he says is as follows:[1]

'Taste in the interior decoration of rooms has undergone several revolutions in France during the lapse of a century. Under Louis XIV it was treated with the same severity as the exterior decoration of buildings. The doors, the windows, the chimney-pieces, the cornices of rooms were all in a grave and serious style; rarely did the architect allow himself to give them forms other than regular, round, oval, right-angled, or of parallelogram shape. Both profiles and ornaments were invariably of the most masculine kind. In the hands of men like Perrault, Mansart and Le Brun, such decorations without doubt had grace, nobility and dignity; they gave a most impressive air to the interior of large suites of apartments, as can be seen from the models which still remain to us in the Tuileries, the Louvre, Versailles and elsewhere. But in the hands of their imitators they soon degenerated and in the long run became insupportably monotonous and heavy. They were overloaded with a multitude of ornaments placed without order and confusedly, and for this reason they came insensibly to disgust.

'About fifty years ago now (i.e. about 1727) we fell into the opposite extreme; regular forms were abandoned and we applied ourselves to tormenting interior decorations in every possible manner under pretext of varying, lightening and enlivening suites of rooms. Men like Lajoux, Pinault, Meissonnier and their copyists made architecture talk nonsense, if the expression may be permitted. Into our decorations were admitted only extravagant contours, a confused assemblage of motifs placed without selection and combined with eccentrically fanciful ornaments in

[1] Blondel, pp. 86ff.; the full French text is given here on pp. 267–8.

which one finds an absurd heap of cartouches placed sideways, rocailles, dragons, reeds, palms, and all sorts of imaginary plants which have for long been the delight of our interior decorations, to such an extent that sculpture had made herself absolute mistress of architecture. The quantity of engravings of these which have been circulated among the public, independently of the large number of apartments decorated in this bad taste which still remain, sufficiently advertise the extravagance of these frivolous compositions.

'It is to Messrs. Servandoni, Cartaud, Boffrand, and to some of our best architects who have not allowed themselves to be carried away by the torrent of fashion that we owe the return to good taste, their productions having made sensible by comparison the absurdity of this monstrous alloy. Little by little we returned to sager, less eccentric forms, and at last the return of the Antique taste having extended its influence over all our decorative arts, especially during the last fifteen years or so, it can be said that the interior decoration of suites of rooms and the style of their furnishings have become in some sense a new art. To the correct style of the last century's decorations has been added less severity, more delicacy, more variety in the forms. Care has been taken to give only a little relief to the projections and profiles in order to take away any heaviness. In adopting regular forms we have at the same time allowed ourselves to assimilate them according to circumstances to contours which are less serious and better able to produce at once an agreeable whole and less uniformity in the disposition of suites. Finally the ornaments that are most admired in the best works of antiquity, like acanthus and laurel leaves, festoons, ovate ornaments, ogees,[1] shells, flutes, guilloche work, Vitruvian scrolls, medallions etc. have been applied to interior decorations so that architecture has recaptured its rights from sculpture.'

By and large there is really very little one need add to Patte's summary and we, who were not present at the time, should hesitate before questioning anything he says—even the curious statement that Boffrand was not influenced by Fashion. The only reason we now find Patte's survey inadequate is that he does not cite examples to support his statements and that he is not very precise about dates. His contemporaries did not need to be told such things since they knew perfectly well what he was talking about. We, on the other hand, need to seek out the evidence and arrange it chronologically so that we can understand more clearly what he was saying.

As far as architecture and the fixed elements of interior decoration are concerned, much of the ground has already been surveyed, the latest major contribution being Michel Gallet's thorough work on the *Demeures parisiennes, l'époque de Louis XVI* (1964), from which source the present author has derived much information included here. Our knowledge of the earliest phases of Neo-Classicism in architecture naturally still remains incomplete for the simple reason that so many of the buildings concerned have been pulled down, and also because many of the designs apparently from that period can still not be securely dated.

Furniture, which Pierre Patte scarcely mentions, has been studied a good deal less thoroughly and presents us with considerable problems. The author has included as much as possible of the information published in Pierre Verlet's fundamental work on the French royal furniture and has borrowed freely from Francis Watson's exceptionally helpful catalogues of the furniture in the Wallace Collection and in the collection of Mr. and Mrs. Charles B. Wrightsman, and also in his useful *Louis XVI Furniture*.[2] Yet, even then the sum of our knowledge is meagre and in-

[1] 'Rais de coeur' in the original. The *Encyclopédie* says of this ornament that 'it is accompanied by *feuilles d'eau* (water-leaves)'.

[2] Francis Watson, *Louis XVI Furniture*, London, 1960.

securely based. Fate, it seems, has decreed that very little royal furniture should survive from the period which most concerns us—the 1760s—while so little of the surviving furniture made for private customers in France can now be dated with much accuracy since we so rarely know for whom or for which house it was made.

In the field of *bronzes d'ameublement*—of bronze furnishings like candelabra, fire-dogs, sconces, clock-cases and so forth—we are rather better informed. Once again it is to Verlet that we are indebted for his pioneer work in discovering the importance of Pitoin who was the principal supplier of such bronzes to the French Court from 1763 onwards.[1] Professor François-Georges Pariset has published numerous drawings, including many for bronzes, which Louis Prieur and Philippe Caffieri supplied in about 1765 for the Warsaw Palace and these provide us with an excellent idea of what the most-up-to-date French *bronzes d'ameublement* looked like at that point.[2]

While the stylistic development in Sèvres porcelain and in goldsmiths' work can be followed comparatively easily on account of the date marks that they normally bear, we are still very ignorant about the other decorative arts—glass, woven silks, and so forth—of which the production was presumably just as extensive and where the stylistic changes must have been equally marked.

So much for illustrating Patte's thesis. What he also fails to tell us are the reasons for the introduction of Neo-Classicism into France. He merely says that it came, and that it came because one was tired of the Rococo! This cannot be the whole truth, for of course everyone knows that Neo-Classicism was the upshot of far-reaching movements affecting the whole of Europe and all the Arts. We know quite a lot about many of the chief characters concerned with its inception, and we are comparatively well informed about those architects who were principally concerned with the introduction of the new style in their own field, partly through Hautecoeur's well-known text-books on the subject and partly through Gallet's excellent work which has already been mentioned.[3] When we come to furniture and most of the other decorative arts, however, it is far from easy to decide which were the most influential people concerned. That is chiefly because works of decorative art are usually created under quite different conditions from those affecting the so-called Fine Arts. An artist like Watteau, for instance, was entirely and solely responsible for the paintings he made: we know exactly whom to praise for the *Embarquement pour Cythère*! It is not nearly so easy to decide who deserves credit for a fine example of decorative art, especially one created for the luxury market. Signatures, if present, often merely mislead and we have to recognise that developments in this field are affected by factors of which one does not usually have to take account in the higher reaches of art history. In the first place, few craftsmen in these fields were so well placed, financially, as to be able to undertake expensive experiments just for the sake of modernity. Another factor was the public's taste. Then there were the middle-men like the *marchands-merciers*, *marchands-tapissiers*, and other dealers who had the capital and could afford to place orders with the craftsmen and thus must have had a certain influence on both their work and on the customers' tastes. The mostly quite anonymous draughtsmen who produced designs for the craftsmen, for the dealers, or for individual customers clearly also played their part. And finally there were the known and the as yet unknown *connaisseurs* and *hommes de goût* whose influence could be enormous. We recognise perfectly well

[1] See Pitoin's biography, p. 213. [2] See Prieur's biography, p. 217.
[3] Michel Gallet, *Demeures parisiennes, l'époque de Louis XVI*, Paris, 1964.

how greatly all these things affected the developments that interest us here but it is none too easy to document their effect. Pierre Patte no doubt thought it unnecessary to mention such matters since they must have been known to all his readers. But, today, we need to throw as much light as possible on these questions, if we are to understand how it happened that, as Patte tells us, the art of interior decoration and the design of furniture came to constitute what was 'in some sense a new art'.

I

TRENDS AND CONCEPTS

1. THE REACTION AGAINST THE ROCOCO

Today most people probably consider the Rococo as one of the most original contributions France has made to the Arts since the Gothic period. It is really not so surprising that it gained such popularity, especially in the field of interior decoration. After the severe and majestic *Louis Quatorze* style, the Rococo must have come as a considerable relief to both the artists and their customers. They could now discard the fetters of Baroque pomp and ceremony, the down-dragging weight of which was surely one of the chief reasons that the new style became so undisciplined. The people of that time—at least, those who lived in some luxury—must have been delighted to pass their days in surroundings that appeared to reflect their own sensibilities rather than in those entirely governed by rigid architectural rules. Furniture, particularly the chair which was also then the class of furniture most used in daily life, was now given forms that suited it perfectly to human use and which in its proportions and organic conception acquired a character related to the human being rather than to the building for which it was designed. Indeed, of all the classes of furniture, it was the chair that yielded most reluctantly to the encroachments of Neo-Classicism and we can be quite sure that much of the criticism which was levelled at the new style was composed by writers comfortably cushioned in a *Louis Quinze* armchair!

The Rococo no doubt had its opponents from the first day it appeared on the scene, but it was not until the 1730s that the criticism began to come into the open, both in conversation and in print. These criticisms of the Rococo phase have often been quoted in our own time, perhaps most extensively in Wolfgang Hermann's excellent book on *Laugier and Eighteenth Century French Theory* (1962) in which they are printed in chronological order. The most subtle is Voltaire's ridiculing of the contemporary taste entitled *Le Temple du goût* of 1733, while the next important contribution is J.-F. Blondel's mockery of the 'amas ridicule de coquilles, de dragons, de roseaux, de palmiers et de plantes, qui font à présent tout le prix de la décoration intérieure'[1] which appears in his famous *De la distribution des maisons de plaisance* of 1737. In 1741, the architect Soufflot addressed the Academy at Lyons on 'toutes ces bizarres nouveautés que la mode

[1] The 'ridiculous jumble of shells, dragons, reeds, palm-trees, and plants which is the be-all and end-all of modern interior decoration'.

authorise aujourd'hui et détruira demain',[1] adding that all right-minded people will look down on these 'frivoles productions'.[2]

As is well known, Soufflot was to be chosen to accompany the young Marquis de Marigny—destined to become France's 'Minister of Culture'—on that epoch-making tour of Italy during the years 1749 to 1751, and it is therefore important to know something of Soufflot's attitude to this question at that early date. The same applies to the Abbé le Blanc and the draughtsman C.-N. Cochin who were selected to be Marigny's two other travel-companions. Although Le Blanc's criticisms were first published in 1745 (*Lettres d'un françois*, letter XXXVI), they were written some time before. The letter concerned is undated but was written in London and we know he was in England between 1737 and 1744.[3] It is addressed to a certain 'Comte de C**' who can hardly be any other than the Comte de Caylus who was to become one of the most energetic exponents of Neo-Classicism.

Le Blanc opens fire with a criticism of the bad taste evinced by the English, but he is soon training his guns on his own countrymen. He points out that in all the decorative arts one has completely lost sight of that 'noble simplicité' which had governed the work of the great masters of Antiquity and which the French themselves had tried to emulate. He deplores that one has turned away from the canons of taste that prevailed under Louis XIV in 'l'âge d'or des Lettres et des Beaux Arts en France',[4] as he called it. He is, furthermore, incensed at the way so many contemporary artists combine motifs that have nothing to do with each other—a Cupid with a dragon, or a sea-shell with bat's wings! He evokes Horace in support of his case, the latter having said, so he claims, that it is an outrage to juxtapose creatures of an unlike nature, adding that modern artists no longer respect either order or plausibility in their works which are now nothing more than haphazard compilations of motifs. The free-ranging ornament of the Rococo has no justification whatsoever in the Abbé's eyes; for him only ornament of an architectural character, based on sound structural principles, has any significance. What on earth is one to make of a clock which is poised on something that seems to have grown out of the wall, he asks. He is of course thinking of those cartel clocks which we have so misguidedly thought were among the more felicitous inventions of the Rococo! Le Blanc of course also has a deep regard for vertical and horizontal lines and abhors the fact that one could draw someone's coat of arms set at an angle. Indeed, everything is so misplaced that he fears it is a sign of mental derangement, and he uses strong words like 'fou', 'ridicule', and 'dépravé' in making his case which are a clear sign of how deep was his revulsion.

Even though Le Blanc does not name any of the particular culprits in his letter, there can be little doubt as to which were the artists he had in mind, for they are pilloried in his review of the *Salon* of 1753.[5] They were Borromini, Meissonnier, and Thomas Germain. He no doubt also had in mind such men as Pineau, Lajoue and possibly Oppenord. The only artist whom Le Blanc praises and mentions by name in his letter from London is the sculptor Bouchardon, a friend of the Comte de Caylus, who had only recently demonstrated that he knew how to employ ornaments which were truly 'nobles' and that were disposed with 'intelligence' in his Fontaine des

[1] 'all those bizarre novelties that fashion permits one day and destroys the next'.

[2] Wolfgang Hermann, *Laugier and Eighteenth Century French Theory*, London, 1962, p. 223.

[3] The full French text is given here on pp. 226–9 (translation pp. 229–32).

[4] 'the golden age for letters and fine arts in France'.

[5] *Observations sur les ouvrages de MM. de l'Académie . . . exposés . . . en l'année 1753*, Paris, n.d., pp. 157–61.

Saisons in the Rue de Grenelle. The Abbé ends up by saying that the current taste is so depraved that it is unlikely to prevail much longer, and that he is sure the recipient of the letter—presumably Caylus, as we have said—will presently bring about this state of affairs by the interest and encouragement he devotes to the Arts.

As far as Caylus' own views about the Rococo are concerned, these are revealed in two papers he read before the Academy in 1749 in which he criticised the 'goût mauvais et mesquin que l'on fait aujourd'hui pour la décoration des maisons'.[1] In modern Parisian houses, he says, one finds nothing but 'de petits ornements aussi déraisonnables que mal placés, de l'or appliqué sans raison'.[2] He says that this fashion has lasted a long time and asks if France cannot remain constant to anything but Bad Taste.[3]

Le Blanc is of course aware that it is not only the artists who are to blame. He says that there are still sensible artists and craftsmen who must blush at the thought of some of the things they are today required to produce if they are to live. A man like Claude Ballin, a goldsmith who had worked for Louis XIV, had subsequently been forced to conform to the prevailing taste but he did all he could to ensure that his work should not be entirely ruined on that account, retaining the elegant proportions and the proper classical profiles of the former style while employing only with the greatest moderation those ornaments his fashion-conscious customers demanded.[4]

Le Blanc's criticisms were entirely negative, and based on a strictly conservative and academic point of view. All the same, they are of interest because they already contain many of the arguments set out less spitefully and with greater skill by Cochin ten years later in his now famous articles in the *Mercure de France* of December 1754 and February 1755. In his *Mémoires*[5] Cochin makes a statement which seems to imply that it was during the journey to Italy with Marigny—that is, in 1749–51—that he first came to realise how *ridicule* was the Rococo taste, but he had been working for a decade or so for the *Menus Plaisirs* (the drawing-office concerned with royal entertainments, etc.) where the Rococo was at the time flourishing merrily, and he did not have a literary background like that of the Abbé Le Blanc, his senior by ten years, that might have affected his attitude which was therefore based entirely on visual considerations.

Cochin's first article[6] is aimed, like Le Blanc's letter, primarily at those practising the decorative arts. He attacks their lack of common sense. It is particularly the goldsmiths who draw his fire. He ridicules the way they decorate their wares with figures which are entirely out of proportion to each other—full-sized vegetables coupled with a rabbit the size of your little finger, and so on. Moreover, he accuses them of sacrificing practical considerations on the altar of Rococo ornament, for example when they make the drip-pans of candlesticks convex instead of concave so that molten wax dribbles on the table.

He accuses the carvers and sculptors of the same crimes but is here rather more specific in his criticisms. He says they entirely eschew regular forms in the panelling of rooms—they neglect the straight line, the rectangle, the circle and the oval—in favour of all kinds of contorted shapes. These things are ludicrous in the first place, he says, and moreover lead to the squandering of good and expensive timber.

[1] 'poor and pitiful taste that is today applied to the decoration of buildings'.
[2] 'small ornaments, unsuitable and incorrectly disposed, with gilding applied for no good reason'.
[3] Hermann, op. cit., pp. 226–7.
[4] 'Éloge historique de Claude Ballin', *Mercure de France*, May 1754, pp. 156–9.
[5] Extract in French is printed here on p. 269 (translation pp. 269–70).
[6] The full French text is given here on pp. 233–5 (translation pp. 235–7).

The architect is counselled by Cochin to go and take an occasional look at some of the beautiful buildings erected in the previous century—the Louvre and the Tuileries, for instance. The same advice had of course been given them by Blondel many years earlier.[1] This might persuade them, Cochin claimed, to cease making buildings with corners that are canted or set at an acute angle, and they might then plan their rooms to be rectangular instead of octagonal. He furthermore urged them to complete their buildings with a decent stone parapet instead of a mansard-roof of slate, which had been one of Blondel's points as well. As he puts it, one is now growing weary of seeing a blue-black house standing on the white one below! Finally he expresses the hope that these good architects will soon tire of having always to think up something new and will gratefully adopt once again the sound principles embodied in the buildings of yesterday.

The second of Cochin's *Mercure de France* articles[2] pretends to be a protest against the first but now it is mostly at the architects he is aiming. He has written the piece wittily and with a sharp sense of the ironic, posing as an indignant Rococo architect speaking up for himself and his colleagues, the carvers and the plasterers.

Cochin in this oblique fashion makes fun of the way large paintings are no longer used for the decoration of walls and ceilings, but sculptured panelling and plasterwork are relied on instead. He then jeers at the way artists have now gone over, encouraged by Meissonnier, Borromini and—to some extent—Oppenord, to a form of architecture which is all light-hearted fun and has lost sight of those rules previously regarded as being the mark of good taste, that is to say, the rules of Classical architecture. And last of all he bemoans the fact that the Classical column has been excluded from fashionable architecture, no doubt, as he says, because our friends consider them dreary features which have the additional drawback of making their other decorations look a bit mean ('elles font paroître mesquin tout ce qui les accompagne').

Cochin in fact maintains that the protagonists of the Rococo now find themselves, to their great surprise, excluded from all commissions from the royal household where of course everything reeks of the old architecture ('tout ce qui s'y fait sent la vieille architecture'), and that the Academy will only award prizes to those architects whose work most closely approaches the Antique taste. To make up for this, the supposed Rococo architect is made to say, he and his friends are so admired by everyone else ('le public nous aime') that it is quite senseless to go on making objections like this, if only because those who can well afford to build new houses also believe they understand about Art and Architecture and 'peut-on manquer du goût quand on a de l'argent?'[3]

The reader will have noticed that Cochin's criticism was rather less negative than Le Blanc's, but both exaggerate grossly—as all good polemicists will do—and both of them are rigidly academic in their approach and totally blind to any of the qualities that we find so delightful in the Rococo today.

A positive and entirely aesthetic, as opposed to ideological, criticism was levelled at the Rococo by that strange architect Pierre Vigné de Vigny which appeared in the *Journal Oeconomique* in March 1752 (pages 68–107), that is to say, more than two years before Cochin's first article. De Vigny has nothing against the style in itself, as we can see from his thumbnail sketch of recent developments. 'On détruit', he writes, 'l'antique pour faire place au moderne, puis on aban-

[1] J.-F. Blondel, *De la distribution des maisons de plaisance*, Paris, 1737, vol. II, p. 67, quoted in Hermann, op. cit., pp. 221–2.

[2] The full French text is given here on pp. 238–44 (translation pp. 244–50).

[3] 'Can one lack taste when one has money?'

donne le moderne pour courir étudier les ruines de l'antique, comme si celui-ci n'avoit aucuns défauts, & que celui-là n'eût aucunes beautés.'[1] His criticisms are aimed at those Rococo architects who have abandoned the style because they were unable to make it sufficiently original and therefore robust enough to serve as a bridge-head from which to make further advances. He considers contemporary painters and sculptors to be talented and original in their art but, of the architects, he says that they 'sont à présent dans une espèce d'esclavage, en s'asservissant à suivre uniquement les anciens monumens des Grecs et des Romains: ils ont besoin d'un génie heureux qui les dégage, comme, entr'autres le Borromini qui en a frayé le chemin en Italie'.[2] De Vigny adds, by way of praise for Borromini and condemnation of his own French colleagues, that Borromini knew all about Classical architecture and its principles, as could be seen from his S. Agnese in Rome which is 'très régulier en son tout et ses parties'.[3] But Borromini grew tired of the 'manière gênante' ('tiresome manner') of the Antique style, and began to create wonders ('des merveilles') without adhering to any of the generally accepted architectural rules of his homeland. This is clearly to be seen, for instance, in his S. Ivo della Sapienza, he says.

Of course neither de Vigny nor the other critics of Rococo art knew what the future held in store. They all hoped things would change. Most of them hoped this would be achieved within the framework of Classical tradition governed by sound principles while others like de Vigny looked for a development in the direction of yet more freedom untrammelled by considerations of 'good sense'.

2. THE CLASSICAL REVIVAL IN ROME

While the Rococo was reigning triumphant in Paris and was spreading all over Europe, artistic enterprises were being undertaken at the French Academy in Rome which did not owe their inception in any way to barren criticism, and it was in Rome that the creed was first substantially formulated that was to impart such an impetus to Classicism that it could once again bear fruit and develop.

The group of young French artists who were living in Rome in the late 1730s and in the 1740s at their King's expense included the painter J.-B.-M. Pierre (who was in Rome between 1735 and 1740), the architect J.-L. Le Geay (1738–42), the sculptor J.-F.-J. Saly (1740–48), the painter C.-M.-A. Challe (1742–49) and his brother Simon Challe (1744–52), also the architect N.-H. Jardin (1744–48), the painter J.-M. Vien (1744–50) and the architects E.-A. Petitot (1746–50) and J.-C. Bellicard (1748–51).

Once these clever young men had demonstrated their outstanding talents at the Académies Royales in Paris by winning the Grand Prix de Rome, they were sent, according to the traditional practice, to Rome to further their training by studying the widely-famed monuments of Classical antiquity as well as the works of famous masters of more recent times. They lived at the Palazzo Mancini, where the French Academy was housed. The director at that period was the painter

[1] 'One discards the old-fashioned to make way for the new, and then one drops the new to scurry off to study the ruins of antiquity—as if the latter were faultless and the former had possessed no beauty whatsoever.'

[2] 'are at present bound in a kind of slavery to copy exclusively the ancient monuments of the Greeks and the Romans; what they need is a genius to come and release them, just as Borromini—among others—had marked out the way in Italy'.

[3] 'entirely regular in sum and in all its parts'.

Jean-François de Troy. He kept an eye on the studies and well-being of the stipendiaries and reported regularly on their progress to Le Normant de Tournehem who was then *directeur général des bâtiments, académies,* etc.[1] From these reports we know just how assiduously the students followed their studies, but we know little of what else occupied them—their interests and their acquaintanceship.

There was plenty to look at in Rome. Apart from the Classical monuments there was a good deal of modern architecture. As Christian Elling has pointed out,[2] Rome was a lively and up-to-date capital city at that time, with much to offer any young artist in a receptive frame of mind. The dominance of the archaeologists, the *ciceroni* and the *scavatori* was still not properly established. Rome was still a living city. Unexcavated, unrestored and covered in vegetation as the ancient monuments then still were, these must have seemed far more exciting and fantastic than they do today when they resemble well-groomed skeletons and only show signs of life when darkness falls. In those days, however, the ruins must have been astonishing phenomena, especially in contrast with the surrounding modern buildings. Important edifices were in fact being erected in the 1730s and 1740s. For example, the Spanish Steps, the Fontana di Trevi, Alessandro Galilei's new façade on San Giovanni in Laterano, and Fuga's Palazzo della Consulta, were all completed by 1740 and all were splendid works in the late Baroque taste which must surely have been of interest to the young architectural students. Indeed, Elling has published a document giving details of exactly which monuments Jardin, one of the young architects already mentioned, had studied and admired while in Rome.[3] Works by Bramante, Michelangelo, Giacomo della Porta and Carlo Rainaldi are mentioned and Jardin places St. Peter's, the Gesù, S. Ignazio and S. Maria dei Miracoli on a par with the most esteemed Classical monuments. And Jardin was probably not alone in making such unprejudiced judgements about the masterpieces in his own field. We also know something of the extent of the sculptor Saly's interests since he not only copied an antique figure of Antinous and drew an ancient tripod[4] but apparently also very much wanted to copy one of Bernini's sculptures.

When the architect Le Geay left Rome in January 1742 at the age of twenty-eight and returned to Paris, de Troy wrote home to say that he was bringing with him a series of beautiful drawings consisting partly of studies of public buildings and partly of his own designs. The latter, said de Troy, were works of spirit and genius ('du feu et du génie'). Although we have unfortunately not yet been able to identify any of these drawings, there must have been something quite outstanding about this man Le Geay of whom we now know so little. Otherwise his fame could hardly have lingered on long after he himself had disappeared from the scene. Cochin, who was one of the Neo-Classical movement's lay-preachers, stated quite positively that Le Geay was responsible for reviving Good Taste. 'On peut donner pour première époque du retour d'un meilleur goust, l'arrivée de Legeay', he says.[5] Cochin and other writers stress how great was his influence on several young artists, notably architects like Boullée, Moreau-Desproux, Peyre and De Wailly. We can hardly ignore such statements merely for lack of drawings with dates. Emil

[1] Cf. *Correspondance des directeurs de l'Académie de France à Rome avec les Surintendants des Bâtiments*, ed. Montaiglon and Jules Guiffrey, vol. X, 1742–53; hereafter abbreviated to *Corr. des Dir.*

[2] *Jardin i Rom*, Copenhagen, 1943, *passim.*

[3] *Documents inédits concernant les projets de J.-A. Gabriel et N.-H. Jardin pour l'Église Frédéric à Copenhague*, Copenhagen, 1931, pp. 32–6.

[4] Plate 294.

[5] 'One can say that good taste started to be regained on the arrival of Le Geay back in Paris.' *Mémoires*, pp. 141–2.

Kaufmann and John Harris, who have both studied Le Geay's work,[1] suggest that certain curious compositions like those shown in Plates 2 to 6 may belong to his Roman period; we must at any rate be content at present to regard these as reflections of the 'feu' and the 'génie' to which de Troy referred, and as some of the 'exaggerations' which Joseph Lavallée spoke of later.[2] In the design for a sepulchral monument (Plate 2) the strictly geometric composition confines the figures in rigid positions. The loose, almost flaccid anatomy of these figures is in marked contrast to the heavy, cubistic architectural feature, the character and size of which is stressed by the stunted trees on the left and the distant ruins on the right. A design by Le Geay for a mausoleum published by Vasi in 1739 incorporated the motif of a great rectangular block pierced by an obelisk which may of course be traced back to Juvara but Le Geay's use of it was entirely uncompromising and cubistic. The two monumental fountains shown in Plates 3 and 4 have been placed to the right in each picture in order to leave room for imaginative views of Rome showing the Pyramid of Cestius and the Palatine. The low perspective and the excessive depth stress the proximity of the fountains and their bulk. While the fountain shown in Plate 3 may recall the work of Bernini, both compositions display originality and a strange romantic quality. Notice how the rectangular plinth of the large urn shown in Plate 4 is formed by a weathered block from some antique monument. Here Le Geay is using ruined masonry in just the way that Carlo Fontana had done at the end of the previous century[3] and as Jardin was to do in the proposal for a monument shown in Plate 11.

Le Geay's series of engravings published in 1768 under the title *Rovine* (Plates 5 and 6) must in fact have been composed many years earlier, as John Harris has pointed out,[4] because Sir William Chambers apparently had access to them at some point during his journey to France and Italy which lasted from 1749 until 1754. These, too, may possibly belong to Le Geay's Roman period, that is, from about 1740, even if they seem to represent a later stage in his development than the projects for monuments and fountains just discussed. Their fantastic and dramatic aspect is strangely reminiscent of Piranesi and it is indeed highly probable that Le Geay knew the great Venetian artist, who arrived in Rome in 1740 and is known to have consorted with the young Frenchmen at the Academy and to have become a close friend of some of them. Le Geay's compositions are anyway couched in the Piranesi idiom, illuminated by a dramatic light which startlingly reveals scenes of ghostly Classical monuments and some rather spooky figures. And while the series is entitled *Rovine*, none of the buildings actually seem to be in ruins; indeed they are so well preserved that one has the impression they have always stood in the cavern where Le Geay found them. These strange pictures have a dream-like quality and have little to do with structures of any reality. They are entirely romantic exercises.

Although we are none too sure about the date of Le Geay's engravings, we are on firm ground when it comes to a series of projects and schemes of decoration carried out in the second half of the 1740s by Le Lorrain, Saly, Vien, Jardin and Petitot, and these bear eloquent witness to the way the wind was blowing. The students at the French Academy had occasionally to fulfil

[1] Emil Kaufmann, 'Three Revolutionary Architects, Boullée, Ledoux and Lequeu', *Transactions of the American Philosophical Society*, N.S. 42, pt. 3 (1952); John Harris, 'Le Geay, Piranesi and International Neo-Classicism in Rome 1740–1750', *Essays in the History of Architecture presented to Rudolf Wittkower*, London, 1967.

[2] See John Harris, op. cit., p. 190.

[3] E.g., his rebuilding of the Temple of Neptune at Piazza di Pietra in Rome, and his proposal for a church in the centre of the Colosseum.

[4] Op. cit., pp. 190–1.

tasks other than that of copying the works of the great masters of yesterday, and some of these tasks gave them the opportunity to demonstrate new ideas which might otherwise have remained as mere doodles in their sketch-books. Especially suited to such experimental treatment were the ornamental edifices needed in connection with festivals of various kinds, of which there were many each year in Rome. These might be as large as a fair-sized house but were of course far cheaper to erect and were constructed of timber and canvas and similar light materials. They only needed to last until the festival concerned was over and, whether they were good or bad, they were torn down afterwards. We only know what some of them were like from descriptions or surviving illustrations. Such gala decorations, although essentially ephemeral in character, at least offered artists and architects a chance to try their wings.

Le Lorrain designed a number of such set-pieces, notably some for the annual Chinea Festival (*Festa della Chinea*). That which he designed in 1744 was a painted backcloth, traditional and of no special interest but the following year he ventured to produce an architectural set-piece in an exceedingly progressive style (Plate 8). This one consisted of a triumphal arch which seems to betray the influence of Bibiena and possibly also of Galilei, and certainly of Michelangelo's *palazzi* on the Capitol which in the next years were to become a popular source of inspiration for architects.

Contemporary Romans can hardly have found Le Lorrain's triumphal arch in any way surprising, when considered as a whole, but important details like his accentuation of the wall-surfaces round the rectangular bas-reliefs and the oval medallions with their weighty garlands must surely have seemed novel. Architects, notably in France, were subsequently to continue to evolve schemes in which the wall-surface itself became a significant element underlining the block-like character of the building. One may, for instance, discern a relationship between this handling of the theme by Le Lorrain and that embodied in the church at Nérac (Plate 59) which was built after designs by Barreau de Chefdeville seventeen years later.

In 1746—that is, a year later—Le Lorrain designed a set-piece in the form of a temple which clearly reveals the influence of Piranesi. Through Louis Hautecoeur's important studies we have long been aware of Piranesi's far-reaching influence on numerous French architects, and Christian Elling has studied how Piranesi influenced Jardin at an early stage.[1] Actually, the engraving illustrating Le Lorrain's Chinea decoration for the year 1746 (Plate 9) is lit in a theatrical manner which probably owes more to Giuseppe Vasi's well-known dramatic style than to Piranesi himself. It is in the architecture that Piranesi's influence is more truly betrayed. Possibly the open body of the building, with its surround of columns, could have been conceived without knowledge of Piranesi's work—perhaps under inspiration of fantasies by Le Geay like those John Harris has published.[2] Yet Piranesi must be the source of inspiration for the strange cupola which is more like a gigantic monolith than a structure of masonry. The boldly modelled profile and the band of reliefs help to stress the impression of enormous weight. Such a Cyclopic concept is entirely in the Piranesian tradition.

These designs by Le Lorrain reflect the ideas which must have been going through the heads of the young French architects and draughtsmen in Rome at that time. Not all of them were given the opportunity of designing settings for the Chinea festivals like Le Lorrain and Petitot had been (Plate 13) but they worked up designs for other kinds of buildings (Plates 10 and 11). All of

[1] *Jardin i Rom*, Copenhagen, 1943, *passim*.
[2] Op. cit., fig. 15, for example.

B. Moreau 'Le Jeune', 1771

them are inspired with an unmistakable streak of romantic Classicism like that revealed in Le Lorrain and Le Geay's compositions, and all reflect to a greater or lesser degree the influence of Piranesi whose character and inventiveness were of a far more impressive stature than those of the young Frenchmen. It is hardly surprising that they admired and were fascinated by this personality of such remarkable genius. He was, one might say, their first love in Rome and he left on them an indelible impression which they carried with them wherever they went, be it Paris or Copenhagen, Parma or St. Petersburg.

Designing ornamental vases or urns seems long to have been a kind of side-line for artists and this was particularly so in the mid-eighteenth century. As a motif, the urn offers as much scope for invention as, for instance, the arabesque or the rocaille. On paper, at any rate, there is no limit to the possibilities! Saly is unfortunately the only artist whose vase-compositions can be securely dated to the period of his stay in Rome (Plates 291 to 293) but it seems probable that the vases drawn by people like Pierre and Le Lorrain (Plates 297 and 298), also date from their sojourn in the Eternal City. Saly actually engraved his vase-designs himself and published them in 1746. They are just as typical of their period as Le Lorrain's decorative settings and reflect similar influences and trains of thought.

Saly was anyway an artist of greater talent than these others and he was, moreover, a sculptor and not an architect, and this makes a considerable difference. His vase-designs show that he was clearly drawn to the art of Classical antiquity but that he had wider sympathies. The influence of Piranesi is once again unmistakable and he owes something to Stefano della Bella and perhaps also to Bernini whom he greatly admired. Indeed, a few of these designs are vaguely reminiscent of Meissonnier's entirely Rococo compositions while others reflect an awareness of Baroque artists like Le Brun and Jean Le Pautre. Saly has nearly always made the bodies of his vases of antique Classical form, or at least that has been his intention, and each is composed of a few, clearly defined elements. They have bold profiles and deep channelling which produces striking effects of light and shade. But this almost architectural clarity is then embellished with rich and often fantastic sculptural ornament of gamboling tritons and nereids, nymphs and merfolk, bucrania and lion-masks, garlands and gaping mussel-shells, reeds, bullrushes and all kinds of dank vegetation—all as if these vases were intended to be set up in the subterranean dwelling of some nymph, with trickling springs and moss-covered walls. A few of these vases can hardly be regarded as truly Neo-Classical in the accepted sense; they lack the dominant clarity of form to be found in urns designed by men like Neufforge, Vien and De Wailly (Plates 310 to 318, and 323 to 328) while several support light-hearted sculptural ornament that is far more characteristic of the Rococo than the Neo-Classical idiom. The architect Jardin, who was a close friend of Saly's, had a large urn that was entirely Neo-Classical in style executed after one of these designs in 1757 and placed as decoration at a focal point in a dining-room in the town house of Count Moltke in Copenhagen (Plate 30). This would seem to indicate that Jardin regarded Saly as no less worthy an exponent of the new style than himself.

Among the works of art which exemplify this early phase of Neo-Classicism in Rome in the 1740s is the high altar at the Cathedral in Vienne which was executed in Rome between 1744 and 1747 by the sculptor M.-A. Slodtz (Plate 12). Of course the altar's essentially sacred nature might to some extent have led to it being conceived in such a severely Classical manner, but the fact that it is formed like a Roman sarcophagus with S-shaped channels and a bold Vitruvian scroll can only be due to Slodtz's own predilection for the Antique and his facility in handling

Classical motifs which he managed to combine in an entirely fresh manner. Slodtz was also the first person to design a Neo-Classical set-piece in France itself. This was a catafalque made in 1760 to stand in Notre-Dame (Plates 42 and 43). It marked a definite change in the style of such ephemeral decorations. We do not know whether Slodtz was influenced by Piranesi. He had himself acquired a thorough acquaintance with Rome and its monuments, having lived there from 1728 until 1746—far longer than any of the other French artists we have been discussing. Moreover, born in 1705, he was a good deal older than the rest.

It is worth noting that all the 'Roman' works of these Frenchmen so far discussed were not only produced before the first systematic excavations had been started (1748) in that area of antique ruins which was later to reveal itself as Pompeii, and well before the 1750s when the scholarly Classicism, heralded by the archaeologist Winckelmann, made its breakthrough, but also long before the future 'Minister for the Arts', the Marquis de Marigny, started out on his oft-mentioned journey to Italy (1749–51), and even longer before the publication of Cochin's polemical essays in the *Mercure de France* (1754–55).

Marigny's tour and Cochin's articles have been cited as turning-points marking the introduction of Neo-Classicism and it was apparently Cochin himself who first made this claim. In 1758, he referred to 'les heureux effets' ('the fortunate results') which Marigny's journey had had, while in his *Mémoires* he states that the return of the Marquis and his companions from Rome constituted the actual moment ('la véritable époque décisive') when Good Taste returned to the scene in France.[1] Cochin, who had of course been one of Marigny's companions on the journey, insisted that the latter had been won over to Classicism, as the young Frenchmen at the Academy in Rome had been, and that Marigny had brought his influence to bear, as soon as he took up his post as cultural minister, in order to bring about the triumph of Neo-Classicism. Cochin's own articles must also have had their effect, as he claimed. We shall say more about this later but we must accept that Cochin knew what he was talking about and, although he says almost in the same breath that Good Taste came back with Le Geay (who returned in 1742), he was really differentiating, and probably rightly so, between the artist's activity on the stylistic level, on the one hand, and the more political action of men like Marigny and himself on the other.

As everyone knows, the Marquis de Marigny was Madame de Pompadour's younger brother and she had been the King's mistress since 1745. It is reported that she immediately took steps to ensure that her brother should succeed Le Normant de Tournehem as Directeur-Général des Bâtiments, Jardins, Arts, Académies et Manufactures Royales which in effect was the equivalent of being Minister of Culture, a concept which Saly recognised in addressing Marigny as 'Ministre des Arts'.[2] It was in order to qualify him for this important post that the young man, still only twenty-two years old, was sent on a study-tour to Italy, in the company of the forty-three-year-old art-critic, the Abbé Le Blanc, and the thirty-six-year-old architect Soufflot, both of whom were known to hold critical views about the Rococo style, and with Cochin, who was a draughtsman then aged thirty-four. This small party set out in December 1749 and first stayed in Northern Italy, notably at Turin where Soufflot took some of the rooms at the Stupinigi Palace 'dans le goût des folies de Meyssonier'[3] as examples with which to demonstrate Bad Taste to Marigny. They went and admired some of Palladio's buildings at Vicenza, notably the Teatro Olimpico,

[1] See p. 269.

[2] Letter dated 31st May 1771, published by J.-J. Guiffrey in *Nouvelles Archives de l'Art Français*, 1878, p. 89.

[3] 'in the same taste as those ridiculous works of Meissonnier'. C.-N. Cochin, *Voyage d'Italie*, vol. I, Paris, 1758, p. 31.

while Florence they found to be the only city where there still reigned 'sage & de bon goût' ('sober and sound taste').[1] Almost everywhere else they found the taste in architecture and ornament 'entièrement corrompu' ('entirely corrupted').[2] Just as in Paris, one had everywhere lost the knack of creating works of true beauty in the headlong rush to invent something novel: 'les caprices les plus extravagans y sont devenus l'architecture à la mode, & la plus applaudie'.[3]

On 17th March 1750 the little group arrived in Rome and took up residence in the Palazzo Mancini where the French Academy was housed. De Tournehem had instructed the Academy's director, who was still de Troy, to make the four gentlemen properly welcome and to make sure that Marigny would see everything in the city that deserved attention. Soufflot already knew the city well and showed Marigny all the famous monuments, both Classical and modern, and pointed out those which he thought most worthy of praise and those which he did not. They also managed to fit in a trip to Naples in order to take in Herculaneum but Marigny seems not to have felt like going on to Paestum in the heat of the summer. On the other hand, he looked into the running of the Academy and was not particularly impressed. Marigny remained the whole of the following winter in Rome and then set out on the return journey on 3rd March 1751—leaving his three mentors in the Eternal City.

In spite of what Cochin tells us, it is not easy to decide exactly what Marigny got out of the journey. We can, however, be sure that he did not come home a confirmed adherent of Neo-Classicism in the same way as Le Geay, Saly, Le Lorrain and Jardin had done. Marigny was a more stolid character than any of these artists! At any rate, he could not see why it was thought necessary for the young trainee-architects in Rome to spend so much time studying the old temples there; they ought rather to devote themselves more to problems bearing some relation to modern taste and requirements! On the other hand, he felt that the painters and sculptors spent too little time copying 'le bel antique' and the works of the great masters.[4] That was what they were sent to Rome to do, he commented rather sharply in 1752 to Natoire, who by then had succeeded de Troy as the Academy's director. They are not meant to be painting little pictures of imaginary subjects, says Marigny, just in order to earn a bit of pocket money! What would have happened if Natoire, Vanloo, Pierre and Bouchardon had not used their time in Rome to 'copier et recopier le bel antique'?[5] All the same, it is clear that Marigny's three companions had at least turned him into an adversary of the Rococo even though he was to become a less rabid opponent of the style than they were.

Cochin stated that 'le ridicule (i.e. the Rococo) nous parut à tous bien sensible . . .'[6] and Marigny asked the Academy of Architecture in Paris in 1756, by which time he had become Directeur-Général as planned, whether they could not include a few questions, in their annual competition for prizes, that concerned interior decoration in order to 'corriger le mauvais goust d'ornemens qui subsiste aujourd'hui'.[7] These utterances indicate that Marigny had learned a good deal more from his journey through Italy and his stay in Rome than merely to speak Italian so he could take on a Florentine mistress! One must not believe the story about his having said to

1 Ibid., vol. II, p. 86. 2 Ibid.

3 'The most extravagant caprices imaginable now constitute fashionable architecture in that city and are mightily applauded.' Ibid.

4 *Corr. des Dir.*, X, p. 417.

5 'to copy and copy again the fine works of Antiquity'. Ibid.

6 'The absurdity appeared perfectly evident to us all.' See p. 269.

7 'to correct the poor taste that at present reigns in the field of decoration'. *Procès-verbaux de l'Académie Royale d'Architecture*, ed. H. Lemonnier, vol. VI, Paris, 1920, p. 262.

Soufflot in 1760 that 'Je ne veux point de chicorée moderne; je ne veux point de l'austère ancien; mezzo l'uno, mezzo l'altro',[1] when Soufflot asked him what kind of decoration he wanted in his new house in the Faubourg du Roule. It just does not ring true and he was in fact talking about some picture frames for portraits of Madame de Pompadour which were to be given as presents and had nothing to do with his own house which was anyway not being built until several years later. On the contrary, he wrote to Soufflot in 1768 that the inside of the house should be in Soufflot's own style. 'Quant à la décoration je m'en raporte entièrement à vous; je vous la demande d'aussi bon goût que la façade que vous m'avez donné'.[2] If we recall that the façade was in the style of Palladio (Plate 76), it will be realised that the interior can hardly have been a half-hearted essay in a transitional style. In fact contemporary witnesses disagree somewhat as to when Marigny became an active opponent of the Rococo. For instance, Dufort de Cheverny, who could not bear Marigny, claimed he was converted at Madame Geoffrin's (i.e. after the return from Italy). All we can now say is that his conversion started in Rome in 1750 but may well not have been completed until sometime between 1755 and 1761 in Paris.

3. THE CLASSICAL HERITAGE IN FRANCE

The restoration of Classicism in the form we now call Neo-Classicism was greatly eased by the very fact that a resilient, if on occasion flagging, Classical tradition had survived in France from the seventeenth century. Awe-inspiring monuments from the Age of Louis XIV were everywhere in evidence. The Louvre, the Tuileries, the Porte Saint-Denis, the Grand Trianon, Versailles and many other impressive structures stood as imposing reminders of a past which had held Classical principles in high regard. Marigny's first great ambition had been to complete Perrault's colonnaded façade of the Louvre which Pierre Patte called the supreme triumph of French architecture. The radiance emanating from the Age of the Sun King was still bright and, when criticising the Rococo, it was this splendid aureole that people recalled, at least as much as that of a more distant Age of Antiquity.

Reading through the minutes of the meetings at the Académie d'Architecture in Paris during the first half of the eighteenth century, it is difficult to find any references to the Rococo style or indeed to a stylistic development of any kind. Artists continued to discuss the Classical orders and listened to readings on the subject from ancient and from modern authorities like Vignola, Palladio, Desgodetz, Perrault, Bullet, Vitruvius, etc. The Académiciens had no doubt that the Classical column was the most august of architectural elements, and its correct proportions and the composition of its capital were judged perfectly suitable subjects for discussion *ad infinitum*.

Of course the impression given by these eternal arguments is entirely misleading. In fact, enormous changes and advances were made in the field of architecture in France during that period, notably in the planning of private houses which made them far more comfortable to live in. The relief of façades came to be less bold, while proportions became more elegant than they

[1] 'I do not want any of those modern chicory-leaves, nor do I want any of that Classical austerity; I seek a happy medium.'

[2] 'As for the interior decoration, I trust you entirely; I would like you to provide something as felicitous and in as good taste as the exterior you have already created.' More about Marigny and his attitude to the modern trends is on page 117, in his biography, p. 204, and in the present author's article 'Marigny and "le goût grec"', *Burlington Magazine*, March 1962, pp. 96–101.

had been in the seventeenth century. They seemed lighter, gayer, more charming and more human. Louis XIV himself had played a part in this development and we may recall his oft-quoted instructions to Mansart shortly before 1700 concerning the interior decoration of the *Ménagerie* at Versailles. 'Il me parait', he wrote, 'qu'il faut qu'il y a quelque chose à changer, que les sujets sont trop sérieux, qu'il faut qu'il y ait de la jeunesse mêlée dans ce que l'on fera . . .'[1]

As soon as there was a need to produce a solemn or awe-inspiring effect, architects relied on the Classical column. This was particularly the case with the façades of churches and certain public buildings. For example, when Servandoni designs stage-settings or set-pieces for some festival he uses the Rococo style, but when it concerns a church, as it did in 1732 when he was working on Saint-Sulpice (Plate 1), he uses the Classical idiom which both satisfied the conservatives and won the admiration of the Neo-Classicists. As Bachaumont said, Servandoni was an excellent architect 'pour les grandes choses dans le goust grec et du bel antique'.[2] To us, a colonnade like that at Saint-Sulpice seems just as much a building in the old-established tradition as the herald of a new style. Contant d'Ivry's project for Saint-Eustache (Plate 7), drawn ten years later, embodies the old seventeenth century Classical tradition in a largely undigested state. Both works at any rate bear witness to the tenacity of this tradition in France.

The Classical orders also remained *de rigeur* for those sections of public and private buildings in which it was hoped to convey an impression of dignity and conjure up feelings of respect in the visitor—namely entrance halls and staircases. An architect might adopt a ground plan of the most eccentric Rococo conformation but could not really do without Classical columns in such places; they were too well established as symbols of dignity. This is why one must regard designs like those of the Brunetti brothers more as a continuation of a Classical tradition than as reflections of a new tendency. Their painted staircase at the Hôtel de Luynes, which is now in the Musée Carnavalet, was executed in 1748 (Plate 14).[3] As will be seen, this is really an example of illusionistic Baroque decoration, owing nothing to either the Rococo or Neo-Classicism, yet created while the Rococo was at its height and while Neo-Classicism was still germinating. There were staircases decorated by the Brunetti brothers at about the same time, and presumably in much the same taste, in such otherwise markedly Rococo buildings as Madame de Pompadour's Château de Bellevue (1751)[4] and the Hôtel de Soubise (about 1750–51).[5] At the Hôtel du Controleur-Général (formerly the Hôtel de Pontchartrain), in 1749–50, the Brunettis decorated the main salon with a scheme dominated by columns of the Tuscan order, painted in fresco.[6] It was probably not long afterwards that they decorated the Great Dining-room at the Hôtel de Rohan with a scheme executed *en grisaille* that was no doubt very like those already mentioned—and this, too, lay side by side with some of the most typical and masterly Rococo interiors ever carried out.[7] These schemes of decoration should be grouped with those at Condé-en-Brie which

[1] 'It seems to me that something needs to be changed; the motifs are too austere, too sober; I would like to see a certain youthfulness, a certain playfulness, introduced into what we are doing . . .'. Quoted from Fiske Kimball, *The Creation of the Rococo*, Philadelphia, 1943, p. 107.

[2] 'for works on a grand scale in the Grecian or Antique taste'. Quoted from Louis Hautecoeur, *Histoire de l'architecture classique en France, tome III, première moitié du XVIIIe siècle, le style Louis XV*, Paris, 1950, p. 270.

[3] See J.-F. Blondel, *Architecture Française*, I, Paris, 1752, p. 255.

[4] See Comte Paul Biver, *Histoire du château de Bellevue*, Paris, 1933, p. 49.

[5] Antoine-Nicolas Dezallier d'Argenville, *Voyage pittoresque de Paris . . .*, Paris, 2nd ed., 1752, p. 198.

[6] See Archives Nationales, Paris, o^1 1921^B (Brunetti's file); Dez. d'Argenville, *Paris*, 3rd ed., 1757, p. 180.

[7] *Almanach des Beaux-Arts*, Paris, 1761, p. 19; Dez. d'Argenville, *Paris*, 3rd ed., 1757, p. 257; the Dining-room is not mentioned in the second edition of d'Argenville's book.

are attributed to Servandoni and are thought to have been executed in the 1740s.[1] These consist of gigantic Ionic pilasters between which are painted *trompe l'oeil* representations of some of the famous seventeenth-century statues in the park at Versailles. In this connection it would be interesting to know more about the Dining-room at the Palais Royal which was designed by Contant d'Ivry and decorated in 1754 by the plaster-worker Louis Mansiaux. We only have the puzzling entry in Mansiaux's account-book where he records having 'fet tout la ditte salle Entucque conposse de sesse collonne et sesse basse quatre pilastre plusse quattre basse les cocles Endesous poure la somme de 4,000 livres';[2] that is, a scheme with sixteen columns and four pilasters of counterfeit marble (scagliola). He does not say whether there were any painted decorations like those at the Hôtel de Luynes and at Condé-en-Brie, but, if there had been, these would surely have been mentioned by Dezallier d'Argenville who, when describing the Palais Royal, certainly draws attention to some decorative painting in a room next to the Dining-room but then goes on merely to say that 'la salle à manger offre une décoration très-agréable par son Architecture de stuc, dont le poli & la fraîcheur imitent le marbre au point d'y être trompé'.[3] At any rate it may well be that this particular room seemed to contemporary eyes quite traditional rather than an expression of a new form of Classicism, but it is worth bearing in mind that a room newly decorated in this way existed in such a prominent Parisian building when we are considering the dining-room Jardin designed for Count Moltke in Copenhagen which was executed in 1757 (Plate 30).

All the above-mentioned rooms, decorated in a Classical vein, remind us that in the houses of the period—and especially the grand ones—there was an accepted sequence of rooms and there was an accepted manner of decorating each class of room. As a general rule, the formality decreased as one progressed from the entrance hall, up the staircase, into a vestibule, through the salon or drawing-room, into the antechamber and then into the bedchamber itself. The *cabinets* or closets were the most informal of all, and it was only in the rooms where formality was not obligatory that the vagaries of Fashion were really tolerated. Ceremonial rooms were to be decorated in a traditional and dignified manner and this implied that the time-honoured Classical elements were used in their decoration.

As far as furniture from the Louis XIV period is concerned, virtually the only type which was admired throughout the eighteenth century was that decorated with boulle-work. As is well known, the chief characteristic of this type of furniture is its rich yet sombre aspect, resulting from the use of ebony veneers (black-stained woods of a less exotic nature were sometimes used) coupled with marquetry decoration in dark tortoiseshell and brass, while the whole is then usually embellished with rich gilt-bronze mounts. Even though André-Charles Boulle, one of Louis XIV's favourite cabinet-makers, did not invent this technique himself, it was very much a speciality of his workshops at the Louvre, which continued production under the direction of the son, Charles-Joseph Boulle, after the father's death in 1732. In his workshop, several young cabinet-makers learned to work in this complicated technique and some of them, like Etienne Levasseur, continued to make boulle-work furniture once they had set up on their own, often

1 Illustrated in *Connaissance des Arts*, January 1967, pp. 36–41.

2 'made the whole of the aforesaid room in stucco, consisting of sixteen columns and bases, four pilasters and bases, with pedestals below, for a total of 4,000 livres'. Archives du Département de la Seine et de la Ville de Paris, Paris, 5 B^{6} 2738, fol. 2 *verso* f.

3 'The Dining-room is pleasingly decorated with architectural motifs in stucco, of which the polish and smoothness so resemble marble that one is quite deceived.' Dez. d'Argenville, *Paris*, 3rd ed., 1757, pp. 71–2.

using the same or closely similar mounts and marquetry templates as those used at the Boulle establishment in the Louvre. The technical similarity is so complete that it is often difficult and sometimes impossible to be certain whether a piece of boulle-work furniture dates from about 1700 or from the late eighteenth century. This is, for example, true of the large so-called 'Londonderry cabinet' in the Wallace Collection[1] which bears the stamp of Etienne Levasseur who became an independent master cabinet-maker in 1760. Yet the bronzes on this piece are punched in a way that had apparently gone out of use by that date and the possibility must therefore be borne in mind that this could be a piece of furniture dating from the early period which Levasseur had subsequently undertaken to adapt or repair.

Boulle furniture presumably retained its popularity throughout the century largely because pieces decorated in this rich technique were regarded as veritable works of art or at least as works of conspicuous luxury. Moreover the black ebony veneer lent such furniture a dignified and sober air, irrespective of whether the contours of a piece were serpentine, as in the case of the famous 'Mazarin commodes' which Boulle made in 1708–09 for the Grand Trianon[2] but which were subsequently much copied, possibly by Levasseur, or whether they were of strictly architectural and rectilinear form like the 'Londonderry cabinet'. Even as late as 1779, when furniture of mahogany had become highly fashionable in Paris, Marigny could write to the cabinet-maker Pierre Garnier that, in his view, furniture decorated with ebony and gilt bronze was far more *noble* than that made of mahogany and he assumed Garnier would agree with him.[3] Marigny himself had a certain number of Boulle pieces, acquired in the 1750s through the dealer Lazare Duvaux.

Authentic Boulle furniture—pieces that could safely be claimed to have been made by *le fameux* André-Charles Boulle himself—were considered the most desirable and therefore the most expensive. The Vicomte de Fonspertius owned several pieces including a pair of tables of serpentine contour that were sold at an auction of his possessions in 1747.[4] When describing this particular lot, the cataloguer—the famous dealer Gersaint—stated that old Boulle's furniture was eagerly sought by collectors even though it was couched in a style very different from that now prevailing. This is confirmed by the Comte de Caylus who stated in 1757 that Boulle's work was keenly admired 'avec raison'.[5] Lalive de Jully, a man of taste, as we shall see, bought a large bookcase for no less than 12,000 livres from Lazare Duvaux in 1756 and it is clear that this must have been similar in size and shape to the 'Londonderry cabinet' already mentioned. He was very proud of this piece of furniture, claiming that it was one of the most beautiful ever made by Boulle 'dont les ouvrages devroient toujours servir de modèles à ceux qui travaillent dans ce genre'.[6]

That we ought to consider furniture in the boulle-work technique as representing the same tenacious and revered tradition from the time of Louis XIV as the classicised architecture we discussed earlier, is made clear by certain comments made about some furniture (Plates 85 to 89 and colour Plate A) designed for Lalive de Jully by Louis-Joseph Le Lorrain—whom we have

[1] F. J. B. Watson, *Wallace Collection Catalogues: Furniture*, London, 1960, F.390.

[2] Pierre Verlet, *Le mobilier royal français, meubles de la Couronne conservés en France*, Paris, 1945, pp. 3–4, Pl. 1.

[3] Bibliothèque historique de la Ville de Paris, MS. N.A. 106, letter dated 5th November 1779. All the letters from Marigny to Garnier were published in the *Journal of The Furniture History Society*, vol. VIII, 1972.

[4] E. F. Gersaint, *Catalogue . . . de M. Angran, Vicomte de Fonspertius*, Paris, 1747, p. 147.

[5] *Tableaux tirés de l'Iliade*, Paris, 1757, p. XXIII, note.

[6] 'whose works ought always to serve as models for those who make this class of furniture'. *Catalogue historique du cabinet . . . de M. De Lalive*, Paris, 1764, p. 106.

already come across in Rome in the 1740s—which is usually regarded as the very earliest Neo-Classical furniture made in France. Mariette, for instance, said that this furniture was 'dans le goût de ceux que Boulle avoit fait autrefois'.[1] We may now think this furniture very different in style from that characteristic of Boulle but both are veneered with black ebony, both are inlaid with brass stringing, and both are furnished with rich gilt-bronze mounts. Moreover, both are designed in a heavy, architectural style. Lalive stated that these pieces of furniture had been 'composés dans le style antique' ('designed in the Antique taste') by Le Lorrain.[2] The architect's imitation of Boulle's style did not satisfy Mariette who felt that the bronze ornaments were too uniform but he conceded that Le Lorrain deserved credit for having made the attempt at all.[3]

Another form of inheritance from the Golden Age of Louis XIV which affected all artists and craftsmen in the middle of the eighteenth century was embodied in the engraved plates which had been used for printing the illustrations in works on architecture and ornament of that period and which several publishers still had on their hands many years later. The most famous of these publishers was the *libraire du Roi* himself, Charles-Antoine Jombert, who is best known for having brought out J.-F. Blondel's classic *L'Architecture Française*. This began to appear in 1752. It was dedicated to the Marquis de Marigny and had a vignette by Cochin in Neo-Classical taste on the title-page (Plate 303). This is of course one of the primary sources of information about French architecture of the seventeenth and eighteenth centuries. The same publisher, Jombert, re-published Jean Le Pautre's *Oeuvres d'Architecture* in 1751. Le Pautre's work had first been published a hundred years before, in 1652, yet it was still pertinent—or perhaps one should say that it had once again become so. In April 1764, Jombert announced in the *Mercure de France* that he was preparing for publication a *Bibliothèque portative d'Architecture élémentaire* in six volumes and containing some 350 illustrations, which was to include examples of the work of Vignola, Palladio and Scamozzi, as well as Chambray's *Parallèle de l'architecture antique et moderne*. In fact only four volumes were produced. They appeared in the following year and were illustrated with only 300 scaled-down copies of the designs of the great Classical architects. Jombert explained that he had brought out this pocket edition of the Classical works which were so essential for young architects who could, however, rarely afford to buy them in the form of full-sized volumes. The price per volume in fact was 7 livres, 10 sols, while each of the corresponding full-sized works would have cost perhaps four or five times as much. Of course the reason Jombert republished these various books was not merely because he had most of the copperplates in his warehouse, handed down from father to son. There must also have been a demand for them. Moreover, he must have been closely associated with Cochin (we saw how he used a vignette by Cochin when he published Blondel's work) and he is therefore likely to have been in touch with the earliest partisans of Neo-Classicism who may well have advised him, if advice he needed, as to what he should do with all those ancient copperplates he had inherited. That Jombert was not ignorant of the new tendencies is proved by the fact that it was he who published off-prints of Cochin's famous articles in the *Mercure de France*, as already mentioned. In 1758 he also published Cochin's report on Marigny's tour of Italy.

What was apparently Jombert's last great re-print of old copperplate engravings appeared in 1765 under the title *Répertoire des Artistes*. The two volumes contained 688 illustrations re-

[1] 'in the taste of that made by Boulle in former times'. P. J. Mariette, *Abecedario*, ed. Ph. de Chennevières and A. de Montaiglon, Paris, 1854–56, 3, p. 124.

[2] *Catalogue historique . . .*, p. 110.

[3] Op. cit., p. 124.

printed from ancient plates dating from the seventeenth and even the sixteenth centuries (many of them were by Jacques-Androuet Ducerceau). The publication presented strange mixtures of architectural designs and others of a purely ornamental character, as well as some designs for urns. The collection has obviously been put together so as to appeal to a wide range of artists and craftsmen. Jombert's sense of what was needed is exemplified by the fact that he included sixteen plates of de la Gourthière's engravings of Raphael's grotesques at the Vatican. In two cases he seems to have felt it necessary to make the title-pages somewhat more up-to-date, so he added the words 'à la grecque' which at that time was something of a modernistic catch-phrase. The *Répertoire des Artistes* therefore offers the very clearest proof that many people at the time considered the traditions handed down from the past as in no way irrelevant to modern needs.

4. MEASURED MODERNISM

Today, we know very well that the Rococo was replaced by Neo-Classicism and that the change took place between 1750 and 1770. In the 1750s, however, no-one of course knew how things would work out. There were plenty of critics and prophets but it cannot have been easy to see just how their ideas might be carried through to fruition. The only thing which seemed certain was that one wanted to be rid of the Rococo with its lack of symmetry and its 'frivolous' ornaments, and people sensed that this would have to be achieved with the aid of formulae culled from Classical antiquity and the great tradition of French seventeenth century architecture and decoration.

There must have been many different views on exactly how this 'renaissance' should be brought about. Those with the clearest notion of the ultimate goal were the creative artists themselves, and particularly the architects who were more fully aware of which side their bread was buttered; yet even among them there must have been divergent views, springing from their different ages and backgrounds. Those who could afford to commission work from the artists and craftsmen—those who had to foot the bill—were just as mixed a bag as they are today. Often bored, often vain, craving luxury, they mostly ask only to be 'in fashion' and care little what the fashion may be. Very few wish, or have the courage or the freedom, to spend their money on modernistic ventures which may not come off. In order to understand the works of art which were produced during the 1750s and 1760s—architecture, furniture, etc.—it is essential to bear in mind that there were two distinct types of 'modernist' seeking to get away from the Rococo. One was cautious and moderate, the other bold and tending towards extreme expressions of the new idiom.

An important statement that helps throw much light on the moderate point of view is J.-F. Blondel's 'Observations générales sur la décoration' which appeared in 1762 in Diderot and d'Alembert's *Dictionnaire des Sciences*. It included illustrations of the Duchesse d'Orléans' recently completed apartments at the Palais Royal which had been redecorated by Contant d'Ivry (Plates 22 and 23). The full text of Blondel's essay and his commentary on the illustrations of Contant d'Ivry's work is given on pages 251-4.

At several points Blondel makes it clear that he is no admirer of the Rococo but, at the same time, he feels that the style of decoration prevailing under Louis XIV, however admirable this may have been in many ways, was really too massive and overpowering—and often a little confused. This is all very banal and every modernist of the period must have been thinking along much the same lines, whether he was a moderate or an extremist. But what Blondel then goes on to say could never have been uttered by an extremist. He takes the new arrangements at the Palais Royal (Plates 22 and 23) as an example of the ideal solution to the problem of replacing the Rococo without returning to the oppressive style of Louis XIV. Blondel draws attention to the Classical columns and motifs which form the principal decorative elements in Contant d'Ivry's schemes. It is these, says Blondel, which prevent the rest of the wall-panelling from appearing 'frivole'. If any one needs convincing, these rooms should be compared with those at the Hôtel de Soubise or, for that matter, elsewhere at the Palais Royal, he continues. Then it will be realised how successfully Contant d'Ivry has managed to bring a sense of calm to these rooms which is in marked contrast to that produced by the plethora of ornament crammed onto the walls of our houses—and even our churches—during the past thirty years or so. The comparison emphasizes how perilous our situation would have been, Blondel adds, if it had not been possible to create a new 'genre de décoration' which would sweep away 'cette frivolité' —the Rococo.

Blondel claims that this new style of decoration, so well exemplified by Contant d'Ivry's recent work, also does away with the ponderous character ('ce caractère de pesanteur') which has long been a weakness of the ornament in most royal palaces. Both the *Louis Quatorze* style and the Rococo have been guilty of exaggeration, he says, but now at last a felicitous compromise—'un juste milieu entre ces deux excès'—has been evolved. Although modern architects have been enthusiastically advocating 'le genre mâle' ('the male style')—that is, the severe style based on a strict imitation of antique Classical architecture—in interior decoration, they have now come to realise that rooms must be decorated in a manner that is pleasing: they must be 'agréables'. Nothing must seem ponderous, nor should there be too much symmetry, for that often produces a rigid and monotonous effect. Indeed, it may sometimes be necessary to enliven the architectural elements with a few contrasting motifs—as long as these are not exaggerated, he adds.

Blondel's views on the golden mean and the requisite degree of contrast in the decoration of rooms are included in his comments on the illustrations reproduced here in Plates 301 and 302. They show sections of the carved panelling, a sofa, and a console-table with a pair of gilt-bronze candelabra from the new rooms in the Palais Royal.

The sofa is one of a pair, standing under large looking-glasses flanked by Corinthian pilasters and seven-branch candelabra. Their symmetrical placing in the salon may be seen in Plate 22. Since these sofas and the other items have serpentine outlines and are devoid of Classical ornament, we would tend to class them as typical examples of Rococo furnishings. And of course Blondel would never have claimed them for 'le genre mâle', but he would have regarded them as acceptable contrasts to the Classical columns and the other strictly architectural elements in the room. Earlier on, when discussing the salon as a whole, Blondel had already drawn attention to the silk material brocaded with gold and silver thread with which these sofas were covered and stated that they helped furnish the room 'avec la plus grande magnificence'.[1] If we look closely, we must agree with Blondel that the sofas are not in any way 'outrés', in spite of their curving forms, and that their carved details cannot be called 'frivoles'. Among the motifs used are none of the rocailles, bat's-wings, or similar figments of the Rococo imagination. There is in fact a mussel-shell on the cresting but this has an almost Classical appearance. The motifs are all arranged symmetrically and the sofas have excellent proportions with which critics like Le Blanc

[1] 'with the greatest magnificence'.

and Cochin would have found it difficult to find fault. The same may be said of the console-table with its five-branch candelabra which stood at one end of the same room opposite the chimney-piece. There seem to have been two similar but smaller tables in the *Salle de Jeu*. Once again the serpentine lines of the table are treated with strict symmetry. The only straight line is that formed by the marble slab. On the stretcher is perched a decorative vase reminiscent of the late-Classical porphyry urns in Julienne's Collection which Frederick the Great bought for such an enormous sum of money in 1767.[1] If one compares Contant's console-table with that produced by Roumier for Versailles in 1737,[2] or that designed by Slodtz in 1739 for Compiègne,[3] one can see how great is the difference. Roumier's table is an example of the most extreme Rococo taste. That by Slodtz is slightly more controlled but still fairly wild in conception and free in its lineaments. Contant's, by contrast, is on a tight rein, well-managed and rhythmically organic.

We must admit, then, that even among the elements which were to provide the desired contrasts, a stylistic change had taken place. The contrasts were still wanted but they must have reference to the rest of the decoration in the room. They must therefore be symmetrical and they must provide an organic foil to the strictly architectural decoration of the room itself.

None of the furnishings from the Duchesse d'Orléans' rooms are known to survive but there luckily exists, by way of compensation, a set of furniture made in Paris for Count Bernstorff's house in Copenhagen in 1755–57. Of especial interest are the console-tables and pier-glasses (Plates 24 to 26) which are virtually indentical to those which were made for the Duchesse's rooms at the Palais Royal. The bronze candelabrum shown in Plate 202 was executed by F.-T. Germain and is dated 1756. It, too, is apparently a copy with only the smallest differences, of one that stood in the Duchesse's apartment. The chimney-piece (Plate 27) at Bernstorff's house is also by Germain and is a direct copy of the one he had made for the Palais Royal.[4]

Presumably many people in the 1750s and 1760s, artists and craftsmen as well as their clients, could see no very good reason why all interior decoration and all the furnishings of a room should suddenly be drawn with a set-square and compasses. They could appreciate that the walls might benefit from being treated architecturally but one can well imagine they had a healthy dislike for furniture designed in an architectural manner, especially seat-furniture—chairs, sofas, stools and daybeds—and occasional furniture that did not necessarily remain standing against the wall. When we today admire French chairs of the Rococo period, we do so not just because they are extremely comfortable but because their contours are as organic as the material from which they are made, and because there is a sympathy, as it were, between the curving lines of their structure and the human frame which relates them to human needs and sensibilities. It is therefore hardly surprising that, as far as furniture was concerned, modernism had to be carefully tempered and make its advances only gradually.

The fact that Blondel, who was quick to find fault with things, fails to draw attention to this problem when discussing the new arrangements at the Palais Royal, shows that it was not really disturbing anyone greatly at that stage—around 1760. With the exception of Lalive de Jully's extremely advanced Neo-Classical furniture, which was conceived in an architectural idiom,

[1] Illustrated in Paul Seidel, *Französische Kunstwerke des XVIII Jahrhunderts im Besitze seiner Majestät des deutschen Kaisers und Königs von Preussen*, Berlin, 1900, pp. 15 and 59.

[2] Verlet, *Mobilier Royal*, I, Pl. XXV.

[3] Ibid., Pl. 26.

[4] More information about the Bernstorff pieces will be found in the relevant Notes to the Illustrations (Plates 24–27).

there can have been very few other pieces couched in this vein at that date and almost certainly no seat-furniture at all. A few years later, however, the situation had changed markedly and Blondel felt impelled to snatch up his pen again and thus provide us with clear documentation of a new and widespread opposition to the new architectural style which now threatened to dominate the scene indoors. In the first volume of his *Cours d'Architecture*, which was published in 1771 but was probably written some years earlier, Blondel reminds his readers that it was not so long ago that the frivolous ornaments of the Rococo had crept all over the exteriors of their buildings, but now people are committing just as serious an error, he says, in having their furniture made in the severe style which is perfectly appropriate for the façade of a house but which experience has long shown us to be unsuitable for the movable items indoors. Their angular corners offend the eye and hinder movement in the room. This has mostly been done in the belief that these shapes were used in Ancient Greece but one forgets, he tells us, that the Greeks only used these forms in their temples and public buildings and that they are never, or at least very rarely, appropriate 'dans les choses d'agrément ou d'un usage journalier'.[1] He goes on to ask the reader whether anything could be more absurd than to decorate a lady's boudoir with the garlands of oak-leaves or laurel that one had used in Ancient Rome as ornament solely on the triumphal arches which were to commemorate the victories of great heroes![2] There is no doubt that all this was meant as a shot across the bows of the extremists.

5. OUTRIGHT MODERNISM

As we have seen, Blondel criticised the extremists among the advocates of the Neo-Classical taste for their lack of common sense and discrimination in the use of antique motifs. Unfortunately we do not know precisely when he actually put his views down on paper; we only know they were published in 1771. We cannot, therefore, be sure exactly whom or what he was criticising. All we can say is that the extreme form of this new style came into existence just as early as the more moderate version—that is to say, in the 1750s. It is also clear that it largely had its roots in the Rome of the 1740s and that its first important expression was embodied in the fashion known as 'le goût grec' which flourished at the beginning of the 1760s.

The originator of the style, or one of them at any rate, was Louis-Joseph Le Lorrain, a painter and amateur architect, whom we have already mentioned several times and who had designed some remarkable Classical set-pieces for the Chinea Festival in Rome (see page 32 and Plates 8 and 9). When back in Paris, he produced some no less modern designs for the Swedish minister Carl Gustav Tessin's country-house, Åkerö, not far from Stockholm (Plate 15).[3] These were sent off to Count Tessin at the end of May, 1754. Comte de Caylus, who had recommended Tessin to go to Le Lorrain instead of to the more famous Jean-Baptiste Oudry for the designs for his house, stated in a letter that he was extremely pleased with the drawings. Although they concerned the decoration of a dining-room, where it was still the tradition to use a Classical idiom, Le Lorrain's proposals were decidedly purer in style and less theatrical

[1] 'for works of decorative art or objects of daily use'.

[2] The French text and an English translation, is given here on p. 266.

[3] For a detailed discussion of Le Lorrain's works for Tessin, the reader is referred to the present writer's article 'Om salen paa Åkerö og dens kunstner Louis-Joseph Le Lorrain', *Konsthistorisk Tidskrift*, Stockholm, 1963, pp. 94–120.

than the schemes the Brunettis had been executing only a short while before, if their work at the Hôtel de Luynes is anything to go by (see pp. 37–8 and Plate 14).

Le Lorrain designed all kinds of furniture for Tessin at this time, and the drawings included designs for chairs, beds, tables and commodes, but they seem to have disappeared and, unlike the proposals for the mural decoration in the dining-room, were apparently not used by Tessin. We now only know that, as Tessin's nephew, Count Frederik Sparre wrote, all the drawings were in the best taste and in a style so entirely new that no one had seen the like of it before let alone seen it carried into practice ('d'un goût admirable et tout à fait nouveau, qui n'a pas même été vû, encore moins exécuté par personne').[1] It is not unreasonable at least to infer that this furniture which Le Lorrain designed in the Spring of 1754 cannot have been couched in the then reigning Rococo style and presumably not even in advanced versions of that style Contant d'Ivry used for the sofas and console-tables in the Palais Royal (see page 43 and Plates 301 and 302). In fact, Sparre's statement seems so categorical that one is strongly tempted to assume that this furniture was very like that which Le Lorrain designed for Lalive de Jully a couple of years later (Plates 85 to 89). To make this assumption is not so audacious as it would at first seem, especially if we recall Le Lorrain's former experience and training in Rome and the circles he moved in after his return home. His relationship with the Comte de Caylus is indeed symptomatic. Sparre tells us that Le Lorrain was 'extrêmement de ses amis'[2] and, from the context, it would seem that Caylus had himself used this phrase when discussing the architect.[3] Mariette states that Le Lorrain was a *protégé* of Caylus, which is perhaps nearer the mark.[4] Caylus was Le Lorrain's senior by some twenty years. He was very learned but this can by no means be said of Le Lorrain, if we may judge from the atrocious spelling in the handful of his letters which survive and the notes he has added on the drawings he sent Tessin! Yet any difficulties which may have arisen over the differences in age and intellectual capacity were apparently subjugated by their common interest in the Classical Age, and we know that they actually collaborated in several schemes concerning archaeological matters. Caylus had studied graphic techniques but he was not really able to draw all that well or to work out compositions on his own. On the other hand, he was conversant with the Classical texts—even if he preferred to read them in translation. He made excerpts from Hesiod and Virgil's descriptions of the shields carried by Hercules and Aenaeas, and then explained it all to Le Lorrain who proceeded to make 'an artist's impression' of the shields. These drawings he later engraved and Caylus then used them to illustrate papers he had written for the Academy's year-book. In the same way they made reconstructions of the paintings by Polygnotus which Pausanias had described. The results of these experiments are hardly inspiring aesthetically and they are only mentioned here to show how close was the link between the two men and that this may well have stimulated Le Lorrain to try and devise furniture in an Antique style. The reader is referred to the biographical notes at the end of the book for more details of the collaboration between these two very different characters.

It is also known that Le Lorrain was in contact with Lalive de Jully already as early as 1754 when he was designing furniture for Count Tessin, and at a point where Lalive himself had sided with the Neo-Classicists and was, moreover, well acquainted with Caylus. Until 1751, at any rate, Lalive does not seem to have had any objection to the Rococo style, judging from his

[1] State Archives, Stockholm, Tessin Papers, letter from Sparre to Tessin written in Paris and dated 3rd March 1754.

[2] 'very much one of his friends'.

[3] See Eriksen, op. cit., p. 104.

[4] *Abecedario*, vol. 3, p. 124.

coat-of-arms which appear on an engraving dedicated to him in that year (Plate 305). It cannot, however, have been long before he changed his views. The epitaph he erected in 1754 over the tomb of his young wife, who had died in 1752, was in the purest Neo-Classical taste (Plate 38). This monument in the church of Saint-Roch was executed by Falconet but people said, probably incorrectly, that Lalive himself had designed it. In view of Lalive's sympathies, it is not surprising that he, a man in his early thirties, should have admired Le Lorrain as an artist, and that he should therefore have commissioned from him a painting that was to hang in the very chapel for which the epitaph was being made. Whether the two had by that time already started to discuss furniture design is not certain, but it cannot have been very long before they were doing so since it must have taken some time for Le Lorrain to work out proposals, and then to make working drawings and models, for the famous pieces of furniture (Plates 85 to 89) which were probably delivered to Lalive in the Spring of 1758, or at any rate in 1759 when Greuze painted a portrait of Lalive showing some of it in the background (Plates 321 and 322). We cannot state categorically that the furniture Le Lorrain designed for Tessin was in much the same style as that he designed for Lalive a few years later, but it would not be surprising if this turns out to have been the case.

The style of Lalive's furniture is markedly different from that of contemporary Rococo furniture. The pieces are massive, monumental and entirely lacking in charm. They are of oak veneered with ebony and decorated with boldly modelled gilt bronze mounts of decidedly Classical form. The side rails of the table are treated as a kind of frieze and are decorated with a dominant band of Vitruvian scrolls. The accompanying *cartonnier* has a similar ornament round its waist, as it were, and a prominent Greek key-fret running along its frieze. Besides these bold features, the two pieces are hung with tightly bound garlands of oak and laurel leaves of the type that Blondel thought should be confined to triumphal arches. At one end of the table there is a bold mount in the form of the mask and hide of the Nemaean lion while the columnar legs end in heavy lion's paws. Blondel must surely have thought these features 'absurde', and only permissible if Hercules himself had ordered the furniture.

We know that Mariette and Lalive saw a certain similarity between this furniture and the venerable furniture of Boulle (see p. 40), but there can be no doubt that Lalive's contemporaries regarded his furniture as ultra-modern. Cochin is our witness that this was so. In his survey of the stylistic development from Rococo to Neo-Classicism, he poured scorn on such uncompromisingly modernistic taste in much the same way as Blondel did, and he actually takes Lalive's furniture as an example, adding that it had become famous largely because the Comte de Caylus had praised it in so fulsome a manner; indeed it was this suite of furniture which had been the cause of the rot.[1]

One might suppose that there had been some connection between Le Lorrain and his contemporary, Jean-François de Neufforge, who was not particularly talented but who, through his *Recueil élémentaire d'architecture* had showed himself to be as extreme an adherent of the Neo-Classical taste as Le Lorrain. However, so far it has only been possible to discover one link between them; they both collaborated in the production of J.-D. Le Roy's famous *Les Ruines des plus beaux monuments de la Grèce* which was published in 1758, sponsored by the Comte de Caylus. Both therefore belonged to Caylus' circle.

Neufforge is thought to have attended Blondel's renowned school of architecture but, if so,

[1] See the extract from his *Mémoires* on p. 269.

the master can hardly have regarded him subsequently as one of his favourite ex-pupils, for few artists can ever have produced Classical designs that were more 'absurde' and uncompromising than Neufforge's. Perhaps Blondel appreciated Neufforge's projected façades for buildings (Plate 37) but he is not likely to have approved of his proposals for interior decoration (Plates 28 and 29) in which he has quite uncritically adopted all the Classical architectural motifs, including the garlands Blondel thought only appropriate for the triumphal arch but which Neufforge hangs in festoons about the walls—even in ladies' boudoirs. Cochin, like Bondel, was highly critical of such misuse of Classical ornament. He particularly blames those architects like Neufforge, who had never been to Italy, but who wished to show they were in the fashion, for handling Classical motifs incorrectly and thereby distorting their proper character. As an example of the numerous howlers ('mille autres bevües') these people would perpetrate, he draws attention to the way they used outsize key-frets forming a dado-rail when a moulding would be correct. But, in Blondel's eyes, Neufforge's designs for furniture must have been even worse (Plates 368, 369, and 434 to 436), with their rectilinear forms and sharp corners, especially as these, too, are mostly bedecked with those infamous garlands. Neufforge claimed that, in these designs, he had tried to imitate the severe lineaments and simple, majestic forms favoured by the ancient Greek, and the best modern, architects ('la manière mâle, simple & majestueuse des anciens architectes grecs & des grands Architectes de nos jours').[1] The Academy, at any rate, decided that there was much to be said for Neufforge's compositions and at a meeting on 16th August 1757, when those present (they included Blondel) studied his engravings, it was recorded that they had won the assembly's approval and been found 'assé bien composées' ('extremely well composed') and, moreover, that it was felt the architect would now be able to undertake more ambitious projects. After having expressed satisfaction with certain sections, Neufforge was urged to continue his work in this vein.[2] On the 5th September, the members of the Academy again considered Neufforge's engravings and agreed that they still approved of the majority. The implication is that some did not come up to the required standard but we do not know which particular ones failed to pass the test, although one suspects Blondel's views affected the decision since he was also present at this meeting. All the same, the Academy recognised Neufforge's talent and agreed to extend official approbation to his *Recueil*[3]—an honour that Neufforge was quick to have recorded on the title-page.

Some of Neufforge's designs for interior-decoration were already on sale by June, 1756;[4] that is to say, more than a year before they were placed before the Academy. Moreover, many more drawings were ready and awaiting engraving.[5] The plates for Neufforge's *Recueil* appeared in series from 1757 until 1772, *but* the drawings for the earliest engravings, which were already couched in the monotonous and *outré* style for which he is now famed, must have been executed by the beginning of 1756 at the latest, and quite possibly in 1755 or even earlier. His style was therefore evolved at about the same time as Le Lorrain's furniture for Lalive was being made, and at a time when Le Lorrain and Neufforge were working together on Le Roy's monograph on the ancient Greek monuments which, as we saw, appeared in 1758.

It is doubtful whether there were any rooms in Paris decorated at this period in the extreme style favoured by Neufforge. It is unlikely that any one went beyond the more moderate but still

[1] *Mercure de France*, June 1756, pp. 176–7.
[2] *Procès-verbaux de l'Académie Royale d'Architecture*, ed. H. Lemonnier, vol. VI, Paris, 1920, pp. 303–4.
[3] Ibid., p. 305. [4] See *Mercure de France*, loc. cit. [5] See Neufforge's biography, p. 207.

entirely classicised style embodied in Jardin's work carried out in 1757 for Count Moltke in Copenhagen (Plate 30) or in that which the young Boullée executed in 1759–60 in the salon of the Hôtel de Tourolles (Plate 35). Unfortunately, we do not know what the interior of Moreau-Desproux's Hôtel de Chavannes (Plate 31) was like although, as Michel Gallet has shown, this was an ultra-modern building put up already in 1758–60.[1] In Lyons, on the other hand, there are several rooms of this date which, if it was not known that they were designed by a certain Toussaint Loyer, one would be tempted to ascribe to Neufforge. These rooms are in the Hôtel de Varey (Plates 32 to 34) which stands at the corner of the Rue Auguste Comte and the Place Bellecour and was erected between 1758 and 1760, for Jean Dervieu du Villars, Seigneur de Varey.[2] All the rooms are decorated in the Neo-Classical style although most have discreetly plain panelling and little ornament. But each apartment has a richly decorated *salon d'assemblé* and that on the main floor is exceptionally rich (Plate 34).

Toussaint Loyer had been a pupil of Soufflot's and subsequently collaborated with him. In 1762 he addressed the Academy at Lyons on the subject of the principles that governed the schemes of decoration he was wont to use indoors.[3] He naturally eschewed all 'formes arbitraires' and determinedly avoided 'contours forcés', by which he presumably means 'affected forms', which, he says, merely weary the eye of a person of true sensibility. He only made use, he told his audience, of the rich repertoire offered by Architecture. Whatever the purpose of the room in question, one must adhere to architectural principles and architectural ornament, he claimed. In this respect he offered no compromise; he says nothing about softening severe architectural features with the kind of late-Rococo ornament that was to provide 'contrasts' of the sort Blondel admired at the Palais Royal. The salon at the Hôtel de Varey (Plate 34) shows how consistently Loyer carried out his own theories. The various outsize Classical motifs, the 'money-moulding' on the dado-rail, and the stiff vertical garlands on the door-cases must all have been examples of extremist modernism in their time. He seems to have been carried away by his excitement over the new style and exaggerated its details out of sheer devotion! He also described another salon he had designed in Lyons. This was couched in the Doric order but was of the same size as the room at the Hôtel de Varey. It would appear to have had a very striking, possibly oppressive, frieze decorated with a continuous band of triglyfs and metopes, each of the latter being decorated with a garland. Instead of an ordinary moulding, this room had a key-fret border as a dado-rail.

6. THE 'GOÛT GREC'

When one comes across the terms 'dans le goût grec' or 'à la grecque' in eighteenth-century writings, it must not be assumed that it invariably means the same thing. It all depends on where it occurs, who is using the term, and in what context. It can certainly be said that 'le goût grec' was mostly used in reference to a particular fashion in furniture and other classes of decorative art that flourished in the early part of the 1760s but it must be stressed that the term was used

[1] Michel Gallet, 'Dessins de Pierre-Louis Moreau-Desproux pour des édifices parisiens', *Bulletin du Musée Carnavalet*, November 1961, pp. 6–15.

[2] See Loyer's biography, p. 204.

[3] The full French text is given here on pp. 257–60 (translation, pp. 260–3); there is a reference to the unpublished manuscript, now in the library of the Lyons Academy, in Marius Audin and Eugène Vial, *Dictionnaire des artistes et ouvriers d'art du Lyonnais*, vol. I, 1918, p. 519.

C. OEBEN'S WORKSHOP, about 1765-67

very loosely indeed. The fashion was sometimes an expression of the ultra-modernistic taste but in other cases it was merely a bi-product of it.

When Louis Petit de Bachaumont, the author of the famous *Mémoires secrets*, stated in 1750 that Servandoni was an 'excellent architecte pour les grandes choses dans le goust grec et du bel antique',[1] we can safely conclude that Bachaumont has in mind one of Servandoni's entirely Classicised projects like that for Saint-Sulpice (Plate 1)—that he was merely speaking of architecture in a Classical vein. That he calls it 'Greek' is presumably due to the fact that the ancient Greeks had long been considered more venerable than the Romans, and that Roman Classical architecture was anyway thought to be just a reflection of that of Greece since comparatively little was at that time known about the surviving architectural monuments of Greece itself. Cochin must have been using the term in the same loose sense when he said of the seventeenth-century portals of Milan Cathedral that they were 'très belles, d'architecture dans le goût grec'.[2]

In these two instances, 'le goût grec' is a term of praise meaning 'classical' in the widest sense and used in much the same way as we speak of 'a classic'. It was as a logical consequence of this use of the term that the ornaments or motifs which were seen on architecture so described should also be labelled as being in 'le goût grec'. This is why Jombert, Cochin's publisher, could publish in 1765 a series of seventeenth-century engravings of all kinds of ornamental details of a vaguely Classical derivation and call them all 'à la grecque' on the title-page.[3] There were hundreds of these details all drawn by Jean Cotelle who had died in 1676. He often gives several variations of forms that are by no means traditional. They are unmistakably Baroque in flavour but one can accept them as freely-interpreted seventeenth-century versions of Classical motifs. To call them 'à la grecque', as Jombert does, is stretching the term to its utmost!

Lalive de Jully's furniture, which was composed entirely of elements culled from Classical Antiquity, could therefore also be described, in the jargon of the day, as being 'dans le goût grec' —as, indeed, it was. Lalive himself actually stated in 1764 that his pieces of furniture had been 'composés dans le style antique, ou, pour me servir du mot dont on abuse si fort actuellement, dans le goût grec'.[4] When a desk in the Lalive-Le Lorrain style was offered for sale in 1767, the advertisement simply referred to the bronze mounts as being 'à la grecque'.[5] It will later be seen that the terms 'goût grec' and 'style antique' were synonymous at this time.

The return of Classicism to the French architectural field was brought about, as we have seen, by a circle of serious-minded artists of varying ages, some of whom were extremely talented. However, just as the Rococo style had finally run riot, so Classicism proved capable of being exaggerated—especially in the hands of less intelligent designers. It was the results of such exaggeration that came to be labelled 'goût grec'. Not only was the style resulting from this high-minded drive towards purification in French architecture and interior-decoration abused; its very name was also borrowed.

Both Lalive and Cochin admitted with regret that people were so taken with Lalive's pieces of furniture that they absolutely had to copy them. Lalive's furniture stood on its own in his

[1] 'a first-rate architect for grand buildings in the Grecian or Antique taste'. Quoted from Hautecoeur, *Histoire, première moitié*, p. 270.

[2] 'very beautiful, and Grecian in style'. C.-N. Cochin, *Voyage d'Italie*, I, Paris, 1758, p. 32.

[3] Part of his *Répertoire des Artistes*.

[4] 'designed in the Antique taste, or to use a term that is today much abused, in the *goût grec*—the Grecian taste'. *Catalogue historique du cabinet . . . de M. De Lalive*, Paris, 1764, p. 110.

[5] *Annonces, affiches et avis divers*, 24th August 1767, quoted from Henry Havard, *Dictionnaire d'ameublement*, II, column 1183.

Cabinet Flamand, a closet decorated in the Classical taste by the architect Barreau de Chefdeville. Lalive said that 'c'est même depuis l'exécution de ce Cabinet que s'est répandu ce goût d'ouvrages à la grecque que l'on emploie maintenant ridiculement à tout, à la vaisselle, aux bijoux, aux étoffes, aux coëffures, &c. & jusqu'aux boutiques, dont maintenant presque toutes les enseignes sont à la grecque'.[1] Cochin adds that it was from Lalive's furniture that we derived 'garlands like well-ropes, and clocks with rotating bands instead of dials and shaped like vessels that the Ancients had made to hold cordials; all very pleasing inventions in themselves but, now that they are imitated by all kinds of ignorant persons, we find Paris flooded with all sorts of stuff in the Greek manner.'[2] Evidently the fashion was widespread; otherwise there could not have been so many contemporary references to it. Let us cite again Baron de Grimm's well-known statement in his *Correspondance littéraire* under the date 1st May 1763, where he says that 'during the past few years we have favoured shapes and ornaments in the antique style. This represents a great advance in taste and the fashion now has so many advocates that everything in Paris today has to be "à la grecque" . . . our ladies wear their hair "à la grecque" and our *petits-maîtres* would be ashamed to parade about without a gold "à la grecque" snuff-box.'[3] Identical sentiments were expressed on the stage in Nicolas-Thomas Barthe's play entitled *L'Amateur*, the first night of which was on 3rd March 1764. From this little comedy, we learn that:

'La mode est pour le Grec; nos meubles, nos bijoux,
Etoffe, coëffure, équipage,
Tout est Grec, excepté nos âmes'.[4]

'Goût grec' and 'à la grecque' were thus just catch-phrases that could be turned to good account commercially by the vendors of anything from coffee[5] to hair-lotion,[6] as one can see from studying the announcements in the *L'Avantcoureur* and the *Annonces, Affiches et Avis divers* of 1763 and 1764. At the end of 1764 some small almanacks appeared reflecting the same craze. One was called *La Grécanicomanie, ou l'amusement des Belles, Étrennes à la Grecque*[7] or the *Almanach à la Grecque*.[8] The composer Papavoine also wrote a *Duo à la Grecque* at this time.[9] In the same year, Saint-Aubin wrote his *Avanture à la Grecque* (Plate 377) but there is nothing very Greek about this poem except for a rather earthy reference to Hebe, the goddess of eternal youth. However, it is all framed in an 'à la grecque' key-fret border and it is noteworthy that the author has written 'mode de 1764' at the bottom. The artist Carmontelle made fun of 'la fureur du goût grec' by drawing some carnival costumes composed of 'à la grecque' elements and

[1] 'It was really only after the creation of this room that the taste for works *à la grecque* started to spread—a taste that is now taken up everywhere in a quite ridiculous manner for silver-ware, jewelry, silks, hair-dresses, and so forth—even shop-signs are now couched in this style!' *Catalogue historique . . . de M. De Lalive, loc. cit.*

[2] See the extract from his *Mémoires*, pp. 269–70.

[3] The French text is given here on p. 264.

[4] 'The Greek taste is the rage; our furniture, our jewelry, our silk materials, our hair-styles, our carriages—it is only our souls that are not Greek!' Quoted from Maurice Badolle, *L'Abbé Jean-Jacques Barthélemy et l'hellenisme en France dans la seconde moitié du XVIIIe siècle*, Paris, 1926, p. 224.

[5] *L'Avantcoureur*, 5th September 1763.

[6] *L'Avantcoureur*, 2nd July 1764, and *Annonces, affiches et avis divers*, 1st August 1764.

[7] *Mercure de France*, December 1764, and December 1765; Bachaumont, *Mémoires secrets*, 30th November 1765.

[8] *L'Avantcoureur*, 24th December 1764.

[9] *Mercure de France*, November 1764.

Baron de Grimm tells us in 1763[1] that these were immediately copied. Perhaps the costumes illustrated in Plates 357 to 364 are some of them. Years later, in 1776, the colourman and Jack-of-all-trades, Jean-Félix Watin, felt it worth saving future scholars the trouble of trying to discover the origin of the term 'Dorure à la grecque' which form of gilding, he explained, had no links with 'l'époque du siège de Troies' but owed its name to the fact that it came into fashion 'durant le règne très court d'une mode qu'on appelloit, il y a 12 à 15 ans, à la grecque'.[2] Incidentally, the inventor of this type of gilding was advertising an odourless paint which he called 'Chipolins à la Grecque' already in 1757.[3]

Sensible people like Lalive, who after all only had a single room in his apartment decorated 'à la grecque', and men like Cochin, Baron de Grimm and Blondel considered 'le goût grecque' a quite ridiculous phenomenon which certainly had very little connection with Ancient Greece. 'But what does it matter?', asks Grimm, 'If one cannot avoid exaggeration, then it is better to exaggerate something good than something bad.'[4] Cochin agreed, adding rather cynically that it really was of no great consequence which taste was dominant, since there would never be more than a few good things being produced at any given moment! Lalive was more confident, maintaining that 'il en résultera cependant toujours que les Artistes qui emploieront & placeront raisonnablement la noblesse & la simplicité de l'antique dans les ouvrages qui l'exigent, mériteront toujours la préférence, de même que les Sculpteurs qui ont le plus approché de la pureté de l'antique ont toujours été préférés.'[5]

So we see that, when Grimm says in 1763 that everything in Paris is 'à la grecque', this should be taken with a grain of salt. It is probably true that the fashion reached its height at about that date, as Watin said and the other evidence confirms. On the other hand, we know that not everyone went in for the more extreme forms of this fashion, as Blondel in particular made clear, even though many people disapproved of the Rococo and wanted to see a regeneration of French art in the light of Reason and under the banner of Classicism. The datable examples that survive from this period—whole buildings, individual rooms, furniture, gold and silver boxes, porcelain, bronzes—confirm that the new style had many nuances, from the most sober and moderate expressions to the most extreme. We shall discuss these tendencies in greater detail in the next chapter but a clearer insight into the problem may be gained from a study of the Plates with their accompanying notes, which are arranged chronologically.

[1] *Correspondance littéraire*, 1st May 1763; the French text is given here on p. 264 (translation pp. 264–5).

[2] 'Grecian gilding' had nothing to do with 'the era of the siege of Troy'; the term came into fashion 'during the very short reign of a fashion which, some 12 or 15 years ago, was said to be *à la grecque*'. *L'Art du peintre, doreur, vernisseur*, 3rd ed., Paris, 1776, p. 163.

[3] *Mercure de France*, June 1757, pp. 169–71. See also *Procès-verbaux de l'Académie Royale d'Architecture*, ed. H. Lemonnier, VI, pp. 314–15.

[4] *Correspondance littéraire*, 1st May 1763; the French text is given here on p. 264 (translation pp. 264–5).

[5] 'It will always be the case that those artists who take up and use with discretion the nobility and simplicity of the Antique taste in the works that require it, will always be preferred, in the same way as sculptors who most closely approach the purity of the Classical style have always been preferred.' *Catalogue historique du cabinet . . . de M. De Lalive*, Paris, 1764, p. 110.

II

EVOLUTION

1. ARCHITECTURAL WORKS AND MURAL DECORATION

In order to understand the stylistic development which led to the adoption of Classicism in French furniture and other forms of applied art, we must study it in relation to the contemporary development in architecture and mural decoration. French Neo-Classical architecture was of course only one prong of a far-reaching European cultural development which deeply affected philosophy, literature and art in general. However, it was the architects who created the Neo-Classical framework within which the applied arts were in turn forced to evolve. For this reason one can say that the introduction of Neo-Classicism into the applied arts in France was really due to the influence of French architects, irrespective of whether they themselves actually provided the designs for such things or whether the various craftsmen and their draughtsmen merely yielded to the new architectural style because their customers were demanding they should do so. We must therefore take a closer look at what the progressive architects actually achieved.

In the work of French architects active during the two middle decades of the eighteenth century—both in their projected designs and those which they executed—one often sees unmistakable if widely differing signs that they were seeking to revise the current taste in architecture in a Classical spirit. The students at the French School in Rome during the 1740s were, as we noted before, determined Classicists, fired by a highly romantic conception of Classical Antiquity and much influenced by the strange genius of Piranesi. Among the next generation of students at the French School—those in Rome during the 1750s and 1760s—this tendency was developed further. It was given further impetus by the excitement which attended the archaeological discoveries that were then being made, and possibly also by the pronouncements of Winckelmann. Moreover, the Academy had introduced a more thorough course of study of the antique monuments in Rome itself. Those attending the Academy at this time included Clérisseau, Barreau de Chefdeville, Moreau-Desproux, De Wailly, Peyre, Victor Louis, Gondoin and Chalgrin.

Back in France, on the other hand, Classicism gained ground in quite a different manner and for very different reasons. Moreover, it did so hesitantly and at an uneven rate. In the field of church architecture, Servandoni's entirely classicised project for the façade of Saint-Sulpice

(Plate 1) could be selected already in the 1730s, in preference to Meissonnier's exuberant Rococo proposal, although it must be said that the interior came to display many ornamental features which are in no way Classical. The design for the front of Saint-Eustache (Plate 7), drawn a decade later by Contant d'Ivry who had never been to Italy, seems strangely old-fashioned when compared with Servandoni's composition. Its somewhat undigested and *mouvementé* Classicism seems to be the fruit of a perusal of old books on architecture. However, if one compares Contant's design with the façade of Mansart de Sagonne's contemporary Cathedral at Versailles, which owes much to Jesuit church-architecture in Rome, then it must be admitted that Contant's project is much more modern with its comparatively sober and lucid composition and the way the wall-faces are allowed to play their part as decorative elements in their own right.

A quite new era in the field of church design opened when Soufflot made the first of his proposals for Sainte-Geneviève, now the Panthéon (Plate 20), in 1757. With its plan in the form of a cross, its elegant colonnade, its temple-like portico and pediment, it established a new concept and, indeed, the doctrinaire theoretician of the Neo-Classical movement, Père Laugier, called Sainte-Geneviève 'a building which will ever remain unique in Europe and will mark the beginning of an epoque in the history of architecture where it will be regarded as the first and most beautiful monument built since the Renaissance.'[1] Not long after this, Contant d'Ivry, who was now over sixty years old and had meanwhile built the Cathedral at Arras (about 1755), made a further advance along the road to Neo-Classicism with his designs for the Madeleine in 1761. However, Laugier disapproved of these most strongly.[2]

A new stage was reached when the young architect, Barreau de Chefdeville, designed the astonishing pure Neo-Classical church of Saint-Nicolas at Nérac (Plate 59) in 1762,[3] shortly before he was to become responsible for the mural decorations in Lalive de Jully's *Cabinet Flamand* which we have already discussed. We can include under the heading 'church architecture' the very advanced monument to Lalive's wife which Falconet had executed for the church of Saint-Roch in 1754 (Plate 38), and Germain Doré's no less classicised altar-rail (Plate 343) which was provided about 1760 for the same church, as well as Pierre Deumier's very similar screen at Saint-Germain l'Auxerrois which was started in about 1762 (Plate 344). In the same way, we can take into account the monument for the King and Queen of Spain (Plates 42 and 43) which Michel-Ange Slodtz designed towards the end of the year 1759 for the memorial service at Notre-Dame, the 'goût antique' of which caused a great stir and won much praise. The decoration of the private chapel of the tax-farmer Marin de la Haye at his country house at Draveil, which was executed in scagliola by the stuccatore Louis Mansiaux after designs provided by the Comte de Caylus himself, must also have been of great interest.[4] The ornaments were ready by 12th December 1760 but we only know that they comprised some twelve-foot high Tuscan columns which were yellow but had white capitals and bases. Finally, mention should be made of Victor Louis' painted mural designs which Gaetano Brunetti executed about 1763–64 in the chapel of Sainte-Marguerite which stands in the middle of the quarter where many of the Parisian cabinet-makers had their premises (Plate 45). These particular decorations are almost

[1] Laugier, *Observations sur l'architecture*, Paris, 1765, p. 182.

[2] See Michael Petzet, *Soufflots Sainte-Geneviève und der französische Kirchenbau des 18. Jahrhunderts*, Berlin, 1961, p. 91.

[3] See F.-G. Pariset, 'Barreau de Chefdeville', *Bulletin de la Société de l'Histoire de l'Art Français*, 1963, pp. 77–99.

[4] Arch. Seine., 5 B^6 2738, fol. 12 verso—13.

as purely Neo-Classical as Barreau's church at Nérac and while Laugier might bemoan the fact that they were only skin-deep, he could not forbear to praise their 'simplicité' and their 'grande manière', conceding that they constituted some of the most beautiful pieces of architectural decoration in the city.[1]

In the field of secular building, we must distinguish between public works and those commissioned by private individuals. Among public buildings one quickly discovers new features that may be called Neo-Classical in Soufflot's early buildings at Lyons—on the façade of the Hôtel Dieu (built after 1741) and the theatre he built between 1754 and 1756 which has long since disappeared (Plate 17). The latter was of course built shortly after his return from the famous tour of Italy with the Marquis de Marigny, Cochin and the Abbé le Blanc. In these buildings, the flat surfaces of the walls are themselves dominant features while the accentuated Classical ornaments are used with economy and precision. The same characteristics are embodied in Servandoni's triumphal arch of about 1754 (Plate 16) and we find them occurring again in the more advanced works of some of the younger architects. In Paris and at royal palaces like Compiègne we find Ange-Jacques Gabriel, a contemporary of Contant d'Ivry's but also belonging to the great dynasty of royal architects, acting as custodian of the grand tradition of the seventeenth century—especially in great schemes like that of the École Militaire (started in 1751) and the Place Louis XV (now de la Concorde; started in 1759). But in buildings where grandeur was not at a premium, for instance at the little hunting-lodge named Le Butard (1750), he cultivated a simple elegance that seems to anticipate Ledoux's Neo-Classicism although the building hardly displays any features of Classical derivation.

In the great twin mansions (Plate 19) forming one side of the Place de la Concorde, Gabriel has evidently had in mind the general principles underlying Perrault's colonnade at the Louvre (1667–74), but Gabriel makes his buildings elegant rather than imposing, while their ornamented details are a good deal lighter than those on earlier works in the royal, Classical tradition. Ledoux was perfectly correct when he said of these twin buildings that 'c'est là, c'est dans ce fastueux édifice que brille le sentiment inépuisable de l'Architecture française.'[2] Originally there were also two guard-houses in the Square but these no longer survive (Plate 21). Their rugged shape seems to anticipate the city-gates (*barrières*) Ledoux was to build many years later. At the same time, Gabriel's gate-houses probably owe much to François Mansart's pavilions at the Château de Balleroy in Normandy which were built a century before, as Sir Anthony Blunt has shown.[3]

An ambitious although not all that revolutionary design from the year 1756 is that of Etienne-Louis Boullée for the new Royal Mint in Paris (Plate 18). This was composed when he was only twenty-eight and long before the open competition was held which resulted in J.-D. Antoine's scheme being chosen. Antoine's design seems in fact to owe something to Boullée's, and Boullée in turn may have been inspired by Gabriel's first projects for the Place Louis XV.[4] While considering public buildings, we should remember the various designs Gabriel produced for the new Opera-building at Versailles (1763 onwards; Plates 61 and 74). He seems to have been hesitant about producing a strictly Classical building although the great auditorium was in

1 Laugier, *Observations sur l'architecture*, Paris, 1765, p. 115; quoted in full in Note to Plate 45.

2 'It is there, in that magnificent building, that the inexhaustible spirit of French Architecture truly shines.' Quoted from Emil Kaufmann, 'Three Revolutionary Architects . . .', *Transactions of the American Philosophical Society*, N.S., 42, pt. 3 (1952), p. 479, note 70.

3 Private communication.

4 See Solange Granet, *La Place de la Concorde*, Paris, 1963, p. 31, fig. 6.

fact couched in this style when it was finally built in 1768. Perhaps at first he met opposition from the more conservative Louis XV and his court-officials who no doubt mostly still felt more at home with the Rococo taste.

In the kind of building carried out for private customers, including those like the Petit Trianon and the Pavillon de Louveciennes which may be classed as such, the development was naturally less restrained than in the public field. It is therefore regrettable that we know so little about it because so many of the private houses concerned have disappeared.

Probably the most severe loss has been the little pavilion which the tax-farmer Charles-François Gaillard de la Boissière had built on the heights of Montmartre and which was famed both for its garden, which Count Sparre (see page 45) said was 'en petit ce que les Thuileries sont en grand',[1] and for its luxuriously furnished rooms in which were two ceilings by Le Lorrain and a series of carved wall-panels painted with scenes described as being 'tant soit peu scandaleuses' ('not a little shocking').[2] The building was designed by Antoine-Mathieu Le Carpentier and was started in 1751. It was completed in 1754 when Blondel called it 'une des plus ingénieuses qui se voyent à Paris & aux environs'.[3] Count Sparre went out to see it in the summer of 1753, when it was not yet finished, and wrote to Carl Gustav Tessin in Stockholm that it 'est bâtie en forme de Temple d'Apollon'.[4] In his *Cours d'Architecture*, Blondel mentions it several times when discussing the concept 'petite maison' and then calls it 'une des plus jolies & des plus estimables productions en ce genre, qui se soit élévée de nos jours . . . dont la disposition, le goût & la beauté des détails, décelent l'intelligence des Architectes qui en ont donné les dessins'.[5] It is difficult to get anything like a correct idea of what this house was originally like because it was soon altered both inside and out, partly by Le Carpentier himself and partly by Couture (see the Note concerning Plate 75). Le Rouge's engravings of the house were probably executed after these changes had been made.[6] However, a plan of the house dated 30th June 1751 is still to be seen in the archives of the Montmartre police[7] and this makes it clear that the twelve free-standing Ionic columns on the garden front, which Le Rouge also shows, were part of the original conception. The metope-like reliefs from the façade, executed by Nicolas-Sébastien Adam *le cadet* and now to be seen at the Musée Carnavalet, must also have been part of the original design because one of them was exhibited at the *Salon* of 1753[8] and they were all described by the Abbé Le Blanc in his review of the Exhibition.[9] There was an oval *salon d'été* (summer drawing-room) facing the garden and screened by the Ionic columns, and one can be sure that both the plan of the house and its decoration was entirely in the Rococo taste, although the columns and a central octagonal hall, lit from above, which Le Rouge illustrates, reflect a new spirit. The Pavillon de la Boissière cannot, therefore, be regarded as a revolutionary piece of architecture but it does seem to have had features which did not become fashionable

[1] 'on a small scale what the Tuileries were on a large'. State Archives, Stockholm, Tessin Paters, letter from Sparre to Tessin dated 31st June 1753.

[2] *Le Plan*, 9th March 1844.

[3] 'One of the most ingenious [buildings] to be seen in Paris and its surroundings.'

[4] 'It is in the shape of a Temple of Apollo.' Letter from Sparre quoted above, p. 45, note 1.

[5] 'one of the prettiest and most highly estimable examples of this class of building [i.e. la petite maison] which has been erected in our day. The disposition, the taste and the beauty of the detailing reveal the ability of the architects responsible for their design.' J.-F. Blondel, *Cours d'Architecture*, vol. 2, Paris, 1771, pp. 251–2.

[6] In the supplement to his *Jardins Anglo-Chinois*, Paris, n.d. (late eighteenth century).

[7] Archives Nationales, Paris, Z² 2458.

[8] Catalogue No. 155.

[9] *Observations sur les ouvrages de MM. de l'Académie . . . exposés . . . en l'année 1753*, Paris, n.d., p. 43.

until 1765–70. Blondel must have been thinking of the classicised garden-front when he praised this building in 1754.[1] When he subsequently praised the house as a whole, he was presumably speaking of the house as altered and furnished with a peristyle on the North Front and with Louis Mansiaux's *Salon de stuc* which has already been mentioned and came into being in 1769 (see page 55; Plate 75).

It was in the very year the Boissière Pavillon was completed that Le Lorrain designed the mural decorations for Count Tessin's Dining-room at Åkerö in Sweden (Plate 15). As we have noted (page 37), it was usual although not obligatory to decorate dining-rooms and the other likewise more formal rooms of a house in a classicised style—even during the Rococo period. All the same, Le Lorrain's sketches embody several essentially Neo-Classical features and there is no doubt that we should regard his proposals as representing a complete renewal of the traditional formula. Quite apart from the relative simplicity of the whole scheme, the manner in which he arranges tight pendant swags round the door-cases and elsewhere is new. Swags of this sort are an unmistakable Neo-Classical motif which had certainly already been used at Soufflot's Hôtel Dieu in Lyons and was to be taken up with such eagerness and used with such frequency that Cochin came to feel that this was altogether too much of a good thing,[2] although he himself had used the motif two years before the Åkerö drawings were completed when composing the vignette for the title-page of Blondel's *Architecture Française* (Plate 303).

It was also in 1754 that Louis Mansiaux decorated the Dining-room at the Palais Royal, after designs by Contant d'Ivry. Of this we now only know that it had sixteen columns and four pilasters, all of scagliola (see page 38). The room was in fact roughly contemporary with Contant's Cathedral at Arras. Was it an essay in traditional Classicism or was it a forward-looking conception, *Neo*-Classical in spirit? We may ask the same question about the dining-room Mansiaux executed for Madame de Pompadour's Château de Crécy-Couvé after designs provided by Jean Lassurance. In his account-book, Mansiaux mentions having provided, amongst other things, sixteen pilasters of simulated Antin marble and four large discs of scagliola imitating *brêche violette*.[3] We also have very little information about the work Mansiaux carried out in the Spring of 1758 at the Marquis de Courteilles' château of the same name, after designs by Le Carpentier. We merely know that he decorated an antechamber there with twelve pilasters of white scagliola and that he provided an ornament described as 'une Entique' to go above each of the doorways, as well as a medallion with figures of the Three Graces.[4]

We have already mentioned the work Mansiaux executed in 1760 after some designs by the Comte de Caylus (see page 53). In 1760–61 he was working for the tax-farmer Hatte, partly at his house in Paris and partly at his country residence, Ermenonville, where Mansiaux decorated a gallery in 1761 with sixteen pilasters 'de lordre conposit' between which were portrait reliefs of Roman emperors and kings of France, each 'attaché par un flot de ruban'.[5] Until recently, when his account-book came to light, nothing was apparently known of the many important commissions Mansiaux carried out. All his work seems to have disappeared but it is clear that his contribution ought not to be ignored since many of his mural-decorations were definitely Classical in character.

[1] J.-F. Blondel, *Architecture Française*, vol. III, Paris, 1754, p. 90. [2] See p. 50.
[3] Arch. Seine, 5 B[6] 2738, fol. 6 (20th November 1756). [4] Ibid., fol. 7f.
[5] i.e. the pilasters were of the Composite order and the portrait reliefs were suspended by 'a knot of ribbon'. Ibid., fol. 15f.

Another private house which has probably also disappeared was that built 'near Dammartin' by N.-H. Jardin no later than 1754 for someone described as 'Mme. la Présidente des Vieux'[1] which was probably in an advanced Neo-Classical taste, since we know that Jardin had been among the French students in Rome in the 1740s and that he was an eager advocate of the Classical style, as his known early work proves. Moreover, he remained of this persuasion and was to introduce the Danes to Neo-Classicism after his arrival in their country in January 1755 (see page 43 and Plate 30).

Another building from this still very obscure phase of Neo-Classicism in the 1750s is Servandoni's own house which still stands on the Place Saint-Sulpice. It was built in 1754 and is therefore contemporary with his triumphal arch (Plate 16) and with Contant d'Ivry's work in the Duchesse d'Orléans' apartments at the Palais Royal (Plates 22 to 23) which we discussed in some detail when considering the more moderate forms of modernistic taste current in France at that stage (see page 42). Jardin must have seen both these exercises before he departed for Denmark where one of his first important tasks was to create a dining-room at Count Moltke's house in Copenhagen (Plate 30). Executed in 1757, this must now be the earliest surviving room decorated entirely in the Neo-Classical taste by a French architect. The Classical style of this room, which is in fact purer than that of his friend Le Lorrain's designs for Åkerö in Sweden, is perhaps not quite so remarkable when considered in the light of the accepted tradition that dining-rooms should be decorated in this general idiom. However, the colour-scheme in this room, confined to white and gold like Contant's decoration at the Palais Royal, must surely be regarded as a relatively new feature which, in conjunction with the cleanly Classical elements of the room, must have seemed very advanced when they were completed, especially when the eye fell on the buffets at each end which sport large decorative urns executed after one of Saly's classicised engravings of vases.

The hundreds of engravings Neufforge started to publish in the summer of 1756 must have fallen like manna from Heaven on the private individuals seeking to erect buildings of a progressive nature. As the years went by and the prints poured from the presses, the series became a kind of architect and decorator's compendium which those about to build could consult and from which they could pick and choose the elements that suited their purpose and their purse. His dry, monotonous style may well have had little appeal for the critical and spoilt Parisians but in the provinces and abroad it no doubt met with wide acceptance and we know, for instance, that important architects and designers like Robert Adam were conversant with Neufforge's work. Toussaint Loyer, at Lyons, may also have sought inspiration from Neufforge when composing the ornaments for the interiors of houses like his Hôtel de Varey (Plate 34) which should date from 1758–60—the very years in which the first three volumes of Neufforge's great work appeared and the engravings reproduced here on Plates 28, 29 and 37 were made public.

On Louis XV's instructions, the court architect, Gabriel, built a small shooting-box named Saint-Hubert for Madame de Pompadour in the Yvelines forest. It was completed in 1758

[1] See Jardin's biography (by Else Kai Sass) in *Weilbachs Kunstnerleksikon*, II, Copenhagen, 1949, p. 27. The house referred to may possibly be the Château de Dammartin-en-Goële (Seine-et-Marne) which, however, according to Hautecoeur, was built to the designs of Michel Tannevot under whom Jardin for a period served as clerk-of-works (see Hautecoeur, *Histoire*, *première moitié*, pp. 171–2). 'Mme la Présidente des Vieux' is presumably identical with Marie Therèse Du Cluzel who in 1735 was married to Philippe-Etienne Desvieux who eventually became *président de la première chambre des requestes du palais*. Conceivably it was the same lady who had her modern desk exhibited at the *Salon* of 1761 (see page 70).

but has long since disappeared. It would be quite incorrect to claim that this charming little building was a Neo-Classical structure, for a single surviving view[1] and the contemporary inventories seem to indicate that it was decorated in a traditional style and furnished in the richest manner.[2] However, two mementoes of Saint-Hubert survive which suggest that there were corners in the house possessed of a rather modern aspect. In the first place there were some large sconces in the form of spiralled hunting-horns, made by Philippe Caffieri, that may be identical with, or closely similar to, those now in the Hall at Floors Castle; they are completely naturalistic in character (Plate 203). Secondly, there is the small chimney-piece which may now be seen at the Petit Trianon (Plate 55) but was originally made for Madame de Pompadour's bedchamber at Saint-Hubert. This displays an advanced taste closely related to some of Neufforge's many designs for chimney-pieces. There is therefore reason to speculate whether the surroundings in which these sconces and chimney-piece stood did not possess a similar character, more advanced than the drawing and the inventories would now suggest.

At Saint-Hubert, there was also a circular *Salon de Compagnie* which *L'Avantcoureur* described on 28th January 1760 as having a certain Classical character. The walls were entirely faced with scagliola put up by the stuccatore Antonio Clerici in 1757–58,[3] after designs by Gabriel, and decorated with sculptural ornament by Michel-Ange Slodtz, Pigalle, Falconet and Coustou. The walls were divided into fields by eight pilasters of the Corinthian order. Four of these pilasters framed an arcade with windows and a door leading out to the garden. The ceiling was painted to resemble the sky. A feature which may well have seemed somewhat old-fashioned, however, was the large coved ceiling supported by brackets above each of the pilasters. Between the pilasters there were various hunting trophies executed in plasterwork. The structural elements were faced with yellow or with green scagliola, but the capitals, bases, and some garlands and animal heads were executed in white stucco. The walls were of scagliola resembling *brêche violette*. The total effect must have been kaleidoscopic, especially if one can imagine that the room also contained a large set of seat-furniture (with cabriole legs, be it noted) covered in crimson damask, window-curtains and portières of the same material, while most of the floor was covered by a large circular Savonnerie carpet which had multi-coloured motifs on a striking black ground and a border resembling a heavy ormolu egg-and-dart moulding.[4] One must, in addition, imagine this room furnished with various gilt-bronze items—including a bracket-clock and a pair of large andirons surmounted by the heads of a lion and a wolf—which were no doubt all Rococo in character. Yet all this marble, albeit an imitation, the Corinthian pilasters, and the circular plan of the room must have lent this salon an elegant and dignified appearance, even though it was only about eighteen feet in diameter, and it must have been markedly different from most other salons of the period. However, it may not have been unlike some of the dining-rooms executed in scagliola by Louis Mansiaux at about this time, which we have already mentioned.

A very modern little private house at this time was the Hôtel de Chavannes on the Boulevard du Temple (Plate 31), the surprisingly early date of which has been established by Michel

1 Reproduced in Hautecoeur, *Histoire, première moitié*, p. 566.

2 The furniture executed for Saint-Hubert is described in the Journal of the *Garde-meuble de la Couronne* in the Archives Nationales, and in particular in the volumes o[1] 3316, fol. 166ff., and o[1] 3317, fol. 138ff.

3 Clerici's estimate is dated 21st August 1757 (Arch. Nat., o[1] 1742).

4 Delivered on 24th May 1760; see Arch. Nat., o[1] 3317, fol. 101 *verso*.

Gallet.[1] It was started in August 1758 and completed in May 1760. It was designed by Pierre-Louis Moreaux-Desproux who had only returned in 1756 from the French Academy in Rome where he had carried out a number of excavations of a genuinely archaeological character together with the architect De Wailly. If the drawing we have of the house is at all faithful, the roof cannot have been visible from the ground, and the building must have looked uncompromisingly cuboidal. This effect was enhanced by the complete absence of the urns or statues which normally grace the parapets of such buildings, and by the manner in which the pilasters and cornice on the façades have been rendered in such shallow relief that they scarcely disturb the severely rectilinear silhouette. The trenchant Père Laugier had several criticisms to make about this building—he would have liked to see proper columns instead of pilasters, for instance—but he could still see that it possessed 'grandeur' in spite of its small size and that it boded well for the architect's future development.[2]

Surviving buildings from this early phase are naturally rare. Moreover, the Seven Years' War, which ended in 1763, must of course have put a damper on building in France but a certain amount of activity still took place, especially in the area round the old ramparts—the *Boulevard*. At any rate, a writer in *L'Avantcoureur* could state on the 28th July 1760 that 'les terreins voisins du Boulevard s'embélissent tous les jours de nouveaux édifices, que la beauté de la situation rend très-agréables'.[3] We know little about the buildings in this area. The architect L.-F. Trouard's own house in the Rue du Faubourg Poissonnière, which Michel Gallet's researches show must have been built in 1758, and which is still standing, certainly had some unmistakable if very discreet Neo-Classical features.[4] The Hôtel de Chavannes, which we have just discussed, was another of these new buildings on the outskirts of the city, as was a house which lay opposite it which *L'Avantcoureur* tells us was built for a certain 'M. de Persan'.[5] The architect's name is not mentioned but it was probably Jean-Louis Blève.[6] This house had a façade decorated 'd'un ordre de pilastres Ioniques' which 'soutient les combles qui sont terminés en baldaquin & relevés de grouppes',[7] as *L'Avantcoureur* tells us, and a projecting balcony on the first floor. We know nothing about the interior of these two houses but it would not be unreasonable to suggest that they were in a Neo-Classical idiom, perhaps less extreme than that reigning in the Hôtel de Varey at Lyons (Plate 34) and more like Boullée's still-surviving although damaged work at the Hôtel de Tourolles (Plate 35) which one can now safely date to just before 1760 and not to the mid-1760s as has previously been suggested.[8]

One feels obliged at this point to explain why it should be necessary to examine at such length and in such detail evidence concerning buildings which have long been forgotten or have long since disappeared, the Classical character of which it is by no means easy to establish! In fact our picture of French, and particularly of Parisian, architecture and mural decoration during the second half of the 1750s and early 1760s is so incomplete for the very reason that most

[1] Michel Gallet, 'Dessins de Pierre-Louis Moreau-Desproux pour des édifices parisiens', *Bulletin du Musée Carnavalet*, November 1961, pp. 6–15.

[2] Gallet, op. cit.

[3] 'The land out by the Ramparts is every day being improved by the erection of new buildings, the beauty and the position of which make them extremely pleasing.'

[4] Michel Gallet, 'Escaliers parisiens du XVIIIe siècle', *Médecine de France*, No. 191, April 1968, p. [14].

[5] *L'Avantcoureur*, 28th July 1760, p. 443.

[6] See Gallet, *Demeures*, p. 174.

[7] 'with pilasters of the Ionic order supporting the roof in the form of a baldachino, enhanced with groups of figures'.

[8] Boullée's salon in the Hôtel de Tourolles is described in *L'Avantcoureur*, 21st January 1760, pp. 13–14.

of it has been destroyed and few illustrations of it survive. This is especially the case with the houses built for private individuals which generally receive less attention from commentators than do public works. It is of course not our intention to imply that a large number of buildings of Neo-Classical character were erected in Paris during these years. Had this been so, the Marquis de Marigny would have had no need, in 1756, to urge the Académie d'Architecture to mount competitions in the field of interior decoration 'pour corriger le mauvais goust d'ornemens qui subsiste aujourd'hui'.[1] Nor would *l'Année Litteraire* in 1762 have made the comment, in connection with a highly favourable report on Ledoux's recently completed Café Militaire in the Rue Saint-Honoré,[2] that 'tout y est riche, grand, simple & respire la belle & saine Antiquité'[3] and that the decorative features were 'nobles & nouveaux' and 'font beaucoup de bruit',[4] adding rather peevishly that it was all so much better than what one saw elsewhere—'ornemens mesquins & frivoles, malheureusement trop analogues au caractère d'esprit de ce siècle'.[5] No, there can be little doubt that buildings and rooms decorated in the Neo-Classical taste were far from common in Paris or anywhere else at this stage and this is why it is important for us to know about the few that were constructed if we are to trace the early developments of the new style. Although Baron de Grimm was surely exaggerating when he wrote in May 1763 that 'tout est à Paris à la grecque',[6] he implies that there had not really been much of this kind of thing before when he tells us that 'depuis quelques années on a recherché les ornements et les formes antiques'.[7]

Mention must be made of a few other private buildings erected before the coming of peace in 1763 which may be said to mark the end of the earliest phase of Neo-Classicism in Paris. In 1760–61, the painter François Boucher designed the mural decoration of a room in a villa belonging to one Pierre de Monlong outside Lyons and this had curious plasterwork on a ceiling which was photographed shortly before it collapsed and was destroyed (Plate 44). The silk-mercer Duboc built a shop in the Rue Saint-Denis which had been designed for him by the sculptor Honoré Guibert. *L'Avantcoureur* of 7th September 1761 described this as being 'd'une architecture Grecque'. The gateway to the Hôtel de Gamaches in the Rue Saint-Lazare is only known to us from an anonymous drawing dated October 1762 but this clearly must be classed among the early essays in Neo-Classicism (Plate 49), as must the villa which was built in 1762 by Marie-Joseph Peyre, De Wailly's close friend at that time, for Madame Leprêtre de Neubourg on the southern outskirts of Paris but which, like almost all the other buildings we have been discussing, has long since disappeared (Plate 48). Peyre himself claimed that he had designed it under the influence of Palladio. We know nothing about the interior but it is reasonable to suppose that this was Neo-Classical in character. This was certainly true of the mural decoration in Lalive de Jully's *Cabinet Flamand* which Barreau de Chefdeville had designed and which provided the background for the famous suite of ebony furniture constructed in about 1756–57 (Plates 85 to 89). We dare not claim that this scheme was of such an early date; it more likely dates from the period when Lalive moved from the Rue Saint-Honoré to the Rue de Menars in 1762. There

[1] 'to correct the bad taste which prevails in the field of ornament today'. See p. 35.

[2] *Année Littéraire*, 1762, vol. VI, pp. 282–3. The wall-panelling from the Café Militaire has recently been acquired by the Musée Carnavalet; it is illustrated in Hautecoeur, *Histoire*, *seconde moitié*. p, 271.

[3] 'Everything there is opulent, spacious, simple and redolent of the beauty and sanity of the Antique taste.'

[4] 'noble and fresh' and 'were extremely impressive'.

[5] 'mean and frivolous ornaments, unfortunately all too representative of the spirit of our times!'

[6] 'everything in Paris is *à la grecque*.'

[7] 'For some years now the ornaments and forms of the Antique have been sought after.' An extract from his *Correspondance Littéraire*, is given here on p. 264 (translation pp. 264–5).

were numerous paintings on the walls of this *Cabinet Flamand* so one can assume the walls presented comparatively large areas unbroken by decorative features, perhaps with a low dado and a cornice, in the manner Barreau was to use shortly afterwards in the Intendant's lodgings at Bordeaux (Plates 56 to 58). Otherwise, we have no information about the decoration of Lalive's apartment except that there was a stove in the form of a Classical column in an adjacent room.[1] This may have been like the stove Dumont illustrates in an engraving of about 1764 (Plate 63).[2]

While the decoration of wall-surfaces at this period is under consideration, the new design for tapestries which Soufflot and Maurice Jacques evolved in 1758 should be mentioned. The basic conception was a simple one, consisting of a symmetrical disposition of suspended garlands and oval frames containing a scene by Boucher (Plate 36). This arrangement was very flexible; individual hangings could have the pattern so adjusted as to fill satisfactorily the space on a given wall. The entirely Neo-Classical picture-frames carved by Honoré Guibert must also have played their part in certain mural schemes of the time. Several frames of this type were to be seen at the *Salon* of 1761 and are discussed more fully on page 126 in reference to Plates 345 to 348.

Once peace had returned in 1763, much more attention was again paid to building which was taken up with renewed vigour all over France. The reduction in military expenditure, the increase in trade, and the resultant optimism in financial circles, all encouraged this development. Moreover, as Michel Gallet has pointed out, regulations were introduced in 1766 which gave greater financial security to architects, builders and craftsmen, as well as those advancing loans to make building possible.[3] It was of course in Paris that the effect of these developments was particularly felt. Luckily we know far more about the buildings of this next phase in French architectural history, as a result of Gallet's systematic researches in many hitherto little-known archives.[4]

The King set the pace by erecting an elegant little *pavillon* for Madame de Pompadour—the Petit Trianon (Plates 50 to 53)—which he had long promised her and for which Gabriel had already provided several designs that were now revised. Fiske Kimball published a design of 1762 for a building with tri-partite façades in which Gabriel had proposed that the Corinthian columns or pilasters on the four façades should have a wider interval between the central pair than between them and the outer ones, so that the whole took on an almost Baroque character[5]—an effect that was to be echoed in the different treatments bestowed on the architraves of the windows and in the rusticated basement. The final design was fundamentally different and had its columns and pilasters equally spaced, its windows alike, and the plain rustication replaced by chamfered rustication. The building came to have a more tranquil aspect after these changes had been made and took on a distinctly cuboidal character which was in keeping with the prevailing tendency. If we also take into account the oval windows with heavy garlands and bold Vitruvian scrolls on the side-walls of the courtyard (Plate 52), it would be difficult to imagine a more advanced or a better example of a Neo-Classical building at that date. The only complaint one might make is that the wall-surface itself has not been allowed to play a sufficiently dominant rôle, especially between each storey, so that the actual volume of the building might become

[1] *Catalogue historique du cabinet . . . de M. De Lalive*, Paris, 1764, p. 16.

[2] The reader is referred to the biographical notes on Lalive (p. 195) for details of furnishings of his rooms.

[3] Gallet, *Demeures*, p. 17.

[4] Ibid., *passim*.

[5] Kimball, *Creation*, figs. 270–1.

more apparent—as was subsequently done so successfully at Madame du Barry's Pavillon de Louveciennes (Plate 79).

Although the interior of the Petit Trianon was not decorated when the whole building had otherwise been completed in 1766 or 1767, it is likely that the designs for the panelling and other interior furnishings were executed beforehand although perhaps not at so early a date that Madame de Pompadour could herself have influenced their style before her death in 1764. Some old *boiseries* in a moderate Rococo idiom were used again in a few of the rooms but the principal rooms, notably the main salon (Plates 66 and 67), were panelled with carved (and subsequently painted) panels executed in the workshops of Honoré Guibert, probably after designs provided by Gabriel or at any rate under his supervision. Guibert had also been responsible for all the decorative work on the exterior—capitals, balustrades, etc.—and we have noted how in 1760–61 he had produced some carved frames of a marked Neo-Classical character, so he was well versed in the repertoire of Classical ornament by the time he came to work on the interior decoration of the Petit Trianon. In the salon, it should be noted, the floral ornaments are just as prominent as the Neo-Classical features, and they seem as luxuriant as those of the Rococo period. However, they are entirely naturalistic and botanically accurate so that each bloom can be identified, yet they are all disposed symmetrically within the framework formed by the architectural decoration of the room. These flowers are not added to provide a 'contraste'; they form an integral part of the classicised whole. The red-flecked marble chimney-piece was likewise Neo-Classical in style (Plate 55), as were the fire-dogs. The seat-furniture, on the other hand, was still of a Rococo form but its carved ornament was in the Neo-Classical taste. Further details of the furnishings in the salon may be found in the Note to Plate 66.

During the time the Petit Trianon was under construction, the architect Claude-Nicolas Ledoux started to alter and modernise the Duc d'Uzès' ancient house in the northern part of the Marais *quartier* (Plate 62). Ledoux was a great admirer of Gabriel's. The house has now been demolished but we can judge how it looked from studying the old photographs of it which give a better impression of its character than Ledoux's own drawings which, many years later, he subsequently altered and brought up-to-date before publishing them, thus misleading his readers and posterity into thinking that he had been an architect with revolutionary ideas already in the 1760s, which was not the case at all![1] In the Hôtel d'Uzès, Ledoux did what Gabriel had not done at the Petit Trianon, namely, he made the wall surfaces important features in their own right, just as Peyre had done at Madame Leprêtre de Neubourg's villa, by making windows without architraves or entablature. However, Ledoux could not avoid having a mansard-roof and this may of course have been a feature of the old house that the Duc wanted to retain. Some of the rich and finely carved white and gold panelling (*boiseries*) from the house has been preserved and one suite was recently installed in the Musée Carnavalet. The walls are divided into rectangular panels, as in the salon at the Petit Trianon, and the large chimney-glass has a rounded top. The individual motifs are rendered in shallower relief than those at the Petit Trianon and are somewhat more elaborate and detailed in their carving. The panels mostly extend to the full height of the wall without the usual break at dado-level. In one, a tree is depicted in which are suspended all kinds of trophies, and the whole composition is reflected symmetrically in the next panel. Having a panel running the full height of the wall and occupied by a single tree was a novel conception published by Neufforge in the first volume of his *Recueil*

[1] *De l'architecture considérée sous le rapport de l'art, des moeurs et de la législation*, Paris, 1804.

d'Architecture (1757) but Ledoux of course carries the idea through in a more logical manner and with greater bravura. The motif itself does not seem to have won wider favour, but this crisp and highly detailed style of ornament was to become a hallmark of the next phase of decorative art in France. Perhaps the most interesting aspect of the panelling at the Hôtel d'Uzès, however, is that provided by some designs which were never executed (Plates 64 and 65). These embody the earliest example so far discovered of the revival in France of the arabesque, which was later to become so popular. These designs are not by Ledoux, as was formerly supposed, but either by Pierre-Noël Rousset or Mathurin Cherpitel, as Michel Gallet has so kindly pointed out to the present writer, and must date from 1765 which probably places them slightly earlier than the designs for *boiseries* in the Petit Trianon.[1] There may, incidentally, be a connection between these rejected proposals and the panelling Ledoux designed for the Hôtel d'Hallwyl a year or so later.[2] As can be seen from the enlarged detail photographs reproduced in Plates 396 to 398, Rousset and Cherpitel also included in these compositions some proposals for furniture of advanced form. We do not know how the house was actually furnished, however.

Another group of designs which do not seem to have been carried out are those drawn in 1766 by Henri Piètre for interior decoration at the Hôtel de Mélusine (Plates 68 and 69) which Gallet was the first to publish.[3] They appear to be for painted rather than carved ornament. In style and general character, they bring to mind the floral ornament on the boxes in the Opera-house at Versailles which was built shortly after.

A more opulent use of painted floral decoration is to be seen in Victor Louis and Jean-Louis Prieur's designs of 1766 for mural treatment in the old palace at Warsaw (Plate 70). The whole place was suddenly to be modernised in accordance with the very latest Parisian fashions. It was an astonishing enterprise reminiscent of our own shipping of complete prefabricated hospitals or factories from Europe out to distant and so-called under-developed countries! Every single item had to be made in France by the most up-to-date artists and craftsmen, although in this case it was the King of Poland, Stanislas-Auguste Poniatowski, who footed the bill. Madame Geoffrin set herself up as artistic adviser for the whole undertaking, further details of which are given in Notes to the relevant Plates.[4] Casimir Czempinski, who held a position of trust with the King, reported on what purchases he had made in Paris during 1764 in connection with this scheme.[5] He claimed that 'dans tous les achats que je fais, je donne la préférence au bel antique, au Grec décidé'.[6] All this of course took place at what would seem to have been the very height of 'le goût grec' (see pp. 48–51). Czempinski even ordered a braid with a Classical pattern of some sort (*galon à la grecque*) in Lyons with which to trim the royal throne. But this was only a beginning. Victor Louis, who had presumably become known in fashionable and progressive circles in Paris because of his work at Sainte-Marguerite (see page 53), was put in charge of the whole enterprise and the entire scheme for modernising the Palace then became his responsibility.

[1] According to Gallet's latest researches there still seems to be some uncertainty about the authorship of the drawings, see Michel Gallet, 'Le Salon de l'Hôtel d'Uzès', *Bulletin du Musée Carnavalet*, 22e année, 1969, No. 2 (1971), pp. 1–22.

[2] Illustrated in *Connaissance des Arts*, October 1970, p. 94.

[3] Michel Gallet, 'Les dessins de l'architecte Henri Piètre pour la décoration du Palais Royal', *Bulletin du Musée Carnavalet*, June 1960, pp. 8–15.

[4] Plates 70–71, 190, 205–7, 213, 241, 402–23.

[5] Stanislas Lorentz, 'Victor Louis et Varsovie', in the catalogue to the exhibition of the same name, held in Paris and Bordeaux 1957–58, p. 9.

[6] 'In all the purchases I am making, I am giving preference to items couched in the Antique taste—to the Grecian style.'

For instance, he supervised the production of furniture, which Le Prieur actually designed, and bronzes which Philippe Caffieri both designed and executed. The designs were made during 1765 and 1766; the works of art themselves were produced between 1766 and 1768.

At the Hôtel d'Hallwyl (Plate 72) which was designed in about 1766 by Ledoux who was then in his late twenties, the architect further simplified the wall-treatment and thus made them seem stronger and more significant. He uses the classical French banded rustication as the dominating motif and this produces a particularly delightful effect on the front facing the narrow street. Gabriel had in fact used this same feature in a less consistent manner at Le Butard almost twenty years earlier. It is surprising that Ledoux provides his windows with bold architraves and entablatures which, however, accentuate the flatness of the walls by their marked relief. Ledoux has also done away with the 'shoulders' that were a traditional feature of French architraving; he may not have been the first to make this simplification but henceforth the feature was to become increasingly widespread. Gabriel was likewise to omit these ornaments on the Hôtel de Saint-Florentin in 1768.

Both at the Hôtel d'Uzès and at the Hôtel d'Hallwyl, then, we find Ledoux embarking on the course which was to prove him such a significantly creative artist. He began to seek a bold and striking form of simplicity through reducing shapes to their essentials and eschewing all unnecessary ornament. It is curious to note that Ledoux, who evolved and carried out his theories in the light of the Classical revival, had in fact never been to Italy. However, his sensitivity towards the Classical idiom had been nourished by study of illustrated works and engravings, and he was especially influenced by Palladio—the Renaissance architect whose buildings adhered most closely of all to the Classical ideal. Ledoux had attended the elementary courses at Blondel's private academy but his real guiding star—apart from Palladio—was Gabriel, and he must also have felt himself in definite sympathy with Piranesi, many years his senior but a man whose work was by this time known all over Europe. Piranesi's sense of gigantic and overpowering scale must have fascinated the young Ledoux.

Ledoux's predilection for an accentuated banded rustication seems to have found an echo in Soufflot when he was designing a 'Palladian' villa for the Marquis de Marigny in 1768. This stood in the Faubourg du Roule but was demolished in the last century. Sir William Chambers sketched the house (Plate 76) and his drawing is so convincing that it presumably shows it as finally built with boldly banded rustication. The better known drawing[1] of the house probably comes from Soufflot's drawing-office and is more likely to represent a projected design. The walls are here treated differently and the roof is hidden by a parapet. As far as the interior was concerned, Marigny merely wanted it to be as tasteful as the exterior[2]—which implies that it was couched in the Neo-Classical style.

It would seem that very few buildings, and hardly any schemes of interior decoration, can have been built in Paris during the 1760s which were not in the Neo-Classical style. It is understandable that, during the 1750s and early 1760s, people wavered between the moderate and the extreme versions of the style but, by 1765 or so, this problem had been resolved and taste had apparently settled down on the path which future development was to follow. Contemporary examples seem to bear this out (Plate 56 et seq.) but we must always remember that our knowledge is now bound to be incomplete. For example, it is a great pity that we do not know what the new mural decoration was like at the Palais Bourbon after its modernisation in the 1760s. Since

[1] Reproduced in Hautecoeur, *Histoire, seconde moitié*, p. 199.

[2] See p. 36.

D. Carlin and Poirier, 1771

the work was directed by Le Carpentier, perhaps after designs presented by Barreau de Chefdeville who was dead by this time, it is probable that the rooms were dressed in an uncompromising form of Neo-Classicism, possibly similar to but richer than the rooms Barreau executed at Bordeaux (Plates 56 to 58). We know, at any rate, that the furniture in the Palais Bourbon was thoroughly Neo-Classical and that the chairs had straight legs (Plates 127 to 130 and 453 to 461).

We know what the rooms in the Duc de Choiseul's partly re-decorated house in the Rue de Richelieu looked like from the views Van Blarenberghe painted in miniature on the famous snuff-box[1] (Plates 81, 463 and 464), but we do not know precisely when this work was carried out. One is tempted to think that some of the rooms were done over in the early 1760s because the panelling seems to be in a heavy style similar to that used at the Hôtel de Varey at Lyons, but the work might quite well have been done rather later although probably not as late as 1770 which is the date of the box itself according to the hall-marks on the parts made of gold.

The young Duc de Chartres was also an early advocate of the new style, or so it would seem, and a man of his position and wealth is not likely to have been particularly modest when it came to doing up a house. Unfortunately all we know about the work he had done at this early stage is that, in August 1767, an anonymous *marchand-tapissier* (upholsterer) provided 173 feet of five inch wide gilded border carved 'à lagreque' and a chimney-glass eight feet high and four feet broad with a frame likewise 'sculpté à lagreque'.[2] This was all for use in a *Salon de Compagnie* in a *Maison de Plaisance* which has not so far been identified. The fact that the border was so wide indicates that, whatever its purpose, it must have been intended for use in a room of some size. In fact, the height of the room must have been at least eleven feet high, judging from the dimensions of the chimney-glass which, incidentally, was of very simple proportions (2:1). Even from these meagre details we can conclude that the Duc de Chartres' salon, which does not seem to have survived, must have been a room of ultra-modern appearance in its day. Indeed, why should it have been any less advanced in style than that of the designs (Plates 68 and 69) Henri Piètre made the year before for Madame de Montesson, the close friend of the Duc's father?

We are told by the Duc de Croy, in his *Mémoires*, that he made a tour of Paris in the company of Soufflot in 1767, and he noted that a great deal of building was going on all over the city. One could see, he said, that there was a lot of money about and that the return of peace had been very welcome.[3] From these very years must date such striking buildings as Boullée's Hôtel Alexandre in the Rue de la Ville-l'Evêque (about 1766) and the Hôtel de Monville which he built round the corner in the Rue d'Anjou-Saint-Honoré at about the same time (from 1764 onwards?). The former still survives. The latter was built for a colleague of the same M. de Tourolles who had been Boullée's very first client (see page 59). Until we can date these buildings more exactly, we shall not be able to decide whether it was Boullée who influenced Ledoux, who was eight years his junior, or vice versa. The buildings they erected at the period have many features in common—windows without architraves or pediments, metope-like reliefs over doors and windows, and sturdy-looking walls. However, it is of course equally possible that these features were 'in the air' as part of the repertoire familiar to all the young

1 All the views are reproduced in F. J. B. Watson, *The Choiseul Box*, 1963.

2 The *marchand-tapissier*'s ledger is preserved in the Archives de la Seine (5 B[6] 1952). For the same room the anonymous dealer delivered a *sultane* and eight arm-chairs which all, like the border and the frame, were described as being 'sculpté à lagrecque'.

3 Quoted from Gallet, *Demeures*, p. 17.

architects of the day. For instance, one finds them introduced with varying degrees of definition in Louis-Marie Colignon's Hôtel de la Vaupalière in the Avenue Matignon, which was probably started in 1768 and still survives, and in Moreau-Desproux's beautiful Maison Carré de Beaudouin (Plate 78) which was built in 1770 and may still be seen in the Rue de Menilmontant where it commands a fine view of Paris. Even such bourgeois buildings as Pierre Desmaison's house in the Rue Dauphine (1769) and his corner-house on the Carrefour Buci (1771) display these features.[1] There is much we still need to know about the stylistic evolution at this stage.

Fate has been cruel to Ledoux's two virtually contemporary and stylistically related masterpieces, the Hôtel Guimard (Plate 77) and Madame du Barry's Pavillon de Louveciennes (Plates 79 and 80 and Colour Plate B) both designed in 1770. The former has been demolished and the latter has been badly mauled—most of the interior decoration having been removed. Moreover, Ledoux's drawings of the buildings, executed long afterwards, cannot really be trusted since he was apt to furnish his buildings with impossibly advanced features retrospectively. However, we can once again fall back on the sketches made by Sir William Chambers (Plates 77 and 79) who can have had no axe to grind in this respect, and he shows that both houses reflect Ledoux's efforts to accentuate the cuboidal structure of a building and to handle the Classical motifs with such precision and economy that the large, reticent wall-surfaces against which they are seen are rendered doubly significant and effective. Features that must have been new in France were the apsoidal entrance halls behind the semi-circular porticoes and the coffered vaults of the 'Roman' ceilings. These two features cause one to speculate where Ledoux actually went on his two-year study-tour about which nothing is known. Could he have gone to England? The plan elevations of the Pavillon de Louveciennes is much more regular than that of the Hôtel Guimard which, on the other hand, had a coffered dome which must have seemed astonishing to Parisians in 1770, although it might not have seemed strange to English eyes. The Pavillon de Louveciennes was lavishly furnished with quite exceptional elegance; it had bronzes by Gouthière and straight-legged chairs from the workshops of Delanois (Plates 172 and 173).

As far as the period under consideration in this book is concerned, a late example of a private house with an interior decorated in an advanced style was the Hôtel Grimod de la Reynière where the main salon, fitted up in the early 1770s, was provided with panels painted by Charles-Louis Clérisseau. The house lay in the Rue Boissu d'Anglas near the Place de la Concorde and was built towards the end of the 1760s by the clever but not especially talented Neo-Classical architect, Nicolas Barré. It is a little difficult to date the panels (the problem is discussed in the Note to Plate 82) but the panels themselves are very probably those now at the Victoria and Albert Museum which come from Ashburnham Place, near Battle in Sussex. Edward Croft-Murray has drawn attention[2] to the considerable resemblance there is between these mural decorations and those James 'Athenian' Stuart had designed in 1759 for the Painted Room at Spencer House in London,[3] but points out how the compositions differ both in handling and in quality. He also shows that both derive, not from a Classical prototype, but from Italian Cinquecento interpretations of Classical Roman wall-painting, notably Raphael and Giovanni da Udine's 'grotesques' or arabesques in the Loggie at the Vatican which were of course widely famed through engravings and had been much copied and imitated by artists and architects throughout the seventeenth and eighteenth centuries. Jacques-Androuet Ducerceau had been

[1] Ibid., figs. 19 and 21. [2] *Apollo*, November 1963, p. 377. [3] Reproduced ibid., p. 379.

greatly inspired by them already in the late sixteenth century, and no doubt renewed emphasis was given to them as a fruitful source of inspiration by Jombert's re-publication of a suite of engravings of them in 1765. For example, Pierre Rousset's proposals for the decoration of the Duc d'Uzès' new house in Paris in that same year may well owe much to these engravings, as we have suggested in the Note to Plate 64.

We do not know whether Clérisseau was responsible for the furnishing of the salon at the Hôtel Grimod. It is unlikely that he designed the candelabra (Plate 483). The pattern of the carpet (Plate 83) is reminiscent of that of the parquet floor at the Hôtel de Choiseul (Plate 81), which is of slightly earlier date, or with that shown in Freudeberg's engraving of 1774 reproduced in Plate 487. Incidentally, a floor of marquetry with a similar design of Neo-Classical type, judging from the description,[1] was delivered to the Prince de Condé's Palais Bourbon by the cabinet-maker J.-F. Leleu in 1775. It was presumably designed by the architect Bellisard (see page 92).

2. VENEERED FURNITURE

Before we embark on a study of the actual furniture made during the first phase of Neo-Classicism in France, it is worth reminding the reader of two features that were peculiar to French, and especially Parisian, furniture-making in the eighteenth century. In the first place, there was a marked difference between the craft of the *menuisiers* and that of the *ébénistes.* A *menuisier* was a joiner who assembled fairly substantial pieces of wood to produce a piece of furniture. He did not concern himself with veneering—the process of facing a piece of timber with a thin layer of another kind of wood. The *menuisier* mostly produced seat-furniture, beds, console-tables and fire-screens. He only made cupboards, tables or chests-of-drawers if they were of the kind that were not veneered. An *ébéniste* or cabinet-maker, on the other hand, produced furniture the carcass of which was faced with a thin veneer of a wood that was more expensive than that of the underlying structure. In the seventeenth century, the veneer has often been of ebony—*ébène*—and the French name for such craftsmen derived from this fact. The *ébénistes* chiefly produced tables, commodes, desks and cabinets of various kinds (and the English name for such a craftsman is of course a 'cabinet-maker'); only very rarely did they produce chairs and the like which were the *menuisiers*' preserve. In England, a firm like that of Chippendale might have both joiners and cabinet-makers on its strength but the Parisian firms normally specialised in one trade or the other. Certain French cabinet-makers, and a few joiners, who were commercially minded and could lay their hands on sufficient capital, set up shops from which to sell their wares. They would then engage other master-craftsmen to work for them. On the other hand, many master-craftsmen produced furniture for dealers, in which case the *menuisiers* usually supplied *marchands-tapissiers*—the upholsterers—while the *ébénistes* worked for *marchands-merciers* who were essentially dealers in luxury furnishings. The majority of Parisian *menuisiers* worked in the Bonne-Nouvelle *quartier* near Montmartre. The *ébénistes* tended to establish themselves in the Faubourg Saint-Antoine although a few, who were especially skilled or had become successful dealers on their own, sometimes established themselves more centrally—unless of course they had been honoured with a royal appointment whereupon

[1] Archives Condé, Château de Chantilly, A.C.7, Leleu's bill for works executed 1775–76, fol. 1–2 *verso*.

they might enjoy the privileges of having their workshops in the Louvre or at the Arsenal or in the Gobelins.

The second fact that needs to be borne in mind is that, at this period, both *menuisiers* and *ébénistes* were as a rule supposed to sign their wares with a stamped mark. They did not place these marks on their work for reasons of pride, except very occasionally; they did so because it was a strictly applied rule of their guild that their wares be distinguished in this way. With their own name they signified that the furniture had been made according to the high traditions of their craft, as far as quality of materials and standards of craftsmanship were concerned. Failure to satisfy the guild's officers that these standards had been maintained could result in confiscation of the piece of furniture and the levying of a fine. We must, at any rate, not regard these stamped marks as in any way corresponding to the signature of an artist on, say, a painting. Indeed, the presence of a stamp does not indicate that the craftsman concerned had designed a particular piece of furniture; it only means that he made it or caused it to be made in his workshops. Moreover, on certain groups of veneered furniture, the stamped name is not even that of the man who applied the veneers but merely of the master in whose workshops the bare carcass was produced. All this means that, while we should never ignore the evidence provided by the stamped marks, we must view it with a certain amount of reservation.

In the field of Parisian veneered furniture, there occurred a change during the second half of the 1750s which to some extent echoes the change we noted when studying the contemporary architecture and interior decoration. The earliest known example of the more extreme form of modernism is in fact Lalive de Jully's famous suite of furniture (Plates 85 to 89 and Colour Plate A) which was designed about 1756 by Louis-Joseph Le Lorrain whom we have mentioned frequently already. It was made about 1757 by an as yet unidentified *ébéniste* while the mounts were produced by the bronze-founder Philippe Caffieri who may indeed have undertaken the whole commission and farmed out the work to be done in wood.

With the exception of the chair, which has apparently disappeared but which can partially be seen in Greuze's portrait of Lalive (Plate 322), this furniture is not the result of an attempt to reproduce Classical Roman or Greek furniture, the general appearance of which was after all known to people like Le Lorrain and Lalive from archaeological publications and, as Roubo—a cabinet-maker who wrote a treatise on furniture-making[1] at this period—pointed out, from Poussin's paintings. This furniture in fact represents a definite attempt to create something new, partly by using the materials—ebony and massive gilt-bronze mounts—which were so much a feature of the old and respected Boulle furniture, and partly by using Classical motifs applied according to Classical principles. Whether one considers the resulting furniture a success or not, there can be no question about the furore it caused. There is a table of this kind in a private collection in England; this may perhaps be one of the set which Le Lorrain wanted to have with him in Russia, where he had hoped to set himself up as a designer of furniture. He had the furniture shipped from Rouen to St. Petersburg in 1758, in the middle of the Seven Years' War, but the ship was unfortunately captured in the Channel by an English privateer. A similar table is to be seen in Drouais' portrait of Prince Dmitri Galitzin (Plate 352) which was painted in 1762, and another in the style is visible in Van Loo's portrait of the Duc de Choiseul (Plate 367). In 1767, moreover, there appeared in Paris an advertisement for 'un très-beau Bureau dans le

[1] André-Jacques Roubo, *L'Art du menuisier*, Paris, 1768–75, p. 605.

goût de celui de M. de Lalive'[1] which suggests that everyone interested would know what Lalive's furniture looked like and that it was of a type that was not at all common.

If one felt Lalive's pieces looked somewhat too awkward and lugubrious but still wanted some new furniture in a style that was not Rococo and which harmonised with the current enthusiasm for anything Greek or Roman, one could of course ask some designer to work out fresh proposals and one could choose some timber for the veneer other than Lalive's sombre ebony; one might even make a few suggestions oneself as to how the furniture should look! Something of the sort seems, anyway, to have taken place, for several pieces of furniture were exhibited at the *Salon* in 1761 which were not only not Rococo in taste but were clearly in a classicising style. Exactly when new forms of this sort began to be developed after Lalive's initial experiments, we do not know. On the other hand, would anyone deny, without other evidence, that the cupboard we can discern in the background of Roslin's portrait of a Russian lady (Plate 308), painted in Paris in 1757, must be a figment of the artist's imagination? Like Lalive's pieces, it is made of materials reminiscent of Boulle furniture, but the simplified ornament, the oval centre, and the garland hanging from a rosette preclude a date for this piece in the early eighteenth century, let alone one in the seventeenth century, and the clock above the cupboard has every appearance of belonging to the second half of the eighteenth century. Roslin was normally meticulously accurate in the rendering of his sitters' clothes so he may equally well have depicted this cupboard quite faithfully. In the following year, Boucher painted his famous portrait of Madame de Pompadour which shows her sitting in front of a looking-glass in which is reflected a bookcase (Plate 309) of straightforward shape, decorated with a Vitruvian scroll and surmounted by a lyre-shaped clock, all of which seem to be of advanced form, judged by the standards of 1758 as we know them. But here again we have absolutely no proof that this piece of furniture actually existed.[2] We only reach more secure ground when we get to the furniture shown at the *Salon* of 1761, which we have just mentioned. These were unfortunately not mentioned in the catalogue so we have no official record of their appearance and Diderot presumably considered it beneath his dignity to mention such 'arts mineurs' in his reviews. Luckily, three other correspondents mentioned them in their articles on the show, one of which appeared in the *Mercure de France*[3] and the other two in *L'Avantcoureur*.[4] Even these references, however, are tangential and not all that enlightening. We do not even know how many pieces were exhibited.

The article in the *Mercure* is the least helpful. The writer merely mentions a 'secrétaire' belonging to 'Madame la Présidente Desvieux'[5] and adds that it is a relief to find a few ladies have now at last forsworn the 'goût petit & mesquin des colifichets, qui, sous prétexte de galanterie, s'étoit introduit dans toutes les décorations intérieures des maisons'.[6] Forthright this may be, but it fails to tell us who the designer or the cabinet-maker may have been. The writer in *L'Avantcoureur* was luckily rather more helpful and mentions the architect Charles De Wailly and the *ébéniste* Pierre Garnier. In the first report in this journal, the writer discussed De Wailly's work on show at the *Salon* and mentions 'une table de lapis, dont le pieds est en bois des

[1] 'a very beautiful desk in the style of that made for Monsieur de Lalive'.

[2] Considering the fact that Boucher in 1760–61 designed the Neo-Classical ceiling for Pierre de Monlong's villa (Plate 44), it would not come as a surprise if the book-case in fact turns out to be Boucher's invention as well.

[3] October 1751, pp. 227–8.

[4] 21st September, p. 605, and 5th October, p. 636, both 1761.

[5] See p. 57, note 1.

[6] 'the tiresome and unworthy taste for trashy gewgaws which, under the pretext of being rather dashingly libertine, is now to be seen in the interior decoration of every house'.

Indes, orné de bronzes dorés. Cette table supporte un vase de granite, dans le goût antique; l'un & l'autre sont d'une belle forme, les ornemens en sont riches & d'un goût très-noble & très-éloigné d'avoir l'air colifichet, qui a regné trop long-temps dans nos meubles.'[1] In the second article he again mentions De Wailly who had apparently sent in a fresh piece of furniture of which 'les connoisseurs trouvent que le meuble qui y a été apporté ces jours derniers, est traité dans le meilleur goût de Boule. Ce meuble a été exécuté par le sieur GARNIER, ébéniste, rue neuve des petits-Champs, vis-à-vis le trésor royal, & la manière dont l'exécution en est traitée, la précision avec laquelle il est fait, le rendent très-supérieur à celui qui a été exposé précédemment & dont nous avons déja parlé.'[2] So one could see at the *Salon* of 1761 a writing-desk made for Madame Desvieux, a table with veneered legs, bronze mounts, and a slab of lapis-lazuli, and a third piece of furniture of unspecified type. At least the last-named was made by Garnier and designed by De Wailly who had also designed the table with the lapis-lazuli slab. We still do not know who was responsible for Madame Desvieux's writing-desk and it is not even certain this was of a Classical form. All we can say is that it was not in the pure Rococo style and it may only have been couched in a moderately advanced taste like that of Louis XV's famous *Bureau du Roi* which will shortly be discussed (Plates 90 to 93). The two pieces drawn by De Wailly, however, must surely have been in something like 'le goût antique'.

None of these pieces has so far come to light but fortunately there exists a series of engravings by De Wailly (Plates 324 to 330), which he executed himself, and which help us form an idea of his tables. The series was advertised in *L'Avantcoureur* on the 30th June 1760, at which point the tables must have been under construction or at least on the drawing-board, if they were to have been ready for the *Salon* in 1761. The series is entitled 'P[re]. Suite de Vases' and is indeed a series of illustrations of urns or vases, some in a Classical style, others in a kind of Chinese taste presumably owing something to Sir William Chambers who was a close friend of De Wailly's, and a few which may have been inspired by Le Geay who had been De Wailly's teacher.[3] However, on the title-page all these vases are reproduced in miniature and shown standing on two tables of highly unusual aspect (Plates 329 and 330) which might well be described as being 'dans le meilleur goût de Boule' or 'dans le goût antique (see pp. 38–40).[4] We cannot tell what these tables were for. Were they writing-desks or dressing-tables? Were these the tables that were exhibited at the *Salon* of 1761? If not, we can at least assume that those which were looked something like those shown in these illustrations. Like Lalive's furniture, these are not attempts to imitate Greek or Roman originals. They derive more from the so-called 'Mazarin desks' which date from the last third of the seventeenth century and are often seen veneered with boulle-work in tortoiseshell, brass and ebony. Like De Wailly's tables, these 'Mazarin desks' also consist of a superstructure containing drawers, a knee-hole conformation with flanking drawers, and two groups of four legs each joined by crossing stretchers. De Wailly takes this

[1] 'A table of lapis lazuli, with legs of an Eastern wood, decorated with gilt bronze mounts. This table supports a huge granite urn in the Antique taste. Both items are of a beautiful shape; their ornaments are rich and in a noble style quite different from that of the fussy gewgaws that have far too long pervaded the field of furniture design.'

[2] 'Connoisseurs maintain that this piece of furniture, which has recently been brought in, is couched in the best Boulle manner. It has been made by M. Garnier, the cabinet-maker, who lives in the Rue Neuve des Petits-Champs, opposite the Treasury. The manner of its execution and the precise workmanship are very much better than was the case with the piece shown previously, of which I have already spoken.'

[3] See Note to Plates 324–30.

[4] 'in the best Boulle manner' or 'in the Antique taste'.

formula and gives it a lighter appearance by altering the proportions of the superstructure and making the legs more slender—so slender that one feels the intention must have been to produce them in metal. Almost all the ornamental details, however, are of Classical inspiration. The figures of sirens, forming the top section of the legs and supporting the table are noteworthy (Plate 329). An unsigned drawing in the Musée des Arts Décoratifs, which is clearly also by De Wailly, shows a similar table to that here reproduced in Plate 330. It differs in having a garland draped over rosettes, instead of an espagnolette head, by the knee-hole.[1]

We do not know whether De Wailly's two designs were ever executed but it is not too fanciful to believe that his style can be recognised in the so-called 'Tilsit table', with its accompanying filing-cabinet and standish, in the Wallace Collection (Plates 101 to 103) which Francis Watson has convincingly suggested must date from the mid-1760s.[2]

As far as Garnier is concerned, we now know that he was in touch at an early stage with a designer who worked in a progressive and pure Neo-Classical style. We do not know if this association continued but the indications are that it did not. None of the furniture we know which bears Garnier's stamped mark is so well conceived as those De Wailly designed. Indeed, Garnier's furniture is always somewhat dilettante and individual in its conception. Perhaps it was his collaboration with De Wailly that inspired him to design furniture in a modernistic style on his own. As we shall show (see page 127), we know that Garnier was able to design furniture himself; in fact, he is one of the few *ébénistes* of whom we can say this for certain. For this reason, we have little hesitation in dating to the early 1760s a type of table of which some exist bearing Garnier's mark (Plate 99). We see tables of roughly the same type in certain drawings by Carmontelle (Plates 349 and 350) which are thought to date from these same years. Garnier's tables of this type possess rather heavy proportions and some characteristic bronze mounts in the form of triglyphs, drawn in a somewhat unorthodox manner, and drawer-handles of a strange rectangular kind with a representation of a burning oil-lamp in the centre. There are two commodes by Garnier with these same handles in the Swedish royal collection at Gripsholm Castle (Plate 97). These are even more massive in their proportions than Lalive's filing-cabinet (Plate 89) but, unlike the latter, the pilasters on the front have an even number of flutes, a solecism which no academically trained draughtsman would have perpetrated. The corner-cupboard bearing Garnier's mark shown in Plate 98 does not embody this rather individual style for it and its pair are direct copies of some corner-cupboards by Oeben (Plate 96) which we shall presently discuss.

As we have said, we know nothing about Madame Desvieux's 'secrétaire' which was shown at the 1761 *Salon*. When unqualified, 'secrétaire' was a word used to describe several types of writing-desk in the mid-eighteenth century, and among them were the so-called 'secrétaires à abattant' which resemble a cupboard or upright cabinet and have a hinged, falling writing-leaf forming the central panel. If Garnier did not make La Presidente's desk, then perhaps Oeben did. We know that when he died in January 1763 he left a large stock of completed and partly finished furniture among which were five 'secrétaires' that fairly certainly looked like the one shown in Plate 94. This is in fact a 'secrétaire à abattant'. The measurements and the descriptions given in the inventory drawn up after Oeben's death[3] more or less agree with those of this group

[1] Reproduced as an anonymous drawing in Léon Deshairs, *Dessins originaux des maîtres décorateurs . . .*, Paris, n.d., Pl. XXXIX, fig. 87.

[2] Watson, *Wallace Collection Furniture*, F. 330. [3] See the reference given in Oeben's biography, pp. 207–9.

of 'secrétaires'; pilasters are specifically mentioned. Like Garnier's furniture, these pieces also show signs of having been designed by someone without an academic training. The triglyphs, for instance, have been made as tall as the interlacing pattern on the frieze, and no architect would have arranged matters in this way. If Oeben, in his efforts to decorate his furniture in an architectural taste that would appeal to his more progressive customers, found he did not have a model or sketch of a triglyph lying around from the days when he worked for Charles Boulle, a descendant of the famous André-Charles Boulle, he probably composed one out of his head.

In an advertisement announcing the sale of Oeben's stock in 1763, it is specifically stated that all the furniture was 'd'un goût nouveau' ('in an entirely new style'),[1] but, while Oeben's secretaires are certainly rectangular and somewhat weighty in appearance, they are very different in style from that of Lalive's furniture (Plates 85 to 89). In the first place, Oeben's pieces are veneered with woods of a lighter tone assembled for the most part in elaborate and delicate patterns, while the gilt bronze mounts never dominate or look heavy even though they are of Classical inspiration.

Like 'secrétaires à abattant', commodes and corner-cupboards are designed to stand against a wall and this circumstance probably explains why the new style seems first to have made its appearance in these classes of furniture. The commode shown in Plate 95, with its frieze inlaid with a Classical fret and its ram's-head mounts at the corners, can also be dated to the first two or three years of the 1760s since furniture answering to this description is mentioned in the inventory (see page 314). It is probable that the several commodes 'à la grecque'[2] which were in Madame de Pompadour's collection on her death in 1764 were like this, for she had been Oeben's principal customer. It should here be pointed out that, although Oeben died in 1763, we still cannot be absolutely sure about the date of furniture bearing his stamped mark for the simple reason that his widow kept the firm going after his death (see page 76). Otherwise we could say quite definitely that any piece bearing his mark and displaying Classical features must have been made in the few years before his death. Unfortunately this is not the case and we have therefore had to fall back on documentary evidence.

Many commodes by Oeben have survived and it will be seen that he usually thrusts the centre-section forward, softens the edges of the break, and rounds off the corners. The 'softened break-front' effect is also to be seen on the corner-cupboard shown in Plate 96. Furniture like this would have earned Blondel's approval for it did not offend the eye by having sharp corners (see page 44). However, it will be noted that it is only *in plan* that this type of furniture has curves; the lines of the front projection are strictly vertical. This formula was to gain great favour and remained popular for a long while, as we shall see.

Oeben himself was clearly fond of commodes like that shown in Plate 95 because he had one, valued at 1,500 livres, standing in his bedchamber. Like the one in the photograph, it had 'testes de bellier' and was veneered with marquetry in 'cinq panneaux remplis de fleurs nauncées'.[3] Floral marquetry was of course not a new kind of decoration; it had been practised all over Europe in the last decades of the seventeenth century. Although it then went out of fashion

[1] Salverte, *Les ébénistes*, p. 239, note 5.

[2] See the references to Jean Cordey's edition of Madame de Pompadour's inventory of chattels in Oeben's biography, pp. 207–9.

[3] 'goats' heads' and 'five panels decorated with flowers'. J.-J. Guiffrey, 'Inventaire de Jean-François Oeben', *NAAF*, 1899, p. 328.

in France and England, it remained in favour in Holland and Germany. It seems that it was reintroduced as a form of decoration on fashionable Parisian furniture shortly before 1750 by immigrant German cabinet-makers like Latz and Oeben. However, the late Oeben pieces in question are embellished with marquetry of a delicacy hitherto unsurpassed since the seventeenth century. The naturalism is such that each flower can be clearly identified. This pictorial marquetry, moreover, is no longer confined to small panels at this stage, but spreads ever more widely across the surface of the furniture. We do not know whether Oeben designed his own floral patterns or followed engraved designs but his compositions remind one of J. B. Le Monnier's well-known engravings of flowers and he had in his bedchamber four over-doors 'représentant des corbeilles de fleurs' ('representing baskets of flowers').[1]

The most magnificent, the most opulent piece of French furniture made in the early 1760s was the *Bureau du Roi*, the famous roll-top desk made for Louis XV (Plates 90 to 93). It was started in 1760 by Oeben and completed by Jean-Henri Riesener who had married Oeben's widow in 1767 and taken over the firm's workshops at the Arsenal. The stages in the creation of this piece are discussed in the Notes to the Plates concerned.

The general shape of this writing-desk would have seemed fairly conventional at the time: the legs are of cabriole form and most of the carcass is *bombé*. Yet the curves are played down and seem tame compared with those on furniture of the High Rococo. In some places there are even quite straight lines. The back face is flat and more flat surfaces are also revealed when the cylinder top is swung back. Only a few true Rococo details are to be seen, notably the superb candle-branches held by female figures. Most of the bronze mounts are naturalistic in form and symbolise the virtues a monarch is supposed to possess—a symbolism, be it noted, entirely derived from Classical sources. There is, for instance, the club of Hercules and the hide of the Nemaean lion, the cornucopia of Plenty, wreaths of laurel, and *fasces*. Moreover, some of the ornaments are derived from Classical architecture. The gallery round the top of the superstructure, for example, consists of a run of pierced ovals linked to form a formal, chain-like border. The interior, hidden by the cylinder-top when closed, is likewise decorated with regular patterns, rectangular mounts, and some small figures which were described in 1763 as being 'quatre Termes, figures dans le goût grec'.[2]

When compared with Lalive's furniture or that designed by De Wailly, or even the 'secrétaires à abattant' Oeben was making at about this same time (Plate 94), the *Bureau du Roi* seems hardly Neo-Classical at all. But this is quite an unreal assessment for we are then taking no account of the setting for which this impressive piece of furniture was designed and its position in the room. Lalive's writing-table must have stood with one end against the wall. This is shown by the fact that the filing-cabinet (Plate 89) on that end has an undecorated back. Furthermore, the table is unusually high and the writing-chair must have been correspondingly tall, so that these pieces must really have been more in the nature of show-pieces in his 'museum' than practical items of furniture. Oeben's upright 'secrétaires' must also have been designed to stand against the wall, as we have said. Not so the *Bureau du Roi*, which was Louis XV's personal writing-desk. It had to serve a utilitarian purpose and, what is more, it was to stand out in the middle of the floor, so one could walk all round it. Last but not least, it had to blend with the existing furnishings—Verbercht's Rococo *boiseries* which can just be seen in the background of the photograph reproduced in Plate 92, Gaudreaux's famous commode of 1738 which is so often

[1] Ibid., p. 316. [2] 'four terminal figures in the Grecian taste'.

given as an example of pure Rococo,[1] Joubert's coin-cabinets of 1755[2] and his red lacquer *bureau plat*[3] which had only been completed the year before the *Bureau du Roi* was begun. If we consider the writing-desk against this background, and remember that Louis XV was fairly conservative in his tastes, then the *Bureau du Roi* must surely be regarded as a notable stride forward and as a very important example of the moderate form of Neo-Classicism we discussed in Chapter I—far more advanced in taste, incidentally, than the console-tables in the Duchesse d'Orléans' rooms at the Palais Royal (Plate 302). That this piece of furniture could have been designed in 1760 for such an important position—at the very heart of the French monarchic systems, as it were—shows how profound had been the change that took place during the second half of the 1750s.

Stylistic experimentation is the key-note of the 1760s in the field of furniture in France; that is at any rate the impression we get from the relatively few datable examples from that decade which survive. The two main trends were pointed out by Lalive's furniture (Plates 85 to 89) and Oeben's *Bureau du Roi* (Plates 90 to 93). These respectively represented the uncompromisingly modernistic approach to the problem in which artists sought to evolve a new style within a rigid architectural tradition and, on the other hand, a moderate form of modernism which rejected the ornamental repertoire of the Rococo yet continued to regard furniture as a creation made for the convenience and comfort of human beings, and which should therefore be composed of forms which at least appear to be as organic as those of the human being—forms which had come to be held in esteem during the Rococo phase.

The tendency to adopt the Classical idiom with moderation was surprisingly tenacious, especially among those classes of small furniture which could be moved about the room at will and which anyway were not intended to stand against the wall. These would normally be veneered on all four sides. It is curious that this inclination applied equally to elaborately-decorated and expensive pieces of furniture and to quite cheap, plain ones. Although even quite substantial pieces, which can scarcely be moved by a single person, will often reflect this convention, it was one which principally affected small pieces of free-standing furniture intended for personal and informal use.

The earliest known piece of furniture of the class decorated with bronze mounts of an entirely Classical character is the table shown in the portrait of Madame de Pompadour which was started shortly before her death in 1764 (Plate 372). Although small in size and intended for a very different purpose, it will be seen that this table is closely related in style to the *Bureau du Roi* (Plate 90). The small lady's writing-table shown in Plate 111 mounted with Sèvres porcelain plaques is the earliest known example of a type which seems to have been turned out almost by series-production methods from 1766 onwards, apparently on the initiative of one man—the *marchand-mercier* Poirier, who did not run a cabinet-making establishment but had an emporium in the fashionable shopping area where he dealt in luxury furnishing goods of all kinds.[4] He knew very well the tastes of the fashion-conscious rich who were quite prepared to buy some decorative object for more than many an ordinary person might earn in a whole year. The table concerned is in fact of the type that was known at the time as a *bonheur-du-jour*. The curves are confined entirely to the legs and body while the superstructure and the plaques are

[1] Watson, *Wallace Collection Furniture*, F. 86. [2] Verlet, *Mobilier Royal*, vol. II, Pl. I.
[3] F. J. B. Watson, 'The Craftsmanship of the Ancien Régime', *Apollo*, September 1969, Pl. III.
[4] See Poirier's biography (p. 215).

rectilinear. The mounts follow the curving outlines on the lower sections but, at the top, are rigidly straight; there are small garlands at the corners. The handles are in the form of rosettes with wreath-like grips and the gallery is pierced with a pattern similar to that on the King's desk. It seems that furniture mounted with Sèvres plaques was a speciality of Poirier's and, in about 1770, he launched two new models—a jewel-coffer on a stand and a small round table (Plates 121 and 122). The coffer has a stand which is not unlike the table but the coffer itself is the dominant feature and is possessed of a simple outline. The mounts are in the same style. The top of the table is a simple circle which is echoed by the circular shelf forming a stretcher between the three 'columns' which form the top section of the legs. The legs below this shelf are of cabriole form, however.

An endless variety of occasional table was produced at this time and the general theme was usually much the same. An exceptional type is Lacroix's *bonheur-du-jour* (Plate 137) in which all the lines are curved yet, notably in the oval top, there is a clarity of form which is underlined by the repetitious nature of the marquetry. Topino's *bonheur-du-jour* (Plate 138) is a less expensive and somewhat less sophisticated version of Poirier's type; it has an inlaid Vitruvian scroll instead of Sèvres plaques, vases of flowers depicted on the doors and Chinese *objets d'art* on the small drawer in the superstructure. Even as late as 1773, the Comtesse de Provence preferred this kind of 'softened' Classicism and the small cylinder-top desk she obtained from Riesener (Plate 141) still has curved forms reminiscent of the *Bureau du Roi*.

As we have noted, the severe, architectural form was principally taken up for stationary furniture which stood against the wall but, even in furniture designed for such positions, many people clearly had a preference for a softer outline and there are not a few examples of curvilinear forms in this class as well. But while such pieces may have some serpentine contours, the inlaid patterns or the bronze mounts (and sometimes all such decoration) invariably embody classicising allusions. An imposing example is the massive desk at Waddesdon Manor which must date from some time in the 1760s (Plates 104 and 105). The outside is japanned with gold figures on a black ground in a close imitation of true Japanese lacquer, but the interior is veneered with various woods of a light hue. The whole interior is bombé like the outside; even the front, which falls to form a writing surface, is bombé. At first glance it is a conventional piece of Rococo furniture of rather large proportions. However, it is from the Classical vocabulary of ornament that the forms of its bronze mounts are taken. Its unusual shape, size and high quality indicate that this must be a specially-commissioned piece of furniture and thus it was very expensive. No cabinet-maker, even in Paris, would have dared to embark on such a *tour de force* on his own account and at his own risk. Stamped marks on the piece show that Dubois and Goyer were involved in its construction but the design for it must presumably have been provided by a third person—someone, it would seem, who thought more in sculptural than architectural terms. Although in general form it may be said to be related to the *Bureau du Roi*, closer inspection shows that there are important differences in style which make it inconceivable that both were designed by the same person. In fact the desk at Waddesdon is not so well conceived as the royal piece; there are numerous incongruities in its decoration which are no less blameworthy than the eccentricities of work in the Rococo style which contemporary critics were then so busy deriding. For example, the eagle at the top is larger than the two allegorical figures of women below, while the leaves of the foliage on the front are larger than the women's faces! The lyre which may be seen when the desk is open is also larger than the ladies, and the lion's mask on the apron is smaller than the four lion's paws which support the desk. It looks as if the paws come from a fully-grown beast but the head comes from a mere cub. Academically-trained artists or architects like Slodtz or De Wailly, or whoever it may have been that designed the King's desk, would never have made mistakes of such an obvious kind. Tradition has it that this desk was made for Catherine the Great of Russia and this may well be correct. The strange character and unusually large size certainly point to its having been made for someone with eccentric and rather vulgar tastes nurtured far from the polished sophistication of Paris.

Another somewhat bizarre type which likewise seems to spring from a dilettante approach to design in a Classical idiom is represented by the secretaire stamped 'L. Boudin' shown in Plate 109 which has a double Greek fret ornament that follows the serpentine top-edge of the falling writing-leaf. Such off-hand treatment of Classical motifs is very frequent in the less expensive classes of Parisian furniture of the 1760s and must be the result of breathless and not particularly inspired attempts by minor cabinet-makers to keep up with the fashion. In this instance, the carcass could easily have been that of a standard model produced ten or even twenty years before which the cabinet-maker then brought up-to-date by veneering it and furnishing it with bronzes of a modern character.

Oeben's wife kept his workshops going after his death in January 1763, as we have already noted. At that point, by far the most important piece of furniture in stock was of course the great desk being made for the King (Plates 90 to 93) which was not in fact completed until seven years later. This does not, however, mean that all the firm's journeymen were engaged exclusively on this single task; other furniture was certainly made concurrently. There were twelve work-benches in the Oeben workshops in 1763 which probably means that he had twelve journeymen—all skilled craftsmen but not able to set up as masters in their own right, either because they had not served long enough as journeymen or because they could not find sufficient capital to go independent. Each journeyman probably also had an apprentice. Apart from these men working in the cabinet-making branch, there must have been craftsmen in the smithy which we know was nearby. Riesener, who was a talented mechanic, presumably worked most of the time in this section. Maybe only a few outstanding craftsmen like Riesener were allowed to work on such an important commission as the King's desk, and this would explain why it took so long to complete. The other craftsmen presumably then produced the less spectacular furniture which secured the firm a turn-over and maintained the working capital.

The monumental secretaire shown in Plate 113 was probably made in the Oeben workshops during these years after the master's death when the King's desk was still under construction. It bears Oeben's stamp which his widow continued to use after his death in 1763 and until she married Riesener, the most capable and talented of her first husband's journeymen, in 1767. We cannot say, however, precisely when between 1763 and 1767 it was made. The general shape had been evolved by the early 1760s when Oeben had several desks of this type in production (Plate 94). A simplified version is illustrated by Diderot in 1765 (Plate 390) and, in 1766, proposals for a richly decorated adaptation were laid before the King of Poland, drawn by Victor Louis or his collaborator Louis Prieur (Plate 410). It is therefore not too bold to suggest that this desk was made between about 1765 and 1767. This piece is much more elaborate than Oeben's prototypes, both in the pictorial marquetry and the bronze mounts. The flat pilasters of Oeben's original conception have been replaced by sculpted terms of Classical mien whose faces are patinated while the bust and hair are gilded. The 'à la grecque' border has also been made more prominent than it would have been in Oeben's lifetime. Indeed, the whole thing seems a little more chunky and angular than Oeben himself would have made it and this leads one to speculate whether Leleu, who was still a journeyman working for the firm at this time, may not have had a hand in designing the furniture made there during this phase; for, after he had established his own workshops in 1764, Leleu produced furniture displaying many of the same characteristics. Of course, the similarities may simply be due to the fact that Leleu became familiar with this style before he left Oeben's firm, and the style itself may have been thought up by someone else. On balance, however, this seems the less likely possibility.

We cannot unfortunately identify positively any furniture produced by J. F. Oeben's brother, Simon Oeben, in the 1760s although he had become a master already in 1764 and had a workshop at the Gobelins. However, a man who is believed to have worked for him as a journeyman, Georg Haupt, executed in 1767 a large writing-desk (Plate 114) which was apparently made for the Duc de Choiseul's country residence, Chanteloup. In general conception it is a simplified version of veneered pieces like Garnier's (Plate 99) and Dubois' (Plate 100) which must belong to the early 1760s but it is not veneered; it is made of solid mahogany which, as far as we can judge from securely dated pieces and surviving documents, was a wood not commonly used in France at this stage. Haupt's desk is in fact somewhat roughly made, notably in the detail work. The same may be said of another desk and filing-cabinet (Plate 115), which also came from Chanteloup. Strikingly rectilinear, it may also perhaps be ascribed to Haupt. Its form may have been inspired by the typical English pedestal desk but its decoration is reminiscent of that on J. F. Oeben's fall-front 'secrétaires' while some of the mounts are almost identical to types used in Oeben's workshops.

Also from the year 1767 comes the long-case clock shown in Plate 116. It is of a kind often found bearing the mark of the *ébéniste* Lieutaud. The mounts on this particular example are signed by Philippe Caffieri who, it will be remembered, had collaborated in the production of Lalive's famous suite of furniture about ten years before and who was in fact one of the most progressive artists working in the French capital at this time. We shall have more to say about his contribution to the Classical revival in France in the chapter on bronzes (see page 93). Lieutaud is known to have turned out numerous clock-cases in a pure Rococo style but we have no evidence as to whether he was responsible for the design of this particular ultra-modern clock or not. On the whole, this seems improbable, however. It is more likely that Caffieri, a highly capable artist, designed them himself, although we can provide no proof of this. None of the mounts described in the inventory of his stock made in 1771 seem to correspond to those on this clock and one can only say that the bronzes are in his style.

Thanks to the researches of Pierre Verlet, it is now possible to identify several magnificent pieces of furniture, of an essentially static character, which were delivered for use by the French royal household in the years around 1770. The two commodes (Plates 119 and 120) provided in 1769 respectively for Madame Victoire and Madame Louise, daughters of Louis XV, are serpentine in plan but the front elevation is composed of vertical lines except in the legs which are of the cabriole type. The form is thus not truly *bombé*. We found this same characteristic embodied in some of Oeben's productions (Plates 95 and 96); indeed, the principle had been adopted already in 1739 by Gaudreaux in the well-known commode-like medal-cabinet[1] which he had designed to stand in Louis XV's study—where Oeben's *Bureau du Roi* now also stood. Joubert had designed

[1] Verlet, *Mobilier Royal*, vol. II, Pl. I.

a pair of corner-cupboards[1] for this very room in 1755 and had then followed the same principle in order to make them conform in spirit with the medal-cabinet. This feature lends an air of dignity to the King's corner-cupboards which sets them apart from typical Rococo furniture, and the same characteristic is present in the commodes made for the King's two daughters. We do not yet know sufficient about Joubert's production to be able to say whether this was a general feature of such of his furniture as was designed to stand against the wall, or whether it reflects a preference of the King's, or whether Joubert was in some way influenced by Oeben who had also worked for the Crown and whose productions, including those in an advanced style made shortly before his death in 1763, must have been well known to Joubert.

The mounts on Joubert's two commodes are in such an individual style that one can only conclude that they were produced specially for Joubert. They are mostly in a classicising style, while their rectilinear and rhythmic forms lend a markedly architectural aspect to these pieces in spite of their curved fronts. The apron mounts, on the other hand, are strangely old-fashioned; they could have been made ten and even twenty years earlier and are in fact described in a much later inventory as 'rinceaux de rocaille'.[2] This brings to mind Blondel's recommendation that one should season the architectural forms with a few discreet contrasts (see page 42). One of the commodes is decorated with naturalistic pictorial marquetry of extreme elaboration resembling that on Oeben's *Bureau du Roi.* On the flanks are reproduced some designs of vases by Maurice Jacques dating from the early 1760s (Plate 392). The marble slabs on both pieces have mouldings of a relatively simple profile; this must have been a strikingly modern feature at the time.

Many commodes and commode-like pieces with cabriole legs were produced in Paris until well into the 1770s. A room might easily contain two or three commodes and a pair of corner-cupboards, at this time; and every grand house, every fine apartment contained numerous pieces of furniture of this class. So the reason that the architectural style took so long to sweep curved forms from the field may well have been that it was feared the effect would be altogether too over-powering unless the monumentality were in some way softened. In the case of upright secretaires and long-case clocks, of which there were only a few in a house, the new style could be allowed to dominate. The records of deliveries to the *Garde-Meuble de la Couronne* show that commodes formed the major part of Joubert's production. In 1765, for instance, he delivered sixty commodes but only four secretaires for royal use. In 1766, the numbers were respectively twenty-three and six, and in 1767 they were forty-two and six. This state of affairs continued during the next few years. An inventory of Joubert's stock in 1771 shows that a similar situation prevailed all along the line and not just in his royal commissions; at that date he had thirty-five commodes and nine secretaires in the workshops.[3]

As we have noted, it was not uncommon to retain the cabriole form of leg on a piece of furniture on which the decoration was couched in the new style. Vanrisamburgh, like Joubert, furnishes his pieces with bronzes of Classical form at this stage, and surrounds his lacquer panels with rectangular frames (Plates 117, 119 and 120). The same principle is followed in the design of the commode set with Sèvres plaques dated 1772 which Poirier caused to be made for Madame du Barry (Plate 125), the commodes Joubert and Riesener produced in 1774 shown in Plates 146 and 147, and in the pieces by Foullet, Roussel, Garnier, Mewesen and Lapie which must date from these same years (Plates 131 to 133, and 148 to 151).

[1] Ibid. [2] Verlet, *Mobilier Royal*, p. 110.
[3] Arch. Nat., Minutier Central, CXVII–852, inventory dated 16th March 1771.

The style used for royal furniture in France was radically changed when an important jewel-cabinet was made for Marie-Antoinette. This has disappeared but was designed in 1769 by François-Joseph Belanger, an architect then only twenty-five years old, and completed on 4th May 1770 (Plate 448). The cabinet work was by M.-B. Evald, the sculpture and carved ornament by A. Bocciardi and the bronze-founder Gouthière. The cabinet was of a type that had not been produced for the best part of a century but ancient examples of which could of course still be seen in many houses. This consisted of a case of small drawers hidden by two large doors, all supported on a stand comprised of eight or more legs. One well-known kind of cabinet of this general type, which must have appealed to connoisseurs of the 1760s on account of its imposing architectural detailing, was that of solid ebony carved in relief, many of which are supposed to have been made in Paris but which were also made in Flanders.[1] The Queen's cabinet was predominantly of walnut, a wood of quite a light colour, richly set with gilt-bronze mounts and the stand was apparently carved and gilded. These materials must have made the cabinet seem far less massive than the seventeenth-century ebony examples, in spite of the fact that it was larger than these usually were (it was about 2.60 metres high—say 8 feet 6 inches). When compared with Lalive de Jully's famous ebony furniture (Plates 85 to 89) it must also have seemed lighter and more elegant, not least on account of the graceful design of the legs and the delicacy of the ornaments which, in this respect, are more reminiscent of the designs for the mural decorations at the Hôtel d'Uzès than the work at the Petit Trianon (Plates 64 to 67). In fact, stylistically the cabinet is not any more advanced than some of De Wailly's projects (Plates 329 and 330) from 1760, or Neufforge's designs of 1763 (Plates 368 and 369), or the furniture made for the King of Poland between 1765 and 1768 (Plates 406 to 416). But, as far as veneered furniture made for use at the French court is concerned, the cabinet marks a water-shed as unmistakable as that represented by the chairs made for Madame du Barry's apartments at Versailles at about the same time (see page 91). These are the first instances of furniture with straight legs making their appearance at Versailles, as far as we know. Even at the Petit Trianon, there was nothing so advanced in the way of actual furniture and it was not until 1771 that the King actually acquired for his own use, two tables with straight legs[2] but, even then, he never condescended to have a chair with straight legs for his personal use!

The radical redecoration which the Prince de Condé carried out at the Palais Bourbon from 1770 onwards was on a par with that which had been completed at the palace in Warsaw, with the difference that Condé acquired a great many pieces of veneered furniture as well as carved furniture (Plates 127 to 130), while the King of Poland had only ordered carved furniture and, at most, a single piece of cabinet-making (Plate 410). The furniture provided for Madame du Barry's famous Pavillon de Louveciennes also seems to have consisted largely of chairs, while the carved furniture in her rooms at Versailles was notably more Neo-Classical in taste than any of her pieces of veneered cabinet-making.

[1] Examples are in the Louvre, in Her Majesty the Queen's collection at Windsor Castle, in The Metropolitan Museum of Art, New York, and elsewhere.

[2] Riesener's table is entered in the Journal of the *Garde-meuble de la Couronne* (Arch. Nat., o[1] 3318, fol. 48 bis) and the legs are described as 'à guaine'. The description in the Journal of Joubert's table, on the other hand, is not very detailed but the description in Joubert's own bill (Arch. Nat., o[1] 3623, fol. 2 *recto*) leaves no doubt about the design: 'Ordre du 19 Fevrier. Livré le 7. May . . . au Château de Fontainebleau Pour le Roy à son passage. Vn Bureau de Cabinet de 4. pieds 1/2. bois violet et rose, très orné de pieds Portans, quartderonds, Chûtes Sur les quatre pans de chaque pied . . . 2450 livres.' ('Order of 19th February. Delivered on 7th May . . . to the Château of Fontainebleau for the King's stay there—a man's writing-desk 4½ feet long, of purple and tulip wood, richly worked, the legs having canted corners and pendant ornaments on the four faces . . . 2,450 livres.')

We do not know anything about the furniture provided for some of the other notable re-decorations carried out in Paris during these years. What was the furniture like in Marigny's house in the Faubourg du Roule, or at the Hôtel d'Uzès or in the Hôtel d'Hallwyl? One may presume that furniture in a Neo-Classical vein of some kind was provided, but we cannot be sure. Nor have we any information about the many pieces of carcass furniture which Leleu, the Prince de Condé's *ébéniste*, executed between 1765 and 1771 for Baron d'Ivry. They may well have been couched in an exceedingly advanced style since we know that the chairs the Baron acquired at this stage (Plate 174) were in just as up-to-date a style as those made for the Palais Bourbon, both of which groups were provided by the *menuisier* L. C. Carpentier.

We owe it to Pierre Verlet's researches in the Condé archives that some of the furniture from the Palais Bourbon has been recognised (Plates 128 to 130).[1] The pieces concerned are now to be found at the Louvre, in the Petit Trianon and at the Wallace Collection. The desk shown in Plate 127 once belonged to Boni di Castellane and is presumably now in some private collection. None of the furnishing bronzes (*bronzes d'ameublement*) have been traced so far (Plates 453 to 461) nor has any seat-furniture been located although we know from the carvers' accounts that this was of a highly up-to-date form (see page 92 f.).

The four pieces by Leleu illustrated here (Plates 127 to 130) were delivered in 1772 and 1773. They were to go in three rooms at the Palais Bourbon and this would probably account for the marked differences in their decoration. All the same, each is an expression of uncompromising Classicism and of course each piece was designed to stand in a particular spot against a wall in the room concerned. The commode shown in Plate 128 now lacks its original marquetry decoration with the Prince's cipher and fleurs-de-lys which resemble the work on the commode, one of a pair, illustrated in Plate 130. These three pieces were made for the Duchesse de Bourbon's bed-chamber. It is noteworthy that the legs of all these pieces are straight, circular in section, and furnished with capitals of the Ionic or the Corinthian order. We know of a few designs for legs of this markedly Classical form which are earlier than this (see page 86) but these are the earliest actual pieces of French furniture with this feature, so far discovered. The crisp and delicate bronze mounts make for a light and elegant form of decoration. According to the bills subsequently rendered by the carver, Lachenait, the bed belonging with this suite was decorated with equally detailed Classical ornament.[2] According to an inventory of the contents of the room made in 1779[3] there were also a chiffonière and two tables in the room which were by no means in such an advanced style as the three commodes, for they are stated to have had 'pieds de biche' which means legs of a cabriole form. However, these pieces were no doubt free-standing and therefore, as we have seen (see page 75), could therefore be less severe in style.

The commode shown in Plate 129 was intended for the Prince de Condé's own bedchamber and the above-mentioned inventory informs us that this was the only piece of veneered cabinet-making in the room. Compared with the three commodes in the Duchesse de Bourbon's bed-chamber, this is a far more obtrusive piece of furniture. It was what the eighteenth century would have called 'plus mâle'. This somewhat aggressive or domineering character—note the lion's paws—would of course have been entirely suitable in the personal room of the head of a princely house. In the rooms set aside for the ladies of the house, a more discreet, retiring style was called

[1] See the references in Leleu's biography, p. 201.

[2] Archives Condé, Château de Chantilly, Bill No. 79, fol. 1ff.

[3] Extracts published in Pierre Verlet, *La maison du XVIIIe siècle en France, société, décoration, mobilier*, Fribourg, 1966, pp. 270–84.

E. Heurtaut, about 1768-69

for. These differences of purpose must be taken into account when trying to evaluate stylistic developments in eighteenth-century furniture.

A small cylinder-top desk (Plate 127) was also made for the Prince's rooms. As in the case of the commode, this was the only piece of cabinet-making in the so-called 'Salon roze'. Like Lalive's furniture (Plates 85 to 89), it has lion's masks to indicate the owner's sex but, otherwise, it is not nearly so positive in its masculinity. In spite of its small size (about 81 cm. wide) it was apparently intended to stand against the wall and Leleu, in his bill, points out that it was only furnished with bronze mounts on the front and sides.[1]

The large writing-table shown in Plate 126 bears the stamp of J. F. Leleu but it does not come from the Palais Bourbon even though it is in the same style as the Prince de Condé's furniture, especially as far as the capitals on the legs are concerned. These closely resemble those on the Duchesse de Bourbon's commodes (Plate 130) and the table is likely to be of the same date as these.

Datable furniture from the early 1770s, other than the Condé pieces, has been difficult to identify. We have certain firmly dated pieces among the royal furniture, thanks to the information provided by the meticulous entries in the Journal of the *Garde-Meuble de la Couronne* (Plates 123, 141 to 143, 145 to 147). We are familiar with many pieces of furniture set with plaques of Sèvres porcelain which are frequently marked with a letter indicating the year they were produced. These date-letters of course help us to establish an approximate date for the piece concerned (Plates 121, 122 and 136 and Colour Plate D). And finally there are a few pieces for which we can produce an acceptable *dato ante quem* or *dato post quem* for one reason or another (e.g. Plates 139, 140, 150 to 152).

After Marie-Antoinette's jewel-cabinet of 1770 (Plate 448) and the King's two tables of 1771, the next royal piece with straight legs of which we have records is the 'Bureau le pied en guaîne' ('desk with straight legs') which Joubert delivered on 27th May 1771 for the apartment of the Comte and Comtesse de Provence at Marly. If it survives, it has not been recognised. It ought to bear the inventory number 2614 and the letter 'M' for Marly.[2] Next comes an expensive little table which Riesener sent round to Fontanieu, the director of the *Garde-Meuble*, on 21st September of the same year (Plate 123).[3] In this piece we see for the first time the new style taken up in its entirety. It has straight legs, a carcass composed of vertical faces, light and elegant proportions in every detail, and a precision and delicacy of craftsmanship which could not be surpassed. It only lacks the legs of entirely square or circular section that were to be so characteristic of the coming style. A correspondingly pure version of the style is to be seen in Poirier's fall-front secrétaire fitted with Sèvres plaques that are dated 1773 (Plate 136), and in the roll-top desk Riesener made for the Comte de Provence in 1774 (Plate 143). The same character could be produced with less costly materials, as is to be seen in the 'table à gradin'[4] made by Evald (Plate 139) which must have been produced before 1774 since this cabinet-maker left Paris in that year.

This delicate little piece has much in common with a design by Besse (Plate 499) which is described as being for a 'Table à gradin à la greque' and is dated 1776. Evald had in fact been the cabinet-maker who executed most of the woodwork for the Queen's jewel-cabinet (Plate 448)

[1] See Leleu's description in Note to Plate 127. [2] Arch. Nat., o[1] 3319, fol. 57.
[3] Identified by Verlet and published in his *Mobilier Royal I*, pp. 18–21, Pl. X.
[4] 'a table with a superstructure with small drawers'.

but his usual customers were apparently people of less extravagant tastes than the members of the royal family. A fall-front desk by him (Plate 140) is in the same neat style as his 'table à gradin' and, if it is compared with an engraving which appeared in Diderot's *Encyclopédie* and is dated 1765 (Plate 390), one might think it was made before 1770; yet the elaborate detail in the marquetry point to a somewhat later date.

Really grand furniture is not often light, either in weight or appearance, especially if it is designed to stand against the wall. The commode and one of its accompanying corner-cupboards (Plate 142) decorated with martial emblems are at any rate no exception to this rule. They were made by Joubert for the Comte d'Artois and delivered in 1773 when the Prince was only sixteen years old. The rule also holds good for the stylistically related fall-front desk shown in Plate 152 which, however, cannot have been made before 1776, for reasons that are set out in the Note to this Plate. In such pieces the classicising spirit is so over-powering that one is reminded of furniture from the time of Louis XIV, and it is only the light colour of the veneers and the complexity of the marquetry-work that temper this impression.

The undoctrinaire tastes prevailing at Court are reflected in the upright secretaire shown in Plate 145 which Joubert handed over to the *Garde-Meuble* in June 1774. In general form and in some of its decoration it is of course quite up-to-date, and the wide 'à la grecque' border at the bottom is no less striking than that on the Prince de Condé's commode (Plate 129). But immediately below this border is a mount of the purest Rococo character which might have been found on furniture made a quarter of a century earlier. The keyhole escutcheons and the mounts on the corners just above the feet display much the same character. The commode (Plate 146) delivered only eight days earlier (the two pieces have consecutive inventory numbers painted on them corresponding to entries in the *Garde-Meuble* records) presumably came from Joubert's stock although it was handed over by Riesener (see page 193 for an explanation of this curious circumstance). The mounts on the feet are likewise of a Rococo type and the legs are of cabriole form. The apron-mount on the commode illustrated in Plate 147, which Riesener delivered in August 1774 and which was ordered shortly after the death of Louis XV, resembles mounts on commodes provided by Joubert in 1769 (Plates 119 and 120). It is interesting to note that these mounts are not unlike the carved ornaments which appear in similar positions on the seventeenth-century ebony cabinets which we have already discussed. One of these cabinets with just such a mount is in the Louvre.[1]

When Louis XV died on 10th May, 1774, the Neo-Classical style was fully established in the field of veneered furniture and had been entirely assimilated by the Parisian cabinet-makers. By then, quite a few pieces of such furniture had been produced in the new style which was to dominate the scene during the next reign. As we have noted, furniture was still being made by even the leading cabinet-makers which displayed old-fashioned Rococo features, especially in its ornamentation. On balance, however, it would seem that, as far as cabinet-making was concerned, Pierre Patte was not wrong when he said in 1777 that 'enfin le retour du goût antique ayant répandu son influence sur nos arts d'agréments . . . on peut dire que la décoration intérieure des appartements, & le style de leurs ameublements sont devenus en quelque sorte un art nouveau'.[2]

[1] Reproduced in Carle Dreyfus, *Musée du Louvre, mobilier du XVIIe et du XVIIIe siècles*, 1922, Pl. 1.

[2] 'In fact, the return of the Antique taste having extended its influence over all our decorative arts . . . it can be said that the interior decoration of suites of rooms and the style of their furnishings have become in some sense a new art.' See p. 24.

3. CHAIRS AND OTHER CARVED FURNITURE

We found it necessary to preface our discussion of veneered furniture with a few general remarks and the same applies here. The joiners who made and assembled the elements of chairs and other kinds of carved furniture like beds were normally called *menuisiers en sièges*, just as in English they might be called chair-makers. The regulations concerning the stamping of wares with the craftsman's name applied equally to the *menuisiers* and signified that the joinery was well executed with good and well-seasoned timber. However, as in the case of veneered furniture, too much weight should not be attached to the names stamped on joined furniture, particularly when it concerns pieces carved with any elaboration. The standard mouldings and small flowers which appear on so much joined furniture of this period could be turned out in the chair-maker's workshop, but more ambitious carving was almost always executed by a carver (*sculpteur*) and he virtually never signed his work, yet it was he who gave the chair much of its character and, since he might accept work from many different chair-makers, it will be appreciated that the presence of their name on the finished article is not necessarily of great significance. The chair-makers apparently worked chiefly for the *marchands-tapissiers*—the upholsterers—rather than for private customers direct, and it was often these middle-men who accepted commissions and thereafter saw to the execution of the orders. If there was a degree of urgency, they might easily farm out an order among several chair-makers. In such cases, each presumably was issued with a model or with working drawings. This explains why we sometimes find sets comprised of chairs, some with the name of one chair-maker and some with that of another stamped on them.[1]

What we actually know about the stylistic development in the realm of chairs in France at this period is quickly told, for we know very little—very much less than we know about veneered furniture. In England one can point to a wealth of surviving and firmly documented chairs and other furniture from the 1760s but, in France, one can hardly find a single chair of which the date is known for certain—at any rate, not chairs made earlier than 1768. So we have to make do with such indirect evidence as can be found in the odd description, and in dated paintings, drawings and engravings.

One curious fact is that seat-furniture was far more resistant to the encroachments of Neo-Classicism than were other kinds of furniture. Chairs with straight legs and oval or rectangular backs, all carved with Classical ornament, were certainly made at quite an early date but chairs with cabriole legs and generous, serpentine forms continued in favour for a very long time—right into the 1780s—even in houses where, for instance, the wall-panelling was decorated entirely in the Neo-Classical style. Take for example the Château de Montgeoffroy, which was modernised by the architect Barré early in the 1770s and entirely refurnished. The walls are decorated in a discreet but purely architectural style. This is reflected in the fire-dogs (Plate 233) and the sconces (Plates 215 and 216). The commodes (Plate 148) are couched in the moderate kind of Neo-Classicism which Oeben had cultivated about 1760. The chairs, however, all of which are simple and virtually without ornament, are entirely of Rococo form. We find the same apparently incongruous contrasts in many engraved illustrations showing interiors of the period. Good examples are Auguste de Saint-Aubin's famous drawing of *Le Concert* which was engraved by

[1] E.g. the chairs on Plates 175 and 176.

Duclos and is dated 1773, in many of Moreau *le jeune*'s illustrations for Laborde's *Choix de Chansons* which appeared in 1773 and the next few years, and most of Moreau's illustrations for the large edition of Rousseau's *Oeuvre* which came out at the end of the 1770s and in the early 1780s. Moreau's apparent predilection for chairs of Rococo form is the more strange when one recalls that he had once studied under Le Lorrain, one of the most *outré* designers of his day, and had even accompanied him to Russia. Moreau must have known Le Lorrain well and must have been fully conversant with the latter's progressive tastes. Moreover, Moreau was one of the younger generation of artists; he was only born in 1741. However, the fact that he depicted mainly Rococo chairs in the 1770s, may simply mean that this kind of chair was much in evidence in fashionable Parisian houses at the time.[1]

Madame Elisabeth, the sister of Louis XVI, who was born in 1764, was only fourteen when she received (in 1778) a luxurious set of chairs which had cabriole legs and wavy contours that might almost have been based on templates of about 1760.[2] It would seem, therefore, that the old Rococo forms remained in favour not merely with aged and conservative people but had an appeal for the young as well. It may in fact simply have been the case that people had come to appreciate the characteristic chair of the Rococo period with its welcoming, accommodating form—to such an extent that they remained loyal to it and not even the dictates of Fashion, to which they otherwise yielded very happily, could prize them away. Blondel had of course been referring to this phenomenon when he criticised those who would introduce angular furniture into a room. As he pointed out, such things offended the eye and hindered circulation in the room. These uncompromising shapes were rarely suitable, he wrote, 'dans les choses d'agrément ou d'un usage journalier' (page 44).[3] Those people who could afford to change their furniture as fashions changed must anyway have known, if only from their experience when listening to the sermon in church, that angular chairs with straight backs could be terribly uncomfortable!

Large numbers of chairs survive which have comfortable Rococo forms but which, on account of their carved Classical decoration, can tentatively be dated to the 1760s. A selection is shown in Plates 155 to 163. The writing-chair by Michard illustrated in Plate 155, which has a narrow garland carved round the outer edge of its back, resembles that one can see on the chair or sofa on which the Comtesse d'Egmont Pignatelli is seated in Alexander Roslin's portrait which is dated 1763 (Plate 371). The rectangular 'scroll' on the upright supporting the arm is like those executed in bronze on the feet of Oeben's secretaire shown in Plate 94 and which must be of about the same date (see page 71f.). A closely similar feature is to be seen on Caffieri's candelabrum of 1760 which is to be seen in Plate 204. On the other hand we have no record of rosettes in square sinkings, like that on the chair, making their appearance before 1765 and 1766, as is explained on page 86, unless the 'plinthes caré' [*sic*] ('squared plinths') which were a feature of some chairs the Marquis de Marigny acquired in 1763 can have been motifs of this kind. The two armchairs (Plates 156 and 157), respectively stamped by Delanois and Letelier, have several features that are also to be seen on the chair in which the Marquis is seated in Roslin's

[1] Some of the furniture which may be seen in Moreau's illustrations to the famous book *Monument du Costume* is in an uncompromising *Louis Seize* style, e.g. the chair in the engraving entitled *N'ayez pas peur, ma bonne Amie*. For this actual engraving, however, a preparatory drawing is preserved (reproduced Pl. XI in the catalogue to the Madame Lucien Guiraud sale, Hôtel Drouot, 14th June 1956) and here the chair is of pure Rococo shape! It is unknown whether Moreau or Eberts, his fashion-minded editor, decided to change the style of the chair.

[2] See Verlet. *Mobilier Royal I*, pp. 69–73, and Pls. XXXIV–XXXVI.

[3] 'for works of decorative art or objects of daily use'.

portrait of him which was painted in 1761—notably in the top corners of the backs but also in their general style (Plate 353). Those by Letelier are said by their owner to come from the Château de Menars which was of course first the summer-residence of Madame de Pompadour and then of her brother—the same Marquis de Marigny. Such a tradition must of course be viewed with reservation but it is certainly worth recording and bearing in mind.

The chair shown in Plate 158, which has no maker's stamp, bears the same inventory mark (an anchor between the initials CP, surmounted by a crown) as the desk and filing-cabinet shown in Plate 115 which we have attributed to Haupt. It must therefore have been at Chanteloup, the Duc de Choiseul's country residence. As we have already noted, the Duc seems to have taken up the new fashion at an early date even though he did not discard all his old furniture. This is apparent from the surviving views of the interior of his house in Paris (Plates 463 and 464). Some of his chairs were very modern, and entirely Classical in spirit, as miniatures show. The unstamped armchair, however, is of Rococo shape although the carved ornament is Classical in style and resembles that to be seen on the chairs by Delanois and Letelier which we have just mentioned (Plates 156 and 157). The rosettes at the top corners of the back, on the other hand, are reminiscent of some on a set of chairs by Heurtaut which, because of their provenance and upholstery, must date from about 1768–69 (Plates 166 and 167 and Colour Plate E). At any rate, the armchair in question must belong to the 1760s and probably to the first half of that decade.

The chair with the mark of Pothier (Plate 159) and the two unstamped chairs shown in Plates 160 and 161 pose similar problems. After reading the detailed description of the chairs 'sculptées à la Grecque' which the Foliot brothers executed for the Petit Trianon in 1767 (see page 335) one feels confident in ascribing them to a similar date but they might be slightly earlier, if one allows for the conservatism that governed taste in French royal circles. Much the same may be said of the chairs by Delanois and Gourdin shown in Plates 162 and 163, but of course chairs such as these could equally well have been made as late as the early 1770s, and their slender proportions rather point to this having been the case. As a general rule-of-thumb, it would seem that chairs with rather bold and striking carving in the Classical taste are likely to be earlier than those in which the ornament is more reticent.

As we noted earlier (see page 45), we do not yet know what the 'modern' chairs that Le Lorrain designed for Carl Gustav Tessin in 1754 looked like. We can only assume that they were not exactly like any furniture then in existence. Let us hope that the drawings for them and the other furniture he designed for the Swedish minister will one day turn up. We do, on the other hand, know what at any rate the top part of the writing-chair he designed some two years later for Lalive de Jully looked like, for it is depicted in Greuze's portrait of the owner (Plate 322). It will be seen that the chair was just as uncompromisingly progressive in its style as the rest of the furniture in Lalive's *Cabinet Flamand* (Plates 85 to 89), with its elements forming severely rectangular shapes, its dark wood and its gilt ornaments 'dans le goût antique' as the auction catalogue of 1770 was subsequently to describe them. The front ends of the arms had a sunken quarter circle carved in them. This is a motif to be seen on some late-Roman thrones of marble or porphyry. The legs can unfortunately not be seen but one can be fairly certain that they were straight and fluted like those of the writing-table although they probably did not end in lion's paws. This chair must have seemed even more striking, on account of its sombre colour and its angular form, than the table or the filing-cabinet because, although people were still fairly familiar with cabinet-work in the majestic style of Boulle and his contemporaries, a chair couched in this idiom had never been seen before. And, although the table was imitated more than once, we never hear of anyone copying the chair; no doubt it was thought altogether too bizarre for that! In fact, it was not until towards the end of the 1760s—a whole decade later—that Neufforge published some designs for chairs in a similar rectilinear style (Plates 434 to 436). Neufforge's proposals were, however, even more ponderous and it would seem that they won little acceptance in the French capital. The proposals made a few years earlier by De la Rue fared no better (Plates 334 and 335). He attempted to get even closer to original Classical forms although he probably based his knowledge of these on seventeenth-century engravings. At any rate, he illustrates what came to be known as the 'sabre leg' which is of course to be seen in representations of Antique Classical furniture. De la Rue's engravings were published posthumously in 1771 but he had died in 1765 and his compositions may well have been drawn several years before his death as he was a member of Lalive de Jully's circle and can hardly have been unaware of the latter's efforts during the late 1750s to contrive new types of furniture based on old principles. However, we have no evidence to support this suggestion.

It is most regrettable that the appearance of the important set of seat-furniture which the Marquis de Marigny acquired in 1763 is only known to us by report. The set was intended for his place out in the Faubourg du Roule where Soufflot was later to build the house here illustrated in Plate 76. In 1763, Marigny had caused a tent-like pavilion designed by Soufflot to be set up there and then ordered twelve chairs (*chaises*), twelve armchairs (*fauteuils*), four 'bergère'-type armchairs (*fauteuils en bergère*) and five sofas (*canapés*) from the upholsterer (*marchand-tapissier*) Antoine Godefroy.[1] The only information of interest in Godefroy's bill, as far as we are here concerned, is that the legs were 'à gaines avec des plintes caré' [*sic*]. The term 'à gaine' indicates that the legs were straight and tapering but it is not certain whether the 'plintes carés' means that these legs had square blocks at the top or at the bottom, or both. The legs of a chair to be seen in Noël Hallé's painting of 1764 (Plate 376) are of the type which would presumably have been so described.

If we only knew more precisely what Marigny's chairs were like, we would probably be able to decide once and for all what form was taken for the models for chairs which at that same time were being prepared at the *Manufacture des Gobelins*. These were chairs that were to be fitted with the tapestry-woven covers *en suite* with the tapestry hangings, for which Soufflot and Maurice Jacques had been working out designs already in 1758 (Plate 36). The principal features of these tapestries consisted of *trompe l'oeil* representations of oval framed medallions containing paintings by François Boucher. The problem is whether the chairs that were to go with the tapestries were also provided with oval backs, and whether they had straight legs. Mrs. Eileen Harris, who has devoted much time to this question in connection with her studies of Robert Adam's furniture[2] has produced some convincing reasons for believing that the oval back was not an invention of Adam's although he was to design a number of chairs with this feature. Mrs. Harris concludes that the pattern originated in Paris. This may well be so but the earliest representation of a chair with an oval back so far discovered is that in Pierre-Antoine Baudouin's engraving entitled *Le Lever* which was published in 1765 (Plate 389). This chair also has straight

[1] See present writer's article 'Marigny and "le goût grec"', *Burlington Magazine*, March 1962, p. 98.

[2] See Eileen Harris, 'Robert Adam and the Gobelins', *Apollo*, April 1962, pp. 100–6. See also Fiske Kimball, 'The Moor Park Tapestry Suite of Furniture by Robert Adam', *Philadelphia Museum Bulletin*, XXXVI, March 1941, p. 29; and Fiske Kimball, 'Les influences anglaises dans la formation du style Louis XVI', *Gazette des Beaux-Arts*, 6th ser., V, 1931, pp. 29–44, 231–55.

legs so the formula was certainly in existence by the mid-1760s. Baudouin was François Boucher's son-in-law and brother-in-law to François' son, the furniture-designer Juste-François Boucher. François Boucher of course had close links with Les Gobelins and, as we have noted, the medallions on the tapestries in question contained reproductions of some paintings by him. The managing director of Les Gobelins was Soufflot. He had been responsible for the general conception of the tapestries. As director of this important establishment, he would have been in daily contact with the Marquis de Marigny who was his immediate superior—it will be remembered that Marigny was in effect a Minister of Culture—and was still his close friend although it was now more than a decade since they had come back from their joint visit to Italy. In fact, Soufflot now acted as Marigny's formal architect and the chairs we have already mentioned, which Marigny acquired in 1763 for his place at Roule, were to stand in a pavilion designed by Soufflot. It will thus be seen that there were numerous close contacts between the characters in this story, all of whom must have been well aware of what was being done at Les Gobelins at this crucial period. Even so, it would be unwise to conclude, without further evidence, that the chairs designed for the tapestries (which had first been projected already in 1758) were furnished with oval backs and straight legs or that Marigny's chairs at Roule were of this type.

A chair of Classical character very similar to those designed by De la Rue (see above, page 86), is to be seen in Vien's painting, *La Marchande d'Amour* (Plate 374) which was executed in 1763. Apparently the time was not yet ripe for chairs of such a novel form to be acceptable in real life and it was not until some twenty-five years later that chairs of this kind were actually produced. Among the earliest were those Georges Jacob made in 1787 for the salon at the 'laiterie' which Louis XVI built for Marie Antoinette at Rambouillet. No less *outré* and equally unrealistic is the *faldestolium* or 'fauld stool' (Plate 373) which is to be seen in the altar-painting by Lagrenée of 1764, which is made to look as if it were made of marble or porphyry. The chair has an 'à la grecque' border, lion's paws and heavy swags very like those on Lalive de Jully's furniture (Plates 85 to 89), and it does not therefore come as a surprise to learn that Lagrenée was one of Lalive's protegées. Another member of this côterie was Noël Hallé who, in the same year, painted a family scene (Plate 376) set in a room of a heavy Neo-Classical character resembling that at the Hotel de Varey (Plate 34). The table and chair in this picture have no carved decoration and are scarcely classicised at all, yet their members are straight and regular—like shaved versions of designs by Neufforge (Plate 368).

A bewildering illustration of some strange furniture is that on the title-page of Thibaud's *Ballade* which Hubert Gravelot drew in 1764 (Plate 375). At first glance, the chairs in the picture seem to be in a pure *Louis Seize* style of about 1780, yet the costumes are roughly of the Louis XIII period while Thibaud, who was Count of Champagne, lived at the time of St. Louis—in the thirteenth century! No doubt Gravelot wanted to illustrate a scene with 'historical' furniture, just as he had put his figures in historic dress. He was of course used to exercises of this kind, for he had been commissioned to execute numerous series of illustrations, not only in France but also in England where he had illustrated Shakespeare and Richardson, for example. Moreover, for the 1764 edition of Corneille's *Oeuvres*, Gravelot produced in 1763 some illustrations of scenes set in fairly faithful reconstructions of a Roman Imperial palace complete with furniture of the right kind. All the same, while Gravelot could certainly turn out scenes in a historicising vein, the fact that these particular pieces of furniture were drawn in 1764—a year in which much experimentation was taking place in this field—is perhaps significant. Gravelot was a highly versatile artist. He designed ornaments of all kinds including patterns for carpets to be made at the Savonnerie factory and tapestries to be woven at the Manufacture des Gobelins—both, incidentally, establishments under the control of the Marquis de Marigny. He could also design costume for the stage and apparently knew something of furniture design for, already during his stay in England, he is said to have provided drawings 'for cabinet-makers and other workmen in upholstery and furniture'[1] and there are certainly many representations of chairs—admittedly of early Rococo form because the illustrations concerned were produced in the years around 1740—in the scenes he executed while in England.[2]

It is perhaps worth bearing in mind that Gravelot, during his stay in England, must have been familiar with the—to French eyes—very strange furniture then being produced in the so-called English Palladian style in which Classical forms and motifs played an important part. The ponderous 'Palladian' style was very different from that of the chairs in Gravelot's drawing of 1764, but it is just possible that this artist's earlier experience may have made him more easily able to assimilate the new style.

The seat-furniture and beds which Jean-Louis Prieur designed in 1766, presumably under the direction of Victor Louis, for the Warsaw Palace (Plates 411 to 416) were completed in 1768. The chair-frames were produced in the workshops of Louis Delanois and the carved ornament in the atelier of the sculptor Denis Coulonjon. The chairs were couched in the same markedly advanced style as the rest of furnishings which were being produced at that time in Paris for the Polish court, under the sponsorship of Madame Geoffrin and with the enthusiastic approval of the Marquis de Marigny. Hardly any traces remain of the serpentine Rococo line; the carved ornament is all of a Classical character. As the Polish king's commissioner, Czempinski, put it, in this furniture the artist had 'donné la préférence au bel antique, au Grec décidé'[3] (see page 63). The richly carved decoration is in fact particularly noticeable and it will be seen that the garlands of flowers are rendered in an entirely naturalistic manner. When one considers the intricacy of this work it is not surprising to discover that Coulonjon's bill for the carving came to ten times as much as Delanois'. It was of course because this furniture was intended for royal use that it was so very elaborate and, like the equally richly ornamented *Bureau du Roi* made for Louis XV (Plates 90 to 93), it was designed to stand in rooms where the walls and all the other furnishings were decorated with the same opulence.

It is of course quite probable that some equally progressive chairs existed in Paris by 1766, at least on paper. We have already noted the chair and bed of advanced form illustrated by Baudouin in 1765 (Plates 388 and 389) and these need not necessarily have been figments of the artist's imagination. Such furniture may well have been made by that date for a few apartments of an advanced character. We know of a design for a sofa produced in that very year by Rousset for the Hôtel d'Uzès (Plate 398; see also page 63) and another by Henri Piètre of 1766 for the Hôtel Mélusine (Plate 399). These two projects have little in common with Prieur's designs but are no less Classical in taste.

Even though we can produce no actual examples of Neo-Classical seat-furniture dating from the years 1766 or 1767, it is obvious that designers were by that time actively engaged in trying

[1] Quoted from H. A. Hammelmann, 'Gravelot in England', *Book Handbook*, Vol. 2, No. 4, December 1951—March 1952, p. 178; I am indebted to Peter Thornton for calling my attention to this interesting article.

[2] See Desmond Fitz-Gerald, 'Gravelot and his influence on English Furniture', *Apollo*, XC, August 1969, pp. 140–7.

[3] 'given preference to items couched in the Antique taste—to the Grecian style'.

to devise chairs of Neo-Classical form that would be as readily acceptable as the graceful and accommodating chairs of the Rococo type. It is not yet possible to define this activity with any great precision but there are several isolated examples that seem to be symptomatic of this development. There is the chair shown in Baudouin's engraving of 1767 (Plate 426) which has fluted legs of columnar form with Ionic capitals, and we know of a large armchair that Godefroy delivered to the Marquis de Marigny on the 12th January 1768, which was 'tout caré par devant et sur tous sens'.[1] Then there are Neufforge's designs (Plates 434 to 436) which were published in 1768 but which must have been drawn some time before (see page 47). There are likewise some designs by Delafosse of a similar character, produced in the same year (Plates 439 and 440). A candlestick curiously resembling a Classical chairleg is shown in Plate 432; this was drawn by Jean-François Forty. He rented rooms in the premises of the chair-maker, Louis Delanois, who in turn was responsible for some of the earliest seat-furniture of Classical form to be made in Paris, as we have just seen. The chairs to be seen in some of Baudouin's undated engravings must at least have been designed before December 1769 when he died, and perhaps well before that. In the same way, the chairs to be seen in Van Blarenberghe's view of the interior of the Duc de Choiseul's house (Plate 464) can very well have been made a few years before the painting was executed in 1770.

From Louis Delanois' account-books we also get the impression that certain new developments were taking place at the very time when he was preparing the furniture that was to go to Warsaw.[2] On the 14th March 1768, a *marchand-tapissier* named Caumont apparently received from Delanois, among other things, 'quatre fauteuils oval sculpté à La grec, une ottomanne pour aller avec les fauteuils oval à la grec, 2 Bergères ovals en bois de noyer sculpté à lantique'[3] while, on the 28th June, Caumont took possession of a 'fauteuil carré les pieds tourné a lantique'.[4] On the same day, a batch of chairs was sent to the Comte d'Orsay, of which some were 'en gros bois' —that is, frames which had not yet received any carved decoration at the hands of a sculptor. Their shape is not described but it would seem that most of the seat-furniture in this order was of a traditional Rococo kind although there were also 'quatre fauteuils en Cabriolet en bois de noyer les dossiers oval et les pieds à gaine'[5] and there can be no doubt that these were in the new style. A few days later, on the 5th July, Delanois delivered a bed to another *marchand-tapissier* named Mallet. This seems to have been the first entirely Neo-Classical bed made in the Delanois workshops: it had 'colonnes cannelés' and was decorated with 'guirlandes de laurier' and 'branches d'olivier noué d'un ruban'.[6] Four days later, a bed of similar description was handed over to Mallet's colleague, Valette.

The seat-furniture of advanced taste intended for the palace at Warsaw was standing ready in Delanois' workshops on the 27th September 1768, but this did not of course mean that he subsequently switched to producing furniture of an entirely Classical nature. For instance, right through October, November and December of that year Delanois was exclusively making chairs in the *Louis Quinze* taste, and it was not until January and February of 1769 that he was

[1] 'entirely rectangular in front and in every detail'. See Godefroy's bill in the Bibliothèque historique de la Ville de Paris, MS., N.A., 106 bis, fol. 421.

[2] Delanois' account-book is in the Archives de la Seine (D^5 B^6 4245).

[3] 'Four oval armchairs carved *à la grecque*, an ottoman to go with the oval armchairs *à la grecque*, two oval *bergère*-type armchairs of walnut carved in the Antique style.'

[4] 'A square armchair with turned legs in the Antique style.'

[5] 'Four armchairs of the *cabriolet* type of walnut, with oval backs and legs of square section.'

[6] 'fluted colums', 'garlands of bay-leaves', 'branches of olive tied with ribbon'.

again producing the occasional piece which, judging from the ledgers, must have been modern in style. We find mention of 'six chaises et le dossier oval sculpté à Lantique',[1] made for the above-mentioned Caumont, and a bed with 'colonnes cannelées' made for Caumont's colleague, David. On the 20th July, he produced for another *marchand-tapissier*, a man named Dizi, two chairs with 'le dossier oval a moulure propre et des rosettes sur les pieds de devant'[2] and these must have been purely Classical in style. In September and October he provided a further handful, always to *marchands-tapissiers*, be it noted. Delanois' extensive production otherwise continued to consist of furniture of traditional form throughout that year.

It was not only at Delanois' that chairs of a modern type were being turned out at this stage. The chair-makers Nicolas Heurtaut and Louis-Charles Carpentier, who lived in the same *quartier* as Delanois, were concurrently producing a certain number of chairs which must have been viewed with considerable interest by their rivals. Unfortunately, the account-books of these two chair-makers do not seem to have survived but we are able to date by other means some large sets of furniture bearing their stamped mark. For instance, the *canapés* (sofas) and accompanying armchairs, covered with Gobelins tapestry, which Heurtaut provided for the Château de La Roche-Guyon (Plates 166 and 167 and Colour Plate E) were constructed in 1768 or 1769, as we have already noted (see page 85). The strange, irregular shape of the *canapés*' backs, which are three times as wide as the back of a single armchair, in no way echo the lineaments of the mural-decoration in the salon where they stand, and one is tempted to conclude that the chairs were designed to fit the expensive coverings and not to agree with the décor of the room.[3] The great question is of course still whether or not the designs for these *canapés* were produced at the Gobelins, under the direction of Soufflot.

It is said that Carpentier provided furniture worth 3,300 livres between 1765 and 1771 for Baron d'Ivry's Château d'Hénonville, and there is no reason to doubt this is true. Among this furniture were two *Louis Seize canapés*, one of which is shown in Plate 174, and sixteen corresponding chairs. All were covered in Gobelins tapestry of almost the same pattern as that on the set made for the Château de La Roche-Guyon.[4] We do not know whether Barré, the architect who altered the house at this stage, designed that set and exactly when they were made is not yet known. Caution prompts one to date them as late as possible—to 1771 or slightly before. The armchair shown in Plate 171 must, however, have been made by 1769 when an identical chair was depicted in the portrait of Bertin, the Minister of Finance, painted by Roslin in that year (Plate 447). The chair is anyway unlikely to have been manufactured more than a year or so earlier. The chair has a gently curved back which is reminiscent of those on Heurtaut's chairs (Plates 167 and 170) and is of a type which Delanois produced around 1765–70.[5] Yet the rest of the chair, and notably all the carved details, are entirely Neo-Classical in taste and the chair itself is imbued with the graceful, slender proportions that were to become so characteristic of chairs produced in the next decade. More of Carpentier's work is shown in Plates 177 and 178.

None of the furniture—a bed, chairs, sofas, firescreens, console-tables, etc.—which was delivered in December 1769 for Madame du Barry's apartment at Versailles seems to have

[1] 'Six chairs with oval backs carved *à l'antique*.'

[2] 'oval backs with plain mouldings and with rosettes on the front legs'.

[3] Three views of the salon of the Château de la Roche-Guyon are reproduced in F. Contet, ed., *Les anciens châteaux de France*, 6th ser., Paris, 1924, Plates 9–11.

[4] The relevant documentation is given in the Note to Plate 174.

[5] See the present writer's *Louis Delanois*, Pl. XXff.

survived but we know something of its appearance from the accounts rendered by the gilder, Jean-Baptiste Cagny.[1] It was made by Delanois and carved by Joseph-Nicolas Guichard. We do not know who designed this furniture, however, although it may conceivably have been the architect Gondoin. The chairs were similar in shape and decoration to those made by Delanois for her Pavillon de Louveciennes which is discussed below but the carving was much richer—almost as elaborate as that on the chairs Louis Prieur had designed in 1766 for the Palace at Warsaw (Plates 411 to 414), the frames of which were also produced by Delanois.

The salon in Madame du Barry's suite of rooms was furnished with a large *canapé*, thirteen armchairs, twelve chairs, a slightly taller chair for the King, a firescreen and a console-table—all gilded. The whole set was carved with the same motifs although the console-table was even more richly decorated. The chairs had oval backs and straight, tapering and fluted legs. There were richly carved garlands of flowers below the seat-rails ('sept guirlandes de fleurs très riches avec leurs chutes tant sur le devant que sur les deux côtés') and the cresting consisted of 'un bouquet très riche dans le milieu du . . . Dossier de plusieurs fleurs différentes liées d'un ruban'.[2] The seat-rails and framing of the backs bore ornaments of a Classical nature which, judging from the descriptions, were as delicately carved as those on the Louveciennes set. There was a large basket of flowers forming an additional carved ornament on the crossing of the stretchers of the table. Each of its legs was surmounted by a cuboidal block—the front face of which displayed a lion's mask. On the frieze was a medallion with a cupid clasping a dove. In general form, this table must have been rather like that designed by Cherpitel in 1765 for the Hotel d'Uzès (Plate 397).

The bed in Madame du Barry's chamber at Versailles—which, incidentally, was only 1.31 metres wide—was a gilded structure with a domed tester supported on converging serpentine 'posts'. Its decoration was similar to that of the furniture in the adjacent salon but had yet more carving—a riotous tumble of amorous symbols and flowers, with garlands twined round the fluted columns. The legs of the bed tapered and had spiralled fluting. The chairs in this bed-chamber, however, were somewhat less richly ornamented than those in the salon; their cresting, for instance, consisted only of a floral scroll (*fleuron*) flanked by volutes—probably similar to the motif on the sofa made by Delanois for the Warsaw palace (Plate 411). The furniture in the remaining rooms of the suite was similar in general style but the sets in each room differed in their ornamentation, and some sets were gilt while others were painted white.

A few of the chairs made for the Pavillon de Louveciennes still exist; two are illustrated in Plates 172 and 173 and more may be seen in Moreau *le jeune*'s drawing reproduced in Plate 474. They are of a shape that was entirely modern in its day, and the decoration is so exquisite and delicately carved that it almost resembles goldsmiths' work. This must have been consonant with the decoration of the other items in the room which included the various *bronzes d'ameublement* by Gouthière whose crisp style we know from surviving contemporary or slightly later works (Plate 243).

Delanois executed 208 pieces of furniture for Madame du Barry, the last of which were delivered in 1770. The majority of the pieces he was producing at this time were in the Neo-Classical taste. On 2nd June 1770, for instance, he provided a certain Monsieur Bufaut with a set of chairs that, judging from the entry in his account-book, was just as up-to-date as Madame du

[1] Cagny's accounts are in the Bibliothèque Nationale in Paris (MSS. fonds français 8158). Comte François de Salverte (*Les ébénistes du XVIIIe siècle, leurs oeuvres et leurs marques*, Paris-Bruxelles, 1923, article on Delanois) first identified some of the furniture made for Madame du Barry and described in Cagny's accounts.

[2] 'an elaborate bouquet of various flowers tied with ribbons in the centre of the cresting'.

Barry's, although it was less richly decorated and was not furnished with any of the intricate foliage on the Louveciennes pieces (Plate 172 and 173). The Prince de Beauveau received a set of chairs from Delanois in December of the same year and these, too, must have been in a less expensive version of the same style. The general form of Delanois' chairs is represented by the chairs shown in Plates 164, 165, 175 and 181. He was delivering furniture of this type in and shortly after 1771 to the Prince de Condé and, in November of that year, to the Duc de Chartres.[1] The sofa shown in Saint-Aubin and Helmann's engraving of Le Peintre's painting of the Duc and his family in 1774 (Plate 498)[2] may in fact be a product of the Delanois workshops.

The descriptions in Delanois' ledgers suggest that he did not provide any furniture of advanced taste for the Palais Bourbon, when that building was being so drastically modernised, and presumably the large amount of furniture he made for the Prince de Condé was intended for use in the Prince's other dwellings—at Chantilly, for instance, and at Versailles. In fact, L. C. Carpentier, to whom we have referred already, was the *menuisier* principally concerned with providing seat-furniture for the Palais Bourbon and we know from the accounts that the sculptural decoration was entirely the work of the carver Charles Lachenait. The designs for this furniture were probably executed by Le Carpentier and Bellisard, the Prince's architects. This furniture was delivered during the years 1772, 1773 and 1774 but we know from a note in Lachenait's accounts that he was already engaged on producing models by the beginning of May 1770.[3] The impressive bed made for the Duchesse de Bourbon was first designed on the drawing-board, after which small-scale models were made. From these Lachenait made a full-scale model. 'Avant de commencer ce lit, on a fait des modeles grands comme l'exécution d'après des Esquisses et Maquettes en petit faites en premier lieu et dont j'ai donné un Mémoire. Au commencement du mois de mai 1770 on recommança led. modele grand comme l'execution, et on y emploia jusqu'au mois d'aoust . . .'.[4] With such a complicated object, it was obviously necessary to make a mock-up first: one could not afford to make mistakes with the final work. It was particularly the upholsterers who needed to try out the immensely complicated drapery that a grand bed of this period would have had. By rigging up a full-scale model it was possible to make accurate patterns for the curtains and valances and thus avoid wasting any of the expensive material of which they would finally be made. Chippendale, writing a decade earlier, certainly advised people to produce a mock-up whenever a really intricate piece of furniture was to be made,[5] and this was no doubt the general practice with special orders.

As was the case with the Prince's veneered carcass-furniture (Plates 126 to 130), each set of joined furniture also differed in its decoration so as to correspond with that of the room for which it was specially designed, but all the sets were couched in a pure Neo-Classical style both with regard to shape and ornament. The chairs had squared or oval backs, while the legs were straight and fluted, and each leg was surmounted by a cuboidal block. The entire repertoire of Classical ornament was employed in various combinations and permutations in the ornamental detail. Judging by the descriptions, it would seem that the chairs were altogether more sober

[1] See the present writer's *Louis Delanois*, pp. 41–2. [2] See Note to Plate 498.

[3] Lachenait's accounts are in the Archives Condé, Chantilly, Accounts Nos. 76 and 79.

[4] 'Before starting to make this bed, full-scale models were made after the sketches. Small-scale models were made beforehand; I have already sent a statement about them. At the beginning of May 1770 the full-scale model was started and work on it lasted until August. . .' Account No. 76, fol. 3.

[5] T. Chippendale, *The Gentleman and Cabinet-Maker's Director*, 3rd. ed., 1762, Note to Plate XLVII: 'A Workman of Genius will easily comprehend the Design. But I would advise him, in order to prevent Mistakes, to make first a Model of the same at large; which save both Time and Expense.'

and more severe in outline than Madame du Barry's. The Prince's chairs were clearly of the highest quality. The carving alone on the ordinary chairs cost anything from 34 to 79 livres per chair, and 200 to 205 livres was charged for the carved work on certain chairs. Charges of this order were normally only involved when it concerned exceptionally fine work for the Crown.[1]

It may not be easy to identify the Prince's chairs, if any survive, because they do not appear to have been so distinctive as Madame du Barry's. All the same, certain ornamental details seem to have been unusual and may help us to recognise any survivors that may exist. For instance, many of the chairs without arms had 'une moulure méplate taillée en feuilles de laurier en losanges'[2] which is a feature that ought to be recognisable. Two *canapés*, on which work was started on 19th January 1771, each had a motif consisting of a large scallop-shell with coral, flanked by recumbent Chinamen holding garlands of flowers to form a framing round the central shell. Moreover, the eight fluted columnar legs of each *canapé* had Ionic capitals. There were four other eight-legged *canapés* which had rectangular backs, the uprights of which had pine-cone finials. One should perhaps also be able to recognise—if they survive—four armchairs and four *chaises* which were delivered in 1774 and which cost so much that they were clearly of quite exceptional quality. The carving of each armchair cost 260 livres and that of each chair 200 livres. The chairs had backs that were rounded at the top but otherwise rectangular. In the centre of the cresting on each was 'un bouquet de fleurs et une branche de Mirthe formant une couronne . . . dans cette Couronne passe un Carquois et une flutte formant un Trophé noués avec des rubans'.[3] Four other chairs with oval backs between uprights each had 'une couronne de fleurs et Branches de Mirthe et une guirlande de fleurs passant entre les feuilles tournantes' on their cresting and their uprights consisted of 'un Cornet rempli d'un bouquet de fleurs. Le Cornet est orné de petites Volutes desquelles sortent des Guirlandes de fleurs et Cannelures torses'.[4] Such features ought also to be striking.

One important feature which is, however, not revealed by the descriptions concerns their proportions. Were these chairs massive and heavy in appearance, or were they light, slender and elegant? If they were the latter—if they were the fore-runners of chairs in the pure *Louis Seize* style—then the furniture made for the Palais Bourbon must have been even more influential than that made for Madame du Barry. Unfortunately we have as yet no proof that the Palais Bourbon seat-furniture *was* slender of line so it is still too early to make any firm pronouncements about its possible influence. All we can safely say is that a great deal of money was spent on the furnishing of this palace and that the Prince enjoyed enormous influence, so the magnificence of the furnishings with which he surrounded himself did certainly not go unnoticed!

4. WORKS IN ORMOLU

The decorative effect of gold was much admired in the eighteenth century. Walls and ceilings

[1] Cf. Verlet, *Mobilier Royal I–II*, *passim*, and Verlet, *French Royal Furniture*, *passim*.

[2] 'with a moulding of a comparatively flat section, carved with bay-leaves arranged in a lozenge-pattern'.

[3] 'a bouquet of flowers with a myrtle branch forming a coronet . . . this coronet encircles a quiver with a flute forming a trophy tied with ribbons'. Archives Condé, Chantilly, Lachenait's account No. 79, fol. 3ff.

[4] 'a coronet of flowers with branches of myrtle and a garland of flowers threaded through spiralling leaves' and 'a cornucopia filled with flowers. The horn is decorated with small volutes from which spring garlands of flowers and with spiral fluting.' Ibid., fol. 4 *verso* ff.

frequently had gilded detailing and much carcass-furniture was furnished with bronze mounts which, if clean and lacquered with a translucent varnish, could almost be mistaken for real gold. In a few instances, bronze mounts were actually gilded (*doré d'or moulu*) by means of the traditional method using quicksilver. Bronze clock-cases, sconces and candlebranches, candelabra, chandeliers, andirons and similar *bronzes d'ameublement* were mostly gilded and constituted striking elements in the decoration of a room.

Most furniture-mounts could be produced with the aid of moulds of sand but a great many *bronzes d'ameublement* needed to be made by the more complicated and expensive *cire-perdue* process. In both cases, the work was carried out by founders (*fondeurs*) and the gilding by *doreurs*. Both the *fondeurs* and *doreurs* were also *ciseleurs* and could execute the essential chasing process by means of which a sharper definition may be imparted to the contours, and various finishes given to the surfaces.

The objects produced by the bronze-founders were reproductions of models which especially talented founders might make themselves but which were mostly provided by others. The founder might commission a model from an artist; alternatively an artist might make a model on his own initiative and then have it reproduced by a founder. Another possible course was for a *marchand-mercier*—a dealer in expensive house-furnishings—to commission an artist to produce a model, whereupon it would be reproduced on the dealer's account by a founder. A clock-maker, or a *marchand-miroitier* (who specialised in mirrors but also dealt in all kinds of items for the dressing-table and the boudoir) might commission bronze-work in the same way; and the *ébéniste* Foullet, who mostly specialised in clock-cases and liked to have in stock some made entirely of metal alongside the wooden ones he himself turned out, also caused bronze-work to be produced in this manner.[1] Goldsmiths, incidentally, might make bronzes on their own account but bronze-founders were not permitted to make castings in gold or silver except when commissioned to do so by a goldsmith.

French bronzes of the eighteenth century are very rarely signed. There was in fact a regulation—a *Sentence de la Chambre civile*, dated 26th May 1651[2]—concerning the marking of bronzes but hardly anyone was observing it by this time. We know of bronzes signed by Caffieri *père* and *fils*, by F.-T. Germain, Jean-Joseph de Saint-Germain, Robert Osmond, Jean-Louis Prieur, François Vion and a handful of other artists but most of the numerous bronze-founders in Paris did not follow this practice.

In some cases the presence of a signature on a bronze may signify that the founder also made the model himself—that he was capable of working as a sculptor, in fact. This was probably the case with many of the bronzes signed by Philippe Caffieri and by Prieur, for example, both of whom had studied at the Académie de Saint-Luc and had presented masterpieces as sculptors before they took up bronze-founding. On the other hand, in cases where the founder is not known to have been trained as a sculptor, as was the case with Saint-Germain and Osmond, for example, it is to be presumed that they bought their models from some sculptor after which they probably had the right to reproduce them at will, and might also sign them as well. As Pierre Verlet has shown,[3] Pitoin, who enjoyed the patronage of the Crown over a long period, is not known to have signed any of the many *bronzes d'ameublement* he provided for the Court, although

[1] See Foullet's biography, p. 181.

[2] Published in René de Lespinasse, *Les métiers et corporations de la Ville de Paris*, 1892, p. 425.

[3] Pierre Verlet, 'The Wallace Collection and the Study of French Eighteenth-Century Bronzes d'Ameublement', *Burlington Magazine*, vol. XCII, June 1950, pp. 154–7.

he was trained as a sculptor and certainly made the models for these bronzes himself, often in collaboration with his father. He was not trained as a *fondeur* and did not in fact cast the bronzes himself; they may well have been made off the premises. Moreover, he probably inherited his title of *doreur du Roi* through his wife and this would have enabled him to have gilders working under him even though he was not trained as a gilder either.[1] Laurent Hubert, who was also a sculptor but not a *fondeur* by training, is not known to have signed any of the many completed *bronzes d'ameublement* he sold. Forestier, Héban and Aze, who were only *fondeurs* by training, but all seem to have been above-average practitioners of this craft, are not known to have signed their work either. Several goldsmiths, like the elder Duplessis, and like Roëttiers, Auguste and Germain, made bronzes but only the last two signed their work as far as we know. The younger Duplessis, who was a *fondeur* but was also an experienced draughtsman and sculptor even though he never became a master *sculpteur*, is not known to have signed his own work either. As if the confusion were not already sufficient, the position might further be complicated by the fact that one founder might hand over a model to another, for all kinds of reasons,[2] while the stock of models left by a founder on his death might be purchased by another craftsman who could then continue to make castings from them and probably had the right to sign them himself, if he wished. From all this it will be clear that there is much uncertainty in this field and we still do not know the identity of the artists who provided the models for most of the famous *bronzes d'ameublement*. Luckily we are at least aware of the magnitude of our ignorance and we realise that we must proceed with the utmost caution in this field!

Our helplessness is not eased by the additional circumstance that plagiarising was all too common among bronze-founders although it was considered as serious an offence as the copying of silk-designs, about which there were strict regulations. This unfair practice was so widespread, and the outcry against it so loud, that the Bronze-Founders' Guild managed to force through an Act governing 'la sûreté des Modèles'[3] which received the Royal approbation on 30th July 1766—in the very period with which we are here concerned. This ordinance must be one of the very first to protect an artist by an Act of Parliament from having his designs stolen by his rivals.[4] It is quoted in full on pages 271–3.

In the preamble to the Act, attention is drawn to the great expenditure of effort which an artist must be prepared to make if he wishes to create a new model. First, we are told, he must make a drawing, then he must make a model in clay or wax or of wood, then he must make one or more moulds from the model, and only then can he make the final castings which then need to be chased and finished. The models are part of the artist's capital and the basis of his livelihood. If he has a good model, he can reproduce it as often as he likes and as long as it will sell. Only in this way can he receive compensation for the time, effort and money he has put into creating the model in the first place. But if others copy his models, he not only loses the rightful fruits of his labours but soon loses the will to think up new forms and his inventiveness withers away! The public is thereby denied new creations and, moreover, it is cheated by being offered copies that are of less value, less beauty and of poorer craftsmanship than the originals.

For this reason the Act absolutely forbids anyone to copy, or cause to be copied, any bronze-founder's model. If anyone is found guilty of doing so, he must not only pay to the owner a sum

[1] The relevant documentation is given in Pitoin's biography, p. 213. [2] See Note to Plate 187.

[3] The security of copyright of designs or models.

[4] Already in 1737 a regulation was issued to protect the works of the Lyons silk-designers, see Peter Thornton, *Baroque and Rococo Silks*, 1965, p. 28.

equal to the estimated value of the model but a fine of 1,000 livres as well. A reward of 100 livres would also be made to anyone reporting a breach of the Act which led to a successful prosecution.[1] Henceforth those *maîtres-fondeurs* who devised, or caused to be devised, a new model were to have a full-sized drawing made of it and deposited at the Hall of the Founders' Guild where it would be properly registered, numbered and filed away in safety, only to be produced again if evidence of authorship were subsequently required. Gold and silversmiths, as well as sculptors, who of course all had the right to create new models for bronze-founding, could all deposit drawings of such models with the Guild if they wished to do so. The same applied to private individuals who had commissioned a new bronze for their private use and wished it to remain unique. This Act remained in force well into the nineteenth century. In the introduction to the sale-catalogue of the bronze-founder Feuchère's stock in 1824[2] it is specifically stated that a buyer of a bronze at this sale did not thereby acquire the right to copy it, 'le sol ou les modèles étant la propriété des fonds, que les lois garantissent'.[3]

Although the above-mentioned Act was only passed in 1766, the copying of bronzes had been forbidden long before, at least among the members of the Guild which exercised a strong hold over the trade. This is made clear by a *Sentence de Police* of 13th December 1765,[4] concerning two *maîtres-fondeurs*, Coisset *le jeune* and Louis Biston, who had been found guilty of plagiarising models belonging to some of their colleagues. The pair were not fined, in this instance, but had the illegal goods confiscated and were made to pay 500 livres—no small sum, this—by way of compensation. In the depositions made in connection with this case, stress is laid on the poor quality of the copies which are described as being 'de mauvaise fonte' and 'mal finies'.[5]

It goes without saying that the prohibition exercised by the Guild and firmly codified by the Act of 1766 had a marked influence on stylistic development within this field. It must have had great advantages for the creative craftsmen, particularly those who had been trained as *sculpteurs* —men like Laurent Hubert, Caffieri, Pitoin and Prieur. But it must have been a hindrance to those *fondeurs* who lacked artistic talent and especially those who could not afford to invest capital in making new models. Another possible result of the Act, unforeseen by its promoters but of enormous potential advantage to us who seek to study their work and that of their colleagues, is that a large body of signed and dated drawings of bronzes must have been made and may still survive. To date, none of these drawings has come to light and this author has still not had the time to search in the vast archives of the Paris police where one could at least expect to find evidence of prosecutions for contraventions of the Act—accompanied, possibly, by the relevant designs. We must at any rate be prepared to have our present meagre and fragmentary knowledge concerning French *bronzes d'ameublement* made after 1766 suddenly enormously expanded, and it is then possible that many of the pieces that we do not at present have the temerity to date earlier than, say, 1755 will turn out to have been a decade older than we had guessed. Having said all this, it must now be admitted that we have a rather clearer idea of the developments that took place in the field of *bronzes d'ameublement* than in that of many of the other applied arts, thanks to the fact that a number of bronzes and designs for bronzes are dated, that there are many

[1] The size of the fine, and of the reward, become impressive when compared with the daily pay (4–5 livres) received by, for instance, some of Gouthière's *ciseleurs* (cf. J. Robiquet, *Gouthière*, 1912, pp. 109 and 113).

[2] Lugt, No. 10766.

[3] 'the copyright of the models being the property of the founder, backed by law'.

[4] Arch. Nat., Y 9468; they were accused of copying fire-dogs, clockcases, sconces and furniture-mounts.

[5] 'poorly founded' and 'badly finished'. Arch. Nat., Y 14092 (18th November 1765), fol. 1.

F. Anonymous, about 1763-64

detailed descriptions in the Journal of the *Garde-Meuble de la Couronne*, and that we now have the interesting information contained in Philippe Caffieri's inventory which has recently come to light and which is quoted in full on pages 277–81.

Although one cannot find any Classical motifs on the candle-branches made by François-Thomas Germain in 1756 and shown in Plate 202 or in those attributed to Philippe Caffieri shown in Plate 203 which must date from about 1758, both sets must have been regarded as being very advanced in taste by contemporary critics. Germain's sconces, which are to be seen in what is believed to be their original positions at the Palais Royal in the engraving reproduced in Plate 23,[1] are each composed of three entirely naturalistic elements—sprigs of bay-leaves—tied together with a bow. Caffieri's, which are of a type that was almost certainly first made for Madame de Pompadour's little hunting-lodge at Saint-Hubert,[2] consist of three hunting-horns, again tied with a bow, and so disposed as to resemble a pendant hunting-trophy rendered in the most naturalistic terms. Neither sets display any feature that we, or contemporary observers, would regard as belonging to the Rococo tradition. Apart from the nozzles on Germain's set, there is no element of 'frivolity' about these compositions, there are no exaggerations, and the various components are in no way disproportionate to one another. In this respect, the Abbé le Blanc's criticism of the Rococo[3] had surely been heeded, and, indeed, these sconces do not appear to grow from the walls like the Rococo cartel-clocks the Abbé specified as being particularly ludicrous to his eyes. There is nothing that he would have called 'fou', 'ridicule', or 'depravé' about these pieces; one can see exactly what they represent and how they are suspended—with ribbons and bows. We will thus not be far wrong if we regard these sets of sconces as representing that moderated version of the new 'modern' taste which Blondel had so enthusiastically praised in 1762.[4]

The furniture made for Lalive de Jully, which expressed an extreme form of the new taste (Plates 85 to 89), was being made at about the same time as these sconces. The bronze mounts were also executed by Caffieri, probably after designs by Le Lorrain, although Caffieri was certainly capable of designing bronzes himself when necessary, as we have already noted. In this case, however, the bronzes were not mere applications to the furniture but were conceived as an integral part of a unified and consistent whole that is clearly the work of an architect. The clock shown in Plate 187 is probably the one which originally stood on top of the filing-cabinet belonging to Lalive's writing-table, or must anyway be identical to it. It has recently been purchased by the Musée Condé and now graces the cabinet again. It will be seen that the clock takes the form of a vase and that all its ornaments are of Classical derivation. Cochin actually mentions the clock in his memoirs when discussing Lalive's furniture and the unfortunate influence he feels it has had. He claims that it is 'de la' that 'nous vinrent . . . les vases, dont l'usage ancien étoit de contenir des liqueurs, devenus pendules à heures tournantes', and that these drug-jars for cordials, with the hours inscribed on a turning band, were 'belles inventions qui furent imitées par tous les ignorans et qui inondèrent Paris de drogues à la grecque'.[5] Lalive's standish has not

[1] See Note to Plate 202. [2] The relevant documentation is given in Note to Plate 203.
[3] See p. 41ff. [4] See p. 26.
[5] 'from this source' . . . 'there came to us . . . clocks with rotating bands instead of dials and shaped like vessels that the Ancients had made to hold cordials' . . . 'pleasing inventions in themselves, but now that they are imitated by all kinds of ignorant persons, we find Paris flooded with all sorts of stuff in the Greek manner.' The full relevant text is given here on p. 269.

so far been rediscovered but a somewhat coarse variation is to be seen in Plate 86. It was really the most *outré* of all the components of this astonishing desk. It is possible that Lalive had some candelabra and sconces made *en suite* with this furniture but we do not know for certain. All we can say is that, in the catalogue of the sale of his effects in 1769, a pair of two-branch candelabra (lot No. 272) accompanied the writing-table and that a pair of sconces, each with three branches and about twenty-three inches high, were listed as lot No. 273. The descriptions suggest they were in the Neo-Classical style. Monsieur Pierre Verlet has told the present author that he has seen some sconces in a private collection which one would at present tend to date about 1765–70 but which actually bear the date 1759 and are signed by Philippe Caffieri. The early date is less surprising if one knows the candelabra which Caffieri produced the year after, in 1760, for the High Altar at Notre-Dame and repeated in 1770 for Bayeux Cathedral (Plate 204). These are based on an older model and are in an advanced taste, especially if one considers the exceptionally sacred nature of the position for which they were made. They marked a great advance on the taste represented by the candelabra (Plate 342) designed by Slodtz for the catafalque erected in the same building in January of that year (Plate 42). The shaft of Caffieri's model resembles that of the central support of a projected table drawn by De Wailly and also published in 1760 (see page 70 and Plate 330). In that year, or the year before, Caffieri also provided two nine-branched candelabra for Notre-Dame which likewise seem to have been in an advanced classicising taste,[1] while the pedestal he made in 1761, now in the Louvre, obviously springs from a careful study of Classical ornament (Plate 236).

Germain and Caffieri were not alone in producing *bronzes d'ameublement* in an advanced style at this stage. A *marchand-mercier*, probably Poirier, commissioned a standish of bronze with Sèvres plaques in 1761 (Plate 235). This is the earliest of many such inkstands which are known to have been sold at Poirier's shop in the Rue Saint-Honoré from 1765 onwards. Laurent Hubert, a bronze-founder whose work has not yet been identified, also produced several pieces 'dans le goût du bel antique', according to an advertisement of February, 1763.[2] In the same year, when the English could once again get to Paris after the end of the Seven Years' War, we find Lord Coventry buying a considerable amount of expensive furnishings including two pairs of sconces 'à l'antique' which he acquired at Poirier's,[3] while the Duke of Bedford also went shopping and bought from some unnamed Parisian dealer 'un beau feu model neuf à la grec à vase forme antique orné de guirlandes de laurier'.[4] The many pieces of porcelain mounted with bronze ornaments 'dans le goût antique' the collector Julienne is known to have possessed (one is shown in Plate 237) must likewise date from the early 1760s.[5] During the summer of 1764 the Parisian dealer, Testard, sent various *bronzes d'ameublement* to the Court at Parma, including eight pairs of sconces and six pairs of fire-dogs. Some of the sconces survive (Colour Plate F); these are in a pure Neo-Classical style and Testard's bill makes it clear that the rest of the consignment was in the same taste. Unfortunately, we neither know who designed these bronzes, nor who executed the order (see the Note to Colour Plate F). It will be seen that the Neo-Classical taste must have

[1] See Note to Plate 204. [2] See Laurent Hubert's biography, p. 191.

[3] Croome Court Archives, Bill No. 14, dated 9th September 1763; I am indebted to Mrs Eileen Harris for having called my attention to this and other interesting documents relating to Lord Coventry's purchases in Paris, and to Mr. Geoffrey Beard for having procured photocopies of the said documents.

[4] 'A fine grate of a new design, *à la grecque*, with a Classical vase decorated with garlands of bay-leaves.' See Joan Evans, 'The Embassy of the 4th Duke of Bedford to Paris, 1762–63', *Archaeological Journal*, vol. CXIII, 1956, p. 144.

[5] The pieces referred to are listed in Note to Plate 237.

been well-established in the field of *bronzes d'ameublement* at a relatively early date—earlier than in most other branches of the decorative arts in France although roughly contemporarily with the parallel development taking place in the field of mural decoration (see pages 52–62).

On reflection, we can appreciate why these 'furnishing' bronzes should reflect the developments in interior architecture, for most of them were destined to be fixed or placed in close proximity to essentially architectural features in a room—notably on the walls and on chimney-pieces. Even the Court was quick to adopt the new fashion when it came to bronzes.

Pitoin, who was appointed bronze-founder to the Court in 1763, was providing pairs of fire-dogs for Versailles by the following March which, according to the descriptions, were embellished with Classical urns, architectural ornament and cupids playing musical instruments.[1] In the years that follow, Pitoin's work for the Court seems to have been couched almost entirely in the new taste. On 6th August 1765, he handed over two pairs of fire-dogs, worth respectively 650 and 700 livres, for the use of Monsieur de Fontanieu, the director of the *Garde-Meuble de la Couronne*. The descriptions of them are unusually detailed and help us envisage their appearance. One consisted of 'une Grille à quatre branches ornée de Pieds d'Estaux et Vazes avec des Rainceaux de feuilles de Refent, Gorges et Baguettes terminés en Volute par le bout, le Vaze orné de Testes de Belliers sur les cotés avec des Postes tournantes au pourtour, le dessus orné de feuilles de Persil, le tout terminé par une flame . . .'.[2] The vase, it will be seen, bore goats' heads and a Vitruvian scroll, as well as a collar of acanthus leaves and a flame on top. The other pair was supported by four fluted brackets ('à volute quarrée'). The vases in this case were trimmed with garlands of bay leaves. Pitoin provided three more sets of fire-dogs in the same year, all of which were definitely Classical in character. One went to Madame Louise's apartment at Fontainebleau and had vases with lion-masks.[3] The other two pairs were used in Louis XV's rooms. Each piece had an urn standing on a 'Colomne tronquée ornée de cannelures' and a 'consolle à volute quarrée'.[4]

The fire-dogs that could be bought in 1767 at Perier's ironmongery on the Quai de la Mégisserie were probably simplified versions of these. An example from Perier's shop is shown in Plate 401. It is interesting to note that it was the fire-dogs only made for royal use which were of Neo-Classical form at this stage; modern sconces were not being provided before 1768, as far as we can judge from the records, and up-to-date clock-cases not before 1769 and 1770.

As is explained in the Note to Plate 188, the chimney-clock there illustrated may already have been made in 1758. This cannot be proved but there is really no feature of its shape or decoration which speaks against such an early dating. Even the patination of the female figure is consonant with such a date in spite of a widespread belief that patination came in later (many clock-cases in the purest Rococo taste have such figures; for example those well-known pieces signed by Saint-Germain sporting elephants or oxen). The Classical calm of the figure, the chased antique ornament on her dress, and the architectural form of the actual case itself must have satisfied every nuance of modernistic taste, especially if the wooden base with its gilt bronze scroll is original! Such a clock could very well have stood on Lalive's filing-cabinet instead of the

[1] Arch. Nat., o[1] 3616[1] (Pitoin's bill), fol. 2–3, and o[1] 3318 (Journal of the *Garde-meuble*), fol. 16 *verso* and fol. 24 *verso*.

[2] Arch. Nat., o[1] 3617 (Pitoin's bill), fol. 3 *verso*, and o[1] 3318 (Journal of the *Garde-meuble*), fol. 91 (No. 3268 and No. 3269).

[3] Arch. Nat., o[1] 3318, fol. 91 *verso*.

[4] 'a short fluted column' and 'a bracket with a squared volute'. Ibid., and fol. 99 *verso*.

vase-like one he actually chose (Plate 187); indeed, we can see from the views of the Duc de Choiseul's rooms that it went very well on top of what would then have been an ultra-modern filing-cabinet (Plate 464). Presumably it was the enormous interest shown in the eighteenth century in anything mechanical, and especially in instruments concerned with the accurate keeping of time, that led to the bestowal of so much expensive artistic effort on the cases made to hold clock movements. Clocks, like public fountains, could become veritable monuments. One can cite many examples of elaborate time-pieces occupying prominent positions in palaces during the eighteenth century (e.g. the Cabinet de la Pendule at Versailles and the Clay clock in the Cupola Room at Kensington Palace). One frequently spent more on the cases for such clocks than on their movement. The King of Denmark ordered a clock in Paris in 1765 (Plate 189) for the movement of which he was charged 1,500 livres. The model for the case was made by the sculptor Pajou and alone cost 1,800 livres. The casting and chasing in Saint-Germain's workshops cost 5,480 livres, and the gilding 2,400 livres.[1] The case of the Marquis de Rochechouart's famous clock in the Wallace Collection[2] which was executed in 1771, cost even more in proportion to its movement.

Pajou's model for the Danish King's clock was exhibited at the *Salon* during the autumn of 1765 and it may well be that it was the source of inspiration for Prieur's design of 1766 which is shown in Plate 406 and must be a preparatory design for the clock which once stood in the palace at Warsaw (Plate 190). The recumbent woman with her attendant cupid of Prieur's project is a much more light-hearted being than the gravely Classical lady on Pajou's model. Indeed, Prieur's girl might well have come, almost unchanged, straight from a clock-case in the Rococo style! The same may be said of the figures on the cases shown in Plates 191 and 192, the second of which is signed by Prieur. However, when it came to the strictly ornamental, non-figurative elements, Prieur adhered to the Classical vocabulary, although, when compared with Caffieri's work at this stage, his style was rather less severe and his forms were more graceful. Caffieri had been an early adherent of the revived taste for Classicism and had been steeped in its most extreme form. He may have found it difficult to moderate the severity of his style whereas Prieur, a decade his junior, had just become a *maître-sculpteur* in 1765 when it is probable that the wilder excesses of the 'goût grecque' were gently on the wane.

Caffieri and Prieur's numerous works for the Court at Warsaw can hardly have gone unnoticed in Paris. Their work for this commission did not in fact represent any abrupt change of direction in the general development but, as far as richness and variety were concerned, they must have been quite exceptional and unlike any earlier essays in the new style. One can imagine how all these new pieces must have made many a bronze-founder cast a critical eye over his existing stock of models and pause to consider what could be done about getting some fresh ones. As it happens, there is a certain amount of evidence that a considerable number of new models were created in the years that followed the completion of the Polish enterprise. There are new clocks—both clocks for the mantel-shelf (Plates 193, 197, 198 and 201) and cartel clocks to hang on the wall (Plates 194 to 196 and 444). There are new barometers (Plates 199 and 200), candelabra and sconces (Plates 208 to 214, 441 and 442), and new types of fire-dogs (Plates 223 to 228). New forms also appear among the bronze mounts that were fitted to so much porcelain and to so many vessels of semi-precious stone during the middle decades of the eighteenth century in France. In this particular field—that of *bronzes d'ameublement*—we may notice a tendency to-

[1] See Note to Plate 189. [2] Watson, *Wallace Collection Furniture*, No. F. 258.

wards increasing elegance of form which embodies a light and graceful kind of Classicism. No doubt this was found more attractive than the doctrinaire rigours of the 'goût grec'; at any rate it was the style destined to triumph in the future.

Once Caffieri had discarded the severe style of his early essays in Neo-Classicism, he seems to have fallen in with the new trend towards a lighter and more graceful idiom. The sconces shown in Plate 213, which seem to be identical with a model listed as being part of his stock in 1770, exemplify his later style. That the large 'chandelier Pascal' he made for the Cathedral at Clermont-Ferrand in 1771 (Plate 217) still retains a strong monumental element is presumably due to the special nature of its intended position.

Even if we ignore the bronzes that the Prince de Condé ordered from Caffieri on 1st March 1770 (Plates 453 to 461)—pieces which mark such a major step forward in the stylistic development, it is clear from the inventory drawn up on 3rd December that Caffieri's stock must have been very extensive and modern at the end of that year. This inventory was made on the death of Caffieri's wife; the text is given in full on pages 277–81. Caffieri was present when the list was being compiled; the valuation was made by the bronze-founder Robert Osmond in collaboration with his colleague Pierre-François Boitard. This inventory is not of course anything like as informative as the collection of signed and dated designs which was deposited at the Guild's offices would be,[1] partly because the descriptions are so brief and partly because we are not told how old the models were when the list was drawn up. All the same, it is of very considerable help and interest. It contains 101 items of which some comprise several pieces. In all, there were some 160 pieces, about twenty of them forming pairs, in the stock-room or in the workshop. This did not include the contents of eighteen crates of discarded models and an unspecified number of unused components.

We may assume that a few items[2] described as being 'dans le goût moderne' and 'à la moderne'[3] were in the Rococo taste, because some of these can be equated with items listed in the inventory of Caffieri's father's workshop, made on the latter's death in 1755, so there can be little doubt that these were in the old taste. We can be fairly certain, on the other hand, that most of the collection was in a progressive style of Neo-Classical character. For instance, the lyre-shaped cartel clock listed as item No. 47 probably resembled that shown in Plate 194. The ornaments of the sconces illustrated in Plate 211 agree with those described under items 67 and 70, while the sconces mentioned as No. 94 must have been very like those now in Warsaw (Plate 213) even if the latter were not included among the goods Caffieri forwarded to the Polish Court in 1766 and 1767. The fire-dogs sporting a dog and a cat (No. 33) may well have been identical to those shown in Plate 223, and those comprising items 38, 40 to 42 and 80, seem to have had much in common with a pair now in the Mobilier National in Paris (Plate 231), and another pair in the Musée des Arts Décoratifs, also in Paris (Plate 232); both pairs are decorated with Classical tripods.

Not a single example of Pitoin's productions from the 1760s has so far been identified for certain. All the same, we have the most detailed descriptions of the work he did for the French Court, both in his own bills and in the Journal of the *Garde-Meuble*. From these documents it becomes apparent that Pitoin did not charge separately for the original drawing or model of a bronze, as Caffieri was to do in the case of the work he did for the Palais Bourbon, and we must

[1] See p. 96. [2] Nos, 1, 3, 4, 6, 23, 28, 48, 49, 51, 56, 58, 72, 79, 92 and 93.
[3] 'in the modern taste', and 'modern'.

therefore conclude that the bronzes Pitoin sold for use at Court were not unique or solely reserved for use in the royal household. If this is so, and he retained the copyright of his models in accordance with the provisions of the Act of 1766, we can assume that he made more than one bronze from each model and that any bronzes agreeing closely with the descriptions in the royal accounts may with reason be attributed to him even though the actual piece in question does not have a royal provenance. Having said this, one should, however, closely inspect the bronze to see if the craftsmanship is of the quality one could expect to find in Pitoin's work; if the piece in question is of inferior quality one may, for this reason alone, suspect it of being spurious, or a copy of the kind the Act of 30th July 1766 was intended to make illegal.[1]

In the Musée des Arts Décoratifs at Lyons there is a pair of fire-dogs that seems to echo the descriptions[2] of two of the items Pitoin delivered to the French Court in 1767 at a cost of 2,200 livres the pair (Plate 224). The Classical derivation of the motifs embodied in these fire-dogs is unmistakable yet the general forms have a Baroque flavour. The vase forming the finial, however, is of an uncompromisingly severe aspect and might almost have been designed by Le Lorrain or Neufforge.[3] These particular pieces are of excellent quality, even if they are ungilded, but inferior specimens of the same model have also come to light and should be viewed with distrust.

Pitoin provided numerous bronzes for use at the French Court. For example, he sent five pairs of gilded fire-dogs for the new Petit Trianon in 1768 and the descriptions indicate that these were similar to the pair just mentioned (Plate 224). He also produced some very expensive and, presumably, elaborate sets—one for the *Salon de Compagnie* in the same little palace, costing 4,800 livres, and one for the large Dining-room costing 4,000 livres. Pitoin went out to the house on 12th April to measure the fireplaces and the orders were issued four days later. He managed to deliver them by 15th June—that is, just two months later. This does seem to indicate that he already had the models in stock and only needed to reproduce them; he could hardly have gone through the whole process of designing a new model, and having it made in that time as well. It seems reasonable to suppose, therefore, that other sets of fire-dogs similar to those he made for the Petit Trianon were produced by Pitoin and sold to slightly less illustrious customers.

It would seem that new sconces were not made specially for the walls of the Petit Trianon (finished in April 1770). The first sconces in what would seem to be a Neo-Classical style that were provided for the French court were those delivered on 4th October 1768 by the *marchand-miroitier*, Claude de la Roüe, who normally supplied the Court with mirrors and chandeliers but was perfectly willing to provide wares of other kinds. The sconces in question were 'à vazes et guirlandes de fleurs' ('with vases and garlands of flowers') and had two branches.[4] They had been made for the Hôtel des Sceaux at Fontainebleau in readiness for a proposed over-night stay by the King of Denmark who was then on a visit to France. They may have resembled those shown in Plate 210. We know that this model was produced in, or shortly before, 1769 because an example may be seen in the background of the portrait of the Marquis de Marigny (Plate 442) which was exhibited at the *Salon* in that year.

In July 1769, Pitoin provided five sconces for Madame Adelaïde's rooms in the Château at Compiègne, although he had not hitherto concerned himself much with sconces. Judging by the descriptions,[5] these particular pieces were not all that Classical in taste; they were chiefly com-

[1] See p. 95. [2] See Note to Plate 224.

[3] E.g. the vases reproduced as Plates 297, 298, 313–318. [4] Arch. Nat., o[1] 3318, fol. 214 *verso*.

[5] Given in full in Note to Plate 214.

posed of naturalistic branches and flowers. They may have looked rather like a set in the Musée Nissim de Camondo (Plate 214). It was not until after 1770 that Pitoin really began to concentrate on the manufacture of sconces. The first set entirely couched in the Neo-Classical taste, with lion's masks and so forth, were sent for Madame du Barry's use at Compiègne on 24th June 1771.[1] These would seem to have resembled a set in the Wrightsman Collection[2] although the latter are known to have been made at a later date.[3] All the same, they may have been taken from a model first produced in 1771. At this same time, Pitoin made some sconces for the Comtesse de Provence and, later in the year, others for Fontainebleau, all of which must have been rather like that shown in Plate 211 although this actual example was almost certainly produced by Caffieri some years before.

A number of pieces of porcelain and objects of semi-precious stones of various kinds were provided with mounts of gilt bronze in the Classical taste during the late 1760s which are often bewildering in their richness and intricacy. It had long been the practice to mount Oriental, and subsequently also European, porcelain in elaborate bronze settings. This tradition was already well established by the sixteenth century but by far the most imaginative mounts of this class were made during the Rococo period and this taste for fanciful settings prevailed through the Neo-Classical phase and right into the early nineteenth century. A famous collection of such mounted *objets d'art* that existed during the period which concerns us here was that of Blondel de Gagny, of which Dezallier d'Argenville wrote in 1770 that 'les montures semblent disputer de prix avec les pieces qu'elles accompagnent'.[4] Another such collection was that of Jean de Julienne.[5] The mounts for many such pieces were made by F.-T. Germain and Duplessis *père* and when one finds one of the Duplessis (it is not certain whether it was the father or the son in this case) buying four rather expensive pieces of unmounted Chinese porcelain at the collector Julienne's sale in 1767[6]—one cost 1,004 livres—one can be fairly sure the intention was to furnish them with mounts of gilt bronze, after which—in their new up-to-date guise—they could be sold to advantage! At the Sèvres porcelain factory, vases of Oriental shape and colour were being turned out at this period specially for mounting in this manner (Plates 238 to 240). It is not yet known whether the Duplessis, who were both attached to the factory as designers, were in any way responsible for introducing this new line. We do, on the other hand, know that such vases were at first sold without mounts, when they were all bought by *marchands-merciers* like Dulac, Lair's widow, and Grouel—and, later, also by Poirier.[7] This suggests that the initiative in this matter may have been taken by the dealers who may have provided the designs for these

[1] Arch. Nat., o[1] 3319 fol. 60 *verso*, 'Vne Paire de bras a 3 branches de bronze doré d'or moulu en forme de guienne ornées de graines montantes Le bas terminé par une plinte faisant resaut orné au milieu d'un masque de lyon portant un soc d'ou sort les branches avec volutes guirlandes et cannelures avec bobeches. au dessus de la plaque est posé un vaze orné de feuilles et flâmes avec des anneaux de chaque coté haute de 24. pouces.' ('A pair of sconces with three branches, of gilt bronze, each in the shape of a term, with a plinth below decorated with corn forming a network in the centre of which is a lion's mask with a socket from which spring branches with volutes, garlands and fluting, ending in nozzles. On top of the plaque is a vase decorated with leaves and flames, with ring handles on each side. 24 inches high.')

[2] F. J. B. Watson, *The Wrightsman Collection*, I–II, New York, 1966, No. 237.

[3] See Pierre Verlet, 'Homage to the Dix-Huitieme', *Apollo*, March 1967, p. 211.

[4] 'the mounts would seem to be of at least as high a value as the pieces they adorn'. Dezallier d'Argenville, *Paris*, ed. 1770, p. 136.

[5] See Note to Plate 237.

[6] See Geneviève Levallet-Haug, 'Jean-Claude Duplessis, orfèvre du roi', *La Renaissance de l'Art Français*, pp. 60–7.

[7] See Note to Plate 238.

vases and then commissioned the mounts from the bronze-founders they habitually patronised. Whatever the case, it will be noted that the mounts are in an advanced taste reminiscent of Caffieri's contemporary work. It is noteworthy that these vases never bear the Sèvres mark and that they are such skilful imitations of the genuine Oriental article that even such eminent connoisseurs as Brongniart, the Director of the Sèvres factory at the beginning of the nineteenth century, once bought a pair of the factory's own products in the belief that they were really Chinese! Indeed, it may well be that the original intention had been to pass off these vases as Chinese. After all, at this period furniture was often veneered with genuine Oriental lacquer or japanned imitations, all trimmed with French bronze mounts, first in the Rococo style and subsequently in the Classical taste, so why not do the same with porcelain? At any rate, the idea quickly caught on and vases were soon being made for the same purpose decorated in the normal Sèvres style (Plate 242). This was a great success and thus a tradition was established which came to last a long while.

None of the *bronzes d'ameublement* that Caffieri made between 1770 and 1772 for the Prince de Condé has so far been identified and it is, indeed, possible that only a single pair of candelabra now survives. All the bronzes are listed in Caffieri's bill which is still preserved in the Archives Condé at Chantilly. Those which were specially designed for the Prince, and were therefore unique, are depicted in the margin (Plates 453 to 461). This would seem to be a form of tacit acknowledgement on Caffieri's part that he no longer had the right to reproduce this model; it probably corresponded to depositing the designs at the offices of the Guild—but on behalf of the customer, not the artist. The remaining bronzes, which were presumably taken from models already in stock and which were therefore not unique, are not illustrated in the bill. In these instances, the Prince did not have to pay the cost of providing a model. The total sum involved was 62,898 livres which was subsequently reduced to 43,457 livres. This is about half what Caffieri received for the bronzes he produced for the Polish Court. The Prince de Condé paid in addition the sum of 704 livres for some models and designs that were never used.

What is remarkable about Caffieri's Condé bronzes is their grace and elegance. They lack all heaviness. This may be due to Prieur's influence, since the bronzes he had designed for the Polish Court in 1766 had been considerably more graceful than anything Caffieri had produced by that time. The sconces and fire-dogs (Plates 453 to 461) Caffieri now made in the early 1770s for the Grande Galerie at the Palais Bourbon, a room where heroic symbolism was after all much in evidence, are totally free of that flamboyant character associated with Caffieri's previous work. The candle-branches are extremely attenuated and curve elegantly. The trumpets—symbols of Fame—are considerably more slender than those on the sconces he made for the Saint-Hubert pavilion about 1758, and the same applies to the laurel wreaths (cf. Plate 203). Likewise, the tall fire-dogs (some 21 cm. high) appear much less monumental than one might expect of pieces designed for these surroundings. When compared with those shown in Plate 224, here attributed to Pitoin, they are far less massive in their proportions. This elegance pervaded all the bronzes Caffieri made for the Palais Bourbon.

If only we had the Bronze-founders Guild's collection of signed and dated designs to guide us, we could so easily judge whether in fact Caffieri's Condé bronzes represent a new tendency or whether they were merely reflections of a more widespread trend. The indications are that the latter was the case. In 1770, for example, Gouthière was engaged in making bronze furnishings for the Pavillon de Louveciennes: they were designed by Ledoux and have now disappeared.

But he was apparently also working at this stage for the Duc d'Aumont who had had him taken onto the staff of the *Menus Plaisirs*, the organisation not concerned with buildings and furnishings in the ordinary way but prepared to conjure up all kinds of occasional arrangements and special equipment for the royal household.[1] There, he would probably have worked from drawings supplied by Belanger. The tripod supporting a jasper bowl (Plate 243) is an example of the work produced by Gouthière for the Duc d'Aumont and can reasonably be dated between 1772 and 1775. Pitoin's bronzes made for Madame du Barry's rooms at Fontainebleau in 1771 and 1772 (Plates 229 and 230) have already been discussed (p. 103). The table-lamp (Plate 220) made by an unknown bronze-founder must date from 1774 or slightly earlier, as is explained in the Note to the Plate concerned. And the younger Duplessis' candelabrum shown in Plate 218 must at any rate belong to the first half of the 1770s. All these pieces embody the slender, elegant variant of the Neo-Classical idiom of which we have been speaking, and it was this form which was to reign supreme in subsequent years. If one considers the forms of the *canapés* and chairs made by Carpentier, which almost certainly came into existence in 1770, and possibly even in 1769 (Plates 171 and 174), or if one studies the projected designs for the mural-decorations of the Hôtel d'Uzès and the Hôtel Mélusine (Plates 64, 65, 68 and 69), it is not so surprising that this new form of the Neo-Classical style makes its appearance in *bronzes d'ameublement* at this stage, for, as we pointed out, these were pieces of furniture normally closely associated with architectural features which, in turn, were the first elements to record a change of spirit. These bronzes, then, as well as the rooms and seat-furniture just mentioned, exemplify Pierre Patte's pronouncement of a few years later—namely that the decoration and furnishing of houses had recently become something of 'un art nouveau'.[2] We shall show how the same development was echoed in the work of the goldsmiths and in the products of the porcelain factory at Sèvres.

5. WORKS IN GOLD AND SILVER

It was at the gold- and silversmiths that Cochin directed his first public attack against what he felt was the bad taste licensed by the misguided permissiveness of the Rococo phase. The first article was published, it will be recalled, in the *Mercure de France* in December 1754 (see pages 233–5 where it is reprinted in full). He particularly begged these craftsmen to cease producing works with components of grossly differing proportions—which was so much a feature of contemporary work. He thought it silly, for instance, to ornament the lid of a soup-tureen with life-sized representations of carrots and then top the whole thing with the figure of a rabbit the size of one's little finger. Claude Ballin is said to have been one of the few Parisian goldsmiths who tried to keep the figurative elements in something like their true proportions, even during the phase when the Rococo spirit was at its most abandoned. Soon after Cochin's criticisms were made, we find Robert-Joseph Auguste and François-Thomas Germain taking very positive steps to rectify the situation. Auguste made some tureens between 1756 and 1760 which have been in the Danish royal collection since the eighteenth century; these have the figures of playing children on their lids, as well as bay-leaves and some ornaments that clearly derive from the

[1] See Gouthière's and Duc d'Aumont's biographies, p. 187 and p. 148 respectively. [2] See p. 24.

Antique. In spite of their ebullient, almost Baroque, form, these tureens represent a definite attempt to break with the turbulent indiscipline of the Rococo. They are early examples of a return to a moderate form of Classicism.[1] Germain favoured a purer Classical style, as the tripod-stands of the large tea-kettles he made already in 1756–57 show (Plate 244). With their goats' heads and garlands, these are far more positively Classical than, for example, the chimney-pieces he made for the Count Bernstorff's house in Copenhagen (Plate 27) or for the Palais Royal. So, as in other branches, there were two streams of progressive taste in Parisian goldsmiths' work—moderate on one hand and extreme on the other—and these two streams were already quite apparent by the late 1750s.

On the other hand, we do not really know how widespread the progressive movement may have been and we never shall for the simple reason that enormous quantities of French silver were sent to be melted down in 1759 and 1760, as a patriotic measure designed to bolster up the nation's finances during the Seven Years' War. The King alone sent silver and silver-gilt objects weighing over 8,000 lb. to the crucibles.[2] Furthermore it is likely that the war itself put a brake on the amount of work being commissioned from the goldsmiths. The Journal of the *Garde-meuble* makes it clear that the King, at any rate, was not ordering much new silver at this period. In 1760, he was obliged to order a certain amount of silver for the young Duc de Berry and also some for a church—but the total only weighed 94 lb. But in 1761 only one single silver egg-cup was ordered for the Court, while the next year the total order comprised a sugar-spoon and linings for two Sèvres soup-tureens. The story was the same in 1763 when orders for a soup-ladle and two more linings for tureens were issued. But once the War was over, in 1764, the orders began to stream from the offices of the *Garde-Meuble*. Silver weighing 179 lb. was bought, and Roëttiers delivered a pair of gold sugar-casters which had been ordered in 1757.[3] In 1765, 1766 and 1767, silver weighing respectively 250, 860 and 1,090 lb. was ordered. It is doubtful whether any of this silver survived the Revolution of 1789 and our knowledge of its appearance is very limited. Nor do we really know to what extent ordinary people commissioned new silver to replace that which they had sacrificed during the War. The comparatively small amount of silver dating from the 1760s, however, rather suggests that the output during this decade was on a reduced scale.

It has so far only been possible to find a few pieces of silver with up-to-date features, dating from the early 1760s. The tureen shown in Plate 245, which was made in Antoine-Jean de Villeclair's workshops in 1762 or 1763, belongs to the moderate category, while the accompanying stand (here shown separately; Plate 246), with its clean oval shape and its purely Classical decoration, is as progressive a piece as one could possibly expect to find at this date. The same applies to Germain's candlesticks (Plate 247) which are dated 1762 and may have been made for Madame de Pompadour, and to the cruet-stand (Plate 248) made in 1763–64 by Jean-Charles Gordière which has a pineapple-like finial and its draperies suspended from some chunky, rectangular objects that resemble blocks of masonry. In this connection it is worth recording that Germain, in 1761, sent off six soup-tureens and six *pots à oille* (another type of tureen) to Russia

[1] The most readily accessible reproduction of one of these tureens is in the catalogue to the exhibition '*Le Danemark, ses trésors, son art*', held at the Musée du Louvre in 1965; the tureens are No. 193 of the catalogue. Another may be seen in Gudmund Boesen, 'L'Argenterie française dans les collections royales danoises', *La Revue du Louvre*, 1965, No. 3, p. 129, fig. 4.

[2] Arch. Nat., o[1] 3317, fol. 44–91.

[3] See Pierre Verlet, 'La vaisselle d'or de Louis XV', *La Revue des Arts*, 1956, pp. 99–104.

for use at the Court in St. Petersburg. *L'Avantcoureur* described them as having 'la forme de ces vases ovales antiques destinés aux sacrifices'.[1]

It is of course hardly surprising that few if any of the costly, bejewelled, gold snuff-boxes (*tabatières*) the King was wont to give as presents have survived. Their obvious intrinsic value must in most cases have tempted an owner to sell them or have them melted down. On the other hand, a number of rather less expensive snuff-boxes have come down to us—mostly those without jewelled decoration but set with plaques of porcelain or enamel instead (Plates 249 to 256). These were hardly worth melting down.

It is not surprising, either, that the veerings of Fashion should be recorded almost immediately in these little boxes which were, after all, so essential a piece of equipment for the man-about-town. Indeed, we are told by numerous contemporary observers how the *tabatière* was regarded as something of a status symbol in the eighteenth century. No less an authority, from our point of view, than l'Abbé Le Blanc has confirmed this,[2] while the wit, Sébastien Mercier, maintained that, if you were the proud possessor of three hundred little snuff-boxes, you could dispense with your library, your cabinet of curiosities and your collection of paintings![3] Baron de Grimm, another of our favourite commentators in the present connection, whose words have already been much quoted above, spoke of how any of the town's young sparks would have been deeply ashamed in 1763 if they had been unable to sport a gold snuff-box which was 'à la grecque'.[4]

Already in the 1750s the fanciful shapes of the typical Rococo snuff-box were giving way to more regular forms—ovals and rectangles—which now made their appearance again in this by-way of the decorative arts. We know of two oval boxes bearing the date-mark for 1753–54 made by Noël Hardivilliers; one in the Louvre and the other in the Rijksmuseum. Both have chinoiserie decoration in enamel and have what appears to be an 'à la grecque' border that, on closer inspection, turns out to be more of a Chinese fret than a Vitruvian one! It is not really until the early 1760s that Parisian snuff-boxes acquire undoubtedly Classical decoration to go with a plain and regular form. Examples from the years 1763 and 1764 are shown in Plates 249–255. It must have been boxes of just this type for which the fashion-conscious Parisian was clamouring when Baron de Grimm made his comment. Boxes of this class are the work of goldsmiths like Jean Fremin, Charles Le Bastier, Mathieu Coiny, Jean George, R.-J. Auguste, Jean Formey, J.-M. Tiron and Louis Roucel. It will, incidentally, hardly come as a surprise to the reader who has followed us this far to learn that one of the very earliest surviving snuff-boxes in the Neo-Classical taste is the work of Robert-Joseph Auguste who had shown sympathy at an early date for the new style, as we have already noted. It is dated 1762–63 (Plate 251). Auguste had, in fact, worked already in 1761 in bronze for the architect De Wailly who was, it will be remembered, a leading exponent of the more uncompromising vein of Neo-Classicism (see page 70). Most of the snuff-boxes in the Neo-Classical taste have scenes in enamel amid the decoration executed in the metal of the box itself. The subjects depicted in enamel might still be in the old Boucher-type style but more up-to-date motifs were equally popular. In the case of the box illustrated in Plate 256, the enamel decoration consisting of arabesques entirely dominates the goldsmith's work.

[1] 'in the shape of those oval Classical urns intended for sacrificial ceremonies'. *L'Avantcoureur*, 13th July 1761, p. 442.

[2] *Mercure de France*, March 1754, pp. 171–2.

[3] *Tableau de Paris*, Chapter 175 (ed. 1782), p. 220.

[4] See p. 50.

Commissions from foreign Courts like those of Spain, Portugal, Russia and Denmark must have done much to keep the Parisian goldsmiths solvent during the Seven Years' War and in the mid-1760s. Enormous quantities of French silver was sent off to these important foreign customers and, while much of it has long since disappeared, some still survives. One item which seems to have disappeared but which must have been ultra-modern in its day was the silver-gilt toilet-set made by Germain *le Romain* and Thomas Chamelier which the King of Spain ordered as a birthday present for the Princess of Asturias in 1765. From the contract, which Guiffrey published,[1] we know it was designed by Philippe Caffieri who was also to supervise its execution. While we are not sure whether the set still survives, we can make a fair guess at what it was like. In the first place, we already know something of Caffieri's Neo-Classical style in the years around 1765, through his work in bronze for Notre-Dame and the Polish Court (see page 98ff. and Plates 204 and 206). And, secondly, we have the report in *L'Avantcoureur* of 9th December 1765, published a fortnight after the set had been dispatched to Madrid, telling us that 'Le goût, l'élégance & la nouveauté des formes regnent de toutes parts dans ce morceau'[2] and that each piece constituting the set was adorned with garlands of flowers as well as cupids. The report goes on to state that 'Cet ouvrage, qui fait honneur au talent & au génie des Artistes, qui l'ont exécuté de concert, leur a procuré le concours & les applaudissemens de tous les Connoisseurs qui en ont vu l'exposition . . .'.[3] From all this, it seems reasonable to conclude that this set was at least as advanced in taste as Caffieri's work for the King of Poland. Presumably it was in much the same style as the toilet-sets made by François-Thomas Germain which are now in Lisbon and Leningrad, one dated 1765–66 and the other 1766 (Plates 257 to 260). In both these sets, some of the pieces—especially some of the boxes—are of a shape that calls to mind silver from the early years of the century. All the same, the Neo-Classical element is undoubtedly present. The 'Roman' heads, the pineapple finials, the tightly-twisted garlands all betray the new spirit. The shape of the dressing-mirror in the Leningrad set is of an architectural conception as severe as the carved picture-frames Guibert made in 1760 and 1761 (see page 61 and Plates 345 to 348). Some candelabra made by Auguste between 1766 and 1768 (Plates 261 and 262) are closely related in style to these two toilet-sets and are, moreover, surmounted by representations of Classical incense-burners like some of Caffieri's bronzes of the same date.

Although little of the work of Germain, Auguste and Roëttiers has come down to us from the mid-1760s, it is clear that Neo-Classicism was well established in their workshops by then —as it may also have been among many less well-known Parisian goldsmiths about whom we at present have all too little information. We only have reports of the magnificent inkstand Germain made in 1766 for the King of Poland but these are quite revealing. *L'Avantcoureur* for 8th September 1766, describes it as follows: 'Cette écritoire a la forme d'un vase antique. Aux deux bouts sont deux enfants dont la partie inférieure se termine en feuilles: elle entoure & décore le vase. Il est lui-meme terminé dans la partie supérieure par un couronnement qui forme une sonnette que l'oeil ne soupçonne pas y être. Ce couronnement est surmonté d'un aigle de la plus extrême vérité. A chaque côté de cette écritoire sont deux serre-papier qui représentent les armes du prince. Ils ont chacun la forme d'un rocher sur lequel est un taureau d'après l'antique. L'un des deux est imité du taureau Farnese.'[4] There can have been no mistaking the Classical

[1] Guiffrey, *Les Caffieri*, p. 143. [2] 'Good taste, elegance and novelty of form radiate from every piece.'

[3] 'This piece of work, which reflects great honour on the talents of the artists who have collaborated on the project, has procured them encouragement and praise from all connoisseurs who have seen the exhibition.'

[4] 'This inkstand is in the form of a Classical urn. On each side is the figure of a child springing from foliage

character of this piece. Handles in the form of children with their nether parts blending into foliage that encircles a vase were motifs which Auguste was to use a decade later on some tureens he made for the Swedish ambassador, Creutz.[1] Germain had exhibited the toilet-set made for the Princess of Asturias at his shop the year before and he now showed the new inkstand, in the same place, together with a toilet-service he had just made for the King of Portugal. It remained on show until the 14th September.

Germain suffered a spectacular bankruptcy in 1764—a misfortune which did not prevent him contriving to work for the French and foreign Courts—after which Roëttiers became principal supplier of works in gold and silver for Versailles. In fact, Roëttiers had already been executing work for the Court for some years. A commission he had completed and delivered by the 14th June 1766 consisted of two inkstands for the personal use of Louis XV which seem to have had at least some Classical features, for the brief description informs us that they were decorated with garlands and had legs in the form of 'canneaux à l'antique',[2] which presumably means 'like fasces'. In the same year, Roëttiers made some silver forks for the King, as M. Yves Bottineau has shown.[3] These were of a Neo-Classical form and must have resembled a fork which he made five years later and is illustrated in Plate 264. Roëttiers is also known to have supplied four large tureens and some *pots à oille* of markedly Classical form 'pour servir dans les differens offices du Roy, de Monsieur Le Dauphin Et de Mesdames de France au Château de Versailles'.[4] These were delivered on 29th February 1768. One of the tureens was described as being 'chantournée sur l'ovale representant un vaze antique cannelé de godrons en relief avec les armes du Roy aussy en relief orné de guirlandes qui s'attachent à des mascarons antiques, d'où sortent les anses mobiles formés par des feuilles de laurier liées de rubans, le couvercle cannelé de godrons creux et de relief chargé d'un groupe'.[5] It is unlikely that these tureens were as advanced in their Neo-Classicism as those Roëttiers made for Catharine the Great in 1770–71 (Plate 263), but the description just quoted suggests they must have had a comparatively modern look about them when they were new.

The famous Orloff set (Plates 263 to 265), which is now dispersed and is to be found in many collections—both public and private, was made in 1770–71. It marks the end of an old, and the beginning of a new, era in the history of French goldsmiths' work. It is couched in a relatively massive architectural style, composed almost entirely of purely Classical motifs. The next stage in the development was to give the forms and motifs greater elegance and more pleasing proportions. Auguste seems to have set the pace and the new idiom can be seen in his tureen of 1771–72 (Plate 266) and in the service he made for the Swedish Ambassador which we have already mentioned—a set, incidentally, which subsequently passed into the hands of Gustavus III.

---

that envelops the urn. On top, the vase is crowned by a capping incorporating a disguised bell. This is surmounted by an extremely lifelike eagle. Flanking the inkstand are two filing-trays decorated with the King's coat-of-arms. Each is in the form of rocks on which stand bulls taken from a Classical source. One is after the Farnese bull.'

[1] Now in the royal Swedish collections, reproduced in Åke Setterwall and Stig Fogelmarck, *Stockholm slott och dess konstskatter*, Stockholm, 1950, p. 163.

[2] Arch. Nat., o[1] 3319, fol. 116 *verso*.

[3] See Note to Plate 264.

[4] 'for use in the apartments of the King, the Dauphin, and the King's daughters [Mesdames] in the Château of Versailles.'

[5] 'oval in profile, representing a Classical vase with gadrooning bearing the Royal Arms in relief and decorated with garlands springing from Antique masks from which also depend swinging handles in the shape of bay-leaves bound with ribbon, the lid being decorated with raised and sunken gadrooning, all surmounted by a group of figures'. Arch. Nat., o[1] 3318 fol. 183 *verso*.

In the main, the stylistic development in French silver ran parallel to that in the field of *bronzes d'ameublement*. Indeed, there must have been a certain amount of mutual influence from one of these two branches of the decorative arts to the other. We have seen how Caffieri designed a toilet-set for Germain *le Romain* to execute. This need not have been an isolated instance of cross-fertilisation. The increasing technical excellence and delicacy that we find in bronzes made in the 1760s, notably in their chasing, may well be the result of the influence of goldsmiths like Auguste and F.-T. Germain who also worked in bronze! It may even turn out to be the case that many bronze-founders employed the same chasers—*ciseleurs*—as the goldsmiths.

6. SÈVRES PORCELAIN

It almost goes without saying that the management of a large enterprise like the soft-paste porcelain factory at Sèvres would feel bound to adopt a cautious stand in the face of a new style, in order to make sure it had staying-power. The total output of the Sèvres establishment was destined for the luxury market; unlike many more-recently established porcelain factories, Sèvres did not turn out a steady flow of standard wares in order to earn its bread-and-butter and help support the luxury range. For this reason, the factory very rarely accepted special orders from private individuals, at least during the period that concerns us, and all capital investment in new models had therefore to be borne solely by the enterprise itself. The factory's economy as a whole was not at all soundly based, so it is hardly surprising that they proceeded with caution, when it came to developing new lines. The factory was particularly reluctant to alter the shapes—requiring new designs and moulds—of the ranges that were the best-sellers, and of which a large stock was held in the white, ready for painting. This applied particularly to the large dinner-services. It was far less risky to experiment with wares like the decorative vases, of which the output was limited. Experiments could also be tried with the painted decoration at no great expense. In this way, new decorative styles could be tried out on the public and the production of new forms adjusted according to their reaction. Such experiments with the painted decoration were often carried out on cups and saucers which came to be eagerly sought by collectors, even at the time.

The first unmistakable, if somewhat insignificant, attempt to introduce a measure of Classicism at Sèvres is embodied in some small rectangular trays which have upstanding edges in the shape of a Vitruvian scroll (Plates 268 and 269). These made their first appearance in 1757. The framing of the painted decoration is of a plain and regular kind, quite unlike the lacy borders normally used by the factory at this period. Moreover, the flowers are rendered in a naturalistic manner; they are no longer entirely imaginary blooms. In fact, Sèvres had already brought out a rectangular tray before 1757 but it had not been furnished with the scrolled Classical edging. Likewise, cups of extremely plain shapes had already been produced by that time. For example, the form known as the 'gobelet litron' (Plate 289), which is still in production, had been developed by this stage.

A similar attempt to bring an old shape up-to-date is to be seen in the pot-pourri vases which are shaped like a masted ship. That shown in Plate 271 bears the date-mark for 1761 and the new feature is the foot which is now of architectural form, replacing the scrolled foot of the earlier model. Moreover, as on the trays just mentioned, the gold trimming is simpler than that which one finds on most Sèvres porcelain of the period. The bronze stand for the 'masted' vase consists of a gilded rectangular block with an oval wreath of bay-leaves and dolphins. It was undoubtedly made at the same time as the vase since the latter has been specially shaped to fit into the base. The original 'masted' vase was presumably designed and modelled by Duplessis *père*, then the factory's chief designer, but it is not known whether he was also responsible for this remodelling.

Many more examples could be given to show how the Sèvres factory had already begun to revise its style by the end of the 1750s. The panels reserved in the painted ground, which were to be painted with bouquets of flowers or with small scenes, began to become more regular in shape at about the same time. The panels were now usually oval and were surrounded with a frame-like border, gilded and incised, which had a bow at the top—a formula reminiscent of that evolved by Soufflot and Jacques for the decoration of tapestries at the Gobelins in these very years (see page 61 and Plate 36).

For some reason, the large ornamental vases produced at Sèvres are rarely furnished with the usual date-letter—indeed, they often lack any marks at all. This may be because it was perhaps thought too risky to turn such pieces upside down when they were freshly painted, merely in order to add a factory-mark and date. At any rate, this lack of a date-letter makes it difficult for scholars to establish a chronology for the stylistic development of such vases, a difficulty in no way alleviated by the fact that the firm's ledgers of this period—about 1760—mostly contain only the briefest description like, for example, 'vase d'ornement'.

The earliest known Sèvres vase of an entirely Neo-Classical shape is in the collection of Her Majesty Queen Elizabeth II (Plate 270). It bears the date-letter 'I' for 1761. With its rectangular handles echoing the shape of the body, this is as uncompromising a piece of Neo-Classicism as Lalive de Jully's furniture (see page 68 and Plates 85 to 89), and all its relief ornaments are of Classical derivation. The oval panel on the side of the ovoid body stresses the regularity of this form, and it is interesting to note that the panel contains a scene painted in the style of David Teniers which serves as a reminder of how popular was the work of such seventeenth-century Flemish painters among French connoisseurs and dilettanti in the eighteenth century. Indeed, it will be recalled that Lalive was soon to have his famous furniture standing in a *Cabinet Flamand* where a number of Flemish paintings were displayed on the determinedly Neo-Classical walls. As we have explained, this admiration for seventeenth-century Netherlandish paintings went hand-in-hand with the current wish to revive some of the sober grandeur and formal circumstance of the French Academic tradition of the Age of Louis XIV, in an effort to bring back good taste and counter the still mounting tide of the Rococo. We do not know for certain who designed this particular vase. Once again, it could have been the elder Duplessis, or his son, or one of his assistants named Jacques-François Deparis. For although one may normally identify the elder Duplessis with the Rococo style, he did in fact possess quite a few engravings of vases and urns in the Classical taste, by Saly (whose suite of *Vases* appeared in 1746), by Beauvais (published in 1760), and by Delafosse (which, however, appeared after 1761, the date that concerns us here). This by no means proves that Duplessis had gone over to the Neo-Classical camp by this date but we can certainly not exclude the possibility that he or his son had a hand in creating the earliest Neo-Classical models at the Sèvres factory. The son, of course, being of the new generation, might very well have been the man responsible. We also know that a vase of a markedly progressive shape which must be quite early in date is inscribed with Duplessis' name.[1] Nor can we exclude the possibility that some of the factory's first Classical vases were based on designs which were provided some years earlier, for there is an entry in the firm's accounts for the year 1754 for a payment on 6th March of 48 livres to a certain 'Sieur Lorain'—a name which one immediately associates with that of the designer of Lalive's furniture—for 'plusieurs Traits de vases antiques'.[2] All the same, it is more likely that it was the sculptor Falconet who actually played the leading role in bringing in the new style at the factory. He was accredited to the establishment in 1758 and the *L'Avantcoureur* of 10th January 1763 tells us that it was he who had designed the vases displayed at the previous annual exhibition which the firm had held at Versailles during December 1762. Falconet's taste for Neo-Classicism is known to us through, amongst other things, his monument to Lalive de Jully's wife which was executed in 1754 (see page 46 and Plate 38), while we know he was well versed in the repertoire of Classical ornament. This is to be seen, for example, in the way he decorated the quiver of his figure of 'L'Amour menaçant' which he produced in marble in 1757 for Madame de Pompadour (now in the Rijksmuseum, Amsterdam).

It is characteristic of the Sèvres factory that none of its vases is a direct copy of an Antique original. The forms are certainly of Classical inspiration and Classical ornament is used logically, yet each type is a new creation in its own right. It must be admitted that the shapes are not all equally pleasing, and the handling is frequently uncertain, but it is clear that great efforts have been made to fall in with 'le goût antique'. One may also perceive how concerned the firm was with the new movement from the names bestowed on its progressive models. These are known from the original plaster models which still survive and some of which bear what appear to be their contemporary designations. The vase of 1763 shown in Plate 274 was thus apparently known as a 'Vaze antique ferré', while that shown in Plate 276, which bears the date-letter for 1767, seems to have been called a 'Vaze cassolette à festons'. Others were merely called by such titles as 'Vaze antique', 'Vaze étrusque', and 'Vaze grec'.

The numerous processes through which an elaborately painted vase had to go before it was finished and ready for sale might take many months to accomplish. If it bears a date-letter, this will only indicate when it was completed, not when the model was first evolved, which could easily have been some years before. When it concerns vases without a date-letter, but of which we know the date of sale, we have to remember that it might have been on the shelves for a while before being sold. This would have applied especially to the more expensive confections. An example is provided by the pair of vases which the Duc de Choiseul bought in December 1766 for 2,880 livres—the top price for vases at Sèvres at the time. In the sales-ledger, these are described as '2 Grands Vazes à serpens'.[3] This pair was apparently one of the show-pieces of the factory's annual exhibition at Versailles at the end of 1766 and was the subject of a short notice in *L'Avantcoureur* for 19th January 1767,[4] where we are told they were two feet high, that they were painted blue 'parsemé d'or' ('sprinkled with gold'), that each handle was in the form of two entwined serpents painted in natural colours, and that they were decorated with cartouches containing paintings after Greuze. Obviously these were large and elaborate pieces which must have

[1] The vase, now in the Rijksmuseum in Amsterdam, is of the same shape as the vase reproduced in Plate 287 (dated 1770) although it was decorated as late as in 1779; the *incised* inscription runs 'Vase Grec duplessi rectifié'. I am indebted to Mr. A. L. Den Blauwen for calling my attention to this inscription.

[2] Sèvres Archives, F 2, liasse 2 (Compte po. 1754).

[3] '2 large vases with serpents'. [4] page 37.

G (i). Barrière, 1766-67

G (ii). Germain, 1764-65

taken a long time to complete. It would appear that these presumably unique vases have disappeared so we do not know what date-letter they bore, if any. However, the factory's records of firing show that '2 Vazes à Serpent' were removed from a kiln in 1765 after having had their ground-colour fired[1]—that is to say, at least a year before the vases were sold. If we further allow time for the forming and first firing of the ware, and for the initial design and model to have been produced before that, it will be seen that the original conception of the Duc's two vases cannot have taken place much later than 1764 or even 1763!

Along with the modernisation of the shapes of Sèvres vases went a renewal of the form of the painted decoration which became ever more regular and balanced. The reserved cartouches were now strictly geometrical in shape although the motifs painted within these panels were not always derived from any Classical source. This development may have been brought about by Jean-Jacques Bachelier who was one of the firm's three *directeurs artistiques*. The number of different patterns evolved during the 1760s for the grounds and gilt borders is astonishingly large. The variety of patterns available is chiefly to be seen in small wares like cups and saucers (Plate 289 and Colour Plate H), and in small tea-sets, but may also be noted on the decorative vases. This development did not really affect the large services until 1766, however, when Louis XV presented the Austrian Ambassador to the French Court, Count Starhemberg, with a service which had numerous small circles, equally spaced, reserved on a blue ground. The next important service decorated in an advanced style was probably that bought by the Duc de Choiseul in December 1769 and which was probably decorated in a manner similar to the Sartine service which was made five years later and still survives.[2] The service provided for Madame du Barry in August 1771 was decorated with a frieze sporting small representations of Classical oil-lamps (Plate 290).

[1] Institut de France, MS. 5675 (not foliated).

[2] Elements of the Sartine service are reproduced in Pierre Verlet, *Sèvres, le XVIIIe siècle*, 1953, Pl. 77. Part of a service decorated with an identical pattern and date-marked for 1769, is in the possession of The Antique Porcelain Co., New York. Presumably this is part of the service which the Duc de Choiseul bought in December 1769 and which in the sales ledgers was described as 'En Rozes Et Mozaique' ('with roses and mosaic').

III

RETROSPECT

1. ARTISTIC ADVISERS AND PROMINENT PATRONS

However great may have been the influence of Lalive de Jully's furniture (Plates 85 to 89), no-one will claim that, without it, Neo-Classicism would have failed to make its appearance in French furniture and other branches of the decorative arts. All the same, we can admit that the development of Neo-Classicism might have taken a rather different, and perhaps slower, path if Lalive had not had this extremely advanced furniture made, or if he had chosen someone other than that not very talented artist, Le Lorrain, to design it. Then we might at least have been spared all those ridiculous sausage-shaped garlands which, as both Cochin and Lalive pointed out, all derived from those on Le Lorrain's furniture. Suppose Lalive had gone to De Wailly, instead, and asked *him* to design it. From what we know of De Wailly's style (Plates 324 to 330), it may well be that we should have seen a far purer and more graceful form of Neo-Classicism evolved at a much earlier date—that is, provided that such designs were received with as much enthusiasm by the Comte de Caylus as Le Lorrain's were to be and were thus likewise praised within Madame Geoffrin's influential circle which could in turn be guaranteed to secure their immediate acceptance among all fashionable people in Paris—as happened with Le Lorrain's designs. Had Lalive presumed to turn to such a well-established artist as Michel-Ange Slodtz for his designs, then we can be sure these would not have received Caylus' approbation, no matter how good they were, because Caylus disliked Slodtz for some reason, and did all he could to cause him discomfort. Finally, if Caylus and Lalive had been enemies, and if Lalive had not been an extrovert who was glad to let anyone at all interested come and see his house, then his furniture would probably not have become at all widely known and its influence would have been negligible. All this goes to show that one should not under-rate the important role played by the rich patron who sponsors something new, and the influential connoisseur whose intrigues and advice can have such a far-reaching effect.

The name of the Comte de Caylus has already been mentioned several times in the preceding chapters. Some of his contributions to the artistic life of the French capital are enumerated in the biographical note on pages 160–3. All we need say here is that no-one was such an energetic and single-minded protagonist of the Neo-Classical cause as he. His high social standing, his self-assurance, and the enjoyment he derived from persuading others to accept his own aesthetic judgements, all ensured for him a position of considerable influence. Already in 1754, Blondel referred to him as one of the most influential among the many *amateurs* in Paris, and eleven years later Diderot called him 'the most malicious *amateur* of all'. Cochin devoted an entire chapter of his *Mémoires* to him, clearly so as to leave a detailed picture for posterity of this man he so hated for the quite unfair treatment he had meted out to numerous artists. Cochin was no admirer of 'le goût grec' as a fashionable manifestation so it was no compliment to Caylus when he tells us that it was Caylus' praise of Lalive's furniture (see p. 269) that led to their being so widely admired! He documents with care the important part Caylus played in introducing 'le goût grec'. Sebastien Mercier actually states that it was Caylus who 'brought back the "goût grec"' but he must here have meant the Classical style generally and not merely the widespread craze that went by that name. Although he was something of a rake, this did not hinder him in the slightest from advocating a severe style when it came to Art, as his early admiration for the work of the sculptor Edmé Bouchardon indicates. Already in the spring of 1749 he was to be found delivering thunderous judgement on the Rococo before the assembled Academy. As early as 1753 he had managed to arrange matters so that Petitot, an architect with Neo-Classical leanings, should go to Parma instead of the architect François-Nicolas Lancret, while in 1754 he saw to it that Le Lorrain was given the task of designing the mural-decorations for the dining-room at Åkerö (Plate 15), a task which should really have fallen to Oudry.

Caylus can hardly be blamed for having done such a great deal to help those artists who shared his ideas and interests but one may be permitted to question the manner in which, for example, he discomfited the young Bachelier merely because the latter had dared to show an interest in a painting technique used in Classical times which Caylus felt he had the sole right to exploit.

Caylus' energetic sponsorship of Le Lorrain may well have ensured that it was this artist who was chosen to design Lalive's furniture. We have no proof of this but Caylus was acquainted with Lalive from 1754 onwards—that is, before the furniture was designed—and we know that Lalive had originally had a taste for the Rococo style (see Plate 305) and for the work of such traditional artists as Oudry who had once painted his portrait. It is very likely that it was Caylus who converted Lalive—over thirty years his junior—and made him take an interest in Classical art. Lalive had just inherited a huge fortune so he was well able to take on the role of a Maecenas in the art field.

Lalive does not seem to have been at all interested in the politics of the art world—Caylus' happy hunting-ground. He was simply a collector who was proud to own works not only of old masters such as Rubens and Rembrandt but also those of young French artists of his own age. Like Caylus, he was an admirer of the 'noble simplicité' of Bouchardon's sculpture and this may perhaps have provided a common meeting-ground when they first became acquainted. He was apparently of a kindly disposition and anyone really interested in art was welcome to come and inspect his collections. Guillaumot, an architect who worked for the Marquis de Marigny, mentions this as a rare trait among the Parisian collectors of his day. Rich or titled people could of course get in anywhere, he says, but the poor and badly-dressed artist is rarely welcome, however worthy may be his reason for wanting to see a collector's treasures. Lalive's generosity was thus appreciated by his less fortunate contemporaries and it will have led, incidentally, to the furniture Le Lorrain designed in such a progressive style becoming known not only among other rich collectors but to many artists and designers, and perhaps also to some of the more astute cabinet-makers. Neo-Classical mural decorations designed by Barreau de Chefdeville for Lalive's apartment in the Rue de Menars (probably executed when he moved from the Rue Saint-Honoré in 1762) must have become widely known for the same reason. Indeed, it was probably largely by the example he set that Lalive came to be of such importance for the early development of Neo-Classicism.

Caylus and Lalive belonged to the group of artists and connoisseurs who regularly attended Madame Geoffrin's famous *salons*. She lived only a few doors away from Lalive. It is more than likely that Caylus expounded on Le Lorrain's talents as a designer of furniture at these assemblies. Caylus and Madame Geoffrin were of about the same age and, as far as we can judge from what we know of their collections, they seem to have had rather similar tastes—tastes shared by Lalive after his 'conversion'. She knew many artists, young ones as well as old, but we cannot really say whether she had any widespread influence in artistic matters although she certainly played an important role on one occasion, as we shall see. The real significance of her *salons* seems more to have lain in the fact that a great number of artists and amateurs of the arts met there and it is evident that there was much animated discussion of the latest developments in the field. The Comte Dufort de Cheverny tells us that Madame Geoffrin took care to see that the Marquis de Marigny was accepted into her circle and insists that it was there the Marquis 'épura son goût' ('clarified his taste'). The occasion on which Madame Geoffrin was undoubtedly able to exert her influence was that on which the King of Poland was about to remodel his palace in Warsaw. In 1753–54, the young prince Stanislas Auguste Poniatiowski had spent some time in Paris and had there come to know Madame Geoffrin very well, although she was very much his senior. They had kept up an active correspondence after the Prince had returned to Warsaw and become King. The old lady did all she could to become the King's sole advisor on artistic matters in Paris, and in this she was to some extent successful, for she did at least manage to ensure that her own favourite painters—men like Van Loo, Vien, Hallé and Lagrenée—were given commissions. But it is clear from the surviving correspondence that she was in no way responsible for the choice of such a determined advocate of Neo-Classicism as Victor Louis to be the architect in charge of the whole enterprise. On the contrary, she seems to have been highly displeased that the King's emissary, Casimir Czempinski, should have taken an independent course and made contact with Victor Louis through the goldsmith François-Thomas Germain. Czempinski was evidently sensitive to fashion. In July 1764 he wrote to the King that 'dans tous les achats que je fais, je donne la préférence au bel antique, au Grec décidé'.[1] However, on 10th August, he was writing that 'Mme Geoffrin veut bien m'honorer de ses conseils que je suivrai pour les appartements futurs'.[2] Perhaps the old lady had managed to pull a string or two and forced Czempinski to toe the line!

Other less scheming women must also have exerted an influence on the course of Neo-Classicism. Madame de Pompadour's role was by no means insignificant. At quite an early date she seems to have found herself in sympathy with the new developments towards a style springing from the Classical tradition. One only has to think of the portrait of her by Boucher, painted in 1758 (Plate 309), which shows a bookcase that need not be imaginary; it has a Vitruvian scroll

[1] 'In all the purchases I am making I am giving preference to items couched in the Antique taste—to the Grecian style.'

[2] 'Madame Geoffrin has been so kind as to offer me her advice which I will follow when it comes to [selecting furnishings for] the next [group of] apartments.' Quoted from Stanislas Lorentz' article 'Victor Louis et Varsovie' in the catalogue to the exhibition of the same name held at the Musée Jacquemart-André in 1958.

and is surmounted by a lyre-shaped clock. Or there is the well-known little table with rams' heads and garlands which may be seen in Drouais' painting of her, made in 1763–64 (Plate 372). And there are the two candlesticks (Plate 247), made by Germain in 1762, which may have belonged to her and display unmistakable Classical features. And finally we know that she possessed quite a few commodes described as being 'à la grecque' when she died in 1764.[1] Although she had been such an ardent admirer of the Rococo style, it ought not really to surprise us to discover that she should gradually have turned to the new taste. For we know she had had a hand in ensuring that the men who were to accompany her brother, the Marquis de Marigny, on that famous journey to Italy (which started in 1749, it will be remembered) were all determined opponents of the Rococo. What is more, she can hardly have avoided hearing something of the propaganda with which these same people, the Abbé Le Blanc, Cochin and Soufflot, as well as her brother, sought to undermine the Rococo once they had returned from Italy. It is also quite possible that Lalive de Jully exerted a certain influence on her in a progressive direction. We know they knew each other quite well. They were of about the same age and both had a rather similar family background in the world of high-finance. Before Madame de Pompadour went to Court, she had lived almost next door to Lalive in the Rue Saint-Honoré, and it was she who in 1756 obtained the post of *introducteur des ambassadeurs* for Lalive. It may have been by way of a return favour that he made two journeys to Switzerland, in 1757 and in 1759, to arrange some private financial matters for her. It seems inconceivable that these two people, who were both so interested in artistic matters and who were both practising artists in a small way, should not have discussed the trends then becoming apparent in Paris and, indeed, in the very street in which they lived!

We should probably also try to discover more about Madame Desvieux—the lady whose unusual secretaire was shown at the *Salon* of 1761[2]—and also about the other ladies, who according to the *Mercure de France*, had foresworn the Rococo by that date.[3] Such patrons must also have exerted a certain influence, if only by commissioning work in the new taste.

One would also think that the Marquis de Marigny, the man Saly called France's *Ministre des Arts*, could not have made a move within the field of the Arts without it being noticed, and one would expect to find that anything he did was liable to be imitated. We have already noted how he had turned his face resolutely against the Rococo in his official capacity already by 1760 and perhaps even some years before.[4] All the same it is rather more difficult to establish just how eagerly he personally embraced Neo-Classicism in his private surroundings at this early date.

Guillaumot, whom we have recently mentioned, had probably forgotten about Lalive's furniture when he wrote in 1768 that Marigny 'a le premier eu le courage d'introduire dans sa maison des meubles de bon goût, & de les décorer d'ornemens sages'[5] but otherwise there is likely to have been a large grain of truth in the statement, even if it is hard to decide exactly what may have constituted furniture 'de bon goût' in Marigny's eyes. In 1761, this would presumably have meant something like the furniture that can be seen in his portrait by Roslin (Plate 353), which means to say chairs of a controlled Rococo form decorated with ornaments of Classical origin, and tables in a simplified version of the Boulle style. As far as picture-frames are

[1] See Madame de Pompadour's biography, p. 216. [2] See p. 69 and p. 57, note 1.
[3] See note 2 above. [4] See pp. 34–6.
[5] 'was the first person to have the courage to introduce furniture of really good taste [i.e. in the new style] into his house, and to have it decorated with sensible ornaments.'

concerned, on the other hand, he seems to have accepted the 'goût grec' in its purest form (Plate 346). Two years later, however, he bought the large suite of furniture of which the most striking feature seems to have been that the legs were straight.[1] This was in 1763 and it was perhaps this set to which Guillaumot was referring when he said, in 1768, that Marigny had been the first to introduce furniture 'de bon goût' into his own home. The set comprised twenty-eight chairs and five sofas, and this suggests that Marigny was used to entertaining rather large parties of people; it is reasonable to suppose that many of those who visited the house were impressed by the advanced taste of the Minister's furniture. But did any of them follow his example? We do not know. One man who did not visit Marigny's house was the King of Poland but he listened to Marigny's opinions—no doubt, to Madame Geoffrin's great chagrin—on the various projected designs that were being worked out in 1765–66 and the following years for the modernisation of the palace at Warsaw. Marigny seems to have approved of most of them, and, on the 22nd April 1767, the King wrote to Victor Louis, the architect in charge of the whole undertaking, that he was exceedingly pleased to have had Marigny's views and that his excellent advice would certainly be heeded.[2] By that time most of the furnishings were ready for dispatch so there cannot have been much chance of making changes, anyway. Caffieri had by then already delivered most of his bronzes, and most of the actual furniture was completed. Marigny cannot have found these things in any way surprising. The Gobelins factory, which came under Marigny's jurisdiction, had perhaps already by then produced the models for chairs in a pure Neo-Classical style[3] and Marigny was at this very time himself a customer of Caffieri's and other no less progressive craftsmen.[4] Moreover, in November of that year (1767) he was to order an ultra-modern carriage which had a Vitruvian scroll round the edge of the roof and emblematic devices in the Classical taste painted on the sides (Plate 430).

We cannot yet say for certain whether we ought to class the Duc de Choiseul among those who first took up Neo-Classicism, but there are several indications that we should. In the first place, he is seen sitting at a desk, reminiscent of Lalive's in the portrait of him by Van Loo painted in 1763 (Plate 367). The inkstand on the desk is in no less an advanced style for that date. Of course we cannot be sure that these pieces belonged to the sitter and not to Van Loo but Choiseul must at least have agreed to their being represented in the portrait, which incidentally, was copied several times. Secondly, there are the two fall-front desks that can be seen in Van Blarenberghe's miniature of about 1770 (Plate 463) which may have come from Oeben's workshops, where such pieces were being produced from about 1760 onwards (Plate 94). Unfortunately, we do not know when Choiseul bought them! We are likewise ignorant of when in the 1760s he had some rooms in his house in the Rue de Richelieu modernised with, amongst other things, wall-panelling and parquet floors in the Neo-Classical taste (Plate 81). The set of seat-furniture made for his *Cabinet à la Lanterne* was likewise of a decidedly Neo-Classical character (Plate 464). In December 1766 he bought the pair of large and very expensive Sèvres vases which we discussed in the previous chapter. It will be remembered that the handles of these impressive vases were in the form of entwined snakes, which suggests they were Classical in spirit. In 1767, the *ébéniste* Georg Haupt made for him the writing-desk shown in Plate 114, which is certainly couched in the Classical taste. All this suggests that the Duc de Choiseul for preference bought works in the new style, at least in the second half of the 1760s, but that he did not discard all his

[1] See p. 86. [2] See the article referred to on p. 116, note 2. [3] See p. 86.
[4] See Marigny's biography, pp. 204–6.

furniture on that account, as the views by van Blarenberghe show.[1] There one may see furniture in the Rococo taste alongside pieces of Classical inspiration. Indeed, if we may believe van Blarenberghe, Choiseul chose to use a writing-desk which is an extreme expression of the Rococo taste as his regular work-table. This is the famous table which was subsequently to belong to Talleyrand and Metternich and is now in a private collection in Switzerland.[2]

Another prominent person about whose tastes and influence it would be interesting to know more was the Duc d'Uzès who had his town house modernised by Ledoux between 1766 and 1769. Thanks to the researches of Michel Gallet,[3] we know a good deal about this house and its mural decorations.[4] Gallet mentions that the *ébéniste* Leleu provided some cabinet-furniture for the house at this period and this rather suggests that the furniture in the Hotel d'Uzès was in just as advanced a taste as the rest of the house. It would seem that Ledoux concerned himself down to the last detail with the new decorations. The designs he made for the wall-panelling were first modelled in wax by the sculptor Métivier before he was allowed to go ahead with the full-scale work. The Duc d'Uzès presumably had to give his approval of Ledoux's designs before Métivier went ahead and made the models which, incidentally, cost the very considerable sum of 4,368 livres. Were similar careful preparations made in connection with the furniture Leleu produced? It would be of enormous interest to know the answer to this question because it might show that Leleu's style, which seems to be such a personal one, in reality had its origins on Ledoux's drawing-board.

Leleu was soon to make a good deal of furniture in an advanced style for the Prince de Condé's Palais Bourbon (see pages 79–81). The Prince was a prominent military leader, like the Duc d'Uzès whom he must have known. Indeed, it is not inconceivable that the Duc's new furniture caught the attention of the Prince de Condé who was currently modernising his own house. The architect who was placed in charge of the renovations at the Palais Bourbon was the identical Le Carpentier who also worked for the Duc de Choiseul. Of course the influences on any potential patron of the Arts at this stage must have been manifold and complex. Paris was not then a very large city and the people who could afford to enjoy luxuries of the kind we are discussing were comparatively few in number and mostly knew each other, or at least knew about each other. It is not surprising, therefore, if we find that the cross-currents are numerous and sometimes bewildering.

The Prince de Condé had in fact shown that he was a man of progressive tastes already in 1764 when he had chosen the architect Barreau de Chefdeville to re-decorate the Palais Bourbon, and this architect was of course an uncompromising advocate of the Neo-Classical style, as we have noted (see page 53). He had been responsible for the decoration of Lalive de Jully's new apartment—including the room made to house the famous writing-desk which had been made some years before (see page 68 and Plates 85 to 89). Barreau died in 1765 and Le Carpentier was appointed to succeed him. The alterations took many years to complete and it was not until 1769 and 1770 that sets of furniture and *bronzes d'ameublement* were ordered from men like Leleu, Caffieri and the chair-maker Carpentier (Plates 127 to 130 and 453 to 461). Everything was in the most advanced taste but the Prince did not take up residence in the house for several years. All

[1] F. J. B. Watson, *The Choiseul Box*, 1963, figs. 5 and 6.

[2] More about Choiseul as a collector in his biography, pp. 165–7.

[3] Michel Gallet, 'Le salon de l'Hôtel d'Uzès', *Bulletin du Musée Carnavalet*, 22e année, 1969, No. 2 (1971), pp. 1–23.

[4] The panelling of one room has recently come to the Musée Carnavalet.

the same, his initiative very probably helped to establish the new style among the craftsmen who worked for him.[1]

It is not difficult to demonstrate that there were links of some kind between one patron or another, as we have said, but it is not often possible to show what result such links may have had, if any. Thus we know, for instance, that the Duc de Richelieu and the Duc d'Aumont were closely associated, as both were *premiers gentilhommes de la chambre du Roi*, and we know that both became enthusiastic admirers of the Neo-Classical style. Whether there is any connection between these two facts, however, we cannot at present say. Richelieu was the elder of the two but this does not necessarily mean that he was the first to take up the new style. The biographies of the two men[2] show that we have no definite information about their views on this subject before 1767 and 1768.

Louis XV was the greatest of all the French patrons of the Arts at this time, as might be guessed, but he was probably one of the most difficult to satisfy. He was unusually interested in architecture. Madame de Pompadour once said that he was not really happy unless he had an architectural drawing in his hands.[3] He did not merely content himself with inspecting and criticising the designs submitted to him by the royal architects; he frequently took up his red crayon and altered details himself. We can therefore be fairly certain that at any rate such pieces of furniture and other items that were produced for his personal use were tailored to suit his tastes very exactly.

The famous commode by Gaudreaux and Jacques Caffieri, now in the Wallace Collection,[4] shows that Louis XV was a passionate admirer of the Rococo style when this piece of furniture was made in 1739, for no more *outré* example of the Rococo is known in the whole field of French furniture. This piece was made in 1739 for the King's private bed-chamber—*not* for the official State Bed-chamber next door—and we can be sure that a piece of furniture destined for a position in this innermost sanctum reflects the King's personal tastes at the time. This piece of furniture remained in that position until his death, and this suggests that he continued to hold in high regard the style which, in France and elsewhere, has come to bear his name.

In 1750, eleven years after Gaudreaux's commode was made, the King commissioned the bronze case for an astronomical clock which is still the focal point of the room named after it—the *Cabinet de la Pendule* at Versailles. The King had rejected the original case made for the elaborate movement designed by Passement, and the *Mercure de France* subsequently informed its readers that His Majesty 'ordonna une nouvelle boite sur le dessein qu'elle choisit, qui a été composée et executée par le s.Caffieri . . .'.[5] This clock-case[6] stands high on four cabriole legs and is surmounted by an armillary sphere. The whole edifice is certainly couched in the Rococo taste but in a version that is restrained when compared with the commode. The curves are still pronounced yet the whole spirit of the composition is quite different from that governing the

[1] More about the Prince de Condé in his biography, pp. 165–7. [2] See p. 148 and p. 218.

[3] 'La Marquise et ses amis disent qu'on ne peut amuser absolument le Roi que de dessins d'architecture, que S.M. ne respire qu'avec des plans et des dessins sur sa table, ce qui ruine les finances.' ('The Marquise and her friends say that the only certain way of entertaining the King is to place before him plans or architectural drawings: he can only live if he has plans and drawings on his desk—all of which ruins the country.') Quotation from the Marquis d'Argenson reproduced in Hautecoeur, *Histoire, seconde moitié*, p. 75.

[4] Watson, *Wallace Collection Furniture*, F. 86, and Plates 40–41.

[5] 'had ordered a new case based on the design he had selected—and drawn by Mr. Caffieri'. Quoted from Jules Guiffrey, *Les Caffieri, sculpteurs et fondeurs-ciseleurs ; étude sur la statuaire et sur l'art de bronze en France au XVIIe et au XVIIIe siècles*, Paris, 1877, p. 76.

[6] Illustrated on page facing p. 80 in Guiffrey, *Les Caffieri*, and in colour in the September 1966 issue of *L'Oeil*.

design of the commode. The ornaments on the commode would have qualified for the term 'frivole' in the jargon of those who were by this time beginning to criticise the Rococo. The ornaments on the clock-case, on the other hand, consist to a large extent of naturalistic elements of a botanical nature that can be recognised—oak-leaves, bay-leaves, and flowers of various kinds. The clock-case may therefore be said to represent a retreat from the wilder excesses of the Rococo, as far as the King's tastes are concerned. But he did not plunge headlong into an espousal of the Classical taste! His hesitation is epitomised by the small commode Joubert delivered to the King's Bed-chamber at Fontainebleau in 1755 which is also in the Wallace Collection.[1] This piece is certainly not as richly decorated as the commode by Gaudreaux and Caffieri, but the bronzes must still be classed as 'frivole'.

In the same year, Joubert delivered to the *Garde-Meuble* the pair of corner-cupboards intended for the King's Study—*Le Cabinet du Roi*—where they were to stand with the commode-like medal-cabinet Gaudreaux had made for the room in 1738, the year before he made the *outré* Rococo commode we have just discussed.[2] The corner-cupboards are couched in a moderate form of Rococo equivalent to that of Caffieri's Passement clock-case. The same may be said of the red-lacquer writing-desk (*bureau plât*) which Joubert also made for the King's Study—in 1759—and which is now in the Wrightsman Rooms at the Metropolitan Museum, New York.[3]

The year before, Caffieri produced the highly naturalistic sconces in the form of hunting-horns for the little hunting lodge, Saint-Hubert, which, as we know, the King had built for his mistress, Madame de Pompadour (Plate 203). These may well echo a definite change in the King's artistic tastes—unless, of course, it was Madame de Pompadour herself who decided how the place should be furnished. The large roll-top desk—the famous *Bureau du Roi*—which was made to stand in the same study as the red-lacquer table of 1759, the medal-cabinet of 1738, and its now accompanying corner-cupboards of 1755, was ordered from Oeben in 1760 and was to be a supreme example of the more measured version of the new style in which restrained but essentially Rococo forms were combined with sculptural and inlaid ornament deriving from the Classical repertoire (Plates 90 to 93). It will be seen from this that the King, by this time a man of fifty, still allowed himself to be swayed by Fashion—even when ordering a piece of furniture which was to cost more than any other he had ever had made for his own use. It needs to be stressed, moreover, that this desk, which was to go in the middle of his Study—as it were, at the very centre of the French monarchic world—must have reflected rather faithfully Louis XV's aesthetic tastes as the 1760s began.

At the same time, or not long afterwards, Louis must have ordered from Joubert the two 'pendules à Equations', one giving information about the sun and the other about the moon, each seven and a half feet high, which were handed over to the *Garde-Meuble* on 29th December 1762.[4] These were placed in the King's private bed-chamber, on either side of the bed-alcove. No indication is given in the inventory as to their style except that each was surmounted by a 'cassolette' with garlands.[5] This rather suggests that they were in the Antique taste,

The fact that Van Loo's large portrait of the King, which was shown at the *Salon* of 1761 (Plate 345), should have had a richly carved frame in the Classical taste is not in itself evidence that the King had by that date gone over entirely to the new style. If anything, its style may reflect

[1] Watson, *Wallace Collection Furniture*, F. 70, and Plate 42.

[2] The corner-cupboards and the medal-cabinet illustrated in Verlet, *Mobilier royal II*, Plate I.

[3] F. J. B. Watson, *The Wrightsman Collection*, vol. III, pp. 42–50.

[4] Verlet, *Versailles*, pp. 521–2. [5] Arch. Nat., o[1] 3317, fol. 186 *verso*.

a wish on the King's part to have this official portrait framed in a manner that would remind the beholder of the days of the Sun King, just as the throne and the *tabouret* shown in the portrait seem to be couched in a style that looks back rather than forward. On the other hand, the frame was executed by Honoré Guibert, who was not only one of the best but also one of the most progressive sculptors of his day.[1] The commissioning of the frame was in fact the Marquis de Marigny's responsibility and he took the opportunity of ordering a frame for his own portrait on the same occasion (Plate 346). The frame was similar to the King's but less ornate and this very simplicity must have made it seem advanced in taste and not an essay in retrospection.[2]

Indeed, these two frames afford an example of how difficult it must have been at this stage to distinguish that strand of Classicism which sought to revive the great tradition that had reached its height under Louis XIV from that strand which sought to create something fresh by reference directly to the Classical monuments. Both derived ultimately from the same source and the motifs were largely the same; it was only the handling which differed. It is of course not at all unlikely that Marigny had a say in the design of the frame for the royal portrait as well.

At any rate, it was not long before the King took up Neo-Classicism wholeheartedly. It may have been the work at the Petit Trianon or at the Opera-hall at Versailles which brought about his final conversion. The King was deeply interested in Gabriel's various proposals for the Opera and, during the course of a few years, was shown increasingly modernistic designs (Plate 61) until he finally approved one which was entirely Neo-Classical in character (Plate 74). We do not know if a similar sequence of projected designs was put before the King in connection with the carved panelling for the Petit Trianon which Guibert was to carve; all we know is that the most prominent series of panels came to be couched in an ultra-progressive style (Plates 66 and 67). We saw, moreover, how most of the *bronzes d'ameublement* produced for the Court in and after 1764 were in the new style; this was particularly true of the fire-dogs. In the silver which was made for Louis XV's personal use in the 1760s the new idiom also made its appearance. It was probably apparent enough in the two inkstands Roëttiers provided for him in 1766[3] and must have been quite unmistakable in the large tureens which he delivered in February 1768, judging by the description we have already quoted.[4]

All the same, Louis XV was curiously stubborn over one point! He could not bear chairs with straight legs. He had to put up with the fact that Madame du Barry ordered chairs of this type—at his expense—for her rooms at Versailles, but he never once bought a chair with straight legs for use in his own apartments. It was perfectly all right for his chairs to have carved ornament in the Classical taste, as was the case with all those made for the Petit Trianon,[5] but he liked chair-legs to be curved in the manner to which he had been accustomed all his life. Even so, he was no doubt perfectly at ease when he visited Madame du Barry's apartments or called on her at her little pavilion at Louveciennes where everything was likewise couched in quite an advanced form of Neo-Classicism. He is anyway said to have been rather taken with the architecture of Ledoux's little pavilion. The architect himself records with pride how the building was greeted with approval by Louis when he first saw it, and the King apparently said to Ledoux, when extending his approbation to the plans for La Saline, that 'on ne peut disconvenir, ces vues sont grandes'.[6] Louis only bought veneered furniture with straight legs very late in life, the first pieces being a

[1] See Guibert's biography, p. 189. [2] See p. 61. [3] See p. 109.

[4] See p. 109. [5] See p. 85.

[6] 'One cannot deny it, these aspects are splendid.' Michel Gallet, 'La jeunesse de Ledoux', *Gazette des Beaux-Arts*, February 1970, p. 86.

little table executed by Riesener and delivered on 5th February 1771,[1] and another table ordered on the 19th of the same month and delivered on the 7th May the same year, by Joubert.[2]

We know very little about Madame du Barry's tastes before she moved into her new apartments at Versailles. She bought a set of furniture from the chairmaker Louis Delanois in September 1768—one presumes that the King had to foot this bill as well, even though she was still at this time living in Paris, as far as we know—but this set was in no way as advanced in taste as those she was later to commission.[3] Admittedly some of this first set was 'sculptés à la grec' but it would seem that the legs were all of the cabriole type and that the forms as a whole were traditional ones, as far as we can judge from Delanois' account-books. Only the decoration was Classical in style. She can scarcely have been unaware of what constituted the height of fashion in the field of furniture, since at this time she was living right in the middle of the Bonne-Nouvelle quarter where a great part of the furniture-making trade was centred. Indeed, if it is true that she had lodgings in the house of the rather suspect Madame Dupressoir, then she was in fact living right next to Delanois in the Cul-de-sac de l'Etoile and he had had an ultra-modern set of furniture at his premises—the pieces he had made for the Palace at Warsaw—in 1768, the very year she procured her first set of furniture from him which was in fact delivered a week before the Warsaw consignment was ready. In June of that year he had also produced some furniture for Grimod d'Orsay of which at least some of the chairs were quite advanced in style, with oval backs and straight legs. She cannot, one feels, have avoided seeing something of this production at the neighbouring premises—at an establishment from which she herself was currently ordering chairs couched in a less adventurous idiom. Delanois' premises opened on to a courtyard with two entrances which everyone used as a short cut from the Cul-de-sac de l'Etoile and the Rue Neuve Saint-Sauveur, and Madame du Barry must surely have cut through this courtyard on her way to visit her mother in the Rue Neuve Saint-Etienne further up the hill. In fact, it is quite likely that she knew Delanois personally. How else can one explain how he suddenly came to be appointed chair-maker to the French Court when, before she had caught the King's eye, he had not provided a single piece of furniture for the Court?

As we saw, the first entirely Neo-Classical seat-furniture to be seen at the Palace of Versailles had been introduced by Madame du Barry in December 1769,[4] while her pavilion at Louveciennes represented the first consistently conceived decorative ensemble cast in a thorough-going form of Neo-Classicism to have been produced for anyone within the innermost circle at Court. But it is worth remembering that, while everything in the Pavillon de Louveciennes had been designed specially for this expensively-appointed little house, nothing there was more advanced in taste than much which could be seen in many Parisian houses at the time and which could even have been bought in the shops. Madame du Barry cannot therefore be considered an innovator or sponsor of a new style. Rather she was remarkable because 'nouveautés' were her delight and because she did not allow her taste for luxury to be restricted by inhibitions of any sort. We are told[5] that she managed to spend over seven million livres during the five years she was at Court.

[1] Arch. Nat., o[1] 3318 fol. 48 bis; it is here stated that the table was made 'pour servir au Roy au Nouveau Pavillon de Trianon' ('for the King's use at the new Pavillon de Trianon').

[2] See p. 79, note 2.

[3] The relevant documentation for Madame du Barry's acquisitions of chairs executed in Delanois' workshops is given in the present writer's book on Louis Delanois, pp. 33–41.

[4] See pp. 90–1.

[5] Charles Vatel, *Histoire de Madame du Barry d'après ses papiers personnels et ses documents des archives publiques*, I–III, 1883.

This was money given her by the King; an even greater sum was spent on building works and furnishings that needed to be provided for her. Since these items were not entered under her name, it is not easy to estimate their total cost.[1]

It seems hardly conceivable that Madame du Barry could have initiated and carried through so many admirable projects merely by exercising her feminine talents; she must have had one or more experienced advisers to whom she could turn or who were in a position to urge her to adopt the path that she should take. We do not know who these people can have been and the problem may never be solved. Francis Watson has suggested that the Duc d'Aumont was one of them.[2] He was the most senior of the King's *premiers gentilhommes* and was in charge of the *Menus Plaisirs*.[3] He was one of Gouthière's principal patrons. Another possible adviser may have been d'Aumont's colleague, the notorious Maréchal Duc de Richelieu, who had been a close friend of Madame du Barry's long before she became the King's mistress. There is good reason to believe that Richelieu had gone over to Neo-Classicism by 1768, if not before. Although rather ugly, few men have ever had such a way with women; whether his powers were ever directed at influencing them in artistic matters, we do not know, however.[4]

2. INNOVATING DESIGNERS

We have a comparatively clear picture of how Neo-Classicism was introduced into French architecture and which were the people primarily responsible for bringing this about. We cannot say the same about the decorative arts. We recognise that, when an object bears a stamp or some other maker's mark, this does not necessarily mean that the maker concerned actually designed the object. In some cases he may have done, but often not. If he was not able to draw, who did produce designs for him and was this designer an innovator? And if the craftsman *could* draw, did he have any original ideas himself? Such questions are difficult to answer and it will be appreciated that the possibilities and permutations are virtually unlimited. There was no accepted general rule even if some working arrangements may have been more common than others.

In the case of Lalive de Jully's famous ultra-progressive furniture (Plates 85 to 89), we know pretty well how this came to be made. The architect Le Lorrain, who was somewhat dilettante in his approach to his subject, designed the pieces while Philippe Caffieri executed the models for the rich bronze mounts and was then responsible for their casting. He may also have supervised the construction of the pieces in the workshop of the cabinet-maker whose identity is not known but whose role, even if we had known his name, must have been a relatively minor one, as far as the design is concerned. We also know that the furniture made for the apartments of the Duchesse d'Orléans at the Palais Royal (Plates 301 and 302), which was couched in a less outspoken version of the new style, was designed by the architect Contant d'Ivry—according to Blondel. In spite of what Blondel says, however, one may question whether Contant d'Ivry was really responsible for the design of features like the chimneypiece (Plate 27) or fittings like the sconces (Plate 203), all of which were produced in the workshops of the famous goldsmith François-Thomas Germain. Germain was after all no mere craftsman. It is apparent from some letters—one from Germain

1 More about Madame du Barry the collector in her biography, pp. 150–3.
2 Watson, *Louis XVI Furniture*, p. 16.
3 See the Duc d'Aumont's biography, p. 148.
4 See the Duc de Richelieu's biography, p. 216.

and one from Czempinski, the Polish emissary responsible for the commissions being made in Paris for the Palace at Warsaw—written in February 1764, that Germain was not only concerned with 'orfèvrerie' (i.e. silver and goldsmith's work) but with 'tout ce qui concerne décoration, sculpture et desseins de toutes espèces'[1] and that he had been in charge of much of the decoration of, among other things, 'les palais des duc d'Orleans et prince de Soubise'.[2] Of course Germain may have been exaggerating a bit and he may not have been referring to the chimneypiece and the sconces just mentioned, but it is by no means inconceivable that these are some of the decorative objects of which he was thinking when he made his claim. We must at any rate bear this possibility in mind, even if we acknowledge that any designs Germain may have produced are likely to have been submitted to Contant d'Ivry for his approval. The fact that Germain was consulted in 1755 about the design of some mirrors which were to be made for the Count Bernstorff's house in Copenhagen (Plates 24 and 25) proves that he was not only a talented craftsman but also a designer of some repute. On the other hand, we also know that he was the director of a very large workshop, employing several hundred people, and it seems improbable that he could possibly have designed all the works of art produced by his own firm. In fact, in the letter of 1764 just mentioned, he states that he is collaborating with certain 'artistes habiles'.[3] Even so, we can be fairly sure that all the designs executed in his workshop had met with his general approval. Thus the candlesticks shown in Plate 247, which are of such a markedly Neo-Classical form, the tea-kettles with their spirit-lamps in the shape of Classical tripods (Plate 244), and the no less advanced toilet-set (Plate 260) show that F.-T. Germain was one of the most talented and inventive creators of the new style, and it is possible that his influence may have extended well beyond the confines of the craft for which he is so justly famous.

We also know that the other goldsmith named Germain—Germain *le Romain*—was capable of executing designs because he published a series of engravings of his own compositions between 1748 and 1751. These were in the Rococo taste, however. The now missing toilet set which Germain made in 1765 in collaboration with Thomas Chamelier, and which was Neo-Classical in style, was, on the other hand, designed by Philippe Caffieri,[4] so we cannot claim at present that this Germain was an innovator in the field even if he certainly knew how to handle a pencil.

We are not in doubt about Philippe Caffieri, at any rate. We have a mass of evidence that he was a fertile artist with original ideas who adopted the Neo-Classical taste at an early date.[5] This famous bronze-founder had learned his trade in his father's workshops and had attended courses at the Académie de Saint-Luc where he subsequently became a teacher. That he clearly considered himself a practitioner of the Fine Arts and no mere craftsman, is shown by the way he joined actively in a dispute within the Académie de Saint-Luc in 1766–67 when some of the members, including Caffieri, protested that certain other members, who, they claimed, did not possess adequate artistic qualifications, were wielding too much power.[6] That Philippe Caffieri

[1] 'everything connected with the decoration, sculpture, and designs of all kinds'.

[2] 'the town houses of the Duc d'Orléans and the Prince de Soubise'; quoted from Stanislas Lorentz' article 'Victor Louis et Varsovie' in the catalogue to the exhibition of the same name held at the Musée Jacquemart-André in 1958, p. 11.

[3] 'skilful artists'. The word 'artistes' could in fact mean designers, skilled craftsmen or artists in the normal English sense.

[4] See p. 108. [5] See p. 97ff.

[6] Jules Guiffrey, *Histoire de l'Académie de Saint-Luc*, *Archives de l'Art Français*, Nouvelle Période, vol. IX, Paris, 1915, pp. 65ff.

did not join the Académie Royale, as his brother did, was probably simply due to the fact he was destined to take over his father's bronze-founding business, an eventuality for which careful preparations had been made by the father.[1]

We can certainly say that Caffieri played a most important role in spreading Neo-Classicism. He was apparently the earliest bronze-founder to take up the new style, his production was extensive, and his example cannot but have influenced many of his colleagues. Indeed, he tells us himself that the sconces he made for Madame de Pompadour's pavilion, Saint-Hubert, and the candelabra he provided for Notre-Dame (Plates 203 and 204) were quickly imitated by other bronze-founders.[2] Moreover, as a teacher at the Saint-Luc Academy he must have had a certain influence on young artists who were presumably not in most cases going to become bronze-founders. Unfortunately, we do not know at what stage of his career he was doing this teaching; all we can say is that by 1766 he was being referred to as 'ancien professeur' ('one-time instructor').

The sculptor Honoré Guibert was also a creative artist who played his part in the early stages in the evolution of the Neo-Classical style in Paris. The picture-frames which were on show at the *Salon* in 1761 (see page 61 and Plates 345 to 348) were carved after his own designs. We know this from *L'Avantcoureur* of 7th September 1761[3] and we also know that when the Marquis de Marigny wanted some frames he asked Guibert to run off some designs for them.[4] Furthermore, the front of the shop of the silk-mercer Duboc in the Rue Saint-Denis, which was 'd'une architecture Grecque', was made in Guibert' workshops in 1761 after designs he had himself produced.[5] It is therefore probable that he was able to make a not inconsiderable artistic contribution to the final appearance of the panelling at the Petit Trianon (Plates 66 and 67) for which he produced models and which were carved in his workshops. Of course the general configuration of the panels must have been laid down by Gabriel but Guibert's share in their conception can scarcely have been minimal.

One of Caffieri's pupils at the Académie de Saint-Luc may have been Jean-Louis Prieur who, in 1765, himself became a member of this Académie and a *maître-sculpteur*, and who, like Caffieri, also became a *maître-fondeur*.[6] We know something of his capabilities from the many designs he produced for the furnishings commissioned for the Palace at Warsaw which included furniture as well as bronzes.[7] He was probably bound to subordinate himself to Victor Louis who was the architect in charge of the whole project but Prieur's personal contribution is likely to have been substantial.

Most people who have studied books on French furniture will be aware that André-Jacques Roubo, a joiner whose business was chiefly concerned with the building trade, was also the author of a lengthy work on the various branches of woodworking entitled *L'Art du menuisier* which appeared in several parts between 1768 and 1775. He waxed indignant over the fact that all too few makers of furniture in his day were able to provide their own designs. He claimed that most of them did purely routine work, using drawings or templates which they would certainly not themselves have been able to draw.[8] One of the exceptions to this rule would seem to have

[1] See Caffieri's biography, p. 157. [2] See Notes to Plates 203 and 204.

[3] The relevant passage is quoted in full in the Note to Plates 345 to 348.

[4] See present writer's article 'Marigny and "le goût grec"', *Burlington Magazine*, March 1962, p. 101.

[5] *L'Avantcoureur*, 7th September 1761, pp. 570–1.

[6] See his biography, p. 217. [7] See Plates 402 to 423.

[8] Page 601. 'While Roubo's work is an extremely valuable source of information, it is necessary in the present connection to draw attention to his tendentious attitude towards cabinet-makers and joiners whom he despised in an almost pathological way. Apparently it went to the young man's head (he was born in 1739) that he, as

been the famous cabinet-maker J.-F. Oeben. The style of his furniture is so individual that it seems reasonable to suppose that he designed it all himself but we have no proof of this. Alternatively he must have had on his staff a very competent draughtsman who worked purely on designs for this one firm. At any rate, Oeben was certainly among the very first *ébénistes* to take an interest in the Neo-Classical style. His upright secretaires, like that shown in Plate 94, which are likely to date from about 1760, exemplify this quite clearly. It is less likely, however, that he was responsible for the design of the *Bureau du Roi*, the writing-desk specially designed for the private use of Louis XV (Plates 90 to 93). This is more likely to have fallen to one of the professional designers working for the Crown—someone like Slodtz—although Oeben may possibly have composed the marquetry patterns himself.

It is not unreasonable to suppose that a man like Oeben could design his own furniture if we remember that Pierre Garnier, a competent although less talented *ébéniste* than Oeben, worked from designs he had turned out himself.[1] Garnier's furniture also displays a highly individual style and is somewhat dilettante in character (Plate 97). It would seem that Garnier had constructed a piece of furniture in a highly progressive style in 1760–61, after designs provided by the architect De Wailly.[2] Maybe it was this commission which encouraged him to try his hand at composing designs in the new taste on his own. In fact what we know about Garnier's ability as a designer of furniture is gleaned from some unpublished drafts of letters addressed to him by the Marquis de Marigny in the year 1779.[3] It is apparent that the latter had been one of Garnier's customers from 1766 onwards and Marigny seems to have had sufficient respect for Garnier's talents as a designer to invite him to produce drawings for several pieces of furniture he needed. On the 4th October 1779 Marigny writes to Garnier describing a table he would like to have made; 'faites moy un petit dessin de ce que je vous demande . . . affin que je voie si mon idée est bien saisie', he says.[4] In the letter he implies that he trusted Garnier so much that he occasionally allowed him to execute furniture for him without first submitting a drawing. When he wanted to have richer mounts added to a dressing-table, he wrote to Garnier saying that 'Vous me feriez grand plaisir de m'envoier à ce Sujet deux dessins, un représentant La Toilette Telle Quelle est aujourdhuy et un autre la représentant telle que vous projettez de L'orner'.[5] Marigny was apparently also quite willing to listen to, and even act on, advice proffered by this talented cabinet-maker. 'Vous me faites Monsieur une observation très judicieuse . . . Je change donc d'avis pour la forme de mes meubles et voicy comme je vous les demande . . .'[6] These letters were written long after Neo-Classicism had ceased to be a novelty in Paris, but there is

a mere journeyman joiner (*compagnon menuisier*), had been allowed to attend courses at Blondel's school of drawing for nothing, and that, thanks to the fact that the Duc de Chaulnes had extended his protection to him, his manuscript was accepted for publication in the series entitled *Description des Arts et Métiers* which was published by the Académie des Sciences.

[1] See p. 71. [2] See p. 69.

[3] These letters form part of the Marigny Papers preserved in the Bibliothèque historique de la Ville de Paris (MSS, Nouvelles Acquisitions, 106, fol. 13–36); they were known by Vial, Marcel and Girodie who referred to them in their book *Les artistes décorateurs du bois*, volume I (article on Garnier), Paris, 1912. The highly interesting Marigny Papers are analysed in Gabriel Henriot, 'Catalogue des manuscrits entrés à la bibliothèque de 1903 à 1905', in *Ville de Paris, Bulletin de la bibliothèque et des travaux historiques*, vol. II (Paris, 1907), pp. 92–104.

[4] 'Make me a small sketch of what I have asked you to do, just so I can be sure you have understood what it is I am after.'

[5] 'You would be doing me a great favour if you would send me two drawings, one showing the table as it is now, and one showing what it would look like decorated in the way you suggest.'

[6] 'Sir, you have made a very true observation . . . accordingly I have changed my mind as regards the shape of my furniture. Here then are my instructions . . .'

no reason to suppose that Garnier only learned to draw at an advanced age. It is difficult to judge what part Garnier may have played in the early spread of Neo-Classicism in France but his role could at least have been of some importance within the field of cabinet-making.

If it had been up to De Wailly, Neo-Classicism would probably have evolved more quickly than it did, in the field of furniture. The drawings reproduced in Plates 329 and 330 show that he was a highly original designer, uninhibited by notions of traditional methods of construction or accepted rules of design. He took no notice of those guild regulations that so often hampered collaboration between members of different trades. He was capable of envisaging constructions in terms of metal as well as wood, and did not merely see a piece of furniture as a wooden core on to which certain metal adornments were screwed. To his way of thinking it was perfectly reasonable that members which were to take a stress greater than that which timber could reasonably withstand should be constructed of metal. We do not know if more furniture was made after designs by De Wailly than the one Garnier executed which was shown at the *Salon* of 1761 and we cannot therefore say whether his contribution had any effect whatsoever.

Soufflot, whose influence on architecture and on the thinking which brought about the rejection of the Rococo is widely recognised, should have been in a strong position to impose the new style on the decorative arts as well, since he was director of Les Gobelins and a friend of the Marquis de Marigny. Once again, however, we cannot yet assess his contribution and we do not even know whether he in fact designed the chairs to take the tapestry covers en suite with the hangings in the new taste he had designed in 1758 (Plates 166 and 167). It seems probable but it is not certain.

The drawing of a bed which Barreau de Chefdeville, Lalive de Jully's decorator who died young, designed for the Intendant's residence at Bordeaux (Plate 58) shows that he was quite a capable furniture designer as well, but we do not know if any furniture was actually made after his designs. The architects Cherpitel, Rousset and Piètre also seem to have had certain talents in this particular field, judging by their designs (Plates 396 to 400) but, again, we do not know whether any of their designs were ever executed, or whether they had any influence. However the energetic architect Ledoux is quite likely to have had a say in the design of the furniture produced for those houses he modernised (e.g. the Hôtel d'Uzès) and, as we have explained elsewhere, he may possibly have had some influence on the work of the *ébéniste* Leleu.[1]

As for the artists who had their designs published, the earliest among those whose work might have affected the decorative arts and brought to them the new style was Neufforge.[2] However, his style is so dry and monotonous, as well as being ponderous and clumsy, that one cannot believe the fastidious Parisian public would have found them at all to their taste, and it seems unlikely that furniture in Neufforge's style was produced in the French capital, even if his designs were found perfectly acceptable in the provinces and abroad (Plates 434 to 436). Delafosse's designs, on the other hand, were far better and more imaginative (Plates 437 to 440 and 479 to 482). The colour-merchant, Watin, who sold Delafosse's engravings, naturally recommended them to his clients but warned that it would be extremely expensive to follow this artist's elaborate proposals and suggested that they might be simplified, notably in the parts that were to be carved.[3]

Another talented designer was Jean-François Forty who was active in the 1760s. The engravings he published were exclusively for metalwork—chalices, choir-screens, candlesticks

[1] See p. 119. [2] See pp. 46–7. [3] See Note to Plates 479 and 480.

H. Sèvres, 1768

(Plates 431 to 433), etc. But it is not unreasonable to suppose that he could also have designed furniture. Indeed, there is a general resemblance between his candlesticks and the kind of leg frequently seen on *Louis Seize* chairs. It may therefore not be entirely irrelevant that Forty was renting rooms in the house of the chair-maker Delanois, just about the time the latter was starting to embrace the Neo-Classical style.[1] It is possible but unlikely that Delanois could draw. He certainly possessed a collection of models (what in English were called 'pattern chairs' because they served as patterns in the workshop), and we know that these were valued more highly than any other chairs in stock when he handed over his workshops to Martin Jullien.[2] The models could very well have been designed by someone else—someone like Forty. In fact, much evidence suggests that Delanois' talents lay in the world of business and administration, but he had the luck or the skill to acquire, at quite an early date, large commissions for furniture designed by first-class draughtsmen like Prieur and the as yet unidentified designer of Madame du Barry's pieces. In this way he quickly became conversant with the new style. The size and prominence of these commissions must in turn have ensured that such furniture was studied with some care by his competitors and by many potential customers.

We are again not certain what role the Court cabinet-maker Gilles Joubert may have played in the creation of the furniture he produced. As far as we can judge, it seems to display such a highly personal style that one must conclude that Joubert designed it himself. But was this really so? At the end of the 1760s, when a stylistic change took place in his production, Joubert was well into his seventies and it is surely more likely that he somehow acquired the services of a younger man who would have been more sympathetic to the new taste than he was himself. Moreover, he must have had access to the services of a sculptor who could provide the models for the exceedingly rich gilt bronze mounts with which his furniture is often embellished (see Plates 119, 120, 145 and 146).

There can be no doubt that Riesener, who took over from Joubert's appointment as cabinet-maker to the French Court, was a capable draughtsmen or he would hardly have allowed himself to be shown in his portrait holding a crayon, with a well-executed drawing in front of him![3] It fell to him to produce the first thoroughly Neo-Classical pieces of cabinet-making for the Court in a style which he had inherited from his former master, Oeben, but which he had subsequently refined considerably. He must have been encouraged in his efforts to introduce the new taste in a more consistent manner by the Director of the *Garde-Meuble de la Couronne*, Pierre-Elizabeth de Fontanieu, who was of a progressive persuasion and is known to have enjoyed sketching and working out compositions in his leisure hours. He made some drawings of vases in the Neo-Classical taste (Plates 449 to 452) which were later copied at the Sèvres factory (Plate 288). The Court must have benefited from the services of several professional designers as well, of course. For instance, the ultra-modern jewel-cabinet (Plate 448) made as a wedding present for Marie-Antoinette was designed by the architect Bellanger in 1769. We do not yet know whether he was responsible for the design of other pieces of furniture but it would be surprising if this were an isolated instance of his working in this field. On the other hand, we know that all the seat-furniture made for use at Court from about 1769 onwards was designed by Jacques Gondoin. It cannot have been his fault that all the chairs made for the Court before the death of Louis XV had cabriole legs because he was a convinced Neo-Classicist of the extremist school; the King

[1] See Forty's biography, p. 181. [2] See present writer's *Louis Delanois*, p. 44.
[3] Reproduced as frontispiece in Salverte, *Les ébénistes*.

himself must have insisted that this old-fashioned feature be retained on the chairs and sofas with which he was to be surrounded.[1] Otherwise Gondoin's and Fontanieu's tastes would surely have prevailed.

As one might have guessed, then, much of the credit for establishing the Neo-Classical style—even in the minor Arts—must be given to the professional architects, since this particular style was essentially based on architectural concepts and motifs. However, we must not overlook the fact that it was not only architects who could receive instruction in the art of drawing and design, even in those days. There were in fact several establishments where ambitious craftsmen, hoping to learn how to design things on their own, could acquire the appropriate training.

Such people could of course not attend courses at the royal academies but painters and sculptors belonged to a guild with the title of Académie de Saint-Luc. All the members were *maîtres* who had qualified as masters in their respective crafts, and they provided courses in drawing, geometry, architecture, painting, sculpture, perspective and anatomy, which their apprentices could attend. With the exception of Honoré Guibert, who was trained in Avignon, it is probable that all the Parisian Neo-Classical sculptors and carvers whose names have so far been mentioned in this book will have attended this academy—men like Babel, Toussaint and François Foliot, Butteux, Lachenait, Coullonjon and Guichard. Draughtsmen like Maurice Jacques, who came to be the Gobelins' designer of ornament, and probably Delafosse (who was also trained by the sculptor, Poulet) are also likely to have been pupils at this academy; in fact, Delafosse later became a teacher there. The goldsmith F.-T. Germain may likewise have attended courses there and we know for certain that both Philippe Caffieri and Jean-Louis Prieur became *maîtres-sculpteurs* after being trained there, whereupon they were made full members—only to go and become *maîtres-fondeurs* (in order to be allowed to practice as bronze-founders). Thanks to their much wider training, these two craftsmen acquired a notable advantage over other bronze-founders. Indeed, as we have noted, they were able to design bronzes, and they were only able to do so without coming into conflict with other artists because they were members of the Saint-Luc Academy.

It would be wise to assume that there were quite a few more draughtsmen than those we know the names of, who were able to provide designs in the modern style at this period. In the final analysis it is the vagaries of chance that have determined what we know about the happenings of two centuries ago! For example, it would be interesting to know more about a man like Antoine Rascalon, a carver (*sculpteur en bois*) who was also a member of the Académie de St. Luc. To date he is to us not much more than a name. We know that, in the 1780s, he did some work for the French Court; and a drawing of 1771 in the Cooper Union Museum, New York, bearing his name shows a scheme of mural decoration of a particularly rich kind, couched in the purest Louis Seize style. As we have seen, Rascalon was a carver but does the presence of his name on the drawing mean that he composed it or merely that it was for him to execute? No one yet knows. But then one suddenly discovers a bill in the Parma archives dated 22 January 1769[2] which shows that Rascalon, '*sculpteur en bois*' to the Court at Parma, had delivered nine drawings for mural decoration, stoves, console-tables, and so forth. We know that everything produced for the Court at Parma in the 1760s was in an advanced Neo-Classical idiom, thanks to the presence there of the French architect Petitot, whose name has already cropped up several times in this survey.

[1] See page 122.

[2] Parma, Archivio di Stato, *Tesoreria en la Corte de Paris y Corresponsales*, Busta 1095, Diverze 12.

Why, then, did one need to order designs from Paris? Could there have been some doubt in Parma that Petitot was right up to date? And why turn to Rascalon, anyway? Was he perhaps known to be a particularly talented designer? We have as yet no means of telling and a document like that bill in Parma underlines the fact that there is a great deal that we still do not know.

Indeed, Rascalon—and others scarcely known to us or as yet unheard of—can very well have been a character of immense importance in the development and spread of Neo-Classicism in France and elsewhere. He need by no means have been an isolated example of our present ignorance of matters.

The courses at the Saint-Luc Academy were reserved for the apprentices of painters, sculptors and carvers who were already members. Where, then, did people like chair-makers and *ébénistes* learn to draw? If we may believe Roubo, the master-joiner who wrote the multi-volume treatise on woodworking, very few such craftsmen were able to give instruction to their apprentices in the art of drawing since they themselves rarely knew how to manage a pencil.[1] However, there were various schools of drawing and independent drawing-masters to whom such apprentices could turn. The painter, Jean-Jacques Bachelier, who was one of the three artistic directors at the Sèvres porcelain factory and who had always had interests of a paedagogic nature, had set up a more or less private drawing-school in Paris in 1753.[2] This acquired official status in 1766 under the title of École gratuite de Dessin and, a year later, royal patronage was extended to it along with a measure of support. The school still exists, having formed the basis for the establishment of the present École des Beaux-Arts. Anyone who wished could attend Bachelier's free-school: 'On y admet indistinctement les ouvriers, les apprentis et même les enfans qui ne sont pas encore engagés dans aucune profession.'[3] The school was established in the Rue Saint-André-des-Arts and remained there till 1776. On Mondays and Thursdays, architecture and geometry were taught, while on Tuesdays and Fridays one could learn how to draw 'figure' and 'animaux'. On Wednesdays and Saturdays, classes were held in the drawing of ornament and flowers. According to Bachelier, there were not less than 1,500 pupils divided into groups of about 125 which could then receive two hours of instruction each week in the discipline for which they had signed on. We cannot say whether the school was actually frequented, as Bachelier claimed, by chair-makers, *ébénistes*, pewterers, bronze-founders, goldsmiths, turners, joiners, etc., etc., because no list of pupils survives, but instruction was available to such people. Moreover, we know that the school was orientated towards the new style, since Bachelier made a speech on the 10th September 1766,[4] when the school was still not officially recognised, criticising the Rococo style which, however, he had practised himself when he was working at the Sèvres factory. Now, on the other hand, he favoured a 'noble symétrie' and an 'heureuse simplicité consacrée par l'approbation et l'admiration de tant de siècles'.[5] For this reason, he thought it best that young people should be instructed in the mysteries of geometry.

It is unlikely that J.-F. Blondel's architectural school could normally have been attended by craftsmen because we are told that it was quite exceptional that the above-mentioned master-joiner, André-Jacques Roubo, should have been permitted to attend classes there. But Blondel

[1] See page 126. [2] See Bachelier's biography, p. 149 and the references given there.

[3] 'It is open to all craftsmen, and to apprentices, and even to children who are not yet engaged in a trade.'

[4] Louis Courajod, *Histoire de l'École des Beaux-Arts au XVIIIe siècle, l'École Royale des Élèves Protégés*, Paris, n.d., pp. 197–212.

[5] 'noble symmetry', 'a felicitous simplicity which has been consecrated by the approbation and admiration extended to it over many centuries'.

states that there were many schools similar to his in Paris.[1] He was presumably referring to private schools. In any case, we know virtually nothing about them. Delafosse called himself 'architecte & professeur pour le dessein'[2] in 1767 when he was living in the Rue Poissonnière which lay right in the centre of that part of Montmartre where many of the Parisian chair-makers were congregated.[3] Out in the Faubourg Saint-Antoine, where many of the *ébénistes* worked, lived a certain Le Meunnié who also gave instruction in drawing, according to his printed trade-card.[4] From this we also learn that he gave lessons on Sundays and holidays 'pour la facilité des ouvriers'[5] and he adds that he could provide the services of an interpreter for 'les Allemands' —for Germans. He must have been referring to all those cabinet-makers and *marqueteurs* of German origin who were living in just that part of town—men like Evald, Weisweiler, Carlin, Mewesen, Benneman and Canabas. Who else could they have been? Unfortunately, we know nothing else about Monsieur Le Meunnié; we do not even know exactly when he was active.[6]

Irrespective of how many schools of drawing and design existed in Paris at the end of the 1760s, we must remember that, by that time, there existed numerous pieces of furniture in the Neo-Classical style, that there were many *bronzes d'ameublement* and works in silver and so forth —all in the new taste, and that one could procure the engravings of men like Neufforge, Forty and Delafosse. This means that any craftsman could acquire models or designs in the new taste that he might copy, without much difficulty and at comparatively small cost, if he wished to be in the swim. Roubo's book, with its fine illustrations of both old-fashioned and up-to-date furniture (Plates 476 to 478), must have been beyond the means of most furniture-makers. It cost 221 livres which was a considerable sum of money. This is no doubt why it sold so badly; in ten years only 200 copies were sold from a printing of 1,500.[7] The price was, after all, the equivalent of two or three months' pay for a journeyman cabinet-maker. The impact this useful book can have made is therefore likely to have been limited.

3. SPECIALISTS, CONTRACTORS AND MIDDLE-MEN

If someone commissioned a house or a piece of furniture, for instance, he was in a strong position to influence its final appearance. But not everything of this kind was made to order in the eighteenth century. There also existed a ready-made market, and the craftsman or dealer who sought to cater for this was obliged to have a stock of finished or half-finished pieces ready in his shop or warehouse. This required considerable capital investment and necessitated having a knowledge of the potential customers' tastes.

Large enterprises like the royal porcelain factory at Sèvres, and no doubt a number of silk-weaving establishments, worked largely for this market. At Sèvres, where a large organisation

[1] *Cours d'architecture*, vol. III (1772), p. LXXXII.

[2] 'architect and teacher of drawing'.

[3] *L'Avantcoureur*, 6th July 1767.

[4] Waddesdon Manor Library, in a volume containing a large collection of old trade-cards.

[5] 'for the benefit of working men'.

[6] He may conceivably be identical with the engraver Le Meunnié who signed some engravings which form part of Delafosse's *oeuvre* (*sér.* TT, *43e cahier*) and of that of Lalonde (*sér.* C, *pieds de meubles*, and *sér.* N, *plafonds*) and which were published in the early 1780s.

[7] Cf. the present writer's article 'En haandvaerkets bog fra det 18. aarhundrede: Descriptions des Arts et Métiers 1760–1788', *Fund og Forskning i Det kongelige Biblioteks Samlinger*, V–VI (1958–59), p. 156.

with a large staff was involved, one had to think very carefully before launching a new model. It was probably for this reason that the factory in 1751, even while it was still at Vincennes, became associated with Lazare Duvaux, one of the principal dealers in *objets d'art* and fine furniture in Paris. He was of course well equipped to give the directors of the factory good advice with regard to any new models they were thinking of putting into production.

We know quite a lot about these Parisian dealers who called themselves *marchands-merciers*, thanks to an important article published by Pierre Verlet, and to the edition of Lazare Duvaux's account-book brought out by Louis Courajod, the introduction to which is a masterpiece of its kind.[1] These merchants dealt in most of the wares discussed in this book and their pleonastic title would seem to underline the fact that they were essentially dealers and not craftsmen. As the great *Encyclopédie* states, a *mercier* was a 'marchand de tout et faiseur de rien'.[2] Savary de Bruslons tells us that their guild was regarded as superior to all others, not merely because its members never worked with their hands but because their business consisted largely of enhancing the beauty of objects which had already been made by others. He uses the word 'enjoliver' in this context, which implies that they were wont to add further decoration to things.

The *marchand-mercier* was thus a middle-man who stood between the craftsmen and the public. He needed to know the latter's tastes and then sought to meet the resulting demand by placing appropriate orders with the craftsmen. In Paris there were several important *merciers* and many smaller ones. The leading members of this fraternity—Hébert, Duvaux, Poirier, Dulac, Julliot, Bazin and so on—had shops at the fashionable end of the Rue Saint-Honoré and in the neighbouring streets—an area where all the best shops lay, and which now corresponds to that round the Place Vendôme and the Rue du Faubourg Saint-Honoré. We know from contemporary writers like Horace Walpole, the Rev. William Cole and Baronne d'Oberkirch that one could spend many a happy hour browsing in these shops,[3] for there was much to see—fire-dogs, sconces, chandeliers, mirrors, decorative vases of Chinese or French porcelain, clocks, cups and saucers decorated in every possible manner, and furniture (though not beds and seat-furniture).[4] Shortly after the Seven Years' War was over, the Earl of Coventry came to Paris and made considerable purchases at Poirier's and when, a few years later, the Duchess of Northumberland drew up a short list of the principal shops where one could buy veneered furniture in Paris, Poirier's name was naturally included.[5]

While Lazare Duvaux can hardly have experienced any diminishing in the admiration for the Rococo in his time (he died in November 1758), Simon-Philippe Poirier does seem to have played a significant role in the early evolution of Neo-Classicism. We would not claim that he had been among the pioneers but he seems to have become aware of which way the wind was blowing before any of his rivals, so that he was quicker to provide furniture and *objets d'art* which would appeal to the more fashion-conscious among his luxury-loving customers. Already

[1] Pierre Verlet, 'Les marchands-merciers à Paris au XVIIIe siècle', *Annales*, January–March 1958, pp. 10–29; *Livre-journal de Lazare Duvaux marchand-bijoutier ordinaire du Roy 1748–1758 précédé d'une étude sur le goût et sur le commerce des objets d'art au milieu du XVIIIe siècle* . . . (by Louis Courajod), vols. I–II, Paris, 1873.

[2] 'dealer in all things, maker of nothing'.

[3] See Watson, *Louis XVI Furniture*, pp. 78–80, and the same author's 'Walpole and the Taste for French Porcelain in Eighteenth-Century England', in: *Horace Walpole, Writer, Politician, and Connoisseur*, New Haven, 1967, pp. 185–94, and 327–36; also the introduction to Watson, *Wrightsman Collection*, p. XLVIIIff.

[4] See p. 136.

[5] I am much indebted to the Lady Victoria Percy for drawing my attention to the relevant passages in her ancestress' notebooks which are in the archives of the Dukes of Northumberland at Alnwick Castle.

on 26th December 1762 he sent to Parma 'Une Table, ou petit Bureau alagrec',[1] and among the furnishings he sold to Lord Coventry in 1763, there were some sconces 'à l'antique' and a 'commode à la grec'.[2] In 1765 he sent the same 'Milord' a 'bureau à la grec' (Plate 100). Poirier specialised in furniture set with plaques of Sèvres porcelain, as Verlet has demonstrated.[3] In 1760 he took a commode of traditional Rococo style and added plaques on all three sides. These were painted with flowers and had a green ground.[4] During 1761 and the following four years he caused eight small serving tables of Rococo form to be fitted with a tray of Sèvres porcelain on top instead of the more usual slab of marble.[5] The trays were of the type that normally served for the sets they called 'déjeuners Courteilles' at Sèvres. It may well have been Poirier, moreover, who commissioned, also in 1761, the first of a special kind of inkstand which has twelve small porcelain plaques set into the bronze body of entirely Neo-Classical form (Plate 235). In 1766, at any rate, Poirier brought out a new type of lady's writing-desk which, in spite of its high cost, sold very well (Plate 111). Such a piece of furniture, which has no less than seventeen porcelain plaques of ten different shapes, can only have been the result of careful organisation and an enormous amount of preliminary work, taking many months and perhaps even a couple of years or so. A full-scale model must certainly have been made and no doubt numerous detail drawings as well. The wooden cabinet-making work had to be executed by an *ébéniste*—in this case, Martin Carlin—while the mounts were cast by a bronze-founder and gilded, and the plaques were made and painted out at Sèvres. Each element had of course to fit and, since the capital investment in the various parts was considerable (such a desk retailed at 1,400 livres), it was essential that mistakes were not made, and we can be sure that Poirier and his draughtsman kept a close eye on the work, especially in its early stages when jigs, moulds, templates and full-scale patterns were being prepared. Poirier must have thought it would be too risky to adopt an ultra-modern and whole-heartedly Neo-Classical shape for this type of desk, especially if he planned to put it into series-production. So he compromised and decided to retain legs of Rococo form but made the superstructure rectangular, furnishing it with mounts of Classical form. These desks thus came to be elegant, but not too extreme, expressions of the new taste. The owner of such a desk made it clear that he was modern in outlook but with respectable moderation!

Poirier repeated his success with this desk when, about 1770, he launched his new jewel-coffer on a stand (Plate 121) and a small circular table (Plate 122)—both elegant little pieces of furniture couched in the same measured modernism as the lady's desks. These were also very expensive objects: the coffer cost 1,800 livres and the table 800. In 1771 or soon after, Poirier took the plunge outright and caused to be made a piece of furniture couched entirely in the new style. The result was the table shown in Colour Plate D. This is also mounted with Sèvres plaques and these must have been considerably more expensive than any we have so far seen on Poirier's furniture. Set on the top is an oval plaque, not visible in the illustration, that must alone have cost something in the region of 1,500 *livres* before mounting—that is, more than the total cost of one of his earlier tables. If we estimate that Poirier must have sold this new model at his shop for 2,500 or 3,000 *livres*, perhaps even rather more, we will probably not be far out. That would be the equivalent of, say, £2,000 in today's money—some would say a good deal more. It would be

[1] Parma, Archivio di Stato, *Tesoreria en la Corte de Paris y Corresponsales*, Busta 1093.
[2] See p. 98.
[3] Pierre Verlet, *Sèvres, le XVIIIe siècle*, pp. 30–1.
[4] Ibid., Plate 39.
[5] Verlet, *Les meubles français du XVIIIe siècle, II, ébénisterie*, 1956, Plate VIII.

interesting to know whether Poirier was commissioned to make this little table or whether he had it made as a speculation, without any particular one of his rich customers in mind. At any rate, with its straight and fluted legs, it is more consistent in its Classicism than any piece of furniture that had so far been sold on the premises; there is no trace of Rococo left in this piece—except in its elegance and grace. In 1773 he put a new desk into production (Plate 136), a development of the table just mentioned with some of the same bronze mounts, and this must have cost two or three times as much as the coffer. By this stage, of course, it was no longer risky to adopt the new taste in its more thorough-going form—even in an expensive line like this!

We know which *ébénistes* worked for Poirier but we have as yet no idea who was his designer. There is no reason to think he himself executed the designs from which the various independent craftsmen worked. Indeed, in a bill sent to Lord Coventry in 1768, one item is for a drawing of a candelabrum and Poirier states explicitedly that he had paid twelve livres 'pour le Dessein que J'ai fait faire'.[1] In fact he probably engaged more than one designer, each a specialist in a certain branch of the decorative arts. For example, the candelabrum just mentioned was 'avec Enfants' ('with children') and these are likely to have been drawn by a designer with a knowledge of sculpture, or by a painter. He probably had quite different artists to design his furniture. He must have had a selection of designs at his shop ready to show to potential customers, and we happen to know that Poirier had a stock of models for bronzes, because Poirier gave Dominique Daguerre, who was to become his partner, some 'modeles de cuivre cizelé'[2] as a wedding present when he got married in 1772.[3] This presumably means that Poirier had borne the cost of having these models made so the copyright was his, and he was now handing over the right to reproduce them to Daguerre. If one then recalls the terms of the Act regulating the copying of bronze-founders' patterns, it seems reasonable also to suppose that furniture like the table shown in Plate 112, which bears mounts of a type found on other known Poirier confections, is likely to have been made for him or for Daguerre who became his partner in 1772 and took over the firm entirely five years later.

Unfortunately we have no descriptions of the models for bronze which Poirier gave Daguerre. They may have been for furniture mounts, for *bronzes d'ameublement*, for clock-cases or cases for barometers like the three shown in Plates 197 to 199 which are known to have come from his shop, or for the body of inkstands. One type known as an 'écritoire Poirier' had porcelain plaques, and figures in the ledgers of the Sèvres factory in 1770 and 1771. Madame du Barry bought one from him in 1770.[4]

Of the *marchands-merciers* active in Paris during the 1760s, Poirier probably had the most extensive business but there were others who seem to have played a certain creative role as well. Others, for instance, were having vases of various kinds set in mounts of gilt bronze. In many cases the vases were specially commissioned and designed for the purpose at the Sèvres factory; they were not part of the regular production, there. Vases like those shown in Plates 238 to 240 were in fact normally sold without mounts to *marchands-merciers*—to people like the widow Lair, to Grouël and Dulac, as well as Poirier—who must then have been in a position to have them mounted.

[1] 'for the design that I have had made'. Croome Court Archives, Bill No. 53.
[2] 'models for chased copper [or bronze] ornaments'.
[3] Arch. Nat., Minutier Central, CXVII–857 (15th April 1772).
[4] *The James A. de Rothschild Collection at Waddesdon Manor, Sèvres Porcelain*, 1968, No. 90.

It must have been on the initiative of these *marchands-merciers* that both the bronze and the porcelain components of such confections were designed, and it was also mainly in their shops that such pieces could be bought. When Horace Walpole went to Paris in the 1760s he went to Dulac, Poirier and Marc Saïd, and not to the Sèvres factory, to buy Sèvres porcelain and bronze-mounted pot-pourri vases like those illustrated in Plate 238, as Francis Watson has shown.[1]

It also seems probable that certain dealers ordered, at their own expense, new models for fire-dogs, sconces and other decorative objects of bronze, instead of relying on what the bronze-founders had in stock. For example, in 1769 and 1770 we find Claude de la Roüe providing several sets of fire-dogs for the *Garde-meuble de la Couronne* including some which were very like, and perhaps even identical to, those illustrated in Plate 225 which were destined for the Dauphin's rooms at Fontainebleau. Where furnishings for prominent positions were concerned, it is unlikely that the Court wanted pieces that anyone could go out and buy in a shop. On the other hand, the dealer who could provide bronzes after a fresh model could not be prevented from running off further copies, if he had orders for such things on his books—unless of course the Court had paid for the design and creation of the original model and could thereby reserve the copyright.

It will thus be appreciated that the more powerful *marchands-merciers* were in a position to influence design, if they chose, and they were bound to be acutely aware of changes in fashion. Another class of business-man who had to keep a close watch on taste were the *marchands-tapissiers* (or upholsterers, as they were called in England) whose sphere of interest to some extent overlapped that of the *marchands-merciers*. They too, dealt in veneered furniture, *bronzes d'ameublement*, and mirrors, for instance, but they did not sell porcelain, clocks and similar luxury wares which the *merciers* handled. The upholsterers sold chairs, sofas, stools, couches and beds. They could also upholster all these things; they undertook the rigging up of intricate curtains and draperies of all kinds round windows, on walls, and on beds; and they could lay carpets. Moreover, they dealt in all the many textile materials that were required for these purposes. Since a *tapissier* could attend to all this, it was often simpler for a customer to go to him for his seat-furniture, for he could then have it upholstered on the premises, and this was particularly important if the chairs and sofas concerned had to match the other furnishings in a room—all of which, incidentally, the *tapissier* could also supply. In an Age when the furnishings of a room were often made *en-suite*, it was of course far easier to leave the co-ordination to one man. It is therefore not so surprising to discover that the famous chair-maker, Louis Delanois, sold more furniture to *marchands-tapissiers* than direct to customers.

An important difference between the *marchands-merciers* and the *marchands-tapissiers* was that the latter were trained as craftsmen (as upholsterers) and therefore belonged to a rather lower social class than the *merciers*. They must therefore have ranked with the cabinet-makers and the makers of chairs etc. Many of them also lived in a different part of town from the *merciers*. For instance, the *marchand-tapissier*, Antoine Godefroy, who was the accredited upholsterer to Madame de Pompadour and her brother, the Marquis de Marigny, and must have been among the most successful men in the business, lived right out in the Rue de Cléry[2] where many of the chair-makers also had their premises and where, incidentally, many of his competitors also had showrooms and workshops. It was naturally very practical for a *tapissier* to be established near

[1] See Watson's article on Walpole referred to on p. 133, note 3.

[2] See his biography, p. 186.

the chair-makers who supplied him with his *bois de sièges* (chair-frames). On the other hand, there were also advantages in living near the customers, as Charles-Antoine Ravary did. His showrooms lay in the Faubourg Saint-Germain, a highly fashionable address. Apart from the *ébéniste* Jean-Mathieu Chevalier, who lived in the Rue du Bac, all Ravary's suppliers of furniture lived far away. The other *ébéniste* who worked for him, Pierre Roussel, lived in the Faubourg Saint-Antoine, while the men who provided him with chairs and beds—well-known chair-makers like Delanois, Sené, Gourdin, Boulard and Tillard—lived up on Montmartre in the Bonne-Nouvelle quarter.[1] But, while some upholsterers may have preferred to live near their customers and others found it advantageous to be near their chair-makers, all had to have the textile materials they needed brought mostly from distant parts of the country—silks from Lyons or Tours, canvas and webbing from Brittany or Flanders, woollen cloth from Rouen or Abbeville, and so forth.

Several *marchands-tapissiers* lived in or near the Rue de la Verrerie which lies on the fringes of the Marais quartier, again a fashionable area, and there seems to have been a congregation of *tapissiers* near the Place Maubert and in the Rue du Four, on the other side of the River Seine. Only a few lived actually in the Rue Saint-Honoré but these included François Labitte who supplied Madame du Barry, and Dubuquoy who was calling himself 'Marchand Tapissier ordinaire de Mgr le Dauphin' in 1770 and who made a speciality of providing chair-covers of *petit-point*.[2] It would be nice to know, incidentally, where Claude-François Capin lived, since he was *tapissier ordinaire* to the Court.

We still cannot say for certain whether *marchands-tapissiers* were generally less prosperous than the *marchands-merciers*, but this was probably the case although both must have required a considerable amount of capital to run their business. *Merciers* like Duvaux and Poirier made a profit of between 9% and 12% on the Sèvres porcelain they sold,[3] whereas the royal upholsterer Capin only made 5% on the items provided for the Court.[4] On the other hand, many a *marchand-tapissier* made a lucrative business hiring furniture to people but, as so often happened in the eighteenth century, the customers did not always pay up and several upholsterers went bankrupt on this account. One Pierre-Henri Lelorin suffered this fate in 1764 even though he reckoned on getting back each year 33⅓% of the value of the furniture he hired out![5] Vildieu, who was declared bankrupt in the same year, used to charge eight sols a day for the hire of a sofa covered with silk damask; this comes to 146 livres per annum which would seem to represent a substantial profit.[6]

The reason we need to know more about the financial standing of the principal *tapissiers* is that we might thereby be better able to judge the degree to which they could govern and finance the production of furniture in an advanced taste. For the moment we can only assume that they were in a stronger position than the average chair-maker to embark on ambitious experiments in this direction. They may even have been better able to sponsor such ventures than a leading chair-maker like Delanois. Indeed, in his case we know that some of the first commissions he received for sets of chairs in the progressive style came from *marchands-tapissiers* like Caumont,

[1] Arch. Seine, D[4] B[6], Carton 58, dossier 3713 (Bilan of 26th June 1776).
[2] See his advertisement in *L'Avantcoureur*, 12th March 1770.
[3] Verlet, *Sèvres le XVIIIe siècle*, p. 45.
[4] This is stated in Capin's yearly accounts preserved in the Archives Nationales.
[5] Arch. Seine, D[4] B[6] Carton 26, dossier 1364, (Bilan of 14th May 1764).
[6] Arch. Seine, D[5] B[6] 3028, Livre-journal de Vildieu (entry dated 23rd May 1764).

David, Mallet, Toussin and so on,[1] and in some cases it is actually recorded in his account books that he has made the chairs in question after designs sent to him by the *marchand-tapissier* concerned. Delanois also occasionally produced the framework for fire-screens which had to fit a screen-cloth—probably an embroidery—of a particular size and shape supplied by a *marchand-tapissier*.[2] Of course the cloth and the designs for the framing may have come from a customer for whom the *tapissier* was acting as go-between, but it seems at least as likely that an enterprising *tapissier* would have a selection of designs and models he could show to customers, and he may well also have had items of this kind produced for stock. It is unlikely that *marchands-tapissiers* were themselves normally able to draw although they certainly needed the services of draughtsmen to set out cutting-patterns for drapery and upholstery of all kinds, and perhaps also for making sketches of proposed work to show to customers. Guillaumot, who was *tapissier ordinaire* both for the City and the University of Paris, was apparently an exception, for he is known to have designed as well as executed the catafalque set up in connection with a memorial service held for the Dauphin in 1766.[3]

If we know all too little about the *marchands-merciers* and the *marchands-tapissiers*, and about the degree to which they were able to influence the evolution of the Neo-Classical style in Paris during this period, we know even less about the other classes of dealer who might have affected the issue. There were certain *ébénistes* who had left the quarter where the cabinet-makers mostly lived and worked—the Faubourg Saint-Antoine—and set up business as *marchands-ébénistes* in more central areas of the city. For example, Denis Genty settled in the Rue de l'Echelle, just off the Rue Saint-Honoré, where the Court cabinet-maker, Gilles Joubert, also lived. According to an advertisement in *L'Avantcoureur* of 18th August 1760, he had in stock a wide selection of furniture of all kinds 'de bon goût'. Léonard Boudin was another cabinet-maker who subsequently set up shop in the fashionable quarter of Paris and, judging by the number of pieces of furniture one still finds bearing his name, he must have been a man of substance and perhaps also of some influence, especially as a number of other well-known *ébénistes* worked for him. However, we do not know whether those who supplied him with furniture provided the designs themselves or whether drawings were supplied by Boudin. He had himself previously worked for the dealer and cabinet-maker, Pierre Migéon, before establishing himself in the Rue Froidmanteau, near the Palais Royal.[4]

The appearance of a banker named Jean-Henri Eberts on our stage presents a curious phenomenon. He was an energetic man who came to Paris from Strasbourg. In about 1773 he devised a completely new type of furniture—a tripod stand which could serve as the base for a washstand, an occasional table, a jardinière, and much else (Plates 186 and 484). It was based on the Classical incense-burner which had a tripod stand—and, for this reason he had the brilliant idea of calling it an *Athénienne*—and it was a highly practical piece of furniture. In England the same classical form had inspired designers like James (Athenian) Stuart and Robert Adam to develop tripod candle-stands and pastille-burners but these retained much of the spirit and significance of the original while the *Athénienne* was a playful adaptation which had none of the mystique of the English versions.

[1] See p. 89.
[2] Arch. Seine, D^5 B^6 4245, Livre des ouvrages, (1st February, 1766).
[3] S. P. Hardy, *Mes Loisirs*, Paris, 1912, p. 48, (entry dated 12th May 1766); *Almanach Royal*, 1775, p. 267.
[4] See his biography, p. 156.

Eberts is otherwise best known for having published *Le Monument de Costume* which is a large work with engravings after Moreau *le jeune's* drawings that give us many charming glimpses into life among fashionable people in Paris in the 1770s. Eberts' contribution to this venture need not have been limited to financial support; he knew how to draw and make etchings, and it was more probably him rather than Moreau who decided that the furniture—including the chairs—depicted in the illustrations should be in the modern taste and not in the Rococo style which Moreau otherwise preferred, as may be seen if one studies the latter's many other compositions made without the guidance of an editor. In the first version of the famous scene entitled *N'ayez pas peur, ma bonne Amie* of 1775, Moreau first included a chair of Rococo form[1] but this was subsequently changed to that of pure Neo-Classical lineaments which one sees in Helman's engravings which were executed the year after. It seems reasonable to suppose that Eberts ordered this alteration to be made.

We have no idea which *ébéniste* made Eberts' first *Athéniennes* but we do know that they were sold by Jean-Félix Watin, the colour-merchant and gilder who has already been mentioned (see page 128). Watin had started off as a *marchand-épicier*[2] but, in 1772, became a *maître peintre-doreur* and a member of the Académie de Saint-Luc. He was then living in the Rue Sainte-Apolline which lay in the chair-makers' quarter near the Porte St. Denis.[3] He set up as a dealer of sorts and hit upon the idea of selling engravings of furniture designs in the modern taste—the work of Delafosse, Boucher *le jeune*, etc.—and undertaking to have furniture based on such designs executed for customers. At the same time, he ran a workshop of gilders and, in this capacity, he worked for the chair-makers Le Normand, Lebas and Georges Jacob, as well as sculptors like Gouffier and Guibert.[4] This does not necessarily mean that Watin went to these same people to have his furniture made. Whether he had in fact had much furniture produced on this basis before he went bankrupt in 1776 is not known but he was an enterprising fellow and his debts totalled well over a quarter of a million livres.[5] The book he published on the art of gilding may well have earned him a certain renown and, with his many contacts, it would not be surprising if it transpired that he had been a man of some influence.

4. FRANCE AND ENGLAND

Louis Hautecoeur and other students of architecture demonstrated that Neo-Classicism evolved in France and in England quite independently although the architects in both countries drew their inspiration from the same wells—Classical Antiquity, Palladio and Piranesi—and, in the case of France, from the great Academic tradition current in the Age of Louis XIV. In this connection, it is amusing to note that Madame de Genlis—that survivor of the *Ancien Regime* who was always lecturing the rather brash society of the Napoleonic era and drawing attention to their ignorance and bad manners—claimed that the landscape-garden, the so-called *Jardin à*

[1] Illustrated Plate XI in the catalogue to the Madame Lucien Guiraud sale, Hôtel Drouot, 14th June 1956 (lot 59).

[2] Arch. Nat., Minutier Central, XXVIII–378 (13th March 1762), Bail de maison, Charles Pierre Mayron à Jean Félix Watin.

[3] See Guiffrey, *Académie de Saint-Luc*, p. 484.

[4] Arch. Seine, $D^4 B^6$, Carton 57, dossier 3638.

[5] See M. Jallut, 'Un cadre royal', *Bulletin des Musées de France*, December 1946, pp. 15–18.

l'angloise, had in fact been invented first in France—by Pierre Daniel Huet, the famous Bishop of Avranches—and that Addison had thought of it later, independently![1]

At any rate, it is clear that neither nation need accuse the other of so serious a crime as having foisted Neo-Classicism on its neighbour! On the other hand, the two nations cannot have remained entirely ignorant of what the other was doing in the field that interests us here, and ideas, in some cases of great importance, must occasionally have been exchanged across the Channel. As far as Neo-Classicism is concerned, such an exchange of ideas is likely to have had an effect on the subsequent development of the style rather than on its conception. In the present context, however, we must confine ourselves to surveying the possible contribution England may have made to Neo-Classicism in France.

In 1753, the Abbé Le Blanc wrote that 'Paris est depuis long-tems le Magasin de L'Europe pour toutes les frivolités que le caprice met à la mode'[2] and he must have been well aware that a constant stream of luxury wares—articles of fashion—flowed from Paris to London, a city he knew well. The English correspondent of the French *Journal Oeconomique* wrote in August 1754 that 'il est indubitable que quelque mode qu'on invente en France, elle sera bientôt adoptée en Angleterre'[3] and one could quote numerous statements in contemporary English publications confirming that this was so. Indeed, an Anti-Gallican Society was founded at about this time 'to oppose the insidious arts of the French Nation', while measures of all kinds were introduced by Parliament to hinder, if not stem, the flow of goods. The English writer in the *Journal Oeconomique* added that, when Englishmen went over to Paris, they tended to come home dressed up like Frenchmen! The French, on the other hand, do not adopt English fashions, he says. However, after the Seven Years' War, things were different, judging by a report which appeared in the *L'Avantcoureur* in April 1764[4] in which we are informed that several shop-signs had recently appeared in the Rue Saint-Honoré and that one of these had been provided by Honoré Guibert, the famous carver. The report continues to explain that such signs are 'un des principaux ornemens de la ville de Londres'[5] and adds that 'Il nous est très-permis d'imiter les Anglois sur ce point comme sur quelques autres. On sçait qu'ils nous rendent quelquefois le change, malgré leur affectation à nous étaler des habits à taille courte et de grands chapeaux'.[6] The conclusion of the Seven Years' War, in which France had lost so much, does not seem to have left her people with feelings of animosity towards England. Already in November 1762, before peace was concluded, there was considerable enthusiasm at the Court at Versailles when a 'contredanse d'Anglais et d'Anglaises'[7] was included with the performance of Favart's play *La Soirée des boulevards*, and Papillon de la Ferté specially draws attention to the fact that the dance 'dans les circonstances présentes, a fait grand plaisir à tout le monde'.[8] Naturally one should not interpret this to mean that the flow of fashionable goods and influences from France to England

[1] Comtesse de Genlis, *Dictionnaire critique et raisonné des étiquettes de la cour . . .*, vol. 1, 1818, pp. 297–8.

[2] 'For a long time Paris has been the warehouse of Europe for all those little frivolities that caprice suddenly makes fashionable.' *Observations sur les ouvrages de MM. de l'Académie . . . exposés . . . en l'année 1753*, Paris, n.d., p. 53.

[3] 'It is indubitable that whatever fashion one invents in France will soon be taken up in England.' Ibid., p. 189.

[4] 16th April 1764, pp. 249–50.

[5] 'one of the chief ornaments of the streets of London'.

[6] 'We may certainly copy the English in this matter, as we do in several others. After all, we know they sometimes beat us to it, even if they do parade before us in short coats and large hats.'

[7] 'a quadrille of English men and women'.

[8] 'In the prevailing circumstances, the dance has been greeted with great enthusiasm on all sides.' *Journal de Papillon de La Ferté*, ed. Ernest Boysse, 2nd ed., 1887, p. 91.

had been reversed. Indeed, we know very well how extensive were the purchases made in Paris by English visitors who came over after the war. Having been largely deprived of French goods for seven years, their eagerness was no doubt heightened, while the recent victory had ensured that their purses were mostly full. Many English country-houses still bear witness to their zeal; much furniture, many tapestries, and huge quantities of porcelain remain as evidence. All the same, these quotations indicate that the flow was no longer one-way and that it was not considered at all repugnant in France at the time to display an interest in what Englishmen had to offer.

In fact, both before and after, and even during, the war some French artists had been in touch with their colleagues in England. Both Sir William Chambers and the Adam brothers had close contacts with artists in France. As John Harris has shown, Chambers was a good friend of the architect Le Roy and of De Wailly. He knew Barreau de Chefdeville, Soufflot and the sculptor Pajou and he was on friendly terms with men like Mique, Antoine, Patte, Peyre and Jardin, and probably also with Belanger. We do not yet know when he first met these various people but it is probable that, in many cases, he made their acquaintance when he was attending J.-F. Blondel's school of architecture in Paris in 1750.[1] At any rate, we know that Chambers stayed for quite a while in Paris although he spent the winter of 1750–51 in Rome. He in fact departed for the second time at the end of October 1752 and not in 1750, as has hitherto been believed. This is proved by a letter from the Swede, Frederik Sparre, dated 10th November 1752 in which he states that Chambers had left for Rome a fortnight earlier after having had his portrait painted by Roslin who[2] had only arrived in Paris the year before, from Italy. So Chambers had had plenty of time to form friendships with people like Barreau and De Wailly. The former only went to Rome himself at the beginning of 1752 and De Wailly did not depart until 1754. They must all three have met in Rome, even though De Wailly left in 1755 to go to England. Chambers may not have met some of the other artists and architects we have mentioned until after his arrival in the Eternal City, however. For example, Le Roy seems to imply that it was in Rome that he met Chambers.[3] In any case, it will be perceived that Chambers belonged, at an early date, to the circle of Frenchmen who were to play the leading role in creating the new Classical style in France. Born in 1723, he was some ten years younger than, for example, Soufflot, Le Lorrain and Le Geay; he was about the same age as Jardin and Barreau de Chefdeville, and seven years older than De Wailly and Pajou.

We also know that both Chambers and De Wailly were interested in the design of furniture and that each was among the very first to design furniture in a Neo-Classical idiom in his own country. Could it be that Chambers influenced De Wailly in this matter? It is by no means impossible. Admittedly we have records of only a single instance of De Wailly borrowing direct from his friend—he copied the vase shown in Plate IV of Chambers' book of *Designs of Chinese Buildings, Furniture . . . etc.* of 1757 and used it in the composition reproduced here in Plate 329, but this Chinese vase was not an original conception of Chambers'. Even so, when two people know each other well and are interested in the same problems, it is virtually impossible to prevent them influencing each other. We know that De Wailly designed some furniture which was exhibited at the *Salon* of 1761,[4] but we have no idea what it was like and we are entirely

[1] John Harris, *Sir William Chambers, Knight of the Polar Star*, 1970, pp. 5–6 and 30.
[2] State Archives, Stockholm, Tessin Papers, letter from Sparre to C. G. Tessin dated 10th November 1752.
[3] David Le Roy, *Les ruines des plus beaux monuments de la Grèce . . .*, 2nd ed., vol. 2, 1770, p. XVIII.
[4] See p. 70.

ignorant of what other furniture he may have designed. On the other hand, John Harris has shown that it was Chambers who, in 1759, designed the ceremonial chair that was to be used by the President of the Royal Society of Arts, and this chair had legs of an unusual form—tapering, circular in section, and with spiral fluting.[1] This characteristic feature is to be seen on a French table which cannot have been produced very many years later (Plate 102) and may quite possibly have been designed by De Wailly. Is there a connection? We certainly cannot exclude the possibility.

We can only speculate about the appearance of the decorations Barreau de Chefdeville designed in about 1762 for Lalive de Jully's *Cabinet Flamand* in the Rue de Menars, the room which was to house the famous furniture made to Le Lorrain's designs a few years before. We know the room was decorated 'à la grecque' but Le Lorrain had nothing to do with this because he had gone to Russia in 1758 and had died in 1759. However, Barreau was a friend of Chambers and, together with Blondel, Pajou, Le Roy and the painter Doyen, had been among the few Frenchmen whose names appeared in the list of subscribers to Chambers' *Treatise on Civil Architecture* which appeared in 1759. Possibly this is irrelevant but the few drawings we possess from Barreau's hand (Plates 56 to 58) show that he at any rate had much the same artistic ideals as Chambers.

Fiske Kimball once put forward the suggestion that Robert Adam had influenced the history of French furniture in the 1760s,[2] but there cannot be many people who still subscribe to this view. Rousset's design for a sofa (Plate 398) may be faintly reminiscent of Adam's design for a sofa intended for Kedleston Hall,[3] but Eileen Harris has put forward weighty arguments to show that the influence in fact flowed in the opposite direction.[4] In view of this, one is rather astonished to discover that, already in 1766, the French publisher, Nyon, opened a subscription for a work which was to be dedicated to 'MM. Robert et Jacques Adam, Architectes Ecossois'. According to Nyon's announcement in that year's July issue of the *Mercure de France*,[5] this was to consist of a collection of illustrations executed by 'des Professeurs & des amateurs de la belle antiquité'[6] and entitled *Journal de Rome, ou Collection des anciens monumens qui existent dans cette Capitale & dans les autres parties de l'Italie*. The scheme seems to have come to nothing but the very fact that one could have the idea of publishing such a work and dedicating it to the brothers Adam at least suggests that the English—or, as the dedication rightly says, Scottish—architects were fairly widely admired in France at that time. Yet who can their admirers have been, and for what, particularly, were they admired?

The only French architect whose works may occasionally make one think of Adam is Ledoux. For example, as Michel Gallet has recently pointed out, there are certain similarities between the ante-room at Syon House (1763) and some of Ledoux's mural decorations at the Hôtel d'Uzès, which was designed a few years later.[7] Moreover, in the two houses he designed in 1770,

[1] See John Harris, 'Early Neo-Classical Furniture', *The Journal of The Furniture History Society*, vol. II, 1966, Plate VI; and the same author's *Sir William Chambers*, 1970, pp. 89–90 and Plate 181.

[2] Fiske Kimball, 'Les influences anglaises dans la formation du style Louis XVI', *Gaz. d. B.-A.*, 6th ser., V (1931), pp. 29–44, 231–55. Kimball's ideas were further elaborated in his book *The Creation of the Rococo*, 1943, pp. 186–8, 198–200, and in his 'The Beginnings of the Style Pompadour 1751–9', *Gaz.d.B.-A.*, 6th ser., XLIV, 1954, pp. 57–64.

[3] Eileen Harris, *The Furniture of Robert Adam*, 1963, fig. 98.

[4] Eileen Harris, 'Robert Adam and the Gobelins', *Apollo*, April 1962, pp. 100–6.

[5] p. 134.

[6] 'scholars and connoisseurs of the Classical Antiquities'.

[7] Michel Gallet, 'Le salon de l'Hôtel d'Uzès', *Bulletin du Musée Carnavalet*, 22e année, 1969, No. 2 (1971), pp. 1–23.

for Madame du Barry and Mademoiselle Guimard respectively, he used a characteristic portico resembling the one that Adam had previously employed with such success at Syon and at Newby Hall. Can this exceptionally intelligent and original French architect have known Adam's works? He does not ever seem to have set foot in Italy, let alone in Rome, yet we know he was abroad for a couple of years although we do not know where he went. Could his journey have taken him across the Channel? If one studies his career, the only period in which he could have been away for that length of time was between 1763 and 1765.

Belanger, the designer of Marie-Antoinette's jewel-cabinet (Plate 448) was in England in 1766 and was probably welcomed there by Chambers, as John Harris has suggested.[1] Gondoin, who was to become furniture-designer to the French Court and responsible for many of the designs for chairs provided for the *Garde-meuble de la Couronne* in the 1770s, was in England that same year. Since these two talented artists bothered to go to England in the first place, it is unlikely that they failed to come away with a number of fresh ideas. If so, it would be interesting to know what they were. The clean lines of Gondoin's École de Chirurgie (Plate 84) seem to reflect a knowledge of Adam's style, for instance. The last word has certainly not been said on the cross-fertilisation of ideas between French and English architecture at this period!

As far as furniture is concerned, on the other hand, much is known about the enormous influence of French designs on English furniture, particularly chairs, during this phase. Several classes of English furniture also became known in France during the 1760s, however. A Parisian furniture-maker (*maître menuisier-méchanicien*) named Dufour advertised in *l'Avantcoureur* on 14th March 1768 that he had some 'pupitres à l'Anglaise' for sale. The description indicates these were reading-desks of the type now known as 'architects' tables'. There was also a certain Madame Blakey who owned a 'Magasin Anglais' in the Rue des Prouvaires.[2] She announced in the same paper in that year, on 21st June, that she could offer various articles of English manufacture including 'des tables de bois d'Acajou pour le thé' ('some mahogany tea-tables'); these tables may well be identical with the 'trois tables de bois d'acajou avec leurs pieds' which passed through the Customs at Péronne, near Saint-Quentin, on 11th March that year, and which were addressed to Madame Blakey. On 3rd April 1769, this lady bought from a certain 'Jacques Granges'[3] in London 'Une Grande Table en 3 pièces de bois d'acajou' for 176 livres and '2 Tables Bois d'accajou de Manger et une ditte à Thé' for 108 livres, as well as some tableware. On 18th November 1769, she obtained from 'Ch. Granges', also of London,[4] 'Une Grande Table de Mahogoney' for 130 livres, while she bought from Oppenheim's in Birmingham some

[1] John Harris, *Sir William Chambers*, 1970, p. 12.

[2] Madame Blakey was née Marguerite Elisabeth Aumerle. She described herself as 'marchande mercière priviligiée du Roi'. Her husband, William Blakey, was English and was the brother of Nicholas Blakey, the painter, who died in Paris in 1758. Blakey seems originally to have been a clockmaker; at any rate, he is known to have made clock-springs. He subsequently went into the truss and belt-makers' trade and then joined in his wife's business. He also wrote an account of springmaking which was published in Amsterdam in 1780. Some documents concerning the Blakeys' firm are preserved in the Archives Nationales (Y. 13701 and 13702).

[3] 'Jacques Granges' is probably identical with James Grange who had an upholstery warehouse at 95 High Holborn, according to the London Directories of 1768 to 1783.

[4] Charles Grange and Son were upholders at the sign of The Royal Bed on Snow Hill, near St. Sepulchre's Church. Their trade-card of about 1760 is to be seen in the Heal Collection at the British Museum. They claimed to make 'after the Newest Fashion all sorts of Four Post and Standing Beds'. Charles Grange was probably identical with the craftsman of the same name who played an important part in the furnishing of the Mansion House in the 1750s (see H. Clifford Smith, 'Two hundred years of the Mansion House, London, and some of its furniture', *Connoisseur*, December 1952).

expensive clocks including '1 Grand cartel doré en Guirlandes' for 1,200 livres and some buttons, snuffboxes and jewellery set with marcasites.

The large writing-desk in the Musée des Beaux-Arts at Tours (Plate 115) which was made in about 1768 for Chanteloup and can reasonably be attributed to Georg Haupt, is of a form commonly found in England even if the detailing is essentially French. If Haupt had anything to do with the design of this piece, it may indicate that he was himself already then interested in English furniture. At any rate, it was not long before he went to England and, in 1769, he made a table to the design of Sir William Chambers.[1] Both of them were Swedes and it may well be that they were in some way in contact while Haupt was still in Paris. However, we have said enough to show that there could be many other reasons why this clever *ébéniste* should at this stage have produced a desk of an English type.

In the 1770s, *l'anglomanie* became widespread and English influence could be detected in all the applied arts. Chairs with lyre-shaped backs,[2] for instance, could then be found in Paris, and furniture executed in solid mahogany—like that made by Garnier in 1778 for the Marquis de Marigny's house in the Place des Victoires.[3] Marigny had bought a pair of mahogany games-tables in London that year and Garnier was given these to copy, as well. However, we must not wander off beyond the proper confines of our subject.

To reward the patient reader who has studied with us all the many pieces which go to make up the incomplete jig-saw puzzle of which we spoke at the beginning of this book, we shall leave him holding what could be an important little English fragment that still needs to be set in its proper place. In Mathew Darly's *A Compleat Body of Architecture*, which appeared in 1773, mention is made in a footnote of a certain 'Mr. Rich. Langcake' who, we are told, has been 'neglected by his own country' but is 'now teaching the French the art of Design, requisite for Commerce etc. etc. they having not his Equal in all France'. Presumably he was identical with the 'Sr. Lancake, Artiste Anglais' who ran a wallpaper factory at Carrières, near Charenton.[4] But who were the Frenchmen he instructed in the gentle art of drawing and what influence, if any, can he have had?

[1] John Harris, *Sir William Chambers*, London 1970, p. 255 (No. 158).

[2] E.g. chairs stamped by Delanois who ceased activity in 1777; see also F. J. B. Watson, *Louis XVI Furniture*, pp. 88–9.

[3] See letters dated 28th October 1778 and 1st November 1779 from Marigny to Pierre Garnier, Bibliothèque historique de la Ville de Paris, MS. N.A. 106.

[4] See *L'Avantcoureur*, 16th January 1769.

SELECT BIOGRAPHIES

Adelaïde de France, Madame. Born in 1732, died in 1800. Daughter of Louis XV and Marie Leczinska. Elder sister of Madame Victoire, Madame Sophie and Madame Louise.

As far as one can judge from the Journal of the *Garde-Meuble de la Couronne*, from the accounts rendered by the various tradesmen appointed to the Court, and from the ledgers of the Sèvres factory, neither Madame Adelaïde nor her sisters seem to have acquired works of art that differed stylistically in any way from those purchased by their father, the King. There is certainly no indication that they might have favoured the Neo-Classical style earlier than he did. However, with the exception of Madame Louise who entered a convent in 1770, the sisters had such luxurious tastes, and their purchases were so extensive, that their example cannot have gone unnoticed and must in fact have done much to help consolidate the new style at the French Court whence it was effectively spread to a far wider circle.

Nouvelle Biographie Générale, vol. I, columns 268–9.[1]
Madame de Campan, *Mémoires*, 2nd ed. 1823, I, pp. 1–22.
Verlet, *Mobilier royal*, I–III, *passim*.
Verlet, *Versailles*, pp. 474–505.

See Plates 119–20, 196, 224, 228, 288.

Auguste, Robert-Joseph. Goldsmith. Born at Mons in 1723, died 1805. Father of Henri Auguste.

Auguste became a *maître* on 19th January 1757, in which year he lived in the Cul-de-sac, Saint-Thomas-du-Louvre; in 1766 he was in the Rue des Cordeliers, in 1773 in the Rue de la Monnoie, in 1781 on the Place du Carrousel in a house he had bought from Jacques Roëttiers; after 1784 he had a workshop in the Louvre as Roëttiers' successor.

Auguste was one of the first of the Parisian goldsmiths to execute work in the Neo-Classical style. The earliest recorded is a gold box in the Louvre (Plate 251) dated 1762–63, a pair of silver candelabra at Woburn Abbey dated 1766–67 (Plate 261), and another pair dated 1767–68 in the Metropolitan Museum of Art (Plate 262).

Auguste delivered numerous pieces to royal or aristocratic customers abroad. Three complete dinner-services were sent to Russia; in 1775–76 he provided Count de Creutz, the Swedish Ambassador to the French Court, with another service which is now in the Royal Swedish Collections. Other early Neo-Classical work by this master is to be seen in two Portuguese private collections. Auguste became the favourite goldsmith of Louis XVI and carried out many commissions for the Court—works since lost, including the crown used at Louis XVI's Coronation which was executed in collaboration with Ange-Joseph Aubert, *jouaillier de la Couronne*, the friend of Pierre Germain and a man who had also co-operated with Gouthière, the bronze-maker.

[1] The literature relevant to each entry is listed at this point throughout the biographical section.

It is known that Auguste also worked in bronze. Thus in 1761 he provided bronze mounts for a column after designs by the architect Charles De Wailly, and at the Blondel de Gagny auction in 1777, we see that lot No. 1033 consisted of 'Une paire de bras à trois branches de bronze doré, très bien exécuté, & de la composition de M. Auguste; le corps de chaque bras représente un therme de femme'. ('A pair of sconces with three branches, of gilt bronze, extremely skilfully executed, the work of M. Auguste; the body of each branch is in the form of a female term').

Jal, *Dictionnaire.*
Thieme and Becker, *Künstlerleksikon.*
Faith Dennis, *Three Centuries of French Domestic Silver*, New York, 1960.
Les grands orfèvres de Louis XIII à Charles X, Paris, 1965, pp. 231ff., text by Yves Bottineau.
A. de Champeau, *Dictionnaire des fondeurs*, pp. 44–5.
Musée du Louvre et Musée de Cluny, *Catalogue de l'orfèvrerie*, Paris, 1958, p. 33.
Museu Nacional de Arte Antiga (Lisbon), *Roteiro da ourivesaria*, Lisbon, 1959.
Henry Nocq and Carle Dreyfus, *Tabatières, boîtes et étuis . . . du Musée du Louvre*, Paris, 1930, p. 22.
Mercure de France, Oct. 1761, pp. 227–8.
Watson, *Wrightsman Catalogue*, p. 418.

See Plates 251, 261–2, 266.

AUMONT, Louis-Marie-Augustin, Duc d'. Peer, Lieutenant-general and *premier gentilhomme de la chambre du Roi*. Born in 1709, died in 1782. Son of Louis d'Aumont de Roche Baron, Duc d'Aumont (died 1723). Father-in-law to the Duchesse de Mazarin.

The Duc who was a year older than the King, was appointed *premier gentilhomme* in 1723 when Louis XV was only thirteen and he held this post until the King died in 1774. He was made a marshal in 1743, and a lieutenant-general in 1748. He was given a knighthood in the Order of the Saint-Esprit in 1745. He fought in the war against England and Holland, notably at the Battle of Fontenoy.

The Duc was one of Louis XV's closest friends and, because of his official position, was in daily contact with the King. His salary was paid through the *Menus Plaisirs* and, together with the three other *premiers gentilhommes*, he was the supreme head of this organisation and was thus one of those responsible for meeting the King's wishes with regard to such matters as the arrangements and settings for banquets and festivities of all kinds, and in connection with presents he was to make to various people. He might thus be concerned with the form and decoration of snuff-boxes—of which the King often made presents—and he was involved in the commissioning of the great jewel-cabinet (Plate 448) made in 1769, designed by Belanger, and fitted with bronzes by Gouthière. He signed the warrants appointing artists to the *Menus Plaisirs* including those of Belanger and Gouthière in 1767.

It is well known that the Duc, who cared little for paintings and other pictorial works of art, on his death left a collection of outstanding pieces of furniture and objets d'art in the purest *Louis Seize* style, including many bronzes by Gouthière. It is difficult to ascertain when he started to go in for Neo-Classicism but it would seem that he had already shown a preference for this new style by 1767 and it seems possible that he played a role of considerable importance in introducing his new taste into circles at the French Court. Francis Watson has suggested that it was the Duc who persuaded Madame du Barry to take up the new style and to commission work from Gouthière. The Duc d'Aumont's career deserves closer study. It would be fascinating if the inventory made on his death could be found, and if the copy of the catalogue of the subsequent auction, with sketches by Saint-Aubin, that rests in a French private collection, were to be published. Both documents would undoubtedly throw much fresh light on the life of this apparently highly influential person.

As a young man, the Duc lived in his father's house in the Rue de Jouy but moved to the Rue de Beaune in the Faubourg Saint-Germain in 1753. In 1775 he rented part of one of the two large buildings on the present Place de la Concorde (No. 10 in the Hôtel Crillon, see page 54) at the corner of the Rue de la Bonne-Morue, which the architect Pierre-Adrien Paris redecorated for him in the *Louis Seize* style.

Granges de Surgères, *Répertoire historique et biographique de la Gazette de France*, vol. I.
Cochin, *Mémoires.*
Guiffrey, *Les Caffieri.*
Hautecoeur, *Histoire*, seconde moitié.
Lazare Duvaux, *Livre-Journal.*
Rapports d'Experts.
Verlet, *Mobilier Royal I–II.*
Verlet, *French Royal Furniture.*
Watson, *Louis XVI Furniture.*
Jean Stern, *A l'ombre de Sophie Arnould. François-Joseph Belanger, architecte des Menus-Plaisirs*, 1930.
Pierre du Colombier, 'Le duc d'Aumont, la pointe de l'avant-garde en 1780', *Connaissance des Arts*, July 1961, pp. 24–31.
Baron Ch. Davillier, *Le cabinet du duc d'Aumont et les amateurs de son temps*, 1870.

See Plate 243.

BABEL, Pierre-Edme. Wood-carver, designer and engraver of ornament. Probably born 1700–10, died 1775.

At an early age Babel was known as a skilful carver in wood. In 1736 an unsuccessful attempt was made by the Swedes to engage his services for the Court in Stockholm. He became a *maître-sculpteur ornemaniste* in 1751. In and after 1763 he delivered work to the *Garde-Meuble de la Couronne* and during the period 1766–75 was paid a total of over 200,000 livres for such work. He was elected a *directeur garde* of the Académie de Saint-Luc in 1765. Like so many Parisian carvers, Babel lived in the Montmartre quarter, first of all in the Rue Montorgueil and then in the Rue Neuve Saint-Eustache. His widow kept the workshop going after his death; it was still operating in 1779.

Babel was also much occupied in engraving the work of others; for instance he engraved the illustrations for books by Boffrand and Meissonnier in the Rococo style. Neufforge's series of *Projets d'autels et de baldaquins* which he engraved in 1747 was in the same style. When Nicolas-Joseph Maria's *Livre de desseins de jouaillerie et bijouterie*, a collection of designs for jewellery, snuff-boxes, etc., appeared in 1765, the engravings by Babel were in the new Neo-Classical style. Presumably Babel's carved work for the Court at Versailles was mostly in the new taste, and probably in the main after drawings by Gondouin.

B. N. Est. Inv., vol. I, pp. 368–82.
Guiffrey, *Académie de Saint-Luc*, pp. 79 and 171.
Verlet, *Mobilier Royal* I.
Lazare Duvaux, *Livre-Journal*, No. 788.
Rapports d'Experts.
Vial, Marcel and Girodie, vol. I, p. 13.
Kimball, *Creation*, pp. 193 and 198.

See Plates 379–87.

BACHELIER, Jean-Jacques. Painter. Born in 1722, died in 1806.

In 1748 he was appointed *directeur artistique* of the porcelain factory at Vincennes which moved to Sèvres in 1758. He was responsible for providing sketches and designs for the other porcelain-painters to follow, and supervised their work and that of the modellers. Between 1758 and 1766, however, Falconet took over the supervision of the modellers—a job which then reverted to Bachelier whose responsibility it remained until 1774, when he was replaced by Boizot. As the years passed, the scale of Bachelier's responsibilities was reduced and, in 1793, when the factory's financial difficulties became acute, he was dismissed.

In 1753 he had opened a private academy of drawing and painting primarily, it would seem, for the benefit of the porcelain-painters engaged at the Vincennes factory. He established a public and free school of drawing in 1766, with the assistance of several private benefactors; this became the École Royale and survives as the École des Beaux-Arts.

Several of the figure-compositions which Bachelier showed at the Paris Salons have come down to us, as have a few animal- or flower-paintings. On the other hand, none of the paintings that were intended for use at the porcelain factory seem to have survived. All the same it seems almost certain that all the floral motifs, at any rate, were executed after models supplied by him, while he was probably responsible for the introduction of the *Louis Seize* designs that appeared in the 1760s.

Bachelier was a friend of François Boucher's but fell out with the Comte de Caylus at an early stage.

Thieme and Becker, *Künstlerleksikon.*
Louis Courajod, *L'École royale des élèves protégés*, Paris, n.d., *passim.*
Charles-Nicolas Cochin, *Mémoires inédits sur le comte de Caylus, Bouchardon, les Slodtz*, publiés . . . par Charles Henry, Paris, 1880, pp. 41–4.
Joubert de l'Hiberderie, *Le dessinateur pour les fabriques d'étoffes d'or, d'argent et de soie*, Paris, 1765, pp. 90–1, and 93.
Robert Rosenblum, 'On a painting of Milo of Crotona', in *Essays in Honour of Walter Friedlaender*, 1965, pp. 147–51.
Svend Eriksen, *Sèvres Porcelain, The James A. de Rothschild Collection at Waddesdon Manor*, Fribourg, 1968, pp. 19–20.
Journal Oeconomique, June 1755, pp. 94.

BARREAU DE CHEFDEVILLE, François-Dominique. Architect. Born in 1725, died in 1765.

A pupil of Boffrand and of the Académie d'Architecture where he won the Grand Prix in 1749. Attended the Académie de France, in Rome between February 1752 and March 1756. In 1765 he was living in the Rue de l'Arbre Sec near the Louvre. He numbered the sculptor Pajou among his friends.

Barreau's few known works include the mural decorations of the *Cabinet flamand* in Lalive de Jully's apartment in the Rue de Menars. These were carried out not earlier than 1762, the year in which Lalive moved from the Rue Saint-Honoré. He drew up a design for the new Mint in Paris, and is known to have provided schemes of interior decoration and other work in Bordeaux after 1762. He designed the church of Saint-Nicolas at Nérac which is now his only surviving work. The drawings for his projected alteration of the Palais Bourbon were approved by the Prince de Condé in 1765.

Gallet, *Demeures*, p. 172.
F.-G. Pariset, 'Barreau de Chefdeville', *BSHAF*, 1963, pp. 77–99.

See Plates 56–9.

BARRY, Jeanne Aimart de Vaubernier, Comtesse du. Louis XV's mistress from 1768 to 1774. Born in 1743 at Vaucouleurs (Département de la Meuse), guillotined in Paris in 1793. Daughter of a seamstress named Anne Bécu. Her father's name is not known.

Jeanne Bécu, as she was called, attended the convent-school of Sainte-Aube in Paris as a child. In 1759 she is known to have been living with her mother, then married to a certain Nicolas Rançon, in the Rue Neuve-Saint-Etienne which lies in the Bonne-Nouvelle quarter where many cabinet-makers resided. In that year she spent some time being trained to become a hair-dresser. But in about 1760 she had become apprenticed to a *marchand de modes* in the Rue Neuve-des-Petits-Champs near the Place des Victoires. In 1764 she moved in with Comte Jean du Barry who was acquainted with two of Louis XV's *premiers gentilhommes de la chambre*, the Duc de Duras and the Maréchal Duc de Richelieu. On 23rd July 1768, however, she married Comte Guillaume du Barry, a brother of the afore-mentioned Comte Jean. The marriage was clearly a *pro forma* arrangement; the church wedding took place on 1st September the same year, at five o'clock in the morning at the out-of-the-way church of Saint-Laurent outside the Porte Saint Martin.

Louis XV's attachment to Madame du Barry seems to have begun during the first months of the year 1768—the year in which, in July, Queen Marie Lesczynska died. Later that year or early in 1769 she was installed in the town of Versailles and, on 22nd April, she was presented at Court. Thereupon she was provided with an apartment in the Palace itself, together with apartments at Fontainebleau, Compiègne and Saint-Hubert. Louis was by now almost sixty years old, she was twenty-five.

On the 24th July 1769, the King gave her his old Pavillon de Louveciennes which Gabriel immediately set about modernising for her use. It was in the grounds of this building that was erected her new little pavilion after designs by Ledoux (Plates 79 and 80).

We know a good deal about Madame du Barry's purchases of furniture, *bronzes d'ameublement*, porcelain, etc. from sources like the Journal of the *Garde-Meuble*, the Sèvres factory's ledgers, and the accounts of the *marchand-mercier* Poirier, of the chair-maker Delanois, of the gilder Cagny, and of bronze-founders like Pitoin and Gouthière. From such sources we know that her earliest suite of furniture she purchased (on 20th September 1768), no doubt with funds provided by the King, was from Delanois and must have been in a markedly transitional style, with cabriole legs but with carved decoration in the Classical taste—probably very like the chairs shown in Plates 156 to 161. We do not know where she was living at this point, whether in Paris or in the town of Versailles, but the price seems to indicate that this furniture was not of the most luxurious kind so she was probably still resident in Paris. On 18th November 1768, she bought a small writing-desk in the transitional style set with Sèvres plaques from Poirier (cf. Plate 111), from whom she also bought a bronze clock (Plate 197). These were both expensive items (respectively 1,440 livres and 912 livres). In December, the Sèvres factory provided her with three vases which very probably resembled that shown in Plate 281. It bears a portrait relief of Louis XV and is entirely Neo-Classical in style.

From 1769 onwards, after she had been presented at Court and after having moved into her apartment at Versailles, Madame du Barry acquired such furniture as she required partly through the *Garde-Meuble de la Couronne* (and therefore paid out of their vote) and partly with her own money direct from various dealers who did not otherwise normally serve the royal household. Judging by the descriptions, much of what she acquired through the *Garde-Meuble* was not apparently very different from that which this organisation was providing for other important members of the Court at this time. The *Garde-Meuble* furnished apartments for Madame du Barry at Fontainebleau (1769–70 and again in 1772) at Saint-Hubert (1769), at Compiègne (1770–72), and at the Petit Trianon (1772). All the seat-furniture provided for these schemes had cabriole legs while the ornaments were of a Neo-Classical character. The commodes she thus acquired seem to have been transitional in style and were probably like those shown in Plates 119 and 120. The principal colours in her apartments were blue and white, and this colour-scheme was carried through from the window-curtains to the chair-coverings and to the painted woodwork of the chairs themselves. The decorative bronzes—sconces and fire-dogs—were mostly provided by Pitoin and were, like other pieces he produced for the *Garde-Meuble*, considerably more modern in style than much other contemporary work (see Plates 229 and 230). In September 1772, Gondoin designed four three-armed candelabra for her Fontainebleau apartment; each was supported by two *putti* standing on a kind of tripod composed of three consoles.

Curiously enough, much of the furniture supplied for the use of Madame du Barry in her Versailles apartment did not come through the *Garde-Meuble* at all but was ordered direct from craftsmen and dealers she already knew or had dealt with before. Among them were Poirier, and Delanois, and the upholsterer, Labitte, who had been patronised by one of her earlier lovers. The apartment set aside for her use was still panelled with *boiseries* decorated in an old-fashioned style but all the chairs she acquired for the rooms—from Delanois, delivered in December 1769—were ultra-modern being furnished with straight legs and Neo-Classical ornament. Even so, the furniture was no more advanced in taste than that which Delanois had made for the Court at Warsaw the year before (Plates 411 to 414). Poirier provided a barometer and a thermometer for her apartment in that same December of 1769; they resembled those shown in Plates 199 and 200. He also supplied a clock like that illustrated in Plate 198, while, on 13th December, Madame du Barry bought from him a jewel-casket set with Sèvres plaques which was probably like that to be seen in Plate 121. On 21st August 1772 he sold her the commode shown in Plate 125 and this was also placed in the Versailles apartment.

The furniture made for the Pavillon de Louveciennes was produced while the building was being erected in 1770–71 and was just as advanced in taste as the house itself. Most of the seat-furniture came from Delanois' workshop and the carving was executed by Guichard (Plates 172 and 173). We do not know who designed it but it may have been Gondoin. The ornamental bronzes—sconces, chimney- and door-furniture—were provided by Gouthière after designs made by Ledoux.

Between 1768 and 1774, Madame du Barry bought no less than 70,000 livres worth of Sèvres porcelain. Her first purchases, in December 1768, were the above-mentioned vases 'à Médaillon du Roy' and these were bought straight from the factory. On the other hand, on 4th September 1770, Poirier sold her a set of three small Sèvres vases mounted in gilt bronze which were presumably like those shown in Plate 242. Otherwise she does not seem to have been a great admirer of the generally rather popular ornamental vases the factory produced. However, she bought a great deal of porcelain, first from the Chantilly works and then from Sèvres, for use on her dining-table. The most famous dinner-service she had was that of Sèvres porcelain, delivered in August 1771, which is now spread all over the world; it has small vases of Antique form, with garlands of flowers and her monogram painted on it. A piece from her set is shown in Plate 290. In August 1773 she bought a small but comparatively expensive dinner-set decorated with 'figures chinoises'—with chinamen. A single plate cost 140 livres which was three times more than the price of one belonging to the monogrammed set just mentioned.

Unlike Madame de Pompadour, who could act, sing and play the harpsichord, and was no mean draughtsman, Madame du Barry seems to have been a woman with neither intellectual nor artistic ambitions. Such paintings as she owned do not suggest that she was particularly discriminating in artistic matters. However, her rejection of a series of canvasses with erotic scenes that Fragonard had painted for Louveciennes (now in the Frick Collection, New York) may have been occasioned by the fact that the identity of the lovers was rather too apparent, and was not necessarily due to the lack of taste on her part. That she had them replaced by some paintings by the popular but dull artist, Vien, would seem to indicate that she had little sense of quality when it came to judging paintings.

Did Madame du Barry have a good eye for the decorative arts or was she simply fascinated by everything that was new and fashionable? The latter is much more likely, on the whole. She never seems to have purchased anything in the way of furniture, bronzes, etc. that was not already available on the market, although the style of what she bought was comparatively advanced. We must, all the same give her credit for having caused to be erected, and for having paid for (even if the money originally came from the King), the Pavillon de Louveciennes which was one of the very first ensembles in an entirely pure version of the Neo-Classical taste. Indeed, perhaps it was *the* first! Moreover, the quality of everything in the house seems to have been of a very high order.

It is probable that Madame du Barry had influential advisers in such matters. Francis Watson has suggested that one such adviser was the Duc d'Aumont, the most senior of the King's *premiers gentilhommes* who controlled the *Menus Plaisirs* and whose modern outlook is proved by the way he engaged the architect Belanger and the bronze-founder Gouthière to work for that organisation, while he himself was one of Gouthière's best patrons. Another candidate could be the infamous Duc de Richelieu who was also one of the *premiers gentilhommes*. He was a close friend of Madame du Barry; indeed, he had known her for many years before she became associated with Louis. Unfortunately we know as yet very little about Richelieu's views on the Neo-Classical taste.

Arch.Nat., 01 3318, *passim*.
Sèvres Archives, Vy, 1768ff.
J. A. Leroi, 'Madame du Barry 1768–1793', *Mémoires de la Société des sciences morales, des lettres, et des arts de Seine-et-Oise*, vol. 5, 1859.

J. A. Leroi, *Curiosités historiques sur Louis XIII, Louis XIV, Louis XV, Mme de Maintenon, Mme de Pompadour, Mme du Barry, etc.*, 1864, pp. 243–376.
Charles Davillier, *Les porcelaines de Madame du Barry*, 1870.
Charles Vatel, *Histoire de Madame du Barry d'après ses papiers personnels et les documents des archives publiques, I–III*, 1883.
Verlet, *Mobilier Royal*, I, pp. 66–7.
Pierre Verlet, 'The Wallace Collection and the Study of French Eighteenth-Century Bronzes d'Ameublement', *Burlington Magazine*, XCII, June 1950, p. 155.
Franklin M. Biebel, 'Fragonard and Madame du Barry', *Gaz.d.B.-A.*, LVI, 1960, pp. 207–26.
Verlet, *Versailles*, 1961, pp. 566–71.
G. Wildenstein, 'Simon-Philippe Poirier, Fournisseur de Madame du Barry', *Gaz.d.B.-A.*, LX, 1962, pp. 365–77.

See Plates 79–80, 121–2, 125, 172–3, 186, 197–9, 229–30, 290, 472 and 474.

BARTHÉLEMY, Jean-Jacques (known as the Abbé Barthélemy). Philologist, numismatist and archaeologist. Born at Cassis, Provence, in 1716; died in Paris in 1795. Son of a well-to-do business man.

As a young man, Barthélemy attended a Jesuit college and subsequently went to the Lazarists' College at Marseilles. He came to Paris in 1744 and was soon taken on as an assistant at the Cabinet des Médailles. In 1747 he became a member of the Académie des Inscriptions. In 1753 he was appointed director of the Cabinet des Médailles. Between 1755 and 1757 he went on an extended tour of Italy lasting twenty-one months, studying architecture in Rome with Piranesi, Moreau-Desproux and others. He also visited Naples and Paestum. On his way to Italy, he stopped at Nîmes where he was so impressed by the Maison Carrée that he put forward proposals for moving the building and re-erecting it in a public square in Paris. He explained how this removal might be carried out technically in a letter to the Marquis d'Argenson.

Barthélemy published many scientific papers and was recognised as a brilliant philologist and numismatist at an early age. He became a close friend of learned men like, for example, the Comte de Caylus, whose experiments with encaustic painting Barthélemy exhibited in Marseilles. He assisted Caylus by making several contributions to the latter's *Recueil d'Antiquités*. In 1760 he published a make-believe Greek tale entitled *Les amours de Carite et Polydore*, a tear-jerking story of two young lovers at the time of Theseus. His better-known and more ambitious novel, the *Voyage du jeune Anacharsis en Grèce vers le milieu du IV siècle avant l'ère vulgaire*, was not published until 1788 and has since been re-published in abridged versions no less than forty-one times and translated into eight foreign languages.

It may well be that Barthélemy's work in the field of Classical archaeology had a certain influence on the early development of Neo-Classicism, since he undoubtedly helped to increase the general interest in Greek and Roman antiquities. He was a very close friend of the Duc and Duchesse de Choiseul with whom he stayed when he visited Rome during the period of the Duc's appointment as Ambassador to the Holy See. It is possible that Barthélemy was in some measure responsible for the fact that the Duc and his wife became early admirers of the Neo-Classical taste.

Maurice Badolle, *L'Abbé Jean-Jacques Barthélemy (1716–1795) et l'hellénisme en France dans la seconde moitié du XVIII siècle*, Paris, 1926.

BAUDOUIN, Pierre-Antoine. Painter. Born in 1723, died on 15th December 1769.

In 1758 he married a daughter of the painter François Boucher and thus became the brother-in-law of Juste-François Boucher, the engraver of ornament and designer of furniture. Baudouin's widow later married E.-G. Cuvillier who collaborated closely with the Marquis de Marigny at the *direction des bâtiments*.

Baudouin, who is known for his frivolous subjects set in rich interiors, has secured himself a place in the history of Neo-Classicism because he was one of the first painters to depict Neo-Classical furniture in his pictures.

Herluison, *Actes*, p. 22.

See Plates 388–9, 426–7, 443–5.

BEAUVAIS, Jacques. Engraver, recorded working in 1760.

Lived in the Montmartre quarter, in the Rue Beaurepaire, leading off the Rue Montorgueil. He drew and himself engraved three series of Neo-Classical vases, the first of which was published in 1760. The third is undated but was dedicated to the painter, Challe. This Beauvais may be identical with the painter of that name who competed for the Grand Prix of the Academy in 1749, and also perhaps with the sculptor, Jacques-Philippe Beauvais who died in 1781.

B. N. Est. Inv., vol. 2, pp. 184–5.
Procès verbaux de l'Académie, vol. VI, p. 163.

See Plates 339–41.

BELANGER, François-Joseph. Architect and designer of furniture. Born in 1744, died in 1818.

At the age of twenty, Belanger was admitted to the Académie Royale d'Architecture under the protection of the Comte de Caylus. His instructors were David Leroy and Contant d'Ivry. He is supposed to have visited England in 1766–67. In 1767 he was appointed *dessinateur des Menus Plaisirs* where he became assistant to Charles-Michel-Ange Challe. He also became *dessinateur du Comte de Provence*, in 1770. He was promoted to *inspecteur des Menus Plaisirs* in 1777 and in addition was appointed *premier architecte du Comte d'Artois*. These important posts, together with his intimate connection with the much-admired actress, Sophie Arnould, gained for him a secure place in the field of architecture and interior-decoration in France. Among Belanger's many buildings are included a pavilion designed for the Comte de Lauraguais and a town-house made for Sophie Arnould (1773). He also designed the Pavillon de Bagatelle (1777) for the Comte d'Artois.

Belanger's contributions to the decorative arts include, amongst other things, the jewel-cabinet made for Marie Antoinette which he designed in 1769. This was executed in the workshops of the *ébéniste* Evald and mounted with gilt bronzes chased by Gouthière. Many of the decorative bronzes made by Gouthière for the Duc d'Aumont and his daughter, the Duchesse de Mazarin, were designed by Belanger. This artist's influence in the field of the applied arts was probably more widespread than is at present appreciated, and a systematic search in the archives of the *Menus Plaisirs* may well produce much fresh information on his activities in this direction. For of course Stern's otherwise exhaustive monograph deals primarily with Belanger's work as an architect.

Jean Stern, *A l'ombre de Sophie Arnould, François-Joseph Belanger architecte des Menus-Plaisirs, premier architecte du comte d'Artois*, vols. I–II, Paris, 1930.
Richard P. Wunder, 'Bagatelle and two drawings by Belanger in the Cooper Union', *The Connoisseur*, vol. 148, 1961, pp. 171–4.
Rudolf H. Wackernagel, *Der französische Krönungswagen*, Berlin, 1966.

See Plates 243, 448, 475.

BELLICARD, Jérôme-Charles. Architect and engraver. Born in 1726, died in 1786. Son of a *maître-menuisier*.

He was a student at the Académie d'Architecture where he won the Grand Prix in 1747. He was in Rome from November 1748 to June 1751. On his return, he collaborated with Nicolas Cochin *le jeune* on the work entitled *Observations sur les antiquités d'Herculanum* which appeared in 1754 and for which he is chiefly famous. For several years he was chief clerk in the Marquis de Marigny's office; subsequently he became *contrôleur* at the Palace in Compiègne and then at Fontainebleau, where he remained until 1777.

Bellicard met the painter Roslin in 1762 and his wife became godmother to one of the latter's children. Bellicard lived in the Rue Neuve des Petits Champs.

References to architectural work by Bellicard mention the town-house of the Marquise de Matharel in the Rue Notre-Dame-des-Champs (1758–59) and a Neo-Classical dining-room at the Hôtel Cassini, 32 Rue de Babylone (1771)—the latter having been executed in stucco by Louis Mansiaux in whose account-book it is described.

Apart from his illustrations for the *Observations*, his engraved work included two views of Rome (1750), four architectural drawings by Petitot, Soufflot's *Loge des Changes* at Lyons, and six engravings showing Soufflot's Église Sainte-Geneviève (1757).

Gallet, *Demeures*, p. 174.
Corr. des Dir.
Guiffrey, *Scellés*, vol. III, pp. 180–1.
Arch. Seine, 5 B6 2738 fol. 52 *verso*.
B. N. Est. Inv., vol. 2, pp. 295–8.

BELLISARD, Claude Billard de. Architect. Probably born 1720–30, died about 1793.

Bellisard worked as an architect for the Prince de Condé between 1765 and 1780, at first as *contrôleur* under Le Carpentier until the latter's death in July 1773, whereupon he succeeded to the principal post. In these positions he was engaged in the alteration and modernising of the Palais Bourbon and the Hôtel de Lassay. While it is scarcely possible that he designed any of the furniture which was provided for the Prince in Le Carpentier's time, Bellisard must have watched the preparation of these pieces which included chairs, beds and fire-screens, the rich carving of which was executed by Charles Lachenait. At the same time, under Le Carpentier, it was Bellisard who verified the accounts rendered by the various tradesmen to the Prince de Condé, including bills from Lachenait and Leleu.

Bellisard only became a member of the Academy in 1776. After leaving the Prince's service, he went to Italy in 1781. In December 1790 he made plans for a journey to Spain where he intended to make measured drawings of Roman and Moorish monuments.

G. Macon, *Les arts dans la maison de Condé, passim.*
Gallet, *Demeures*, p. 173.

BLÈVE, Jean-Louis. Architect. Born about 1725, died after 1801.

Active between 1766 and 1792 as *architecte-expert bourgeois*. His earliest known work was a house erected in the Faubourg du Temple for a certain Monsieur Persan. The house lay opposite the Hôtel de Chavanne (by Moreau-Desproux) and was presumably in much the same style. Persan's house is discussed in *L'Avantcoureur* of 20th July 1760, where it is stated to have been built 'depuis peu' ('recently'). The correspondent goes on to say that 'les dehors & les dedans sont ornés avec la plus grande recherche. Un ordre de pilastres Ioniques, soutient les combles qui sont terminés en baldaquin & relevés de grouppes . . .' ('both inside and out the house is decorated with the greatest refinement. Pilasters of the Ionic order support the roof which is in the form of a *baldachino* decorated with groups of figures . . .'). Of Blève's other work, mention may be made of the surviving house, Nos. 7–9 Rue Bonaparte, built in 1771 for a Monsieur Doublet de Persan who may well be identical with the client just mentioned.

Gallet, *Demeures*, p. 174.
L'Avantcoureur, 28th July 1760, p. 443.

BLONDEL, Jacques-François. Architect. Born in Rouen in 1705, died in Paris in 1774. Perhaps a nephew of Jean-François Blondel the architect.

Blondel arrived in Paris around 1729 and acquired considerable influence as an instructor for young architects and craftsmen. In 1739 he started a private École des Arts in the Rue de la Harpe where the lessons began at four o'clock in the morning. In 1756 he became a member of the Académie d'Architecture and taught as a professor in the Academy's rooms at the Louvre.

Blondel carried out various now-demolished houses in Paris. Between 1764 and 1774 he built the Hôtel de Ville in Metz, while about 1768 he made a theatre and the Town Hall at Strasbourg; he also erected some barracks and some bridges. However, his most famous work is embodied in his writings, especially in his work *De la distribution des maisons de plaisance et de la décoration des édifices en général* (1737); his *L'Architecture française ou recueil des plans, élévations, coupes et profils des églises, maisons royales, palais, hôtels et édifices les plus considérables de Paris* (1752–56), and his *Cours d'architecture civile* (which was completed by Pierre Patte, 1771–77). Moreover, he wrote the article on Architecture in Diderot and d'Alembert's great *Encyclopédie*.

Emil Kaufmann, *Three Revolutionary Architects, Boullée, Ledoux, and Lequeu*, Philadelphia, 1952, pp. 436–46.
Robert Middleton, 'Jacques-François Blondel and the Cours d'Architecture', *Journal of the Society of Architectural Historians*, XVIII, 1959.
Wolfgang Hermann, *Laugier and Eighteenth Century French Theory*, London, 1962.

See Plates 343–4.

BOUDIN, Léonard. Cabinet-maker and furniture dealer. Born in 1735, died about 1804.

Boudin became a *maître* in 1761 after having worked for Migéon and other cabinet-makers. He thereupon moved into the Rue Traversière, a side-street leading off the Rue du Faubourg Saint-Antoine. A few years later he bought up a shop selling furniture in the Rue Froidmanteau, opposite the Palais-Royal. This business moved to the Cloisters of Saint-Germain-l'Auxerrois behind the Louvre in 1777.

Boudin's stamp is found on much furniture of widely differing character although most of it is of good quality and is in the transitional style. His stamp is frequently found together with that of other cabinet-makers on the same piece; for instance with that of Topino, Antoine Foullet, Pierre-Antoine Foullet, François Bayer and G. Cordié. It would seem that the reason for the presence of two stamps on such pieces must in most cases be that Boudin, who already in 1775 called himself *marchand-ébéniste*, stamped furniture which other craftsmen had delivered to him for sale at his shop.

Salverte, *Les Ébénistes*, pp. 39–30.
Arch. Nat., Y 13402 (24th September 1775).

See Plates 109, 131 and 138.

BOULLÉE, Etienne-Louis. Architect. Born in 1728, died in 1799. Son of the architect Claude-Louis Boullée who was *architecte-expert des bâtiments du roi*.

Boullée first wanted to be a painter and studied under Lancret and J.-B. Pierre. Later he became a student of his father, then of P.-E. Lebon, and subsequently of Le Geay and of J.-F. Blondel. He does not appear to have studied at the Académie d'Architecture or in Italy. In 1762 he became a member of that Academy, however, and in 1775 was appointed *intendant des bâtiments du comte d'Artois*. He was living in the Rue du Mail, near the Place des Victoires, in 1777.

Boullée's earliest known essay in architecture is a project for the Hôtel des Monnaies, couched in the style of Gabriel, which he designed in 1756 on the instruction of Chauvelin who was *intendant des finances*. The scheme came to nothing but is known through an engraving dedicated to the Marquis de Marigny, executed in 1760. In 1759 he composed some wall-decorations for a salon in the Hôtel de Tourolles which were completed in January 1760: these are now in the Cercle Interallié in Paris. Between 1772 and 1779 he built the Hôtel de Brunoy in the Rue du Faubourg Saint-Honoré. His other work is listed by Gallet, among others, in his *Demeures*.

Boullée was also a teacher. At the early age of nineteen he started to give instruction at the École des Ponts et Chaussées, while his somewhat romantic Neo-Classical theories are said to have had a considerable influence on several young architects, notably Taraval and Brongniart.

Unpublished letter from Schreiber to Wasserschlebe dated Meudon, 24th June 1756, Royal Library, Copenhagen, Ny kgl. saml. 2152.
Année Littéraire, 1759, pp. 21–8.
L'Avantcoureur, 21st January 1760, and 20th October 1760.
A. de Champeaux, *L'Art décoratif dans le vieux Paris*, Paris, 1898, p. 191.
Contet, *Vieux hôtels de Paris*, vol. XX, p. 12.
Emil Kaufmann, *Three Revolutionary Architects, Boullée, Ledoux and Lequeu*, Philadelphia, 1952.
Silvestre de Sacy, *A-T. Brongniart*, Paris, 1940, pp. 8–10.
Gallet, *Demeures*, pp. 174–5.
Jean-Marie Pérouse de Montclos, *Etienne-Louis Boullée (1728–1799), de l'architecture classique à l'architecture révolutionnaire*, Paris, 1969.

See Plates 18 and 35.

BRONGNIART, Alexandre-Théodore. Architect. Born in 1739, died in 1813.

After a thorough schooling, Brongniart became a pupil of J.-F. Blondel and of the young Boullée. He furthermore attended the courses supervised by the architect Hubert Pluyette at the Académie d'Architecture.

Among Brongniart's early works are the theatre at Caen (1765), the Hôtel de Montesson in the Chaussée d'Antin (1770–73), the Hôtel du Duc d'Orléans in the Rue de Provence (1772), the Hôtel Taillepied de Bondi, at the corner of the Rue de Richelieu and the Boulevard Montmartre (1771), and the still-surviving Hôtel de Monaco (No. 59 Rue Saint-Dominique, 1777).

Brongniart designed many houses in Paris, and these are discussed in works listed below.

Silvestre de Sacy, *Alexandre-Théodore Brongniart 1739–1813, sa vie—son oeuvre*, Paris, 1940.
Gallet, *Demeures*, pp. 175–6.

BUTEUX, François-Charles. Wood-carver. Born about 1730, died after 1787. Probably son of the carver Jean-Charles Buteux and presumably related to the members of the Buteux family who worked at the porcelain factories at Chantilly and Sèvres who are known to have come from the Beauvais area. He lived in the Rue de Sépulcre.

Buteux worked for the Royal Family from 1760. Like Honoré Guibert, he was principally responsible for supplying numerous picture-frames, most of which were in the *Louis Seize* style, according to the accounts. A single drawing from his hand is in the Archives Nationales. Between 1765 and 1769 he supplied a wooden relief for the West Door of the Church of Saint-Thomas d'Aquin, as well as other work including the carving on the organ-case.

Arch. Nat., o^1 1921 A (dossier Buteux).
Vial, Marcel and Girodie, vol. I, p. 77.
Verlet, *Mobilier Royal* II, pp. 38 and 40.

CAFFIERI, Philippe, known as Caffieri *l'aîné*. Sculptor and bronze-founder. Born in 1714, died in 1774. Son of the bronze-founder Jacques Caffieri, who held the title of *sculpteur et ciseleur ordinaire du Roy*. His younger brother was the sculptor Jean-Jacques Caffieri. In 1751, he married Antoinette-Rose Lambert Rolland, whose father and brother were successively *premier valet de chambre* in the household of the Prince de Condé.

Caffieri lived with his parents who owned two houses backing on to each other in the Rue des Cannettes and the Rue Princesse near Saint-Germain des Près. Philippe Caffieri inherited the latter house while his brother received the other.

Caffieri studied under his father and also attended the drawing-school of the Académie de Saint-Luc. In 1743, his parents managed to have transferred to him the privilege hitherto granted to his mother, of being 'marchande doreur graveur damasquineur suivant la Cour' 'pour faciliter son établissement' ('to help set him up'). In 1747, he and his father formed a partnership. He became a *maître-sculpteur* in 1754 and was made a member of the Académie de Saint-Luc where he was later to become a *juré*. His father died in December 1755 and he became proprietor of the workshop in the Rue Princesse and took over the family concern's stock of models, for which he paid compensation to his brother. A month later (on 16th January 1756) he was accredited *maître-fondeur en terre et sable* without having had to produce a masterpiece, simply because his father had been a *maître-fondeur*.

Judging from the inventories drawn up on the death of the father and then of Philippe himself, it seems that the latter enlarged the establishment to some extent after having taken it over. In 1770, there were six work-benches whereas in his father's day there had been but four. For comparison, it may be noted that Pitoin had only two benches in his workshop in 1777. Apart from bronze-casting equipment, Caffieri also possessed taps and dies for the production of screw-threads. Furthermore, four sculptor's stands (*établis*) and an easel are listed. The establishment was valued at 400 livres as against the 60 livres of Pitoin's workshops. Caffieri's prosperity is also reflected by the not inconsiderable quantity of table-silver he owned—totalling 74 *marc* in weight and valued at 3,774 livres as bullion, i.e. almost twice as much as his father had possessed, and very much more than poor Pitoin could boast of. Caffieri also had 6,000 livres in cash when he died.

When his wife died in 1770, Caffieri had an impressive stock of fire-dogs, sconces, candlesticks, candelabra, etc., partly in the form of models and partly as finished goods. In all, there were something like a hundred pieces, valued at 16,154 livres. The descriptions show that only a small proportion of this stock was in the Rococo taste, and that some of these pieces were in fact produced during the father's life-time. The rest were clearly in the Neo-Classical style. It is noteworthy that the stock did not apparently include ordinary mounts for furniture.

Among the sculptor's independent work, produced after the father's death, were the rich bronze mounts for Lalive de Jully's furniture (about 1756–57), executed after designs by Le Lorrain. Then there were some sconces in the form of hunting-horns for the Palace of Saint-Hubert (1758), fire-dogs made for the Marquis de Marigny (1758), an altar-set for Notre-Dame (started in 1760), various works for the Polish Court at Warsaw (1766–68), some designs for a silver toilet-service intended for the Princesse des Asturies (1765, executed by Pierre Germain and Thomas Chamelier), some chandeliers, fire-dogs, etc., for the Prince de Condé (1769–70), an altar-set for the Church of Saint-Nicolas du Chardonnet (about 1770), a 'girandole à cinq branches' for the Comte d'Orsay (1770–71), and an altar-set for the Cathedral at Bayeux (1771).

Most of the gilding of Caffieri's work seems to have been carried out by Pierre-François Carpentier to whom he owed 14,580 livres in 1774. The fathers of the two men had incidentally worked together in the same way. Other craftsmen who collaborated with Caffieri were the bronze-founder Pierre-François Boitard to whom he owed 8,181 livres in 1774, and the bronze-founder Louis-Barthelemy Hervieu who was owed 6,313 livres. There was also Georges-Alexandre Moreau, a bronze-founder, who was Caffieri's creditor to the tune of 2,118 livres.

Our picture of Philippe Caffieri is filled in when we study the contents of his respectable art-collection and library. Among his oil-paintings were five by Chardin, two by Lagrenée *l'aîné* and one by Le Geay—an oval painting entitled *Fragment du Temple de Jupiter, et le Tombeau de Sextius*. He possessed works by Saly, Falconet and Challe, along with drawings by Pajou, François Boucher and Fragonard. Among his works on architecture were the engraved designs of Marot, Palladio, Vignola, Le Pautre, Vitruvius and Le

Roy's *Les Ruines des plus beaux monuments de la Grèce*, as well as the Comte de Caylus' compilations. He had Roman *Vedute* by Piranesi, Le Geay and others, together with 188 engravings of 'vases' and 170 of 'ornemens'. And it comes as no surprise that he also possessed some engravings of Vien's works.

Arch. Nat., Y 9327 (25th October 1754) and Y 9328 (16th January 1756).
Arch. Nat., Minutier Central, XXVII, 277 (1st December 1755).
Ibid., XCVIII, 589 (3rd December 1770).
Ibid., XXXIV, 697 (14th October 1774).
Guiffrey, *Les Caffieri*, *passim*.
Guiffrey, *Scellés*, vol. III, pp. 52–8.
Stanislas Iskierski, *Les bronzes du château royal et du Palais de Lazienski à Varsovie*, Warszaw, 1929, *passim*.
René Dubosq, 'Les richesses de la Cathédrale de Bayeux, l'oeuvre de Philippe Caffieri', *Revue Illustrée du Calvados*, 1911, Nos. 4 and 5.

See Plates 85–9, 116, 187, 203–4, 206, 213, 217, 223, 236, 424–5, 453–61.

CARLIN, Martin. Cabinet-maker. Born about 1730, supposedly in Freiburg in Breisgau, in South-west Germany; died in Paris in 1785. Son of a carpenter. In 1759, he married a sister of the cabinet-makers J.-F. Oeben and Simon Oeben. Carlin was also a friend of Roger Vandercruse *dit* Lacroix (the cabinet-maker who stamped his wares 'R.V.L.C.'), who was best-man at his wedding and whose sister was married to J.-F. Oeben.

Carlin presumably arrived in Paris in the 1750s. It seems probable that he first came to work in J.-F. Oeben's workshops in the Arsenal, since he had married this master's sister by the end of that decade and he lived on the Quai des Célestins, only a few minutes' walk from Oeben's house and workshops. And when Oeben died in 1763, Carlin was one of his creditors. By that time he was living in the Rue du Faubourg Saint-Antoine, where he remained for the rest of his life. He became a *maître* on 30th July 1766. In the same or the next year, he must have come into contact with the *marchand-mercier*, Poirier, whose premises were in the Rue Saint-Honoré, and for whom both his friend Lacroix and Bernard Vanrisamburgh were already providing furniture, apparently after designs supplied by Poirier. As Verlet has demonstrated, Poirier made a speciality of, among other things, furniture set with Sèvres plaques and it was to Carlin he turned to have commissions in this line executed. The earliest datable example bearing Carlin's stamp is a *bonheur-du-jour* in the Musée Nissim de Camondo, set with Sèvres plaques bearing the date-letter for 1766. This piece is in the transitional style, as are the other examples dating from the next few years. Carlin also worked for Daguerre, Poirier's successor; and since both these *marchands-merciers* supplied furnishings to the royal household, furniture by Carlin was not infrequently bought for royal use, and especially by the ladies of the Court.

When he died in 1785, Carlin had seven benches in his workshops, apart from some machinery for working metal. In his store-rooms was a certain amount of completed furniture, 6–700 livres weight of bronzes in various stages of 'finishing', and a small collection of models in metal. Carlin left a small debt (679 livres) owing when he died to a *ciseleur* named Prevost—who was probably identical with Joachim Prevost—for 'ouvrages de sa profession' ('products of his trade'). Presumably he was Carlin's regular supplier of bronze-mounts.

Salverte, *Les ébénistes*, pp. 46–7.
Pierre Verlet, 'Le commerce des objects d'art et les marchands merciers à Paris au XVIIIe siècle', *Annales*, January–March, 1958.
Comte de Salverte, 'Documents inédits sur les ébénistes Martin Carlin et Georges Jacob', *BSHAF*, 1928, pp. 84–111.

See Plates 111–12, 121–2, 125, 136 and Colour Plate D.

CARPENTIER, Louis-Charles. Chair-maker. Active during the third quarter of the eighteenth century.

Carpentier became a *maître* in 1752 and was a *juré* of the Guild during the period 1765–67. His workshop was in the Rue de Cléry.

At a comparatively early date, Carpentier produced chairs in an almost pure *Louis Seize* style, including an armchair (Plate 178) which may well be identical with that depicted in Alexandre Roslin's portrait of the Minister, Bertin, which was shown at the *Salon* of 1769. Between 1765 and 1771, he provided the Baron d'Ivry with furniture to the value of 3,300 livres, all said to have been in the *Louis Seize* style. About 1770, he executed various orders for the Prince de Condé, probably after designs by the architect Le Carpentier; the carved ornament for these pieces was carried out by Charles Lachenait. Louis Delanois, who lived barely three minutes' walk from Carpentier, was at the same time providing seat-furniture for the same Prince, probably after the very same designs. It is therefore not surprising that their chairs often resemble each other. Carpentier was later patronised by the Duc Philippe d'Orléans.

Gustave Macon, *Les arts dans la Maison de Condé*, Paris, 1903, p. 136.
Salverte, *Ébénistes*, pp. 47–8.
Paul Eudel, *L'Hôtel Drouot et la curiosité en 1883–1884*, 1885, pp. 329–30.

See Plates 171, 174, 177–8.

CAUMONT. A family of *marchands-tapissiers* who were active from about 1760. The eldest was Louis Caumont who, in 1763, was elected *syndic des tapissiers*. Jean-Jacques Caumont became a *maître* in 1760 and was presumably Louis' son, while a Jean-Baptiste-François Caumont became a *maître* in 1766.

It must have been one of these three who bought furniture from the chair-maker Louis Delanois in 1768. The chairs concerned were partly in the transitional style and partly in a pure *Louis Seize* style. Between 1764 and 1771, Delanois sold Caumont furniture to the value of 11,130 livres. In 1778 Jean-Baptiste-François Caumont was calling himself *valet de chambre et tapissier du Roi*, a title he still used in 1782.

Arch. Nat., Y 9328 (31st December 1760, 7th December 1763, 28th February 1766).
Jean Stern, *François-Joseph Belanger*, vol. I, Paris, 1930, p. 55, note 2.
Almanach de Versailles, 1782, p. 89.

CAYLUS, Anne-Claude-Philippe de Tubières Grimoard de Pestel de Levis, Comte de. Archaeologist and writer on art. Born in 1692, died in 1765. Son of a niece of Madame de Maintenon.

At the age of fifteen, Caylus joined the army and is said to have distinguished himself at the battle of Malplaquet (1709) and later at the Siege of Fribourg in Brisgau (1713). He left the military service in 1715 and immediately paid a short visit to Italy. Later that year he set out on a longer journey which took him to places like Smyrna, Ephesus and Constantinople, where he stayed a couple of months. He was back in Paris in 1717. In 1722 he went to Holland and England. His wide knowledge of the Arts earned him election as an *amateur* at the Académie de Peinture et Sculpture in 1731. In 1742 he was made an honorary member of the Académie des Inscriptions et Belles Lettres. He built himself a house in the Rue Saint-Dominique (now No. 109) but later moved into an apartment at the Tuileries, on the Cour de l'Orangerie.

Caylus, who enjoyed adequate private means and did not need to earn a living, devoted most of his time to the study of Classical archaeology, while continually showing a lively interest in both contemporary and earlier art. He was not steeped in traditional book-learning and apparently his knowledge of Latin and Greek was slender. In spite of this, he is regarded as the French counterpart of the great German scholar, Winckelmann, in the field of Classical archaeology. In the course of time, he amassed a very considerable collection of Egyptian, Greek and Roman antiquities. At first he bought such things in Paris but later he acquired them through contacts in Italy, notably through Father Paciaudi, the Italian with whom the Abbé Barthélemy had put him in touch and with whom he carried on an extensive correspondence over the years. He drew and described meticulously every single piece in his collection and published it all in his famous *Recueil d'antiquités* which appeared in seven volumes between 1752 and 1767. By stages he presented his collection to the King and one may still see it in the Cabinet des Antiques in the Bibliothèque Nationale.

Apart from undertaking this large enterprise, Caylus wrote numerous shorter dissertations on archaeological matters. He twice endeavoured to reconstruct antique objects on the basis of descriptions given by Classical authors. One case concerned the ornamental shields carried by Hercules and Aeneas which are described by Hesiod and Virgil; his other had to do with some paintings by Polygnotus discussed by Pausanias. Caylus explained the meaning of the texts to the painter Louis-Joseph Le Lorrain who then drew his conception of the designs which were subsequently published with Caylus' treatises.

Caylus' interest in antiquities was essentially practical; he was not particularly concerned with artistic merit. Through a study of antiquities he acquired knowledge of the customs and practices current in Classical times—he learned about costume and took a special interest in the techniques used by artists of the period. In his *Mémoire sur la peinture à l'encaustique* (1755), he sought to establish on the basis of Plinius' description, the method used for this technique much favoured in the late-Classical period. He persuaded Vien to paint a head of Minerva in this technique which became a source of much interest, both in France and abroad—notably in Genoa to which city the Abbé Barthélemy took the painting. Le Lorrain executed several paintings in this technique including two ceiling-paintings in the Comte de l'Islebonne's Hôtel d'Harcourt in the Rue de l'Université, and one with the head and shoulders of a girl, dated 1755, which is still preserved at Bregentved, the country-house of the Counts Moltke in Denmark. Caylus was convinced that the reintroduction of this technique would revolutionise contemporary painting, just as the Van Eyck's techniques had done four centuries earlier, and he was sorely vexed that so few young French artists showed any interest in his discovery.

Caylus was a competent engraver. He had learned the technique from Watteau (died 1721) who was one of his earliest artist-friends. Caylus in fact engraved many of Watteau's drawings as well as works by earlier French and foreign masters—especially the landscapes of Paul Bril, compositions by the Carracci, Charles Coypel, Claude Gillot, Rembrandt, Raphael, Van Dyck, Titian, Leonardo etc. as well as of Bouchardon who became his close friend. Moreover, he engraved all the plates for his own great work, the *Recueil.* Some 600 engravings by him are recorded.

He also seems to have tried his hand at designing ornaments, for, according to Dezallier d'Argenville (*Paris*, ed. 1757, page 12) he was responsible for the drawings after which the decorations in the Chapelle d'Harcourt at Notre-Dame were executed 'dans toute la noblesse de ce beau simple de l'Antiquité' ('in the full nobility that springs from the glorious simplicity of the Classical style'). According to the same authority (ibid., page 380) Caylus designed a pedestal for the church of Saint-Germain des Près on which was placed Bouchardon's model for the head of his famous equestrian statue of Louis XV. Furthermore, in 1760, the stuccador Mansiaux produced some mural decorations for the *fermier-général*, Marin de la Haye's Château de Draveil 'sous la conduitte de Mr. le conte de quelusse' ('under the guidance of the Count de Caylus'). These included the altar-table and two twelve-foot high Tuscan columns in scagliola made to resemble yellow marble (cf. Arch. Seine, 5 B^6-2738, fol. 12 v.–13).

For many years after he had become a member of the French Academy, Caylus only rarely attended meetings—once a year, at the most. Rocheblave concludes that he was at that stage more interested in his own collection of antiquities and in the jolly life he led which provided material for his *Oeuvres badines.* But, from about 1746 or so, when Caylus was over fifty, we find him turning up for the Academy's meetings with praiseworthy regularity and he soon became one of its most energetic members.

Caylus persuaded the Academy to revive the ancient tradition of sponsoring instructive lectures which had fallen into abeyance, and delivered many of these himself. By this time he had become a serious-minded person and, moreover, had unfortunately grown convinced that true *cognoscenti* like himself were better equipped than other people to decide on the course Art should take to ensure a healthy future, and proceeded to shower young artists with good advice. As a consequence of this belief, he instituted the offering of prizes in various disciplines—perspective, anatomy, facial-expression—in order to counteract what he regarded as the prevailing indifference to such matters among contemporary artists. He also revived a number of ancient themes which he proposed the painters and sculptors might take up—publishing, with this aspect in mind, a series of extracts from Homer and Virgil (1757) together with a foreword on which he had much to say about the correct rendering of costume and the trappings of everyday life in Classical times.

Such an energetic man as the Comte de Caylus, who was passionately interested in Classical Antiquity and especially in its more practical aspects, and who enjoyed a social position of some significance, was almost bound to have a certain influence at a period like that prevailing in the middle decades of the eighteenth century when a sober, classicising spirit was already widespread and there were many who were prepared to listen to ideas of the kind he sought to propagate.

We have much contemporary evidence of Caylus' fame, and the authority with which he spoke on artistic matters. The *Procès Verbaux* of the Academy of course reveal much, but J.-F. Blondel's statement, in his *Discours sur la nécessité de l'étude de l'architecture* (1754, page 53) is quite definite. 'Enfin', he says 'que ne devons-nous pas à M. le Comte de Caylus, M. Vatelet, M. Hulst, amateurs nés des Arts, qui par leurs conseils, leurs importants avis, leurs soins infatigable pour le bien de la société, non contens de s'intéresser à tout ce qui contribue à l'embellissement de l'intérieur de la Capitale, étendent leur attention et leurs lumières jusques dans les Provinces les plus éloignés, et ne le refusent pas même aux Nations étrangères?' ('What do we not owe to the Count de Caylus, M. Watelet and M. Hulst, all born connoisseurs of the Arts, who, by their good advice, by voicing their opinions, by the indefatigable manner in which they have looked after the welfare of our society, and not content with having been involved in everything that contributes to the embellishment of our capital, extend their help and enlightenment to the most distant provinces and to foreign countries as well?'). Cochin confirms Blondel's statement when writing about a statue of Louis XV which was to be commissioned by the city of Rheims. Cochin, who could not bear Caylus, points out rather spitefully that 'M. de Caylus avoit été consulté, car il s'étoit fait une réputation dans la province et chés l'étranger, telle que l'on croyoit ne pouvoir rien faire de bien sans son attache' ('M. de Caylus has been consulted, since he has made such a reputation for himself in the provinces and abroad that one believes nothing can be carried out without his approval'; *Mémoires*, page 53).

A striking practical result of Caylus' intervention in artistic matters was the mural-decorations which were designed for Åkerö, the country-house in Sweden owned by Count Carl Gustav Tessin (see Plate 15). Tessin hoped to have these designed by Oudry but Caylus arranged matters so that the young artist, Le Lorrain, was chosen instead. For this room, Le Lorrain composed a scheme couched in entirely Neo-Classical terms which was drawn in April or May 1754 and was subsequently carried out by a local Swedish decorator.

It is by no means improbable that Caylus also had a say in the conception of Lalive de Jully's furniture (Plates 85 to 89) which the same Le Lorrain designed in about 1756 or slightly earlier. We have no proof of this but we know that Lalive was elected to the Academy as an *honoraire associé* on 27th April 1754 at a meeting attended by Caylus who subsequently praised the furniture in enthusiastic terms. Cochin says of his furniture that 'Ils firent d'autant plus de bruit que M. de Caylus les loua avec enthousiasme' ('They caused an even greater stir because M. de Caylus praised them so enthusiastically'; *Mémoires*, page 142). It would seem from this that Caylus at any rate contributed to the resulting success of this set of strictly Neo-Classical furniture. Mercier, incidentally, confirms the impression one gets of Caylus' influential position in the *Tableau de Paris* when he writes that 'Le comte de Caylus a ressuscité parmi nous le goût grec et nous avons enfin renoncé à nos formes gothiques' ('Count de Caylus has revived the Grecian taste among us and we have now turned away from all those terrible out-moded shapes'; quoted from Hautecoeur, *Histoire, seconde moitié*, page 6).

It was anyway certainly Caylus who intrigued with such success to get Petitot invited to Parma to become the official court architect there, instead of a certain Lancret whose name had been put forward by Contant d'Ivry (cf. Henri Bédarida, *Parme et la France de 1748 à 1789*, 1928, page 501).

It is not surprising to discover that Caylus also had his antipathies! Among the better-known casualties of his disapproval were Michel-René Slodtz, Pierre and Bachelier. The last probably suffered because he independently experimented with the encaustic technique of painting for which Caylus clearly felt he owned a virtual patent (see above).

Caylus remained active until his death in 1765. He dreamed of his sepulchral monument which was to be in the Classical taste. 'M. de Caylus en mourant avoit souhaité qu'on mît sur son tombeau à St. German l'Auxerroie, sa paroisse, un monument antique de porphyre très cher et très précieux. Le Curé de la paroisse a fait des difficultés: il a témoigné des scrupules de faire d'entrer dans son église cet ornement profane.' ('M. de Caylus had hoped that one would raise a precious and extremely costly Classical monument above his tomb in his parish church of St. Germain l'Auxerrois, but the vicar made difficulties. He had scruples about allowing such a profane ornament to be set up in his church . . .'; Bachaumont, *Mémoires secrets*, 9th March 1766).

After Caylus' death Diderot, who had been wont to tease the old man, wrote that 'La mort nous a délivré du plus cruel des amateurs' ('Death has delivered us from this most malicious of connoisseurs') and it is thought that Diderot was also responsible for the following mocking epitaph:

> 'Ci-gist un antiquaire acariâtre et brusque.
> Ah! qu'il est bien logé dans cette cruche étrusque'.
> ('Here lies an Antiquary peevish and rude.
> How suitably lodged he is in this Etruscan urn!')

Samuel Rocheblave, *Essai sur le comte de Caylus*, 1889.
Dictionnaire de biographie française, VII, 1956.
Jean Babelon, *Choix de bronzes de la collection Caylus donnée au Roi en 1762*, 1928.
Cochin, *Mémoires*, 1880, *passim*.

See Plate 294.

CHALGRIN, Jean-François-Thérèse. Architect. Born in 1739, died in 1811. Married a daughter of Joseph Vernet, the painter.

A pupil of Boullée and Servandoni, Chalgrin won the Grand Prix in 1758 and attended the French Academy in Rome between November 1759 and May 1763. On his return to Paris, he was appointed *inspecteur des travaux de la Ville de Paris* then under the directorship of Moreau-Desproux. In this capacity he supervised the building of the Hôtel de Saint-Florentin in the Rue Saint-Florentin in 1767, the pavilions of which were designed by Gabriel while Chalgrin himself designed the Classical gateway. About 1764 he designed the church of Saint-Philippe-du-Roule which was actually built in 1772–84. Among his later works were the Pavillon de la Comtesse de Provence at Versailles and the Arc de Triomphe in Paris. In 1775 he became *premier architecte du Comte de Provence* while in 1779 he was appointed *intendant des bâtiments du Comte d'Artois.*

Hautecoeur, *Histoire, seconde moitié*, pp. 212–19.
Gallet, *Demeures*, p. 177.

CHALLE, Charles-Michel-Ange. Painter and architectural-draughtsman. Born in 1718, died in 1778. Brother of the sculptor Simon Challe. In 1762 he married a daughter of the painter Natoire.

Challe spent three years studying architecture and then went over to painting which he studied first under François Lemoine and then under François Boucher. In 1741, he won the Grand Prix de Peinture and travelled to Rome the year after, where he installed himself at the French Academy, staying there until October 1749. After returning to Paris he continued to paint and exhibited pictures on several occasions at the *Salon*,—in most cases, scenes from Roman history. He was living in the Rue Thevenot in 1777.

In 1762, Challe became Professor of Perspective at the Académie Royale. After the death of Michel-Ange Slodtz in 1765, he was appointed *dessinateur de la chambre et du cabinet du Roi* and in this post was responsible for designing a number of decorative schemes for occasions of various kinds, all of an architectural nature and all in the Neo-Classical taste. Among these were the catafalques of the Duke and Duchess of Parma (1766), Marie-Josephe de Saxe (1767) and Louis XV (1774). He also created the decoration for the façade of Notre-Dame for that monarch's funeral. Challe's assistants included the architect François-Joseph Belanger.

During his stay in Rome, Challe was strongly influenced by Piranesi, like so many of the Frenchmen who came in contact with this important Italian artist. Several architectural fantasies in the style of Piranesi are among Challe's *oeuvre*.

Henry de Chennevières, 'Michel-Ange Challe, dessinateur du Cabinet du Roi', *Gazette des Beaux-Arts*, 1882, pp. 505–23.
Richard P. Wunder, 'Charles-Michel-Ange Challe, a study of his life and work, *Apollo*, January 1968, pp. 22–33.
Almanach des artistes, 1777, p. 56.
Jean Locquin, *La peinture d'histoire en France de 1747 à 1785*, 1912, pp. 198–201.

CHALLE, Simon. Sculptor. Born in 1719, died in 1765. Brother of Charles-Michel-Ange Challe.

In 1743, he won the Grand Prix de Sculpture and went to Rome in December, 1744. He remained there, staying at the Académie de France, until March 1752. He became a member of the Academy in Paris in 1756.

The only known decorative work of Simon Challe is the now much-altered pulpit in Saint-Roch in Paris, which was set up between 1752 and 1758 at the expense of Pâris de Monmartel. Its original appearance is, however, known from an engraving by Etienne Fessard. On account of its massive proportions and pompous Roman style, the pulpit was both much criticised and much praised; it was claimed that it resembled a box at the opera and that its style 'tient à l'italique' ('is firmly Italic').

Challe incidentally designed a suite of six 'vases' or urns; these were engraved and published by the architect Gabriel-Pierre-Martin Dumont in 1765.

Thieme and Becker, *Künstlerleksikon.*
Grimm, *Correspondance littéraire*, ed. M. Tourneux, vol. 4, p. 52 (November 1758).
Année Littéraire, vol. VIII (1758), pp. 186–93.
Mercure de France, December 1760, p. 152.
Bachaumont, *Mémoires secrets*, 24th November 1765.
L'Avantcoureur, 29th June 1767, p. 405.

CHARTON, Jean. Silk-manufacturer in Lyons. Probably identical with Jean-François Charton who was born on 15th June 1728, the son of Jean-François Charton, one-time *maître-ouvrier en droit de soie* but who, by the time the son was christened in the church of Saint-Nicaise at Lyons, was described as a *marchand-fabricant*.

According to Pierre Verlet, who first drew our attention to this man's existence, Charton was the principal supplier of woven silk furnishing materials. In 1763–64 alone, he delivered silks to the value of more than 125,000 livres to the Court at Versailles. Nevertheless, it has not yet been possible to identify any of these materials. A few of the patterns he delivered at this period are known only from brief descriptions—a green silk 'brochée d'or à cornets d'abondance' ('brocaded with silver-gilt thread in a pattern of cornucopiæ') was used in 1764 for Louis XV's *chambre* at Versailles, for instance. It was designed by Alexis Peyrotte. And there was a 'damas cramoisi fin dessein à Ananas' ('light-weight crimson damask with a pineapple design') which was bought in 1764 and used by Capin, the *marchand-tapissier*, for hanging the apartments of Mesdames in the little Palace of Saint-Hubert.

Charton was certainly still active in 1779.

Verlet, *Mobilier Royal I–III, passim.*
Verlet, *Versailles*, p. 522.
Arch. Nat., o[1] 3616[1]; 3318 fol. 5 *verso*; 3319 fol. 12.

CHARTRES, Louis-Philippe-Joseph d'Orléans, Duc de. Later known as Philippe Egalité. Born in 1747, guillotined in 1793. Son of Louis-Philippe, Duc d'Orléans. Elder brother of Louise-Marie-Thérèse-Bathilde d'Orléans who married the son of the Prince de Condé in 1770. In 1769, he himself married Louise-Marie-Adélaïde de Bourbon (born in 1753), a daughter of the Duc de Penthièvre. They had three sons of which one, Louis-Philippe, became King of France in 1830.

The Duc de Chartres' later career is no concern of ours in the present context, and we need not consider the *anglomanie* that possessed him in later years. Of direct interest to us, on the other hand, is the fact that, already in 1767 when he was only twenty, he acquired some furniture decorated with Classical ornament (see page 65). On 6th November 1771, he received from the chair-maker Louis Delanois a set of furniture which, according to the account, must have been conceived in an entirely Neo-Classical style with legs which are described as being 'à gaîne' ('straight and tapering'). In the portrait of the Duc and his family (by C. Le Peintre), painted about 1775–76, a sofa may be discerned which could well be an example of Delanois' work (Plate 498).

In all sorts of ways the Duc seems to have had a taste for novelty, even when he was quite young. This predilection may well have made him especially ready to adopt the new style of ornament. His *lecteur* from 1759 onwards was the artist, Carmontelle, who drew many of the visitors to the Duc's country residence, Saint-Cloud, and one often notices tables in an advanced taste depicted in these little pictures (Plates 349 and 350). Thus it would seem that the Duc had examples of furniture in a classicising style before him, long before he himself began to buy such things off his own bat. One should also remember that at the Palais Royal, the family's town seat which he was given in 1769, there were several rooms in an ultra-modern taste including a staircase built between 1763 and 1768 by Contant d'Ivry with wrought iron banisters embodying a pure version of the *Louis Seize* style. The Duc's two architects were Henri Piètre and Victor Louis, the latter particularly being a firm adherent of the new movement. Whatever the reasons, the Duc seems to have been early to patronise Neo-Classical artists and his royal example can hardly have gone unnoticed.

Amédée Britsch, *La Jeunesse de Philippe Égalité*, 1926.
Present author, *Louis Delanois*, 1968.
Arch. Seine, 5 B[6] 1592.

See Plates 186 and 498.

CHOISEUL, Etienne-François de Choiseul de Stainville, Duc de. Minister from 1758–1770. Born in 1719 died in 1785. Son of the Comte François-Joseph de Choiseul de Stainville. In 1750 he married Louise-Honorine Crozat du Châtel. He was a first cousin of César-Gabriel de Choiseul, Duc de Praslin.

Choiseul, while still Comte de Stainville, earned the gratitude and goodwill of Madame de Pompadour in 1752 by coming to her aid (in a financial matter) in a situation which might have brought her downfall. As a result of her support, he was first appointed Ambassador to the Holy See (in 1754) and, after having been created Duc, then to Vienna (in 1757). He was recalled in 1758 to become Foreign Secretary. In 1761 he became, in addition, Minister for War and of the Navy. In 1760 he had also been appointed Governor of Touraine. He lost no favour with Louis XV after Madame de Pompadour's death in 1764 but he fell from grace during the 'reign' of Madame du Barry, whom he seems to have disliked for some reason, and on 24th December 1770 he was dismissed and commanded to remain at his country residence, the Château de Chanteloup near Blois.

In Louis-Michel Van Loo's portrait of Choiseul, which is dated 1763 (Plate 367), we see him seated at a desk very reminiscent of Lalive de Jully's (Plate 85) and before him is an inkstand in no less marked a Neo-Classical style. The chair in which he sits, however, is couched in the traditional Rococo style. While one cannot be absolutely certain that Choiseul owned the desk shown in the portrait, we can be sure that he must have given his approval for such an ultra-modern object to have been depicted there at all. Thus we may deduce that, by 1763, this powerful minister wished to have himself portrayed as a man of advanced tastes. There is reason to believe that the desk in the portrait was made early in the 1760s so must have been new when Van Loo depicted it (see page 68).

Choiseul's next known acquisition of a work of art in the new style took the form of a pair of expensive Sèvres vases bought in 1766 which have since disappeared (see page 112). In 1767, Georg Haupt made the desk shown in Plate 114 for Choiseul's residence at Chanteloup; it is entirely Neo-Classical in style and the fact that it is of solid mahogany would have been a comparatively advanced feature in France at this date. In December 1769, Choiseul bought a dinner-service of Sèvres porcelain with a decoration described as being 'en rozes et mosaïque' ('with roses and mosaic-pattern') which was one of the factory's very latest patterns. It is not known when the table shown in Plate 115 was produced but it, too, was made for Chanteloup.

We know what the Duc de Choiseul's house in the Rue Richelieu looked like in 1770 from Louis-Nicolas van Blarenberghe's miniatures (Plates 463 and 464). It will be seen that the house seems to have presented a curious mixture of the old and the new. Several rooms—the *Premier Cabinet*, the *Cabinet à la Lanterne* and the bed-chamber—seem to have been strikingly more modern than others. In these three rooms the inlaid floors seem to be sparklingly new and two of them have panelling and chimney-pieces which seem to be in the new taste. Other rooms look as if they had not been touched for a score of years or more. It seems probable that the modernisation of the Hôtel de Choiseul, which was carried out early in 1760s, was handled by the same architect who was to renovate the Prince de Condé's Hôtel de Bourbon from 1765 onwards—namely A.-M. Le Carpentier. Dezallier d'Argenville says in the fourth edition of his *Voyage pittoresque de Paris* (1765) that Choiseul's house had been extended by Le Carpentier whereas in the third edition (1757) he says nothing about the house which was then still known as the Hôtel Crozat.

The furniture shown in these views of the rooms at the Hôtel de Choiseul in 1770 was equally mixed in style. Most of the chairs were in the Rococo taste with serpentine forms and cabriole legs although those in the re-decorated *Cabinet à la Lanterne* had straight legs and seem to present a definite Neo-Classical aspect. The writing-desk in this room is entirely Neo-Classical in style and brings to mind that made by Haupt for Chanteloup in 1767 (Plate 114). The Duc's usual writing-desk (illustrated by Watson, fig. 5, see bibliography below) was of a marked Rococo form, on the other hand the secretaire and the book-case in the bed-chamber (Plate 463) seem very like the early Neo-Classical secretaires Oeben produced shortly before his death (Plate 94). On the chimney-piece stands a clock in an equally advanced style.

Choiseul's collection of paintings, comprising works by Dutch, Flemish and contemporary French artists, was spread throughout the house. The older pictures mostly had ancient frames but in the *Premier Cabinet* were two large paintings by Teniers in frames that are not unlike those Honoré Guibert exhibited at the *Salon* in 1761 (Plates 345 to 348). All the contemporary French paintings, by artists like Greuze, Vien, Vernet, Hubert Robert and so on, are furnished with Neo-Classical frames. It is interesting, in this connection, to note that the above-mentioned portrait of Choiseul, painted in 1767 by Van Loo, was engraved by Etienne Fessard in 1769 and provided with an engraved framing in a ponderous Neo-Classical style (Plate 462) echoing that of the book-case and secretaire that have just been discussed.

It is also noteworthy that Choiseul and his wife were close friends of the Abbé Jean-Jacques Barthélemy who was keeper of the King's *Cabinet des Médailles*. The Abbé and the Duchesse spent many hours studying Classical antiquities together while she and her husband were stationed in Rome between 1755 and 1757.

Gaston Maugras, *Le Duc et la Duchesse de Choiseul*, 1924.
Geneviève Levallet, 'Notes inèdites sur la collection de Choiseul', *BSHAF*, 1925, pp. 201–11.
Emile Dacier, 'La curio sité au XVIIIe siècle, Choiseul collectionneur', *Gaz.d.B.-A.*, pp. 47–74.
Maurice Badolle, *L'Abbé Jean-Jacques Barthélemy (1716–1795) et l'hellénisme en France dans la seconde moitié du XVIIIe siècle*, 1926.
F. J. B. Watson, *The Choiseul Box*, 1963.

See Plates 81, 94, 114–15, 158, 367, 462–4.

CLÉRISSEAU, Charles-Louis. Architect and painter of ruins. Born in 1721, died in 1820.

Clérisseau was the son of Rousselot Clérisseau, 'le plus grand parfumier aux gants de Paris' ('the leading merchant dealing in perfumed gloves in Paris'). He became a pupil of J.-F. Blondel and won the Grand Prix d'Architecture in 1746. He received a stipendium to study at the French Academy in Rome, where he remained from June 1749 until the Spring of 1754 and was instructed by, among others, Gian Paolo Pannini, the Academy's 'professeur de perspective' ('teacher of perspective drawing'). From Rome he set out for France but stopped in Florence where he met Robert Adam in 1755. Clérisseau collaborated with Adam and his brother James, during the next eight years, in Rome and elsewhere in Italy. He also befriended the painter Mengs, and Winckelmann, the archaeologist.

In about 1766 he decorated a 'Ruin Room' for the Abbé Farsetti which still survives in the monastic buildings in Rome belonging to the Order of the Sacred Heart, which lie above the Spanish Steps between the church of Trinità dei Monti and the Villa Medici.

Clérisseau returned to France in 1767 and became a member of the Académie Royale de Peinture in 1769. On the way, he stopped at Marseilles where, before September 1767, he designed a *maison de campagne* for a Monsieur Borrély which, according to contemporary reports, was of a markedly Classical character. He visited England in 1771. In about 1775–76 he designed the wall-decorations 'dans le style arabesque' ('in the arabesque style') for a salon in the Hôtel Grimod de la Reynière, the panels of which are now in the Victoria and Albert Museum (for some time, these were thought to have been the work of James 'Athenian' Stuart since they somewhat resemble the decoration he designed for Spencer House in London in 1758–59).

The Palais de Justice at Metz was erected between 1776 and 1789 after designs by Clérisseau, while in 1778 he published his *Antiquités de la France* on which he had already started to work in 1767. Clérisseau lived in Auteuil and was a neighbour of Hubert Robert, the painter.

AAF, 28th October and 4th November 1767; and 20th and 27th January 1768.
Almanach historique et raisonné des architectes, peintres, sculpteurs . . ., Paris, 1777, pp. 84–6.
Jeanne Lejeaux, 'Charles-Louis Clérisseau architecte et peintre de ruines', *Revue de l'Art ancien et moderne*, 1928, pp. 125–36, 225–31.
Thomas J. McCormick and John Fleming, 'A Ruin Room by Clérisseau', *The Connoisseur*, vol. 149 (1962), pp. 239–43.
John Fleming, *Robert Adam and his Circle*, London, 1962.
Edward Croft-Murray, 'The Hôtel Grimod de La Reynière: The Salon Decorations', *Apollo*, November 1963, pp. 377–83.
Gallet, *Demeures*, p. 178.

See Plates 82–3, 218 and 483.

COCHIN, Charles-Nicolas. Engraver and designer. Born in 1715, died in 1790. The son of a painter of the same name.

Studied under his father and then under Philippe Le Bas. In 1739, at the age of only twenty-four, he was appointed *dessinateur et graveur des Menus Plaisirs*, while in 1741 he became *agréé* at the Academy and a full member in 1751. He was chosen by Madame de Pompadour to accompany her brother, Abel Poisson (later M. de Vandières but best known as the Marquis de Marigny) on a study tour in Italy between 1749 and 1751, on which journey they had as companions the architect Soufflot and the Abbé Le Blanc, the historiographer and art-critic. In 1752 he was appointed 'garde des dessins du Roi' and in 1755 to the post of 'secrétaire perpétuel et historiographe' ('curator of the King's drawings', and 'secretary and historiographer in perpetuity') at the Académie de Peinture et de Sculpture, at which point he was charged with the vaguely-defined but far-reaching and influential task of supervising 'le détail des arts', which he shouldered until 1770.

The most important collection of Cochin's work, some 400 engravings, presumably assembled by himself, are in the Bibliothèque Nationale. Cochin was also an author. Together with the architect J.-C. Bellicard, he published *Observations sur les antiquités de la Ville d'Herculanum* in 1754. He also brought out his *Voyage d'Italie* in 1758. But his most interesting writings are the famous articles which first appeared in the *Mercure de France* (1754–55) in which he condemns the more extreme forms of the Rococo style, especially as used in the decorative arts. On his death, he left some manuscript notes which were published as *Mémoires inédits* in 1880: these mainly concern Bouchardon, the Slodtz brothers, and the Comte de Caylus (the latter's malicious character is most emphatically portrayed by Cochin, incidentally).

Cochin was a close friend of Soufflot and the Marquis de Marigny. This triumvirate exerted a considerable influence which did much to bring about the triumph of Neo-Classicism.

S. Rocheblave, *Charles-Nicolas Cochin, graveur et dessinateur*, Paris-Bruxelles, 1927.
B.N. Est. Inv., vol. 5, pp. 7–113.
See Plates 303 and 378.

CONDÉ, Louis-Joseph de Bourbon, Prince de. Born in 1736, died in 1818. Son of Louis-Henri-Auguste de Bourbon, seventh Prince de Condé (died in 1740) who, amongst other things, established the porcelain factory at Chantilly. Great-grandchild of Louis de Bourbon, famed as Le Grand Condé, one of Louis XIV's great generals. In 1753 married Charlotte-Elisabeth-Godefride de Rohan-Soubise who died in 1760. Their son, Louis-Henri-Joseph de Bourbon (born in 1756) was married in 1770 to Louise-Marie-Thérèse-Bathilde d'Orléans (born in 1750) whose elder brother was the Duc de Chartres (see his bibliographical note above).

The Prince de Condé was given a thorough military and literary education, and he distinguished himself greatly in the Seven Years' War in spite of his tender age, notably at the Battles of Hastenbeck and Johannisberg (July 1757 and October 1762 respectively). He was appointed Governor of Burgundy and, in this capacity, his interests in such matters as highway improvement, bridge-building, scientific questions, as well as in art and literature, proved a great advantage. He left France with his family after the fall of the Bastille in 1789, and became leader of the emigrants' military forces, distinguishing himself in several important operations against the Revolutionary armies. In 1801, he came to England where his son had already settled. He returned to France with Louis XVIII, the former Comte de Provence. He died at the age of eighty-two in Paris and was buried in the crypt at Saint-Denis among the tombs of the Kings of France.

Condé inherited the castle of Chantilly and the long-since demolished Hôtel de Condé in Paris. In 1764, he bought the Palais Bourbon from Louis XV at an advantageous price. This lies on what is now the Quai d'Orsay and had previously belonged to his family. In 1768 he bought the neighbouring property, that of the Hôtel de Brancas (also known as the Hôtel de Lassay) which belonged to the Comte de Lauraguais, and promptly joined this building with the Palais de Bourbon.

Already in 1764, the Prince had shown his modern outlook by mounting a competition, on Soufflot's advice, for the extension and redecoration of the Palais de Bourbon and inviting architects of advanced tastes such as Barreau de Chefdeville, Chevotet, Peyre, Le Carpentier and the young Boullée to take part. The task was finally given to Barreau who, however, died in 1765 when the work had only just commenced. He was succeeded by Le Carpentier, assisted by Bellissard who, on Le Carpentier's death in 1773, took over the post of architect to the Prince.

During the modification of the Hôtel Brancas and the renovation of the Palais de Bourbon (in which, incidentally, an apartment was set aside for the Prince's son and daughter-in-law who were married in 1770), the Prince showed himself to be a man of progressive inclinations. He seems to have preferred furnishings of a distinctly modern kind. He patronised craftsmen like the ébéniste J.-F. Leleu, the bronze-founder Ph. Caffieri, and the chairmakers L. Delanois and L. C. Carpentier. Meticulous accounts indicate that Carpentier's furniture was unmistakably *Louis Seize* in style, although many of the chairs provided by Delanois had cabriole legs and were more traditional in style (see page 92). It is reasonable to suppose that the Prince's own architects designed most of the furniture but we know that Caffieri provided models of his own for the bronzework he was to make for the Prince, although of course even these had to be passed by the Prince or his architects before they could be cast (see page 104 and Plates 453 to 461). All the furnishings for this great house seem to have been commissioned by the end of 1769 or early in 1770.

Several pieces of case-furniture made for the Prince de Condé, and for his daughter-in-law's apartment about 1770, have survived and have been identified by Pierre Verlet (Plates 128 and 130). No seat-furniture has as yet been located but the *canapé* by Carpentier shown in Plate 174 probably gives us a good idea of its general appearance.

Nouvelle Biographie générale, vol. II, columns 422–7.
G. Macon, *Les arts dans la Maison de Condé*, 1903.
Hector Lefuel, *Georges Jacob*, 1923.
Verlet, *La maison*, 1966, *passim.*
Watson, *Wallace Collection Furniture*, pp. 114–15.
The present author's *Louis Delanois*, 1968, *passim.*

See Plates 127–30, 453–61.

CONTANT, Pierre, known as Contant d'Ivry. Architect. Born in 1698 at Ivry-sur-Seine, died in Paris in 1777.

Contant lived in the Rue du Harlay on the Ile de la Cité and was *premier architecte* to the Duc d'Orléans as well as being *contrôleur* at the Hôtel des Invalides.

Among Contant's many important works, one may single out for mention his project for the façade of the church of Saint-Eustache (1744) and the great dining-room, long since dismantled, at the Palais Royal which was furnished with sixteen columns and four pilasters executed in scagliola by the stuccator, Louis Mansiaux (1754). He also provided the large and surviving *escalier d'honneur* (great staircase) in the same Palace between 1763 and 1768; this had wrought iron banisters executed by Corbin in collaboration with Philippe Caffieri. In 1764, the foundation-stone was laid for the subsequently much-altered Madeleine church which Contant originally designed, with a nave flanked by aisles and with a crossing.

Arch. de la Seine, 5 B^6 2738 fol. 2 *verso* (15th October 1754).
Dezallier d'Argenville, *Voyage pittoresque de Paris*, 3rd ed., Paris, 1757, pp. 71–2.
A.A.A., 28th May 1766.
L'Avantcoureur, 11th May 1767 and 18th January 1768.
Hautecoeur, *Histoire*, *seconde moitié*, *passim.*

See Plates 7, 22–7, 301–2.

COULLONJON, Denis. Carver. Active between 1743 and 1786.

He became a *maître-sculpteur* in 1743 and in the same year was made a member of the Académie de Saint-Luc, of which he became *directeur garde* in 1751. He was living in the Arsenal in 1748 and is recorded as being in the Rue de Bourbon in 1764 and in the Rue Saint-Benoît between 1775 and 1786.

Coullonjon is at present only known for the carved work he carried out on the chairs made for the Court at Warsaw between 1766 and 1768 by Louis Delanois, who provided the joined frames.

Guiffrey, *Académie de Saint-Luc*, p. 237.
Vial, Marcel and Girodie, I, p. 121.
Arch. Nat., Y 9327 (19th October 1751), and Z[1j] 921 fol. 103 *verso*.

DELAFOSSE, Jean-Charles. Architect and designer. Born in 1734, died in 1791. The son of a wine-merchant living in the Rue du Roi-de-Sicile.

In 1747 he was apprenticed to the carver Jean-Baptiste Poulet who was *directeur garde* at the Académie de Saint-Luc. However, he seems not to have completed his apprenticeship. In 1767 he was calling himself 'architecte et professeur pour le dessein' ('architect, and teacher of drawing') while in 1775 he was 'adjoint à professeur de géométrie et perspective' ('assistant professor of geometry and perspective') at the same Academy. In 1768 he was living in the Rue Poissonnières but had moved to the Rue Neuve-Saint-Martin by 1775. He became a member of the Academy in Bordeaux in 1781.

In 1768, Delafosse published 111 engravings under the title *Nouvelle Iconologie Historique*. All the plates were ready and printed by July 1767 although 'les explications' (*lit*. 'the explanations'; notes to the illustrations) were still lacking. According to *L'Avantcoureur* (6th July 1767), he had been working on the suite 'for several years'. It cost 48 livres, and comprised series of trophies in a severe Neo-Classical style. He expanded the series and then included designs for all kinds of furniture, stoves and fireplaces, vases, cartouches, etc., issued in batches. By 1773 he had issued 258 plates; by 1776, a further 42 were finished, and in 1785 a further 78. Each set of six plates cost 1 livre, 6 sols, and these were sold partly by Daumont in the Rue Saint-Martin and partly by Chereau in the Rue des Mathurins. One could also procure them from the painter and gilder Jean-Félix Watin who offered his assistance to anyone who sought to have furniture made after Delafosse's engraving. However, Watin drew attention to the fact that one would have to simplify Delafosse's designs if the price of the finished article was not to be prohibitively high!

It was recently noted by Michel Gallet that Delafosse was also the architect of two Parisian houses which still survive—the Hôtel Titon and the Hôtel Goix in the Rue du Faubourg Poissonnière (1776–83). In 1780, he built a house in Pantin and another in the Rue Sainte-Apolline, together with two sets of barracks in Paris.

Arch. Nat., étude XXXVIII, 10th November 1747.
L'Avantcoureur, 6th July 1767.
Jean-Félix Watin, *l'Art du peintre, doreur, vernisseur*, Paris, editions 1773, 1776 and 1785.
Geneviève Levallet Haug, 'l'Ornemaniste Jean-Charles Delafosse', *Gaz.d. B.-A.*, 1929, pp. 158–69.
Michel Gallet, 'Jean-Charles Delafosse, architecte, *Gaz.d.B.-A.*, March 1963, pp. 157–64.

See Plates 152, 154, 437–40, 479–82.

DELANOIS, Louis. Chair-maker. Born at Savignies near Beauvais, in 1731, died in Paris in 1792.

Delanois became a *maître* in the Parisian Guild of Joiners and Cabinet-Makers in 1761. He had possibly been working in the workshop of the widow of Jean-Baptiste Lerouge the year before. In 1777 he sold his stock and the tools of his trade to Martin Jullien to whom he then also let his workshop premises. At the same time he gave up his right to practise the craft of chair-making. He set up as a dealer in timber and became involved in speculative building. In 1790 he went bankrupt and his debts amounted to about

400,000 livres. Delanois lived in the Rue Saint-Denis in 1753, then in the Rue Saint-Nicolas in the Faubourg Saint-Antoine (1761), subsequently (from 1764) in the Rue Bourbon-de-Villeneuve, which ran parallel to the Rue de Cléry, and finally in the Cul-de-sac de l'Etoile close by, where he lived from 1768 until he died.

Delanois' output was enormous. During the short period of sixteen years in which he was active as a *menuisier*, he produced over 14,000 items of furniture—chairs, beds, etc. In 1768 alone, he delivered 2,000 pieces to his customers. He sold his products primarily to *marchands-tapissiers* but he also served the aristocracy and the wealthier bourgeoisie: Mme. du Barry, the Prince de Condé and the King of Poland were among his clientele.

This craftsman was among the very first of the Parisian chair-makers to adopt the *Louis Seize* style, probably as a result of the commissions he received from customers with avant-garde tastes in this direction.

Salverte, *Les ébénistes*, pp. 80–2.
Vial, Marcel and Girodie, pp. 141–2.
S. Eriksen, *Louis Delanois menuisier en sièges*, Paris, 1968.
Verlet, 'Un mobilier par Delanois couvert en tapisserie de Beauvais', *Bulletin des Musées de France*, April 1946, pp. 13–14.

See Plates 156, 162, 164–5, 172–3, 175–6, 181.

De la Rue, Louis-Félix. Sculptor. Born about 1725–30, died in 1764.

De la Rue won the Deuxième Prix de Peinture at the Académie Royale de Peinture et Sculpture in 1748, while the next year he won the 2nd Prize and in 1750 the 1st Prize in Sculpture. He frequented the 'École royale des élèves protégés'. In 1754 he was granted permission to attend the French Academy in Rome where he arrived on about 1st November. But he had to leave Rome on account of ill-health early in May of the next year, much to the annoyance of the Marquis de Marigny. Five years later, he became a *maître-sculpteur* and was elected to the Académie de Saint-Luc where, from 1762 until his death, he was a teacher. He lived in the Rue de la Verrerie.

De la Rue is known for, amongst other things, the eight drawings he made of vases or urns in the Neo-Classical taste which are now in the Musée des Arts Décoratifs (the twelve other drawings exhibited under his name in the same place are unlikely to be from his hand; two are signed by Le Lorrain who would appear to have also drawn the rest). De la Rue is also known for the eight suites of drawings of vases, monuments, furniture, etc. 'dans le goût antique' which were engraved by Ph. L. Parizeau and published in 1771 and 1775. Lalive de Jully owned four terracotta vases by De la Rue which may be those which can be seen in G. de Saint-Aubin's engraving of *Four Vases* produced in 1754 (E. Dacier, Plate X).

Mercure de France, 1771 and 1775 (Index by E. Deville).
Guiffrey, *Académie de Saint-Luc*, p. 253.
Procès verbaux de l'Académie de peinture, *passim*.
Corr. des Dir., *passim*.

See Plates 54 and 333–8.

Deumier, Pierre. Executor of fine metal work, the son of a smith of the same name. Active in Paris in the 1760s.

In 1763, Deumier was registered as a *maître-serrurier* (locksmith) and later was granted the title of *serrurier des bâtiments du Roi*. His workshops were in the Rue du Carrousel.

Deumier put an advertisement in *L'Avantcoureur* in 1763 in which he offered for sale 'un pied pour porter une table de marbre à double consolle, avec volutes en cornes de bélier, enrichie d'avantcorps & moulures prises, sur les masses, surmontées d'une frise avec rond entrelassé & rosettes. Le bas est terminé par un vase antique de ronde bosse avec branches de chêne. Les consolles sont garnies de différentes pièces d'ornements, & dans le milieu est une tête de femme coëffée à l'antique; des branches de laurier forment guirlande au pourtour . . .' ('the support for a marble table consisting of two consoles with rams-head volutes, a richly carved and pierced apron. The frieze is decorated with a running interlaced pattern with rosettes. At the base is an urn in high relief with oak leaves. The consoles are decorated with various motifs and in the centre is a female head with a Classical hair-dress. Bay-leaves form garlands all round'). Between 1763 and 1767 he executed the Neo-Classical choir-screen, which still survives, for the church Saint-Germain l'Auxerrois; on completion of this task he invited the Marquis de Marigny to come and inspect the screen. Between about 1766 and 1768 he provided works to the value of 25,714 livres for the Polish Court at Warsaw: these may have been after designs by Victor Louis and included console-tables similar to those described in *L'Avantcoureur* advertisement. Among his customers was the Duc de Richelieu who paid him 4,000 livres in 1768.

Arch. Nat., Y 9328 (10th January 1763), Z^{1j} 921, o^{1} 3044 *pièce* 370.
Arch. Nat., Minutier Central, II–627.
J.-F. Blondel, *Cours d'architecture*, vol. V, Pl. XXIII.
L'Avantcoureur, 8th August 1763, pp. 503–4.
NAAF, 1902, p. 66.
BSHAF, 1921, p. 241.

See Plate 344.

DE WAILLY, Charles. Architect and furniture-designer. Born in 1730, died in 1798.

Student of J.-F. Blondel, Servandoni and Le Geay. Won the Grand Prix d'Architecture in 1752. Held a study-grant at the French Academy in Rome from September 1754 until December 1756. A member of the Académie d'Architecture from 1767 and of the Académie de Peinture from 1771. He was successively *contrôleur de bâtiments* at Versailles and at the royal residence at Choisy.

De Wailly drew and engraved a series of vases and tables in 1760. At the 1761 *Salon*, he exhibited 'une table de lapis, dont le pieds est en bois des Indes, orné de bronzes dorés ('a lapis lazuli table, with legs of an Eastern wood, decorated with gilt bronze mounts') together with a 'vase de granite, dans le goût antique; l'un & l'autre sont d'une belle forme, les ornemens en sont riches & d'un goût très-noble & très-éloigné d'avoir l'air colifichet, qui a regné trop long-temps dans nos meubles' ('a granite vase in the Antique taste, both of exquisite form, their decoration being rich and in an exceedingly noble style very different from that which has prevailed so long in the field of furniture, with its fussy gewgaws'). At the same *Salon* was shown a marble column with gilded bronze mounts executed by the goldsmith R.-J. Auguste after drawings by De Wailly.

Among his later work may be mentioned the decorations he provided for rooms in the Palazzo Serra at Genoa (1772–73) and at the Théâtre Français (Odéon) in collaboration with M. J. Peyre (1773–85). He also designed two houses in the Rue des Pepinières in about 1776, for himself and his friend, the sculptor Pajou.

L'Avantcoureur, 30th June 1760, 21st September and 5th October, 1761.
Mercure de France, October 1761, pp. 227–8.
Gallet, *Demeures*, p. 181.

See Plates 101–3, 324–30 and 489.

DORÉ, Germain. Executor of fine metalwork. Registered as a *maître-serrurier* in 1760. His brother, Pierre Doré, was likewise registered in 1765. Their father was also a locksmith. Doré's workshops were in the Rue l'Evêque, now part of the Avenue de l'Opéra.

Doré is now only known for the now lost wrought-iron choir-screen which he made in 1760 for the church of Saint-Roch and which J.-F. Blondel illustrates in his *Cours d'Architecture*. It would appear from the contemporary description in *Affiches, Annonces et Avis Divers* that Doré also designed the choir-screen.

Arch Nat., Y 9328 (26th March 1760 and 27th February 1765).
Mercure de France, January 1761 bd. I pp. 144–5 and bd. II p. 175.
A.A.A., 4th February 1761, p. 19.

See Plate 343.

DOUBLET, Simon-Hubert. Painter. Born about 1730–35. Presumably son of the painter Jean-Hubert Doublet and grandson of Hubert Doublet, who was also a painter.

Doublet was elected a member of the Académie de Saint-Luc as a *maître-peintre* in 1753. He lived in the Rue Sainte-Anne, off the Rue Saint-Honoré. A painter of this name competed for the Académie de Peinture's Grand Prix in 1768, while in the Paris Musée des Arts Décoratifs is a volume of engravings of antique friezes and vases signed 'Lhuillier et Doubley, Romae delineaverunt' and with a title-page reading 'Livre d'ornements à l'usage des artistes dessiné par l'Huillier et gravés par Doublet et [sic] Romae'; possibly 'Doubley' is identical with our Doublet. A clock and a calendar in the form of a pair of marble vases with bronze mounts are at Waddesdon Manor; one is inscribed as having been made in 1774 by 'Julia' after a design by 'Doublet'.

Herluison, *Actes*, p. 117.
Guiffrey, *Académie de Saint-Luc*, p. 268.
BSHAF, 1907, p. 69.
Procès-Verbaux, vol. VII, p. 384.
Hautecoeur, *Histoire, seconde moitié*, p. 479.

See Plate 201.

DUBOIS, Jacques. Cabinet-maker. Born about 1693, died in 1763. Father of René Dubois.

Dubois, who first became a *maître* in 1742 at the ripe age of about fifty, had probably practised his trade as an *ouvrier libre* in Faubourg Saint-Antoine where he lived in the Rue de Charenton. In 1752 he was elected a *juré* of the cabinet-makers' guild for two years, and in 1763 he was chosen to make the valuation of Oeben's stock and effects after the latter's death.

Dubois' stamp (I. DUBOIS) may be found on furniture ranging from the simple to the highly ornate, in both the pure Rococo style and in the *Louis Seize* taste, as well as in transitional forms. The son, René, continued to use his father's stamp when he took over the direction of the family firm, and he may be presumed to have made most of the non-Rococo furniture bearing this stamp.

Salverte, *Les ébénistes*, pp. 95–6.

See Plates 100–6, 108.

DUBOIS, René. Cabinet-maker. Born in 1737, died in 1799. Son of Jacques Dubois, also a cabinet-maker.

René Dubois became a *maître* in 1755. He continued to work in his father's workshop which he then took over and directed, in company with his mother, after his father's death in 1763. About 1780, he seems to have ceased cabinet-making and set up as a dealer in furniture, opening a shop in the Rue Montmartre, at the corner of the Rue Neuve Saint-Eustache. When he died he was living in the Rue des Orfèvres by the Quai de la Mégisserie.

This cabinet-maker continued to use his father's stamp (I. DUBOIS) and must have produced most and perhaps all the furniture bearing this stamp which is in the *Louis Seize* and transitional styles, while the father probably produced all or most of those pieces which are in the Rococo taste. Many of René

Dubois' products are unusually ornate and are mounted with exceptionally elaborate bronze mounts, which indicates that he had close connections with skilful designers and competent bronze-workers. A certain amount of his furniture is veneered with Oriental lacquer panels, while a few are painted with scenes *en grisaille*, especially with landscapes in the style of Vernet.

Salverte, *Les ébénistes*, pp. 96–8.

See Plates 100–6, 108.

DUMONT, Gabriel-Pierre-Martin. Architect and engraver. Born about 1715, died sometime after 1790.

Dumont won the Grand Prix d'Architecture in 1737 and went to Rome in 1742 where he lived at the French Academy on a stipendium until June 1746. He apparently visited Paestum in 1750 together with Soufflot. He became a member of the Italian Academies of Art in Rome, Florence and Bologna, as well as of the Académie de Saint-Luc in Paris. In 1765, however, he was living in the Rue des Arcis, near the beginning of the Rue Saint-Martin.

He is principally known for his many publications dealing with Classical monuments, notably that on the temples at Paestum which appeared in 1764 and was based on measured drawings made by Soufflot. He also engraved measured drawings of St. Peter's in Rome (1767) and of French and Italian theatres, together with a series of urns after drawings provided by the sculptor, Simon Challe.

Jean Monval, *Soufflot*, Paris, 1918, p. 23.
Gallet, *Demeures*, p. 182.

See Plates 10 and 63.

DUPLESSIS, Jean-Claude Chambellan, known as. Silversmith, bronze-worker and designer of porcelain-ware. Probably born in Turin about 1690–95, died in Paris 1774. His Italian name was Giovanni Claudio Chiamberlano; he had acquired the name Duplessis already by the year 1720 when he married Gioanna Ludovica Caronina, who died at Sèvres in 1768, aged about seventy-two. Their son was Jean-Claude-Thomas Chambellan Duplessis who also became a bronze-worker. A daughter married the miniature-painter J.-B. Letellier, while another married the engraver A.-F. Vanquetin.

Duplessis first practised as a silversmith in Turin and probably worked for Amadeo, Duke of Savoy, amongst others, since the latter acknowledged a debt to Duplessis of 2,000 livres in 1739. This craftsman came to Paris about 1740. In 1742 he designed and made two large bronze braziers which Louis XV presented to Saïd Mahmet Pasha, the Ambassador of the Sublime Porte to the Court of Versailles. One of these is still in Istanbul. In 1745 or 1747 he became connected with the porcelain factory at Vincennes (which later moved to Sèvres) as a designer—a post he held until 1773. At the same time he worked as a free-lance designer and maker of bronzes in Paris itself. In 1758, he was granted the privilege of calling himself *orfèvre du Roi*. He included amongst his customers the famous *marchand-mercier* Lazare Duvaux, and also Madame de Pompadour and the Marquis de Voyer d'Argenson. He is said to have executed a massive lectern in the form of an eagle for Notre-Dame in Paris, and he is also believed to have provided the models for the rich bronze ornaments on Louis XV's roll-top desk (known as the *Bureau du Roi*) in about 1760. However, a surviving document would seem to suggest that it was in fact the son who carried out this work. Perhaps they worked together on this task, since the son was already assisting his father by 1752.

The majority of the forms Duplessis devised for the porcelain factory—ornamental vases, table-services, etc.—were in the Rococo idiom. It is conceivable that he also designed some of the vases which first came off the production-line early in the 1760s and which betray a nascent Neo-Classicism similar to that of the decorative bronze mounts on the *Bureau du Roi*.

In March 1764, Duplessis moved to a small apartment in the Rue Sainte-Marthe in the Enclos du

Cloître Saint-Germain-des-Près, where he does not seem to have had any real workshop. When he died, there was listed as being in a basement-room, a portable forge 'sans soufflet' ('without bellows'), three benches and a table for soldering 'garnie de son soufflet' ('with its bellows'). In the kitchen stood 'un tour à guillocher' and two 'tours à lapidaire' (a machine for producing lengths of guilloche pattern, and a spindle for lapidary work). Apparently he was still active as a worker in bronze and silver, and he left both completed and half-finished fire-dogs, sconces, and mounted porcelain objects, including a large bronze *surtout* with figures of Meissen porcelain and flowers executed in silver which the son contracted to complete. Duplessis also left materials for painting together with some 200 papier-mâché snuff-boxes, all of which suggests he had been dabbling in side-lines of the minor arts in his old age.

Duplessis had a collection of engraved ornaments, including work by Saly, Babel, Beauvais, Delafosse, Petitot and the younger Boucher.

Geneviève Levallet-Haug, 'Jean-Claude Duplessis, orfèvre du roi', *La Renaissance de l'art français*, 1920, pp. 60–7.
Torino, Archivio di Stato, Sez. II, Atti d'insinuazione notarili, 1720, libro 12, vol. III, fol. 1206–1208.
Arch. Nat., Minutier Central, étude I, liasse 558 (27th October 1774).

See Plates 90–3.

DUPLESSIS, Jean-Claude-Thomas Chambellan, known as Duplessis *fils*. Bronze-worker. Born about 1730, died in 1783. Son of Jean-Claude Duplessis.

The earliest information we have about the younger Duplessis is that he was already assisting his father make models for the Vincennes porcelain factory in 1752, in which year he received 648 livres for his pains. On 12th June 1765, he was registered as a *maître fondeur en terre et sable* 'suivan larrest du consul du 24 janvier . . . et par chef d'oeuvre' ('by order of the Council given on 24th January . . . and having produced a satisfactory master-piece'). He was a co-signatory of the bronze-founders' copyright resolution which was accepted on 30th July 1766. In 1763, before he became a *maître*, he is recorded as being owed an unspecified sum of money by the famous cabinet-maker, J.-F. Oeben, on the latter's death. In this connection he is styled *sculpteur*. On the engravings of vases that he published about 1775–80, on the other hand, he calls himself *sculpteur cizeleur*. The *Almanach des Artistes* for the year 1777 states that this 'bon dessinateur, travaille d'après ses dessins' ('an excellent designer who can work from his own drawings'). He then lived in the Rue du Four, Faubourg Saint-Germain. Later, he moved to the Rue Sainte-Marine, in the neighbourhood of Notre-Dame.

It is not certain whether the models for the bronzes on Oeben and Riesener's famous *Bureau du Roi* (about 1760) were made by the elder or the younger Duplessis and the relevant document, dated 1767, merely mentions 'M. Duplessis, modeleur', who was paid 1,500 livres. Considering the father's advanced age and that he had already moved to a small flat without any proper workshop in 1764, it seems far from certain that it was the father who executed the models. And, as we have just noted, the son was one of Oeben's creditors in 1763. Perhaps the father and son collaborated over this important commission.

About 1775–76, Duplessis *fils* made four large bronze candelabra for Grimod de la Reynière, the *fermier-général* (Plate 218). These can be dated because they are mentioned in the 1777 *Almanach des Artistes*, the manuscript for which was ready for press by 23rd November 1776.

Sèvres, Archives of the Manufacture Nationale, Compte pour 1752, F 1, liasse 7.
Arch. Nat., Y 9328 (12th June 1765) and H 2118 (1787).
Wildenstein, *Rapports d'experts*, pp. 129–30.
J. J. Guiffrey, 'Inventaire de J. F. Oeben', *NAAF*, 1899, p. 301.
Verlet, *Mobilier Royal II*, p. 68.

See Plates 90–3 and 218.

DURFORT-DURAS, Emmanuel Félicité, Duc de. Marshal of France and *premier gentilhomme de la chambre du Roi.* Born in 1715, died in 1789.

In 1752, after many years' active service in the Army, the Duc de Durfort-Duras was appointed French Ambassador to the Court of Spain. In 1757, he was created a *pair de France* and *premier gentilhomme de la chambre du Roi*, as a result of which—like the Duc d'Aumont and the Duc de Richelieu—he came to belong to Louis XV's closest entourage. Moreover, like the other *premiers gentilhommes*, he became a controller of the *Menus Plaisirs*. In this capacity, he concerned himself particularly with matters related to the theatre but was also specially responsible for the arrangements connected with court mourning, and was thus involved in the preparations for the memorial service for the King and Queen of Spain which was held at Notre-Dame on 15th January 1760, when the catafalque, designed by M.-A. Slodtz, was unmistakably Neo-Classical in character (Plates 42 and 43). This structure was greatly praised at the time for its classicising style (see the Note to the above-mentioned illustrations) but it is not at present certain whether the Duc de Durfort-Duras had any determining influence on its stylistic conformation.

Nouvelle Biographie Générale, vol. 15.
Journal de Papillon de la Ferté, 1887, *passim.*

EVALD, Maurice-Bernard. Cabinet-maker. Active between 1765 and 1774.

Evald was of German origin and became a *maître* in 1765. He settled in the Rue du Bac, far from the traditional centres of cabinet-making. He found himself ruined in August 1774 and thereafter completely disappears from the scene.

Evald is principally known for having executed the cabinet-work of the entirely Neo-Classical jewel-cabinet which the architect F.-J. Belanger designed for Marie-Antoinette in 1769—the piece for which Gouthière chased the mounts. At Saltram there is a drop-front desk by Evald which is also in the Neo-Classical style (Plate 140).

His name is rendered without a final 'e', contrary to statements made elsewhere.

Salverte, *Ebénistes*, pp. 109–10.
Geoffrey Wills, 'Robert Adam at Saltram', *The Connoisseur Year Book*, 1958, p. 7.

See Plates 139 and 140.

FALCONET, Etienne-Maurice. Sculptor. Born in 1716, died in 1791. The son of a chair-maker living in the Rue de Bourbon-Villeneuve. In 1739 he married a daughter of Pierre Moulin, *ébéniste du roi.*

Between about 1734 and 1745, Falconet was a pupil of J.-B. Lemoyne. In 1744, he became *agréé* at the Academy and in 1754 a full member. He never visited Italy. From 1757 until 1766 he was *directeur des travaux de sculpture* at the Royal Porcelain Factory at Sèvres. Between 1766 and 1778 he was in St. Petersburg. Later he went to Holland and finally returned to Paris in 1780 where he remained until his death.

Falconet's most celebrated work is the equestrian statue of Peter the Great at St. Petersburg which was unveiled in 1782. In 1754 he executed for Lalive de Jully a sepulchral monument in the Neo-Classical style which was to be placed over the tomb of the latter's first wife who had died in 1752. This was probably the monument that was later moved to the church of Saint-Roch and of which there is a drawing in the Röhsska Museet, Göteborg. Between 1753 and 1760 he carried out decorative work on two chapels in Saint-Roch. While he was associated with the Sèvres porcelain factory he modelled many small figures and groups which were executed in biscuit porcelain. Apart from this, he is supposed—according to *L'Avant-coureur*—to have provided designs for vases which were then carried out in soft-paste porcelain and thus displayed at Versailles in December 1762. He is also said to have produced drawings or a model for the salt-cellar which the silversmith R.-J. Auguste made for Madame de Pompadour in 1755. In 1761 he modelled the female figures for a pair of candelabra, which the silversmith F.-T. Germain produced in bronze. A number of clock-cases and other objects decorated with graceful female figures, notably the *Pendule des Trois Grâces* in the Louvre, have been ascribed to Falconet without convincing reason.

Falconet's most important patrons were Madame de Pompadour, the Empress Catherine II, Lalive de Jully and the Abbé Marduel, who was the prime mover behind the work of decoration being carried out at Saint-Roch during the third quarter of the century.

Amongst his friends, Falconet numbered the well-known painters François Boucher and Pierre.

Falconet lived first of all in the Rue Montmartre; in 1753 he was living in the Cour du vieux Louvre, and in the 1760s he had bought a house in the Rue d'Anjou.

Louis Réau, *Etienne-Maurice Falconet*, Paris, 1922.
L'Avantcoureur, January, 1763.

See Plate 38.

FOLIOT. Three generations of chair-makers and sculptors had this name. The biographical details previously published concerning this family can give rise to confusion, while their work—often the result of collaboration in what must have been well-nigh a partnership—makes it difficult or impossible (in spite of stamped marks and other documentation) to distinguish between the various individuals. It is hoped that the biographies which follow do not contain too many mistakes, however. They are based on information given by Salverte and Verlet, supplemented by certain hitherto-unpublished data culled from documents not previously studied in this connection.

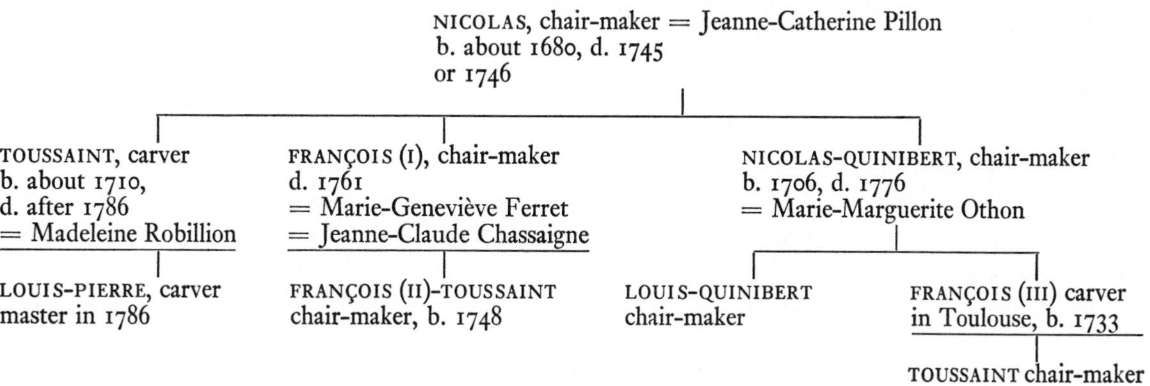

Salverte, *Ebénistes*, pp. 113–16.
Verlet, *Mobilier Royal I–III, passim.*
Arch. Nat., o^1 3315ff., o^1 3619ff.
Arch. Nat., Minutier Central, XX (10th March 1746; 27th August 1761; 14th October 1761; 9th March 1763); XXXVIII (5th August 1748); L (22nd May 1776).

See Plates 179 and 180.

FOLIOT, Nicolas. Chair-maker. Born about 1680, died in 1745 or 1746. Married to Jeanne-Catherine Pillon who was still alive in 1763. They had four sons: François and Nicolas-Quinibert, who became chair-makers, Toussaint who became a carver, and Michel, the fourth son, who became *entrepreneur des ponts et chaussées.* (See above.)

Nicolas, the senior member of the family, had a workshop in the house he owned in the Rue de Cléry which was 'at the sign of the Duc de Bretagne'. He is known to have supplied furniture to the *Garde-Meuble du Roi* from 1723 onwards. He bought a house at Belleville in 1736. His business was kept going by his widow, but after 1749 the management was taken over by the son François, who assumed the royal appointment. It is possible that Nicolas' widow again managed the business after her son François' death in 1761.

FOLIOT, François, also known as Foliot *le jeune*, or as François I Foliot. Chair-maker. The date of his birth is not known but he died in 1761. He was the son of the afore-mentioned Nicolas Foliot. His first wife was Marie-Geneviève Ferret (who died before 1755). Their son, born in 1748, was François-Toussaint Foliot, who also became a chair-maker. Foliot married again in 1755; his wife's maiden name was Jeanne-Claude Chassaigne and she died in 1758. (See page 177.)

François Foliot became a *maître* in 1749 and took over the management of his late father's workshop in the house in the Rue de Cléry in 1749 (at the sign of the Duc de Bretagne) which was owned by his mother and from whom he had rented an apartment. He also assumed the father's appointment as *menuisier ordinaire du Garde Meuble du Roi*. The inventory drawn up after his death in 1761 informs us that the workshop contained ten workbenches and that the completed stock comprised 149 chairs, twelve folding stools and eight beds. The timber-stock consisted of beechwood worth 2,115 livres, and 216 livres worth of oak, but there was no walnut. It is known that François Foliot collaborated with two carvers—mainly with his own brother Toussaint but also with Charles Regnier.

FOLIOT, Nicolas-Quinibert. Chair-maker. Born in 1706, died in 1776. Son of Nicolas Foliot. In 1729 he married Marie-Marguerite Othon (Hotton). A daughter, Marie-Catherine, married the joiner Jacques-François Roblin. A son, François, became a *maître-sculpteur*, while another son, Louis-Quinibert, became a *maître-menuisier*. (See page 177.)

Nicolas-Quinibert Foliot probably became a *maître* in about 1730. It is not certain where he first lived but in 1752 he bought a house in the Rue de Bourbon Villeneuve, a street running parallel to the Rue de Cléry where his father's house lay, although his father's chair-making business was by this time being managed by his brother François. In 1761, he bought a second house in the street, while in January 1768 he rented an apartment on the second floor of a house in the Rue de Cléry owned by his brother Michel: this was possibly the house which had been the father's. In 1768 he also acquired a *maison de campagne* at Argenteuil, while in 1775 he was letting out two houses he owned in the Rue de Bourbon. He died in the Rue de Cléry apartment in 1776.

No mention is made of any workshop in the inventory drawn up on Nicolas-Quinibert Foliot's death and it may well be that he had retired from active business a few years earlier, allowing others to manage the firm in his name. The house at Argenteuil was also noticeably more richly furnished and equipped than the Rue de Cléry apartment, (this is particularly obvious when one compares the contents of the two cellars!), suggesting that he had moved out to the country towards the end of his life and only kept on the flat in Paris as a *pied-à-terre*. Can it be that the work executed by the family for the *Garde-Meuble* during the later years was in fact produced in the workshops of the brother François Foliot who by this time was already dead? All that is certain is that François' son, François-Toussaint Foliot, was owed 156 livres by Nicolas-Quinibert in 1776 for furniture supplied to the *Garde-Meuble* in 1774, and that Nicolas-Quinibert's own son, Louis-Quinibert was also owed money for similar work.

Over many years, Nicolas-Quinibert Foliot delivered great quantities of furniture to the *Garde-Meuble du Roi*. The last account but one was for work delivered in 1774 amounting to 17,044 livres, while the last account of all was for 5,874 livres in 1775. Presumably most of the work supplied for use at the Court was decorated with carving by the brother Toussaint. This was notably the case with the Petit Trianon furniture of 1767. The part Foliot played in the introduction of Neo-Classicism is hard to define. The Royal accounts show that the first chairs with straight legs that he sent to the *Garde-Meuble* were delivered in October 1775 but he may well have made chairs with such features for private customers before this.

FOLIOT, Toussaint. Carver. Born about 1710, died sometime after 1786. Son of the aforementioned Nicolas Foliot. Married to Madeleine Robillion who was perhaps a daughter of the carver Antoine Robillion. Toussaint Foliot was probably the father of Louis-Pierre Foliot who became a *maître-sculpteur* in 1786. (See page 177.)

Toussaint Foliot became a *maître-sculpteur* in 1732 and later a member of the Académie de Saint-Luc of which he became *directeur* in 1757. By 1786 he is described as 'ancien maître'. Like so many other carvers, he lived in the Rue Meslée in a house which he had bought in 1757.

It seems probable that Toussaint Foliot was already working for the *Garde-Meuble du Roi* in 1757 and perhaps even before that, since a console-table executed in that year for the Palace at Compiègne should perhaps be ascribed to him rather than to Nicolas-Quinibert's son François (François III, who was only twenty-four at this date; see Verlet, *Mobilier Royal*, I, p. 55). Amongst his many later works for the French Court, special mention should be made of the carving on all the chairs, etc., which he delivered for use at the Petit Trianon on 9th May 1767, the frames of which had been produced in the workshops of Nicolas-Quinibert Foliot. The frames were in the *Louis Quinze* taste but the carving, according to Toussaint Foliot's bill, was in a Classical vein and would therefore appear to have been the very first items of seat-furniture displaying Neo-Classical features to have been made for the *Garde-Meuble*. We do not know if any of these chairs still exist. In 1769 he made a series of richly carved *gueridons* for the Galerie des Glaces at Versailles after a model supplied by Jacques Gondoin. Until at any rate 1784, Foliot continued to execute carving on furniture intended for use at the French Court, probably always after models or drawings provided by Gondoin.

FOLIOT, François-Toussaint, alias François II Foliot. Chair-maker. Born in 1748, the year of his death is not known. The son of François Foliot and Marie-Geneviève Ferret. (See page 177.)

François-Toussaint Foliot lost his parents in 1761. His grandmother, the widow of Nicolas Foliot, became his ward and arranged for him to be apprenticed to the chair-maker François-Moïse Borel. He did not become a *maître* until 1773. He probably took over the management of the parental workshop in the Rue de Cléry which his grandmother or someone else had presumably kept going in the meantime. In 1774 he is found delivering furniture to his uncle, Nicolas-Quinibert Foliot and in 1776 he seems to have taken over the latter's obligations in connection with deliveries to the *Garde-Meuble du Roi*, and continued to provide furniture for royal use until a few years before the Revolution. His furniture was decorated with carved ornament by his uncle, Toussaint Foliot, as had been the case with the furniture made by his other uncle, Nicolas-Quinibert. He did, however, also go to P.-E. Babel for such work. By far the largest proportion of furniture in the *Louis Seize* style made by this family came from the workshops managed by François-Toussaint and most of this was executed after designs by Gondoin.

FOLIOT, François (III). Carver. Born in 1733, the date of his death unknown. The son of Nicolas-Quinibert Foliot. He had a son christened Toussaint. (See page 177.)

François III Foliot was apprenticed to the carver Antoine Robillion in 1748, and became a *maître* in 1754, in which year he also became a member of the Académie de Saint-Luc. He settled in Toulouse, probably before 1764. It appears that his son may have been apprenticed to Nicolas-Quinibert Foliot. Nothing is known about François III Foliot's work but he presumably first practised in one of the family's workshops before departing for Toulouse.

FONTANIEU, Pierre-Elisabeth de. Administrator-General of the Royal Wardrobe. Born about 1730, died in 1784. Son of Gaspard-Moÿse-Augustin de Fontanieu who had been Administrator General before him (1757–67).

Fontanieu took over the post, known as that of *intendant et contrôleur général des meubles de la Couronne*, on his father's death in 1767 and occupied that office until 1783 when he sold it to Thierry de Ville d'Avray. He was elected a member of the Académie des Sciences and Académie d'Architecture. During most of his life as a Court official, he lived in an official apartment in the house occupied by the *Garde-Meuble* which lay on what is now known as the Place de la Concorde. He was also provided with apartments at Versailles, Compiègne and Fontainebleau.

Apart from being an administrator, Fontanieu was something of an artist and was interested in chemistry and mechanical matters. He had his own laboratory and a workshop in which the tools and equipment—which included several lathes—must have been rather special because Louis XVI bought the complete outfit in 1780 for 50,000 livres. In 1770, he published a folio-volume of designs for vases in a somewhat ponderous Neo-Classical style. He envisaged these vases as having been first turned on a lathe, whereafter they were embellished with ornament of various kinds. He therefore illustrated each vase twice—first in its pure form straight from the lathe, and then provided with its decoration (Plates 449 to 452). The title-page informs us that 'Cette collection a été faite, pour servir aux tourneurs et à ceux qui ornent les vases, comme fondeurs et cizeleurs, &c' ('This collection has been made for the assistance of turners at the lathe and for those, like chasers and bronze-founders, who have to decorate vases and urns'). Shortly after the publication of this work, the Sèvres factory put a couple of Fontanieu's designs into production (Plate 288) and, even during the Empire period, the case of a certain form of chimney-clock, of which many examples were to be manufactured, was based on one of his vase designs.

In the introduction to his book, Fontanieu claims that Louis XV, who was himself no mean mechanic and enjoyed working a lathe, had expressed an interest in the designs when some had been shown to him. Fontainieu also wrote a book entitled *L'Art de faire les cristaux colorés imitant les pierres précieuses* (1778–86), and he is said to have left a manuscript for a work *Sur les couleurs en émail.*

The fact that Fontanieu produced his book of vase-designs in 1770 is proof enough of his positive attitude towards Neo-Classicism by that year. To this we may add the little mechanical table which Riesener produced for him in 1771 (Plate 123) and which could very well have been designed by Fontanieu himself, as Pierre Verlet has suggested. On 23rd December of the same year, Fontanieu received a fall-front desk from this same workshop. From the description in the Journal of the *Garde-Meuble*, it would appear that it resembled the one illustrated in Plate 113. From the same source, we learn that Fontanieu obtained some *bronzes d'ameublement* of Neo-Classical form from Pitoin, resembling the fire-dogs shown in Plate 228 which were delivered in February 1772, while he acquired a table-lamp from the workshop of the silversmith, Roëttiers, in March 1774 which must have looked like that shown in Plate 220. As far as his tastes in the realm of seat-furniture is concerned, we only know that Fontanieu acquired a suite with cabriole legs for his new flat on 27th May 1768, so there is no indication that he was responsible for instigating anything new in this particular field.

It fell to Fontanieu to supervise the transition from Rococo to Neo-Classicism in the furnishing of the French Royal palaces. From occasional observations made in accounts rendered by various craftsmen —for example, Peyrotte, Gondoin, Pitoin and the Foliots—it becomes clear that they were in direct contact with Fontanieu and that they received commissions for work direct from him. As an example, one may cite a bill from Gondoin which includes an item for designs and a model for the Dauphine's bed, executed in 1769. From this we learn that 'Le Modelle à deux pouces pour pieds tant Sculpture que peinture et autres ornements y compris les changements faits par ordre de Mr de fontanieux' ('The model has been made to the scale of two inches to the foot, for both the sculpture and the painted decoration, as well as the other ornaments. It incorporates the alterations by M. de Fontanieu'; Arch. Nat., o[1] 3621).

It becomes apparent, moreover, that the designs for all the furnishings produced for the *Garde-Meuble* were kept at Fontanieu's house. Indeed, everything points to the fact that he was no mere administrator of the Royal Wardrobe who ran his office from on high but, rather, that he supervised every detail with great interest. One cannot of course be sure whether or not Fontanieu personally furthered the cause of Neo-Classicism within the field of French Court furnishings, but, from what we know, it seems extremely likely that he did. It is anyway likely, as Verlet pointed out, that he was responsible for the rapid rise of Riesener who of course became the principal cabinet-maker to the French Court and was, moreover, a particularly skilful mechanic.

Verlet, *Mobilier Royal I–III, passim.*

See Plates 123, 220, 228, 288 and 449–52.

FORESTIER, Etienne. Bronze-founder. Born about 1712, died in 1768.

He became a *maître-fondeur en terre et sable* in 1737 and settled in the Rue de la Verrerie, 'at the sign of the Arms of France'. After his death, his widow continued the business which was subsequently taken over by the sons, Etienne-Jean and Pierre-Auguste. The former became a *maître* in 1764.

Forestier is known to have provided bronzes for the famous royal cabinet-maker, André-Charles Boulle, and also mounts for a *table-volante* (a retractable table) made by Joubert for the Château de Choisy. He is also known to have worked with yet another royal cabinet-maker, the famous J.-F. Oeben. Indeed, he cast some of the bronze mounts (to the value of 4,179 livres) for the *Bureau du Roi* after models by Duplessis: these were finished by the time Oeben died in 1763. It would appear, moreover that Forestier was Joubert's regular supplier of bronzes, because among Joubert's creditors in 1771 there was only one bronze-caster, namely Forestier's widow. At that juncture she was owed 734 livres by Joubert.

Arch. Nat., Y 9324 (1st October 1737), Y 9328 (11th November 1764), Minutier Central, CXVII–852 (16th March 1771).
Granges de Surgères, *Artistes Français*, p. 78.
Guiffrey, 'Inventaire de Jean-François Oeben 1763', *NAAF*, 1899, pp. 308 and 354–5.
Salverte, *Ebénistes, passim.*
Watson, *Wrightsman Collection Catalogue*, p. 566.

See Plates 90–3 and 119.

FORTY, Jean-François. Designer and engraver. Perhaps born at Marseilles about 1730–40, died after 1793. Possibly a brother of the painter Jean-Jacques Forty.

Forty is known for his designs for bronze- and wrought-iron work, which he engraved and published as *Oeuvre d'orfèvrerie* and *Oeuvres de serrurerie*. These must have appeared sometime before 1768, for he gives his address as 'Rue de Bourbon proche celle du petit carreau, chez Mr. delanois' and we know that Louis Delanois moved from that address in 1768. About 1790–93, when he published drawings for his *Projet de deux toilettes*, Forty was living in the Rue de l'Hirondelle, near the Place Saint-Michel.

It is claimed that Forty designed the wrought-iron railings of the École Militaire (about 1755), as well as those of the choir in Saint-Germain l'Auxerrois (1763–67) and those at the Palais Royal.

Thieme and Becker, *Künstlerleksikon.*
Watson, *Wrightsman Collection*, p. 567.

See Plates 431–3.

FOULLET, Antoine. Cabinet-maker. Born about 1710, died 24th September 1775. In 1730 or 1731 he married Geneviève Bailleul. One son, Antoine-André, became a clock-maker while the other, Pierre-Antoine, became a cabinet-maker (see separate entry). The daughter Marie-Geneviève married a bronze-founder named André César Vallée.

Foullet was not registered as a master until 1749 when he was almost forty years old. In 1756 he was elected a *juré* in the Guild of Cabinet-Makers. His workshops lay in the Rue Faubourg Saint-Antoine, opposite the junction with the Rue Saint-Nicholas.

According to two inventories made after his death in 1775, Foullet's workshops were comparatively large. They contained at least seven benches and two vices as well as a marquetry-donkey (*scie de marqueterie*).

These inventories show that Foullet had many completed and partly finished pieces of furniture in stock when he died, including forty clock-cases of which several were entirely of bronze without any cabinet-work. He also owned models for making several such bronze cases. From this it would seem that he specialised in the provision of cases for clocks. From a record of debts it is clear that he had provided goods of some kind for the clock-maker Louis Musson in 1775 and for the Swiss clock-maker Abraham Louis Humbert Droz in 1767. Moreover, it appears that the bronze-founder Caron *père* worked for him, as did Claude-Bernard Héban's widow, and a *ciseleur* named Boullanger.

Most of Foullet's known work is in *Louis Quinze* style, but Watson has shown that a commode in the transitional style in the Nationalmuseum in Stockholm bears his stamp and not that of his son, Pierre-Antoine, as had hitherto been supposed. This piece is embellished with mounts of a characteristic form which otherwise are only known on works bearing the son's mark. One may therefore conclude that it was the father who caused these bronzes to be made in the first place; the comparatively large stock of models for bronzes (totalling some 412 lb.) in his stock-room would seem to confirm this. Among this stock were 'cinquante Livres de fonte servant en partie de modèle pour Lunettes postes et autres'; 'lunettes' were presumably the metal rings that retained the glass over clock-faces while 'postes' are Vitruvian scrolls. (The entry may be translated as '50 lb. of castings partly models for lunettes, Vitruvian scroll-patterns, and so forth'.)

From these inventories, it appears that Foullet's clock-cases bore designations deriving from the figures with which they were decorated. For example, we find names like *La dormeuse*, *Le gros enfant*, *La Prudence et la Fidelité*, *Louis Seize*, *Le Repos de Chasse*, *César Auguste*. The clocks are rarely described in any greater detail, however; occasionally we learn that one was 'à la grecque' and another 'à l'antique'.

Arch. Nat., Y 13402 (24th September 1775), and Minutier Central, étude XXVIII (30th September 1775).
Salverte, *Ebénistes*, p. 118.
Watson, *Wallace Collection Furniture*, pp. 147–9.
Watson, *Louis XVI Furniture*, Plate 26.

See Plate 131.

FOULLET, Pierre-Antoine. Cabinet-maker. Active during the third quarter of the eighteenth century. Son of Antoine Foullet (see above) and brother of the clock-maker, Antoine-André Foullet.

Foullet became a *maître* in 1765 and settled in the Rue Faubourg Saint-Antoine. In January 1769 he declared himself bankrupt but was solvent again by the early 1770s. Later he is known to have been in debt to the furniture dealer, Leonard Boudin, to the tune of 5,000 livres; since he was unable to settle this debt, Boudin took him to court and he was sent to the debtors' prison, from which he did not emerge until his father died in 1775, whereupon his share of the inheritance was made over to Boudin by order of the court.

From the bankruptcy papers of 1769, it is clear that Foullet had a considerable stock of models for bronzes and that the founder Claude-Bernard Héban was his regular supplier of mounts. (Héban's widow is known to have worked for the father: see the previous entry.)

Pierre-Antoine Foullet's stamp is well-known from a large number of commodes in the transitional style which have characteristic mounts of Neo-Classical form but, as was pointed out in the previous entry, it may well be that it was his father who was responsible for introducing these models. An exceptionally rich drop-front bureau in the Wallace Collection (Plate 152) must, however, have been made by the son, at least as far as the marquetry is concerned, because the design is taken from an engraving by Delafosse which was not published until after his father's death.

Salverte, *Ebénistes*, p. 118, and Arch. Nat., Y 13402 (24th September 1775).
Watson, *Wallace Collection Furniture*, pp. 147–9.
Geoffrey de Bellaigue, 'Engravings and the French Eighteenth-Century Marqueteur', *The Burlington Magazine*, July 1965, pp. 357–62.
Arch. Nat., Minutier Central, étude XXIV (24th September 1775).
Arch. de la Seine. D^4B^6 carton 34, dossier 1809 (13th January 1769).

See Plates 132, 152–3.

GABRIEL, Ange-Jacques. Architect. Born in 1698, died in 1782. Son of the architect Jacques V. Gabriel.

Gabriel studied under his father and then worked alongside him, inheriting from him the post of *premier architecte du Roi* in 1741. He became Director of the Académie d'Architecture in 1742, in which office he also followed his father. He retired in 1774.

A detailed catalogue of Gabriel's work is to be found in Gallet, *Demeures* (pages 183–4) and elsewhere. Here, we will merely mention those which concern our theme—the Opera building at Versailles (1748–70), the Petit Trianon (1761–68), the École Militaire (1751 et seq.), the Place Louis XV and adjacent buildings (1755 et seq.) and Saint-Hubert (1755–57).

Comte de Fels, *Ange-Jacques Gabriel, Premier architecte du Roi*, Paris, 1924.
Yves Bottineau, *l'Art d'Ange-Jacques Gabriel à Fontainebleau*, Paris, 1962.
Solange Granet, *La Place de la Concorde*, Paris, 1963.
Pierre Verlet, 'Gabriel et la construction de l'Opéra de Versailles', *Le Jardin des Arts*, July 1957, pp. 555–61.
Pierre Pradel, 'Les projets de Gabriel pour l'Opéra de Versailles', *Gaz.d.B.A.*, 1937, pp. 109–25.
Alain Gruber, 'L'Opéra de Versailles est-il l'oeuvre de Gabriel?', *Revue de l'Art*, No. 13, 1971, pp. 87–97.

See Plates 19, 21, 50–3, 55, 61 and 66–7.

GARNIER, Pierre. Cabinet-maker. Born about 1725, died in 1800. Son of François Garnier who was also a cabinet-maker.

Garnier became a *maître* in 1742. His workshops were in the Rue Neuve des Petits Champs.

He was one of the craftsmen who is definitely known to have turned out furniture of a Neo-Classical character at a very early date. According to a notice in *L'Avantcoureur* of 5th October 1761, it was Garnier who had executed a piece of furniture designed by the architect Charles De Wailly which was exhibited at the *Salon* in that year. De Wailly had of course marked classicising tastes at this period. It is also known, from letters written by Marigny to Garnier, that this cabinet-maker had a talent for designing bronze mounts, and indeed Marigny asked Garnier to design some for a piece of furniture he had. Marigny bought several items of furniture from Garnier, including copies of a games-table that Marigny had bought for himself in London.

Salverte, *Ebénistes*, pp. 125–6.
Vial, Marcel and Girodie, p. 205.
S. Eriksen, 'Early Neo-Classicism in French Furniture', *Apollo*, November 1963, pp. 344–51.

See Plates 97–9.

GEOFFRIN, Madame Marie-Thérèse, née Rodet. Born in 1699, died in 1777. In 1713, she married François Geoffrin (1653–1749), administrator and part-owner of the royal glassworks at Saint-Gobain. Her daughter became Marquise de la Ferté-Imbault.

It was in the 1740s that Madame Geoffrin first set up as hostess of a *salon* for writers and men of learning. Every Wednesday, those invited came to her house in the Rue Saint-Honoré (the present No. 372) to take part in gatherings over which she presided, where reading aloud and high-brow conversation were the principal items in the programme, although the guests were also provided with refreshments. About 1750, she extended her activities by starting to hold similar gatherings on Mondays, to which she invited artists, sculptors and architects. She also invited distinguished foreigners who lived in Paris or happened to be passing through the French capital; these apparently might attend either the Monday or the Wednesday *salons*, presumably depending on their special interests. Her house, at any rate, became a cultural centre of an extremely cosmopolitan nature—a *bureau d'esprit* which has since been described as 'le royaume de la rue Saint-Honoré' ('the Kingdom of the Rue Saint-Honoré') of which Madame Geoffrin was the uncrowned queen. As Bachaumont wrote, 'Les étrangers surtout croiroient n'avoir rien vu en France, s'ils ne s'étoient fait présenter chez cette Virtuose célèbre . . .' ('It is above all foreigners who feel they have seen nothing in France unless they have been taken to meet this virtuous and celebrated woman'; *Mémoires secrets*, 4th May 1766). Among the important foreign guests was Stanislas-Auguste Poniatowski who, as a young man stayed in Paris in 1753–54 and subsequently became King of Poland (1764). Madame Geoffrin kept up a correspondence with him for many years and appointed herself his artistic adviser when the young King planned to modernise the Palace at Warsaw, with the aid of French artists, after his ascension to the throne.

The list of names of those attending Madame Geoffrin's *salons* is almost endless and includes many famous names. Among those of interest to us in the present connection, one should mention the Marquis de Marigny, Lalive de Jully and the Comte de Caylus. The last was a friend of long standing and, according to Madame de la Ferté-Imbault, was responsible for persuading Madame Geoffrin to confine her Monday gatherings to people with artistic interests. It was probably at one of these *salons* that Caylus so loudly praised Lalive de Jully's Neo-Classical furniture (Plates 85 to 89), and it is claimed (by Dufort de Cheverny, *Mémoires*, page 117) that it was there that the Marquis de Marigny 'acquit un jugement sûr et que, malgré lui, il épura son goût' ('acquired his good eye and, in spite of himself, he clarified his taste').

Madame Geoffrin seems to have had a special weakness for the work of François Boucher—she owned nine of his paintings—but, otherwise, her tastes in artistic matters seem to have coincided more with that of Lalive and Caylus. Thus she had ten paintings by Vien in her collection, eight by Vernet, six by Drouais, five by Lagrenée and eleven by Hubert Robert. Most of these painters were among her Monday guests, as was the sculptor Bouchardon—a close friend of Caylus—and also the architect Soufflot.

From a perusal of Lazare Duvaux's *Livre-Journal*, in which Madame Geoffrin's name occurs every now and then between 1749 and 1760, it would appear that she did not have particularly unusual tastes for that period. She bought a certain amount of Vincennes and Sèvres porcelain from him, as well as some Meissen and some Chinese pieces. She also bought a pair of bronze candelabra, a clock with a boulle-work case, a commode with a pair of *encoignures* 'Plaquées en ancien lacq' ('veneered with ancient Oriental lacquer') and embellished with gilt bronzes.

Thanks to some well-known drawings and a painting by Hubert Robert (reproduced in *L'Oeil*, September 1957, pages 54 and 57), we know that at least two of the rooms in her house about 1770 were decorated in a Neo-Classical spirit although the *décor* was extremely simple. All her paintings had frames in the *Louis Seize* taste. The sconces in one room seem to be in the Rococo style as are some of the chairs. A contemporary eye-witness said her furniture was 'tous de forme ancienne, artistique et commode â la fois' ('all of a Classical form, graceful and comfortable at the same time'). The chairs depicted by Hubert

Robert may of course have been old by the time he illustrated them and they may have been made by the chair-maker J.-B. Le Rouge who was her regular supplier. His workshop closed down in 1763. After that she dealt with Georges Jacob, who was to become famous. She also dealt with cabinet-maker Pierre Garnier who sometimes worked for the Marquis de Marigny. He worked in the Neo-Classical taste at an early date but could equally well turn out pieces in the Rococo style.

We know very little about the lay-out of her apartment as yet. However, by 1752 she had a *salle à manger*—a dining-room—which was quite exceptional a phenomenon in Paris at that date (not so, in England, where dining-rooms had been common in even quite modest houses from the mid-seventeenth century onwards). This room was faced with scagliola by the stuccador Louis Mansiaux who is known to have carried out several commissions elsewhere in the Classical taste.

Madame Geoffrin is known to have supervised the ordering of paintings for the new rooms in the Warsaw Palace and these were supplied by artists like Boucher, Van Loo, Vien, Hallé and Lagrenée, all of whom belonged to her circle!

It is interesting to note that, on 19th March 1774, the Parisian *ébéniste* Topino sent his colleague Héricourt a piece of furniture which he described in his ledger as 'un secraitaire en pente a la geofrin'. It is not certain in what way this particular form distinguished itself from other 'bureaux en pente' or why it was named after Madame Geoffrin.

Nouvelle Biographie Générale, vol. 20, columns 1–6.
Charles de Mouy, ed., *Correspondance du Roi Stanislas-Auguste Poniatowski et de Madame Geoffrin* (1764–1777) . . . , 1875.
Marquis de Ségur, *Le royaume de la rue Saint-Honoré, Madame Geoffrin et sa fille*, 1925.
Georges de Lastic Saint-Jal, 'La reine de la rue Saint-Honoré', *L'Oeil*, September, 1957, pp. 50–7.
Stanislas Lorentz, 'Victor Louis et Varsovie', in the catalogue to the exhibition of the same name held at Bordeaux and in Paris, 1958.

See Plates 297–8.

GERMAIN, François-Thomas. Goldsmith and bronze-worker. Born in 1726, died in 1791. Son of Thomas Germain, the famous goldsmith of the Rococo period.

Germain first learned his trade under his father, whose title of *orfèvre et sculpteur du Roi*, and whose workshops in the Louvre he took over in 1748—the year in which he himself became a *maître* at the age of only twenty-two. He went bankrupt in 1764 yet somehow managed to continue working both for the French and foreign courts.

At one stage Germain had 120 men working for him and his production was enormous. Many pieces survive; the largest collections are in Lisbon and Leningrad. Much of this work is in the Rococo style but he was also one of the first, perhaps even *the* first, Parisian goldsmith to accept Neo-Classicism.

Germain is also known to have worked in bronze. In Count Bernstorff's very splendid house in Copenhagen, which was furnished with many works of decorative-art imported from Paris, stands an elaborate chimney-piece with bronze ornaments dated 1756. According to contemporary documents, this was partially copied from a chimney-piece executed by Germain two years earlier for the Palais Royal. There were also four large bronze sconces bearing the date 1756 in the Rosebery sale (Sotheby's, 17th April 1964, lot 18) which bore the inventory mark of the Château de Compiègne. And at the Louvre is a pair of fire-dogs dated 1757. All these works in bronze bear François-Thomas Germain's full signature. Moreover, in 1766 several announcements appeared in the *Mercure de France* stating that Germain was offering for sale various ornamental vases with ormolu mounts.

G. Bapst, *Les Germain*, Paris, 1887.
Mario Krohn, *Frankrigs og Danmarks kunstneriske Forbindelser i det 18. Aarhundrede*, vol. I, p. 77ff., Copenhagen, 1922.
V. Champier and G. Roger Sandoz, *Le Palais-Royal*, Paris, 1900, vol. I., p. 362.

See Plates 27, 202, 244, 247 and 257–60 and Colour Plate Gii.

GERMAIN, Pierre, called *le Romain*. Goldsmith and engraver. Born in 1703 at Villeneuve-les-Avignon, died in Paris in 1783. Son of a baker and apparently not related to the famous family of goldsmiths.

He was apprenticed in his home-town but went to Paris about 1726 and was immediately taken into the workshop of Thomas Germain (father of François-Thomas Germain), the *orfèvre du Roi*, where he worked on such important commissions as the toilet-set made for Queen Marie Leczinska. He left Paris in September 1729 and went to Rome, where he remained some three years. On his return, he came to work for Jacques Roëttiers and later for the latter's father-in-law, Nicolas Besnier. Germain became a *maître* in 1744 and was then living in the Place du Carrousel; he was living on the Quai des Orfèvres by 1759. In July 1757, he was elected *garde* of the Corps des Marchands Orfèvres for the usual two years. A close friend was Ange-Joseph Aubert, *jouaillier du roi*.

Between 1748 and 1751, he published a number of engravings of goldsmiths' work, all in the Rococo style. In 1765, however, he collaborated with Thomas Chamelier in producing a toilet-set for the Spanish Court in the Neo-Classical taste, after designs by Ph. Caffieri.

A. Marcel, 'L'Orfèvre Pierre Germain dit de Romain', in *Mémoires de l'Académie de Vaucluse*, 1916, pp. 229–60.
G. Bapst, *Les Germain*, Paris, 1887.
Arch. Nat., Y 9328 (4th July 1757).

GODEFROY, Antoine. Upholsterer and furniture-dealer.

In 1760, he became a *maître et marchand-tapissier* and in 1764 *petit juré* of his Guild. He lived in the Rue de Cléry by Montmartre.

No work of Godefroy is now known but he delivered some chairs to the Marquis de Marigny in 1763 and these chairs had legs 'à gaines avec des plintes caré [sic]' (i.e., with tapering legs, either with square blocks on top or with square, plinth-like feet) which would seem to suggest they were in the Neo-Classical style. Godefroy was also patronised by Madame de Pompadour between 1762 and 1764, during which short period he sold her furniture to the value of some 150,000 livres for her various houses. He would seem to have been a man of some importance.

Arch. Nat., Y 9328 (15th November 1760 and 7th September 1764).
Jean Cordey, *Inventaire des biens de Madame de Pompadour*, Paris, 1939, pp. 236–7.
Svend Eriksen, 'Marigny and "le goût grec" ', *The Burlington Magazine*, March 1962, p. 98.

GONDOIN, Jacques. Architect and furniture-designer. Born in 1737 at Saint-Ouen, died in Paris in 1818.

He won the 2nd Prix d'Architecture in 1758 and was in Rome between 1761 and 1763. In 1766 he went on a study-tour in Holland and England. He worked for the *Garde-Meuble de la Couronne* in Paris from 1767 and became, probably on the death of Alexis Peyrotte in 1769, *dessinateur du mobilier de la Couronne*, a post he held until 1784. He was paid anything from 200 to 1,500 livres for each design or model that he provided. In 1769, he was living in the Rue de la Harpe, the present Boulevard Saint-Michel.

Gondoin's most outstanding architectural work is the Neo-Classical École de Chirurgie in Paris, built between 1769 and 1775. He also designed the column in the Place Vendôme (1806).

Judging from the surviving accounts, it seems clear that while Gondoin did not provide designs for cabinet-furniture, he was responsible for every ornamental detail of the carved furniture—notably chairs, *canapés*, and beds—which were executed for the Court from the time of his appointment as a royal designer in 1769 and possibly even as early as 1767, in which case he may also have designed the furniture required for the Petit Trianon. As far as the art of furniture in eighteenth-century France is concerned, Gondoin can thus be seen to have filled a place of the greatest importance. He not only provided full-scale and detailed designs '*nécessaire au Sculpteur Menuisier &c*' ('of the sort required by the carver, joiner, etc.') but also models in wood and in wax, usually to a scale of 1:6. He also drew patterns for both woven and embroidered chair-covers, etc., and actually went to Lyons for a month in 1769 in order to compose designs for some silk-materials. Gondoin's first major commission in this line was the complete suite of furniture for Marie Antoinette, who was to be the new Dauphine, in 1769–70. In 1769, he also designed one of a series of twenty-four *guéridons* to go in the Galerie des Glaces at Versailles. The best-known of his surviving works are the six chairs, now at Fontainebleau, which Verlet has shown were produced in the Foliot workshops in 1774 for the Salon des Jeux at Versailles. It is also likely that Gondoin designed the chairs Louis Delanois made in 1775 for the École de Chirurgie (see above), of which a handful are still preserved *in situ*.

Guiffrey, 'Congés accordés à des artistes français pour travailler à l'étranger', *NAAF*, 1878, p. 45.
Guiffrey, 'Correspondance des artistes français travaillant à l'étranger', *NAAF*, 1878, p. 76.
Verlet, *Mobilier Royal I–III.*
Gallet, *Demeures.*
Kimball, *Creation*, p. 212.
Arch. Nat., o^{1} 3619, 1 (Bardou's accounts for 1767); o^{1} 3621ff. (Gondoin's accounts 1769ff.); o^{1} 3279, 2–3.

See Plates 84 and 180.

GOURDIN, Jean-Baptiste. Chair-maker. Active in the third quarter of the eighteenth century. Son of the chair-maker, Jean Gourdin, and brother of Michel Gourdin.

Gourdin became a *maître* in 1748 and had a workshop in the Rue de Cléry. Characteristic of his production are chairs of Rococo form but decorated with Neo-Classical carved ornament.

Salverte, *Ebénistes*, p. 137.
Watson, *Wrightsman Catalogue*, p. 547.

GOURDIN, Michel. Chair-maker. Active in the third quarter of the eighteenth century. Brother of Jean-Baptiste Gourdin.

Michel Gourdin became a *maître* in 1752 and, like his brother, also established himself in the Rue de Cléry. He may in fact have inherited his father's house in this street, which was situated between the Rue du Petit Carreau and the Rue Saint-Philippe. Michel Gourdin is likewise known for his chairs of Rococo form that are decorated with Classical carved ornament. A set of chairs in the Wallace Collection (F. 179–84), together with a similar chair now in the Museum at Saint-Omer, provide clear proof of the high quality of his workmanship.

Salverte, *Ébénistes*, p. 137.
Watson, *Wallace Collection Catalogue*, pp. 100–1.
Preston Remington, *Metropolitan Museum Studies*, November 1929, p. 68.
Connaissance des Arts, ed., *Les Ebénistes du XVIIIe siècle*, Paris, 1963, pp. 170–3.

See Plate 163.

GOUTHIÈRE, Pierre. Maker of bronzes. Born in 1732 at Bar-sur-Aube, between Chaumont and Troyes, died in Paris in 1813 or in 1814.

Three days before becoming a *maître doreur-ciseleur* in April 1758, Gouthière married the widow of the gilder François Cériset over whose shop was at the sign of the Golden Buckle ('à la boucle d'or') on the Quai Pelletier, now the Quai de Gesvres, he thereby gained mastery. In 1780 he built an ultra-modern house, designed by the architect Joseph Metivier, in the Rue Pierre Bullet. However, he was declared bankrupt in 1788 and died in poverty in a home for the aged—the Hospice des Petits-menages, in the Faubourg Saint-Germain.

The first record we have of work by Gouthière refers to gilding—to the tune of 18,000 livres—executed for the goldsmith, F.-Th. Germain in 1764–65. This concerned a commission for the Portuguese Court—probably the toilet-set now in the Museum in Lisbon. In 1767, Gouthière was appointed *doreur ordinaire des Menus Plaisirs*. In 1769–70, he is found making the bronze mounts for Marie Antoinette's jewel-cabinet which had been designed by F.-J. Belanger.

In 1770–71, he delivered gilt bronze ornaments, after designs by Ledoux, for Mme du Barry's Pavillon de Louveciennes, for sums totalling over 100,000 livres; while between 1772 and 1774 he delivered a wide range of objects designed by A.-J. Gabriel for the same lady's rooms at Fontainebleau.

The principal private patron of Gouthière was the Duc d'Aumont, director of the *Menus Plaisirs*, who commissioned work from this craftsman to the value of over 100,000 livres in the period between 1772 and 1782—the year the Duc died. In 1773 the Duc tried to have a couple of tables shown at the *Salon* but without success: these were of porphyry set with gilded mounts made by Gouthière. The Duc's daughter, the Duchesse de Mazarin (died 1781), was also among Gouthière's chief patrons, so many of whom were notoriously bad at paying their bills.

Some, at any rate, of the first bronzes made by Gouthière for the Duc d'Aumont were drawn by Bellanger and modelled by a certain De la Planche. The bronzes he executed for the Duchesse de Mazarin were modelled after drawings by Bellanger.

NAAF, 1906, p. 4.
Arch. Nat., Y 9328 (13th April 1758).
Jacques Robiquet, *Gouthière*, Paris, 1912.
Watson, *Wallace Collection Catalogue*, pp. 86 and 121–4.
Guiffrey, *Les Caffieri*, Paris, 1877, pp. 156–65.
Jean Stern, *F. J. Bellanger*, vol. I., Paris, 1930, pp. 8, 46, 153–4.
Rudolf H. Wackernagel, *Der französische Krönungswagen*, Berlin, 1966.
Geneviève Levallet-Haug, *Claude-Nicolas Ledoux*, Paris, 1934, *passim*.

See Plate 243.

GOYER, Jean. Cabinet-maker. Probably born about 1725–30; date of death unknown. Son of the cabinet-maker, François Goyer (d.1763) and his wife, Marie-Barbe-Charlotte, née Ledoux (d.1768). Cousin of the clock-maker Gabriel-François Goyer who worked at Mannheim.

Salverte, in his biography of François Goyer and the son Jean, confused the careers of the two men because he did not know when the father died. The indictment Salverte discovered in the Archives Nationales (Y 14092, 28th November 1765), in which no Christian names are given, in reality concerns the son and not the father. Young Goyer was accused by the Guild of Bronze-Founders of wrongfully engaging bronze-founders in his workshops—which was in fact the case. He was also on bad terms with his mother who called him 'un fils ingrat' (a wickedly ungrateful son) and reported that he had had her imprisoned for several weeks; it is not stated on what grounds but she disinherited him as a result. The father also seems to have been a trouble-maker (cf. Arch. Nat., Y 10989, 4th May 1745).

Goyer was serving an apprenticeship with the founder, Jean-Joseph de Saint-Germain in 1745. He must subsequently have left that trade because he became a *maître-ébéniste* in 1760. He set up business at a workshop in the Rue de Charenton, opposite the Hôtel des Mousquetaires. It was there that, in 1765, the police called on him in connection with the case just mentioned. They did so on the instigation of, among others, his former master, de Saint-Germain, who was now a *juré* of the Bronze-founders' Guild. The police found various mounts of bronze at Goyer's workshops which he maintained had been made by reputable founders, masters of the Bronze-founders' Guild—including Héban and the two Carons, father and son. Nonetheless—the police arrested several people including a *cizeleur* named Jean-Pierre Le Marchant who was found working on a 'guirlande de fonte à usage de Pendule' on Goyer's account.

Jean Goyer's stamp is to be found on, amongst other furniture, the strange secretaire shown in

Plate 105 and on the clock illustrated in Plate 107. We do not know if he was responsible for the design of these pieces. However, considering their unusual mounts and his close connection with the bronze-founding business, it is not inconceivable that he had a hand in their conception.

Salverte, *Ebénistes*, p. 138.
Arch. Nat., Minutier Central, étude XXVIII (29th August 1763; 21st November 1764; 21st January 1768).

GUIBERT, Honoré. Sculptor and wood-carver. Born at Avignon about 1720, died in Paris in 1791. He married a sister of the painter Joseph Vernet in 1744.

Guibert is referred to as 'sculpteur du duc de Parme' about 1752. While still living in Avignon, in 1755, he was given commissions by the *Bâtiments du Roi* on the recommendation of Vernet who arranged that Guibert should carve the frames for six of Vernet's views of French harbours. Guibert worked in Paris from 1760 and became *sculpteur ordinaire des bâtiments du Roi*. In 1763 he became a *maître-sculpteur* in the Parisian guild and a member of the Académie de Saint-Luc. He lived in the Saint-Sulpice quarter.

Guibert carried out a great deal of work for the Court—mostly picture-frames and *boiseries* (carved wall-panelling). It is clear that most of these works, apart from the frames made for Vernet's paintings and a few other early productions, were in the Neo-Classical taste. This was at any rate the case with the frames he executed in 1760 or 1761 which are known from sketches by Gabriel de Saint-Aubin. Judging by a notice in *L'Avantcoureur*, it appears that Guibert had himself designed the frames. Amongst other commissions executed for the royal palaces, mention should be made of the carved stone ornaments he made for the façades of the Petit Trianon (1764–65), and the *boiseries* of the *Salon de Compagnie* in the same building (1766–67). He also carved decorations in wood for Madame de Pompadour's Château de Menars (before 1764), for the Opera at Versailles (1768–69), the Château de Choisy and the Château de Bellevue—the latter two both, of course, used by the Marquise. Most, if not all, of the works for the Court must have been executed under the direction of the architect Gabriel and perhaps even after sketches provided by him. According to Verlet, it would seem that Guibert carried out the carving on the large cupboards in the *Garde-Meuble de la Couronne* buildings in the Place Louis XV (now the Place de la Concorde) in 1773–74. These were to house the Garde-Meuble's most precious treasures. From about 1768–70, Guibert worked on the Hôtel de Lassay for the Prince de Condé.

Very much less is known about the work Guibert executed for private patrons. He is known to have made a shop-front in the Rue Saint-Denis in about 1761 where the doorway was 'd'une architecture Grecque'. He produced a sign for a shop in the Rue Saint-Honoré in 1764 which consisted of an obelisk some forty feet high decorated with hieroglyphs, and he is said to have made a case for a clock, the movement of which was produced by Le Paute in 1765. Moreover, he provided *boiseries* and picture-frames for the Court at Warsaw between 1765 and 1768, partly in collaboration with Coulonjon, to a value of 110,457 livres.

A portrait of Guibert by Greuze was shown at the *Salon* in 1765 (No. 119).

L'Avantcoureur, 7th September 1761, 16th April 1764, 4th March 1765.
Vial, Marcel and Girodie, vol. I, p. 231 and vol. II, pp. 240–1.
Thieme and Becker, *Künstlerleksikon*, vol. XV.
Hautecoeur, *Histoire, seconde moitié*, p. 115.
NAAF., vol. VIII, pp. 234–9.
Verlet, *Mobilier Royal II*, p. 31.
Verlet, *Versailles*, pp. 444 and 589.
Author's article, 'Marigny and "le goût grec"', *Burlington Magazine*, March 1962, pp. 96–101.
F. Souchal, *Les Slodtz*, 1967, pp. 687–8.
Arch. Nat., Y 9328 (26th November 1763) and Z[1J] 921.

See Plates 66–7, 345–8.

GUICHARD, Joseph-Nicolas. Wood-carver. Active between 1765 and 1786.

He was registered as a *maître-sculpteur* in 1765 and became a member of the Académie de Saint-Luc. He was living in the Rue Bergère in the Faubourg Montmartre in 1786.

In 1770 he carved decoration on seat-furniture and panelling made for Madame du Barry's Pavillon de Louveciennes: the frames of the furniture had been made in the workshops of Louis Delanois. Nothing else is known of his work.

Arch. Nat., Y 9328 (7th November 1765).
Vial, Marcel and Girodie, vol. I, p. 232.
Charles Vatel, *Histoire de Madame Du Barry*, vol. II, Paris, 1883, pp. 517–49.

See Plates 172–3.

HAUPT, Georg. Cabinet-maker. Born in Stockholm in 1741, died there in 1784. Son of the carpenter, Elias Haupt, whose father was likewise a carpenter of German origin.

Haupt became a journeyman in 1759. Early in 1760, he set out to study his trade in Germany—as was the common practice among Swedish journeymen. In 1763, he was in Holland and, that year or the next, found himself in Paris, where he is thought to have worked for Simon Oeben. At the Institut Géographique National in Paris is a Neo-Classical writing-desk inscribed 'George Haupt Suedois a fait cet bureau à Chanteloup 1767' ('The Swede Georg Haupt has made this desk at Chanteloup 1767') and bearing an inventory mark which may be that of the Duc de Choiseul. One may thereby conclude that Haupt, like Simon Oeben, was in the Duc's service. Moreover, it is clear that he had lived at Chanteloup the year before, since he signed the register in the capacity of god-father at Saint-Denis d'Amboise, the local parish church at Chanteloup, on 18th December 1766.

In January 1768 he went to London where he is stated to have made furniture after designs by his countryman, Sir William Chambers. A small satinwood table is recorded as bearing the inscription 'Cette table a été commandé et desinée par Mr. Chambers. Premier Architect de sa Majesté Brittanique, et Executée par son très humble serviteur—George Haupt, Swedois London le 4 de Fevrier 1769' ('This table has been ordered and designed by M. Chambers, Premier Architect to His Britannic Majesty, and was made by his humble servant—the Swede, Georg Haupt, London 4th February 1769'), but its present location is not known. About New Year 1770, he returned to Stockholm, where he became the principal royal cabinet-maker. In 1773–74 he produced the large cabinet for mineral specimens executed after a drawing by the Swedish Court Designer, J. E. Rehn, which the King of Sweden presented to the Prince de Condé and which can still be seen in the Musée Condé at Chantilly.

Marshall Lagerquist, *Georg Haupt, ébéniste du Roi*, Stockholm, 1952.
Marshall Lagerquist and Madeleine Jarry, 'Note sur une table de l'ébéniste suédois George Haupt découverte en France', *Revue de l'Art Français*, 1953, pp. 239–40.
Marshall Lagerquist, 'Haupt i Paris', *Fataburen Nordiska Museets och Skansens årsbok*, 1954, pp. 97–104.
Raoul de Broglie, 'Le meuble minéralogique suédois de Chantilly', *Gazette des Beaux-Arts*, 1963, pp. 2–16.
Tours, Archives Départementales, Registre de la paroisse de Saint-Denis d'Amboise, 18th December 1766.
R. Edwards and P. Macquoid, *Dictionary of English Furniture*, 1954 edn., article on Haupt.
R. Edwards and M. Jourdain, *Georgian Cabinet-Makers*, 1944, p. 105.
John Hayward, 'Christopher Fuhrlogh, an Anglo-Swedish cabinet-maker', *The Burlington Magazine*, December 1969, pp. 648–55.
John Harris, *Sir William Chambers*, London, 1970.

See Plates 114–15.

HERVIEU, Louis-Barthelemy. Bronze-founder and -chaser (*ciseleur*). Active during the second half of the eighteenth century.

In 1749 Hervieu became a *maître-fondeur en terre et sable*; while in 1761, together with Philippe Caffieri, he was elected a *juré* of the Parisian Guild of Bronze-casters for a period of two years. He was co-signatory of the Bronze-workers' Copyright Resolution of 21st April 1766. He had a workshop on the second floor of a house in the Rue de Buci.

Hervieu is famed for having carried out the delicate chasing of many of the bronzes on Oeben and Riesener's *Bureau du Roi* which had been cast by Etienne Forestier after models by Duplessis. Later, he collaborated with Philippe Caffieri who, at his death in 1774, owed Hervieu 6,313 livres. In 1779 he was engaged in chasing bronzes intended for the Chapelle de la Vierge in the church of Saint-Sulpice.

Arch. Nat., Y 9326 (24th March 1749), Y 9328 (14th July 1761).
Ibid., Minutier Central, XXXIV, liasse 697 (14th October 1774).
Guiffrey, 'Inventaire de Jean-François Oeben 1763', *NAAF*, 1899, pp. 298–367.
Journal de Paris, 23rd April 1779 (index by Granges de Surgères).
Lespinasse, *Les métiers et corporations de la Ville de Paris*, vol. II, p. 433.
Verlet, *Mobilier Royal II*, pp. 68–9.

See Plates 90–3.

HEURTAUT, Nicolas. Chair-maker. Born in 1720; the year of his death is not known, but he was still active in April 1771. Presumably the father of the chair-maker Pierre-Nicolas Heurteaux.

Heurtaut became a *maître* in 1755 and established himself in the Rue de Bourbon Villeneuve where Louis Delanois later also set up his workshop.

Most of Heurtaut's richly-carved pieces of seat-furniture are in the Rococo style (e.g. chairs in the Metropolitan Museum, the Frick Collection and at Blenheim Palace). However, in some few cases his work displays marked Neo-Classical features, albeit with Rococo undertones—e.g. four arm chairs in the Wrightsman Collection, and seat-furniture supplied for the Château de la Roche-Guyon covered with Gobelins tapestry. Part of the latter set was recently acquired by the Musée du Louvre.

Salverte, *Ébénistes*, pp. 153–4, and Arch. Nat., Y 12058 (19th April 1771).
Watson, *Wrightsman Collection*, pp. 16, 20, 547–8.
Connaissance des Arts, ed., *Les ébénistes du XVIIIe siècle français*, pp. 122–7.
Serge Grandjean, 'Département des objets d'art', *La Revue du Louvre et des musées de France*, 1967, p. 326.
Pierre Verlet, information supplied personally to the author.

See Plates 166–7, 170, 182 and Colour Plate E.

HUBERT, Laurent. Sculptor and bronze-maker. Born about 1720–30, still active in 1776 and dead before 1786.

Hubert became a *maître-sculpteur* in 1749, and showed works at the Académie de Saint-Luc's exhibitions in 1752, 1753 and 1756. Several of his drawings are known, amongst which is one datable to about 1764: these are all in an early version of the Neo-Classical style. In 1763 he put an advertisement in *L'Avantcoureur*, in which he announced he had in stock 'bronzes pour la décoration des appartements' which were 'dans le goût du bel antique' ('ornamental bronzes for the decoration of apartments . . . in the best Antique Taste'). And in the *Mercure de France* in 1767 he ran an advertisement for bronzes 'pour servir à la décoration des appartemens, soit en girandoles, en bras de cheminées, feux & flambeaux de toute espèce & de toute grandeur, ornés avec des figures' as well as 'boëtes de pendules' ('for the decoration of apartments, including candelabra, candle-branches for the chimney-piece, candle-sticks of every kind and size, [some ?] decorated with figures . . . clock cases'). Moreover, he claimed that he 'fournit les Ambassadeurs pour la partie des bronzes, & décore les appartemens dans le dernier goût' ('furnishes ambassadors with their requirements in the way of bronze ornaments, and decorates apartments in the latest fashion'). He lived on the Ile Saint-Louis, on the Quai d'Orléans.

A large centre-piece (*surtout-de-table*) of gilded bronze in the Ashmolean Museum, Oxford, may be tentatively ascribed to Hubert on the basis of a comparison with his extant drawings.

Guiffrey, *Académie de Saint-Luc*, pp. 325–6.
L'Avantcoureur, 21st February 1763, pp. 125–6.
Mercure de France, January 1767, p. 191, and April 1767, pp. 160–1 (index by E. Deville).
Almanach des Artistes, 1777, p. 100.
Richard P. Wunder, *Architectural and ornamental drawings of the 16th to the early 19th century in the collection of the University of Michigan Museum of Art*, Ann Arbor, 1965, nos. 32–33.

JACQUES, Maurice. Painter. Born in 1712, died in 1784.

Jacques became a *maître-peintre* in 1755 and was then elected to the Académie de Saint-Luc. From 1756 (and perhaps even earlier), he was working as a designer of ornament for the Manufacture des Gobelins, where he was responsible for many of the tapestry border-patterns, often in close collaboration with François Boucher and under the supervision of Soufflot. Amongst his most important compositions were the cartoons for the famous tapestries with oval medallions containing scenes drawn by Boucher, the general conception of which had been Soufflot's. These cartoons were used in the low-warp ateliers at the Gobelins which were run by a Scotsman named Jacques Nielson. He was a friend of Robert Adam's and it was partly due to this connection that so many sets of these particular tapestries found their way into English country-houses. Jacques published (before 1766) a series of engravings of vases which were frequently copied on furniture, gold boxes, etc., not only in France but also in England and elsewhere.

Fenaille, *Etat général des tapisseries de la Manufacture des Gobelins.*
Guiffrey, *Académie de Saint-Luc*, p. 330.
Jean Mondain-Monval, *Correspondance de Soufflot avec les directeurs des Bâtiments concernant la Manufacture des Gobelins* (1756–1780), Paris, 1918, *passim.*
Eileen Harris, *Robert Adam and the Gobelins*, *Apollo*, April 1962, pp. 100–6.
Arch. Nat., Y 9328 (22nd October 1755).
Edith Appleton Standen, *The Croome Court Tapestries, and Decorative Art from the Samuel H. Kress Collection at The Metropolitan Museum of Art*, New York, 1964, pp. 16–17.
Geoffrey de Bellaigue, 'English Marquetry's Debt to France', *Country Life*, 16th and 20th June 1968.

See Plates 36, 119, 132, 135, 140, 153 and 391–5.

JARDIN, Nicolas-Henri. Architect. Born in 1720 at St. Germain des Noyers, died in Paris in 1799.

Jardin won the Grand Prix d'Architecture in 1741 and, from December 1744 until November 1748, stayed as a stipendiary at the French Academy in Rome. On his return to Paris he worked as assistant to the architect Tannevot. He was in Denmark from 1755 until 1771, a visit interrupted by journeys to Paris in 1762–63, and to England, Holland and Belgium in 1768–69. From 1771 until he died he lived in Paris.

While in Rome, he came under the influence of Piranesi. He introduced the Neo-Classical taste to Denmark where, already in 1757, he executed a dining-room of Classical character in the town-house of Count A. G. Moltke, one of the four buildings now comprising the Amalienborg Palace in Copenhagen. In Denmark, he also built Marienlyst, a summer-residence near Elsinore (1759–62), and some military barracks in Copenhagen (1765–69). After returning to Paris, he was responsible for the Hôpital de Lagny (1772–86), amongst other buildings.

Weilbachs Kunstnerleksikon, vol. II, Copenhagen, 1949, pp. 27–9.
C. Elling, *Jardin i Rom*, Copenhagen, 1943.
Hautecoeur, *Histoire*, *seconde moitié*, pp. 209–12.
Mercure de France, June 1766 (laudatory poem in Jardin's honour).

See Plates 11 and 30.

JOUBERT, Gilles. Cabinet-maker. Born in 1689, died in 1775. Son of Pierre Joubert, a joiner and of Antionette Thérèse Delanois, or Lanois. Married Michelle, daughter of Edmond Collet, also a cabinet-maker, in 1714. Joubert had a younger brother, Pierre, who was a joiner like his father, and had a daughter married to the cabinet-maker Louis Peridiez.

In 1702, at the age of about thirteen, Joubert was apprenticed to Pierre Dasneau for two and a half years. Dasneau was a *marqueteur en pieces de rapport* (marquetry maker). When Joubert married in 1714, he called himself *tabletier* (lit. maker of tablets but, in fact, a branch of cabinet-making producing games-boards, fitted dressing-cases, canteens and other small wares usually involving especially delicate crafts-manship in wood, metal, ivory etc.). It is not known when Joubert became a *maître*, but it must have been in about 1715. He was elected to act as a *syndic* for his Guild and in 1771 was entitled *doyen de la commu-nauté des ébénistes* (doyen of the Parisian cabinet-makers). During his apprenticeship, he lived with his parents in the Rue Saint-Nicolas in the Faubourg Saint-Antoine. In 1714 he was living in the Rue de la Savaterie on the Ile de la Cité, and in 1749 at the corner of Rue Traversine (now the Rue de l'Echelle) and the Rue Saint-Honoré. In 1757 he rented a house nearby—in the Rue Sainte-Anne, where he lived for the rest of his life.

Joubert was the leading supplier of furniture to the French Court during the second half of the reign of Louis XV. The first delivery was made by him in 1748 and he worked for the Royal Household for well-nigh twenty-five years, delivering in that time over 4,000 pieces of furniture of various kinds, ranging from simple bidets to richly-decorated desks and commodes. During the decade 1763–73, which appear to have been especially busy years for him, he delivered about 2,200 pieces for use at Court, including 44 writing-desks, 544 commodes, 1,018 small tables, and 513 bidets and close-stools.

An enterprise working on such a scale must of course have a considerable stock. An inventory drawn up in 1771 in fact mentions 250 completed or partly completed pieces of furniture, including 135 tables of various sizes, 35 commodes, and 9 writing-desks (including a 'secrétaire à cilindre sans être garni'), as well as several marble slabs and 357 lb. of bronze mounts. Joubert's total stock was valued at 17,746 livres at this time.

The same inventory of 1771—when Joubert was an old man of eighty-two shows that he had only five benches in his workshops and four marquetry-donkeys (*montures de scie en marqueterie*). Perhaps by this date he had disposed of some of his workshop equipment. At any rate, many of the items of furniture he provided—or at least the unadorned carcasses and simpler elements—must have been made by other cabinet-makers, as Pierre Verlet has demonstrated. It is thus known that A.-M. Criaerd and N.-J. Marchand worked for Joubert during his early period as a royal purveyor, while later, in 1771, Roger Vandercruse Lacroix, Leonard Boudin, Pierre Denizot, Pierre Macret, François Bayer and Joubert's own brother, Pierre, were all owed sums of money for having provided him with furniture. It is also thought possible that Riesener collaborated with Joubert; the former's mark is anyway to be found on a roll-top desk which was delivered in Joubert's name in December 1773 to the Comtesse de Provence (now in the Gulbenkian Collection in Portugal). On his retirement as *ébéniste du Roi*, in October 1774, Joubert handed over to Riesener furniture worth 4,770 livres intended for the *Garde-Meuble de la Couronne*; this was pre-sumably incomplete work.

It seems likely that Etienne Forestier was Joubert's chief source of bronze mounts. They had worked together at an early stage on the large *table volante* of the Château de Choisy (a table that rose through a hole in the floor into the small and intimate dining-chamber, obviating the need for servants in the room). Moreover, Joubert only had one single bronze-founder among his creditors in 1771 and this was Fores-tier's widow who was by then running her late husband's business. The only *ciseleur* among the creditors was a man named Godille, and the supplier of marble slabs was a certain Jouniaux.

Only a few specimens of Joubert's work have been identified because he rarely marked his furniture.

However, Pierre Verlet has identified a number of pieces which Joubert delivered to the *Garde-Meuble* in the 1760s and early 1770s. Amongst the most elaborate are the two surviving medal-cabinets made in 1755 for Louis XV's *Cabinet* at Versailles, and a writing-desk veneered with red lacquer made for the same room and now in the Wrightsman Collection in New York. Two large and richly decorated clocks, made for the King's Bed-chamber in 1762, have however not been traced. Joubert also provided a certain amount of furniture in 1768 for the newly-built Petit Trianon, including two commodes—one of black and one of red lacquer—for the King's apartment.

Joubert's grandest productions show that he had very much a personal style. Already at an early date, he betrayed a tendency to go along with the reaction against the Rococo—e.g. in his medal-cabinets of 1755 which were based on designs by one of Slodtz brothers, and more particularly the furniture from the late 1760s which has a marked transitional character. It needs to be stressed that Joubert was an old man by the time he came to play such a prominent part, as the principal cabinet-maker to the Royal Household, and he had of course grown up in a period when the Classical traditions as expounded by the Academy were still dominant and when the more light-hearted spirit that was to produce the Rococo was still a new phenomenon.

It is relevant to our theme to record that amongst the furniture Joubert provided for Madame Adelaïde's rooms at Versailles in 1771 was an eight-leaf screen of solid mahogany, of which the lower section was pierced with 'antique' open-work ('découpé a jour à la grecque').

Arch. Nat., o[1] 3317–3319, *passim*.
Arch. Nat., Minutier Central, CXVII–852 and 872; XXVIII–64 which last document is Joubert's certificate of apprenticeship (I am much indebted to M. Daniel Alcouffe for drawing my attention to this item and for providing me with a photocopy).
Arch. Nat., Minutier Central, VI-751 and LXII-209.
Guiffrey, *Scellés*, III, p. 251.
Salverte, *Ébénistes*, pp. 167–9.
Verlet, *Mobilier Royal I–III*, *passim*.
Verlet, *Versailles*, pp. 521–2.
Robert Cecil, 'A Secretaire made for the French Crown', *The Burlington Magazine*, January 1960, pp. 35–6.

See Plates 119, 120, 141–2, 145–6.

JULLIENNE, Jean de. Dyer and art-collector. Born in 1686, died in 1766. Son of Claude Jullienne de Francoeur who was *marchand de draps*. Nephew of the dyer Jean Glucq.

Jullienne became a *maître-teinturier* in 1719. He first joined, and later became owner of, the family firm which enjoyed the protection of the Crown and comprised a weaving-establishment and dye-works for the production of fine woollen cloth and which lay next to the famous seat of the tapestry-weaving ateliers in the Hôtel Royal des Gobelins. In recognition of his services, Jullienne was ennobled in 1736 and made a knight of the order of Saint-Michel. In 1739, he was elected to the Académie Royale de Peinture et Sculpture as an *amateur honoraire*.

Jullienne had had ambitions of an artistic nature since he was quite young. He attended courses at the Academy and became the friend of many artists including Antoine Watteau (died 1721) who was two years his senior, and whose extensive oeuvre he caused to be engraved and published. Jullienne became very prosperous and amassed a collection of works of art which came to be regarded as one of the most important in the whole of Paris. He had in fact started to collect when still of a tender age. As is well known, he owned several now famous paintings by Watteau but he also acquired the paintings and drawings of many younger artists including Louis-Joseph Le Lorrain, Noël Hallé, Lagrenée, Pierre and Bachelier, as well as terracottas by De la Rue.

After his death in 1766, Jullienne's great collection was sold at an auction which was held at the Louvre by special permission of the Marquis de Marigny. From the printed catalogue, in which many of the descriptions are exceedingly detailed, we learn that part of his extensive collection of Chinese porcelains was furnished with rich bronze mounts of which several were definitely in the Neo-Classical taste (see Plate 237). Moreover, he possessed a gold snuff-box by Auguste in the same style. Jullienne owned many pieces of boulle-work furniture, some dating from the time of Louis XIV and some made in his own time.

Pierre Remy, *Catalogue raisonné des tableaux, desseins & estampes, et autre effets curieux, après de décès de M. de Jullienne . . . on a joint a ce catalogue celui des porcelaines, tant anciennes que modernes, des laques les plus recherchées, des riches meubles du célebre ébéniste Boule, & autres effets, par C. F. Julliot*, Paris, 1767.
Emile Dacier and Albert Vuaflart, *Jean de Jullienne et les graveurs de Watteau au XVIIIe Siècle*, vol. 1, *Notices et documents biographiques*, by Jacques Herold and Albert Vuaflart, Paris, 1929.

LACHENAIT, Charles. Sculptor and wood-carver. Known to have been active between 1764 and 1777.

Member of the Académie de Saint-Luc from 1764. Worked as a *sculpteur en meubles* for the Prince de Condé between 1770 and 1774 and carried out the carving on a great deal of furniture for the Palais Bourbon under the direction of the architects Le Carpentier and Bellisard. All this furniture was decorated with 'antique' ornament, of which detailed descriptions may be found in Lachenait's bills that are preserved in the Archives Condé at Chantilly.

Lachenait was living in the Rue Neuve Saint-Martin in 1772 and the extension of this street, named the Rue Notre-Dame-de-Nazareth in 1774. The latter was the next street running parallel to the Rue Meslay where Georges Jacob lived—amongst others.

Guiffrey, *Académie de Saint-Luc*, p. 338.
G. Macon, *Les arts dans la maison de Condé*, Paris, 1903, pp. 136 and 138.

LALIVE DE JULLY, Ange-Laurent de. Art-collector and chief of protocol at the French Court. Born in 1725, died in 1779. Son of the *fermier-général* Lalive de Bellegarde (d. 1751), the brother of another *fermier-général* named Lalive d'Epinay. In 1749 he was married to Louise-Elisabeth Chambon (died 1752) and subsequently to Marie-Louise Joseph de Nettine.

It is said that Lalive started his career as *substitut de procureur général.* In 1754 he was elected an honorary member of the Académie de Peinture et Sculpture in recognition of his knowledge of art and his enterprise as a collector. In 1756 he purchased the post of *introducteur des ambassadeurs à la Cour de France.* He obtained this post through the influence of Madame de Pompadour who had lived almost next door to the Lalive family in the Rue Saint-Honoré before she had gone to live at Versailles. It is certainly to be presumed that they were acquainted, if only because Lalive twice went to Geneva (in 1757 and 1759) to manage some private business for her. Lalive seems to have begun to suffer from some kind of mental illness in 1766 for, in that year, he drew up his will and did not attend any of the Academy's meetings. It would seem that he was enjoying better health by the beginning of 1767 because he went to a meeting of the Academy on 7th February and again on 28th—but that was the last time. On 3rd March he added a codicil to his will and he then seems to have retired from his Court post completely, for he is no longer listed as *introducteur* in that year's *Almanach Royal.* On 17th July 1769 Diderot wrote to Falconet that 'votre bon ami M. de La Live, n'est pas devenue imbécile, mais fou' ('your excellent friend M. de La Live has become not merely imbecile, he is quite insane'). In February 1770, Baron de Grimm wrote that '. . . M. de La Live se trouve depuis quelques années dans un état de santé si déplorable que sa famille a pris le parti de faire vendre son cabinet au profit de ses enfants mineurs. C'était un homme aimable et généralement aimé. Il n'avait pas beaucoup d'esprit, il n'avait pas un grand fonds, mais il était doux et aimable dans la société; riche d'ailleurs et d'une figure intéressante, un peu dévot, un peu musicien, un peu graveur, il n'en faut pas davantage pour être à la mode, à la cour et à Paris. A l'âge de quarante ans, remarié à une femme qu'il aimait entouré de petits enfants dont il raffolait, il est tombé dans un état de mélancolie qui a affecté sa tête et l'a séquestré de la société . . .' ('M. de La Live has been for some years in such a deplorable state of health that his family has been forced to sell part of his collection for the maintenance of his young children. He was a pleasant man who was widely liked. He was not a man particularly brilliant or profound but he was gentle and agreeable; he was rich, however, and had an engaging appearance, he was mildly devout, a bit of a musician, a bit of an engraver—it takes no more to make one fashionable at Court or in Paris. At the age of forty, married for the second time to a woman he dearly loved, and surrounded by small children that he adored, he fell into a state of melancholia which affected his brain so that he was forced to retire from society . . .').

During his first marriage, Lalive lived in his paternal home in the Rue Saint-Honoré. The house no longer survives but lay where there is now access to the Place Vendôme (No. 364). When he married again, in 1762, he moved to the Rue de Menars, a road leading off the Rue de Richelieu. This house has also disappeared.

Lalive inherited a large fortune from his father who died in 1751. This enabled him to indulge his passion for collecting works of art, and his collection soon became so impressive that it was mentioned in the *Mercure de France* when his election to the Academy was announced. A summary description of the collection was published already in 1757, in the third edition of Dezallier d'Argenville's *Voyage pittoresque de Paris* (pages 149–54). Apart from his Italian and Flemish paintings, which were hung in his so-called *Cabinet Flamand*, he had an unusually large number of works by French painters of all periods including many young artists. The list includes names like those of Saly, Le Lorrain, Falconet, Lagrenée, Greuze, Vien, Pierre, Chardin and Servandoni.

Lalive was quite a capable draughtsman and enjoyed handling the buren. In 1754 he executed a group of engravings of vases from drawings by Saly, and Dezallier d'Argenville (op. cit., page 110) claims that Lalive himself designed the fully Neo-Classical monument to his first wife erected in his parish church, which Falconet executed in 1754 (Plate 38).

As far as Lalive's furniture is concerned we know that, in 1756, he bought from Lazare Duvaux an unusually rich book-case, fifteen feet long, veneered with ebony and inlaid with metal. According to Lalive it was supposed to be the work of Charles-André Boulle himself. In October of that year he also purchased a commode of boulle-work. It was at about this time that Lalive commissioned Le Lorrain to design the now famous suite of furniture 'à la grecque' (Plates 85 to 89) which was to stand in his *Cabinet Flamand* and which may be discerned in Greuze's portrait of Lalive which was exhibited at his *Salon* in 1759 (Plates 321 and 322).

Lalive transferred his art-collection to his new apartment in the Rue de Menars, which was presumably re-decorated before he moved in, in 1762. As before, his foreign paintings were hung in a new *Cabinet Flamand*. Unlike so many collectors, Lalive kept open house to anyone interested and, for the benefit of visitors, he compiled a guide to the collection with the aid of Mariette. It was entitled a *Catalogue historique du cabinet de peinture et sculpture françoise de M. De Lalive . . .* 1764. He explained that the *Cabinet Flamand* had been decorated by 'M. Baros', by which he must mean Barreau de Chefdeville, and that the room—it seems to have been a cross between a large closet and a study—was provided with furniture 'composés dans le style antique, ou, pour me servir du mot dont on abuse si fort actuellement, dans le goût grec' ('designed in the Antique style, or to use a term that is greatly abused at the moment, in the *goût grecque*'). He adds that the furniture had been designed by the late 'M. Le Lorain'; that is, Louis-Joseph Le Lorrain. While we do not otherwise know anything about the appearance of this room, we can assume that it was in much the same style as those designed by Barreau for the residence of the Intendant at Bordeaux at about the same time (Plates 56 to 59). We know even less about the other rooms in Lalive's house but they may well have been decorated in a similar style to the *Cabinet Flamand*; one room, we know, had a tiled stove in the form of a Classical column surmounted by a terracotta figure of Iphigenia modelled by Michel-Ange Slodtz (cf. *Catalogue historique*, page 16). The description calls to mind the stove which is illustrated in an engraving by Dumont of about 1765 (see Plate 63).

A far more detailed list of the items in Lalive's collection, which includes those not in the four rooms normally accessible to visitors, is to be found in the catalogue of the auction which his family arranged in 1771 after his mental illness had taken complete hold of him. From this it can be seen that he owned several other pieces of boulle-work, apart from those already mentioned, including two large writing-desks, a long-case clock, and a pair of pedestals (lots 759 to 762 and 767). He also had a pair of console-tables, one with a porphyry and one with a green marble slab, which must have been Neo-Classical in style, judging by their description (lots 270 and 271). About some sconces (lot 272), the cataloguer wrote that 'Le bon goût à l'antique qu'il y a dans ces morceaux, & la belle execution, les rendent distingués' ('The sound Classical taste embodied in these pieces, and the high quality of their execution, make them objects of real distinction'), and that they were 'composée de canaux creux, platte-bandes & ornemens, le haut est terminé par un vase, & le bas par une pomme de pin' ('with fluting and the top being surmounted by an urn, the lower extremity terminating in a pine cone'). He also possessed two decorative vases with bronze mounts which were said to be 'de forme antique'.

Unlike the Comte de Caylus, Lalive de Jully is not known to have become involved in the higher politics of art. His importance in the history of Neo-Classicism in France lies in the fact that he caused his furniture 'à la grecque' to be designed and constructed, and that he then placed them on what amounted to public view along with the other riches of his great art-collection.

Arch. Nat., Minutier Central, Étude XLVIII, 24th August 1766.
Mercure de France, June 1754, p. 146.
Almanach Royal, 1761 and 1762.
J. J. Rouseau, *Oeuvres completes*, 1959, p. 501.
Annales J. J. Rousseau, XXIX, 1941–42, pp. 261–75.
Correspondance générale de J. J. Rousseau, II, 1924, p. 37.
Baron de Grimm, *Correspondance littéraire*, VIII, 1879, p. 465.
Dufort de Cheverny, *Mémoires*, I, pp. 116, 192, 273 and 282.
Duc de Luynes, *Mémoires*, XIV, 1864, p. 396.
Comte de Cobenzl, *Correspondance artistique* (1753–66), 1895, *passim*.
Horace Walpole, *Paris Journals*, 1939, pp. 291 and 295.
A. Boppe and M. Delavand, *Les introducteurs des ambassadeurs*, 1901, p. 60.
Louis Réau, *Histoire de l'expansion de l'art français moderne*, 1924, pp. 221–2.
Lucien Perey and Gaston Maugras, *La jeunesse de Madame d'Epinay*, 1891, *passim*.
Lucien Perey and Gaston Maugras, *Dernières années de Madame d'Epinay*, 1884, *passim*.
Fiske Kimball, 'Les influences anglaises dans la formation du style Louis XVI', *Gazette des Beaux-Arts*, 6th ser., 1931, pp. 29–44, 231–55.
Fiske Kimball, 'The Beginnings of the Style Pompadour 1751–59', *Gazette des Beaux-Arts*, 6th ser., 1954, pp. 57–64.
F. J. B. Watson, *Louis XVI Furniture*, 1960, pp. 9–10.
Present author, 'Lalive de Jully's Furniture "à la grecque"', *Burlington Magazine*, August 1961, pp. 340–7.

See Plates 38, 85–9, 187, 305–7, 321–2, 349 and Colour Plate A.

LAPIE, Nicolas-Alexandre. Cabinet-maker. Born in about 1740, died on 8th February 1775. Elder brother of Jean Lapie, also a cabinet-maker. Married to a daughter of the faïence-manufacturer Louis Bazin.

Lapie became a *maître* in 1764, and had a workshop in the Rue de Charenton. At the time of his death, this contained eight work-benches with their tools, as well as four marquetry donkeys (*scies de marqueterie*). Amongst the completed furniture he left behind were twenty *chiffonières*, two *toilettes* and one *commode à tombeau* (small cabinets of drawers, two dressing-tables, and a deep-bodied commode). His belongings were sold on 2nd March 1775.

Most of Lapie's known furniture is in the transitional style and is no more outstanding than that of many other contemporary cabinet-makers. He is of interest, however, partly because he died at a critical point in the stylistic development of the period, so that his marked furniture—and thus other related pieces—can be securely dated prior to the date of his death,

Guiffrey, *Scellés*, III, p. 251, and Arch. Nat., Y 13402 (8th February 1775).
Salverte, *Ébénistes*, p. 182.

See Plate 150.

LA REYNIÈRE, Gaspard Grimod de. *Fermier-général* and *administrateur général des postes* for the Limousin and Haut Languedoc. Born about 1737, died about 1790. Married to Elisabeth-Françoise de Jarente. Father of Grimod de la Reynière, the famous gastronome and cousin of Grimod Comte d'Orsay whose biography is given here (see Orsay).

Grimod de La Reynière is said to have been interested in music and painting. He was elected an *honoraire associé libre* of the Académie de Peinture et Sculpture in 1787. From 1769 onwards he built a house on the Place Louis XV (now the Place de la Concorde). His architect was Nicolas Barré and the great salon was decorated with panels painted by Clerisseau 'dans le style arabesque'—a room for which Duplessis *fils* executed four large bronze candelabra (Plates 82, 83 and 483).

Gustave Desnoiresterres, *Grimod de La Reynière et son groupe*, Paris, 1877.
Louis Réau, 'La décoration de l'hôtel Grimod de La Reynière', *BSHAF*, 1937, pp. 7–16.
Edward Croft-Murray, 'The Hôtel Grimod de La Reynière; The Salon Decorations', *Apollo*, November 1963, pp. 377–83.

See Plates 82–3, 218, 483.

LE BLANC, Jean-Bernard; known as Abbé Le Blanc. French poet, art-critic and man of letters. Born at Dijon in 1706, died in Paris in 1781. The son of a prison warder.

Le Blanc attended the Jesuit Collège des Godrans at Dijon—a school which included the famous naturalist Buffon among its pupils at this very same time. In Dijon, Le Blanc became secretary to the learned président Jean Bouhier and there he made his début as a poet—at the tender age of twenty. In 1728, he moved to Paris where he made numerous friends among literary people and in fashionable circles. He included Madame Geoffrin among his friends and came to know many of the frequenters of her *salons*, notably the Comte de Caylus. In 1737–38 he spent some while in England where he wrote a series of letters, many of which were published in France in 1747 under the title *Lettres de Monsieur L'Abbé Le Blanc, concernant le Gouvernement, la Politique et les Moeurs des Anglois et des François*. These letters brought him considerable renown and it is said that they caught the attention of Madame de Pompadour. It was quite possibly she who chose Le Blanc to accompany her young brother, the future Marquis de Marigny, on the famous study-tour to Italy—an extended journey made together with Soufflot and Cochin. On 20th November 1749, Le Blanc was appointed *Historiographe des Bâtimens du Roy* and the small party set out that December.

Le Blanc was an early and energetic opponent of the Rococo as a decorative style; he criticised it in strong terms more than once. The first public attack was couched in the form of a letter (quoted in full on pages 226–9) to a 'Comte de C*' who is likely to have been identical with the famous Comte de Caylus. In his review of the *Salon* of 1753, he expressed his admiration for the artist Louis-Joseph Le Lorrain who was shortly to design the Classical dining-room for Åkerö (Plate 15) and, subsequently, the famous suite of furniture for Lalive de Jully (Plates 85 to 89). He presumably knew Le Lorrain personally since the latter executed the frontispiece and a vignette for the fifth edition of Le Blanc's *Lettres*, published in 1758. In his review of the 1761 *Salon*, Le Blanc drew attention to a piece of furniture which was clearly not in the Rococo style and he praises some unspecified ladies who had apparently shown their independence of mind by breaking away from the Rococo in the field of interior-decoration (see page 69).

While Le Blanc was not a gifted writer, he must have had a certain importance in bringing about the rejection of the Rococo and thus in the early history of Neo-Classicism. Moreover, together with Cochin and Soufflot, he had a formative influence on the young man who was to become Marquis de Marigny and virtual dictator of all official art from 1751 to 1773—the crucial period in this connection. Some of the credit for the fact that Marigny was to become such an energetic advocate of the Neo-Classical style must surely go to the Abbé Le Blanc and his two colleagues who made sure the young man was instilled with a progressive outlook.

Helène Monod-Cassidy, *Un voyageur-philosophe au XVIIIe siècle, l'Abbé Jean-Bernard Le Blanc*, Cambridge, Mass., 1941.
Wolfgang Hermann, *Laugier and Eighteenth Century French Theory*, London, 1962, *passim.*

LE CARPENTIER, Antoine-Mathieu. Architect. Born on 15th July 1709 at Rouen, died on 13th July 1773 in Paris.

He was a pupil of Jacques V. Gabriel. Member of the Academy from 1755. He designed a Town Hall for the City of Rouen in 1750 which was never built. Between 1751 and 1754, he built for Charles-François Gaillard de la Boissière a pavilion near the present Place Clichy. Between 1754 and 1758 he built the Château de Courteilles (Eure) for Dominique-Jacques de Barberie, Marquis de Courteilles, where the *antichambre* had twelve pilasters executed by the stuccador Louis Mansiaux in 1758. He also built a house for the *fermier-général* Bouret in about 1757 in the Rue Grange Batelière, among many other buildings in or near Paris.

Between 1765 and 1773, Le Carpentier was *architecte des bâtiments* to the Prince de Condé and in this capacity directed the work at the Palais Bourbon and at the Hôtel de Lassay, partly on the basis of drawings supplied by Barreau de Chefdeville and partly to his own designs. He was, moreover, responsible for the interior decoration in these buildings and it is possible that he provided designs for anyway some of the furniture, particularly the chairs, beds, etc., supplied by L. C. Carpentier and Louis Delanois, the decoration of which was executed by the *sculpteur en meubles* Lachenait.

Macon, *Les arts dans la maison de Condé*, pp. 124–6.
L.-M. Michon, *Le château de Courteilles*, BSAF, 1941–44, pp. 59–72.
Livre-journal de Louis Mansiaux (MS), Arch. Seine, 5 B^6 2738, fol. 7–8.
Arch. Nat., Z^2 2458 (plans and planning-permission for the Pavillon de la Boissière).
J.-F. Blondel, *Architecture Française*, III, 1754, p. 90.
Le Carpentier's obituary is published in *Revue Universelle des Arts*, XII (1860–61), pp. 352–6.
J.-F. Blondel, *Cours d'architecture*, I (1771), pp. 388–9, and II (1771) pp. 251–2.
Arch. Nat., Z^{1j} 1214, 30th March 1791 (estimation of damage caused to the Pavillon de la Boissière).
Le Plan, 9th March 1844 (concerning the Pavillon de la Boissière which is to be sold for demolition).

LEDOUX, Claude-Nicolas. Architect. Born in 1736 at Dormans, near Rheims, died in Paris in 1806.

Ledoux was a pupil of J.-F. Blondel in 1757 and of L.-F. Trouard in 1760. He is not known to have visited Italy. He became a member of the Academy in 1770. In 1778, he was living in the 'Rue Basse (des Remparts) entre les portes St. Martin et St. Denis'.

All Ledoux's works are in the *Louis Seize* style. His earliest works in Paris include the interior-decoration of the Café Militaire (1762), a project for the Hôtel d'Hallwyl (1766), the Hôtel d'Uzès (*c.* 1764–1767), the Hôtel Hocquart de Montfermeil (1765–67), the Hôtel de Montmorency (1770–71), the Hôtel Tabary (1771–73), and the Pavillon de Mlle Guimart (1770–73). Madame du Barry's own Pavillon de Louveciennes was also executed to his designs; it was started in 1771 and completed in the summer of

1773. For this, Ledoux also designed bronze ornaments like fire-dogs and sconces, which were then made by Gouthière. Ledoux of course carried out much work after this famous commission.

Like so many architects, Ledoux wanted to publish his *Oeuvre* in a large illustrated volume and, indeed, he prepared for this by writing a text and making drawings of his buildings. The whole was, however, not published until long after his death, as is well known. This work is naturally highly informative for those seeking to evaluate Ledoux's artistic achievement, but illustrations should be treated with considerable circumspection as has been most clearly shown by W. Hermann and L. Langner in their articles which were published in 1960 (see bibliography below). This is particularly the case with the drawings of some of his earliest buildings (e.g. the Hôtel d'Uzès, the Hôtel d'Hallwyl, Mlle Guimard's house and the Pavillon de Louveciennes) which Ledoux has depicted in a more modern guise than was correct, in such a manner as to give a false impression and suggest that Ledoux was a more revolutionary architect than was really the case—at least, as far as his earlier work is concerned. Ledoux would seem to have wished to draw a veil over the debt he owed, like so many of his contemporaries, to the classical French tradition and to some of his older colleagues like Soufflot and, more especially, A.-J. Gabriel of whose twin houses of the Place de la Concorde he said 'C'est là, c'est dans ce fastueux édifice que brille le sentiment inépuisable de l'Architecture française' ('It is there, in that magnificent edifice, that the inexhaustible spirit of French Architecture shines forth').

Bibl. Nat., Dép. des Mss., Fonds français, 8158.
Geneviève Levallet-Haug, *Claude-Nicolas Ledoux*, Paris-Strasbourg, 1934.
Marcel Raval and J. Ch. Moreux, *Claude-Nicolas Ledoux*, Paris, 1945.
Emil Kaufmann, 'Three Revolutionary Architects, Boullée, Ledoux and Lequeu', *Transactions of the American Philosophical Society*, New Series, vol. 42, part 3, Philadelphia, 1952.
W. Hermann, 'The Problem of Chronology in Claude-Nicolas Ledoux's Engraved Works', *The Art Bulletin*, September 1960.
Johannes Langner, 'Ledoux' Redaktion der eigenen Werke für die Veröffentlichung', *Zeitschrift für Kunstgeschichte*, 1960, pp. 136–66.
Gallet, *Demeures*, pp. 188–9.
Michel Gallet, 'La jeunesse de Ledoux', *Gaz.d.B.A.*, February 1970, pp. 65–92.
Pierre Kjellberg, 'L'Architecte "maudit" Ledoux rélévé en tant que décorateur', *Connaissance des Arts*, October 1970, pp. 92–9.

See Plates 62, 72, 77, 79–80.

LE GEAY, Jean-Laurent, Architect. Born about 1710, died after 1786.

Gained the Grand Prix d'Architecture in 1732 and stayed as a stipendiary at the French Academy in Rome from about 1st December 1738 until 9th January 1742, whereupon he went back to Paris. In 1745 he seems to have gone to Berlin where, in 1747, he published a set of engravings of projects for the St. Hedwigkirche which, however, was not built until 1773. He carried out works in Schwerin, Rostock and Potsdam, leaving the last-named place in 1763. He then seems to have gone to England where he anyway was established in 1766 and 1767. Between 1767 and 1770, he published—presumably in Paris—several series of engravings representing bizarre Neo-Classical vases, ruins, etc., which were probably based on drawings he made in Rome. There is then no trace of him until 1786 when he is found applying to the Duke of Mecklenburg from the South of France for a pension to enable him to spend his old age in Rome.

According to contemporary sources, particularly Cochin, Le Geay is supposed to have had an enormously important part to play in the development of Neo-Classical architecture in France already immediately after his return from Italy (in 1742). Yet, since Le Geay is not known to have built anything in France, it would seem that his influence must have been exerted by personal contact and through his drawings which owed much to Piranesi and which are said to have been quite extraordinary.

He numbered among his pupils E.-L. Boullée, Charles De Wailly, P.-L. Moreau-Desproux, and Peyre.

Thieme and Becker, *Künstlerleksikon.*
John Harris, 'Le Geay, Piranesi and International Neo-classicism in Rome 1740–1750', *Essays in the History of Architecture presented to Rudolf Wittkower*, London, 1967, pp. 189–96.

See Plates 2–6.

LELEU, Jean-François. Cabinet-maker. Born in 1729, died in 1807.

Leleu worked first of all alongside Riesener and others in J.-F. Oeben's workshops, which were managed by the widow after Oeben's death in 1763. In 1764 he became a *maître* and settled in the Chaussée de la Contrescarpe in the Faubourg Saint-Antoine. He later moved to the street now known as the Rue Birague near the Place des Vosges. About 1792 he made over his workshops to his son-in-law, C. A. Stadler.

Between April 1772 and June 1776, Leleu enjoyed the patronage of the Prince de Condé for whose Palais Bourbon he provided furniture worth over 40,000 livres, including two 'secrétaires à abattant', two 'bureaux à cylindre', seven commodes, two writing-desks, twenty-seven games-tables and eleven screens of various kinds (both 'paravents' and 'écrans'—presumably implying large folding screens and fire-screens). Some of this furniture has survived and is now in the Louvre, the Petit Trianon and the Wallace Collection. This furniture was for the most part of an elaborate Neo-Classical nature. He provided a floor of marquetry-work for the *petits appartements* which was probably designed by the architect Bellisard and cost 7,320 livres.

Leleu also made furniture destined for Mme du Barry—for example, a commode set with Sèvres plaques. These commissions were executed to the orders of the marchand-mercier, Poirier. According to Salverte, Leleu also made furniture for the Château de Marais and many other recently-built houses of the period. Verlet maintains that Leleu also provided furniture for the Marquis de Marigny's Château de Menars.

Leleu's stamp is to be found underneath a writing-desk in the Musée Condé at Chantilly which is thought to have been made about 1757 for Lalive de Jully (Plates 85–89)—that is, seven years before Leleu became a *maître*. However, his mark is not to be found on the accompanying *cartonnier* and it would therefore seem that he may have stamped his mark on the desk at some later date when he perhaps had the desk in his workshop undergoing repairs. Between 1765 and 1771, he provided Baron d'Ivry with furniture worth 4,902 livres for the latter's Château d'Hénonville.

Salverte, *Les ébénistes*, pp. 192–5.
Verlet, *La maison*, pp. 166–7.
Verlet, 'La commode de la chambre du Prince de Condé au Palais-Bourbon', *La Revue des Arts*, March 1954, pp. 47–8.
Paul Eudel, *L'Hôtel Drouot et la curiosité en 1883–1884*, Paris, 1885, pp. 329–30.
Verlet, 'Two pieces of furniture by Leleu', *Burlington Magazine*, April 1949, pp. 110–13.
Watson, *Wallace Collection Furniture.*
Watson, *Wrightsman Collection*, pp. 304–5.
Chantilly, Archives Condé, A.-C.7.

See Plates 118, 126–30.

LE LORRAIN, Louis-Joseph. Painter and designer of furniture. Born about 1714, died in St. Petersburg in 1759.

Le Lorrain was a pupil of the painter Dumont *le Romain*. In 1739 he won the Grand Prix de Peinture and was at the same time granted a stipendium for a stay at the French Academy in Rome where he arrived in December 1740. He remained in Rome for eight years, during which time he copied paintings in the Vatican. For five successive years he designed the architectural settings for the annual Chinea Festival. He seems to have been a friend of Piranesi.

On his return to Paris, Le Lorrain became a protégé of the Comte de Caylus who, amongst other things, ensured that Le Lorrain was given the task of designing some ultra-modern wall-decorations and furniture for the Swedish Count C. G. Tessin's country-house, Åkerö, in 1754 (Plate 15). He became a member of the Academy in 1756. He designed a suite of furniture for Ange-Laurent de Lalive de Jully, the art-collector and *introducteur des ambassadeurs* (Plates 85 to 89) which caused something of a sensation at the time since it was the first group of furniture to break away from the then dominant Rococo taste, thus establishing the so-called 'goût grec' in the field of furniture. The exceptionally rich bronze mounts were executed by Ph. Caffieri.

At the request of the Comte de Caylus, Le Lorrain corrected and re-drew some of the drawings Julien David Le Roy had brought back from Greece and which were then subsequently published in 1758—engraved by Neufforge—under the title *Les ruines des plus beaux monuments de la Grèce*.

In 1758, Le Lorrain went to Russia to work at the newly-established Academy of Art at St. Petersburg. He had hoped to be able to concentrate on designing furniture and, with this in mind, he sent the furniture he had designed for himself to Russia, but this valuable cargo was lost on the way. Le Lorrain was anyway not able to achieve much in Russia because he fell ill and died within a few months of his arrival.

C.-N. Cochin, *Mémoires inédits*, ed. Charles Henry, Paris, 1880, pp. 142–3.
P. J. Mariette, *Abecedario*, ed. Ph. de Chennevières, Paris, 1854–56, vol. 3, p. 124.
C. Elling, *Jardin i Rom*, Copenhagen, 1943.
S. Eriksen, 'Lalive de Jully's Furniture "à la grecque" ', *Burlington Magazine*, 1961, pp. 340–7.
S.Eriksen, 'Om salen paa Åkerö og dens kunstner Louis-Joseph Le Lorrain', *Konsthistorisk Tidskrift*, Stockholm, 1963, pp. 94–120.
John Harris, *Le Geay, Piranesi and International Neo-classicism in Rome 1740–1750*, Essays in the history of architecture presented to Rudolf Wittkower, London, 1967, pp. 189–96.
John Harris, 'Early Neo-Classical Furniture', *The Journal of the Furniture History Society*, vol. II, 1966, pp. 1–6.

See Plates 8–9, 15, 85–9, 187, 297–8, 321–2, and Colour Plate A.

LEPINE, Jean-Antoine. Clock-maker. Active in the second half of the eighteenth century.

Became a *maître-horloger* in 1762. He made the movement of the clock on the *Bureau du Roi* which was completed in 1769. In 1771, he provided the Comtesse de Provence with a mantel clock which was described as being 'portée sur un socle d'architecture orné sur les faces de guirlandes de Laurier ayant à droite une figure de femme qui represente l'astronomie appuyée à gauche sur un Rouleau et tenant de la main droite une plume et à droite un genie sur un globe et sur des livres qui regarde l'heure' ('supported by a plinth, the faces of which are decorated with garlands of bay-leaves. It is flanked on the right by the figure of a woman emblematic of Astronomy leaning over a scroll, with a pen in her right hand; on the left is another figure, standing with a globe and a pile of books, who is reading the hour'). Another ormolu clock was delivered to Madame Clotilde in 1774; this consisted of a vase of flowers against which 'est apuyé d'un coté une femme debout qui offre des fleurs à l'amour etant de Lautre coté du vaze sur un nuage portant un carquois, un flambeau et une couronne' ('on one side leans the standing figure of a woman who offers flowers to a cupid; on the other side of the vase are to be seen a quiver, a flaming torch and a coronet resting on a cloud'). Lepine delivered a cartel clock intended for the Château of Versailles in 1770; the description of it corresponds closely to a type which often bears the name of the bronze-founder, Osmond (cf. Plate 196). He also sold clocks which had been made by others, e.g. clocks by Caron and Julien le Roy. Lepine's workshops were in the Rue Saint-Denis.

Arch. Nat., Y 9328 (13th March 1762); o[1] 3319 fol. 76 *recto*, and fol. 147 *verso*.
Verlet, *Mobilier Royal II*, p. 66.

LIEUTAUD, Balthazar. Cabinet-maker. Born early in the eighteenth century, died in 1780. Probably the son of the cabinet-maker François Lieutaud.

Lieutaud became a *maître* in 1749 and settled in the Rue de la Pelleterie on the Ile de la Cité. In 1772, he moved to the Rue d'Enfer on the same island.

Lieutaud specialised in clock-cases and is included here principally because his stamp is found on cases of Neo-Classical form, of which an example is in the Frick Collection that has bronzes by Philippe Caffieri which are dated 1767 (Plate 116).

Salverte, *Ebénistes*, pp. 202–3.
Watson, *Wallace Collection Catalogue*, pp. 134–5.

LOUIS XV, King of France (1715–74). Born 15th February 1710, died 10th May 1774. Son of the Duc de Bourgogne, the grandson of Louis XIV, and Marie-Adelaïde of Savoy. In 1725, married Marie Leczinska (died 1768), the daughter of Stanislas Leczinski, King of Poland from 1735, Duc de Lorraine et de Bar.

Among their children Adelaïde (born 1732), Louise (born 1737) and Victoire (born 1733) are of interest in so far as our present subject is concerned. From 1745 to 1764, the Marquise de Pompadour was the King's official mistress. The Comtesse du Barry occupied this position from 1768 to 1774.

Louis XV's tastes and his attitude to the Neo-Classical style are discussed on pages 120–3.

Pierre Gaxotte, *Le siècle de Louis XV*, Paris, 1933.
Comte de Fels, *Gabriel.*
Hautecoeur, *Histoire*, *première* (*-seconde*) *moitié.*
Verlet, *Mobilier Royal I–II.*
Verlet, *French Royal Furniture.*
Verlet, 'Gabriel et la construction de l'Opéra de Versailles', *Le Jardin des Arts*, July 1957, pp. 555–61.
Verlet, *Versailles.*

See Plates 90–3.

LOUIS, Louis Nicolas Victoire, known as Victor Louis. Architect. Born in 1731, died in 1807.

Victor Louis won the Grand Prix d'Architecture in 1755 and then proceeded to the French Academy in Rome where he remained from September 1756 to November 1759. He never became a member of the Académie d'Architecture, probably on account of his somewhat difficult nature. He became architect to the King of Poland in 1764, on the recommendation of Madame Geoffrin, and was in Warsaw in 1765. In 1762, Louis was living in the Rue Neuve des Petits-Champs, behind the church of Saint-Roch; while in 1767, he bought a house in the Rue de Grammont, not far away.

In the 1760s Louis designed, among other things, the painted decoration for a chapel in the church of Sainte-Marguerite in 1764; this was executed by Gaetano Brunetti (an Italian stage-designer who also drew some designs for chairs in the Baroque taste, which were published in London in 1736) and was of an architectural character. He also projected a design, now lost, for uniform façades for the Rue de Grammont (1766), designs for decorative work in the Palace at Warsaw (1765–66), architectural settings at the Théatre des Italiens in connection with a gala performance celebrating the Peace of 1763, the wrought-iron screen for the choir of Chartres Cathedral (1767), and a project for the 'Vaux-Hall' in the Bois de Boulogne which is known to us through an engraving by Taraval (1770). Louis was incidentally also responsible for the design of the theatre at Bordeaux (1772–80).

Hautecoeur, *Histoire*, *seconde moitié*, pp. 260–70.
Gallet, *Demeures*, pp. 192–3.
Stanislas Lorentz, 'Victor Louis et Varsovie', in the Catalogue of the exhibition of the same name, Bordeaux-Paris, 1958.
F. G. Pariset, 'Jeszcze o pracach Wiktora Louisa dla zamku Warszawskiego', *Biuletyn Historii Sztuki*, Warsaw, 1962, pp. 135–55.
L'Avantcoureur, 26th October 1761; 9th August 1762; 24th February 1766.
Sèvres, Municipal Archives, Church Register for 18th April 1762 (for Louis' full name).

See Plates 45, 70, 407–10.

LOUISE DE FRANCE, Madame. Born in 1737, died in 1787. Daughter of Louis XV and Marie Leczinska. Sister of Madame Adélaïde, Madame Victoire and Madame Sophie.

See Adelaïde de France, Madame.

LOYER, Toussaint-Noël. Architect. Born at Lyons in 1724, died in 1807 in the same city.

Loyer went from Paris to Lyons in about 1747 in order to assist Soufflot with, amongst other commissions, the building of the dome on the Hôtel Dieu. He became a member of the Academy at Lyons and was appointed architect to that city in 1803.

Among the houses that Loyer built in Lyons, the most interesting is the earliest—the Hôtel de Varey. This still survives in the Place Bellecour at the corner of the Rue Auguste Comte; it was built for Jean Dervieu du Villars, Seigneur de Varey, in 1758. The extensive Neo-Classical panelling is also still preserved *in situ*. In 1762, Loyer read a paper before the Lyons Academy 'Sur la manière de décorer les appartements' which provided virtually a blue-print for Neo-Classical interior decoration; the manuscript is still to be found in the Academy's archives and its text is reprinted here (see pages 257–60).

In April 1767, Loyer designed wall-decorations for a bath-room for a certain Monsieur Charton who was probably identical with Jean Charton (1701–76), an eminent official in the King's service, living in Lyons and, like Loyer, associated with the La Charité Hospital. The drawing for this scheme is in the École des Beaux-Arts in Paris (Plate 73).

Lyons, Archives du département du Rhône, Minutier du notaire François Perrin, Acte de reconnaissance (1st September 1758); Monsieur François Regis Cottin, who is preparing a detailed study of the architecture and topography of Lyons, has most generously sent me an extract from the important document in which appears proof of the date of the Hôtel de Varey.
Lyons, Archives du département du Rhône, 2 Q 59, Sommier des maisons des condamnés, fol. 27 *verso*, ff.
Rogatien Le Nail, *Lyon, architecture et décoration aux 17e et 18e siècles*, Paris, n.d., pp. 45–6.
Marius Audin and Eugène Vial, *Dictionnaire des artistes et ouvriers d'art du Lyonnais*, vol. I, Paris, 1918, p. 519.

See Plates 32–4, 73.

MARIA, Nicolas-Joseph. Wood-carver and designer of ornament. Probably born about 1710–20, died in 1802.

Maria was elected a *garde* of the Académie de Saint-Luc. He lived in the Rue du Temple. He is only known for his *Livre de desseins de jouaillerie et bijouterie* of 1765 which was engraved by Pierre-Edme Babel. The designs in this work are all in the Neo-Classical taste.

Guiffrey, *Académie de Saint-Luc*, p. 380.

See Plates 379–87.

MARIGNY, Abel-François de Vandières, Marquis de, also known as the Marquis de Menars. Essentially 'Minister for the Arts'. Born in 1727, died in 1781. Son of François Poisson, one of the French Army's forage-contractors. Brother of Madame de Pompadour and her junior by six years. In 1766, he married Marie-Françoise-Julie-Constance Filleul, the daughter of a one-time wine-merchant at Falaise.

Marigny was educated at one of the boy's colleges under royal patronage. In 1745, at the age of only eighteen, it was decided that he should ultimately succeed Le Normant de Tournehem as *directeur général des bâtiments, jardins, arts, académies et manufactures royales*, a post of very considerable importance. While Tournehem was certainly a friend of Marigny's mother and was an uncle of Madame de Pompadour's husband, Le Normant d'Etoilles, this startling appointment can hardly have been due to anything other than the direct influence of Madame de Pompadour on the King, which at this time was very great.

With his future in mind, Marigny was sent on a study-tour of Italy. He set out in December 1749 and the tour lasted twenty-one months. He was accompanied by three mentors, all of whom were substantially older than him—the forty-three-year-old Abbé Le Blanc, the thirty-six-year-old architect Soufflot, and the thirty-four-year-old draughtsman Cochin (see pages 34–6 and their respective biographies here).

Of the three, the first two were known to be active opponents of the Rococo long before the party left Paris and Cochin may already have been highly critical of the prevailing taste as well; at any rate, he had certainly become so within a few months of his return. One may presume that these three companions, who became close friends of Marigny's, exerted a powerful and formative influence in an anti-Rococo direction on the future 'Minister for the Arts', who was not by nature possessed of any very definite views on art. Moreover, we can be sure Marigny often listened to the advice of his old friends, particularly to that of Soufflot and Cochin, with whom he was on especially intimate terms and whom he saw daily.

When Tournehem died in November 1751, Marigny succeeded him as planned. He was by then twenty-four. He enjoyed a salary of 300,000 livres per annum. Louis XV seems to have approved of him, for, after Madame de Pompadour's death in 1764, Marigny's position seems to have remained unaltered except that he had rather more difficulty in obtaining the grants he needed for his department. However, when Madame du Barry stepped into his late sister's shoes he began to meet real opposition and, in 1773, he was finally forced to retire in favour of Terray, a *contrôleur des finances* who belonged to the du Barry faction. After Louis XV's death in 1774, however, Terray was removed and his place was taken by the Comte d'Angivillier.

Marigny was energetic and ambitious. In the course of his career, which lasted almost twenty years, he was responsible for a number of important architectural enterprises—for which he may in several cases have taken the initiative. One of his first grand conceptions involved restoring and completing the Louvre, partly on the basis of old drawings and partly with some new plans produced by Soufflot. He was especially keen to see the famous colonnade finished off, and it is a plan for this that he is seen holding in his portrait by Roslin, painted in 1761. Work on the great Place Louis XV—now de la Concorde—was started in 1755, after designs by Gabriel. The Champs-Elysées and surrounding area were tidied up in Marigny's time, the church of Sainte-Geneviève was built by Soufflot, then Gondoin's École de Chirurgie was begun, and so on. It is difficult to determine what part Marigny played in launching these enterprises although we can be sure he supported the projects for which Soufflot was the architect. In cases where the King was personally concerned, as at the Petit Trianon and the Opera at Versailles, the monarch probably dealt directly with the Court Architect, Gabriel, and Marigny's task would have consisted principally in warding off other work while these special commissions were under way.

The various royal manufactories (with the exception of the porcelain factory at Sèvres) also came under Marigny's jurisdiction. In 1755, he managed to get Soufflot appointed director of Les Gobelins and the Savonnerie factory. He also took a close personal interest in what was being done at these two important establishments, and especially that at Les Gobelins which was thoroughly modernised in the 1760s.

There can be no doubt that Marigny disapproved of the Rococo style—at least, from about 1760 onwards and perhaps several years earlier. On 18th May 1756 he recommended that the Academy should consider holding competitions concerning 'des décorations d'intérieur de palais pour corriger le mauvais goust d'ornemens qui subsiste aujourd'hui' ('the interior decoration of grand residences, in order to correct the poor taste in ornamental design which prevails today'). On the other hand Marigny was no romantic; he was in no way obsessed by the Antique. First and foremost, he was a realist. This is made very clear from the instructions he gave Natoire, the Director of the French School in Rome. He insisted that '. . . je voudrois que nos architectes s'occupassent plus qu'ils ne font des choses relatives à nos moeurs et à nos usages que des temples de la Grèce. Ils s'éloignent de leur object en se livrant à ce genre d'architecture. Je ne juge point cette étude aussi favorable pour cultiver et augmenter leurs talens qu'ils peuvent penser' ('I should like our architects to concern themselves more with matters related to our customs and way of life today and not so much with Greek temples. They get away from their main purpose by devoting too much attention to buildings of that kind. I really do not believe such a study anything like as advantageous for the cultivation and development of their talents as they imagine').

The various contemporary opinions on Marigny's character and views which have come down to us are not entirely trustworthy because one suspects most of the writers concerned were biased. Dufort de Cheverny could not endure him, Cochin was both a close friend and his subordinate, Guillaumot also worked for him, and Patte probably saw some advantage in flattering him. All the same, there are apparently sufficient grounds for believing that Marigny, also as a private individual, was among the earliest of the 'modernists' in France, even if his tastes were of the moderate kind. He was no extremist. (This question has been explored in greater detail by the present author in an article mentioned in the bibliography given below, and on page 36).

Marigny lived in the Rue Saint-Thomas-du-Louvre, in a house placed at his disposal by the King. In the mid-1760s, he had it modernised by Soufflot and Godefroy, the *marchand-tapissier*, provided the seat-furniture, curtains and so forth and it is all described as being 'festonées dans le goût antique'. In 1759, Marigny had bought a house and grounds in the suburb of Roule, where the Rue du Faubourg Saint-Honoré meets the Rue de Monceau. For this, Godefroy provided in 1763 some seat-furniture which must have been noticeably different from the common Rococo style then current, for it is described in the bills as having straight legs. Between 1768 and 1771, the house out at Roule was completed and redecorated in the most modern taste, after designs by Soufflot (Plate 76). Marigny acquired three other notable houses on the death of his sister in 1764; from her he inherited the Château de Menars, the Eremitage at Versailles and the Hotel d'Evreux in Paris. During his later years he lived in a house on the Place des Victoires.

From what remains of his private papers, now in the Bibliothèque Historique de la Ville de Paris, we know the names of some of the other craftsmen who worked for him. They include such well-known figures as the bronze-founder Philippe Caffieri (1758-65), the *ébénistes* Pierre Garnier (1766–79) and Simon Oeben (1768–69), and the carver Honoré Guibert (1766–79). These were of course all men who are known to have produced important works in the Neo-Classical taste (see their respective biographies here).

Bibliothèque Historique de la Ville de Paris, Manuscrits, Fonds Marigny.
Corr. des Dir., vols. X–XII.
Cochin, *Mémoires, passim.*
Dufort de Cheverny, *Mémoires*, ed. 1886, vol. I, p. 117.
C.-A. Guillaumont, *Remarques sur un livre intitulé; Observations sur l'architecture . . .*, Paris, 1768, p. 75.
Alfred Marquiset, *Le Marquis de Marigny*, Paris, 1918.
Hautecoeur, *Histoire, seconde moitié, passim.*
The present author's 'Marigny and "le goût grec"', *Burlington Magazine*, March, 1962, pp. 96–101.
Marc Furcy-Raynaud, 'Correspondance de M. De Marigny avec Coypel, Lepicie et Cochin', *Nouvelles Archives de l'Art Français*, 1903–04.
Emile Campardon, *Madame de Pompadour et la cour de Louis XV au milieu du dix-huitième siècle. Ouvrage suivi . . . du catalogue des objets d'art et de curiosité du marquis de Marigny . . .*, 1867.
Lazare Duvaux, *Livre-Journal*, 1873.
Jean Mondain-Monval, *Correspondance de Soufflot avec les directeurs des Bâtiments concernant la Manufacture des Gobelins (1756–1780)*, 1918, *passim.*
Jean Monval, *Soufflot*, 1918, *passim.*

See Plates 76, 157, 346, 442, 495–6.

MOREAU-DESPROUX, Pierre-Louis. Architect. Born in 1727, died in 1793. He was a nephew of the architect Jean-Baptiste-Augustin Beausire who was *maître des bâtiments de la Ville de Paris.*

Moreau-Desproux never succeeded in winning the Grand Prix d'Architecture, although on three occasions he gained the Second Prize (1750, 1751 and 1752). Charles De Wailly offered to share his own prize with Moreau-Desproux so that the two friends might at least spend eighteen months each (instead of the usual three years) at the French Academy in Rome, which they did between September 1754 and

December 1756. Together they studied Classical Roman architecture and sought to reconstruct the Baths of Diocletian—a project which caught the interest of Piranesi. Between 1763 and 1787 Moreau-Desproux was *maître des bâtiments de la Ville de Paris*.

Already by 1758 Moreau-Desproux had designed the entirely Neo-Classical Hôtel Chavannes by the Porte du Temple on the outskirts of Paris, which was completed in May of that year and which, according to Dezallier d'Argenville, was his first commission. He built the Fontaine des Haudriettes at the junction of the Rue des Archives and the Rue des Haudriettes; this was likewise in the Neo-Classical style. Between 1763 and 1770, he was responsible for the new theatre being built in the Palais Royal. His Pavillon Carré de Beaudouin in the Rue de Menilmontant dates from 1770. Among his other works should be mentioned the Hôtel de Gontaut in the Rue Louis-le-Grand (1772) and the extensive decorations used for festivals in 1762, 1763 and 1782. He acted as *maître des bâtiments* to the City of Paris between 1763 and 1787.

It is worth noting that one of his sisters married the architect Peyre.

Michel Gallet, 'Dessins de Pierre-Louis Moreau-Desproux pour des édifices parisiens', *Bulletin du Musée Carnavalet*, November 1961, pp. 6–15.
Dezallier d'Argenville, *Paris*, ed. 1770, p. 251.
A.A.A., 28th May 1766.

See Plates 31, 60, 78.

NEUFFORGE, Jean-François de. Architect and engraver. Born in 1714 at Comblain-au-Pont near Liège, died in 1791 in Paris.

Neufforge is said to have studied under the architect J.-F. Blondel, and under P.-E. Babel, the wood-carver and engraver who, in 1747, was to engrave seven of Neufforge's designs in the Rococo style published in his *Nouveaux livres de plusieurs projets d'autels et de baldaquins*.

Neufforge's most important work was his *Recueil élémentaire d'architecture* comprising nine volumes with a total of 900 plates which appeared between 1757 and 1772. It would seem that he had intended to entitle the work the *Livre d'architecture contenant différens desseins pour la décoration intérieure* since the publication was advertised thus in the *Mercure de France* in June 1756, where it is also announced that 'l'auteur de ces desseins en a composés un grand nombre qu'il continue de graver' ('the author of these compositions has drawn many more which he proposes to engrave'). The first and second volumes received the approbation of the Académie d'Architecture on 5th September 1757. The fifth volume was 'sous presse' (at the printers) in 1761; a copy of this was presented to the Marquis de Marigny on 25th May 1763 and the work received great praise. The last volume appeared in 1772. The plates could also be bought in unbound sets of six.

Of the twenty-eight plates in J.-D. Le Roy's work on *Les ruines des plus beaux monuments de la Grèce* (1758), Neufforge engraved eighteen after Le Roy's drawings had been improved by L.-J. Le Lorrain. He also engraved several plates for G.-M. Dumont's *Recueil de plusieurs parties d'Architecture* (1766). Neufforge lived in the Rue Saint-Jacques at the sign of the Golden Chariot (*Au Chariot d'Or*).

Thieme and Becker, *Künstlerleksikon.*
Cochin, *Mémoires*, p. 78.
Mercure de France, June, 1756.
Année Litteraire, 1761, p. 284.
L'Avantcoureur, 15th August 1763, pp. 521–2.

See Plates 28–9, 37, 46–7, 310–18, 368–9, 434–6.

OEBEN, Jean-François. Cabinet-maker. As recently discovered by Frau Rosemarie Stratmann, Oeben was born in 1721 at Heinsberg near Aachen where his father was *maître de poste* or *voiturier*. Oeben's brother Simon was also a highly competent cabinet-maker in Paris. Their sister, Marie-Catherine, married the cabinet-maker Martin Carlin in 1759. In 1749, he himself married Françoise-Marguerite Vandercruse, the daughter of the cabinet-maker François Vandercruse called Lacroix and brother of the cabinet-maker Roger Vandercruse (also called Lacroix) who used the stamped mark 'R.V.L.C.'. Roger's other sister married J.-F. Oeben's brother, Simon. Oeben died on 21st January 1763; his widow married the cabinet-maker J.-H. Riesener in 1767.

Oeben is thought to have arrived in Paris about 1740 and lived at first in the Grande Rue du Faubourg Saint-Antoine. In November 1751 he started to work as a journeyman (*compagnon*) for Charles-Joseph Boulle (a son of the eminent cabinet-maker André-Charles Boulle) who let some of his workshops in the Louvre to Oeben. After Charles-Joseph Boulle's death in June 1754, Oeben was granted (actually, in December) the privilege of residing and establishing his workshops in the Manufacture Royale des Gobelins and of bearing the title *menuisier-ébéniste du Roy* which, however, he had used for several months beforehand. Before October 1756, he had moved his home and workshops to the Arsenal; these premises were formally made over to him and his wife for their lifetime in May 1760. Oeben resided at the Arsenal until he died, early in 1763, whereafter his widow kept the business going with the aid of Riesener and some extremely competent journeymen including Leleu. Riesener married the widow Oeben in 1767 and therefore acquired the business.

The inventory drawn up on Oeben's death in 1763 tells us much about his affairs. There were twelve benches in his workshops, together with many hundreds of implements, some of them connected with the working of metals (e.g., two *montures de scie à fendre des vis* or screw-cutting lathes, a large lathe, two polishing-spindles, etc.); he also had a well-equipped smithy in a separate building.

When Oeben died, his stock of completed and partly completed furniture was by no means insignificant. Apart from the cylinder-top *Bureau du Roi*, which was under construction (begun in 1760 and not delivered until 1769 when the firm was under Riesener's direction), there were sixty small tables, six larger writing-desks, nine cupboards, thirteen fall-front desks, fourteen bidets, thirteen commodes, five bookcases, ten embroidery frames, two clock-cases, and forty other pieces of various types, as well as ten items awaiting delivery to Madame de Pompadour. In the subsequent announcement advertising the sale of Oeben's stock, it is explicitly stated that all the furniture was 'd'un goût nouveau' ('in a new taste'). He also had a large stock of more or less finished bronze mounts, weighing 738 pounds in all—that is, more than twice the quantity that Joubert had in his workshops in 1771.

A comparatively large number of *ébénistes* must have worked in Oeben's workshops at one time or another, but we only know for certain the names of four—Simon Oeben, Leleu, Riesener and Winant Stylen. There must have been quite a few more, if the number of work-benches is taken into account. It is, moreover, not known if Martin Carlin, Oeben's brother-in-law who lived only a few minutes' walk away, also worked in Oeben's shops but he certainly made furniture in his own workshops for Oeben. Similar arrangements were made between Oeben and Simon Ledoux, Jacques Porquet and Mathieu Criaerd.

There is no evidence in the inventory drawn up after Oeben's death that he had the means of producing his own bronze mounts. On the contrary, it is clear that he was provided with mounts by the bronze-founders Hervieu and Forestier, and also that Pierre Caron and Anne-François Briquet, who were both *doreurs-ciseleurs* (gilders and bronze-chasers), executed orders for Oeben. A certain Poulain, *maître-marbrier*, and a sculptor named Laurent-Joseph Bouttée provided the marble slabs Oeben required for his furniture. To what extent the other craftsmen whose names appear among Oeben's creditors on his death actually worked for him, or merely lent him money, is not known.

Throughout the period Oeben was active on his own account, the established royal cabinet-maker was of course Joubert. It is not known whether it was J.-F. Oeben or his brother, Simon, who, through the dealer Lazare Duvaux, provided Madame de Pompadour with twelve picture-frames in 1752. Nor do we know which of them provided the cabinet in the form of a commode for the *Garde-Meuble de la Couronne* in 1756. On the other hand, it was certainly Jean-François Oeben who made the invalid-chair in 1760—

the 'fauteuil méchanique'—required for the young Duc de Bourgogne, for J.-F. Oeben's mechanical skill was outstanding and he was indeed on this occasion granted a gold medal worth 200 livres in recognition of his talent.

We also know that Madame de Pompadour ordered many pieces of furniture from him in 1761, that she paid him 17,400 livres on account and provided him with thirty-four planks of mahogany which were to be used for these pieces. It is likely that the sixteen 'commodes à la grecque' listed in the inventory drawn up on her death, the origins of which cannot otherwise be established, were part of this order.

Oeben's most famous piece is the *Bureau du Roi* and, even though it remained for Riesener to complete it, one can assume that it was Oeben who devised the intricate mechanism.

A number of pieces of furniture bearing J.-F. Oeben's stamp must have been made after his death and before Riesener took over the firm—the period when Oeben's widow was in control. All the same, certain pieces displaying exceptionally advanced forms bearing his mark must in fact have been made during his lifetime because furniture of the types concerned is described in the inventory compiled after his death (e.g. Plate 94). It is all the same difficult to establish whether it was Oeben or Joubert who was stylistically the more advanced.

André Boutemy, 'Les tables-coiffeuses de Jean-François Oeben', *BSHAF*, 1962, pp. 101–16.
André Boutemy, 'Jean-François Oeben méconnu', *Gaz.d.B-A.*, April 1964, pp. 207–24.
Ch. Séné, 'Contrat de mariage de Riesener avec la Veuve Oeben et documents sur l'ébéniste Oeben', *NAAF*, 1878, pp. 319–38.
J.-J. Guiffrey, 'Inventaire de Jean-François Oeben, *NAAF*, 1899, pp. 298–367.
Vial, Marcel and Girodie, vol. II, pp. 57–9.
Salverte, *Les ébénistes*, pp. 237–41.
Jean Cordey, *Inventaire des biens de Madame de Pompadour rédigé après son décès*, Paris, 1939, Nos. 569, 1938, 1981, 2004, 2020, 2031, 2056, 2075, 2085, 2106, 2128, 2139, 2168, 2202, 2209, and 2339, and p. 266.
Verlet, *Mobilier Royal II*, pp. 65–75.
F. J. B. Watson, 'French eighteenth-century furniture in the collection of Sir Harold and Lady Zia Wernher', *Antiques*, August, 1957, pp. 147–51.
Rosemarie Stratmann, *Der Ebenist Jean-François Oeben*, Heidelberg dissertation, 1971.

See Plates 90–6, 113 and Colour Plate C.

OEBEN, Simon-François. Cabinet-maker. Probably born about 1725 at Heinsberg near Aachen (see J.-F. Oeben's biography), died in Paris in 1786. Younger brother of Jean-François Oeben and, like his brother, married to a daughter of François Vandercruse, called Lacroix, who was also a cabinet-maker, as was his son, Roger Vandercruse.

Oeben first worked with Charles-Joseph Boulle, as did his elder brother. From January 1755, he worked alongside the latter in the workshops at the Gobelins. When the brother left the Gobelins in 1755 or 1756, Simon Oeben took over his workshops there, whereupon he was appointed *ébéniste ordinaire du Roi*. On 28th January 1764, he joined the Parisian Guild of Cabinet-Makers and became a *maître* officially, after the Marquis de Marigny had issued him with the required *brevet*, making it unnecessary for Oeben to make the otherwise obligatory masterpiece as proof of his skill. In the same year he was provided with new and much larger premises at the Gobelins.

Oeben's activities at the Gobelins in the royal service did not prevent him from working for private customers as well. In particular, he is believed to have worked for the Duc de Choiseul, while between 1764 and 1769 he supplied Marigny with furniture worth 4,000 livres. Moreover, in an advertisement he also claimed that he 'tient fabrique et magazin considérable de meubles et ébénisterie, fait des envois en province et chez l'étranger' (runs a considerable manufactory and show-rooms where various classes of furniture and cabinet work may be seen; dispatches goods to the provinces and foreign parts).

Simon Oeben's mark is rarely found but is to be seen under a table in the Neo-Classical style at the Victoria and Albert Museum (Plate 144).

Vial, Marcel and Girodie, vol. II, p. 60.
Salverte, *Les ébénistes*, p. 241.
Jean-Mondain-Monval, *Correspondance de Soufflot avec les directeurs des Bâtiments concernant la Manufacture des Gobelins*, Paris, 1918, pp. 144–6 and 152–3.
Verlet, *Mobilier Royal II*, pp. 59–60.
Arch. Nat., o^1 1542–211 and 333.
Bibliothèque Historique de la Ville de Paris, MSS. Fonds Marigny, vol. I, fol. 150, 212 *verso*, 261 *verso*, and 319 *verso*.

See Plate 144.

ORSAY, Pierre-Gaspard-Marie Grimod Comte d'. Captain of dragoons. From 1778, *premier maréchal des logis* to the Comte de Provence. Born in 1748, died in 1809. Son of Pierre Grimod du Fort, Seigneur d'Orsay, who was *fermier-général* and *intendant des postes et relais*. Nephew of Gaspard Grimod de La Reynière.

On 27th May 1768, at the age of twenty, Grimod d'Orsay, who had acquired an immense fortune, bought the Hôtel de Clermont in the Rue de Varenne (now No. 69). Here and in his house near Versailles (the Château d'Orsay), he is said to have had an impressive art-collection, amassed entirely by himself. There can be little doubt that he is identical with the 'comte Dorset' to whom the chair-maker Delanois sent along a large consignment of seat-furniture on the 28th July 1768, including at any rate four arm-chairs which as we can see from the entry in Delanois' ledger, must have been in an outright *Louis Seize* style (see page 89). These were the first entirely Classical chairs to issue from Delanois' establishment as far as we know. Comte d'Orsay is also mentioned in the list of items (Nos. 60 and 61) in Philippe Caffieri's stock in 1770 where we read that there were four large *girandoles* in course of preparation for him. These were presumably in the new taste, as well. Neither the chairs nor the *girandoles* have so far been identified.

Ferdinand Boyer, 'Les hôtels parisiens et les châteaux des Grimod d'Orsay au XVIIIe siècle', *BSHAF*, 1951, pp. 107–17.
Ferdinand Boyer, 'La collection d'antiques du comte d'Orsay à la veille de la Révolution', *Comptes-rendus de l'Académie des Inscriptions et des Belles-Lettres*, 1953, pp. 439–43.
The present author's *Louis Delanois*, 1968, pp. 23, 32–3, 52.

OSMOND, Robert. Bronze-founder. Born about 1720, died in 1789. Presumably the father of the bronze-founder Louis-Charles Osmond.

In 1746, Osmond became *maître-fondeur en terre et sable*. In 1756, he was elected *juré des fondeurs* for two years. He was one of the co-signatories of the Bronze-Casters' Copyright Resolution which came into force on 21st April 1766. He seems to have been a friend of Philippe Caffieri since the latter chose Osmond to make the valuation of his wife's effects after her death. Osmond lived in the Rue Macon, near the site of the present Place Saint-Michel.

The name Osmond is found on a number of clock-cases of high quality—notably some cartel clocks like that shown in Plate 196. A cartel clock of this type was delivered for use at Versailles on 12th May 1770 by the clock-maker, Lepine. The same signature is found on some clock-cases made in the form of a short column with a vase containing the movement superimposed, and also on some small clock-cases where the face is in the column itself while cupids frolic at its foot. Such clocks have movements by clock-makers like Montjoie, Hilgers, Frédéric Duval, Julien Le Roy, etc.

The son, Louis-Charles Osmond, became a *maître* in 1757. The Jean-Baptiste Osmond who became a *maître* in 1764 was apparently not a son of Robert Osmond although he may well have been a relation.

Arch. Nat., Y 9328 (10th January 1757 and 7th June 1764), Y 9326 (17th January 1746).
Guiffrey, *Scellés*, III, p. 269.
Lespinasse, *Les métiers et corporations de la Ville de Paris*, II, p. 433.

See Plates 193 and 196.

PAJOU, Augustin. Sculptor. Born in 1730, died in 1809. Son of the carver Martin Pajou and his wife, the daughter of a sculptor named Eustache Pithoin. In 1761, he married the daughter of another sculptor, Claude Roumier. Their daughter, Flore, married the famous sculptor Clodion.

Pajou was a pupil of J. B. Lemoyne. He won the Grand Prix de Sculpture in 1748 and was granted a stipendium to enable him to attend the French Academy in Rome from January 1752 until May 1756. He is known to have visited Naples and Paestum. He became a member of the Académie de Peinture in 1760.

Lalive de Jully was among Pajou's first patrons; from him Lalive commissioned two allegorical figures —*La Paix* and *La Peinture*, in 1759 and 1763 respectively—as well as a portrait-bust in 1765. Pajou made drawings for the model of a large bronze clock for the King of Denmark in 1765; the clock was executed by the bronze-founder, J.-J. de Saint-Germain in 1766–67. Between 1767 and 1769, Pajou delivered a number of sculptures to the Palais Royal, while in 1769–70 he and his sixteen assistants created all the figure-sculpture required for the Opera building at Versailles. Amongst Pajou's other work should be mentioned the portrait-busts he executed of the Royal Family and the several he made of Madame du Barry. He is said to have produced the model for a clock-case that was to be made on the occasion of the marriage between the Dauphin and Marie-Antoinette; this clock was later in the San Donato Sale (lot Number 768, illustrated in the catalogue) and in the Paul Leroi sale (Paris, 16th December 1907; lot 16, illustrated on page 7 of the catalogue). In 1775, Pajou modelled the figures for a bronze clock-case commissioned by the Prince de Condé. It is interesting, moreover, to note that a drawing by him in the Cooper Union in New York showing a tomb in the Neo-Classical style for the Maréchal de Belle-Isle is dated as early as 1761.

Pajou lived in the Rue Froidmanteau by the Louvre for most of his life but he also owned a house in the Rue de la Pépinière which had been built by De Wailly about 1770. He included not only De Wailly among his friends but also two other architects—namely Moreau-Desproux, and Barreau de Chefdeville —and the painters Le Prince, Pierre and Baudouin.

Henri Stein, *Augustin Pajou*, Paris, 1912.
Michel N. Benisovich, 'Drawings of the sculptor Augustin Pajou in the United States', *The Art Bulletin*, vol. 35, 1953, pp. 295–8.

See Plates 39, 74 and 189.

PETITOT, Ennemond-Alexandre. Architect. Born at Lyons in 1727, died at Parma in 1801.

Petitot, whose father was also an architect and engineer, was first of all a pupil of Soufflot's in Lyons, and then studied at the Academy in Paris where he won the Grand Prix d'Architecture in 1745. From May 1746 until April 1750 he was in Rome as a stipendiary at the French Academy. During this period, in 1749, he was chosen to design the extensive architectural settings required for the annual Chinea Festival at the French Academy: on this occasion he created a circular mausoleum-like structure in Le Lorrain's classicising style. After his return to Paris he is known to have designed decorative schemes for a chapel for the d'Harcourt family in Notre-Dame. In 1753, Petitot was appointed *architetto delle fabbriche ducali* in the service of the Duke of Parma, on the recommendation of the Comte de Caylus. He remained in Parma for the rest of his life.

Petitot introduced the Neo-Classical taste to Parma. There, he was responsible for the façade of S. Pietro (1761), the interior of the Biblioteca Palatina (begun in 1763), and extensions to the Palazzo Ducale (1767), among much else.

Before leaving for Parma, Petitot engraved some of the plates for the Comte de Caylus' great work, the *Recueil d'Antiquités*. In Parma, he published an engraved series entitled *Suite de Vases* (1764) and a book, *Mascarade à la Grecque* (1771), which was a satire of 'le goût grec' not dissimilar from one produced by Carmontelle.

Thieme and Becker, *Künstlerleksikon.*
Henry Bedarida, *Parme et la France de 1748 à 1789*, Paris, 1928, pp. 500–14.
John Harris, 'Le Geay, Piranesi and International Neo-classicism in Rome 1740–1750', in *Essays in the History of Architecture presented to Rudolf Wittkower*, London, 1967, p. 195.

See Plate 13.

PEYRE, Marie-Joseph. Architect. Born in 1730, died in 1785. He was the elder brother of the architect Antoine-François Peyre. He was married to a sister of the architect Moreau-Desproux.

Peyre won the Grand Prix d'Architecture in 1751 and studied in Rome, as a stipendiary at the French Academy there, from mid-May 1753 until early in 1756. In Rome, he became friends with De Wailly with whom he later collaborated on the building of the new Théâtre-Français (l'Odéon). In 1772, he was appointed architect at Fontainebleau.

Of special interest in connection with the rise of Neo-Classicism, is Peyre's entirely Palladian (here used in the strict sense) building, the Hôtel de Neubourg (1762), which lay near the Gobelins and is known to us from engraved views in his *Oeuvres d'Architecture*. Among his later works—apart from the Odéon (1773–85)—one may mention the Hôtel de Nivernais in the Rue de Tournon and the Hôtel de Luzy in the Rue Férou.

Hautecoeur, *Histoire, seconde moitié*, pp. 225–31.
Gallet, *Demeures*, p. 197.

See Plate 48.

PEYROTTE, Alexis. Painter, textile-designer and designer of furniture. Born in 1699, died in 1769. He had a son, Augustin-Laurent, who lived in Avignon and was also a painter.

Peyrotte was appointed *peintre et dessinateur du Garde-Meuble de la Couronne* on 25th January 1749, and in this capacity is known to have been especially concerned with designing patterns for embroideries and woven silks, presumably mostly in the Rococo style, and often with chinoiserie themes. These materials were used for curtains, wall-hangings and upholstery in the many royal residences. One of his designs would seem to have embodied an early hint of Neo-Classicism, for we read that the silk was to be 'brochée d'or à cornets d'abondance' ('brocaded with a pattern of cornucopiae in silver gilt thread'); it was woven after the design in 1757 at Jean Charton's silk manufactory in Lyons and used in 1764 for Louis XV's *appartements* at Versailles. Whether Peyrotte was acquainted with the particular techniques of designing complex patterns for the loom is not known but, if not, an intermediary specialist silk-designer would have had to translate his designs into ones suitable for weaving. Since the Lyons silk-designers already excelled in the producing of patterns incorporating naturalistic motifs in the Rococo vein, it may well be that Peyrotte was brought into the scene to devise patterns of a rather different nature.

Peyrotte also designed carved furniture and provided models for the same executed in wax on frame-works of wood (which were provided by the chair-maker Foliot). As far as one can judge from the surviving bills, Peyrotte was not paid nearly as well for his pains as his successor, the architect Gondoin.

Peyrotte's studio was in the Rue du Faubourg-du-Temple. He worked also for private clients and had two assistants. He published a series of engraved designs of chinoiseries.

Guiffrey, *Scellés*, II, pp. 434–5.
Guiffrey, *Académie de Saint-Luc*, p. 417.
Verlet, *Versailles*, p. 522.
Courajod, *Lazare Duvaux*, p. CCI, and Arch. Nat., o^1 93 fol. 11.
Arch. Nat., o^1 3616, 3617, 3619, 3620 and 1922 B.

PIERRE, Jean-Baptiste-Marie. Painter. Born in 1713, died in 1789.

Studied under J.-F. Detroy, François Lemoyne and Natoire. Won the Grand Prix de Peinture in 1734 and attended the French Academy in Rome between 1735 and 1740. Back in Paris, he became a member of the Académie de Peinture (1742) and a professor in 1744. He was appointed *premier peintre* to the Duc d'Orléans in 1752, and became Director of the Academy in 1770 when he also succeeded François Boucher as *premier peintre du Roi.*

Although Pierre's talents were not great he concerns our theme because he belonged to that group of young artists who turned away from the Rococo style at an early date. He was well acquainted with people like Lalive de Jully, the Comte de Caylus and Watelet who all admired him. The Abbé le Blanc also praised his work and he even became the protégé of Madame de Pompadour and the Duc de Choiseul. In 1749, Watelet engraved a series of vases that Pierre had drawn; in 1759 we find Pierre designing frames of a Neo-Classical nature for Watelet's *L'Art de Peindre*. Pierre was among those Neo-Classical artists who devised decorative schemes for the church of Saint-Roch in 1756. But, by 1763, Diderot could write of Pierre that '. . . son talent s'est perdu; c'est aujourd'hui le plus vain et le plus plat de nos artistes' ('his talent has evaporated; today, he is the most ineffectual and dull artist we have').

Jean Locquin, *La peinture d'histoire en France de 1747 à 1785*, Paris 1912.

PIÈTRE, Henri. Architect. Born about 1725, died after 1785.

Piètre was a pupil of Jean-Sylvain Cartaud and later became his collaborator. He later worked with Contant d'Ivry, on whose death in 1777 he took over the latter's post as *premier architecte* to the Duc d'Orléans.

Among Piètre's early work is the interior decoration in the Neo-Classical taste which he carried out at the Palais Royal (Hôtel Mélusine); this is known through plans in the Archives Nationales which can be securely dated to the year 1766. According to Piètre's holographic *curriculum vitae*, he built a circular dining-room decorated with twelve Ionic pilasters at the Château de Raincy in 1768.

Michel Gallet, 'Les dessins de l'architecte Henri Piètre pour la décoration du Palais Royal', *Bulletin du Musée Carnavalet*, June 1960, pp. 8–15.
Gallet, *Demeures*, p. 197, and Arch. Nat., o[1] 1913–204.

See Plates 68–9, 399–400.

PITOIN, Quentin-Claude. Sculptor and bronze-founder. Born about 1725, died in 1777. In 1752 he married Elizabeth Lelièvre (died 1774), daughter of Antoine Lelièvre, a *maître-doreur*. They had three children: a daughter, Germaine-Elizabeth, who married Jean-Antoine Dangé, a *maître-serrurier*, a second daughter named Marie-Elizabeth who married Louis-Pierre Fixon, a *maître-sculpteur*, and a son named Claude-Jean who was later described as a *doreur sur métaux*.

It is not easy to distinguish the branches of the Pitoin family tree but the family included several sculptors and painters. It can, however, be established that Quentin-Claude Pitoin was the regular supplier of *bronzes d'ameublement* to the French Court from 1763 onwards; this is clear from the inventory taken after his death on 11th June 1777 which is preserved in the Minutier Central des Notaires. On the other hand, we cannot be sure of the identity of his father although we know he was a *maître-sculpteur* and that he was not the *maître-sculpteur* named Jean-Baptiste Pitoin *père*, who owned a house in the Rue Boucherat, was director of the Académie de Saint-Luc, and died in 1767.

Our Quentin-Claude Pitoin became a *maître-sculpteur* and a member of the Académie de Saint-Luc in 1752. He was elected a *directeur-garde* of this academy in 1762 for a period of three years. In July 1763 he rented an apartment with workshops in his father-in-law's house in the Rue des Deux Portes Saint-

Sauveur. In 1769 he purchased a house nearby in the Rue des Petits Carreaux, diagonally opposite the house of the chair-maker Louis Delanois, where he remained for the rest of his life.

Judging from the inventory drawn up on 11th June 1777, Pitoin's workshops were not large. He had only two work-benches and a couple of vices or clamps (*étaux*), apart from 'outils et ustanciles propres à la dorure' ('the tools and utensils required for gilding'). In all, these were valued at a mere 60 livres. However, it may well be that Pitoin's fortunes had declined during his later years, since his workshop had been valued at 272 livres when his wife died in 1764, and he had then had fourteen clamps as well as the two work-benches. For comparison, it is interesting to note that Philippe Caffieri had six benches with eight clamps in 1770, valued at 400 livres in all. Pitoin does not seem to have had his own equipment for the casting of bronzes and, curiously enough, the last inventory does not mention any stock of models, similar to Caffieri's. However, it is apparent that he collaborated with several bronze-founders, e.g. Nicolas Henry, Bernard Douet and Louis-Gabriel Feloix, as well as Louis Agy and Nicolas Franche, and also a certain Sieur Villemsens who cannot yet be identified. A Sieur Benoist carried out the silvering of bronzes for Pitoin and is known to have thus treated sixty-three pairs of 'flambeaux à la Royalle' ('candlesticks of the Royal pattern') which Benoist only delivered some days after Pitoin's death. Moreover, Pitoin acknowledged in 1764 that he owed his father 3,806 livres 'pour des travaux de sculptures faits en société entreux' ('for the works of sculpture they had together produced'); that is, they collaborated, so it is possible that the models Pitoin may be expected to have needed for this work in fact remained in the father's workshops.

Pitoin fell ill in 1775 and in 1776, barely a year before he died, he apprenticed his son, Claude-Jean, to a *maître-sculpteur* named Martin so that he should learn the trade of modelling in clay and in wax ('à modeler tant en terre qu'en cire'). It is not known whether the son ever became a *maître* in this or some other trade, but he does seem to have kept the family firm going until 1786 or 1787 when he left the business to become a partner with a certain Pierre-Louis Fockedey, apparently to establish a straightforward commercial enterprise. In 1791 he went bankrupt.

Pitoin claims our interest because he was the principal supplier of *bronzes d'ameublement*—ornamental bronzes—to the *Garde-Meuble de la Couronne* from 1763 until he died in 1777. He probably inherited the post from his father-in-law, Antoine Lelièvre, who had supplied numerous bronzes to the Court before 1760 and styled himself *doreur du Roi.* The existence and importance of Pitoin was first re-discovered by Pierre Verlet. It is now known that Pitoin also supplied bronzes for the use of Madame de Pompadour, while he numbered among his private customers illustrious courtiers like the Prince de Constantin, the Duc d'Orléans and the Duc de Gesvres; he provided the last-named with bronzes worth a great sum in the early 1770s. The son continued to provide bronzes for the Court and included the Prince de Salm amongst his private customers.

Pitoin supplied the Royal Household both with purely practical items such as gilt curtain-rings, and with *bronzes d'ameublement*—works of artistic importance like fire-dogs, sconces and chandeliers. Indeed, during the period 1763–1775 he delivered eighty-three pairs of fire-dogs, forty-five pairs of sconces, and three chandeliers. Of this extensive production only two pairs of fire-dogs have so far been identified—a pair decorated with a wild boar and a stag, made in 1772 for Madame du Barry's apartments at Fontainebleau, and a pair ornamented with lyres made in the same year for Fontanieu who was then director of the *Garde-Meuble de la Couronne*. Both were recognised by Verlet and are now in the Louvre. Verlet has also identified some candlesticks which were executed when the son was in charge of the business, delivered in 1781 for use in Marie-Antoinette's apartments at Versailles.

According to the descriptions given in Pitoin's bills and in the protocol-inventories of the *Garde-Meuble*, it is clear that almost all the bronzes he supplied for the Court were in the Neo-Classical style including all those intended for the recently-erected Petit Trianon.

Pierre Verlet, 'The Wallace Collection and the Study of French Eighteenth-Century Bronzes d'Ameublement', *Burlington Magazine*, vol. XCII, June 1950, pp. 154–7.

Guiffrey, *Scellés*, vol. III, pp. 73–5.
Arch. Nat., Y 9327 (14th June 1752) and Y 9328 (19th October 1762); o[1] 3616 ff and o[1] 3318–3319 *passim*.
Arch. Nat., Minutier Central, III–1195 (23rd November 1788); III–1213 (24th January 1791); XLII–488 (24th January 1764); LXXVIII–823 (11 June 1777).
Arch. Seine, D 4 B^6 carton 112, dossier 8000.
Watson, *Wallace Collection Furniture*, p. 94.

See Plates 214, 224, 227–9, 230.

POIRIER, Simon-Philippe. Dealer in works of art and furniture. Born about 1720, died in 1785. He was a nephew of Thomas-Joachim Hébert, the famous dealer. In 1742 he married Marguerite-Madeleine Hécéguerre who was a daughter of the dealer Michel Hécéguerre; their son François Alexandre became a *marchand d'étoffes*.

Poirier became a *marchand-mercier grossier jouailler* in 1742. His shop, 'at the sign of the Golden Crown' (*A la Couronne d'Or*), lay in the Rue Saint-Honoré near the Rue du Roule and not far from the shops of other important dealers like Dulac and Bazin. It seems that Poirier dealt in all kinds of luxury furnishing wares with the exception of chairs, carpets and tapestries. He handled clocks, porcelain, commodes, tables, chandeliers, and decorative bronzes (fire-dogs, sconces, etc.). The Guild regulations forbade a *marchand-mercier* like Poirier having the goods he was to sell made in workshops of his own: he had to obtain his wares from independent craftsmen. Thus he commissioned furniture from Bernard Vanrisamburgh and, after 1766, from Martin Carlin, as well, apparently, as from Roger Vandercruse (known as Lacroix) who was Oeben's and then Riesener's brother-in-law. Furthermore, it transpires that Poirier engaged designers to produce models for such craftsmen to follow; this can be deduced from an account he sent to Lord Coventry in 1768 and from a letter written by Horace Walpole in 1766.

Poirier must have been one of the Sèvres factory's main customers. We know that between December 1758 and December 1770 he bought about 700,000 livres worth of Sèvres porcelain. One of his special lines was furniture set with plaques of Sèvres porcelain. As Verlet has shown, the first piece of furniture on which this form of decoration was used was the *Louis Quinze*-type commode provided in about 1760 for the Prince de Condé. Later, such ornament was more usually applied to small tables and writing-desks. However, it is important to note that he bought only about 1,400 plaques of various shapes and sizes, for a total of 42,000 livres. And hardly anyone else was purchasing plaques from the Sèvres factory, so it is safe to assume that most of the genuine furniture decorated with such plaques must have passed through Poirier's hands.

Verlet has made it quite clear what an important position Poirier held as an arbiter of taste in the field of the decorative arts. He adopted the Neo-Classical idiom at an early date—for instance, he sent a 'commode à la grec' and some sconces 'à l'antique' to Lord Coventry in September 1763, and some other items in the same taste followed during the next year.

Among Poirier's principal customers was Madame de Pompadour and, on her death in 1764, he acted as valuer of her property. Afterwards, he acquired Madame du Barry as an important client; during the period 1764–74, she bought goods to the value of almost 99,000 livres from him. Among his other illustrious clients were the Duc de Parme, the Duchesse de Mazarin, the Duc d'Orléans, the Duc de Choiseul, the Comtesse de Duras, the Vicomte de Noailles, the Comte de Hautefort, the Duc de Bouillon, the Duc de Caylus and the famous collector Louis-Jean Gaignat.

In 1772, Poirier went into partnership with Dominique Daguerre, who took over the whole business in 1777. Daguerre was a cousin of Madame Poirier's. When Daguerre married in 1772, Poirier gave him as part of his wedding present, a certain amount of 'modelles de cuivre cizelé' (models of chased bronze, or models for chased bronzes).

After having retired from business Poirier became a *consul et administrateur des hôpitaux des petites Maisons et de la Trinité*.

Pierre Verlet, *Sèvres, le XVIIIe siècle*, Paris, 1953.
Pierre Verlet, 'Les marchands merciers à Paris au XVIIIe siècle, *Annales*, January–March 1958, pp. 10–29.
F. J. B. Watson, 'Walpole and the Taste for French Porcelain in Eighteenth-Century England' in *Horace Walpole: Writer, Politician, and Connoisseur*, New Haven, 1967, pp. 185–94 and 327–36.
Jean Cordey, *Inventaire des biens du Madame de Pompadour rédigé après son décès*, Paris, 1939.
Charles Vatel, *Histoire de Mme du Barry d'après ses papiers personnels*, Versailles, 1883.
Georges Wildenstein, ed., 'Simon-Philippe Poirier, fournisseur de Madame du Barry, *Gaz.d.B.-A.* 1962, pp. 365–77.
Arch. Nat., Y. 9325 (9th November 1742).
Arch. Nat., Minutier Central, CXVII (9th November 1742; 15th April 1772; 14th May 1772; 9th September 1785).

See Plates 111, 118, 121–2, 125, 136, 197–9, 235, and Colour Plate D.

POMPADOUR, Jeanne-Antoinette Marquise de. Louis XV's official mistress from 1745 to 1764. Born on 29th December 1721, died on 15th April 1764. Daughter of François Poisson, one of the contractors of forage to the French Army who also enjoyed a position of trust in the service of the banker-family Pâris. In 1741, she married Charles-Guillaume-Borromée le Normant d'Étoilles, a nephew of Le Normant de Tournehem who was to become *directeur général des bâtiments*. Sister of the Marquis de Marigny, and his senior by six years.

While it is well known that during much of her life Madame de Pompadour favoured the style that was called after her royal lover, *Le Style Louis Quinze*, there can be little doubt that she also seems to have played her part in the early development of Neo-Classicism in France. In the first place, in 1749, she sent her younger brother on a tour of Italy to help prepare him for the post of *directeur général des bâtiments* which he was to take over from Le Normant de Tournehem in due course. On this tour, the young man was accompanied by three men, two of which, the Abbé Le Blanc and Soufflot—and possibly also the third, Cochin—were outspoken critics of the Rococo style. She can hardly have been ignorant of their views and the fact that she despatched her brother in their care suggests she was to some extent in sympathy with them.

In the second place there are two portraits of her, painted respectively in 1758 and in 1763–64 (Plates 309 and 372), which shows her amid some pieces of furniture that are unmistakably couched in a Classical idiom, even at that early date. It is to be presumed that she owned these pieces; at any rate she allowed herself to be portrayed with them alongside so they must have met with her approval. What is more, we learn from the inventory made after her death in 1764 that she possessed no less than sixteen commodes 'à la grecque', most of them standing at her Château de Menars (see the references in J.-F. Oeben's biography, page 209). These are likely to have been in the same style as that illustrated in Plate 95. It bears J.-F. Oeben's marks and he was of course famed for his furniture 'à la grecque'. None of these commodes are mentioned in the Journal of the *Garde-Meuble*, nor in Lazare Duvaux's *Livre-Journal* which runs up to March 1762. Probably Oeben supplied the commodes to Madame de Pompadour direct since he was her cabinet-maker by appointment.

Madame de Pompadour had apartments placed at her disposal in almost all the royal palaces—Versailles, Fontainebleau, Choisy, Saint-Hubert etc. Moreover, the King's intention had been to give her the Petit Trianon which, however, was not completed until after her death. When she died she was possessed of several private residences to which she could have retired if she had had to withdraw from Court life. In Paris, for instance, she owned the Hôtel d'Évreux (now the Elysée Palace) and a flat in the Couvent des Capucines. At Versailles, she owned the Hôtel des Réservoirs and an *hermitage* that was a small but most elegantly furnished retreat. She also had homes at Fontainebleau and Compiègne. She owned the Château de Menars in the Loire Valley, a house that the Marquis de Marigny was to inherit from her, and she at various times also owned the Château de Crécy, the Château de Bellevue, and two *pavillons* on the way out to Versailles from Paris. What is more, for three years, she had the use of the Château de Champs.

Emile Compardon, *Madame de Pompadour et la cour de Louis XV au milieu du dix-huitième siècle*, 1867.
Jean Cordey, *Inventaire des biens de Madame de Pompadour rédigé après son décès*, 1939.
Lazare Duvaux, *Livre-Journal.*
Edmond et Jules de Goncourt, *Madame de Pompadour*, *Nouvelle édition, revue et augmentée de lettres et documents inédits*, 1888.
J.-J. Guiffrey, 'Inventaire de Jean-François Oeben', *NAAF*, 1899, pp. 298–367.

See Plates 247, 309 and 372.

PRIEUR, Jean-Louis. Sculptor, furniture-designer, and founder and chaser of bronzes. Born about 1725, died after 1785.

Prieur became a *maître-sculpteur* and member of the Académie de Saint-Luc in 1765. In 1769 he became a *maître-fondeur en terre et sable*. In the *Almanach des Artistes* for the year 1777, he is described as *sculpteur en ornemens*, *modeleur et ciseleur*, while in 1783 he calls himself *sculpteur*, *ciseleur et doreur du Roi*. In 1776 he was living in the Rue du Faubourg Saint-Denis; later he moved to the Enclos du Temple. He went bankrupt in 1778. This J.-L. Prieur should not be confused with another sculptor with the same Christian and surnames who was residing in the Rue Frepillon in 1758.

Prieur's earliest known work is the series of drawings he executed for furniture, bronzes, etc., in the Neo-Classical style intended for the Polish Court at Warsaw in 1766, for which he was paid the not inconsiderable sum of 57,500 livres. Perhaps this included payment for the actual manufacture by Prieur of some of the bronzes—those not being made by Philippe Caffieri. In about 1775, Prieur provided the bronze mounts for the coach made for the coronation of Louis XVI after designs by Bellanger. During the 1780s he produced numerous engravings of ornament, principally proposals for arabesque wall-decoration. Among Prieur's many drawings in the University Library in Warsaw, is a series of *Vases et Fontaines* and another of *Dessins de Diferentes Bordures*. A bronze bracket-clock included in the Albert von Goldschmidt-Rothschild sale (Berlin, 14th March 1933; lot 36) was inscribed 'Prieur Sculpteur Paris'.

Jean Stern, *François-Joseph Bellanger*, I, Paris, 1930, p. 50.
Stanislas Lorentz, 'Victor Louis et Varsovie', in the catalogue of an exhibition with the same title, Bordeaux-Paris, 1958.
F.-G. Pariset, 'Jeszcze o pracach Wiktora Louisa dla zamku Warszawskiego', *Biuletyn Historii Sztuki*, Warsaw, 1962, pp. 135–55.
Arch. Nat., Y 9328 (5th November 1765), Y 9331 (13th July 1769) and Z[1J] 921 (13th August 1768).
Arch. Nat., Minutier Central, XXVIII (20th November 1756).
Archives de la Seine, D 4 B[6] cart. 68, dossier 4505.
Rudolf H. Wackernagel, *Der französische Krönungswagen*, Berlin, 1966.

See Plates 71, 190–2, 205, 207, 402–6, 408, 410–23.

PROVENCE, Louis-Stanislas-Xavier, Comte de. Born in 1755, died in 1824. Son of Dauphin Louis (died 1795) and Marie-Josèphe de Saxe (died 1767), grandson of Louis XV, brother of Louis XVI and Comte d'Artois. In 1771 he married Marie-Josephine de Savoie. In 1814 he became King of France under the title of Louis XVIII.

When the Comte de Provence was married in 1771 at the age of sixteen, apartments were put at his disposal at Versailles and Compiègne and the furnishings were provided at the King's expense through the *Garde-Meuble de la Couronne*. It is not known whether the Comte had had any say in the choice of these furnishings but we know that they were comparatively modern in style, even if they were no more advanced in taste than other furniture then being provided by the *Garde-Meuble*. Only a single piece of furniture from these apartments has so far been identified, namely the commode that was sold as lot 147 in the

Vicomtesse Vigier sale held at the Palais Galliéra in Paris on 2nd June 1970 (illustrated in the catalogue). Although signed by Roger Vandercruse Lacroix, this commode was delivered by Gilles Joubert on 30th September 1771 (Arch. Nat., o[1] 3319, fol. 69 *verso*); the commode, which at the time of writing belongs to Messrs Frank Partridge and Sons, bears the inventory number 2636 which leads to the identification, while another mark, a crowned F and the figure 707, shows that the commode eventually was transferred to the Duc de Coigny's apartment at the Château de Fontainebleau (Arch. Nat., o[1] 3398, p. 348).

The little writing-desk Joubert made for the Comte de Provence in 1771, which is mentioned in the Note to Plate 143, and which had straight legs, was probably the most advanced in taste of the furniture that went into these rooms. The sconce shown in Plate 214 is probably not unlike those with which he was provided for his apartment at Compiègne in 1771. From Pitoin's accounts, we know that the other *bronzes d'ameublement*—sconces and fire-dogs—which he supplied for the Comte de Provence's use, were all couched in the Neo-Classical style. The cylinder-top desk shown in Plate 141, which has cabriole legs, was delivered in 1773 for the personal use of the Comtesse. The Comte received the desk shown in Plate 143 during the following year; this has straight legs. As far as is known, however, none of the chairs provided for their use at this early stage had straight legs.

Nouvelle Biographie Générale, vol. 31, columns 907–39.
Gerard Walter, *Le comte de Provence*, 1950.
Verlet, *French Royal Furniture*, pp. 117–19.

See Plates 141 and 227.

RICHELIEU, Louis-François-Armand du Plessis, Duc de. Marshal of France and *premier gentilhomme de la chambre du Roi*. Born in 1696, died in 1788. Great-nephew of Cardinal Richelieu.

Richelieu, who was as famed for his military exploits as he was notorious for his amorous adventures, was appointed *premier gentilhomme de la chambre du Roi* in 1744. In 1745, he was appointed Governor of both Guienne and Gascony, and in 1748 he became a Marshal of France. He distinguished himself at the Battle of Fontenoy and, during the Seven Years' War, at the Battle for Port-Mahon. As a *premier gentilhomme* he belonged to the inner circle round Louis XV and, like the Duc d'Aumont, was a controller of the *Menus Plaisirs* where he concerned himself principally with matters that had to do with his theatres.

The Duc had known Madame du Barry for many years before Louis XV made her acquaintance; in fact, he was one of her most trusted friends and supported her in her intrigues against the Duc de Choiseul. It is possible that it was Richelieu, perhaps supported by the Duc d'Aumont, who encouraged Madame du Barry to espouse the Neo-Classical cause with such enthusiasm.

For most of his life, Richelieu lived in surroundings of the utmost luxury and he was extremely conscious of changes in fashion. At first he lived in a house on the present Place des Vosges, where he had, amongst other things, a *cabinet chinois* of which sections are now in the Musée Carnavalet. In 1757, he built the Pavillon d'Hanovre which is said to have been furnished with great splendour—presumably in the Rococo style, like almost every other room in Paris at that date. However, in the late 1760s Richelieu's tastes seem to have altered. He appointed Victor Louis his personal architect and commissioned him to carry out various modifications to the Pavillon d'Hanovre which must have been in the new style. Unfortunately we do not know when Richelieu met Victor Louis, nor when he started to alter the Pavillon. The earliest hint we have that Richelieu had turned to the new taste is probably contained in a document dated 3rd May 1768 concerning the payment of the sum of 4,000 livres for some unspecified work to the smith, Pierre Deumier, who was known for his work in the Neo-Classical style including the wrought-iron choir-screen in the church of Saint-Germain l'Auxerrois. In 1771 Richelieu supported Victor Louis' proposal for a theatre in Paris, which came to nothing. However, he succeeded in getting Louis selected to design the Bordeaux theatre instead. At Waddesdon Manor, Buckinghamshire, there are three sets of wall-panels of which one is in the Neo-Classical taste, that are supposed to have come from a house belonging to Richelieu although this tradition has not been confirmed.

Nouvelle Biographie Générale, vol. 39, column 163.
Journal de Papillon de la Ferté, 1887, pp. 291 and 315.
Paul d'Estrée, *La vieillesse de Richelieu*, 1921.
Michel Gallet, 'Le grand cabinet chinois de l'hôtel de Richelieu, Place Royale', *Bulletin du Musée Carnavalet*, June 1967.
Arch. Nat., Minutier Central, étude II, liasse 627 (3rd May 1768).

RIESENER, Jean-Henri (occurs as Joan-Henrich, derived from Johann Heinrich). Cabinet-maker. Born in 1734 at Gladbeck near Essen, died in Paris in 1806. Son of a chair-maker, Herman Riesener, who was known by the name of Marcks. In 1767, J.-H. Riesener married the widow of the famous cabinet-maker, J.-F. Oeben, who was also the sister of the cabinet-maker Roger Vandercruse, called Lacroix, as well as being a sister of the wife of Simon Oeben, J.-F. Oeben's brother, who was also a cabinet-maker. He also came to be related by marriage to Martin Carlin whose wife was a sister of the two Oeben brothers!

Riesener presumably came to Paris in the 1750s. He is known to have been the foreman in charge of the late J.-F. Oeben's workshops at the Arsenal in 1765 when Oeben's widow was directing the business after her first husband's death in 1763. But it is probable that Riesener had started to work there long before, probably well before Oeben died. In 1765 Riesener was living in the Rue de la Contrescarpe, on the far side of the old moat lying between the Bastille and the Arsenal, and thus close to Oeben's establishment. When he had married Oeben's widow, he moved into the Arsenal itself, and took over the direction of the firm. It was not until January 1768 that he became a *maître* in the Cabinet-makers' Guild. At this stage the *Bureau du Roi*, which Oeben had begun in 1760, was still not finished. Very little of the stock left when Oeben died (see Oeben's biography above) remained unsold when Riesener took over. Moreover, five of Oeben's twelve work-benches had been sold in the intervening period.

The *Bureau du Roi*, which represents a transitional style lying between the true Rococo of *Louis Quinze* and the Neo-Classical idiom, was delivered to the *Garde-Meuble* in May 1769. At about the same time—or shortly after—Riesener must have made the rather simpler version now in the Wallace Collection—the *Bureau du Roi Stanislas*.

In 1771 Riesener provided a small writing-desk for the use of Louis XV. This was apparently of the form much favoured by Oeben but with much more complicated mechanical fittings and with straight legs ('pieds à guaîne'). Later in the same year, he provided a fall-front desk ('secrétaire à abattant') and a small table, both of them highly elaborate and very expensive, for the use of Fontanieu the director of the *Garde-Meuble de la Couronne*. A year later, Fontanieu acquired from Riesener a large writing-table and two corner-cupboards. In December 1773, Riesener delivered a cylinder-top writing-desk *with curved legs* to the Comtesse de Provence, and in March of the next year another with straight legs for the Comte—both intended for use in their apartments in the Palace at Versailles.

In the months that followed, the flow of deliveries increases fast. The eighty-five-year-old Gilles Joubert seems by this time to have ceased to execute any more work in his capacity of royal cabinet-maker. During the rest of the year—that is, from March 1774—Riesener delivered no less than three hundred pieces of furniture, some quite plain and others of extreme richness, for use at the Court. This number included fifty-eight commodes, 126 small tables, ten fall-front desks, one cylinder-top desk and one hundred 'chaises d'affaires' ('close-stools') and bidets. By this stage, Riesener seems to have gone over entirely to the Neo-Classical style. Riesener inherited the post of royal cabinet-maker from Joubert in 1774 and continued to hold this position until the mid 1780s. He and David Roentgen were Marie-Antoinette's favourite cabinet-makers.

Vial, Marcel and Girodie, vol. II, pp. 116–19.
Salverte, *Les ébénistes*, pp. 268–74.
Ch. Séné, 'Contrat de mariage de Riesener avec la Veuve Oeben et documents sur l'ébéniste Oeben', *NAAF*, 1878, pp. 319–38.
Josef Giesen, 'Ehret Eure deutschen Meister', *Gladbecker Volkszeitung*, 1st December 1935.
Verlet, *Mobilier Royal I–III, passim.*
Pierre Verlet *Möbel von J.H. Riesener*, Darmstadt, 1955.

See Plates 90–3, 123, 141, 143, 146–7, 149.

ROËTTIERS DELATOUR, Jacques-Nicolas. Goldsmith. Born in 1736, died sometime after 1784. Son of Jacques Roëttiers, *orfèvre ordinaire du Roi*, and his wife who was a daughter of the goldsmith Nicolas Besnier.

Roëttiers first worked under his father and became a *maître* in 1765. He retired in 1777. The father and son between them seem to have taken over the task of providing the greater part of the silver required at Court after F.-T. Germain's bankruptcy in 1765 and until 1774. The father had in fact worked for the Court on occasions before that, however; already in 1756 he was executing work for Versailles, while in 1761 he provided a number of *girandoles* in gilt bronze, and in 1764 he delivered a pair of sugar-castors (*sucriers*) for the personal use of the King. In 1767, Roëttiers made eight tureens with their accompanying spoons and forks for Louis XV: two of the forks of this pattern dated 1770–71 are now in the Louvre. Roëttiers furthermore provided a complete dinner-service in the *Louis Seize* style consisting of 842 pieces for the use of Count Grégoire Orloff, the Empress Catherine's lover; parts of this set are still in Leningrad and Moscow while the odd piece is to be found in various European and American museums. Some tureens like those in the Orloff service were also made for the daughters of Louis XV.

Arch. Nat., o[1] 3317 (30th December 1761).
Mercure de France, November 1764, p. 155.
Victor Advielle, *Notice sur les Roëttiers*, Reunion des Sociétés des Beaux-Arts des Départements, 1888, pp. 446–571.
Musée du Louvre et Musée de Cluny, *Catalogue de l'orfèvrerie*, Paris, 1958, p. 125.
Les grands orfèvres de Louis XIII à Charles X, Paris, 1965, p. 206ff. (text by Yves Bottineau).

See Plates 263–5.

ROSLIN, Alexander. Swedish portrait painter. Born in Malmö in 1718, died in Paris in 1793.

After being trained in Sweden, Roslin went to Italy in 1747 and stayed in Naples until 1749. Thence he went to Rome for half a year in 1750, and was in Parma in 1751 where he came to know Petitot. In 1751 he went to Paris where he became acquainted with, amongst others, the Comte de Caylus who became his enthusiastic supporter. He was at that time in close contact with the Swedish Count Frederik Sparre who was responsible for putting Carl-Gustav Tessin in touch with Le Lorrain (see pages 56–7). Roslin also became a close friend of Boucher and Vien and knew both Soufflot and Taraval. In 1753 he became a member of the Académie de Peinture. He was living in the Rue de la Feuillade, near the Place des Victoires, in 1756 and from 1772 had lodgings in the Louvre.

Roslin not only painted portraits of several members of the French Royal Family but was patronised by a number of people who are known to have favoured the Neo-Classical taste—for example, the Marquis de Marigny (1761), Lalive de Jully (1763), Grimod de La Reynière (*c.* 1764) and Nicholas Cochin (*c.* 1774). Apart from this, he earns a place in the history of Neo-Classicism because, at an early date, he not infrequently included representations of some ultra-modern pieces of furniture in his portraits. The earliest instance of this in his portrait of Marigny.

Gunnar W. Lundberg, *Roslin, liv och verk*, Malmö, 1957.

See Plates 308, 346, 348, 353, 355–6, 371, 428, 447.

SAINT-GERMAIN, Jean-Joseph de. Bronze-founder. Born in 1719, died sometime after 1787. Son of the cabinet-maker, Joseph de Saint-Germain. In 1749, he married Anne Legrand, the widow of a cabinet-maker named Jean-Paul Mathieu. A son, Jean de Saint-Germain, also became a bronze-worker.

Saint-Germain first worked as an *ouvrier libre* in the Faubourg Saint-Antoine where he had a workshop in the Rue de Charenton. Among his apprentices was a certain Jean Goyer who later became a cabinet-maker. However, on 15th July 1748, Saint-Germain was registered as a *maître-fondeur en terre et sable*—'suivant l'arrêt du Conseil d'état du Roy du 27 décembre 1746 et par chef d'oeuvre' ('by order of the *Conseil d'état du Roi* of 27th December 1746 and by virtue of a master-piece'). In 1765 he was elected *juré* of the Bronze-founders' Guild for two years, and, in this capacity, actively campaigned for the Bronze-founders' Copyright Resolution, which was finally ratified on 21st April 1766, and on which his name appears as co-signatory. Saint-Germain's son was made a *maître* in that same year—while the father was *juré* and the son a mere sixteen years of age!

A number of high-quality bronze clock-cases are signed 'ST. GERMAIN'. Most of these are in the Rococo style but a few are in the Neo-Classical taste. The largest and most elaborate—the one made in 1766–67 for the King of Denmark after models by Pajou—is still preserved in the Royal Danish Collections at Amalienborg Palace in Copenhagen.

Saint-Germain also made mounts for furniture and in this connection it is worth noting that in 1755 he obtained a loan of 3,000 livres from the widow of François Vandercruse, the cabinet-maker who, like his more famous son, was known as Lacroix. This rather suggests that the two men may have collaborated at some stage.

Arch. Nat., Y 10989 (24th March and 4th May 1745), Y 14092 (18th November and 28th November 1765), Y 10995 (3rd April 1753), Y 9326 (15th July 1748), Y 9328 (11th July 1765 and 17th February 1766); Minutier Central, XXVIII–341 (12th April 1755).
Lespinasse, *Les métiers et corporations de la Ville de Paris*, vol. II, 1892, p. 433.
Granges de Surgères, *Artistes français*, pp. 185–6.
Mario Krohn, *Frankrigs og Danmarks kunstneriske forbindelser i det 18. aarhundrede*, vol. II., 1922, pp. 205–6.

See Plate 189.

SERVANDONI, Giovanni Niccolo. Architect, theatre-designer, and painter. Born in Florence in 1695, died in 1766 in Paris.

Studied under G. P. Pannini and Gius. Ignazio Rossi in Rome. Went to Paris in 1724 and became *premier peintre décorateur* of the Académie Royale de Musique in 1728. In 1731 he became a member of the Académie de Peinture as a painter of landscapes. He lived in the Place du Palais-Royal, at the corner of the Rue Saint-Thomas du Louvre until 1731, whereupon he moved to the Place Saint-Sulpice where he remained until his death.

Servandoni executed a large number of schemes for gala-settings and stage-scenery but he became famous in his day as the architect responsible for the façade of Saint-Sulpice (1732–54) in which was combined 'la grandeur, la magnificence, ce caractère mâle & élégant de l'antique, ces belles proportions, & ce repos majestueux des anciens édifices' ('the grandeur, the magnificence, the forthright and elegant character of Classical architecture, with the good proportions and majestic serenity of those ancient buildings'; *Mercure de France*, July 1758). Bachaumont said of Servandoni that he was an 'excellent architecte pour les grandes choses dans le goust grèc' ('an excellent architect for works on a grand scale in the Grecian or Antique taste'). He also built a private house on the Place Saint-Sulpice (1754) and designed a private chapel in the house in the Rue Saint-Honoré belonging to Lalive de Jully.

Among Servandoni's pupils were the architects De Wailly and Chalgrin, as well as Morand who settled and worked in Lyons.

Thieme and Becker, *Künstlerleksikon.*
Hautecoeur, *Histoire, première moitié, passim.*
Emile Malbois, 'Projets de place devant Saint-Sulpice', Gaz.d.B.-A., 1922 II, pp. 283–92.

See Plates 1 and 16.

SLODTZ, René-Michel, known as Michel-Ange. Sculptor and designer of ceremonial-decorations. Born in 1705, died in 1764. Son of the sculptor Sébastien Slodtz and his wife who was a daughter of the royal cabinet-maker Domenico Cucci. Two of his brothers became sculptors, while two became painters; a sister married the painter Carel Van Falens.

Studied under his father and at the Academy. Although he had won no Grand Prix, he was given the opportunity of staying at the French Academy in Rome, where he arrived in November 1728 and remained until January 1736. He then stayed a further ten years in Rome at his own expense. There are various works by Slodtz preserved in Roman churches as witness of his stay in that city. While there, he executed a mausoleum for the archbishops of Vienne to be set up in Vienne Cathedral. He also produced a high altar for the Cathedral, between 1744 and 1747. Both these works are in a heavy Classical style. Between 1756 and 1760 he produced several pieces of sculpture in Paris for the sacristy of Notre-Dame which had been designed by Soufflot. He also provided models for Honoré Guibert and Louis-Pierre Fixon to follow. In 1757–58 he made models for the carved decoration of the circular salon in the little Palace of Saint-Hubert.

Slodtz was chosen to succeed his brother, Paul-Ambroise Slodtz, as *dessinateur des Menus-Plaisirs* in 1758. In this capacity, he designed and arranged several funerals and lyings-in-state including that of the King of Spain which took place at Notre-Dame in January 1760 and was entirely in the Neo-Classical style.

In Rome, Slodtz had struck up a friendship with the architect Soufflot. He was also a friend of the Caffieri family who were near neighbours, living in the Rue des Canettes. On the other hand, he was on bad terms with the Comte de Caylus who managed for a time to discredit him in the eyes of the Marquis de Marigny.

François Souchal, *Les Slodtz sculpteurs et décorateurs du Roi 1685–1764*, Paris, 1967.

See Plates 12, 42–3, 90–3, 342.

SOUFFLOT, Jacques-Germain. Architect. Born at Irancy, near Auxerre, in 1713; died at Paris in 1780.

Soufflot left his home-town at the age of eighteen and journeyed to Rome via Lyons: he arrived at his destination in 1731. In December 1734, he joined the French Academy in Rome and remained there until March 1738. He then went back to Lyons where he became the City Architect. He gained a high reputation as a result of the buildings he erected there, and Madame de Pompadour chose him to accompany her young brother, Abel Poisson (later Monsieur de Vandières but best known as the Marquis de Marigny), on a study-tour of Italy, together with the draughtsman Charles-Nicolas Cochin and the Abbé Le Blanc. They set forth in December 1749 and visited Milan, Parma, Modena and Rome. In May 1750, Poisson returned home while Soufflot went on to Naples and to Paestum where, together with the architect G.-P.-M. Dumont, he made measured drawings of the Classical temples.

By February 1751, we find Soufflot back in Lyons where he took up his old appointment again. In 1755, however, he was called to Paris to build the church of Sainte-Geneviève and in the same year he was appointed *contrôleur des travaux de Paris*, a post under the jurisdiction of the *bâtiments du Roi*. The post carried with it the task of being *directeur des manufactures royales des Gobelins et de la Savonnerie*. In 1776, Soufflot was promoted to *intendant général des bâtiments du Roi.*

Among his works at Lyons should be mentioned the Hôtel Dieu's river-façade overlooking the Rhone (1741–48), the Loge du Change (1747–49) and the theatre (1754–56).

In Paris, his most important work was the church of Sainte-Geneviève (now known as the Panthéon, 1756–60), the sacristy at Notre-Dame (1756 et seq.), the Hôtel de Marigny in the Rue Saint-Thomas du Louvre (*c.* 1767) and de Marigny's country-seat in the Faubourg du Roule.

Jean Monval, *Soufflot. Sa vie. Son Oeuvre. Son esthétique*, Paris, 1918.
Jean Mondain-Monval, *Correspondance de Soufflot avec les directeurs des Bâtiments concernant la manufacture des Gobelins* (1756–1780), Paris, 1918.
Hautecoeur, *Histoire, seconde moitié, passim.*
F. Souchal, *Les Slodtz*, 1967.
Michael Petzet, *Soufflots Sainte-Geneviève und der französische Kirchenbau des 18. Jahrhunderts*, Berlin, 1961.

See Plates 17, 20, 36, 76.

STANISLAS II (Stanislas Augustus Poniatowski), King of Poland 1764–95. Born in 1732, died in 1798. Son of General Stanislas Poniatowski and the Princess Constance Czartoryski.

In 1748, at the age of sixteen, Poniatowski was sent abroad for the sake of his education. In Berlin he became acquainted with the English Ambassador, Sir Charles Hanbury Williams, whom he accompanied to France and England. When Williams was posted to St. Petersburg, he made Poniatowski his secretary and the latter thus came to know the Empress Catherine II. In 1764, after the death of Augustus III, he was elected King of Poland with the Empress' support. In 1773, Poland was forced to sign the treaty that entailed the first partitioning of Poland and in 1793 he had to agree to a second partitioning of his country.

Stanislas was an ardent francophile and, after his succession to the throne, he had the Palace at Warsaw modernised with the aid of French artists and craftsmen.

In this task he was aided by Madame Geoffrin who set herself up as his unofficial adviser, on artistic matters. The numerous luxurious items that were produced in Paris for the Polish Court at this time no doubt made a considerable impression in the French capital (Plates 70, 71, 190, 205 to 207, 213, 402 to 423).

TARAVAL, Louis Gustave. Architect and engraver. Born in 1738 in Stockholm, died in Paris in 1794. Son of Guillaume Taraval, a French painter who had been called to Sweden in the 1730s to work for the Swedish Court. He had a brother, Hugues Taraval, who was also a painter.

He was a pupil of Boullée. Already in 1760, at the early age of twenty-two, he was calling himself 'architect' on a trade-card couched in the Neo-Classical style, where he announced that he gave instruction in architecture, and was willing to execute engravings—in which field his *forte* was 'principalement l'architecture'. We know of no buildings by Taraval but he frequently engraved the architectural drawings of others—for example, he engraved several plates for Contant d'Ivry's *Oeuvre* (1766), and others for G.-P.-M. Dumont's *Recueil d'Architecture* as well as some of Soufflot's drawings for the Panthéon (1781). Taraval also engraved some of his own drawings under the title *Plusieurs Portails et Portes.* He also engraved a portrait drawn by L.-G. Moreau of the Comte de Caylus.

Taraval lived in the Rue des Maçons near the Sorbonne in 1760; in 1764, he had moved to the Rue de la Huchette on the Quai Saint-Michel, while in 1794 he was residing in the Rue Saint-Merry on the opposite bank of the Seine.

Jal, *Dictionnaire.*
Thieme and Becker, *Künstlerleksikon.*

See Plate 332.

VANDERCRUSE, Roger; known as Lacroix. Cabinet-maker. Born in 1728, died in 1799. Son of François Vandercruse, also a cabinet-maker. His brother, Jacques-François, became a clock-maker. He had five sisters, three of whom married cabinet-makers—the eldest married J.-F. Oeben and then J.-H. Riesener, the second married Simon Oeben (J.-F. Oeben's brother), and another married Simon Guillaume who is less famous. Roger Vandercruse himself married a daughter of the cabinet-maker, Mathieu Progain; J.-F. Oeben gave the bride away at the wedding.

Vandercruse became a *maître* on 6th February 1755 and took over the direction of his father's workshops in the Rue du Faubourg Saint-Antoine. Already in 1751 he had been working for the cabinet-maker Pierre Migéon; between 1751 and 1759 he supplied Migéon with goods to the value of 21,700 livres. He would appear to have worked mostly for *marchands-merciers* and after designs provided by them. He seems to have been particularly associated with Poirier, to whom he supplied a good deal of furniture from about 1760 onwards, mostly small tables set with Sèvres porcelain plaques. It is apparent that he was greatly influenced by his brother-in-law J.-F. Oeben's work during the earlier part of his career; the marquetry patterns and bronze mounts on his furniture are often closely similar to those on Oeben's work. It may be that Vandercruse borrowed or bought patterns and models for such ornament from Oeben. It is perhaps worth noting, however, that Vandercruse's father was in some way associated with the bronze-founder, J.-J. de Saint-Germain. Vandercruse also worked for Joubert, as Verlet has suggested; Vandercruse's stamp ('R.V.L.C.' = Roger Vandercruse Lacroix) is at any rate found on a commode in the transitional style which was delivered to the *Garde-Meuble* by Joubert in 1769 for the use of Madame Victoire at Versailles.

Salverte, *Les ébénistes*, pp. 177–9.
Verlet, *Mobilier Royal III*, pp. 6–7.
Archives de la Seine, D. 5. B6–5491, *passim*.
Arch. Nat., Minutier Central, XXVIII–316 (12th April 1750).

See Plates 119 and 137.

VANRISAMBURGH, Bernard III. Cabinet-maker. Born about 1731 (or 1721?), died in 1800. Son of the cabinet-maker Bernard II, and grandson of Bernard I a joiner who came from Groesen in Holland late in the seventeenth century and got married in Paris. The spelling of the family name varies: Bernard I wrote it 'Van Risen Burgh', while Bernard II wrote 'Vanrisemburgh'. When the marking of Parisian furniture became general, the members of this family stamped their products 'B.V.R.B.'.

The well-made and usually beautiful products marked with this stamp caused earlier specialists to refer to their maker simply by the initials 'B.V.R.B.'. The true identity of this craftsman—or, as it turned out, dynasty of craftsmen—was established by the late Jean-Pierre Baroli. The results of his studies of this family and its products can only be judged from a brief article he published in 1957, supplemented in some degree by the writings of James Parker and F. J. B. Watson cited below. Both these authors have had access to Baroli's as yet unpublished monograph on 'B.V.R.B.'.

Bernard III never became a *maître* as his father and grandfather had been before him. He contented himself by remaining a journeyman (*compagnon*) in the family's workshops in the Faubourg Saint-Antoine. He presumably took an active part in the running of the family business after his father's death in 1765 or 1766 and up to the time when his mother died (about 1773–75). After that, he left the cabinet-making trade in order to set up as a *mouleur en plâtre*—modeller in plaster. It was in this capacity that he was involved in the bankruptcy proceedings of a bronze-founder in 1786. On his death, he was described as a *sculpteur*.

Most of the furniture stamped 'B.V.R.B.' is in the Rococo style. The few that are in the transitional or fully-developed *Louis Seize* style may be ascribed to Bernard III who, considering his interest in sculpture, was probably also responsible for modelling the bronze mounts on them.

J.-P. Baroli, 'Le mystérieux B.V.R.B. enfin identifié', *Connaissance des Arts*, March 1957, pp. 56–63.
James Parker, 'Furniture with porcelain plaques from the Hillingdon Collection', *Decorative Art from the Samuel H. Kress Collection at the Metropolitan Museum of Art*, New York, 1964, p. 164.

Vial, Marcel and Girodie, vol. II, p. 182, *sub voce* Vannesamburgh.
F. J. B. Watson, *Wrightsman Collection*, pp. 560–1.

See Plate 117.

VICTOIRE DE FRANCE, Madame, Born in 1733, died in 1799. Daughter of Louis XV and Madame Leczinska.

Sister of Madame Adélaïde, Madame Sophie and Madame Louise.

See Adélaïde de France, Madame.

WATELET, Claude-Henri. French financier, art-collector, poet, and engraver. Born in 1718, died in 1786. Son of Nicolas-Robert Watelet who was *receveur général des finances de la Généralité d'Orléans.*

In 1740, after attending the Collège d'Harcourt, Watelet took over his father's lucrative but not excessively demanding post—it only required his attention every second year! In 1747 he was elected a member of the Académie Royale de Peinture et Sculpture; and, in 1760 of the Académie Française. He lived in the Rue Charlot, off the Boulevard du Temple.

In 1749 Watelet engraved a series of designs for vases drawn by Jean-Baptiste-Marie Pierre whom he calls 'suo amico' on the title-page. In 1752, he executed a further series after drawings by L.-J. Le Lorrain which he dedicated to Madame Geoffrin. He engraved some vignettes by Pierre in 1759 for a book he had written on *L'Art de Peindre* which was published in 1760 (Plates 319 and 320).

J.-F. Blondel mentions Watelet already in 1754 as being an influential connoisseur of the arts. Watelet in fact was well acquainted with numerous artists and *cognoscenti* in the Parisian art world and he was almost the only person of whom virtually everyone spoke well! Among his friends he numbered such important figures as Lalive de Jully, Madame Geoffrin, Comte de Caylus and, apparently, the Marquis de Marigny. Unlike Caylus, he seems to have been a tactful patron to those young artists he took under his wing.

Watelet travelled a lot during his lifetime, he was in Italy in 1763–64; this was apparently not the first time he had visited that country.

J.-F. Blondel, *Discours sur la nécessité de l'étude de l'architecture*, 1754, p. 53.
Maurice Henriet, 'Un amateur d'art au XVIIIe siècle l'académicien Watelet', *Gaz.d.B.-A.*, 1922, pp. 173–9.
Corr. des Dir., *passim.*

See Plates 297–8, 319–20.

APPENDIX I

Abbé le Blanc: Letter to le Comte de C**, 1737-44, about Architecture in England, etc.

Abbé le Blanc, *Lettres . . . concernant le gouvernement, la politique et les moeurs des Anglois et des François*, I-III, 1747 (letters written between 1737 and 1744), vol. II, pp. 41–52.

FRENCH TEXT

Lettre XXXVI
A Monsieur le Comte De C** (Caylus ?). De Londres

Monsieur,

Vous connoissez le *Vitruve Anglois*; & comme vous possédez nonseulement les Regles de tous les Arts, mais ce goût sûr bien supérieur aux Regles mêmes, puisqu'il en est le Principe caché, ne vous semble-t-il pas que l'Auteur de cet Ouvrage ait fait exprès dessiner & graver tout ce qu'il y a de Bâtimens remarquables en Angleterre, pour nous apprendre que l'Architecture est un Art qui n'y est pas naturalisé; il est de ceux qui dépendent du Gout, ainsi il peut être encore long-tems étranger dans cette Isle. Ce n'est pas que l'Architecture n'ait des Principes connus & des Regles certaines, fondées les unes sur la nature, telle est celle-ci, par exemple, que le plus fort doit porter le plus foible; les autres établies successivement, & convenues unanimement comme le résultat de l'expérience de ceux qui nous ont précédés; mais la partie la plus difficile & la plus étendue, celle de la Décoration & des Ornemens dont elle est susceptible; le Gout seul peut la donner, & le Gout ne donne rien ici.

L'Architecture est une des choses qui annoncent le plus la magnificence d'une Nation; & de la magnificence, on conclut aisément la grandeur. Quand nous ne pourrions juger des Romains que par ce qui nous reste de leurs superbes Amphithéâtres, ne seroient-ils pas encore l'objet de notre admiration? Tout ce que l'Histoire rapporte des Egyptiens, fait moins d'impression que ces Pyramides immenses qui subsistent dans leur Pays depuis tant de Siécles. Quelle idée ne laissera pas à la Postérité la Façade du Louvre, de la Puissance du Monarque qui l'a fait élever & du point de perfection où les Arts ont été portés sous son Regne!

Le Pays de l'Europe où l'Architecture Moderne a produit le plus de Chefs-d'oeuvre, c'est l'Italie. Les Anglois n'ont encore que le mérite d'en avoir copié quelques-uns. L'Architecte[1] qui a bâti leur fameuse Eglise de Saint Paul de Londres, aux proportions près qu'il a très-mal observées, n'a fait que réduire le Plan de Saint Pierre de Rome aux deux tiers de sa grandeur: pour peu que l'on ait de con-

[1] Christopher Wren.

noissance, il est aisé de s'appercevoir, que partout où il s'est écarté de son Modéle, il a commis les fautes les plus grossiéres.

La plûpart des Maisons de Campagne, car il est peu de Bâtimens à Londres qui méritent qu'on en parle, sont encore ici dans le goût Italien; mais on ne l'a pas toujours appliqué juste. Un des premiers soins d'un Architecte, doit être d'avoir égard au climat où il bâtit; ce qui convient à un Pays aussi chaud, & dont l'air est aussi pur que celui de Naples, devient incommode dans un climat beaucoup plus froid, & dont le Ciel n'est pas aussi serein. Les Italiens dans leurs Maisons doivent se défendre du trop grand jour; les Anglois, qui ne voyent pas le Soleil aussi souvent qu'ils le voudroient, doivent le chercher. La Maison de Plaisance qui orne une Vigne de Rome, n'est pas un Modéle pour une Maison de Campagne des Environs de Londres.

On prétend qu'il en coûte beaucoup ici aux Anglois qui veulent passer pour avoir du Gout; ils sont forcés de contraindre le leur en tout, & d'en affecter un qui leur est étranger. Ils payent, dit-on, fort cher pour entendre une Musique qui leur déplaît. Ils ont leur Table couverte de Mets auxquels leurs Palais ne peuvent s'accoutumer; ils portent des habits qui les gênent, & habitent des Maisons où ils ne sont point à leur aise. Ce Pays n'est pas le seul où l'on trouve des Hommes qui sont la dupe de cette espece de manie, qui sacrifient leurs commodités aux usages du bel air, & le plaisir réel à ce qui n'en est que l'ombre. Combien une pareille folie n'apprête-t-elle pas à rire aux véritables Philosophes?

Le célebre Inigo Jones a orné Londres de quelques Edifices qui ont du gout, & entr'autres de cette magnifique Salle de White-Hall, l'un des plus beaux Morceaux d'Architecture qui soient en Europe. D'un autre côté, Mylord Burlington, qui a joint les exemples aux préceptes, soit par l'Hôtel qu'il s'est bâti lui-même à Londres, soit par quelques Ecrits sur l'Architecture, a tâché d'en communiquer le gout à ses Compatriotes. Mais ces Modéles n'ont pas rendu les Architectes Anglois plus habiles; & toutes les fois qu'ils veulent être autre chose que de simples Copistes, ils n'élevent encore que de pesantes masses de Pierre, telles que le Château de Blenheim, dont vous trouverez le Plan & la Façade dans le *Vitruve Anglois*.

Bien plus souvent encore, les Anglois dans les Décorations de leurs Bâtimens, affectent un gout véritablement puérile. On a construit pour la Reine dans le Parc de Richemond, un petit endroit, où l'on a placé sa Bibliothéque de Campagne. On l'appelle la Grotte de Merlin, ce n'est autre chose qu'un Pavillon octogone, dont la Voute est Gothique. Rien n'y répond à l'idée qu'on peut s'en former sur le nom. On n'y voit pour toute curiosité, que cet Enchanteur, & quelques autres Figures en Cire grandes comme nature. Loin qu'en ce Salon il y ait rien qui ressente l'enchantement & la puissance du Magicien, il n'est pas possible d'imaginer un Spectacle de plus mauvais gout.

Les Anglois ne sont pas toujours heureux dans leurs Inventions; mais en quelque chose que ce soit, ils ne connoissent ni la justesse des Proportions, ni l'élégance des Formes; aussi ne réussissent-ils pas mieux dans le goût des Meubles, que dans celui des autres Ornemens de leurs Maisons. Nous regardons les Italiens comme nos Maîtres pour l'Architecture & la Décoration extérieure des grands Edifices, mais pour la distribution & les proportions intérieures, les François paroissent s'y entendre mieux qu'aucune Nation de l'Europe, & c'est précisement où le mauvais goût des Anglois se fait le plus sentir.

L'Amour de la vérité ne me permettra pas néantmoins de flatter mes Compatriotes, jusques dans leurs défauts. J'oserai avouer & condamner les effets pernicieux de notre inconstance naturelle. Aujourd'hui parmi nous dans tout ce qui dépend du Dessein, de même que dans les Ouvrages d'esprit, on commence à s'écarter de cette noble simplicité que les grands Maîtres de l'Antiquité ont suivie en tout, & que les nôtres ont tâché d'imiter. Ce n'est pas par stérilité que les uns & les autres l'ont adoptée, & ceux qui affectent de s'en éloigner, prouvent moins leur fécondité que leur mauvais gout. Quoi qu'ils disent pour couvrir leur ignorance ou leur manque de talent, il est bien plus aisé de courir après l'esprit & de coudre des Epigrammes les unes aux autres, que d'imaginer une belle Scene, & d'y rendre la nature dans toute sa vérité. Cette abondance apparente est une stérilité réelle. Celui qui a tout-à-la-fois un génie fécond & un gout sûr, se fait un devoir de sacrifier toute beauté superflue. Mais en ce genre de richesses comme dans les autres, il faut en avoir beaucoup, pour n'avoir pas regret à celles que l'on a mal employées. Le plus médiocre Dessinateur invente des Ornemens de toutes formes, & les entasse les uns sur les autres: un homme comme Bouchardon, n'en imagine que de nobles, & les distribue avec intelligence. Les Goths en ont été aussi prodigues que les Grecs en ont été avares, & l'exemple de ces derniers nous fait voir que l'effort du Génie, & la perfection de l'Art, sont de parvenir à cette heureuse simplicité.

Je suis certain, Monsieur, que vous voyez avec regret, qu'en plus d'un genre on affecte déja de s'éloigner du gout du Siécle de Louis XIV, l'âge d'or des Lettres & des beaux Arts en France. Rien n'est plus monstrueux, comme le remarque Horace, que de marier ensemble des Etres d'une nature opposée; c'est cependant ce que grand nombre de nos Artistes se font aujourd'hui gloire de pratiquer. Ils contrastent un Amour avec un Dragon, & un Coquillage avec une aile de Chauve-Souris. Ils ne suivent plus aucun ordre, aucune vraisemblance dans leurs Productions. Ils entassent avec confusion des Corniches, des Bases, des Colonnes, des Cascades, des Joncs, des Rochers; dans quelque coin de ce Cahos, ils placeront un Amour épouvanté, & sur le tout, ils feront regner une Guirlande de fleurs. Voilà ce qu'on appelle des Desseins d'un nouveau Gout. Ainsi pour avoir passé le terme, nous sommes revenues à la barbarie des Goths. Peut-être est il des choses où trop de symmétrie est un défaut, mais c'en est d'ordinaire un plus grand, que de n'en observer aucune, elle doit toujours régner dans les Masses, & non dans le détail des parties. Elle est dans l'Architecture d'une nécessité indispensable. Un Bâtiment quel qu'il soit, est un tout composé de parties qui doivent se répondre. C'est dans le Détail des ornemens qu'on doit chercher la variété. Des Statues placées en regard dans une niche font un mauvais effet, si elles n'offrent à peu près aux yeux la même masse, mais elles ne choquent pas moins, si l'attitude de l'une est absolument semblable à celle de l'autre. Ainsi dans un Parterre; des plattes bandes doivent avoir les mêmes proportions, & soit dans les milieux, soit dans les extrémités des points marqués qui se répondent: observer scrupuleusement le même ordre dans l'arrangement de chacune des fleurs qui sont faites pour en varier le coup d'oeil, c'est affecter une symmétrie aussi froide que puérile. Mais qu'en fait d'ornemens nous sommes aujourd'hui loin de ce défaut! nous ne voulons plus rien de symmétrieque. Si l'on orne le Frontispice d'un Hôtel des Armes de celui qui le fait bâtir, on pose l'Ecu en ligne diagonale, & la Couronne sur l'un des côtés, de façon qu'elle paroisse prête à tomber. On s'éloigne le plus qu'on peut de la ligne perpendiculaire & de l'horisontale: on ne met plus rien à plomb, ni de niveau.

Nos Architectes du tems passé étoient trop sages pour se permettre ces Ecarts que ceux d'aujourd'hui trouvent si ingénieux. Dans ce Siécle plus hardi, on veut que tout le paroisse, & l'on renverse tellement les choses, que je ne sçais si ce mauvais gout ne prouve pas quelque renversement dans les têtes. Ceux de nos Artistes qui ont quelque sens, rougissent souvent des choses qu'ils sont obligés de faire, mais le torrent les entraîne; il faut, pour être employés, qu'ils fassent comme les autres. On leur demande du goût nouveau, de ces Formes qui ne ressemblent à rien, & ils en donnent.

Cette maniere se fait sentir surtout dans ceux de nos Meubles qui sont les plus consacrés à l'ornement, & réellement le Gout qui se permet tout aujourd'hui, s'égare aussi peut-être plus qu'il n'a jamais fait. A qui ressemblent ces Pendules devenues si à la mode, qui n'ont ni base ni console, & qui paroissent sortir du Lambris où elles sont appliquées! Ces Cerfs, ces Chiens & ces Piqueurs, ou ces Figures Chinoises qu'on distribue d'une façon si bizarre autour d'un Cadran, en sont-ils les ornemens naturels? Ces Cartouches qui soit en haut, soit en bas, soit dans les côtés, n'ont aucunes Parties qui se répondent, sont-ils en effet de bon gout? Loin qu'une Forme soit heureuse lorsqu'elle est vague, pour ainsi dire, & qu'elle s'eloigne de toutes les Formes connues, on ne peut imaginer rien d'élégant qui ne soit terminé, & qui ne doive ressembler à quelque chose. Il est dans tous les genres un vrai sans lequel il ne peut rien subsister de beau, & c'est le sentiment de ce vrai qui constitue le Gout.

Quoi de plus ridicule que d'appliquer le Vernis de Martin aux Bronzes dont on orne les Feux d'une Cheminée! Quoi de plus fou que d'y attacher des Pagodes de Porcelaine! C'est ainsi que pour trop varier les Formes nous donnons dans l'extravagant, & qu'en voulant mettre trop de richesses dans les Ornemens, nous tombons dans le papillotage. A peine évitons-nous un excès, qu'un autre plus vicieux s'introduit à sa place. Rien n'est si difficile que de détruire entiérement le mauvais gout. C'est une espéce d'Hidre à plusieurs têtes, on n'en a pas plutôt coupé une, qu'il en renaît une autre. Il est des Mortels heureux, qui par une force supérieure viennent à bout d'en triompher. Ainsi Moliere de son tems, par les beautés de ses Piéces, força le Public à renoncer aux mauvaises Plaisanteries, aux Jeux de mots & aux Equivoques auxquels il étoit accoutumé. Ainsi le Puget de notre Siécle peut, par les productions d'une imagination aussi sage que féconde, & d'un jugement exquis, ramener le vrai gout dans le Dessein, & en nous rappellant à la belle nature, faire tomber dans le mépris tout ce que l'ignorance & le mauvais gout ont enfanté depuis peu. Celui d'aujourd'hui, Monsieur, est si dépravé, que je ne pense pas qu'il puisse durer encore long-tems, & l'attention & l'encouragement que vous donnez aux Arts, ne peuvent manquer d'en accélérer la chûte.

J'ai l'honneur d'être, Monsieur,

Votre très-humble, &c.

ENGLISH TRANSLATION[1]

Letter XXXVI
To the Count of C** (Caylus?). From London

Sir,

You are acquainted with the *Vitruvius Britannicus*; and as you are not only a master of the rules of all the arts, but have that exquisite taste, which is much superior to the rules themselves, because 'tis the hidden principle of them; don't you think the author of that work has had all the remarkable buildings in England, design'd and engrav'd on purpose to shew us, that architecture is a science, which is not yet naturalised here? It is one of those that depend on taste, and therefore may be still a long time foreign in this island. 'Tis not that architecture is void of known principles and certain rules, some of them, founded on nature; as this, for example; *That the strongest ought to support the weakest*; and others successively established and unanimously agreed to, as the result of the experience of our predecessors: but the most difficult and most extensive part of it, that of decoration, and the ornaments it is capable of receiving, taste alone must give; and taste gives nothing in this country.

Architecture is one of those things, which most particularly indicate the magnificence of a nation; and from magnificence, we easily conclude grandeur. Though we would only judge of the Romans, by the ruins which are left us of their stately amphitheatres, would they not nevertheless be the object of our admiration? All that history relates of the Aegyptians, makes less impression on us, than those vast pyramids, which have subsisted in their country for so many ages. What an idea, will the front of the Louvre leave to posterity, of the power of that monarch who erected it, and of the degree of perfection, to which the arts were carried, in his reign!

Italy, is the country of Europe, that has produc'd the most masterpieces of modern architecture. The English have yet only the merit of having copied some of them. The architect,[2] who built their famous church of St. Paul, at London, has only reduced the plan of St. Peter's at Rome, to two thirds of it's size; the proportions excepted, which he has very ill observed: and a man, who understands but little of architecture, may easily perceive, that throughout the whole, wherever he deviates from his model, he has committed the greatest errors.

[1] The translation here used is taken from that published in London in 1747 (I, pp. 279–87). It was customary for such translations to be farmed out as hack-work by eighteenth-century booksellers; for this reason the original translation has been compared with the French text, and one or two mistakes corrected. These and other alterations are noted where they occur. R.W.L.

[2] Sir Christopher Wren.

The greatest part of the country houses, for there are few at London, that deserve to be spoke of, are also in the Italian taste; but it has not been always justly applied. One of the first things an architect should consider, is the climate where he builds; what is proper for a country as hot, and where the air is as clear as that of Naples; is improper in a much colder climate, and where the sky is not so serene. The Italians in their houses, ought to screen themselves from the excessive heat, the English, who do not see the sun so often as they would, ought to admit it, as much as possible. A pleasure-house for a *Vigna*[1] at Rome, is not a model for a country-house, in the neighbourhood of London.

They pretend the English, who will pass for men of taste, do many things against the grain; they are forc'd in every thing to constrain their own taste and affect a forreign one. They pay very dear, say they, to hear musick that displeases them; their tables are covered with meats to which they cannot accustom[2] their palates; they wear cloaths that are troublesome to them, and live to houses where they are not at their ease. This is not the only country where we find men who are the dupes of this sort of madness, who sacrifice their ease to the fashions of a genteel air, and real pleasure to what is only the shadow of it. How must this folly make true philosophers laugh!

The celebrated INIGO JONES, has adorned London with some edifices of taste, and amongst the rest, with the magnificent Banqueting-house at Whitehall, one of the finest pieces of architecture in Europe. On the other hand my lord BURLINGTON, who has joined example to precept, by the fine house which he has built for himself at London, and some things which he has published concerning architecture; has endeavour'd to give his countrymen a taste for it. But these models have not made the English architects more expert; for whenever they attempt to do any thing more than barely to copy, they erect nothing but heavy masses of stone, like that of Blenheim-Palace,[3] the plan and front of which you will find in the *Vitruvius Britannicus*.

The English also, in the ornaments of their buildings, very often affect a taste that is perfectly childish. They have built for the queen in Richmond-park, a small structure to place her country library in; which they call Merlin's-cave. 'Tis only an octogon pavilion, with a Gothick arched roof; and has nothing in it answerable to the idea, it's name gives us of it. You find no other curiosity there, except that sorcerer and some other figures in wax, as large as life. So far from finding any thing in this building that favours of enchantment and the magician's power, it is impossible to conceive any thing of a worse taste.

The English are not always happy in their inventions; but are unacquainted with the exactness of proportions, and elegancy of forms in every thing: and therefore succeed no better in the taste of their furniture, than in that of the ornaments of their houses. We regard the Italians as our masters in the architecture and external ornaments of large buildings; but the French seem to understand the distribution and internal proportions, the best of any nation in Europe; and the bad taste of the English particularly shews itself in these.

However, the love of truth does not permit me to flatter my countrymen in their faults. I shall be bold enough to own and condemn the pernicious effects of our natural levity. We now a-days in every thing that depends upon design, as well as in the productions of the understanding, begin to deviate from that noble simplicity which the great masters of antiquity followed in all things; and ours have endeavour'd to imitate. 'Twas not for want of invention, that both the one and the others adopted this; and those who affect to deviate from it, prove their bad taste much more than the fruitfulness of theirs. Whatever they say, to hide their ignorance or want of capacity, 'tis much easier to follow our own humour, and tack scraps of verses together, than to contrive a fine scene, and represent nature truly in it. This seeming abundance is a real sterility. He that has both a fruitful genius and fine taste, thinks he ought to reject all superfluous beauty. But in this sort of riches as well as others, a man must be rich indeed, not to regret the

[1] In the original translation, *garden*. R.W.L.
[2] In the original translation, *disagreeable to*. R.W.L.
[3] In the original translation, *castle*. R.W.L.

loss of those, he has ill employed. A bungling designer invents ornaments of all forms, and crouds them on one another; a man of BOUCHARDON's genius, invents only noble ones, and distributes them with judgment. The Goths were as prodigal of them, as the Greeks avaricious; but the example of the last shews us, that the force of genius, and perfection of art, are to arrive at this happy simplicity.

I am certain, sir, you see with regret, that we already affect in several instances to deviate from the taste of LEWIS XIV's time; the golden age for letters[1] and fine[2] arts in France. Nothing is more monstrous, as HORACE observes, than to couple together beings of different natures; and yet 'tis what many of our artists at this time glory in doing. A cupid is the contrast of a dragon; and a shell, of a bat's wing; they no longer observe any order, any probability, in their productions. They heap cornices, bases, columns, cascades, rushes and rocks, in a confused manner, one upon another; and in some corner of this chaos, they will place a cupid in a great fright, and have a festoon of flowers above the whole. And this is what they call designs of a new taste. Thus by going beyond the due limits, we are returned to the Gothick barbarity. Perhaps there are things, where too much symmetry is a fault, but 'tis commonly a greater, to observe none; there should always be a symmetry in the whole mass, tho' not in all it's parts. 'Tis indispensably necessary in architecture. A building, of whatsoever sort, is a whole compos'd of parts, that ought to correspond with each other; and 'tis in the ornaments we should use variety. Statues placed facing each other in a niche, have a bad effect, if they do not appear very nearly of the same size; but they offend the eye as much if their attitudes are exactly the same. Thus in a flower-garden; the beds,[3] both in their middles, and at their ends, should have the same proportions and points which answer to each other[4] but to observe exactly the same regularity, in the disposition of every one of the flowers, which are planted there to vary the prospect, would be to affect a symmetry equally childish and insipid. But how far are we at present, with regard to ornaments, from this defect! We will have nothing that looks like symmetry. If they adorn the frontispiece of a house, with the arms of the person who built it; they place the escutcheon in a diagonal line, with the coronet on one side of it, so that it looks if it were going to fall down. They forsake the perpendicular and horizontal lines as much as possible; and place nothing now, either upright or level.

Our architects in time past were too wise to take those liberties, which the moderns think so ingenious. In this more adventurous age, they would have every thing make a shew, and turn things topsy-turvy in such a manner, that I am afraid this ill taste may prove their heads are topsy-turvy likewise.[5] Our sensible artists, often blush at things they are obliged to do; but the torrent bears them down, and they are forced to do like the rest, to get employment. They ask them for things of the new fashion; of those shapes, which bear no resemblance to any thing; and they let them have them.

This fashion is most visible in that part of our furniture, which is designed chiefly for ornaments; and indeed taste[6] which admits of every thing at this time, runs perhaps more ridiculous lengths than ever it did. What do those pendulum-clocks, so much in fashion, resemble; which have neither basis nor console,[7] but seem to spring out of the wainscot, to which they are fasten'd? Those stags, dogs, huntsmen, or Chinese figures, which they dispose in so odd a manner about the dial-plate; are they it's natural ornaments? Those cartouches,[8] whether at the top, the bottom, or on the sides, which have nothing to answer them; are they really of a good taste? A shape that is, as we may say, undetermined, and unlike all known shapes, is so far from being pleasing; that we can't conceive any thing elegant, which is not terminated, and does not resemble something. There is in all sorts of things, a *Right*, without which there can be no beauty; and 'tis the sense of this *Right*, that constitutes taste.

[1] In the original translation, *learning*. R.W.L.
[2] In the original translation, *elegant*. R.W.L.
[3] In the original translation, *borders*. R.W.L.
[4] Incorrectly translated in the original.
[5] The original omitted *may* and substituted *turn'd* for the second *topsy-turvy*. R.W.L.
[6] *the* omitted, R.W.L.
[7] In the original translation, *corbel*, R.W.L.
[8] In the original translation, *cartridges*, R.W.L.

What is there more ridiculous, than varnishing[1] the brasses[2] which are placed for ornament in a chimney?[3] What more absurd, than fastening pagods of China-ware to them? Thus by varying shapes too much, we run into extravagance; and by crowding too much riches into ornaments, fall into foppery. We hardly avoid one excess before we are guilty of a greater. Nothing is so difficult as to eradicate bad taste: 'tis a hydra with many heads, one of which you have no sooner cut off, but another springs up. There are some happy mortals, who by superior strength compass the destruction of it. Thus MOLIERE, in his time, by the beauty of his plays, forc'd the people to abandon the silly jests, playing with words and double-meanings to which they were accustomed. Thus the *Paget* of our time, may, by the productions of an invention as wise as fruitful, and an exquisite judgment, restore the true taste to design, by recalling us to beautiful nature; and make every thing, that ignorance and bad taste has lately produced, fall into contempt. That of this time, sir, is so deprav'd, that I do not think it can continue much longer; and the attention and encouragement which you give to the arts, must necessarily hasten its fall.

I have the honour to be,

Sir, your most humble, &c.

[1] In the original French, *appliquer le Vernis de Martin*, R.W.L.

[2] In the original, *bronzes*. During much of the eighteenth century *brass* still sometimes did duty in English for both metals. R.W.L.

[3] The modern translation would be *fire-place*. R.W.L.

APPENDIX II

C.-N. Cochin: Petition to the Goldsmiths, Chasers and Carvers of Wood for Apartments and others by a Society of Artists, 1754

Charles-Nicolas Cochin in *Mercure de France*, December 1754

FRENCH TEXT

Supplication aux Orfevres, Ciseleurs, Sculpteurs en bois pour les appartemens & autres, par une société d'Artistes

Soit très-humblement représenté à ces Messieurs, que quelques efforts que la Nation Françoise ait fait depuis plusieurs années pour accoutumer sa raison à se plier aux écarts de leur imagination, elle n'a pu y parvenir entiérement: ces Messieurs sont donc suppliés de vouloir bien dorénavant observer certaines regles simples, qui sont dictées par le bon sens, & dont nous ne pouvons arracher les principes de notre esprit. Ce seroit un acte bien méritoire à ces Messieurs, que de se prêter à notre foiblesse, & nous pardonner l'impossibilité réelle où nous sommes de détruire, par complaisance pour eux, toutes les lumieres de notre raison.

Exemple. Sont priés les Orfevres, lorsque sur le couvercle d'un pot à ouille, ou sur quelqu'autre piece d'orfévrerie, ils exécutent un artichaut ou un pied de céleri de grandeur naturelle, de vouloir bien ne pas mettre à côté un lievre grand comme le doigt, une allouette grande comme le naturel, & un faisan du quart ou du cinquieme de sa grandeur; des enfans de la même grandeur qu'une feuille de vigne; des figures supposées de grandeur naturelle, portées sur une feuille d'ornement, qui pourroit à peine soutenir, sans plier, un petit oiseau; des arbres dont le tronc n'est pas si gros qu'une de leurs feuilles, & quantité d'autres choses également bien raisonnées.

Nous leur serions encore infiniment obligés, s'ils vouloient bien ne pas changer la destination des choses, & se souvenir, par exemple, qu'un chandelier doit être droit & perpendiculaire pour porter la lumiere, & non pas tortué, comme si quelqu'un l'avoit forcé; qu'une bobeche doit être concave pour recevoir la cire qui coule, & non pas convexe pour la faire tomber en nappe sur le chandelier, & quantité d'autres agrémens non moins déraisonnables, qu'il seroit trop long de citer.

Pareillement, sont priés Messieurs les Sculpteurs d'appartemens d'avoir agréable, dans les trophées qu'ils exécutent, de ne pas faire une faux plus petite qu'une horloge de sable, un chapeau ou un tambour de basque plus grand qu'une basse de viole, un tête d'homme plus petite qu'une rose, une serpe aussi grande qu'un rateau, &c. C'est avec bien du regret que nous nous voyons obligés de les prier de restreindre leur génie à ces loix de proportion, quelque simples qu'elles soient. Nous ne sentons que trop qu'en s'assujettissant au bon sens, quantité de personnes qui passent maintenant pour de beaux génies, se trouveront n'en avoir plus du tout: mais enfin il ne nous est plus possible de nous y prêter. Avant que de jetter les hauts cris, nous avons enduré avec toute la patience possible, & nous avons fait des efforts incroyables pour admirer ces inventions, si merveilleuses, qu'elles ne sont plus du ressort de la raison: mais notre sens commun grossier nous excite toujours à les trouver ridicules. Nous nous garderons bien cependant de trouver à redire au goût régnant dans la décoration intérieure de nos édifices: nous sommes trop bons citoyens pour vouloir tout d'un coup mettre à la mendicité tant d'honnêtes gens qui ne sçavent que cela. Nous ne voulons pas même leur demander un peu de retenue dans l'usage des palmiers qu'ils font croître si abondamment dans nos appartemens, sur les cheminées, autour des miroirs, contre les murs, enfin partout: ce seroit leur ôter leur derniere ressource. Mais du moins pourrions-nous espérer d'obtenir que lorsque les choses pourront être quarrées, ils veuillent bien ne les pas tortuer; que lorsque les couronnemens pourront être en plein ceintre, ils veuillent ne les pas corrompre par ces contours en S, qu'ils semblent avoir appris des Maîtres Ecrivains, & qui sont si fort à la mode, qu'on s'en sert même pour faire des plans de bâtimens. On appelle cela des *formes*, mais on oublie d'y ajouter l'épithete de *mauvaises*, qui en est inséparable. Nous consentons cependant qu'ils servent de cette marchandise tortue à tous provinciaux ou étrangers qui seront assez mauvais connoisseurs pour préférer notre goût moderne à celui du siecle passé. Plus on répandra de ces inventions chez les étrangers, & plus on pourra espérer de maintenir la supériorité de la France. Nous les supplions de considérer que nous leur fournissons de beaux bois bien droits, & qu'ils nous ruinent en frais en les faisant travailler avec toutes ces formes sinueuses; qu'en faisant courber nos portes pour les assujettir aux arrondissemens qu'il plaît au bon goût de nos Architectes modernes de donner à toutes nos chambres, il nous font dépenser beaucoup plus qu'en les faisant droites, que nous n'y trouvons aucun avantage, puisque nous passons également par une porte droite, comme par une porte arrondie. Quant aux courbures des murailles de nos appartemens, nous n'y trouvons d'autre commodité que de ne sçavoir plus où placer, ni comment y arranger nos chaises ou autres meubles. Les Sculpteurs sont priés de vouloir bien ajouter foi aux assurances que nous leur donnons, nous qui n'avons aucun intérêt à les tromper, que les formes droites, quarrées, rondes & ovales régulieres, décorent aussi richement que toutes leurs inventions; que comme leur exécution exacte est plus difficile que celle de tous ces herbages, aîles de chauve-souris, & autres miseres qui sont en usage, elle fera plus d'honneur à leur talent. Qu'enfin les yeux d'un grand nombre de bonnes gens, dont nous faisons partie, leur auront une obligation inexprimable de n'être plus molestés par des disproportions déraisonnables, & par cette abondance d'ornemens tortueux & extravagans.

Que si nous demandons trop de choses à la fois, qu'ils nous accordent du moins une grace, que dorénavant la moulure principale qu'ils tourmentent ordinairement, sera & demeurera droite, conformément aux principes de la bonne architecture. Alors nous consentirons qu'ils fassent tortiller leurs ornemens autour & pardessus tant que bon leur semblera: nous nous estimerons moins malheureux, parce qu'un homme de bon goût, à qui un tel appartement écherra, pourra avec un ciseau abattre toutes ces drogues, & retrouver la moulure simple, qui lui fera une décoration sage, & dont sa raison ne souffrira pas.

On sent bien qu'une bonne partie des plaintes que nous adressons aux Sculpteurs pourroient, avec raison, s'adresser aux Architectes: mais la vérité est que nous n'osons pas. Ces Messieurs ne se gouvernent pas si facilement: il n'en est presque aucun qui doute de ses talens, & qui ne les vante avec une confiance entiere. Nous ne présumons pas assez de notre crédit auprès d'eux, pour nous flatter qu'avec les meilleures raisons du monde, nous puissions opérer leur conversion. Si nous nous étions sentis assez de hardiesse, nous les aurions respectueusement invités à vouloir bien examiner quelquefois le vieux Louvre, les Tuileries, & plusieurs autres bâtimens royaux du siecle passé, qui sont universellement reconnus pour de belles choses, & à ne nous pas donner si souvent lieu de croire qu'ils n'ont jamais vu ces bâtimens qui sont si près d'eux. Nous les aurions priés de nous faire grace de ces mauvaises formes à pans, qu'il semble qu'ils soient convenus de donner à tous les avant-corps, & nous les aurions assurés, dans la sincérité de nos consciences, que tous les angles obtus & aigus, (à moins qu'ils ne soient donnés nécessairement, commn dans la fortification,) sont désagréables en architecture, & qu'il n'y a que l'angle droit qui puisse faire ue bon effet. Ils y perdroient leurs sallons octogones: mais pourquoi un sallon quarré ne seroit-il pas aussi beau ? On ne seroit pas obligé de supprimer les corniches dans le dedans, pour sauver la difficulté d'y bien distribuer les ornemens qui y sont propres: ils n'auroient pas été réduits à substituer des herbages, ou de pareilles gentilesses mesquines, aux modillons, aux denticules, & autres ornemens inventés par des gens qui en sçavoient plus qu'eux, & reçus de toutes les Nations, après un mûr examen. Nous les aurions priés de respecter la beauté naturelle des pierres qu'ils tirent de la carriere, qui sont droites & à angle droit, & de vouloir bien ne les pas gâter pour leur faire prendre des formes qui nous en font perdre la moitié, & donnent des marques publiques du dérangement de nos cervelles. Nous les aurions priés de nous délivrer de l'ennui de voir à toutes les maisons des croisées ceintrées, depuis le rez-de-chaussée jusqu'à la mansarde, tellement qu'il semble qu'il y ait un pacte fait de n'en plus exécuter d'autres. Il n'y a pas jusqu'au bois des chassis de croisées qui veulent aussi se faire de fête, & qui se tortuent le plus joliment du monde, sans autre avantage que de donner beaucoup de peine au menuisier, & de l'embarras au vitrier, lorsqu'il lui faut couper des verres dans ces formes baroques.

Nous aurions bien eu encore quelques petites représentations à leur faire sur ce moule général, où il semble qu'ils jettent toutes les portes cocheres, en faisant toujours retourner les moulures de la corniche en ceintre, sans que celles de l'architrave les suivent, tellement que cette corniche porte à faux, & que s'ils mettent leur chere console, toute inutile qu'elle y est, ils ne sçavent où la placer. Hors du milieu du pilastre elle est ridicule; au milieu elle ne reçoit point la retombée de cet arc. N'aurions-nous pas pu, en leur accordant que la mansarde est une invention merveilleuse, admirable, digne de passer à la postérité la plus reculée, si on pouvoit la construire de marbre; les prier néanmoins de vouloir bien en être plus chiches, & nous faire voir quelquefois à sa place un attique, qui étant perpendiculaire & de pierre, sembleroit plus régulier & plus analogue au reste du bâtiment ? Car enfin on se lasse de voir toujours une maison bleue sur une maison blanche.

Combien de graces n'aurions-nous pas eu à leur demander! Mais nous espérerions vainement qu'ils voulussent nous en accorder aucune. Il ne nous reste à leur égard que de soupirer en secret, & d'attendre que leur invention étant épuisée, ils s'en lassent eux-mêmes. Il paroît que ce temps est proche; car ils ne font plus que se répéter, & nous avons lieu d'espérer que l'envie de faire du nouveau, ramenera l'architecture ancienne.

ENGLISH TRANSLATION

Petition to the goldsmiths, chasers, carvers of wood for apartments and others from a Society of Artists

Be it most humbly represented to these gentlemen that however great the efforts made by the French nation for several years past to accustom its reason to bend to the waywardness of their fancy, it has not been entirely able to succeed. Wherefore these gentlemen are petitioned to be so obliging as to observe henceforward certain simple rules dictated by good sense, from which we cannot tear the principles of our understanding. It would be a very meritorious act on the part of these gentlemen if they would condescend to our weakness and pardon us the real impossibility in which we find ourselves of extinguishing all the lights of our reason out of complaisance towards them.

Example. Goldsmiths are prayed that whenever they execute a life-size artichoke or celery stalk on the lid of a *pot à oille* or on some other piece of plate, to be good enough not to set beside it a hare as big as a finger, a lark as large as life and a pheasant about a quarter or a fifth of its real size; children of the same size as a vine leaf, or figures supposed to be life-sized which are borne up by an ornamental leaf that could hardly support a little bird without bending; trees whose trunks are not as big as a single one of their leaves, and a quantity of other things of an equal force of reasoning.

We should also be infinitely obliged to them if they would be good enough not to alter the intention of things and to remember, for instance, that a candlestick ought to be straight and perpendicular in order to support its light, not twisted as if someone had forced it out of shape; that its pan ought to be concave so as to hold the wax that runs down and not convex so as to let it drop in a sheet on the candlestick, besides a quantity of other charming devices no less unreasonable which it would take too long to mention.

Similarly Messrs the carvers of panelling in the trophies that they carve are prayed to be pleased not to make a scythe smaller than an hour-glass, a hat or a tambourine larger than a bass viol, a man's head smaller than a rose, a bill-hook as large as a rake, &c. It is with much regret that we find ourselves obliged to beg them to confine their genius within these laws of proportion, however simple they may be. We are but too conscious that in subjecting themselves to good sense quite a number of personages who now pass for great geniuses will find themselves without any genius at all, but it is now no longer possible for us to lend them our countenance. Before uttering loud protests we have endured with all possible patience and made unbelievable efforts to admire these inventions which are so marvellous that they are beyond the province of reason, yet our coarse commonsense invariably excites us to find them ridiculous. But we shall restrain ourselves from raising objections to the taste that reigns in the interior decoration of our buildings. We are far too good citizens to desire to reduce to sudden beggary so many honest folk who know nothing else. We do not even wish to ask them for a little restraint in the use of those palm trees which they cause to grow so abundantly in our apartments, on chimney-pieces, round mirrors, against walls, in fact everywhere; this would be to deprive them of their last resource. But perhaps we may at least hope to obtain from them that when things can be made right-angled they will be kind enough not to twist them, that when arches can be semi-circular they will be kind enough not to vitiate their outlines by those serpentine contours which they seem to have learnt from the writing masters and which are so fashionable that they are used even in making plans of buildings. They are called 'forms' by those who use them, but they forget to add the epithet 'bad' which is inseparable from them. We give our consent nevertheless to their serving up this twisted merchandise to all provincials and foreigners who shall be poor enough connoisseurs to prefer our modern taste to that of the last century. The more these inventions are scattered among foreigners the more we may hope to maintain the superiority of France. We beg them to consider that we furnish them with fine straight wood and that they ruin us with expense by working it into all these sinuous forms, that in bending our doors in order to subject them to the circularities which it pleases the good taste of our modern architects to give to all our rooms, they make us expend much more than if they were to make them straight, and that we find no advantage in them since we pass just as well through a straight door as through a rounded door. As for the curves of the walls of our apartments we find no other convenience in them save that we no longer know where to place or how to arrange our chairs or other furniture against them. The carvers are begged to be kind enough to put faith in the assurances we give them, we who have no interest in deceiving them, that regular straight, right-angled, round and oval forms are as rich a decoration as all their inventions and that since to execute them precisely is more difficult than to execute all those grasses, bats-wings and other paltry ornaments which are in current use, they will do more honour to their talents. And that finally the eyes of a great many honest folk, of whom we are one, will be under an inexpressible obligation to them if they are no longer annoyed by irrational disproportion and by so great an abundance of twisted and extravagant ornaments.

And if we ask too many things at once, let them at least grant us this one grace, that from henceforth the principal moulding which now ordinarily they torment, shall become and shall remain straight in conformity with the principles of good architecture. We shall then consent to their making their ornaments twist about and above it as much as meets their good pleasure, and we shall consider ourselves the less unfortunate because a man of good taste, should such an apartment fall to his lot, will be able to knock away all such stuff with a chisel, and rediscover the plain moulding, which will provide him with a sensible decoration that will cause his reason no suffering.

Our readers will readily perceive that a fair number of the complaints we have addressed to the carvers might with good reason also be addressed to the architects, but the truth is that we do not dare do it. These gentlemen are not so easily ruled; there is hardly one of them who entertains any doubt of his talents and does not boast of them with entire confidence. We do not presume sufficiently on our credit amongst them to flatter ourselves that even with the best reasons in the world we might work their conversion. Had we felt boldness enough we should respectfully have invited them to be kind enough to examine from time to time the old Louvre, the Tuileries and several other royal buildings of the last century which are universally recognised as fine things, and not to give us occasion so frequently for thinking that they have never seen these buildings, which yet are so near them. We should have begged them to spare us those wretched angled forms upon which it seems they are agreed for the salient part of all façades and we should have assured them in the sincerity of our conscience that all obtuse and acute angles (unless introduced from necessity, as in fortifications) are disagreeable in architecture, and that only the right angle produces a good effect. They would lose thereby their octagonal saloons, but why should a right-angled saloon not be as beautiful? It would no longer be necessary to suppress cornices in interiors so as to evade the difficulty of distributing the ornaments proper to them successfully. They would not have been reduced to substituting grasses or similar miserable fancies for the modillions, denticules, and other ornaments invented by persons who were more learned than they and since received of all nations after mature examination. We should have begged them to respect the natural beauty of the stones that they draw from the quarry straight and with right angles, and to be kind enough not to spoil them in order to make them assume forms which cause us the loss of half of them and give public proofs of the derangement of our brains. We should have begged them to deliver us from the tediousness of seeing arched windows on every house from the ground floor to the garrets, in such fashion that it seems as if a pact had been sworn to make no others. Even the window-frames desire to join in the parade and twist themselves about in the prettiest manner in the world with no other advantage save that of giving a great deal of trouble to the carpenter and difficulty to the glazier when he has to cut panes into these Baroque forms.

We should also have had some small representations to make to them on the subject of that general mould into which it seems they cast all carriage-gates by making the moulding of the cornice always turn up into an arched form without being followed by those of the architrave, so that the cornice tells falsely and if they add their cherished console, useless though it be, they do not know where to place it. Beyond the middle of the pilaster it is ridiculous, in the middle it does not receive the fall of the arch. Even while granting them that the mansard roof is a marvellous and wonderful invention, worthy of being transmitted to our remotest posterity could it but be constructed of marble, we should none the less have been able to beg them to be kind enough to be a little more sparing of it, and in its place to offer sometimes an attic storey, which being perpendicular and of stone would appear more regular and more in keeping with the rest of the building. For at last one becomes tired of always seeing a blue house on top of a white.

How many favours should we not have had to ask from them, but in vain should we hope they might be willing to grant us even one. So far as they are concerned all we can do is to sigh in secret and wait until such time as their invention is exhausted and they themselves become tired of it. It seems that this time is approaching, for they do nothing but repeat themselves and there is room for us to hope that the desire to do something novel will bring back the old style of architecture.

APPENDIX III

C.-N. Cochin: Letter to M. l'Abbé R** about a Very Poor Pleasantry from a Society of Architects, 1755

Charles-Nicolas Cochin, in *Mercure de France*, February 1755.

FRENCH TEXT

Lettre à M. l'Abbé R** sur une très-mauvaise plaisanterie qu'il a laissé imprimer dans le Mercure de Décembre 1754; par une société d'Architectes, qui pourroient bien prétendre être du premier mérite & de la premiere réputation, quoiqu'ils ne soient pas de l'Académie

Nous sommes surpris, Monsieur, qu'un homme d'esprit, & un aussi bon citoyen que vous, ait autorisé un écrit satyrique, dont le but est si évidemment de renverser l'architecture moderne, & de détruire la confiance que l'on accorde au Architectes, en mettant le public à portée de juger par lui-même du bien ou du mal des ouvrages que nous faisons pour lui. Pouvons-nous croire que vous n'ayez pas apperçu cette conséquence? ou que l'ayant vue, vous n'ayez pas eu quelque scrupule de vous prêter à décrier des inventions qui depuis tant de temps font les délices de Paris, & qu'enfin les étrangers commencent à goûter avec une avidité singuliere?

Il est aisé de deviner d'où partent ces plaintes, & nous ne croions pas aussi facilement que vous que ce soient simplement les idées d'un seul artiste. C'est un complot formé par plusieurs qui, à la vérité, ont du mérite dans leur genre, mais qui feroient mieux de s'y attacher, que de se mêler d'un art qui est si fort au dessus de la sphere de leurs connoissances. Nous soupçonnons avec raison quelques Peintres célebres de tremper dans cette conjuration: malheur à eux si nous les découvrons! Ils ont déjà pu remarquer que pour nous avoir fâché, nous avons supprimé de tous les édifices modernes la grande peinture d'histoire. Nous leur avions laissé par grace quelques dessus de porte; mais nous les forcerons dans ce dernier retranchement, & nous les réduirons à ne plus faire que de petits tableaux de modes, & encore en camayeux. Qu'ils fassent attention que nous avons l'invention des vernis: le public a beau se plaindre de leur peu de durée, il sera verni & reverni. Cependant nous voulons bien ne pas attribuer ces critiques à mauvaise volonté, mais plutôt au malheur qu'ils ont de s'être formé le goût en Italie. Ils y ont vu ces restes d'architecture antique, que tout le monde est convenu d'admirer, sans que nous puissions deviner pourquoi. C'est, dit-on, un air de grandeur & de simplicité qui en fait le caractere. On y trouve une régularité symmétrique, des richesses répandues avec économie, & entremêlées de grandes parties qui y donnent du repos. Ils s'en laissent éblouir, & reviennent ici remplis de prétendus principes, qui ne sont dans le fonds que des préjugés, & qui, grace à la mode agréable que nous avons amenée, ne peuvent leur être d'aucun usage. Nous nous sommes bien gardés de faire pareille folie; & tandis que nos camarades sont allés perdre leur temps à admirer & à étudier avec bien des fatigues cette triste architecture, nous nous sommes appliqués à faire ici des connoissances, & à répandre de toutes parts nos gentilles productions.

On nous a des obligations infinies: nous avons affaire à une nation gaie qu'il faut amuser; nous avons répandu l'agrément & la gaieté partout. Au bon vieux temps on croyoit que les églises devoient présenter un aspect grave & même sévere; les personnes les plus dissipées pouvoient à peine y entrer, sans s'y trouver pénétrées d'idées sérieuses. Nous avons bien changé tout cela; il n'y a pas maintenant de cabinet de toilette plus joli que les chapelles que nous y décorons. Si l'on y met encore quelques tombeaux, nous les contournons gentiment, nous les dorons partout, enfin nous leur ôtons tout ce qu'ils pourroient avoir de lugubre: il n'y a pas jusqu'à nos confessionnaux qui ont un air de galanterie.

Si l'on a égard à l'avancement de l'art, quelle extension ne lui avons-nous pas procuré? Nous avons multiplié le nombre des Architectes excellens, à tel point que la quantité en est presque innombrable. Ce talent qui, dans le systême de l'architecture antique, est hérissé de difficultés, devient dans le nôtre la chose du monde la plus aisée; & l'expérience fait voir que le maître Maçon le plus borné du côté du dessein & du goût, dès qu'il a travaillé quelque temps sous nos ordres, se trouve en état de se déclarer Architecte &, à bien peu de chose près, aussi bon que nous. Nous ajouterons, à la gloire de la France, & à son avantage, que les étrangers commencent à adopter notre goût, & qu'il y a apparence qu'ils viendront en foule l'apprendre chez nous. Les Anglois même, si jaloux de notre supériorité dans tous les arts, en sont devenus si foux, qu'ils en ont abandonné leur *Inigo Jones*, & leur habitude de copier exactement les ouvrages de *Palladio*. Ce qui pourra peut-être nuire à cet avantage, c'est l'imprudence qu'on a eu de laisser graver quelques-unes de nos décorations de portes & de cheminées, qui d'abord ont apprêté à rire aux autres nations, parce qu'ils n'en sentoient pas toute la beauté, mais qu'ensuite ils n'ont pu se refuser d'imiter. Malheureusement ces estampes dévoilent notre secret, qui d'ailleurs n'est pas difficile à apprendre, & l'on peut trouver en tout pays un grand nombre de génies propres à saisir ces graces légeres. Au reste, si cela arrive, nous nous en consolerons en citoyens de l'univers, & nous nous féliciterons d'avoir rendu tous les hommes architectes à peu de frais. Ces grands avantages nous ont coûté quelques peines; on ne détruit pas facilement les idées du beau, reçues dans une nation éclairée, & dans un siecle qu'on se figuroit devoir servir de modele à tous ceux qui le suivroient. Il étoit appuyé sur les plus grands noms; il falloit trouver aussi quelques noms célebres qui pussent nous servir d'appui. On avoit découvert presque tout ce qui pouvoit se faire de beau dans ce genre, & les génies ordinaires ne pouvoient prétendre qu'à être imitateurs: deux ou trois personnes auroient paru avec éclat, & les autres seroient demeurées dans l'oubli. Il falloit donc trouver un nouveau genre d'architecture, où chacun pût se distinguer & faire goûter au public des moyens d'être habile homme, qui fussent à la portée de tout le monde: cependant il ne falloit pas choquer grossiérement les préjugés reçus, en mettant tout d'un coup au jour des nouveautés trop éloignées du goût régnant, & risquer de se faire siffler sans retour. Le fameux *Oppenor* nous servit dans ces commencemens avec beaucoup de zele. Il s'étoit fait une grande réputation par ses desseins: la touche hardie qu'il y donnoit, séduisit presque tout le monde, & on fut long-temps à s'appercevoir qu'ils ne faisoient pas le même effet en exécution. Il se servit abondamment de nos ornemens favoris, & les mit en crédit. Il nous est même encore d'une grande utilité, & nous pouvons compter au nombre des nôtres ceux qui le prennent pour modele. Cependant ce n'étoit pas encore l'homme qu'il nous falloit: il ne pouvoit s'empêcher de retomber souvent dans l'architecture ancienne, qu'il avoit étudiée dans sa jeunesse. Nous trouvâmes un appui plus solide dans les talens du grand *Meissonnier*. Il avoit à la vérité étudié en Italie, & par conséquent n'étoit pas entiérement des nôtres: mais comme il y avoit sagement préféré le goût de *Borromini* au goût ennuyeux de l'antique, il s'étoit par-là rapproché de nous; car le *Borromini* a rendu à l'Italie le même service que nous avons rendu à la France, en y introduisant une architecture gaie & indépendante de toutes les regles de ce que l'on appelloit anciennement le bon goût. Les Italiens ont depuis bien perfectionné cette premiere tentative, & du côté de l'architecture plaisante ils ne nous le cedent en rien. Leur goût n'est pas le nôtre dans ce nouveau genre, il est beaucoup plus lourd: mais nous avons cela de commun, que nous avons également abandonné toutes les vieilles modes pour lesquelles on avoit un respect superstitieux. *Meissonnier* commença à détruire toutes les lignes droites qui étoient du vieil usage; il tourna & fit bomber les corniches de toutes façons; il les ceintra en haut & en bas, en devant, en arriere, donna des formes à tout, même aux moulures qui en paroissoient les moins susceptibles; il inventa les contrastes, c'est-à-dire qu'il bannit la symmetrie, & qu'il ne fit plus les deux côtés des panneaux semblables l'un à l'autre; au contraire ces côtés sembloient se défier à qui s'éloigneroit le plus, & de la maniere la plus singuliere, de la ligne droite à laquelle ils avoient jusqu'alors été asservis. Rien n'est si admirable que de voir de quelle maniere il engageoit les corniches des marbres les plus durs à se prêter avec complaisance aux bisarreries ingénieuses des formes de cartels ou autres choses qui devoient porter dessus. Les balcons ou les rampes d'escalier n'eurent plus la permission de passer droit leur chemin; il leur fallut serpenter à sa volonté, & les matieres les plus roides devinrent souples sous sa main triomphante. Ce fut lui qui mit en vogue ces charmans contours en S, que votre auteur croit rendre ridicules, en disant que leur origine vient des maîtres Ecrivains; comme si les arts ne devoient pas se prêter des secours mutuels: il les employa partout, & à proprement parler ses desseins, même pour des plans de bâtimens, ne furent qu'une combinaison de cette forme dans tous les sens possibles. Il nous apprit à terminer nos moulures en rouleau, lorsque nous ne sçaurions comment les lier les unes aux autres, & mille autres choses non moins admirables, qu'il seroit trop long de vous citer: enfin l'on peut dire que nous n'avons rien produit depuis dont on ne trouve les semences dans ses ouvrages. Quels services n'a-t-il pas rendus à l'orfévrerie? Il rejetta bien loin toutes les formes quarrées, rondes ou ovales, & toutes ces moulures, dont les ornemens répétés avec exactitude donnent tant de sujétion: avec ses chers contours en S il remplaça tout. Ce qu'il y a de particulier, c'est qu'en moins de rien l'orfévrerie & les bijoux devinrent très-aisés à traiter avec génie. En vain le célebre Germain voulut s'opposer au torrent, & soutenir le vieux goût dont il avoit été bercé dans son enfance; sa réputation méme en fut quelque peu éclipsée, & il se vit souvent préférer *Meissonnier* par l'appui que nous lui donnions sous main. Cependant le croiriez-vous! ce grand *Meissonnier* n'étoit pas encore notre homme; il tenoit trop à ce qu'ils appellent grande maniere. De plus il eut l'imprudence de laisser graver plusieurs ouvrages de lui, & mit par-là le public à portée de voir que ce génie immense qu'on lui croyoit, n'étoit qu'une répétition ennuyeuse des mêmes formes. Il se décrédita, & nous l'abandonnâmes d'autant plus facilement, que malgré les secours que nous lui avions prêtés pour l'établissement de sa réputation, il ne vouloit point faire corps avec nous, & nous traitoit hautement d'ignorans: quelle ingratitude!

Nous fîmes enfin la découverte du héros dont nous avions besoin. Ce fut un Sculpteur qui n'avoit pas pu se gâter à Rome, car il n'y avoit point été, bien qu'il eût vu beaucoup de pays. Il s'étoit formé avec nous, & avoit si bien goûté notre maniere, & si peu les prétendues regles anciennes, que rien ne pouvoit restreindre l'abondance de son génie. Il sçavoit assez d'architecture ancienne pour ne pas contrecarrer directement ceux qui y tenoient avec trop d'obstination; mais il la déguisoit avec tant d'adresse qu'il avoit le mérite de l'invention, & qu'on ne la reconnoissoit qu'à peine. Il allégea toutes ces moulures & tous ces profils, où *Oppenor* & *Meissonnier* avoient voulu conserver un caractere qu'ils appelloient mâle; il les traita d'une délicatesse qui les fait presque échapper à la vue; il trouva dans les mêmes espaces le moyen d'en mettre six fois davantage; il s'affranchit tout d'un coup de la loi qu'ils s'étoient follement imposée de lier toujours leurs ornemens les uns aux autres; il les divisa, les coupa en mille pieces, toujours terminées par ce rouleau qui est notre principale ressource; & afin que ceux qui aimoient la liaison ne s'apperçussent pas trop de ces interruptions, il fit paroître des liaisons apparentes par le secours d'une fleur, qui elle-même ne tenoit à rien, ou par quelque légéreté également ingénieuse; il renonça pour jamais à la regle & au compas: on avoit déja banni la symmétrie, il renchérit encore là-dessus. S'il lui échappa quelquefois de faire des panneaux semblables l'un à l'autre, il mit ces objets symmétriques si loin l'un de l'autre, qu'il auroit fallu une attention bien suivie pour s'appercevoir de leur ressemblance. Aux agraffes du ceintre des croisées, qui ci-devant ne représentoient que la clef de l'arc décorée, il substitua de petits cartels enrichis de mille gentilesses, & posés de travers, dont le pendant se trouvoit à l'autre extrêmité du bâtiment. C'est à lui qu'on doit l'emploi abondant des palmiers, qui à la vérité avoient été trouvés avant lui, & que votre auteur blâme si ridiculement. Il établit solidement l'usage de supprimer tous les plafonds, en faisant faire à des Sculpteurs, à bon marché, de jolies petites dentelles en bas-relief, qui reussirent si bien, qu'on prit le sage parti de supprimer les corniches des appartemens pour les enrichir de ces charmantes bagatelles. C'est notre triomphe que cette proscription des corniches; rien ne nous donnoit plus de sujétion que ces miseres antiques dont en les ornoit, & auxquelles votre écrivain paroît si attaché. Il y falloit une exactitude & une justesse qui, pour peu qu'on y manquât, se déceloit d'abord à des yeux un peu séveres. Nous regrettons encore ce grand homme, quoique ses merveilleux talens aient été remplacés sur le champ par quantité de Sculpteurs non moins abondans que lui dans cette sorte de génie. C'est à lui que nous avons l'obligation de cette supériorité que nous avons acquise, & que nous sçaurons conserver; & on peut dire à sa gloire que tout ce qui s'éloigne du goût antique lui doit son invention ou sa perfection.

En suivant ses principes, nous avons absolument rejetté tous ces anciens plafonds chargés de sculptures & de dorures, qui à la vérité avoient de la magnificence, & contre lesquels nous n'avons rien à dire, si ce n'est qu'ils ne sont plus de mode. En dépit des cris de toute l'Académie de Peinture, nous avons sçu persuader à toutes les personnes chez qui nous avons quelque crédit, que les plafonds peints obscurcissent les appartemens, & les rendent tristes. Inutilement veut-on nous représenter que nous avons justement dans notre siecle des Peintres dont la couleur est très-agréable, & qui aiment à rendre leurs tableaux lumineux; qu'en traitant les plafonds d'une couleur claire, ils n'auroient point le désagrément qu'on reproche aux anciens, & qu'ils auroient de plus le mérite de représenter quelque chose d'amusant par le sujet, & d'agréable par la variété des couleurs. Les Peintres n'y gagneront rien; ils nous ont irrité en mésprisant nos premieres productions, & nous voulons d'autant plus les perdre que nous n'espérons pas de pouvoir les gagner: ils ne se rendroient qu'avec des restrictions qui ne sont pas de notre goût. Les Sculpteurs de figures seront aussi compris dans cette proscription; ils seroient encore plus à portée de nous faire mauvaises chicanes. Notre Sculpteur favori nous a donné mille moyens de nous passer d'eux. Au lieu de tout cela il a imaginé une rosette charmante, qu'à peine on apperçoit, & qu'il met au milieu du plancher, à l'endroit où s'attache le lustre: voilà ce qu'on préfere avec raison aux plus belles productions de leur art. Il y a encore un petit nombre de criards qui répandent partout que le bon goût est perdu, & qu'il y a très-peu d'Architectes qui entendent la décoration qui fait le caractere essentiel de l'Architecte. Nous détruisons tous ces argumens, en soutenant hautement que ce qui distingue l'Architecte est l'art de la distribution. Ils ont beau dire qu'elle n'est pas aussi difficile que nous voulons le faire croire, & qu'il est évident qu'avec un peu d'intelligence chaque particulier peut arranger sa maison d'une maniere qui lui soit commode, relativement au besoins de son état; que la difficulté que le particulier ne sçauroit lever, ni nous non plus, & qui demande toutes les lumieres d'un grand Architecte, est d'ajuster cette distribution commode avec une décoration exacte, symmétrique, & dans ce qu'ils appellent le bon goût, soit dans les dehors, soit dans les dedans: voilà justement ce qui nous rendra toujours victorieux. Comme notre architecture n'a aucunes regles qui l'astreignent, qu'elle est commode, & qu'en quelque façon elle prête, nous nous sommes faits un grand nombre de partisans qui, satisfaits de notre facilité à remplir toutes leurs fantaisies, nous soutiendront toujours. Nous voudrions bien voir ces Messieurs de l'antique entreprendre de décorer l'extérieur d'un bâtiment avec toutes les sujétions que nous leur avons imposées. Comme les plus grands cris avoient d'abord été contre nos décorations extérieures, parce qu'elles étoient exposées à vue de tout le monde; que d'ailleurs le vuide ne coûte rien à décorer, & ne donne point de prise à la critique, nous avons amené la multitude des fenêtres, qui a parfaitement bien réussi: car il est infiniment agréable d'avoir trois fenêtres dans une chambre, qui jadis en auroit eu à peine deux. Cela donne à la vérité plus de froid dans l'hyver, & plus de chaleur dans l'été: mais que nous importe? Il n'en est pas moins sûr qu'à présent chacun veut que sa maison soit toute percée, & que nos Messieurs du goût ancien, qui ne sçavent décorer que du plein, n'y trouvent plus de place. Qu'ils y mettent, s'ils le peuvent, de leurs fenêtres décorées, qu'ils tâchent d'y placer leurs frontons à l'antique, qui, disent-ils, décorent la fenêtre, & mettent à couvert ceux qui y sont: nous y avons remédié en élevant les fenêtres jusques au haut du plancher. Rien n'est si amusant que de voir un pauvre Architecte revenant d'Italie, à qui on donne une pareille cage à décorer, se tordre l'imagination pour y appliquer ces chers principes, qu'il s'est donné tant de peine à apprendre; & s'il lui arrive d'y réussir, ce qu'il ne peut sans diminuer les croisées, c'est alors que nous faisons voir clairement combien sa production est triste & maussade. Vous ne verrez pas clair chez vous, leur disons-nous, vous n'aurez pas d'air pour respirer, à peine verrez-vous le soleil dans les beaux jours: ces nouveaux artistes se retirent confus, & sont enfin obligés de se joindre à nous pour trouver jour à percer dans le monde. Nous n'avons pas encore entiérement abandonné les frontons dont les anciens se servoient pour terminer le haut de leurs bâtimens, & qui représentoient le toit, quoique nous aimions bien mieux employer certaines terminaisons en façon d'orfévrerie, qui sont de notre crû. A l'égard des frontons nous avons du moins trouvé le moyen de les placer où on ne s'attendoit pas à les voir; nous les mettons au premier étage, & plus heureusement encore au second; & nous ne manquons guere d'élever un étage au dessus, afin qu'ils aient le moins de rapport qu'il est possible avec ceux des anciens. Nous avons, ou peu s'en faut, banni les colonnes, uniquement parce que c'est un des plus beaux ornemens de ce triste goût ancien, & nous ne les rétablirons que lorsque nous aurons trouvé le moyen de les rendre si nouvelles qu'elles n'aient plus aucune ressemblance avec toutes ces antiquailles. D'ailleurs elles ne sçauroient s'accomoder avec nos gentillesses légeres; elles font paroître mesquin tout ce qui les accompagne. Beaucoup de gens tenoient encore à cette sorte d'ornement, qui leur paroissoit avoir une grande beauté; mais nous avons sçu persuader aux uns que cela coûtoit beaucoup plus que toutes les choses que nous leur faisions, quoique peut-être en économisant bien, cela pût ne revenir qu'à la même dépense; aux autres, que cette décoration ne convenoit point à leur état, & qu'elle étoit réservée pour les temples de Dieu, & les palais des Rois; que quelques énormes dépenses que nous leur fissions faire chez eux, personne n'en sçauroit rien, quoiqu'ils le fîssent voir à tout le monde, au lieu qu'une petite colonnade, qui ne coûteroit peut-être guere, feroit un bruit épouvantable dans Paris. Nous avons accepté les pilastres jusqu'à un certain point, c'est-à-dire, lorsque nous avons pu les dépaïser par des chapiteaux divertissans. Les piédestaux sont aussi reçus chez nous; mais nous avons trouvé l'art de les contourner, en les élargissant par le bas, comme s'ils crevoient sous le fardeau, ou plus gaiement encore, en les faisant enfler du haut, & toujours en S, comme s'ils réunissoient leur force en ce lieu pour mieux porter. Mais où notre génie triomphe, c'est dans les bordures des dessus de porte, que nous pouvons nous vanter d'avoir varié presque à l'infini. Les Peintres nous en maudissent, parce qu'ils ne sçavent comment composer leurs sujets avec les incursions que nos ornemens font sur leur toile; mais tant pis pour eux: lorsque nous faisons une si grande dépense de génie, ils peuvent bien aussi s'évertuer; ce sont des especes de bouts-rimés que nous leur donnons à remplir. Il auroit pu rester quelque ressource à la vieille architecture pour se reproduire à Paris; mais nous avons coupé l'arbre dans sa racine, en annonçant la mode des petits appartemens, & nous avons sappé l'ancien préjugé, qui vouloit que les personnes distinguées par leur état eussent un appartement de représentation, grand & magnifique. Nous espérons que dorénavant la regle s'établira que plus la personne sera élevée en dignité, plus son appartement sera petit: vous voyez qu'alors il sera difficile de nous faire désemparer. Ceux qui pourront faire de la dépense, ne la feront qu'en petit, & s'adresseront à nous. Il ne restera pour occuper ces Messieurs, que ceux qui n'ont pas le moyen de rien faire.

Voyez, je vous prie, l'impertinence de votre auteur critique; il s'ennuie, dit-il, de voir partout des croisées ceintrées, mais il n'ose pas disconvenir que cette sorte de croisée ne soit bonne. Peut-on avoir trop d'une bonne chose? Et pourquoi veut-il qu'on aille se fatiguer l'imagination pour trouver des variétés, lorsqu'une chose est de mode, & qu'on est sûr du succès? Ne voit-il pas que toutes nos portes, nos cheminées, nos fenêtres, avec leur plat-bandeau, sont à peu-près la même chose: puisqu'on en est content, pourquoi se tuer à en chercher d'autres? Il blâme nos portes où les moulures se tournent circulairement:

invention heureuse, que nous appliquons à tout avec le plus grand succès. Il faut qu'il soit bien étranger lui-même dans Paris, pour ne pas sçavoir de qui nous la tenons. C'est d'un Architecte à qui les amateurs de l'antique donnent le nom de grand. Le célebre François Mansard l'a employée dans son portail des Filles de Sainte Marie, rue Saint Antoine: voilà une autorité qu'il ne peut récuser. Pour vous faire voir combien cette sorte de fronton réussit quand elle est traitée à notre façon, & combien elle l'emporte sur l'architecture ancienne, comparez le portail des Capucines de la place de Louis le Grand, morceau si admirable qu'on vient de la restaurer, de peur que la postérité n'en fût privée; comparez-le avec le portail à colonnes de l'Assomption, qui n'en est pas loin, & vous toucherez au doigt la différence qui est entre nous & les Architectes du siècle passé.

Mais laissons là ce critique: ce seroit perdre le temps que de s'amuser à lui démontrer en détail l'absurdité de ses jugemens. Nous ne vous dissimulerons pas que nous sommes actuellement dans une position un peu critique, & qu'une révolution dans le goût de l'architecture nous paroîtroit prochaine, si nous la croyions possible. Il se rencontre actuellement plusieurs obstacles à nos progrès. Maudite soit cette architecture antique! Sa séduction, dont on a bien de la peine à revenir, lorsqu'une fois on s'y est laissé prendre, nous a enlevé un protecteur qui auroit peut-être été pour nous l'appui le plus solide, si nous avions été chargés du soin de l'endoctriner. Pourquoi aller chercher bien loin ce qu'on peut trouver chez soi? Nous amusons en instruisant. Ne peut-on pas se former le goût en voyant nos desseins de boudoirs, de garde-robes, de pavillons à la Turque, de cabinets à la Chinoise? Est-ce quelque chose de fort agréable que cette église démesurée de Saint-Pierre, ou que cette rotonde antique, dont le portail n'a qu'un ordre dans une hauteur où nous, qui avons du génie, aurions trouvé de la place pour en mettre au moins trois? Il n'est pas concevable qu'on puisse balancer. Cependant cette perte est irréparable: cela est désolant; car tous les projets que nous présentons, paroissent comiques à des yeux ainsi prévenus. Nous avons même tenté de mêler quelque chose d'antique dans nos desseins, voyez quel sacrifice! pour faire passer notre marchandise par ce moyen: tout cela sans succès, on nous devine d'abord.

Autre obstacle qui est une suite du premier. Les bâtimens du Roi nous ont donné exclusion totale; tout ce qui s'y fait sent la vieille architecture, & ce même public, que nous comptions avoir subjugué, s'écrie: voilà qui est beau! Il y a une fatalité attaché à cette vieille mode: partout où elle se montre, elle nous dépare; l'Académie même a peine à se défendre de cette contagion; il semble qu'elle ne veuille plus donner de prix qu'à ceux qui s'approchent le plus du goût de l'antique. Cela nous expose à des avanies de la part même de ces jeunes étourdis, qui se donnent les airs de rire de notre goût moderne. Cette conspiration est bien soutenue; car, à ne vous rien céler, il y a encore plusieurs Architectes de réputation, & même qui n'ont pas vu l'Italie, mais qui par choix en ont adopté le goût, que nous n'avons jamais pu attirer dans notre parti. Il y a plus; quelques-uns que nous avons cru longtemps des nôtres, à la premiere occasion qu'ils ont eu de faire quelque chose de remarquable, nous ont laissé là, & se sont jettés dans l'ancien goût.

Vous êtes, sans doute, pénétré de compassion à la vue du danger où nous nous trouvons, & nous vous faisons pitié: mais consolez-vous, nous avons des ressources; nous sçaurons bien arrêter ces nouveaux débarqués d'Italie. Nous leur opposerons tant d'obstacles que nous les empêcherons de rien faire, & peut-être les forcerons-nous d'aller chez l'étranger exercer des talens qui nous déplaisent. Ils aiment à employer des colonnades avec des architraves en plate-bande: nous en déclarerons la bâtisse impossible. Ils auront beau citer la colonnade du Louvre, la chapelle de Versailles, & autres bâtimens dont on ne peut contester la solidité, qui est-ce qui les en croira? Leur voix sera-t-elle d'un plus grand poids que celle de gens qui ont bâti des petites maisons par milliers dans Paris? Mais voici l'argument invincible que nous leur gardons pour le dernier. Nous leur demanderons ce qu'ils ont bâti: il faudra bien qu'ils conviennent qu'ils n'en ont point encore eu l'occasion. C'est là où nous les attendons: comment, dirons-nous, quelle imprudence! Confier un bâtiment à un jeune homme sans expérience? Cette objection est sans réplique. On ne s'avisera pas de faire réflexion qu'un jeune homme de mérite, & d'un caractere docile, peut facilement s'associer un homme qui, sans prétendre à la décoration, ait une longue pratique du bâtiment, & qui lui donneroit les conseils nécessaires, en cas qu'il hazardât quelque chose de trop hardi; que d'ailleurs il y auroit dans Paris bien des maisons en ruines, si le premier bâtiment de chaque Architecte manquoit de solidité.

Au reste ne croyez point que ce soit dans le dessein de nuire à ces jeunes gens que nous leur ferons ces difficultés: c'est uniquement pour leur bien, & pour leur donner du temps, pendant quelques années, d'apprendre le bon goût que nous avons établi, & de quitter leurs préjugés ultramontains: nous avons l'expérience que cela a rarement manqué de nous réussir.

Si donc vous connoissez cette société d'Artistes, qui prend la liberté de nous blâmer, avertissez-les d'être plus retenus à l'avenir: leurs critiques sont superflues. Le public nous aime; nous l'avons accoutumé à nous. D'ailleurs chacun de ceux qui font bâtir, même des édifices publics, est persuadé que quiconque a les fonds pour bâtir, a de droit les connoissances nécessaires pour le bien faire. Peut-on manquer de goût quand on a de l'argent? Nous sommes déja sûrs des Procureurs de la plûpart des Communautés, des Marguilliers de presque toutes les Paroisses, & de tant d'autres, qui sont à la tête des entreprises. Enfin soyez certains que nous & nos amis nous serons toujours le plus grand nombre. Nous sommes, &c.

ENGLISH TRANSLATION

Letter to the Abbé R. . . on a very poor pleasantry which he has allowed to be printed in the *Mercure* for December 1754. By a Society of Architects who might well claim to be of the first merit and of the first reputation even though they are not members of the Academy.

We are surprised, Sir, that a man of wit and so good a citizen as yourself should have authorised a satirical writing whose purpose is so evidently to overthrow modern architecture and to destroy the confidence placed in architects by enabling the public to judge for itself of the excellence or badness of the works that we execute for it. Can we believe that you did not perceive this consequence, or that having perceived it you felt no scruple in lending yourself to the denigration of inventions which have for so long been the delight of Paris and which foreigners too are beginning to taste with singular avidity?

It is easy to divine the source whence come these complaints and we do not credit so easily as you that they are merely the ideas of a single artist. It is a plot formed by several persons who are, it is true, of some worth in their line but who would do better to apply themselves to it rather than meddle with an art which is so far above the sphere of their knowledge. We have reason to suspect some famous painters are mixed up in this conspiracy: woe betide them if we discover who they are! They have already been able to observe that because they have offended us we have suppressed the grand style of history painting in all modern buildings. We had as a favour left them a few overdoors to paint, but we shall force them out of this last trench and reduce them to paint nothing more than little pictures of the fashions and those only in monochrome. Let them note well that we possess the secret of varnishes. In vain the public complains of how short a time they last; it will be varnished and revarnished. Yet we are willing to attribute these criticisms not to ill-will, but rather to their misfortune in having formed their taste in Italy. There they have seen those remains of Antique architecture which all the world is agreed to admire without our being able to divine the reasons. There is an air, so it is said, of grandeur and simplicity which characterises it; in it are found symmetrical regularity, richness distributed with economy and intermixed with grandiose forms which give repose to the eye. They allow themselves to be dazzled by it and return here full of pretended principles which at bottom are only prejudices and which can be of no use to them thanks to the agreeable fashion introduced by us. We have taken good care to avoid such folly and whilst our comrades have gone off to waste their time in admiring and studying with many fatigues this melancholy architecture, we have applied ourselves to making useful acquaintances here and to scattering our pretty productions on all sides.

The public are under infinite obligations to us. Our business is with a gay nation which has to be amused and we have scattered charm and gaiety everywhere. In the good old days it was believed that churches ought to present a grave, even a severe aspect. The most dissipated persons could hardly enter them without finding themselves impressed by serious ideas. We have quite changed all that. Now there is no lady's dressing-room prettier than the chapels we decorate. If some tombs are still put into them we curve their outlines prettily, we gild them all over, in fact we take from them anything lugubrious they might otherwise have. Even our confessionals have an air of gallantry.

If the advancement of the art is considered, what great extension have we not given to it? We have multiplied the number of excellent architects to the point where they are almost innumerable. A line of talent which bristles with difficulties under the system of ancient architecture becomes under ours the easiest thing in the world. Experience shows that even a master-mason of the most limited gifts in drawing and taste, after he has worked for some time under our orders, is fitted to declare himself an architect and as good as we are, bating only a very little. Let us add that to the glory of France and to her advantage foreigners are beginning to adopt our taste and there is every appearance that they will come here in crowds to learn it from us. The English themselves, so jealous of our superiority in all the arts, have become so wild after it that they have abandoned their Inigo Jones for it and their habit of copying exactly the works of Palladio. What may perhaps injure this advantage is the imprudence which has permitted some of our decorations for doors and chimney-pieces to be engraved, for at first they gave matter for laughter to the other nations of Europe, because they did not feel all their beauty, but since then they have been unable to resist imitating them. Unfortunately these prints disclose our secret which in any case is not difficult to learn, and a great number of geniuses able to catch these light graces may spring up in all countries. Yet should this happen, as citizens of the world we shall console ourselves and congratulate ourselves on having turned all men into architects at very little expense. These great advantages have cost us some pains; it is not easy to destroy the ideas of beauty received in an enlightened nation and in a century which men once imagined would be taken as a model by all to follow. Those ideas rested on the support of the greatest names, and so it was necessary to find some famous names which might serve as a support to us. Almost all that is beautiful that can be done in the old style had been discovered, and ordinary geniuses could only claim to be imitators. Two or three persons would have shone in glory whilst the rest would have remained in oblivion. It was necessary then to find a new style of architecture in which every man might distinguish himself, and to make the public take pleasure in ways of being a skilled artist that should be within the comprehension of everyone. Yet it was necessary too not to give a rude shock to common prejudices by suddenly bringing into view novelties too remote from the reigning taste and so risk being hissed off without hope of return. In those early days the celebrated Oppenort served us with great zeal. He had made a great reputation for himself by his designs; the bold touch he gave them seduced almost everyone and it was long before men perceived that when executed they did not produce the same effect. He made abundant use of our favourite ornaments and brought them into repute. He is still of great use to us and we can count those who take him for their model as being of our numbers. Yet he was still not the man we needed: he could not prevent himself from falling back into the old manner of architecture which he had studied in his youth. We found a solider support in the talents of the great Meissonnier. It is true that he had studied in Italy and hence was not completely one of us, but, since while there he had wisely preferred the taste of Borromini to the tedious taste of the Antique, he drew to our side, for Borromini rendered Italy the same service that we have rendered France by introducing there a style of architecture which is gay and independent of all those rules that formerly were called good taste. Since then the Italians have greatly perfected his first attempt and in respect of the pleasant style of architecture they yield to us in nothing. Their taste in this new genre is not ours, it is much heavier, but we both have one thing in common, for we have both equally abandoned all the old fashions for which there was once a superstitious regard. Meissonnier began the destruction of all the straight lines of the old manner; he bent and swelled out cornices in every possible fashion, he arched them above and below, in front, behind, gave forms to everything, even to those mouldings which seemed least susceptible of receiving them. He invented the art of contrasts, that is to say, he banished symmetry and no longer made the two sides of a panel alike. On the contrary each side seemed to challenge the other as to which of them should draw further and in the most singular manner from the straight line to which until then they had been subservient. Nothing is more wonderful than to see the way in which he invited cornices of the hardest marbles to lend themselves with complacency to the ingenious oddities of form of the cartouches or other things that were to rest on them. Balconies and staircases no longer had permission to go straight along their road; they were obliged to wind according to his will, and the most rigid substances became supple under his triumphant hand. It was he who brought into fashion those charming serpentine lines which your author hopes to make ridiculous by saying that they take their origin from writing masters, as if the arts ought not to be of mutual assistance to one another. He used them everywhere, and to speak precisely, his designs, even for plans of buildings, were only combinations of this form in every possible way. It was he who taught us to terminate our mouldings in a scroll whenever we found ourselves at a loss to link them with one another. He taught us too a thousand other not less wonderful things which it would take too long to mention to you. In fact it may be said that we have produced nothing since whose seeds are not to be found in his works. What services did he not render to goldsmith's work? He rejected all right-angled, round and oval forms, and all those mouldings whose ornaments when repeated with exactitude impose so much respect. He replaced them all with his cherished serpentine contours. What is especially remarkable is that in less than no time it became extremely easy to treat goldsmith's work and jewellery with genius. In vain did the celebrated Germain attempt to oppose the torrent and uphold the old taste in which he had been cradled during his infancy. His reputation was even a little eclipsed by his opposition and he frequently saw Messonnier preferred to himself by means of the support we gave him underhand. Yet would you credit it? Even the great Meissonnier was not yet our man: he was still too attached to what they call the grand manner. In addition he committed the imprudence of allowing several of his works to be engraved and so made it possible for the public to see that the immense genius he was believed to possess was merely a tedious repetition of the same forms. He discredited himself and we deserted him all the more readily because in spite of the help we had afforded him in establishing his reputation he was unwilling to make common cause with us and loudly spoke of us as dunces. What ingratitude!

At last we discovered the hero we needed. He was a sculptor who had not been able to spoil himself in Rome since he had never been there, though he had seen many countries. He had formed himself with us and had so well tasted our manner and so little the pretended ancient rules that nothing could restrain the abundance of his genius. He knew enough of ancient architecture not to cross directly those who were too obstinately attached to it. But he disguised it with such skill that he had all the merit of invention and only with difficulty could it be recognised. He lightened all the mouldings and all the profiles in which Oppenort and Meissonnier had sought to preserve a character they called masculine. He treated them with a delicacy which makes them nearly escape the sight and found means to put six times the number in the same amount of space. He freed himself at one blow from the law which they had foolishly imposed on themselves of always linking their ornaments with each other. He divided them, cut them into a thousand pieces, each ending in that scroll which is our principal resource, and in order that those who liked connection should not perceive these interruptions too clearly he made apparent connections by the help of a flower which itself was attached to nothing or by some equally ingenious piece of airy lightness. He renounced the ruler and compass for ever. Symmetry had already been banished; he did even more in that line. If at times he slipped into making panels resemble each other, he placed these symmetrical objects so far apart that a very continous attention would have been necessary to remark their similarity. For the ornamental keystone of the window arch which in former days merely represented the decorated key of the arch, he substituted little cartouches, enriched with a thousand small prettinesses and set on their sides, whose pendants were to be found only at the other end of the building. It is to him we owe that abundant use of palm trees which truth to say had been discovered before him and which your author so absurdly blames. He established solidly the custom of suppressing all ceilings by having carvers make cheaply pretty little bits of lacework in relief which succeeded so well that the wise plan was adopted of suppressing cornices in rooms so as to enrich them with these charming trifles. This proscription of cornices is our great triumph, nothing subdued us more than that wretched antique stuff with which they were ornamented and to which your contributor seems so attached. They required such exactitude and precision that if one failed in these qualities ever so little it was immediately evident to eyes ever so little severe. We still regret this great man, although his marvellous talents have been immediately replaced by a quantity of sculptors no less fertile than he in this line of genius. It is to him that we are obliged for the superiority we have acquired and which we shall know how to keep, and it may be said to his glory that everything which is far removed from the Antique taste owes to him either its invention or its perfection.

Following his principles we have absolutely rejected those old ceilings loaded with sculpture and gilding which, to say truth, were of some magnificence and to which we make no objection other than that they are no longer the fashion. In spite of the cries of the entire Academy of Painting we have found means to persuade all those persons with whom we enjoy some credit that painted ceilings darken rooms and make them gloomy. In vain are representations made to us that it is precisely in this our own century that we have painters whose colour is very pleasing and who like to make their pictures bright, and that if clear colour were used on ceilings they would not have the unpleasantness which is objected against the old ceilings, and that in addition they would have the merit of representing something amusing in subject and pleasing in variety of colour. The painters will gain nothing from such pleas; they have irritated us by their contempt for our first productions and we are all the more desirous of ruining them because we have no hope of winning them over; they would only surrender themselves under restrictions which are not to our taste. Sculptors of figures will also be included in this proscription; they would have it even more in their power to pick unpleasant quarrels with us. Our favourite sculptor has given us a thousand ways of doing without them; instead of all their things he has imagined a charming rosette which can scarcely be perceived and which he sets in the middle of the ceiling in the place where the lustre is suspended. This is preferred, and with reason, to the finest productions of their art. There yet remain a few grumblers who spread it abroad everywhere that good taste is lost and that there are very few architects who understand that sort of decoration which essentially characterises the architect. We destroy all these arguments by affirming loudly that what distinguishes the architect is the art of distribution. In vain do they urge that distribution is not so difficult as we wish to make men believe and that it is quite obvious that any private person with a little intelligence can arrange his house in a manner convenient to himself according to the requirements of his rank, and that the difficulty which a private person cannot remove, nor we either, and which demands all the knowledge of a great architect is to adjust convenient distribution to a decoration which is exact, symmetrical and in what they call good taste, both outside and inside. But here precisely is the point which will always make us the victors. As our style of architecture has no rules to bind it, as it is convenient and, so to speak, docile we have acquired a large number of partisans who will always support us because they are gratified by the facility with which we satisfy their fancies. We should very much like to see the gentlemen of the Antique school undertake to decorate the outside of a building under all the conditions which we have imposed on them. Since at first the loudest protests were directed against our exterior decorations, because they were exposed to the sight of everyone, and since empty space costs nothing to decorate and leaves no point on which criticism can fasten we brought in the mode for a multitude of windows, which succeeded perfectly, for it is infinitely agreeable to have three windows in a room which formerly would hardly have been given two. It is true that this makes for more cold in winter and more heat in summer, but what does that matter to us? It is not the less certain that everyone at present wants his house pierced all over by windows and that our gentlemen of the Antique taste who only know how to decorate the solid parts find no room for their work. Let them if they can put in their decorated windows, and try to crown them with the Antique pediments which, so they say, ornament the window and shelter those beneath. We have found out the remedy by raising windows to the full height of the ceiling. Nothing is more amusing than to see a poor architect just returned from Italy who has been given such a cage to decorate torture his imagination in order to apply to it those cherished principles which he has given himself so much trouble to learn. And should he happen to succeed, which he cannot do without reducing the windows, then this is the moment we choose to point out how gloomy and dull his work is. You will not be able to see clearly in your house, we say to their patrons, you will have no air to breathe, you will hardly be able to see the sun on fine days. These new artists retire in confusion and at last are obliged to join with us to find an opening through which to make their way in the world. We have not yet entirely abandoned the pediments which the ancients employed to terminate the tops of their buildings and which represented the roof, although we very much prefer to use certain terminations in the style of goldsmith's work which are of our own manufacture. With regard to pediments we have at least discovered how to set them in places where no-one expected to see them before: we put them on the first storey, and with even happier results on the second, and we hardly ever fail to raise another storey above in order that they may have as little relationship as possible to those of the ancients. We have banished columns, or very nearly so, solely because they are one of the finest ornaments of the gloomy Antique taste, and we shall only restore them when we have discovered a means of making them so new that they no longer bear any resemblance to all that lumber of antiquity. Besides they cannot accommodate themselves to our light and airy prettinesses; they make everything that accompanies them seem mean. Many persons still held by this type of ornament which seemed to them one of great beauty, but we found means to persuade some that they cost far more than all the things we made for them, though perhaps with due economy they might well cost no more, and we persuaded others that this sort of decoration was unsuitable to their state of life and was reserved for the temples of God and the palaces of kings, and that however vast the expense to which we put them for their houses no one would realise it though they were to exhibit them to all the world, whereas a small colonnade which might perhaps cost little or nothing would make a terrible noise in Paris. We have accepted pilasters up to a certain point, that is to say, whenever we have been able to denaturalise them by amusing capitals. Pedestals too are received by us, but we have discovered the art of curving them by enlarging them towards the base as if they were bursting under their burden or, with even gayer effect, by swelling them at the top, always in an S curve as if they were collecting their strength in that place the better to give support. But it is in the borders of overdoors that our genius triumphs, that we can boast of having introduced an almost infinite variety. The painters curse us for them because they are at a loss how to compose their subjects among the incursions that our ornaments make on to their canvas. But so much the worse for them: when we put ourselves to so great an expense of genius they too may bestir themselves. The borders are as it were a set of rhymes fixed by us for which they must supply the lines. Perhaps there might still have lingered in Paris some resource for the old style of architecture to reproduce itself, but we have cut the tree at its root by announcing the fashion for small rooms and we have sapped that ancient prejudice which demanded that persons of distinguished rank should have a large and magnificent state suite. We hope that henceforth it will be an established rule that the greater the dignity of the person the smaller his suite of rooms: you see that then it will be difficult to loosen our grip. Those who are able to lay out money lavishly will lay it out only on small-scale work and will apply to us. To occupy these other gentlemen there will remain only those without means to undertake anything.

Consider I beg you the impertinence of your critic author. He says he is wearied of seeing arched windows everywhere, but he dare not disagree that this kind of window is good. Can one have too much of a good thing? And why does he want us to go and weary our imaginations to find variations when a thing is in fashion and we are sure of success? Does he not see that all our doors, chimney-pieces, and windows with their platbands are pretty much the same thing, and since people are happy with them why should we kill ourselves searching for others? He blames our doors because their mouldings turn in circular fashion, a happy invention which we apply to everything with the greatest success. It must be the case that he is very much of a stranger in Paris since he does not know from whom we derive it. It is from an architect to whom the lovers of the Antique give the name of great. The famous François Mansard employed it in his portal of the Filles de Sainte Marie, Rue Saint Antoine. There is an authority which he cannot challenge. In order to make you see how well this sort of pediment succeeds when it is treated in our fashion and how superior it is to the old style of architecture, compare the portal of the Capucines of the Place de Louis le Grand, a work so admirable that it has just been restored for fear that posterity might be deprived of it; compare it we say with the columned portico of the Assomption which is not far away, and you will put your finger on the difference between us and the architects of the last century.

But here let us quit this critic. It would be a waste of time were we to amuse ourselves by demonstrating the absurdity of his judgements to him in detail. We shall not conceal from you that at the present moment our position is a little critical and that a revolution in architectural taste might well seem close at hand to us, could we believe it possible. At the present moment we encounter several obstacles to our progress. Accursed be Antique architecture! Its seductions, from which a man has great difficulty in escaping once he has allowed himself to be entrapped by them, have torn from us a protector who might perhaps have been our most reliable support had we been entrusted with the care of his indoctrination. Why fare far afield to seek something that can be found at home? We amuse while we instruct. Is it not possible to form a taste by seeing our designs for boudoirs, for closets, for Turkish pavilions, for Chinese cabinets? Is there anything very agreeable in that outsize church of St. Peter's or that ancient rotunda whose portal offers only one order in a height where we geniuses would have found room to accommodate at least three? It is inconceivable that any one should hesitate. And yet this loss is irreparable; it is also very distressing, for all the plans we present seem comical in eyes so prepossessed. We have even attempted to infuse something of the Antique into our designs—see what a sacrifice!—in order to pass our merchandise through by this means, but all without success, we are at once divined.

There is another obstacle which is a consequence of the first. We have been totally excluded from the royal buildings. Everything done in them savours of the old architecture, and that same public on whose complete subjugation we used to reckon, cries: Now that is something fine! There is a fatality attached to this old fashion; wherever it appears it throws us into the shade. Even the Academy finds it difficult to escape the infection: it seems as if it wished to award prizes only to those who approach most nearly to the Antique taste. This exposes us to insults from those thoughtless young fellows who give themselves airs of laughing at our modern taste. This conspiracy is well supported, for to conceal nothing from you, there are also several architects of reputation who have not even been to Italy and yet have adopted this taste from choice and we have never been able to attract them into our party. Worse still, some whom we long believed to be with us, have deserted us at the very first opportunity they had of doing something remarkable and have thrown themselves into the old taste.

Doubtless you are pierced with compassion at the sight of the danger in which we find ourselves and doubtless we cause you pity, but console yourself, we have resources, we shall be well able to arrest the progress of these persons newly landed from Italy. We shall oppose so many obstacles to them that we shall prevent them from doing anything and perhaps force them to go abroad in order to exercise those talents which displease us. They like to use colonnades with horizontal architraves; we shall declare them impossible to build. In vain will they cite the colonnade of the Louvre, the Chapel of Versailles and other buildings whose solidity is incontestible, who will believe them? Will their voices carry greater weight than those of men who have built thousands of intimate little houses in Paris? But here is the one invincible argument which we are keeping as our last resource against them. We shall ask them what they have built: they will have no alternative but to concede that they have not yet had an opportunity to build. This is the point at which we lie in wait for them. Indeed, we shall say, what imprudence! Confide a building to a young man without experience? This objection admits of no reply. No one will think to make the reflexion that a young man of merit and of docile character can easily take into partnership a man with no claims to be a decorator but with long experience of building who will be able to give him the necessary advice in case he should risk something too bold, and that besides there would be a great many ruinous houses in Paris if the first building of every architect were wanting in solidity.

For the rest, do not think that we shall raise these difficulties with the design of injuring these young men. It is solely for their good and in order to give them time, for the space of some years, to learn that good taste which we have set up and to leave off their ultramontane prejudices. It is our experience that this means has rarely failed us of success.

Should you then be acquainted with that society of artists which takes the liberty of blaming us, warn them to be more guarded in future. Their criticisms are superfluous. The public likes us, we have accustomed it to us. Besides all those who commission buildings, even public edifices, are convinced that whoever has the funds to build has as of right the knowledge required to do it well. Can one lack taste when one has money? We are already certain of the *procureurs* of most communities, of the church wardens of almost every parish and of all the other sorts of men who are at the head of such undertakings. Rest certain in fact that we and our friends will always be the greater number. We are, &c.

APPENDIX IV

J.-F. Blondel: General Observations on Interior Decoration, 1762

J.-F. Blondel: *Observations générales sur la décoration intérieure appliquées en particulier à un appartement de parade* (*Palais-Royal*), from 'Architecture et parties qui en dépendent' in Diderot and d'Alembert's *Dictionnaire des Sciences*, published in 1762.

FRENCH TEXT

Nous avons parlé, *tome IV. page* 702 &c. de la décoration en général. Il s'agit ici de la décoration des appartemens en particulier: nous ne rappellerons point les écarts de l'imagination de la plûpart de nos artistes à cet égard. La quantité de gravures qui s'en sont répandues dans le public, font assez connoître combien il étoit essentiel que ces compositions frivoles passassent de mode, pour faire place à des compositions moins bisarres sans doute. Nous sommes arrivés à cette époque, à en juger par quelques productions des architectes de nos jours. Pour nous convaincre de ce que nous avançons, nous allons en citer plusieurs de l'un & l'autre genre, & nous finirons ces observations par donner les décorations faites dernierement dans les appartemens du palais-royal, pour feue madame la duchesse d'Orléans, sur les desseins de M. Contant, architecte du Roi, de qui nous avons quantité d'ouvrages du premier mérite, & qui en plus d'une occasion a donné des preuves de son goût dans l'architecture, & de son génie dans les choses d'agrément.

Les décorations intérieures qui tiennent le premier rang, n'entendant pas parler ici de celles du dernier siècle d'un genre admirable (telle que celle du Louvre, des Tuileries, de Versailles, du Palais-royal, de Vincennes &c.), & à qui on ne peut reprocher qu'un peu de pesanteur & peut-être un peu de confusion, les décorations, dis-je, qui tiennent le premier rang sont celles du palais-royal que nous venons de citer, de l'hôtel de Toulouse, de l'hôtel de Biron, de la maison de M. Bourette, de la maison de campagne de M. d'Argenson à Neuilly, de la galerie de l'hôtel de Choiseul, &c. qui, comparées avec celles du palais Bourbon, celles de l'hôtel de Soubise, de l'hôtel de Rohan-Chabot, de la maison de M. Dionis, de la maison de campagne de M. de la Valliere à Montrouge, de la galerie de l'hôtel de Villars, &c. montrent assez la préférence que les unes doivent avoir sur les autres, & combien il eût été dangereux que les artistes les plus célebres de notre tems n'eussent pas créé un nouveau genre de décoration qui anéantît pour ainsi dire cette frivolité qui seule faisoit le mérite des appartemens du palais Bourbon, &c. ainsi que ce caractere de pesanteur que nous avons reproché aux anciennes décorations de la plûpart de nos maisons royales. Entrons dans quelque détail à ce sujet à-propos des desseins que nous allons offrir, & qui, comme nous venons de le remarquer, ont été exécutés sous la conduite de M. Contant, par les plus habiles artistes, qui ont secondé ce sçavant architecte dans les embellissemens du palais-royal.

PLANCHE XXIX (*reproduced as Plate* 22)
Elevation en face des croisées du salon, au premier étage des nouveaux appartemens du palais-royal.

Cette décoration toute de menuiserie peinte en blanc, & dont tous les ornemens sont dorés d'or mat & d'or bruni, offre le plus grand éclat. La porte à placards est revêtue de glaces, & les deux côtés occupés par des sophas (*Voyez* le dessein en grand d'un de ces sophas Pl. XXXVI.) au-dessus desquels sont aussi des glaces qui toutes répondent aux axes des croisées qui sont en face, & répetent le spectacle des jardins du palais-royal. Ces sophas sont couverts par des campanilles d'étoffe or & argent ajustées avec goût, qui meublent cette piece avec la plus grande magnificence. Le plafond de ce sallon est peint par M. Pierre, dont le nom seul dit tout. Les deux colonnes qui se voient ici sont engagées pour symétriser avec celles isolées qui leur sont opposées, & qui ont été introduites ainsi, pour racheter l'inégalité de cette piece anciennement bâtie avec assez d'irrégularité. (*Voyez* le plan de cette piece, Pl. XXXV.)

PLANCHE XXX
Elévation du côté de la cheminée de la même piece.

Les portes de cette décoration sont de glaces, comme celles de la piece précédente, & ne different que dans leur attique; le dessein de la cheminée est de bon goût. Il est aisé de s'appercevoir combien sa beauté réelle l'emporte sur les tiges du palmier, les guirlandes, les rocailles, les palmettes, &c. qu'on a vû si long-tems faire toute la ressource de nos sculpteurs en bois dans ce genre de décoration. Le chambranle de cette cheminée est aussi d'une belle forme, & est revêtu de bronze doré d'or moulu, traité de la plus grande maniere. Des girandoles avec des génies enrichissent ses angles; ces girandoles correspondent à de pareilles qui sont posées sur une table de marbre placée en face de la cheminée, & dont on voit le dessein dans la Planche XXXVI.

Les pilastres corinthiens qui décorent cette façade & son opposée, ont autorisé ici des membres d'Architecture qui l'ont empêché de devenir frivole, comme cela se pratiquoit précédemment; en sorte que toute cette ordonnance d'un bon style paroît convenable à la dignité du prince qui habite ce palais; considération plus intéressante qu'on ne s'imagine, & qui devroit être la premiere regle de toutes les productions des artistes.

PLANCHE XXXI
Elévation de la salle de jeu du côté de la porte qui donne entrée au sallon.

Cette décoration d'ordre ionique est composée de grandes parties, & ornée d'excellens détails. Pour s'en convaincre, on n'a qu'à comparer cette production avec la plûpart de celles du palais Bourbon, gravées dans l'Architecture françoise, ou avec celles de l'hôtel de Soubise, insérées dans les oeuvres de M. Boiffrand, & on verra combien les repos qui se remarquent ici, sont préférables à cette multitude d'ornemens qu'on a prodigués avec excès pendant trente années dans tous nos bâtimens, & dont même la décoration intérieure de nos temples n'est pas toujours exempte. Cet ordre est ionique, pilastres & colonnes; ces dernieres sont engagées pour occuper moins de place dans l'intérieur de la piece, & pour corriger l'irrégularité de la bâtisse, nos anciens architectes ayant presque toujours sacrifié les dehors au-dedans des appartemens. (*Voyez* le plan de cette piece, Pl. XXXV.)

PLANCHE XXXII (*reproduced as Plate* 23)
Elévation du côté de la cheminée de la même piece.

Cette facade, du même style que la précédente, fait voir de côté de la cheminée placée entre deux pilastres; de belles tapisseries occupent les deux espaces qui déterminent le grand diametre de cette piece. Ces deux espaces sont d'inégale grandeur, à cause de la premiere disposition du plan, qui n'étant pas régulier, a occasionné ce défaut de symétrie dans cette ordonnance. Deux pans coupés dans l'un des côtés de la profondeur de cette salle de jeu, lui donnent une forme assez agréable, & ont produit la facilité d'y poser des glaces; ressourse ingénieuse que l'homme de mérite sçait se permettre quelquefois, mais dont l'homme subalterne abuse presque toujours, ainsi qu'on le remarque dans la plûpart des bâtimens que nous avons cités. L'abus des glaces n'est jamais une beauté dans les appartemens; la prodigalité de ces corps transparens annoncent plûtôt la stérilité que le génie de l'architecte. Les beaux appartemens du château de Richelieu, de celui de Maisons, de celui de Versailles, la gallerie de Meudon, celle de Clagny, tous ces chefs-d'oeuvre n'en ont point; ils auroient occupé moins utilement la place des trésors qu'ils contiennent, & part conséquent auroient privé l'homme de goût des productions des grands maîtres qui s'y remarquent. Il est vrai qu'il n'en est pas de même d'un appartement d'habitation, principalement de celui destiné à une princesse. Aussi M. Contant en a-t-il usé, mais avec cette discrétion qui décele l'homme de génie & l'homme instruit de la convenance de son art & des grands principes de sa profession.

PLANCHE XXXIII
Elévation du côté de la cheminée de la chambre de parade.

Cette décoration est du meilleur genre. De belles parties, des détails heureux, des matieres précieuses, des étoffes de prix, tout concourt à procurer à cette piece une très-grande magnificence; les ornemens d'ailleurs nous ont paru assez intéressans, pour que nous en donnaissions la plus grande partie dans les Planches XXXVI. & XXXVII. mais ce que nous n'avons pu rendre, sont les beautés de l'exécution considérées séparément dans chaque genre, & qui doivent exciter la curiosité des amateurs & des artistes éclairés.

PLANCHE XXXIV
Elévation du côté du lit de parade.

Cette Planche fera connoître une des meilleures décorations en ce genre, qui se soit vûe jusqu'à présent dans l'intérieur de nos appartemens. Les quatre colonnes qui se remarquent ici, dont deux placées sur un plan différent, donnent à cette ordonnance un caractere grave, qui n'ôte cependant rien à son élégance. La forme du plan (voyez ce plan, Pl. XXXV.) contribue même à ajouter de la beauté à cette décoration, & à contenir le lit avec la dignité qui lui convient; d'ailleurs la forme de ce lit, la richesse de ces étoffes, la balustrade qui le renferme, les glaces qui sont placées dans les pans coupés, la forme ingénieuse des chapiteaux & des cannelures de l'ordre, enfin l'exacte régularité de chaque partie, tout dans ce dessein fait le plus grand plaisir. Cette belle piece est terminée par une corniche composée d'ornemens d'un excellent genre, & dont on trouvera les desseins pour la plus grande partie, Planche XXXVII.

PLANCHE XXXV
Plans des trois pieces qui composent une partie de
l'appartement de parade dont nous venons de parler

La forme des plans contribuant essentiellement à la beauté de la décoration intérieure, nous avons rassemblé sur la même Planche les trois plans des décorations précédentes. Ces trois plans font connoître les difficultés que M. Contant a été obligé de vaincre, pour rendre ces décorations régulieres dans autant de cages irrégulieres; obstacle qui exige dans un architecte le génie de son art, pour procurer en particulier à chacune de ces pieces les commodités qui leur sont nécessaires; commodités qui font aujourd'hui une des parties essentielles de notre distribution.

PLANCHES XXXVI (*reproduced as Plates* 301–302) & XXXVII
Développemens des principaux ornemens répandus dans
la décoration des trois pieces précédentes.

Le genre mâle que la plûpart de nos architectes cherchent aujourd'hui à donner à nos ornemens, leur a semblé néanmoins ne pas devoir exiger ce caractere de pesanteur que nos anciens ont affecté dans les dedans des appartemens, ni cette prodigalité de petites parties que nous avons déjà reprochée à la plûpart de nos sculpteurs en bois, mais un juste milieu entre ces deux excès, parce qu'ils ont senti enfin que les décorations intérieures doivent être agréables; que rien n'y doit paroître lourd ni dans les masses ni dans les détails; que même il étoit nécessaire de reveiller leur ordonnance par un peu de contraste, pourvu qu'il ne fût point outré; le contraste dont plusieurs ont abusé quelquefois, n'ayant engendré que des chimeres, & qu'ils ont senti que trop de symétrie à son tour ne produisoit souvent que des compositions froides & monotones. Les ornemens de ces deux Planches sont également exempts de ces deux défauts, en fixant, pour ainsi dire, le véritable goût & le style propre à cette partie de l'art.

ENGLISH TRANSLATION

We have already treated (vol. IV, p. 702 &c) of decoration in general. Here our subject is the decoration of rooms in particular. We shall not recall the flights of fancy of most of our artists in this respect. The great number of engravings of them which have been circulated among the public reveal quite clearly how essential it was that these frivolous compositions should go out of fashion in order to make room for compositions without doubt less bizarre. We have now reached this epoch, to judge from some productions of the architects of our day. In order to convince of what we here advance we shall cite some examples of the one genre and the other and we shall close these observations by giving the decorations lately executed in the apartments of the Palais Royal for the late Duchesse d'Orléans after the designs of Monsieur Contant, architect to the King, from whose hand we have a quantity of works of the first merit, and who has given proofs of his taste in architecture and of his genius in the charms of ornament on more than one occasion.

The decorated interiors which hold the first rank, excluding here those of an admirable kind dating from the last century (like that of the Louvre, of the Tuileries, of Versailles, of the Palais Royal, of Vincennes, &c.) which can only be criticised for a little heaviness and perhaps for a little confusion, the interior decorations, I say, which hold the first rank are those just mentioned of the Palais Royal and those of the Hôtel de Toulouse, of the Hôtel de Biron, of M. Bourette's house, of M. d'Argenson's country house at Neuilly, of the gallery of the Hôtel de Choiseul, &c, which when compared with those of the Palais Bourbon, those of the Hôtel de Soubise, of the Hôtel de Rohan-Chabot, of the house of M. Dionis, of M. de la Vallière's country house at Montrouge, of the gallery of the Hôtel de Villars, &c, sufficiently demonstrate the preference that the first ought to be accorded over the second, and how dangerous it would have been if the most famous artists of our time had not created a new style of decoration which has so to speak annihilated that frivolity which was the sole merit of the apartments of the Palais Bourbon, &c., and also that character of heaviness we have criticised in the older decorations of most of our royal palaces. Let us enter into some detail on this subject in connexion with the designs we are about to exhibit, and which, as we have just remarked have been executed under the guidance of M. Contant, by the most skilful artists, who have seconded that learned architect in the embellishment of the Palais Royal.

PLATE XXIX (*reproduced here as Plate* 22)
Front elevation of the windows of the Saloon, on the first floor of
the new apartments of the Palais Royal.

This decoration, entirely of woodwork painted white, with all its ornaments gilded with matt gold and burnished gold, is of the greatest splendour. The panelled door is set with mirrors and has a sofa on either side (see the large-scale drawing of one of these sofas on Plate XXXVI). Above these, mirrors are again placed, set on the axis of the windows facing them and repeating the spectacle of the gardens of the Palais Royal. These sofas are covered by *campanilles* of gold and silver stuff, which are adjusted with taste and furnish this room with the greatest magnificence. The ceiling of this saloon is painted by M. Pierre whose name speaks its own praise. The two columns seen here are engaged in order to match the isolated columns which are opposed to them and which have been introduced in this manner in order to remedy the want of symmetry of this room which was built in former times with considerable irregularity (see the plan of this room, Plate XXXV).

PLATE XXX
Elevation of the chimney-piece wall of the same room.

The doors of this decoration are set with mirrors like those of the preceding and differ only in their upper part. The design of the chimney-piece is in good taste. It is easy to see how superior is its real beauty to the palm branches, garlands, rocaille ornaments, palmettes, &c. which have for so long constituted the sole resource of our woodcarvers in this kind of decoration. The casing of this chimney-piece is also of a fine form, and is faced with ormolu treated in the grandest manner. Girandoles with geniuses enrich its corners and correspond to similar girandoles set on a marble table placed opposite the chimney-piece; the design of this table can be seen in Plate XXXVI. The Corinthian pilasters decorating this wall and that opposite have authorized the use here of architectural members which have prevented it from becoming frivolous, as in the former manner, with the result that the good style of this entire disposition appears suitable to the dignity of the Prince who inhabits this palace, a consideration of greater interest than is apt to be imagined, and which ought to be the first rule in all the works of artists.

PLATE XXXI
Elevation of the Card Room: the wall with the door that gives entrance into the Saloon.

This decoration, in the Ionic order, is composed of large members and ornamented with excellent details. To convince oneself of this fact one has only to compare this production with most of those of the Palais Bourbon as engraved in the *Architecture française* or with those of the Hôtel de Soubise, inserted among the works of M. Boiffrand, and it will be seen how preferable are the intervals of repose observed here to all that multitude of ornaments which for thirty years has been lavished with such excess in all our buildings and from which even the interior decoration of our temples is not always free. This order is Ionic, both in the pilasters and columns; the latter are engaged so as to take up less space in the interior of the room and to correct the irregularity of the construction, our old architects having almost always sacrificed appearances in interiors of rooms (see the plan of this room, Plate XXXV).

PLATE XXXII (*reproduced here as Plate* 23)
Elevation of the chimney-piece wall of the same room.

This façade, in the same style as the preceding shows the wall with the chimney-piece which is placed between two pilasters. Handsome tapestries occupy the two spaces which terminate the full-length of this room. These two spaces are of unequal size on account of the original design of the plan, which not being regular has occasioned this want of symmetry in the disposition. Two recesses cut into one of the deep sides of this card room give it a pleasantly agreeable form and have produced space for placing mirrors, an ingenious device which an artist of merit knows he can sometimes allow himself, but which the lesser man almost always abuses, as may be noticed in the majority of the buildings we have cited. An excess of mirrors is never a beauty in rooms; a prodigality of these transparent members advertises the sterility rather than the genius of the architect. The fine rooms of the Château de Richelieu, of the Château de Maisons, of the Château de Versailles, the gallery of Meudon, that of Clagny, all masterpieces, have none; they would have taken up much less usefully the space occupied by the treasures contained in them and as a result would have deprived the man of taste of the productions of the great masters which are admired there. It is true that things are not the same in a suite of living-rooms, especially in one intended for a princess. Hence M. Contant has made use of them, but with a discretion that reveals the man of genius and the man instructed in the proprieties of his art and the great principles of his profession.

PLATE XXXIII

Elevation of the chimney-piece wall of the State Bedchamber.

This decoration is in the best manner. Handsome members, happy details, precious materials, valuable stuffs all unite to confer on this room very great magnificence. The ornaments moreover seem to us sufficiently interesting for the greater part of them to be given in Plates XXXVI and XXXVII, but what we have not been able to render are the beauties of the execution in each genre separately considered. These must excite the curiosity of connoisseurs and of enlightened artists.

PLATE XXXIV

Elevation of the wall with the state bed.

This Plate will make known one of the best decorations of the kind which has been seen up till now in the interior of our suites of apartments. The four columns which are here seen—of which two are placed on a different level—give this disposition a grave character which yet in no way detracts from its elegance. The form of the plan (for this plan see Plate XXXV) in fact contributes additional beauty to this decoration and encloses the bed in a framework of suitable dignity. Moreover, the form of the bed itself, the richness of the stuff, the balustrade which encloses it, the mirrors which are placed in the recesses, the ingenious form of the capitals and of the fluting of the order, and finally the exact regularity of each member, everything in fact in this design gives the greatest pleasure. This handsome room terminates in a cornice composed of ornaments of an excellent style, designs for most of which will be found on Plate XXXVII.

PLATE XXXV

Plan of the three rooms which compose part of the state suite just discussed.

As the form of the plans contributes essentially to the beauty of interior decoration we have assembled on the same Plate the three plans of the preceding decorations. These three plans exhibit the difficulties that M. Contant has been obliged to overcome in order to produce regular decorations in as many irregular settings. This is an obstacle demanding from an architect the genius of his art so as to provide each of these rooms with the particular conveniences necessary for them, conveniences which today form one of the essential parts of our art of distribution.

PLATES XXXVI (*reproduced here as Plates* 301 *and* 302) *and* XXXVII

Details of the principal ornaments employed in the decoration of the three preceding rooms.

The masculine style which the majority of our architects strive nowadays to give to our ornaments has yet in their view not necessitated that character of heaviness which our ancestors affected in their interiors, nor that prodigality of small members for which we have already criticised the majority of our woodcarvers, but rather a just medium between these two excesses; they came at last to feel that interior decorations ought to be pleasing, that nothing in them ought to appear heavy either in the masses or in the detail, and even that it was necessary to enliven their disposition by a little contrast, always provided it was not exaggerated, that sort of contrast which has been used too freely by several persons having only engendered idle fancies. They also realised that too much symmetry in its turn often produced compositions which were merely cold and monotonous. The ornaments on these two Plates are equally free from both these faults and fix so to speak the true taste and the proper style for this branch of art.

APPENDIX V

T.-N. Loyer: Continuation of First Dissertation on the Manner of Decorating Apartments, 1762

T.-N. Loyer, 'Suite de ma première dissertation Sur la manière de décorer les apartements', 1762 (MS in Académie des Beaux-Arts, Lyons).

FRENCH TEXT

Messieurs,

Dans le discours que J'eus l'honneur de vous presenter lors que vous me fites la grace de m'admettre au nombre des membres de votre illustre compagnie, J'eus celuy de vous Entretenir Sur les decorations intérieures Et Exterieures des maisons particulières; Je fis connoitre la difference qu'il y avoit dans la maniere dont decoroient les anciens architectes, dans (?) celle dont les modernes avoient fait usage jusques à present. Vous mêmes reconnutes, Messieurs, les abus dans les quels on etoit tombé, Et jusques ou l'on avoit poussé l'Excès du mauvais goût En ce genre. Vous parûtes voir avec beaucoup de satisfaction que quelques artistes de cette ville, piqué d'Emulation faisoient tous leurs Efforts pour ramener le bon goût Et rétablir cette sage simplicité dans les formes Et dans la distribution de toutes les parties qui doivent Entrer dans une decoration.

Le goût du bon est toujours En acord avec la raison, Et c'est sur ce premier principe que toutes les bonnes regles ont Ete Etablies. Il faut un Ensemble dans tout ce qui doit se presenter agréablement a notre vüe, Et pour y parvenir, il faut en connoître les moyens. Il n'y avoit que ce qui sera porté à la bonne architecture qui pût nous faire arriver a ce but.

En Effet nous nous apercevons que toute les fois que l'on voudra decorer avec quelque goût un apartement pour tel usage qu'il puisse être on sera toujours obligé de se raprocher des principes que la seule architecture nous fournit. Elle nous donne pour tous les besoins les formes qui peuvent être nécessaires, Elle nous previent sur toutes les convenances, Elle a receuilli tout ce qui Est Suceptible de donner du gracieux a ce que l'on veut representer, En fin Elle s'est Enrichie pour notre propre avantage, Et nous ne manquerons d'aucunes resources quand nous serons fidels à la consulter.

C'est cette route prudente que les anciens architectes ont suivi avec le plus grand scrupule, Et sans rien ôter au génie dont ils Etoient partagés, ils marchoient toujours d'un pas assuré tendant au vray, se renfermant dans la regle adoptée par les hommes les plus Eclairés.

Nous jugerons tous de cette verité quand nous voudrons Examiner avec attention les ouvrages faits dans les beaux Siecles de la Grèce Et de Rome; nous En jugerons de même En voyant les ouvrages des deux derniers Siecles. Et maintenant nous voïons renaitre, Et nous le voïons avec joye ce même goût pour le vray beau, pour le male Et le simple, Et pour tout ce qui a un vray raport aux besoins, Et aux convenances.

Dans ce principe, Et après avoir Examiné Et reflechi sur plusieurs ouvrages de l'Espece dont je parle, j'ay crû qu'on ne pouvoit mieux faire, que de se raprocher de nos anciens modeles, Encouragé d'ailleurs par l'Exemple de ce que nous avons aujourdhuy de plus habile, j'ay cherché l'ancienne route, Et dans le cas ou je me suis trouvé d'avoir quelques maisons a decorer, J'ay puisé dans les principes de l'architecture même tout ce qui a pû Servir a mon Entreprise. J'ay fait des desseins rélativement à mes projets, je les ai Communiqués à differentes personnes de goût qui les ayant approuvés, m'ont Engagé par leurs Suffrages à les faire Exécuter; le dernier de ces desseins fut celuy d'un salon d'ordre dorique, dont je vay, Messieurs, avoir l'honneur de vous faire la description.

Ce Salon dont le plan Est de dixneuf pieds de largeur Sur vingt deux de profondeur Est percé sur deux faces par quatre croisées, Et de deux portes sur les deux autres faces, l'une des quelles forme l'Entrée principale, Et l'autre sert de communication a une partie de l'apartement, la cheminée Est placée au milieu d'une de ces faces du coté de la porte d'Entrée, Et vis avis un des trûmeaux qui se trouve entre les fenêtres, ce trûmeau ainsi que la cheminée sont garnis par des glaces qui En repetant les objets, procurent un air de richesse, Et l'illusion des deux percés très agréables à la vüe, ces glaces contribuent Encore à Etendre les plans, a repeter les Simmetries, Et a rendre plus nombreuses En aparence les Sociétés qui peuvent S'y rassembler. Les autres parties du Salon sont ornées de Seize pilastres d'ordre dorique dont il y En a deux accouplés dans chaque des quatre angles qui forment une tour creuse Et les huit autres servent a accompagner les chambranles des portes Et des croisées.

Avant d'Entrer plus avant dans cette description, l'on me permettra de faire une observation sur les angles rachettés En tours creuses.

Je suis du sentiment que les plans quarés sont toujours la meilleure forme que l'on puisse mettre en usage dans quelque decoration que ce soit, sur tout dans les pieces regulières destinées aux peristiles, aux vestibules, aux Salons d'assemblées &c. Je conviens qu'il seroit ridicule, Et que ce seroit pecher contre les bonnes regles, que determiner les angles de ces pieces par des plans circulaires ou par d'autres formes qui paroissent toujours postiches et deplacées; mais quoyque les plans terminés quârement soient les plus aprouvés, et qu'ils soient effectivement d'une decoration plus noble et plus conformes aux regles de l'art, je crois cependant que les tours creuses dans les angles doivent être tollerées, et qu'elles sont même necessaires pour coriger le mauvais effet que produiroit le biais d'une piece irreguliere ainsi qu'est celle dont il est question.

Je reviens à mon sujet. Les pilastres qui decorent ce Salon ont treize pouces & six lignes de largeur, un pouce trois quarts de saillie et dix pieds six pouces de hauteur compris la baze et le chapiteau, cette hauteur relativement à la largeur du pilastre fait un sixième de plus que les proportions determinées, mais cette disproportion bien loin de faire un mauvais effet, donne plus de legereté et plus d'elegance à cet ordre qui par luy même deviendroit un peu lourd, surtout dans une decoration interieure ou les planchers semblent absorber les objets.

Mais cette licence bonne dans de certains cas, peut aussi être très desavantageuse dans d'autres, c'est à quoy tout artiste jaloux des belles proportions doit prendre garde à bien connoitre les occasions ou il peut, et ou il doit en faire usage. Il faut avant l'execution de son projet qu'il en compare l'ensemble et qu'il se rende compte des raisons qui l'engagent à s'écarter des regles, sans quoy il s'exposeroit de tomber souvent dans le trop lourd, ou dans le trop maigre.

Chaque pilastre est cannelé de cinq cannelures rudentées avec des roseaux et un filet de retraitte à l'extremité de chaque cannelure, quoyque la regle soit que tous les pilastres doivent en avoir sept, j'ay crû devoir ne m'y pas assujettir dans la crainte qu'en me fixant aux nombres et aux proportions, elles ne fussent trop etroites, et alors ne pas être en raison avec les moulures des panneaux qui sont dans l'intervalle des pilastres.

La baze attique et le chapiteau de l'ordre dorique dont les pilastres sont ornés n'exigent pas que j'en fasse aucun detail, ils sont asses connus des artistes pour que je me borne seulement à dire qu'ils sont l'un et l'autre dans les proportions relatives au diametre du pilastre et que pour donner plus de richesse au chapiteau j'ay fait tailler des ornements a ses principales moulures.

Les alettes en arriere corps qui accompagnent les pilastres, ont un tiers de la largeur de ces derniers. Elles se traversent sous l'entablement, sur le socle et environ au premier tiers de leur hauteur. Sur cette derniere traverse, il y a une petite frize de six pouces de hauteur, qui se termine à l'extremité interieure des alettes, cette frize qui est ornée de guillochis à l'antique tient lieu de la cimaise, et sert à partager les panneaux superieurs de ceux du soubassement, qui sont aussi l'un et l'autre en arriere corps d'un pouce sur l'alignement des alettes; ces panneaux sont de forme rectangle ornés d'une moulure de trois pouces et six lignes de largeur, detaché des alettes par un champ de deux pouces et six lignes, cette moulure et ce champ, joint à un quart de rond entre deux filets qui reignent sur toute l'arête des alettes font paroitre une double moulure aux panneaux qui les rendent d'une decoration male et dans une bonne proportion.

Les Chambranles des portes et des croisées ont un septième de la largeur de leur baÿe, et sont saillants sur le nud du cinquième de leur largeur, les venteaux des portes ont chaqu'un deux panneaux dont un dans le soubassement est d'une forme oblongue terminé quarement. Le panneau superieur quoyqu'il conserve aussi le quarré, est orné par le haut d'un médaillon formé par le moulure interieure dans le quel est une rosette à l'antique, ces médaillons sont entourés exterieurement d'une guirlande de feuilles de chêne qui en se reünissant tombe en chutte dans le milieu du panneau. Les deux panneaux dont je viens de parler sont aussi separés par une frize ornée de guillochis semblable à celles des entrepilastres dont j'ay cydevant parlé.

Dans les attiques audessus des portes il y a une table saillante d'un pouce sur le fond qui porte sur le chambranle avec des goûtes en ornements, et qui se termine jusques au dessus de l'architrâve; mais comme cette table quoique decorée d'un panneau, auroit été trop simple, je me suis determiné à y placer deux guirlandes de feuilles de chêne qui en se reunissant avec un ruban forment une chutte dans le milieu du panneau, chaque guirlande en faisant une demy elipse se termine à l'extremité de la table ou elle passe à travers le champ pour retomber au long des montans jusques dessus le chambranle, et par ce moyen lier ces deux parties ensemble.

Le corps de la cheminée dont le plan est quarré est revettüe sur les cotés d'une table saillante de six lignes d'epaisseur detachée par un champ regnant de deux pouces de largeur. La face principale est decorée d'un pilastre de neuf pouces de largeur, ravale et formant un double cadre qui s'eleve depuis le socle de dessus la tablette, jusques au dessous de l'architrave de l'entablement, ou il se traverse, et se termine contre l'attique; la glace qui est en proportion au corps de cette cheminée est aussi d'une forme rectangle ayant en hauteur une fois et trois quarts de sa largeur; elle est encadrée avec une moulure de quatre pouces de largeur dont les principeaux membres sont taillés d'ornemens à l'antique. Cette glace est surmontée d'une table saillante servant à former l'attique qui porte avec des gouttes pendantes sur la traverse du pilastre, et qui s'eleve quarement par dessus l'architrave et la frize jusques au dessous de la corniche, dont les premières moulures luy servent de couronnement ainsi qu'a chaque triglyphe qui est à l'extremité et a plomb des pilastres. Dans le panneau de cette attique il y a une guirlande dans le même goût, et semblable a celles des dessus des portes dont j'ay parlé il y a un moment.

Lentablement qui passe lisse sur l'aplomb des pilastres, est composé de son architrave, de sa frize, et de sa corniche; il est dans les proportions relatives au diametre des pilastres, mais pour donner un peu plus de richesse à l'architrave, j'ay divisé la grande face en deux parties, dont une inferieure, et l'autre superieure, m'étant conformé d'ailleurs aux regles de cet ordre.

Les triglyphes qui decorent la frize y sont distribués dans une distance égale; et quoique j'aye forcé leur largeur de pres que un dixieme il m'est encore resté des metoppes plus larges d'un sixieme que les proportions ordinaires, mais une guirlande a festons attachée avec deux cloux dont chaque metope est orné, corrige cette disproportion et fait en même temps une décoration agréable, riche, et sans confusion.

La division des triglyphes a toujours été l'eceuil de ceux qui ont fait usage de l'ordre dorique surtout lorsque les colonnes, ou les pilastres ont été accouplés par la raison que tous les metopes qui sont dans les intervales doivent être selon la regle exactement quaré, et qu'il n'est pas possible que celuy qui se trouve entre les deux colonnes le soit; ce qui ordinairement fait un très mauvais effet. Quelques architectes pour obvier a ce deffaut ont donné plus d'élévation à leur frize, mais en voulant éviter un inconvenient, ils sont souvent tombés dans un plus insuportable, soit en rendant leur architrave et leur corniche trop maigre ou tout leur entablement trop lourd et en disproportion. Les grecs plus sages que nous sans doute ont bien prévû cette difficulté, car nous n'avons aucuns exemples qu'ils ayent employé les colonnes accouplées; mais puisque les romains, et nous, à leur exemple les avons admises, je crois que lorsqu'il n'y a point de mûtules à la corniche, il vaudroit beaucoup mieux que tous les metopes d'une ordonnance fussent égaux.

La corniche est composée de toutes ses moulures, et de ses denticules; mais j'ay retranché un sixième de la largeur du sophite, afin d'éviter la grande saillie que cette partie auroit eu en suivant à la rigeur les proportions de l'ordre; d'ailleurs les yeux étant accoutumés à ces decorations légeres, ou à peine l'on pouvait distinguer les moulures qui y étoient employées, leur manque de saillie, et leur peu de largeur avoient comme forcé les artistes d'avoir recours aux differentes nüances de couleurs pour les detacher des fonds. Il étoit donc apropos qu'en cherchant à me raprocher de la regle je pusse conserver ce goût mâle que nous donne la bonne architecture et cependant luy concilier cette legereté dont on a encore de la peine à se detacher mais que l'usage du bon bannira entierement.

Cette corniche qui se termine exactement sous le plafonds, fait un meilleur effet et convient mieux de cette maniere que les gorges ou voussures, car les gorges que l'on a introduites aux plafonds ne peuvent bien s'accorder selon moy que dans les apartements d'une grande elevation, ou dans ceux qui sont destinés à n'être revettus qu'avec des lambris a simples panneaux; il est un cas où elles deviennent indispensables, c'est dans les pieces qui sont voûtées avec les nouvelles voutes en briques si ingenieusement inventées par M. le Comte Despie qui a donné un traitté très bien detaillé sur la maniere de les construire.

Voila Messieurs ce que j'ay cru devoir introduire dans la decoration dont j'ay entrepris de vous entretenir. Je me suis enfermé à ne faire usage que des richesses de l'architecture; j'ay suivi la regle et les formes vraiment regulieres pour ne prendre de licences que dans ce qui est de necessité et dans ce cas, les licences, et la regle ne se detruisent point; j'ay banni toutes les formes arbitraires qui ne presentent souvent que des ecards de génie et peu de savoir. Enfin j'ay evité soigneusement les contours forcés qui ne sont propres qu'a fatiguer les yeux de l'homme de goût et du connoisseur delicat.

ENGLISH TRANSLATION

Gentlemen,

In the discourse which I had the honour of delivering to you when you did me the favour of admitting me to make one of the number of the members of your illustrious body, I had that of speaking to you on the interior and exterior decorations of private houses. I made known the differences between the manner of decoration practised by the ancient architects and that used up till now by the moderns. You yourselves recognised, gentlemen, the abuses into which we had fallen and the degree to which the excess of bad taste in this genre had been pushed. You appeared to see with much satisfaction that some artists of this city, stung by a noble emulation, were making every effort to bring back good taste and to restore that grave simplicity in the forms and in the distribution of all the parts which ought to enter into a scheme of decoration.

A taste for what is good is always in accord with reason and it is on this first principle that all correct rules have been founded. In all that is intended to present itself agreeably to our sight, unity of effect is required, and in order to attain to this it is essential to know the means of doing so. Only the course which leans to good architecture is capable of bringing us to this goal.

For we perceive in effect that on all occasions when a man wishes to decorate an apartment with some taste, whatever the use it serves, he is always obliged to turn to principles which architecture alone furnishes. She gives us the forms which may be required for all needs, she apprises us of all the proprieties, she has collected everything which is susceptible of imparting grace to whatever it is desired to represent, she has in fact enriched herself for our advantage and we shall lack no resources if we consult her faithfully.

This prudent road is the one that the ancient architects followed with the greatest scruple, and without in any way diminishing the genius which was their portion, they ever advanced on it with steady step towards the truth, confining themselves within the rules adopted by the most enlightened of mankind.

We shall all judge of this truth if we are willing to examine with attention the works executed during the great centuries of Greece and of Rome, and we shall make the same judgement of it when we see the works of the last two centuries. And now we see, and see with joy, the rebirth of that same taste for true beauty, for the masculine and the simple, for everything which bears a true relation to necessity and propriety.

Following this principle and having examined and reflected on several works of the kind of which I speak I have formed the opinion that it is impossible to do better than to draw closer to our ancient models. Encouraged too by the example of all the most skilful artists of the present day I have sought the ancient road and when I have found myself with some houses to decorate I have taken from the principles of architecture everything that could be of use to my enterprise. I have made designs for my projects, I have communicated them to different persons of taste whose approval and suffrage have engaged me to execute them. The latest of these designs is that for a saloon of the Doric order of which, gentlemen, I am about to have the honour of giving you a description.

This saloon whose ground-plan is nineteen feet wide by twenty two deep is pierced on two of its sides by four windows and on the other two sides by two doors one of which forms the principal entrance and the other serves as a communication to another room of the suite. The chimney-piece is set in the middle of one of these sides next to the entrance door and opposite one of the piers between the windows. This pier and also the chimney-piece are decorated with mirrors which by their repetition of objects produce an air of richness and an illusion of two vistas which are very pleasing to the sight. These mirrors also help to extend the dimensions, to repeat the symmetrical effects and to render apparently more numerous any social gatherings which may assemble in the room. The other parts of the saloon are ornamented with sixteen pilasters of the Doric order, of which two are coupled in each of the four corners, so giving them a smooth turn, while the eight others accompany the framework of the doors and of the windows.

Before continuing further with this description I may perhaps be allowed to make an observation concerning angles softened by smooth turns.

I am of the opinion that a right-angled design is always the best form which can be employed in every sort of decoration, above all in rooms of regular shape intended for peristyles, vestibules, assembly rooms etc. I agree that it would be ridiculous and an offence against the correct rules to terminate the angles of these rooms by a circular design or by other forms which always seem artificial and misplaced. But although plans with right-angled terminations are the most approved, and though in actual fact they are the nobler decoration and conform more to the rules of the art, yet I believe that smooth turns for angles ought to be tolerated, that they are necessary even to correct the ugly effect produced by the obliquity of an irregular room like that which is the subject of discussion.

I return to my subject. The pilasters which decorate this room are thirteen and a half inches wide, project an inch and three quarters, and are ten feet six inches high including the base and the capital. The height in relation to the width of the pilasters is a sixth more than the correct proportion, but this disproportion, far from creating an unpleasant effect gives more lightness and elegance to this order which by itself would be a little heavy especially in interior decorations, where the ceiling seems to absorb the features beneath.

But this licence, though laudable in certain cases can also be very disadvantageous in others. This is something of which every artist jealous for fine proportions must take note so as to mark well those occasions when he can and when he ought to make use of them. Before the execution of his project he must study it as a whole and be fully conscious of the reasons which urge him to depart from the rules, otherwise he would expose himself frequently either to making his work too heavy or too meagre.

Each pilaster is fluted with five cabled flutings with reeding and a recessed fillet at the bottom of each fluting. Although it is the rule that all pilasters ought to have seven flutings, it was my opinion that I ought not to subject myself to it for fear that if I remained too fixed to numbers and proportions the flutings would be too narrow and so not in keeping with the mouldings of the panels which fill the intervals between these pilasters.

The Attic base and the capitals of the Doric order with which the pilasters are ornamented require no details from me; they are well enough known to artists for me to confine myself simply to saying that both the one and the other are proportioned relative to the diameter of the pilaster and that in order to give more richness to the capitals I have had ornaments carved on their principal mouldings.

The recessed frames which accompany the pilasters are a third of the width of these last. They cross over under the entablature, above the socle and at about the first third of their height. Along this last crossing runs a small frieze six inches high which terminates at the inner extremity of the frames: this frieze which is decorated with guilloche ornament in the Antique manner takes the place of a dado and serves to divide the upper panels from those of the under part; both sets of panels are in addition recessed an inch from the line of the frames. These panels are of rectangular form and ornamented by a moulding three and a half inches wide which is separated from the frames by a band two and a half inches wide. Moulding and band together with a quarter-round moulding between two fillets which runs along the entire edge of the frames make it seem as if the panels had a double moulding, so rendering them a masculine decoration and of good proportion.

The casings of the doors and the windows are a seventh of the width of the bay and project a fifth of their width from the ground. The leaves of the door each have two panels of which the one in the base is of oblong form terminating in right-angles. Although the upper panel also retains the right-angled form it is decorated in the upper part with a medallion formed by the inner moulding and containing a rosette of Antique form. These medallions have outer frames composed of a garland of oak leaves which from its point of junction descends into the middle of the panel. The two panels of which I have just spoken are also separated by a frieze decorated with guilloche work like those in the intervals between the pilasters of which I have previously spoken.

In each of the attics above the doors is a rectangular member which projects an inch from the wall. It rests on the casing with drops as ornaments and terminates just above the architrave. As this member, though decorated with a panel, would have been too simple by itself I have decided to relieve it by two oak leaf garlands which are united by a ribbon and then descend into the middle of the panel. Each garland forms a half ellipse and terminates at the extremity of the member, whence it passes over the ground and falls along the uprights to a point just above the casing, and by this means links these two parts together.

The chimney-breast is of right-angled design relieved at the sides by a flat projecting member half an inch thick on a continuous ground two inches wide. The front face is decorated with a pilaster nine inches wide recessed in the wall and forming a double frame which rises from the socle above the mantelpiece to a point just below the architrave of the entablature where it crosses over and terminates along the attic. The mirror which is proportioned to the chimney-breast is also of rectangular form and in height is one and three-quarter times its width; it is framed by a moulding four inches wide whose principal members are carved with Antique ornaments. This mirror is surmounted by a projecting member which forms the attic. It rests with pendant drops on the crossing of the pilaster and rises in right-angled form above the architrave and frieze to a point below the cornice whose first mouldings serve to crown its upper edge. They perform the same service for each of the triglyphs placed at either end perpendicular to the pilasters. In the panel of this attic is a garland in the same taste and similar to those of the overdoors of which I spoke a moment ago.

The entablature which runs transverse on the perpendicular of the pilasters is composed of architrave, frieze and cornice. Its porportions are relative to the diameter of the pilasters, but in order to give greater richness to the architrave I have divided the large surface into two parts, one above and one below, in conformity however with the rules of this order.

The triglyphs which decorate the frieze are distributed at equal intervals and although I have compressed their width by almost a tenth I am still left with metopes a sixth wider than those of the ordinary proportion, but the garland with swags suspended from two nails with which each metope is ornamented corrects this disproportion and at the same time provides a decoration which is agreeable, rich and without confusion.

The division of the triglyphs has always been the stumbling block of those who have employed the Doric order, above all when the columns and pilasters are paired because according to the rule all the metopes placed in the intervals ought to be exactly square, and it is not possible for that between the two columns to be made so, which ordinarily produces a very bad effect. In order to counter this fault some architects have raised the height of their frieze, but in trying to avoid one impropriety they have often fallen into another which is even more insupportable, either by making their architrave and cornice too slender or else the entire entablature too heavy and disproportionate. The Greeks, without doubt wiser than we, foresaw this difficulty clearly for we have no instances of their employing paired columns, but since the Romans and, after their example, we too have allowed them, it is my belief that whenever there are no mutules on the cornice it is far better to make all the metopes in a composition the same size.

The cornice is composed of all its proper mouldings and denticules, but I have cut off a sixth of the width of the soffit in order to avoid the great projection which this member would have offered had I rigorously followed the correct proportions of the order. In any case our eyes have been accustomed to light decorations in which one could hardly see the mouldings employed. Their want of projection and their narrowness practically forced artists to have recourse to different shades of colours in order to detach them from their ground. It was therefore proper that in seeking to adhere more closely to the rules I should preserve that masculine taste which good architecture supplies, yet reconcile it with that lightness which men still find it difficult to give up, though the practice of correct style will banish it completely.

The cornice which terminates exactly under the ceiling produces a better effect and suits this manner better than concave mouldings or coving, for the concave mouldings which have been introduced into ceilings in my opinion only suit apartments of great height, or else those which it is intended should be covered only with a wainscotting of plain panels. There exists one case in which they become indispensable, that is in rooms which are vaulted with the new brick vaults so ingeniously invented by Monsieur le Comte Despie who has given us an admirably detailed treatise on the manner of their construction.

Here gentlemen you have what I have thought it proper to introduce into the scheme of decoration of which I have undertaken to speak. I have limited myself to employing only the riches of architecture. I have followed the rules and forms which are truly regular, only permitting myself licence in cases of necessity and in such cases license and the rules are not mutually destructive. I have banished all arbitrary forms which often display only the waywardness of genius and little knowledge. Finally, I have carefully avoided all affected contours, which are fit but to weary the eyes of the man of taste and of the refined connoisseur.

APPENDIX VI

Baron de Grimm: Extract from 'Correspondance Littéraire', 1763

Baron de Grimm, *Correspondance littéraire*, le 1 mai 1763

FRENCH TEXT

Il faut remarquer les révolutions favorables aux arts, comme celles qui contribuent à leur corruption et à leur perte. La bizarrerie dans les ornements, dans les décorations, dans les dessins et les formes de bijoux, était arrivée à son comble en France; il fallait en changer à chaque instant, parce que ce qui n'est point raisonné ne peut plaire que par sa nouveauté. Depuis quelques années on a recherché les ornements et les formes antiques; le goût y a gagné considérablement, et la mode est devenue si générale que tout se fait aujourd'hui à la grecque. La décoration extérieure et intérieure des bâtiments, les meubles, les étoffes, les bijoux de toute espèce, tout est à Paris à la grecque. Ce goût a passé de l'architecture dans les boutiques de nos marchandes de modes; nos dames sont coiffées à la grecque; nos petits-maîtres se croiraient déshonorés de porter une boîte qui ne fût pas à la greque. Cet excès est ridicule, sans doute; mais qu'importe? Si l'abus ne peut s'éviter, il vaut mieux qu'on abuse d'une bonne chose que d'une mauvaise. Quand le goût grec deviendrait la manie des nos perruquiers et de nos cuisiniers (car enfin il faudra bien que d'aussi grands Grecs que nous soient poudrés et nourris á la grecque), il n'en sera pas moins vrai que les bijoux qu'on fait aujourd'hui à Paris sont de très-bon goût, que les formes en sont belles, nobles et agréables, au lieu qu'elles étaient toutes arbitraires, bizarres et absurdes, il y a dix ou douze ans.

M. de Carmontelle, lecteur de M. le duc de Chartres, qui dessine avec beaucoup d'esprit et de goût, a voulu se moquer un peu de la fureur du goût grec en publiant un projet d'habillement d'homme et de femme, dont les pièces sont imitées d'après les ornements que l'architecture grecque emploie le plus communément dans la décoration des édifices. Ces deux petites estampes auraient pu fournir l'idée d'une Mascarade pour les bals du carnaval. C'est une très-bonne plaisanterie que a été copiée tout de suite par des singes qui ne savent que contrefaire; ils ont publié une suite d'habillement à la grecque, sans esprit et d'un goût détestable.

ENGLISH TRANSLATION

Those revolutions which are favourable to the arts ought to be noticed as well as those which contribute to their corruption and fall. Eccentricity in ornaments, in decorations, in the designs and forms of jewels had reached its height in France. It was necessary to change them every moment because anything that is not rational can only please by its novelty. For some years now the ornaments and forms of the Antique have been sought after, taste has gained considerably thereby and the fashion for them has become so general that today everything is made in the Greek manner. The exterior and interior decoration of buildings, furniture, stuffs, jewellery of all kinds, everything in Paris is in the Greek manner. The taste has passed from architecture into the shops of our vendors of fashions; our ladies all have hair styled in the Greek manner, our fops would think themselves disgraced if they carried a snuffbox not in the Greek manner. Such exaggeration is doubtless absurd, but what does that matter? If abuse cannot be avoided, it is better if a good thing is abused rather than a bad. Even if the Greek taste were to become a mania with our wig-makers and our cooks (for in the end it will be essential for such thorough Grecians as we are to be powdered and fed in the Greek manner) it would be not the less true that the jewels now made in Paris are in excellent taste and that their forms are handsome, noble and agreeable, whereas ten or twelve years ago they were all arbitrary, eccentric and absurd.

M. de Carmontelle, reader to the Duc de Chartres, who draws with great wit and taste, desiring to laugh a little at this rage for the Greek taste, has published designs for men and women's dresses whose parts are imitated from the ornaments most commonly employed by Greek architecture in the decoration of buildings. These two small prints could well have furnished an idea for a masquerade at the carnival balls. His is an excellent piece of pleasantry which has been immediately copied by apes who only know how to imitate. They have published a set of dresses in the Greek manner without wit and in a detestable taste.

APPENDIX VII

J.-F. Blondel: Extract from 'Cours d'Architecture', Vol. I, 1771

J.-F. Blondel, *Cours d'Architecture* . . . vol. I, Paris, 1771, pp. 136–7

FRENCH TEXT

. . . N'avons-nous pas vu les ornements frivoles des dedans passer dans les dehors? abus qui a subsisté long-temps. Aujourd'hui par une inconséquence tout aussi condamnable, on applique le style grave des dehors, dans l'intérieurs des appartements: on donne à nos meubles, ce que l'expérience nous avoit appris à éviter, je veux dire, les formes quarrées dont les angles blessent l'oeil, nuisent à la circulation des personnes assemblées dans nos demeures; & souvent on s'appuie du prétexte que ces formes sont imitées des Grecs, sans refléchir que ces peuples ne les employoient que dans leurs Temples ou dans la décoration extérieure de leurs édifices publics, & qu'elles ne conviennent jamais, ou que très rarement, dans les choses d'agrément ou d'un usage journalier. Quoi de plus absurde par exemple, que de charger les lambris d'un boudoir, des mêmes festons composés de feuilles de chêne & de laurier, dont on décoroit à Rome les Arcs de Triomphe destinés à faire passer à la postérité les victoires du Héros? inadvertance peut-être plus révoltante encore, que les rocailles & les ornements Chinois, qu'on a prodigués pendant vingt années dans tous nos bâtiments, & même jusques dans l'interiéur de nos Temples.

ENGLISH TRANSLATION

. . . Have we not seen the frivolous ornaments of interiors pass from thence to exteriors, an abuse which long subsisted? Today, with an illogicality equally to be condemned, the grave style of exteriors is applied to interiors. Our furniture is given what experience has taught us to avoid, I mean those right-angled forms whose corners hurt the eye and impede the movement of persons who are assembled in our dwellings. Often men adduce the pretext that these forms are imitated from the Greeks, without considering that those peoples only employed them in their temples or in the exterior decoration of their public buildings and that they are never, or only very rarely suitable for works of decorative art or objects of daily use. What can be more absurd for instance than to load the panelling of a boudoir with the same festoons of oak and laurel leaves with which triumphal arches, intended to transmit to posterity the victories of a hero, were adorned in Rome. This is an inattention which is perhaps even more disgusting than the rocailles and Chinese ornaments which for twenty years have been lavishly employed in all our buildings and even within the interiors of our temples.

APPENDIX VIII

P. Patte: Extract from 'Cours d'Architecture', Vol. V, 1777

J.-F. Blondel, *Cours d'Architecture . . . continué par* P. Patte, vol. V, Paris, 1777, pp. 86 ff.

FRENCH TEXT

Le goût de la décoration intérieure des appartements a subi plusieures révolutions en France depuis un siécle. Sous Louis XIV, on la traitoit avec la même sévérité que la décoration extérieure des bâtiments. Les portes, les croisées, les cheminées, les corniches des appartements étoient toutes d'un style grave & sérieux: rarement se permettoit on de leur donner d'autres formes que réguliéres, rondes, ovales, quarrées ou paralellograme: les profils & les ornements étoient toujours du genre le plus mâle: entre les mains des Perrault, des Mansart, & de le Brun, ces sortes de décorations avoient sans doute de la grace, de la noblesse, de la dignité: elles donnoient l'air le plus important à l'intérieur des grands appartements, ainsi qu'on en peut juger par les modèles qui nous en restent dans les Châteaux des Tuileries, du Louvre, de Versailles & ailleurs. Mais sous leurs imitateurs, elles dégénérèrent bientôt; elles devinrent à la longue d'une monotonie & d'une pésanteur insupportables: on les accabla sous une multitude d'ornements placés sans ordre & avec confusion; ce qui fit qu'on s'en dégoûta insensiblement.

Il y a environ 50 ans que l'on donna dans un excès tout opposé; on abandonna les formes réguliéres; on s'appliqua à tourmenter les décorations intérieures de toutes les manières, sous prétexte de les varier, de les alléger & d'égayer les appartements. Les Lajoux, les Pinault, les Meissonier & leurs Copistes firent, si l'on peut s'exprimer ainsi, déraisonner en quelque sorte l'Architecture. On n'admit plus dans nos décorations que des contours extraordinaires, qu'un assemblage confus d'attributs placés sans choix, & alliés avec des ornements d'une imagination bisare, où l'on trouve un amas ridicule de cartouches de travers, de rocailles, de dragons, de roseaux, de palmiers, & de toutes sortes de plantes imaginaires qui ont fait pendant long temps les délices de nos décorations intérieures; tellement que la Sculpture s'étoit absolument rendue maitresse de l'Architecture. La quantité de gravures qui s'en sont répandues dans le public, indépendamment du grand nombre d'appartements qui subsistent encore avec ce mauvais goût de décoration, font assez connoître l'extravagance de ces compositions frivoles.

On doit à MM. Servandoni, Cartaud, Boffrand, & à quelques-uns de nos meilleurs Architectes qui ne s'étoient pas laissés entraîner par le torrent de la mode, le retour du bon goût, en faisant sentir par la comparaison de leurs ouvrages, l'absurdité de cet alliage monstrueux: peu-à-peu on revint donc à des formes plus sages, moins bisares; & enfin le retour du goût antique ayant répandu son influence sur nos arts d'agréments, sur-tout depuis environ 15 ans, on peut dire que la décoration intérieure des appartements, & le style de leurs ameublements sont devenus en quelque sorte un art nouveau. On a ajouté au bon genre des décorations du dernier siécle, moins de sévérité, plus de délicatesse, plus de variétés dans les formes: on a affecté de donner à leurs saillies & à leurs profils peu de relief pour en ôter la pesanteur. En adoptant des formes réguliéres, on s'est permis en même-temps, suivant les circonstances, de les assimiler à des contours moins sérieux, plus capables de produire à la fois, & un ensemble agréable, & moins d'uniformité dans l'ordonnance des appartements. Enfin l'on a appliqué aux décorations des dedans, les ornements que l'on admire le plus dans les meilleures ouvrages antiques, tels que les feuilles d'achante, de laurier, les festons, les oves, les rais-de-coeur, les grains d'orge, les canaux, les guillochis, les postes, les médaillons, &c. de sorte que l'Architecture a repris ses droits sur la Sculpture.

. . . . .

[For the English translation, see Introduction, page 21.]

APPENDIX IX

C.-N. Cochin: Extract from Memoirs, *c.* 1780-90

Charles-Nicolas Cochin, *Mémoires inédits* (written about 1780–90) . . . , ed. Charles Henry, Paris, 1880, pp. 142–3

FRENCH TEXT

. . . Depuis, la véritable époque décisive, ç'a été le retour de M. de Marigny d'Italie et de sa compagnie. Nous avions vu et vu avec réflexion. Le ridicule nous parut à tous bien sensible et nous ne tûmes point. Nos cris gagnèrent dans la suitte que Soufflot prêcha d'exemple. Il fut suivi de Potain et de plusieurs autres bons élèves architectes qui revinrent de Rome. J'y aiday aussi comme la mouche du coche. J'écrivis dans le Mercure contre les folies anciennes et les couvris d'une assés bonne dose de ridicule.

Enfin tout le monde se remit, ou tâcha de se remettre sur la voye du bon goust du siècle précédent. Et comme il faut que tout soit tourné en sobriquet à Paris, on appella cela de l'architecture à la grecque et bientôt on fit jusqu'à des galons et des rubans à la grecque; il ne resta bon goust qu'entre les mains d'un petit nombre de personnes et devint une folie entre les mains des autres.

Nos architectes anciens qui n'avoient pas sorti de Paris voulurent faire voir qu'ils feroient bien aussi dans ce goust grec; il en fut de même des commerçans et même des maîtres maçons. Tous ces honnêtes gens déplacèrent les ornemens antiques, les dénaturèrent, décorèrent de guillochis bien lourds les appuis des croisées et commirent mille autres bevües. Le Lorrain peintre, donna des desseins bien lourds pour tous les ornemens de l'appartement de *M. de la Live*, amateur riche et qui dessinailloit un peu. Ils firent d'autant plus de bruit que M. de Caylus les loua avec enthousiasme; de là nous vinrent les guirlandes en forme de corde à puits, les vases, dont l'usage ancien étoit de contenir des liquers, devenus pendules à heures tournantes, belles inventions qui furent imitées par tous les ignorans et qui inondèrent Paris de drogues à la grecque. Il s'en suivit ce qui sera toujours, c'est que le nombre de bonnes choses sera toujours très-petit dans quelque goust que ce soit et que l'ignorance trouvera toujours le moyen de dominer dans l'architecture; mais quoiqu'il se fasse toujours de bien mauvaises choses, elles sont du moins plus approchantes du bon que le mauvais goust qui les a précédées et que quiconque aura du goust naturel, sera moins éloigné de la voye qui conduit au bon qu'on ne l'étoit cy-devant, si touttefois ce goust ne devient (par la faute de ceux qui en font la parodie), si décrié qu'on ne puisse plus le souffrir.

ENGLISH TRANSLATION

. . . Later the truly decisive epoch was the return of M. de Marigny and his company from Italy. We had seen and reflected on what we had seen. The absurdity appeared perfectly evident to us all and we were not silent. Our protests won so far in the sequel that Soufflot preached by his example. He was followed by Potain and several other good architects who returned from being pupils in Rome. I helped too—like the fly that stung the coach horse. I wrote in the *Mercure* against the late extravagances and covered them with a quite sufficient share of ridicule.

At last everybody turned or attempted to turn back to the path of the good taste of the previous century, and since everything has to be twisted into a nickname in Paris it was called architecture in the Greek manner. Soon even braids and ribbons were made in the Greek manner: it remained as good taste only in the hands of a small number of people and became extravagance in the hands of all the rest.

Our old architects who had never been out of Paris also wanted to show that they could work well in the Greek taste, and it was the same with beginners and even with master-masons. All these worthy people misplaced the ornaments of antiquity, distorted them, decorated window-sills with extremely heavy guilloche work and committed a thousand other blunders. The painter Le Lorrain made extremely heavy designs for all the ornaments in the suite of M. de la Live, a rich amateur who dabbled in drawing. They caused an even greater stir because M. de Caylus praised them so enthusiastically: it was from this source that there came to us garlands like well-ropes, and clocks with rotating bands instead of dials and shaped like vessels that the Ancients had made to hold cordials; all very pleasing inventions in themselves but, now that they are imitated by all kinds of ignorant persons, we find Paris flooded with all sorts of stuff in the Greek manner. There ensued what will always happen, which is that the number of good things in whatever taste may prevail will always be very small and that ignorance will always find means to lord it in architecture. Yet although very bad things are still executed at least they are closer to what is good than the bad taste which preceded them, and whoever has some natural taste will be less far from the path which leads to what is good than men were before, always provided that this taste does not become (by the fault of those who travesty it) so cried down that it can no longer be tolerated.

APPENDIX X

Decree of the Cours de Parlement about the Safeguarding of Bronze Models, 1766

FRENCH TEXT

Arrêt de la Cour de Parlement, portant homologation d'une Délibération de la Communauté des Maîtres Fondeurs, pour la sûreté des Modèles. Du 30 Juillet 1766.

Louis, par la grace de Dieu, Roi de France et de Navarre: Au premier Huissier de Notre Cour de Parlement, ou autre Huissier ou Sergent sur ce requis, sçavoir faisons; que vû par Notredite Cour la Requête présentée par les Jurés en Charge de la Communauté des Maîtres Fondeurs en terre & sable, Sonnetiers, Bossetiers, Racheveurs, Ingénieurs & Fabricateurs d'Instrumens de Mathématique de la Ville & Fauxbourgs de Paris, à ce qu'il plût à Notredite Cour homologuer la délibération faite en l'assemblée de la Communauté des Suppliants le 21 Avril 1766, contenant sept articles de Réglement pour les Modèles, laquelle a été homologuée par Sentence de la Police du Châtelet de Paris du 16 Juillet 1766, pour être ladite Délibération, contenant Réglement pour les Modèles, exécutée selon sa forme & teneur; en conséquence ordonner que l'Arrêt qui interviendra, dans lequel sera transcrite ladite délibération, sera imprimé, lu, publié & affiché par tout où besoin sera; & copie imprimée d'icelui distribuée & envoyée à tous les Maîtres . . .

Reglement pour les Modèles

Aujourd'hui ce 21 Avril 1766, en l'Assemblée de la Communauté des Maîtres Fondeurs, tenue en leur Bureau, sis rue de la Vannerie à Paris, & convoquée par Billets en la manière accoutumée.

Messieurs les Jurés en Charge de ladite Communauté ont représenté à la Compagnie que depuis nombre d'années il a été porté des plaintes à la Communauté de la part de plusieurs Maîtres d'icelle, au sujet des vols & pillages qui se font journellement des Modèles, non-seulement par les Marchands Merciers, Bijoutiers, Miroitiers & autres qui ont droit de vendre des Bronzes; mais comme il est à craindre, & même il ne faut point dissimuler qu'il arrive & est arrivé à quelques-uns de nos Maîtres de profiter de ces sortes de vols & pillages de Modèles, tel qu'il en est arrivé depuis peu à deux de nos Maîtres, qui ont été condamnés par deux Sentences de Police du 13 Décembre 1765, pour pillage de Modèles, cependant aucun des Maîtres de la Communauté n'ignore les peines & les dépenses qu'un Modèle coute à l'Artiste qui se propose d'en faire un; ils doivent sçavoir qu'il faut commencer par faire un dessein, le dessein fait, il faut qu'il fasse le Modèle en terre, en cire ou en bois; cette opération faite, il faut le mouler en plâtre, en jetter une cire pour le tirer d'épaisseur, ensuite le mouler en sable pour le jetter en fonte, qu'il faut ensuite réparer. Le Modèle fait & parfait est un fond qui reste à l'Artiste pour en faire dessus autant qu'on lui en commande, & par-là il trouve dans le bénéfice de la vente, de quoi se dédommager du tems qu'il a employé à la construction de son modèle, & des dépenses qu'il a faites pour y parvenir. Mais si l'on continue de souffrir qu'on lui pille & vole les Modèles, il s'ensuivra que l'Artiste perdra tout le fruit de son travail, se dégoutera, que son imagination ne travaillera plus, & que le Public se trouvera privé des nouvelles choses, & trompé n'ayant que de mauvais surmoulés: cependant c'est ce qui arrive journellement; & voici comme s'y prennent tous ceux qui ont droit de vendre ou d'employer des Bronzes: Connoissant un beau Modèle, ils achetent ou font acheter la premiere piéce d'après le Modèle, ensuite ils la donnent à un Fondeur, ou autre Ouvrier sans qualité, pour lui en faire faire des surmoulés qu'ils font ciseler, soit par un Maître Fondeur, soit par un Ouvrier sans qualité; & le Maître ou Ouvrier sans qualité à qui le Marchand donne la Piéce pour la copier & fondre dessus, qui n'ignore point que c'est une Piéce pillée, en tire aussi des Copies pour lui en faire mouler dessus, & par ce moyen la Piéce dont l'Inventeur n'a encore vendu qu'une Copie, ou très-peu, devient si commune qu'il n'en vend plus, & que tout le fruit de son travail & de son imagination est perdu, ce qui le dégoute & l'empêche d'inventer de nouvelles choses, ce qui fait tort à l'Artiste, & est préjudiciable à l'Etat & au bien Public, qui n'ayant souvent point assez de connoissance pour sçavoir si la Piéce qu'on lui vend est faite d'après le premier Modèle, n'achete que des surmoulés, qui ont dégénéré beaucoup de leur valeur, beauté & solidité. Ce ne sont pas seulement les Marchands qui volent & pillent les Modèles, les Doreurs entre les mains de qui presque tous les Ouvrages des Maîtres de la Communauté passent, en font un usage assez commun, ainsi que les Ebénistes & autres. Non-seulement les différentes Communautés volent & pillent les Modèles des Maîtres de la Communauté des Fondeurs, mais ils font encore notre Etat, ayant chez eux & dans leurs Chambres des Compagnons Ciseleurs, quoique cela leur soit expressément défendu par tous les Arrêts & Réglemens de la Communauté.

De tels abus méritent toute l'attention de la Compagnie, & Messieurs les Jurés ont représenté qu'il étoit de leur devoir de proposer des moyens de les réprimer; qu'ils croyent que les plus efficaces étoient de faire un Reglement à ce sujet, & de proposer à la Compagnie les articles qui suivent.

Article premier

Défenses seront faites à tous Marchands Merciers, Bijoutiers, Miroitiers, Doreurs, Ebénistes, & à tous autres de quelque qualité qu'ils soient, de piller ou faire piller les Modèles des Maîtres Fondeurs, ni faire mouler sur les Modèles desdits Maîtres; & à tous Maîtres Fondeurs & autres Ouvriers de les mouler & finir, qu'ils ne soient sûrs que ce n'est point une Piéce pillée, à peine par les uns & par les autres solidairement, de payer le prix du Modèle, & de mille livres d'amende, applicable moitié au profit du Roi, & l'autre moitié au profit de la Communauté des Maîtres Fondeurs, qui donneront cent livres à celui qui avertira de la fraude & de la Contravention au présent article.

Article II

Pour découvrir & empêcher dorénavant le vol & pillage des Modèles, les Maîtres Fondeurs qui en font ou feront faire de nouveaux tels qu'ils soient, seront tenus de faire ou faire faire un dessein de la Piéce très juste & très-conforme au Modèle & de même grandeur.

Article III

Les Desseins & Modèles seront apportés au Bureau de la Communauté des Maîtres Fondeurs, & présentés aux quatre Jurés en charge les jours de Bureau . . .

Article IV

Qu'il y aura au Bureau un Registre pour enregistrer les Modèles & les Desseins. Le Dessein sera numéroté & restera au Bureau pour servir de témoin en cas de difficulté . . .

Article V

Sera libre aux Orfèvres & Sculpteurs qui ont droit de faire des Modèles, & qui ont intérêt d'en empêcher le pillage, & même à tous Particuliers qui voudront avoir une Piéce unique, d'en déposer le Dessein au Bureau de la Communauté, en payant les droits ci-après.

Article VI

Chaque Dessein qui sera apporté & déposé au Bureau coutera trente sols pour la garde . . .

Article VII

Que si celui qui aura déposé le Dessein au Bureau vouloit faire quelque changement, soit qu'il le fît plus grand ou plus petit, il sera obligé de faire faire un autre Dessein de la même grandeur & forme dudit modéle, & de le déposer au Bureau & de payer trente sols comme dessus pour l'enregistrement.

. . . . .

Fait & arrêté en ladite Assemblée les jours & an que dessus & ont signé; ainsi signés

J. F. Aubry
Medard Aubry
Aze
Baillot
Barrois
Bernier
Berrurier
Bertrand
Bion
Biston
Blondel
Bouquet
Bouquet l'aîné
Brosse
Caussin
Charbonnier
Charmoulue
Cheron
Chevalier
Chibout
Coissé l'aîné
Couturié
Crevier
Dangeville
Daniel
Degruchet
Delacroix
Denoireterre
Deschamps
Dubloc
Duplessis fils
Foncier
Foucaut
B. Fournier
Fournier
Gagniéson
Gaulier
Gendre
Gorlier
Gremaut
Guichon
Guinand
Guy
Harivel
Heban
F. Hébert
Hervieu
Lagrange
Laigné
Lallemand
Leclair cadet
Leclair père
Lefebvre
Leger
Legrix
Leguillier
Leriche
Maillard
Mallassy
Marie l'aîné
Mary
Maurisset
Michel
Mité
Monceaux
Mondon l'aîné
J. Mondon
Morel j.
Morlay
Oblet
R. Osmond
Paffe
Pecour
Raveché
Regnault
Roy
de Saint-Germain
Saublin
Sauveur
F. Sellier
Thury
Vassoult
C. N. Vatinelle
J. B. Vatinelle
Vauchery
Woillet

ENGLISH TRANSLATION

Decree of the Cour de Parlement (Court of Parliament) granting confirmation of a Resolution of the Communauté des Maîtres-Fondeurs (Corporation of Master Founders) for the safeguard of models, dated 30th July 1766.

Louis, by the grace of God, King of France and Navarre, to the First Usher of Our Court of Parliament or to any other Usher or Serjeant summoned for this cause, we make known that whereas Our said Court has seen the Petition presented by the Wardens in Charge of the Corporation of Master Founders in clay and sand, Small Bell-Makers,[1] Boss-makers,[2] Finishers, Mechanicians and Makers of Mathematical Instruments of the Town and Suburbs of Paris, and whereas it has pleased Our said Court to confirm the Resolution made at the meeting of the Corporation of the Petitioners on 21st April 1766, containing seven articles of Regulations concerning models, which resolution was confirmed by Decree of the Police du Chatelet of Paris on 16th July 1766, in order that the said Resolution, containing Regulations for models may be executed in due form and tenor, we hereby ordain that the decree which next follows, in which the said resolution shall be transcribed, is to be printed, read, published and posted up wheresoever need shall be, and that a printed copy thereof shall be distributed and sent to all Masters. . . .

Regulations for Models

This day 21st April 1766, at a meeting of the Corporation of Master Founders, held at their office seated in the Rue de la Vannerie in Paris, and called by circulars written in the customary manner.

Messrs. the Wardens in Charge of the said Corporation represented to the Company that for some years past complaints have been brought before the Corporation by several of the Masters thereto belonging concerning the thefts and plagiaries which are daily made of their models, not only by the Merchant Haberdashers, Jewellers, Looking Glass Makers and others who have the right to sell bronzes, but it is to be feared, and even must not be concealed, that it happens and has happened that several of our own masters profit by these sorts of theft and plagiary of models, as has happened only a short time since with two of our Masters who have been condemned in two sentences of the Magistrate of 13th December 1765 for plagiary of models. And yet none of the Masters of the Corporation is ignorant of the pains and expense which a model costs the artist who proposes to make one. They must know that it is necessary to begin by making a design and that when the design is made it is necessary for him to make the model in clay, in wax or in wood. When this operation has been completed he has to take a mould of it in plaster, then cast a wax from this to obtain its thickness, then take a mould of it in sand to cast it in metal, which then has to be mended. The model when finished and perfected remains the property of the artist as a basis on which he can make as many copies as are ordered from him and thereby find in the profits of his sales a means to recompense himself for the time he has spent in the making of his model and for the expenses he has incurred to succeed in it. But if we continue to suffer his models to be plagiarised and stolen without authorization it will ensue that the artist shall lose all the fruit of his labours, shall take a disgust, that his imagination shall labour no more, and that the public shall find itself deprived of new inventions and deceived in being supplied only with bad after-casts. Yet this is what happens daily. Here is the manner in which all those who have the right of vending or using bronzes go about it. Learning of a fine model they buy or get someone to buy for them the first cast taken from that model and give it to a founder or to an outside workman, and get him to make aftercasts which they then have chased either by a master founder or by an outside workman. The master or outside workman to whom the merchant gives the piece to be copied and to have a cast taken therefrom is well aware that it is a stolen piece and also takes copies for himself to take casts therefrom, and by this means a piece whose inventor has as yet sold only one or very few copies becomes so common that he has no more sale for it and all the fruits of his labour and imagination are lost to him, which gives him a disgust and prevents him from inventing new

[1] In the original, *Sonnetiers*. The *Encyclopédie* explains that a *sonnetier* is 'a workman who belongs to the Corporation of Founders and who makes toy bells and little bells for mules'. R.W.L.

[2] In the original, *Bossetiers*. J. Savary de Bruslons, *Dictionnaire universel de commerce*, i, Paris, 1723, s.v. explains 'This is a title which the Founders of Paris give themselves in their Statutes, in which they are called Master Founders, Mould-Makers in clay and sand, Boss-Makers, Small Bell-makers, etc. This name is theirs because they make works in the round (i.e. *ronde bosse*) and because they are allowed to make copper bosses to put on horse-bits.' R.W.L.

things. This injures the artist and is prejudicial to the State and to the public good, since the public often has insufficient knowledge to recognise if a piece sold to it is made after the first model, and so only buys aftercasts which have greatly degenerated in value, beauty and solidity. It is not only the merchants who steal and plagiarise models without authorization, the gilders through whose hands pass almost all the works of the Masters of the Corporation also make pretty common use of them, as do the cabinet-makers and others. Not only do the different Corporations steal and plagiarise the models made by the Masters of the Corporation of Founders, but they also practise our trade having journeymen chasers in their employ and in their workrooms even though this is expressly forbidden them by all the Decrees and by the Regulations of the Corporation.

Abuses of this sort deserve the entire attention of the Company and Messrs. the Wardens represented that it was their duty to propose means of suppressing them. That they believed the most efficacious were to make regulations on this subject and to propose the following articles to the Company.

Article I

It shall be forbidden to all Merchant Haberdashers, Jewellers, Looking-Glass Makers, Gilders, Cabinet Makers and all others of whatsoever quality to plagiarise or to cause to be plagiarised the models of the Master Founders, or to take moulds from the models of the said Masters. And all Master Founders and other workmen shall be forbidden to take moulds from or to finish them unless they are sure that the piece has not been plagiarised, under penalty laid on the ones and the others jointly and severally of paying the value of the model and a fine of a thousand livres, one half of which shall be applied to the benefit of the King and the other half to that of the Corporation of Master Founders who shall give a reward of a hundred livres to any man advising them of any fraud and contravention of the present article.

Article II

In order to discover and prevent from henceforth the theft and plagiarisation of models all Master Founders who make or shall make new ones of whatever sort shall be bound to make or to cause to be made a drawing of the piece which is very exact and in close conformity with the model and of the same size.

Article III

The designs and models shall be brought to the Office of the Corporation of Master Founders and presented to the four Wardens in charge on office days. . . .

Article IV

That a register shall be kept in the Office in which the models and drawings shall be registered. The drawings shall be numbered and shall remain in the Office to be produced in evidence in case of difficulty . . .

Article V

It shall be open to the goldsmiths and sculptors who have the right of making models and whose interest it is to prevent their unauthorized borrowing and even for all private persons who shall desire to have a unique piece to deposit a drawing of it in the office of the Corporation on payment of the dues hereinafter laid down.

Article VI

On every drawing which shall be brought to the Office and there deposited shall be paid thirty sols for its safe keeping.

Article VII

That if anyone who has deposited a drawing at the Office desire to make some change in it, making it either larger or smaller, he shall be obliged to have another drawing made of the same size and form as the said model and to deposit it in the Office and to pay thirty sols as above for its registration.

. . . . .

Enacted and decreed in the said Meeting on the days and year above recited and duly signed; the signatures as follows.

J. F. Aubry
Medard Aubry
Aze
Baillot
Barrois
Bernier
Berrurier
Bertrand
Bion
Biston
Blondel
Bouquet
Bouquet l'aîné
Brosse
Caussin
Charbonnier
Charmoulue
Cheron
Chevalier
Chibout
Coissé l'aîné
Couturié
Crevier
Dangeville
Daniel
Degruchet
Delacroix
Denoireterre
Deschamps
Dubloc
Duplessis fils
Foncier
Foucaut
B. Fournier
Fournier
Gagniéson
Gaulier
Gendre
Gorlier
Gremaut
Guichon
Guinand
Guy
Harivel
Heban
F. Hébert
Hervieu
Lagrange
Laigné
Lallemand
Leclair cadet
Leclair père
Lefebvre
Leger
Legrix
Leguillier
Leriche
Maillard
Mallassy
Marie l'ainé
Mary
Maurisset
Michel
Mité
Monceaux
Mondon l'aîné
J. Mondon
Morel j.
Morlay
Oblet
R. Osmond
Paffe
Pecour
Raveché
Regnault
Roy
de Saint-Germain
Saublin
Sauveur
F. Sellier
Thury
Vassoult
C. N. Vatinelle
J. B. Vatinelle
Vauchery
Woillet

APPENDIX XI

List made in 1770 of the Stock of Bronzes and Models belonging to the Bronze-founder, Philippe Caffieri

The list is taken from the inventory of goods and chattels belonging to Madame Rose Caffieri, dated 3rd December, 1770. (Original MS in the Archives Nationales, Minutier Central des Notaires, étude XCVIII, liasse 589).

The numbering of the inventory has here been altered so that it begins at '1.' instead of '125.' as in the original. After the first item, the words 'prisé la somme de' have been omitted. The sums are here given in figures instead of in the original words.

FRENCH TEXT

		livres
1.	It. Vn grand bras moderne à quatre branches prisé la so(mme) de quatre vingt Livres cy	80
2.	It. Vn bras a cor de chasse formant trois branches avec une tête de loup	200
3.	Vne paire de bras à trois branches dans le gout moderne	78
4.	It. Vn bras dans le gout à la moderne à quatre branches	55
5.	It. Vn petit modele de bras a deux branches formant des Rouleaux, dans lequel est agraphée une guirlande de laurier attachée d'un clou sur la plaque, fini en partie	30
6.	It. Vne paire de bras a trois branches finie en partie, dans le gout moderne	52
7.	It. Vne paire de bras a trois branches dans le gout antique avec une noble guirlande de lauriers noues d'un noeud De rubands attaché d'un cloud sur la plaque, entierement finit prêt a dorer	250
8.	It. Vne paire de bras à deux branches avec deux consoles formant chacune un rouleau portant un Vase à guirlandes de fruits entierement fini prête a dorer	200
9.	It. Vn modele de bras a trois branches avec une grosse tête de Belier formant la plaque, à la quelle est attachée une guirlande de vignes, propre a mettre dans un paneau de boiserie dans un sallon	160
10.	It. Vn modele de bras a trois branches a branches à rouleaux, avec des doubles Guirlandes de lauriers agraphées dans les trois branches, et nouées d'une draperie qui attache les trois branches à la plaque	175
11.	It. Vne paire de bras à deux branches attachées par un ruban formant le neud au haut de la plaque avec un vase, et une guirlande de lauriers, dans le gout antique	144
12.	It. Vn modele de bras à trois branches dans le gout antique avec une double guirlande de lauriers noues d'une neud de ruban attaché d'un cloud sur la plaque	150

13. It. Vn modele de bras à deux branches, avec des Narselles à la plaque, avec des grandes guirlandes de lauriers agraphées dans les rouleaux des branches et attachées d'un cloud sur la plaque avec un ruban formant le neud dans le haut de la plaque, fini en partie 150
14. It. Vn modele de bras à deux branches dans le gout antique, avec une tête et une peau de Lion agraphée dans lesd. branches 160
15. It. Vn modele de bras à trois branches dans le gout antique avec deux trophées en contrepartie composées de differents attributs 100
16. It. Vne plaque avec des gaudrons dans le haut, avec un Vase dont il sort un bouquet de fleurs et une branche ronde avec une feuille d'eau et des paquets de lauriers 75
17. It. Vn petit modele de bras a deux branches dans le gout antique avec un ruban formant un noeud dans le haut de la plaque, avec une plaque à jour, et des branches à doubles rouleaux 50
18. It. Vne paire de bras antique à deux branches, Modele de Paffe 90
19. It. Vne paire de bras a deux branches à Rouleaux, plaques à jour, à noeuds de ruban dans le haut de la plaque, avec un trophée sur chacune 110
20. It. Vne paire de bras à une branche antique pour un cabinet de toilette 30
21. It. Vne paire de bras modele à trois branches à lys, non finie 60
22. It. Vne paire de bras modele a deux branches à lys 60
23. It. Vne paire de bras modernes à deux branches croisées sortant du bas de la plaque avec des paquets de fleurs sur les branches 18
24. It. Vn modele de bras à palmes, à trois branches avec une palmette de feuille dans le bas formant la plaque 36
25. It. Vn modele de bras à deux branches ou il manque des assortiments, avec trois côtés de bras à une branche sans bassins, et un autre bras à trois branches, avec une chute de feuilles de chesne sur chaque branche et un noeud de ruban à la plaque, et trois autres bras à une branche avec des mascarons sur les plaques, dont deux sont en couleur, et de plus une plaque de bras à rubans, le tout sous le même No. 51
26. It. Vn modele de bras à enfans portant un Vase qui sert de bobeche, et un autre modele de bras à une branche avec des Narselles à la plaque, et une pomme de pin sur la plaque, et un autre modele de bras a une branche en deux parties d'architecture, formans des rouleaux avec une tete de negre dans le bas de la plaque le tout sous le Même No 72
27. It. Vn petit modele de bras à deux branches à fleurs pour un cabinet 48
28. It. Deux plaques de bras a la moderne avec des branches desassorties, le tout sous le même N° 17
29. It. Vn petit modele de plaque à feuilles d'ornemens et une branche ronde, avec des feuilles d'eau 8
30. It. Deux feux à chasseur, dont un modele et l'autre surmoulé sous le même No. 508
31. It. Vn feu a Renard d'un côté et deux coqs de l'autre, pied dans le gout moderne et modeles 150
32. It. Vn modele de feu antique à grosses colonnes garni d'une Guirlande de chêne, avec un gros Vase, avec des têtes de Belier, et une guirlande de fleurs, et un feu complet surmoulé pareil, le tout 150
33. It. Vn feu a chien et à chat, et un autre feu a terrasses avec un Renard et un lapin desassorties, le tout sous le même No. 144
34. It. Vn côté de feu à Vase regulier 30
35. It. Vn modele de feu à terrasse avec un cheval et deux autres terrasses plus petites le tout sous le même No. 120

36. It. Vn feu à pieds quarrés avec des Narselles, et une terrasse avec des chevaux antierement fini prêt a dorer 150
37. It. Vn modele de feu avec deux terrasses, et un socle quarré avec deux chevaux 120
38. It. Vn modele de feu à colonnes avec une cassolette dessus portée par trois consoles avec trois tetes de Lionnes antiques dont la colonne n'est point fini 180
39. It. Vn modele de feu à colonnes avec des canneaux entrelassés et des fleurons de feuilles entre avec un Vase uni 60
40. It. Vn modele de feu avec une cassolette, avec une grosse flamme dessus, soutenue par trois consolles, avec des tetes de bouc avec des guirlandes de laurier, le tout porté sur un socle en triangle, modele a trépied 200
41. It. Vn modele de feu à colonnes avec deux consoles d'architecture ornées d'une guirlande de lierre, avec des têtes de bélier, et une draperie sur le Vase 96
42. It. Vn feu à cassolettes à jour avec trois consolles, avec des tetes lionnes, monté sur son fer 300
43. It. Vn autre petit feu a Vase à draperie avec des têtes de bouc, et à colonnes, avec une guirlande de lierre, monté sur son fer 150
44. It. Vn autre petit feu de cabinet a colonnes, Vase uni, avec son fer 110
45. It. Vn modele de feu à enfans pour un cabinet de toilette, et un autre feu pareil surmoulé dont la figure de la fille tient un oiseau, sous le même N°. 250
46. It. Vn modele de feu à colonnes avec une grosse pomme de pin 48
47. It. Vn grand cartel représentant une lyre pour une pendule, avec un Moufle et une peau de Lyon dans le bas, pour modele qui n'est qu'en partie ébauché 150
48. It. Vn écritoire dans le gout moderne finie en partie 30
49. It. Cinq modeles de pendules dans le gout de moderne, point finis et desassortis prisés sous le même N°. 130
50. It. Quatre pendules à pied, et une moîtié, avec deux petits cartels, le tout desassorti, et en partie fini, prisés sous le même N°. 106
51. It. Vn feu a pieds modernes uni avec des perroquets finis et deux autres pieds de feu moderne point finis, le tout sous le même N° 75
52. It. Vn feu à perroquet et Ecureuil point fini, avec un autre feu a ornement sous le même N°. 40
53. It. Vn modele de chandelier dans le gout grec, d'environ trois pieds deux pouces de haut, avec des têtes de cherubins, et différens medaillons, sous le même No. 153
54. It. Vn autre chandelier d'Eglise d'Environ quatre pieds et demi de hauteur dans le gout antique avec des têtes de cherbins et des medaillons 300
55. It.Vn modele de chandelier dans le gout grec, d'environ trois pieds neuf pouces, avec trois têtes d'anges, et des medaillons 280
56. It. Vn grand chandelier d'Eglise dans le gout moderne, d'environs quatre pieds de hauteur 82
57. It. Vn petit aigle pour un lutrin 180
58. It. Vne paire de flambeaux modernes en couleur, et une autre paire pareille finies en partie et point montées sous le même N°. 30
59. It. Vne paire de flambeaux à la grecque finis et prêts à dorer, et le modele pareil sous le même N°. 120
60. It. Trois Grandes figures en fonte brute, dont deux representent deux Vents, et l'autre represente Bellone, le tout avec leurs accessoirs et leurs attributs pezant cent quatre Vingt dix neuf Livres deux onces à un Sou la livre, revenant en argent à la so. de 597.7.6.

61. It. Vne grande Girandole à cinq branches pour une encoignure d'apartement, portant environ trois pieds et demie de hauteur avec son pied orné d'une tete et d'une peau de Lyon pour M^r le Comte d'Orsay 1000
62. It. Trois grandes Guirlandes pour le même Comte d'Orsay avec leurs pendans représentans trois saisons et entierement finis pour etre employées à trois Girandoles point commencées qui doivent être pareilles à la précédente, les trois guirlandes 200
63. It. Plusieurs branches de laurier en fonte brute pour être employées aux trois précédentes girandoles pezant en total dix sept livres treize onces à trente six sols la livre, revenant pour le total en argent à la so.de 32.1.3.
64. It. Vn grand feu à globes avec son recouvrement orné d'une draperie 500
65. It. Vn Bras à cinq branches regulier, avec ses accessoires 300
66. It. Vn bras à quatre branches orné de guirlandes de fleurs avec un bouquet et un soleil dans le milieu 500
67. It. Vn autre bras aussi à quatre branches, orné de guirlandes de fleurs avec un bouquet et un pavot dans le milieu 320
68. It. Vn autre bras à quatre branches à feuillages sans bassin ni bobeches 220
69. It. Vn bras chinois à cinq branches monté en partie et surmonté d'une pagode, et une autre pagode pour faire le pendant avec des bassins et point de bobeches 300
70. It. Deux paires de bras à quatre branches ornés de guirlandes à fleurs, avec un bouquet et un pavot dans le milieu le tout sous le même N°. 800
71. It. Vne paire de bras à quatre branches à feuillages finie 320
72. It. Quatre petits feux Modernes contrepartie, dont deux avec des figures ou il manque les bras, et un feu ou il manque Les attributs, et un autre ou il ne faut pas d'attributs, et de plus un côté de feu regulier avec deux petits bustes d'enfans, dont il manque les bras, le tout sous le même N°. 90
73. It. Vn feu Rochers avec une figure de Mars avec son pendant monté en partie 278
74. It. Vn feu à Lions non fini, avec un petit recouvrement desassorti, sous le même N°. 80
75. It. Deux socles quarrés unis avec dix vases et cinq pieds de recouvrement, et un autre pied quarré avec des cannaux, le tout sous le même N°. 102
76. It. Quatre enfans dont il manque partie des accessoires sous le même N°. 80
77. It. Sept figures d'enfans et un Arlequin avec son pendant, le tout sous le même N°. 90
78. It. Vn côté de feu à Colonnes avec un Vase en forme de bouteilles point finis, avec vnze figures, animaux et autres, et une grande figure de Lione, et des accessoirs dependans de différens morceaux, le tout sous le même No 94
79. It. Différents croissans dans le gout moderne avec des accessoirs de différentes figures et plusieurs pendans de laurier, avec une branche de bras antique, le tout sous le même N°. 40
80 It. Vn coté de feu à trepied, console a tete de Lionne, avec la cassollete non fini 220
81. It. Différents bassins pieds de chandeliers, et plusieurs autres morceaux de non valeur sous le même No. 42
82. It. Différens accessoirs et piéces desassorties, le tout dans trois boëtes sous le même No. 50
83. It. Deux portes de tabernacle et trois enfans sur un pied de bois portant un globe, et un grand bras dont la plaque est une rosette, et deux boëtes contenans différens modeles non assortis sous le même No. 140
84. It. Sept boetes contenans differens modeles et accessoirs et des enfans, le tout non assorti, sous le même No. 154
85. It. Cinq boëtes contenans différens modeles et accessoirs finis et non finis dessassortis,

avec un bordure de miroir et quatre frises, avec des entrelas et des postes, une petite figure d'Evêque, le tout sous le même No. 151

86. It. Deux figures, une de Vulcein et une autre de Venus 62

87. It. Vn socle uni quarré en deux Morceaux, et une draperie non finie sous le même No. 58.10

88. It. Trois boëtes contenans divers Morceaux en fonte brute sous le même No. 84.12

89. It. Différens articles en fonte brute sous les mêmes Nos 144

90. It. Vne paire de bras à enfans portant un Vase pour bobeches non monté et un Medaillon d'Henry quatre monté dans son cadre, et trois autres medaillons, dont un représente le grand Condé, et les deux autres un Turenne sous le même No. 114

91. It. Trois Cent quatre Vingt dix Sept livres huit onces de fonte brute contenant différens Morceaux à raison de trente six sols la livre sous le même No. 715.10

92. It. Vn feu avec des chinois sur les piés Modernes en couleur 80

93. It. Vne boete de pendule moderne en couleur avec un enfant dessus tenant une lunette d'aproche et une console non en couleur aussi dans le gout moderne prisé sous le même No. 100

94. It. Vne paire de grands bras a trois branches en couleur avec des grandes Guirlandes de laurier agraphées dans les rouleaux des branches et nouées d'une draperie en noir de fumée avec un Vase dont le corps est aussi en noir de fumée 650

95. It. Vne petite figure representant une Vestale 3

96. It. Vn petit model de feu à colonnes avec un Vase uni 55

97. It. Quatre livres et demi de fonte Brute à trente six sols la livre revenant en argent à 8.2

98. It. Trois cent treize livres quatre onces de plomb, partie de vieux Modeles infructueux et lingots sous le même No. 62.13

99. It. Deux Creuse de Vierge avec leurs pieds, petits modeles des Chartreux sous le même No. 63

100. It. Plusieurs parties de cuivre non assorties provenant d'un petit chandelier d'Eglise 4.8

101. It. Vne cuvette et un pot a laver les mains 18

ENGLISH TRANSLATION

Livres

1. It. (i.e., item) A large modern sconce with four branches valued at the sum of eighty of our livres 80

2. It. A sconce, hunting-horn form, making three branches with a wolf's head 200

3. It. A pair of sconces with three branches in the modern taste 78

4. It. A sconce in the modern taste with four branches 55

5. It. A small model for a sconce with two branches forming scrolls, to which is fastened a garland of laurel attached to the plate by a nail, partly finished 30

6. It. A pair of sconces with three branches which is partly finished, in the modern taste 52

7. It. A pair of sconces with three branches in the Antique taste with a noble garland of laurels tied by a bow of ribbons which is attached to the plate by a nail, entirely finished and ready for gilding 250

8. It. A pair of sconces with two branches with two consoles each forming a scroll bearing a vase decorated with garlands of fruit, entirely finished and ready for gilding 200

9. It. A model for a sconce with three branches and a large ram's head forming the plate to which is attached a garland of vine leaves, suitable for fixing in a panel of wainscot in a saloon 160

10. It. A model for a sconce with three branches, the branches of scroll form, with double garlands of laurels fastened to the three branches and tied by a drapery which attaches the three branches to the plate — 175
11. It. A pair of sconces with two branches attached to each other by a ribbon forming a bow at the top of the plate with a vase and a garland of laurels, in the Antique taste — 144
12. It. A model for a sconce with three branches in the Antique taste with a double garland of laurels tied by a bow of ribbon which is attached by a nail to the plate — 150
13. It. A model for a sconce with two branches, with scallop shells on the plate, with large garlands of laurels fastened in the scrolls of the branches and attached by a nail to the plate with a ribbon forming a bow at the top of the plate, partly finished — 150
14. It. A model for a sconce with two branches in the Antique taste, with a lion's head and skin fastened to the said branches — 160
15. It. A model for a sconce with three branches in the Antique taste with two contrasting trophies composed of different attributes — 100
16. It. A plate with gadroons in the upper part with a vase from which rises a bouquet of flowers and a round branch with a water-leaf and bunches of laurels — 75
17. It. A small model for a sconce with two branches in the Antique taste with a ribbon forming a bow in the upper part of the plate, with a pierced plate and branches of double scrolls — 50
18. It. A pair of sconces with two branches in the Antique taste, Paffe's model — 90
19. It. A pair of sconces with two scroll branches, pierced plates, with bows of ribbon in the upper part of the plaque, and with a trophy surmounting each plate — 110
20. It. A pair of sconces with one branch of Antique form, for a dressing-room — 30
21. It. A pair of sconces, a model with three branches of lilies, unfinished — 60
22. It. A pair of sconces, a model with two branches of lilies — 60
23. It. A pair of modern sconces with two crossed branches rising from the lower part of the plate with bunches of flowers on the branches — 18
24. It. A model for a sconce, of palms, with three branches and a palmette of leaves at the bottom forming the plate — 36
25. It. A model for a sconce with two branches from which some of the fittings are missing, together with three sides of a sconce with one branch without pans, and another sconce with three branches, with a pendant of oak-leaves on each branch and a bow of ribbon on the plate, and three more sconces with one branch and masks on the plate, of which two are lacquered, and in addition a sconce-plate with ribbons, all valued as one number — 51
26. It. A model for a sconce with children bearing a vase which serves as a nozzle, and another model for a sconce with one branch and having scallop shells on the plate and a pinecone surmounting the plate, and another model for a sconce with one branch shaped as two architectural members, forming scrolls, with a negro head in the bottom part of the plate, all valued as one number — 72
27. It. A small model for a sconce with two branches of flower form, for a study — 48
28. It. Two sconce plates in the modern manner with branches, not assembled, all valued as one number — 17
29. It. A small model for a plate with ornaments of leaves and a round branch with water-leaves — 8
30. It. Two pairs of fire-dogs of huntsman form of which one is a model and the other an aftercast valued as one number — 508

31. It. A pair of fire-dogs with a fox on one side and two cocks on the other, the foot in the modern taste and the models 150
32. It. A model for a pair of fire-dogs in the Antique style with heavy columns garnished with an oak-leaf garland, with a large vase, with rams' heads and a garland of flowers, together with a complete pair of fire-dogs, aftercast from the first, all valued at 150
33. It. A pair of fire-dogs with a cat and a dog, and another with banks of earth with a fox and a rabbit, the banks not assembled, all valued as one number 144
34. It. A fire-dog, regular vase shape 30
35. It. A model for a pair of fire-dogs with a bank of earth with a horse and two other smaller banks of earth all valued as one number 120
36. It. A pair of fire-dogs with right-angled feet with scallop shells and a bank of earth with horses entirely finished ready for gilding 150
37. It. A model for a pair of fire-dogs with two banks of earth and a right-angled socle with two horses 120
38. It. A model for a pair of fire-dogs with columns with a perfume-pan above resting on three consoles and with three heads of lionesses of Antique form; the column is not finished 180
39. It. A model for a pair of fire-dogs with columns with spiral flutings and with stems of leaves between, with plain vase 60
40. It. A model for a pair of fire-dogs with a perfume-pan having a large flame above the pan, supported by three consoles, with three goats' heads and with garlands of laurel, the whole resting on a triangular socle, a tripod model 200
41. It. A model for a pair of fire-dogs with columns, with two consoles of architectural form ornamented with a garland of ivy, with rams' heads, and a drapery on the vase 96
42. It. A pair of fire-dogs with pierced perfume-pans, with three consoles, with lions heads, mounted on its iron base 300
43. It. Another small pair of fire-dogs with a vase decorated with drapery, with goats' heads, and on columns, with a garland of ivy, mounted on its iron base 150
44. It. Another small pair of fire-dogs for a closet with columns, plain vase, with its iron base 110
45. It. A model for a pair of fire-dogs with children for a dressing-room, and another similar pair of fire-dogs aftercast, in which the figure of the girl holds a bird, all valued as one number 250
46. It. A model for a pair of fire-dogs with columns, with a large pinecone 48
47. It. A large dial-case representing a lyre for a timepiece, with a lion mask and a lion skin in the bottom part, for a model which is only partly roughed out 150
48. It. A standish in the modern taste, partly finished 30
49. It. Five models of timepieces in the modern taste, unfinished and not assembled, valued as one number 130
50. It. Four timepieces on feet and half of one, with two small dial-cases, the whole not assembled and partly finished, valued as one number 106
51. It. A pair of fire-dogs on modern feet, plain with parrots which are finished and two other feet for fire-dogs in the modern style, not finished, all valued as one number 75
52. It. A pair of fire-dogs with a parrot and squirrel, unfinished, with another pair of fire-dogs which is ornamented, valued as one number 40
53. It. A model for a candlestick in the Greek taste about three feet two inches high, with cherub heads and different medallions, valued as one number 153

54. It. Another church candlestick about four and a half feet high in the Antique taste with cherub heads and medallions 300
55. It. A model for a candlestick in the Greek taste about three feet nine inches high, with three heads of angels and medallions 280
56. It. A large church candlestick in the modern taste about four feet high 82
57. It. A small eagle for a lectern 180
58. It. A pair of lacquered modern portable candlesticks, and another similar pair partly finished and not mounted, all valued as one number 30
59. It. A pair of portable candlesticks in the Greek manner finished and ready for gilding and a model similar, all valued as one number 120
60. It. Three large figures rough-cast, of which two represent two Winds and the other represents Bellona, all with their accessories and their attributes, weighing a hundred and ninety-nine pounds two ounces at one sol the pound which comes in money to the sum of 597.7.6
61. It. A large girandole with five branches for the corner of a room rising about three feet and a half in height with a foot decorated with a lion head and a lion-skin for M. le Comte d'Orsay 1000
62. It. Three large garlands for the same Comte d'Orsay with their pendants representing three of the Seasons which are entirely finished and to be employed in three girandoles not yet begun which are to be similar to the preceding, the three garlands 200
63. It. Several laurel branches rough cast which are to be employed in the three girandoles preceding weighing in all seventeen pounds thirteen ounces at thirty-six sols the pound which comes in all in money to the sum of 32.1.3
64. It. A large pair of fire-dogs with globes with their front ornamented by a drapery 500
65. It. A sconce with five branches of regular form, with its accessories 300
66. It. A sconce with four branches, decorated with garlands of flowers with a bouquet with a sun-burst in the middle 500
67. It. Another sconce also with four branches, decorated with garlands of flowers and a poppy in the middle 320
68. It. Another sconce with four branches with leaf decoration without nozzle or pans 220
69. It. A Chinese sconce with five branches partly mounted and surmounted by a mandarin and another mandarin to make the pendant, with pans and no nozzles 300
70. It. Two pairs of sconces with four branches ornamented with garlands of flowers, with a bouquet and a poppy in the middle, all valued as one number 800
71. It. A pair of sconces with four branches decorated with leaves, finished 320
72. It. Four small modern pairs of fire-dogs of contrasting form of which two have figures whose arms are missing together with a pair of fire-dogs whose attributes are missing and another where no attributes are needed and in addition a fire-dog of regular form with two small busts of children whose arms are missing, all valued as one number 90
73. It. A pair of fire-dogs, rocks with a figure of Mars, together with pendant, partly mounted 278
74. It. A pair of fire-dogs with lions, unfinished, together with a small cover not assembled, valued as one number 80
75. It. Two right-angled bases of plain form together with ten vases and five feet for covers and another right-angled foot decorated with fluting, all valued as one number 102
76. It. Four children part of whose accessories are missing, valued as one number 80
77. It. Seven figures of children and a Harlequin with his pendant, all valued as one number 90

78\. It. A fire-dog with columns, with vase of bottle form, unfinished together with eleven figures, animals and others, and a large figure of a lioness, and accessories belonging to different pieces, all valued as one number 94
79\. It. Different crescent andirons in the modern taste with accessories of different figures and several pendants of laurel, together with a branch for a sconce in the Antique taste, all valued as one number 40
80\. It. A fire-dog, with tripod, console and the head of a lioness, with a perfume-pan, unfinished 220
81\. It. Different pans, feet for candlesticks together with several other pieces of no value, all valued under the same number 42
82\. It. Different accessories and parts, not assembled, the whole in three boxes, valued as one number 50
83\. It. Two tabernacle doors and three children bearing a globe on a wooden pedestal and a large sconce whose plate is a rosette and two boxes containing different models not assembled, all valued under the same number 140
84\. It. Seven boxes containing different models and accessories and children, the whole not assembled, valued as one number 154
85\. It. Five boxes containing different models and accessories finished and unfinished, not assembled, together with a mirror-frame and four friezes with pieces of guilloche and Vitruvian scroll ornament, a small figure of a bishop, all valued as one number 151
86\. It. Two figures one of Vulcan and the other of Venus 62
87\. It. A plain right-angled base in two pieces and an unfinished drapery, valued as one number 58.10
88\. It. Three boxes containing different pieces in rough casting, valued as one number 84.12
89\. It. Different articles in rough casting, valued as one number 144
90\. It. A pair of sconces with children bearing a vase for the nozzles, not mounted, and a medallion of Henry IV mounted in its frame, and three other medallions of which one represents the Great Condé and the other two Turenne, valued as one number 114
91\. It. Three hundred and ninety-seven pounds eight ounces of rough-cast work comprising different pieces, valued as one number at the rate of thirty-six sols a pound 715.10
92\. It. A pair of fire-dogs with Chinese on the feet, in the modern taste in colour 80
93\. It. A case for a timepiece in the modern taste in colour, with a child above holding a telescope, together with a console not in colour also in the modern taste valued as one number 100
94\. It. A pair of large sconces with three branches in colour with large garlands of laurel attached to the scrolls of the branches and knotted by a drapery of smoke-black colour with a vase whose body is also smoke-black 650
95\. It. A small figure representing a Vestal 3
96\. It. A small model for a pair of fire-dogs with columns and a plain vase 55
97\. It. Four pounds and a half of rough-cast work at thirty-six sols a pound which in money comes to 8.2
98\. It. Three hundred and thirteen pounds four ounces of lead, partly old models no longer profitable and ingots, valued as one number 62.13
99\. It. Two hollow moulds for the Virgin with their pedestals, small models of Carthusian monks, valued as one number 63
100\. It. Several pieces of copper not assembled originating from a small church candlestick 4.8
101\. It. A basin and jug for washing the hands 18

NOTES ON ILLUSTRATIONS

THE COLOUR PLATES

Plate A

WRITING-TABLE, FILING-CABINET AND CLOCK. Designed by Louis-Joseph Le Lorrain; made about 1757 for Ange-Laurent de Lalive de Jully. *Chantilly, Musée Condé.* See Notes on Plates 85–89 and 187. (*Frontispiece*)

Plate B

DINING-ROOM OF THE PAVILLON DE LOUVECIENNES. Coloured drawing by J.-M. Moreau *le jeune*, executed in 1771. *Musée du Louvre, Cabinet des Dessins.* See Note on Plate 474. (*Facing page 32*)

Plate C

TRAVELLING WRITING-DESK. Stamped *J. F. Oeben*; about 1765–67. *French private collection.* (*Facing page 48*)

The decoration executed in marquetry on the falling leaf, comprising a heavy Neo-Classical garland and a medallion with emblems symbolising Poetry, is to be seen (with minor variations) on a secretaire stamped by Riesener (Guérault sale, Paris, 2nd March 1935, lot 94; illustrated). The motif within the medallion is again reproduced, but in a rectangular framing, on the back of the Comte de Provence's roll-top desk (Plate 143) which Riesener delivered to the Garde-Meuble in March 1774. (This panel is illustrated by Verlet, *French Royal Furniture*, 1963, Fig. 10b.) The comments on dating made in the Note to Plate 113 (below) apply equally to this box.

Plate D

SMALL WRITING-DESK. Stamped *M. Carlin.* The oval Sèvres porcelain plaque on the top is signed by Charles-Nicholas Dodin and dated 1771. *Lisbon, Museu Calouste Gulbenkian.* (*Facing page 64*)

This desk bears on the underside the inventory mark C.R. under a closed crown and the number 6238. 'C.R.' is thought to stand for '*Casa Reale*' (The Royal Household) and is not infrequently to be found on furniture that is thought to have come from Italian royal collections. As James Parker has shown, this desk probably belonged to the Queen and must have come from the Royal Palace at Naples (*Metropolitan Museum of Art Bulletin*, January 1966, No. 4). Pierre Verlet has suggested that the oval plaque may have been identical with that which the dealer Poirier bought from the Sèvres porcelain factory in 1772. There can be no doubt that the table must have been designed before the large plaque and the eighteen smaller plaques were ordered from the Sèvres factory. The lower part of the desk has many features in common with the desk illustrated in Plate 136 which can be dated 1773 and must also have come from Poirier's shop. See also pages 81 and 134.

Plate E

ARMCHAIR. Stamped *N. Heurtaut*; about 1768–69. *Musée du Louvre*. See Note on Plates 166–167. (*Facing page 80*)

Plate F

SCONCE, one of a pair. About 1763–64. Gilt bronze. *Palazzo del Quirinale, Rome*. (*Facing page 96*)

According to Signora Chiara Briganti, who first identified and published these sconces, they were delivered to the Bourbon Court at Parma in 1764 by the Parisian dealer Testard (see *Curioso itinerario delle collezioni ducali parmensi*, Milan 1969, pp. 100–101). It is not known who actually made them.

Plate G (i)

SNUFF-BOX. Gold and enamel. Paris hall-mark for 1766–67. Maker's mark of Jean-Joseph Barrière. *Nationalmuseum, Stockholm*. (*Facing page 112*)

This box belonged to the famous Swedish botanist, Carl von Linné, to whom it was given by Lord Baltimore about 1770. On the lid is an oval medallion with a cupid copied from a well-known figure by Falconet. On the bottom face is another medallion with a representation of a vase taken from the engraving by Maurice Jacques reproduced in Plate 393.

Plate G (ii)

EGG-CUP. Gold. Paris hall-mark for 1764–65. Maker's mark of François-Thomas Germain. *Lisbon, Museu Nacional de Arte Antiga*. (*Facing page 112*)

Note the finely chased Vitruvian scroll round the rim.

Plate H

CUP AND SAUCER. Sèvres porcelain bearing theda te letter 'P' for 1768. *Copenhagen, The Danish Museum of Decorative Art*. (*Facing page 128*)

As stated in the Note to Plate 289, cups of this shape were already being made in 1753, when the royal French porcelain factory was still at Vincennes. The simplicity of this form can therefore not be regarded as an early manifestation of Neo-Classicism. On the other hand, the geometric ornament on this and related examples reflects the efforts made at the factory to modernise its wares during the 1760s.

THE MONOCHROME PLATES

Plate 1

DESIGN FOR THE FAÇADE OF SAINT-SULPICE. Drawn about 1732 by Giovanni Niccolo Servandoni. *Bibliothèque Nationale, Cabinet des Estampes*.

The foundation-stone for the façade was laid in 1733. Servandoni altered parts of the design himself in 1740, notably in connection with the towers and the pediment, which was made considerably wider. The pediment was hit by lightning in 1770 and had to be demolished. Even so, the present façade enables one to appreciate how original was Servandoni's conception and why it was considered epoch-making in its day—a sound example for those seeking a new formula based on Classical principles. The dominating role played by the columns is particularly noticeable, and the simple unity pervading the composition must have struck contemporary beholders as quite unusual. Servandoni was of course Italian and had been trained in Italy. But, while this façade may call to mind certain sixteenth- and seventeenth-century Italian churches, it is not impossible that Servandoni was to some extent inspired by the West Front of Wren's St. Paul's, as Hautecoeur has suggested.

Bachaumont wrote in 1750 that Servandoni was an 'excellent architecte pour les grandes choses dans le goust grec et du bel antique' ('excellent architect for works on a grand scale in the Grecian or Antique taste'). A writer in the *Mercure de France* in July 1768 maintained that the modified project for the façade combined 'la grandeur, la magnificence, ce caractère mâle & élégant de l'antique, ces belles proportions, & ce repos majestueux des anciens édifices s'y trouvent réunis avec éclat & intelligence' ('the grandeur, the magnificence, the forthright and elegant character of Classical architecture, with the good proportions and majestic severity of those ancient buildings'). See also pages 37, 49 and 53.

Plate 2

DESIGN FOR A SEPULCHRAL MONUMENT. Drawn and engraved about 1740 (?) by Jean-Laurent Le Geay.

One of a series of six plates, all illustrating such monuments. It is very likely that these designs date from the three years or so which Le Geay spent in Rome, between 1738 and 1742, although it has not so far been possible to prove this. The composition, with its obelisk and uncompromisingly rectangular block, is reminiscent of Piranesi's *Mausoleo antico* (published in his *Opera varie*, 1750) and of Juvara's project for a royal mausoleum which was published by Vasi in 1739 (see J. Harris, 'Le Geay, Piranesi and International Neo-Classicism in Rome, 1740–50', *Essays in the History of Architecture presented to Rudolf Wittkower*, 1967, fig. 17).

In his *Mémoires*, Cochin wrote that 'On peut donner pour première époque du retour d'un meilleur goust, l'arrivée de Legeay architecte, qui avoit été pensionnaire à Rome. C'étoit un des plus beaux génies en architecture qu'il y ait eu' ('One can say that good taste started to be regained on the arrival of Le Geay back in Paris after he had been a stipendiary in Rome. He was one of the most fertile geniuses in the field of architecture that we have ever had'). De Troy, the Director of the French School in Rome, informed his superiors in Paris, when Le Geay was about to return home, that 'il emporte une quantité de fort beaux desseins, tant des études qu'il a fait d'après des édifices publics que de sa propre composition; dans ces derniers, il y a du feu et du génie' ('he will be bringing back a quantity of extremely fine drawings, both studies which he has made of public buildings [here in Rome] and compositions of his own; the latter display both spirit and genius'). Other contemporaries recognised the seminal character of Le Geay's strange genius, as Harris has pointed out (op. cit.). See also page 31.

Plates 3 and 4

DESIGNS FOR FOUNTAINS. Drawn and engraved about 1740 (?) by J.-L. Le Geay.

From a series of seven plates, all showing proposals for fountains.

Plate 5

TITLE-PAGE TO THE SERIES OF 'ROVINE'. Drawn by J.-L. Le Geay about 1740 (?). Published in 1768.

Ascribed by Kaufmann and Harris to Le Geay's stay in Rome (see Note to Plate 1). The inscription is in Italian, not Latin—or French. See also page 31.

Plate 6

ETCHING FROM THE 'ROVINE' SERIES. See Note to Plate 5, above.

Plate 7

DESIGN FOR THE FAÇADE OF A CHURCH. Designed in 1744 by Contant d'Ivry and published in his *Oeuvres d'Architecture* in 1758.

The original drawing for this scheme, in the possession of Mr. John Harris, bears the inscription 'projet presenté pour le portail de St. Eustache' ('the design for the façade of St. Eustache which was submitted'). When compared with Servandoni's project for the front of Saint-Sulpice of a dozen years earlier (Plate 1), this design seems somewhat antiquated. The virtually free-standing columns each merely support a single piece of sculpture and this lends the façade a theatrical appearance which may owe something to such late-Classical edifices as the Arch of Constantine in Rome—works which French architects had admired far more in the seventeenth century than in the eighteenth. Contant's knowledge of Classical architecture was in fact second-hand, since he never visited Italy. See also pages 37 and 53.

Plate 8

A TRIUMPHAL ARCH. Designed and engraved by Louis-Joseph Le Lorrain. Erected outside the Palazzo Colonna in Rome for the Chinea Festival in 1745.

At this annual festival, the Prince Colonna, as ambassador from the King of Naples, delivered his monarch's tribute to the Holy See in a casket carried by a white mare—*la Chinea*. A firework display was mounted to mark the occasion each year and this took place against an architectural set-piece. For many years, the students at the French Academy in Rome designed these decorations and thereby had the opportunity of demonstrating their talents. As a rule, the designs for these structures were engraved and published. An almost complete set of these engravings, bound in chronological order, is in the Library of the Kunst-industrimuseum in Copenhagen (a microfilm copy may be seen in the Library of the Royal Institute of British Architects in London).

The rotunda crowning Le Lorrain's triumphal arch owes much to Borromini's S.Agnese in Rome but the portals at the side, with the bold entablature supported by two columns, derive from Michelangelo's palaces on the Capitol. The latter motif was to become a great favourite with later French architects, as were the reliefs set in rectangular frames above these openings and the large oval panels with their heavy pendant swags. While Le Lorrain's arch does not reveal any great talent on his part, it embodies features representing trends that were to assume great importance in the future.

There can be little doubt that this composition was a prime source of inspiration for the Slodtz brothers when they were designing a triumphal arch that was to form the central feature of a set-piece which was erected in front of the Palace of Versailles during the celebrations in honour of the Duc de Bourgogne in December 1751 (see F. Souchal, *Les Slodtz*, Plate 59b). See also page 32.

Plate 9

A TEMPLE OF MINERVA. Designed and engraved by Louis-Joseph Le Lorrain. Erected for the Chinea Festival of 1746 (see the Note to Plate 8).

The drum-like dome is so monolithic in character that one can hardly conceive it as being a hollow structure of masonry. The undercut profile and wide band decorated with carvings in relief underline the impression of solidity and massive weight. Cyclopic conceptions of this kind were of course typical features of

Piranesi's work, and it is difficult to believe that Le Lorrain was not at this stage influenced by the young Venetian architect who was living across the road from the French Academy in Rome and was a friend of Le Lorrain and many of the other Frenchmen staying there.

Plate 10

DESIGN FOR A TEMPLE OF THE ARTS. Designed in Rome in 1746 by Gabriel-Pierre-Martin Dumont who also executed this engraving. The original drawings for the scheme were offered by Dumont as his reception-piece at the Accademia di San Lucca.

Like Le Lorrain's triumphal arch of the previous year (Plate 8), this composition has portals of a characteristic form which must derive from Michelangelo's *palazzi* surmounting the Capitol. Le Lorrain's rectangular panels with reliefs are also found here but Dumont's dome is shallow and less ponderous, and is decorated with a dominant band of Vitruvian scrolls.

Dumont became a professor of architecture in Paris. He published the drawings for this project in the 1760s, by which time they were some twenty years old. That he did so, shows that he still felt them relevant although he published some revised versions at the same time. The modernisations consisted principally of removing the pilasters, which he may have done as a result of the fierce controversy that had raged during the early 1750s over the question of whether or not pilasters were a legitimate architectural form. The trimmed version is illustrated by Wolfgang Hermann in his *Laugier and Eighteenth-Century French Theory* (1962, Plate 15). See also page 32.

Plate 11

DESIGN FOR A SEPULCHRAL CHAPEL. Designed and engraved in Rome by Nicolas-Henri Jardin in 1747 or 1748.

Jardin has here adopted the size and proportions of the Pyramid of Cestius for his central feature which he here shows as a well-preserved ruin—the only signs of age being disposed like so many 'beauty spots'. Jardin's pyramid, like that of Cestius, is conceived as a brick structure while the other features of this design are clearly constructed of ashlar. The contrast would appear to have been made on purpose. Can Jardin have intended that this monument should in fact have had the actual Cestius Pyramid as its centre? A similar use of an antique building had been made by Carlo Fontana when he embodied the Temple of Neptune on the Piazza di Pietra in a Customs House, and when he drew up proposals for erecting a church inside the Colosseum, using the old building as a highly theatrical setting. See also page 31.

Plate 12

THE HIGH ALTAR IN THE CATHEDRAL AT VIENNE (ISÈRE). Executed in Rome between 1744 and 1746 by Michel-Ange Slodtz. Erected in 1747.

The sarcophagus-like altar is largely made of a mottled dark green marble but the ornaments, including the Vitruvian scroll, which look as if made of gilt bronze, are in fact of a yellowish marble. The cost of providing this altar was borne by Cardinal Henri de la Tour d'Auvergne who, before commissioning the work from Slodtz, had consulted Soufflot who was at that time domiciled in Lyon. Soufflot submitted proposals for the altar's dimensions and proportions but the designs were executed entirely by Slodtz himself. Soufflot gave Slodtz a similar measure of support when the latter was executing the sepulchural monument for the archbishops of Vienne which he also produced at this period (see F. Souchal, *Les Slodtz*, pages 673–4). See also page 33.

Plate 13

A RECONSTRUCTION OF THE AMPHITHEATRE AT HERCULANEUM. Drawn and etched by E.-A. Petitot and executed as the set-piece for the Chinea Festival of 1749.

The decorative pavilions erected for the annual Chinea Festival (see Notes to Plates 8 and 9) often embodied allusions to the then recently discovered ruins of Herculanium. Petitot's very free interpretation also seems to owe much to Piranesi, particularly to his *Mausoleo antico* which was published just before 1749. The playful portals, on the other hand, spring from the Roman Baroque tradition of architects like Borromini. Petitot's design was published twice; first by himself in 1749 and then by Pierre Patte in 1755 after Petitot had been appointed Court Architect in Parma. See also page 32.

Plate 14

MURAL-DECORATION FOR THE STAIRCASE AT THE HÔTEL DE LUYNES. Executed about 1748 by Gaetano Brunetti. Now erected in the Musée Carnavalet.

More or less Baroque schemes of decorations such as this were probably not uncommon in the houses of wealthy Parisians at this date. The Brunetti family of painters were specialists in this kind of decoration and it is unlikely that they felt themselves in any way to be innovators paving the way to Neo-Classicism. On the other hand, their work may well have been a source of inspiration for later artists. The Classical character of such decoration reflected an old tradition in that rooms where a certain formality was considered proper—in halls, staircases and dining-rooms for instance—the Classical style was most appropriate. See also page 37.

Plate 15

DETAIL OF THE DESIGN FOR THE MURAL-DECORATION OF THE DINING-ROOM AT ÅKERÖ, SWEDEN. Drawn in May 1754 by Louis-Joseph Le Lorrain and executed on canvas a year or two later by a local Swedish painter.

Åkerö is a country house, lying some sixty miles west of Stockholm which was built for the great Swedish minister C. G. Tessin, son of Nicodemus Tessin, and former ambassador to the Court of Versailles. Work on the house started in 1752.

Tessin had originally intended to commission designs for this room from the painter, Oudry. However, the Comte de Caylus, whom he had known in Paris, persuaded him to engage the young designer Le Lorrain who then provided the essentially Neo-Classical design shown here. Tessin was not at first pleased with the radically new taste embodied in this composition, so Caylus made Le Lorrain design a new scheme couched in Oudry's style—that is, in the Rococo taste. Tessin finally decided he preferred the first proposal. Could he in the meantime have read Cochin's now famous article in the *Mercure de France* (see page 233) which had appeared in the December issue?

Le Lorrain's design must undoubtedly be classed as an essay in Neo-Classicism, especially as we know of his preference for this idiom (cf. Plates 8 and 9). However, it must not be forgotten that the style traditionally favoured for formal rooms—like dining-rooms—was the Classical one, as has been explained in connection with the previous illustrations. See also pages 44 and 56.

Plate 16

A TRIUMPHAL ARCH. Designed by G. N. Servandoni. Erected in the square in front of Saint-Sulpice, in connection with the ceremony of laying the foundation-stone of the new church on 2nd October 1754. Engraved by Pierre Patte.

In this composition Servandoni, perhaps inspired by the works of Piranesi, has sought to combine the Classical form of triumphal arch with an opening based on the 'Venetian' window made popular by Palladio. The two consoles, supporting trophies emblematic of War, are decorated with Vitruvian scrolls which are as bold as that crowning François Blondel's Porte Saint-Denis, then some eighty years old (see illustration e.g. in L. Hautecoeur, *Histoire de l'architecture classique en France*, II, page 513). The inscription and the symbolic decorations glorify Louis XV's prowess as a military leader, and his role as protector of the Church and the City of Paris. The two medallions reproduce the front and reverse of the medal struck by Roëttiers *fils* to commemorate the occasion. The left-hand medal shows a bird's eye view of Servandoni's church and the square in front—but without the present arch standing there. The square was to have been surrounded by rows of identical houses but only one (No. 6) was built and the square was never achieved.

Servandoni made proposals for the planned Place Louis XV (now de la Concorde) at about this time. His amphitheatre-like scheme was said to be 'plein des beautés de l'antique'. See also page 54.

Plate 17

THE THEATRE AT LYONS. Drawn in 1754 by Jacques-Germain Soufflot. Completed in 1756 and demolished in 1827. Engraved by Jean-François de Neufforge and published in G.-P.-M. Dumont's *Recueil de plusieurs oeuvres d'architecture.*

In this façade, Soufflot retained the simple lineaments he had used for the Hôtel-Dieu in the same city some years before, but his handling is less heavy—no doubt on account of the building's purpose. No concessions are made to the Rococo in the detailing; even the design of the wrought-iron balustrade is based on Classical ornament. The two side doors on the balcony are surmounted by cartouches flanked by pendant garlands of a type which were to become so common in the next phase of early Neo-Classicism. The chamfered corners reveal Soufflot's debt to contemporary Italian, and particularly Roman architecture; he used the same feature for his *Loge au Change* at Lyons (built between 1747 and 1750, and now demolished) but this accentuates it on the upper storey. See also page 54.

Plate 18

DESIGN FOR A NEW MINT IN PARIS. Drawn by Etienne-Louis Boullée before June 1756. Engraved by Claude Poulleau in 1760.

This design by the twenty-eight year old Boullée owes much to Gabriel's style and is perhaps based on one of the latter's proposals for the pavilions on the Place Louis XV which was not executed (see Solange Granet, *La Place de la Concorde*). Boullée's predilection for plain surfaces and simple cuboid shapes, to which he was later to give full rein, is already to be discerned in this composition. This is especially obvious in the terrace which rises uncompromisingly like a bastion and was conceived as opening on to the Seine—where La Monnaie was in fact later erected. The two pavilions, with their four Ionic pilasters and banded rustication, speak the same language. The bold consoles supporting the cornice are reminiscent of certain Italian buildings, notably some *palazzi* in Genoa.

This project is usually thought to date from the year it was published (1760) or from the year it was placed before the Academy (this event took place on 8th February 1762). However, a Danish cleric was already discussing the designs in a letter to a friend in Copenhagen on 24th July 1756 (Royal Library, Copenhagen, MSS. New Royal Collection 2152, C 11). From this and from an announcement in *L'Avant-coureur* of 20th October 1760, it is clear that Chauvelin, the *intendant des finances*, had invited several architects to submit designs for a new Mint and these were all subsequently exhibited at the Hôtel de Moras. Lack of funds prevented work on the building being started and a fresh competition was then held some years later, as a result of which J. D. Antoine's scheme was accepted in 1768 and executed. See also page 54.

Plate 19

ONE OF THE PAIR OF BUILDINGS ON THE NORTH SIDE OF THE PLACE LOUIS XV (NOW THE PLACE DE LA CONCORDE). Drawn by Ange-Jacques Gabriel in 1755. Completed in the early 1760s. Engraving by Pierre Patte.

Gabriel's final project for a square in honour of Louis XV was conceived after the previous proposals, submitted by himself and other architects, had failed to meet with the King's approval. Gabriel's problem was then to combine the best elements of the various schemes. The City of Paris had set aside a site for a *place royale* in 1748 so the matter had presumably become pressing by 1755. In the centre of this square was to stand the equestrian statue of Louis which Bouchardon was busy preparing, and the square had of course to offer a worthy setting for this monumental representation of the King of France. The colonnade was primarily intended to form a frame for the view up to the Madeleine (not, of course, the temple we see there today) and it was only afterwards that anyone gave much thought as to how the two buildings should be used. In fact the right-hand building came to house the *Garde-Meuble de la Couronne* (it was taken over by the French Admiralty in 1806) while that on the left was occupied by various private individuals and was finally, in 1788, sold to the Comte de Crillon.

Gabriel must have taken Perrault's famous colonnade at the Louvre as the basis for this conception, even if it differs from the great seventeenth-century edifice in so many ways. His personal style is felt in the way he stresses the cuboidal form of the building, and in the relationship between the two houses and the other parts of the scheme—the square and the road leading to the Madeleine. As far as the details are concerned, they all derive from the Classical Roman repertoire but are used in a less dominating manner and with greater economy than in Perrault's building. In this respect, Gabriel reveals himself as one of the earliest proponents of a new form of Classicism, yet he was older than any of the other Neo-Classical architects and had never visited Italy.

An excellent survey of the building of the square will be found in Solange Granet, *La Place de la Concorde*, 1963. See also Plate 21 and page 54.

Plate 20

DESIGN FOR SAINTE-GENEVIÈVE, PARIS. Drawn by Jacques-Germain Soufflot in 1757. Engraved by François-Philippe Charpentier.

This church, now known as the Panthéon, was not completed until long after Soufflot's death in 1780. Its present appearance is the result of several modifications, most of them carried out in Soufflot's time. He started work on this design in 1755 after having been selected for the task on the recommendation of the Marquis de Marigny. This design of 1757 shows a central block of regular conformation on a cruciform plan, with a portico surmounted by a pediment resembling that of a Classical temple. A dome rests on a drum with grouped columns above the crossing, and has a 'broken' entablature. The most important alteration subsequently made by Soufflot was to the drum and dome which thus lost some of its rather incongruous Baroque character. The feature was made taller while the drum was composed of a regular open colonnade of Corinthian columns supporting an unbroken entablature and a balcony. These changes can have been the result of influences from many directions, for Soufflot travelled extensively and was familiar with all the main illustrated works on architecture. At any rate, the present building seems to reflect a knowledge of the works of Bramante, Michelangelo and Wren. The important point to remember in the present connection, however, is that this project of 1757 represented a totally new concept in the field of church architecture in France. See also page 53.

Plate 21

GUARD-ROOM AT THE ENTRANCE TO THE PLACE LOUIS XV. Drawn by Ange-Jacques Gabriel between 1755 and 1757, and completed by 1759.

Gabriel planned to have four such buildings at the two entrances to his square from the Champs Elysées, but only two were built—one on the Cours de la Reine, which led to Versailles, and one on the Rue de la bonne Morue. The bold quoins were presumably thought particularly suitable for para-military buildings like these, especially as they were being erected on what was then the edge of the city and thus had the character of city gates. Ledoux used the same motif for the guardhouses (*barrières*) he later erected at the other entrances to the city. See also the Note to Plate 19 and page 54.

Plates 22 and 23

DECORATION OF THE SALON IN THE DUCHESSE D'ORLÉANS' APARTMENT AT THE PALAIS ROYAL. Executed about 1755–57 after designs by Contant d'Ivry. Engraved by Le Canu and published as illustrations to J.-F. Blondel's article 'Architecture et parties qui en dépendent, septième partie: Observations générales sur la décoration intérieure appliquées en particulier à un appartement de parade' in Diderot and d'Alembert, *Encyclopédie . . . Recueil de planches, sur les sciences, les arts liberaux et les arts méchaniques . . . première livraison*, Paris 1762.

The mural ornaments were made of wood and painted white; the decorative details were finished with burnished gilding. The sofas and console-tables (not shown in these views) were probably also gilded. These sofas were covered with a silk material, brocaded with gold and silver thread. The candle-branches were of gilt bronze. The large wall-panels and the doors were faced with mirror-glass which reflected the rich decorations of the room and, in daytime, the view of the garden.

J.-F. Blondel said in 1762 that these rooms were a clear demonstration that, at last, one was turning from the Rococo style in interior-decoration (see pages 41–3). He pointed out that the 'frivole' appearance of Rococo interiors had here been avoided by the use of proper architectural features. However, he was pleased that the architect had also managed to find a formula less ponderous and oppressive in character than that of the time of Louis XIV in palaces like Versailles. Indeed, for him, Contant d'Ivry's decorations represent the Golden Mean. A room must be pleasant, he says, and neither the total effect nor the detail ornaments must be in any way overbearing. However, one may allow oneself to counterpoint the architectural components by adding a few contrasts (e.g. the serpentine sofas, candelabra, and chimney-piece, in this case), so long as one did not exaggerate (see page 42).

Plates 24 to 27

ORNAMENTS IN THE SALON OF COUNT BERNSTORFF'S HOUSE, COPENHAGEN. Made in Paris between 1755 and 1757 presumably after designs by Contant d'Ivry.

The house was built between 1750 and 1755 for the francophile Danish Foreign Secretary, J. H. E. Bernstorff, who had formerly been ambassador to the Court of Versailles. The principal objects in the salon were the four Beauvais tapestries representing *Les Amours des Dieux*, a marble chimney-piece with gilt-bronze candle-branches and a chimney-glass in a richly carved frame which was echoed on the opposite side of the room by three pier-glasses, with similar frames, and console-tables—all gilt.

We know for certain that the chimney-piece, mounts and candle-branches were executed by François-Thomas Germain and that these were contemporary replicas of the ensemble provided by him for the

Palais Royal (cf. Plate 23) to the designs of Contant d'Ivry. That replicas were ordered would of course have saved the expense of having fresh models made. Unfortunately we do not know who executed the mirror-frames and tables, but comparison with those produced for the Palais Royal (illustrated by Blondel, but not reproduced here) suggests that Contant d'Ivry also designed those intended for Bernstorff's house (Plates 25 to 27). Contant was the architect regularly employed by the powerful Crozat family and it was a prominent member of that family, Baron de Thiers, who supervised the creation of the decorations and furnishings for Bernstorff. The ascription of these to Contant can hardly be doubted although it is known that Germain also was consulted about the mirror-frames (Plate 24).

There are not many Neo-Classical features to be seen in these pieces yet there are some, especially in the cresting of the mirror-frames. The shape of the chimney-piece is traditional enough but the very static heads at the corners, which have a truly Classical bearing, and the bay-leaves flanking the central shell, betoken a new spirit. Moreover, there is now a strict symmetry even in the Rococo forms which seem more placid than hitherto; there is a frozen quality about the curving forms. The baskets of flowers and vases on the sketches of the console-tables also reveal a new idiom. As Blondel explained, this new style represented a mid-course between the ponderous Classicism of the Age of Louis XIV and the intemporate Rococo of the first half of his own century—'un juste milieu entre ces deux exces' ('a happy medium between these two extremes'; see pages 41–3). To Blondel, these decorations seemed like an amalgam of Classicism with Modernism; to us, with hindsight, they seem to be a compromise or, at any rate, only moderately 'modern'. Baron de Thiers promised Bernstorff that the décor of his new room would be 'dans le goût de notre dernière volupté' ('entirely in the latest manifestation of fashionable taste') but imbued with 'noblesse' and 'sagesse' ('nobility' and 'measured good sense').

Bernstorff's friend, the connoisseur Joachim Wasserschlebe, had suggested that the medallions on the mirrors should contain portraits of the King and Queen of Denmark executed in the wax technique 'rediscovered' by the Comte de Caylus (see letters from Klingraff to Wasserschlebe, dated Paris, 17th September 1755, Royal Library, Copenhagen, MS. NKS. 2152^{c}). It is not known whether the proposal was carried through but the existing portraits can hardly be original (Plate 24).

For a full history of Count Bernstorff's house, see Mario Krohn, *Frankrigs og Danmarks kunstneriske Forbindelser i det 18. Aarhundrede*, vol. I, Copenhagen, 1922, pages 66–84. See also pages 43 and 124.

Plates 28 and 29

PROPOSALS FOR MURAL-DECORATIONS. Drawn about 1755 by J.-F. de Neufforge; engraved by him and published in the first volume of his *Recueil Elémentaire d'Architecture* (1757).

The style of Neufforge's numerous compositions is pervaded by a certain lack of imagination, which allowed him to draw his motifs in a banal manner, often over-large, and to organise them so that the proportions of a complete scheme turned out somewhat ponderous. In an announcement in the *Mercure de France* of June 1756 (pages 176–7), which was presumably composed by Neufforge himself, we were informed that in the engravings which were to be published (the first volume came out in September 1757 but this announcement makes it clear that one could purchase loose plates by this date), the artist had sought to imitate 'la manière mâle, simple & majestueuse des anciens Architectes Grecs & des grands Architectes de nos jours'. As far as we know, Neufforge had never visited Italy or Greece and he must therefore have had to rely on information he could obtain from books and engravings. Neufforge's style is of course related to that espoused by Le Lorrain, as we know it from his design for Åkerö (Plate 15) and from Lalive de Jully's furniture (Plate 85 to 89). In fact Neufforge and Le Lorrain were of about the same age and it is reasonable to suppose that they knew each other, since they had both assisted with the engraving of the illustrations for J. D. Le Roy's famous book on the antiquities of Greece which appeared in 1758. See also page 47.

Plate 30

DINING-ROOM AT COUNT MOLTKE'S HOUSE, COPENHAGEN. Decorated in 1757 after designs by Nicolas-Henri Jardin.

The panelling is painted white and the ornamental details are gilded. The plasterwork ceiling is likewise white and partially gilded. At each end of the room is a buffet with a basin and a cistern in the form of an urn which is based on an engraving by Saly. The ends of the room are divided off by pairs of free-standing columns. These, and similar columns in the corners add greater prominence to the buffets with their urns. The walls are otherwise adorned with Ionic pilasters and gilt trophies. Moltke's Palais was one of the four identical buildings forming part of the Amalienborg complex which is now the Royal Palace in Copenhagen. It was built between 1750 and 1754 by the Danish architect Niels Eigtved. The exterior of the buildings is couched in a delightful version of the late Baroque style. With the exception of this dining-room, the other rooms in the house Count Moltke occupied were decorated in a rather loose rendering of Cuvilliés' Rococo. The cool, early Neo-Classical room illustrated here was designed by Jardin soon after his arrival in Denmark early in 1755 and after Eigtved's death. Work on the room was started in March 1757 and was completed by December.

This room in Copenhagen is discussed and illustrated here because it was designed by a French architect who had attended the French Academy in Rome alongside several artists who were involved in the early stages of the development of Neo-Classicism in France, and because no rooms of this character seem to have survived in France itself. The Duc d'Orléans had had a dining-room created for himself by Contant d'Ivry in his Palais Royal. It was completed by 15th October 1754, but we know nothing more about it than can be gleaned from the accounts of the stuccador Louis Mansiaux. These reveal that the room had sixteen columns and four pilasters, executed in scagliola (see page 38). Knowing that it was customary to decorate certain state-rooms—entrance-halls and dining-rooms, for instance—in a more formal manner than others, we may surmise that the Duc d'Orléans' new dining-room was the more markedly Classical in character than the other rooms Contant d'Ivry was decorating in the Palais Royal (e.g. Plates 22 and 23). We cannot exclude the possibility that the Duc's new room had considerable influence on Jardin, since it would have been the most recently-completed grand interior he could have seen in Paris before he departed for Copenhagen early in the New Year, 1755. Jardin was also a friend of the painter Le Lorrain who, already in May of the previous year, had designed the Åkerö dining-room (Plate 15) but there is no reason to suppose that a professional architect like Jardin, who had been through the same schooling in Rome, should have been much influenced by so slender a talent as that of Le Lorrain.

For further information about the history of this room see Mario Krohn, *Frankrigs og Danmarks kunstneriske Forbindelse i det 18. Aarhundrede*, vol. I, Copenhagen, 1922, pages 118–29, and C. Elling, *Amalienborg Interiører*, Copenhagen, 1945, pages 57–62. See also pages 33, 38, 48 and 57.

Plate 31

THE HÔTEL DE CHAVANNES, PARIS. Built between August 1758 and May 1760 after designs by Pierre-Louis Moreau-Desproux. *Drawing in the Musée Carnavalet, Paris.*

Michel Gallet has established the exact date of this house which lay between the Boulevard du Temple and the Rue Amelot (see pages 58–9). It was Moreau-Desproux's first commission after returning from Rome. The Père Laugier, the author of the essay on architectural theory entitled *Observations sur l'architecture* published in 1765, was inspired by this building which was extremely advanced for its date. Yet, while praising the architect's undoubted talents, he criticised him for having used a frieze of key-fretting to mark the separation between the two storeys and for using pilasters instead of columns. Dezallier d'Argenville drew attention to the building in the fifth edition of his guide to Paris (*Voyage pittoresque de Paris*, 1770) and remarks on 'l'élégance de sa décoration & la pureté de ses ornemens' ('the elegance and the purity of style adopted in its decoration'). The building was demolished in 1846.

Plates 32 and 33

THE COURTYARD FRONT AND A DETAIL OF THE STABLE BLOCK AT THE HÔTEL DE VAREY, LYONS. Designed by Toussaint-Noël Loyer and begun in 1758.

A document dated 1st September 1758 and kindly communicated to me by Monsieur F. R. Cottin (see Loyer's biography, page 204) shows that the house was then under construction, while a second document dated 1st May 1760 reveals that it was by then completed.

In its entirety, this house in Lyons must have seemed strikingly modern, when it was newly built, although the front facing the street was considerably less advanced in style than the interior and the façades in the courtyard. For instance, the street fronts had balconies with wrought-iron balustrades in the purest Rococo taste. The scrolled terminals of the hinge-plates on the stable door (Plate 33) was certainly intended to be a novel feature, and the six rather out-size *guttae* under the window-surround also betray a quite new spirit. The Classical detailing of the steps, terrace and doorway (Plate 32) is also rather exaggerated and perhaps rather dilettante. Loyer had studied under Soufflot, during the latter's stay in Lyons, and had assisted with the erection of the Hôtel Dieu. His knowledge of Classical ornament was probably derived from this second-hand source and not from genuine Classical monuments. See also page 48.

Plate 34

THE SALON AT THE HÔTEL DE VAREY, LYONS. Decorated about 1760 after designs by Toussaint-Noël Loyer.

The room is 7.35 metres long and 6.07 across. It is on an elevated ground-floor with French-windows opening on to small balconies—two facing the Place Bellecour and two facing the Rue Auguste Comte. The wall-panelling is of wood, painted white and partially gilt. However, the medallions are executed in white stucco. The chimney-piece is of mottled red marble and the parquet of oak. One does not know how the ceiling originally looked.

The decoration of this room is closely knit and has much in common with the seventeenth-century tradition for tightly-packed mural ornament. However, there are fewer elements and each is drawn on rather a large scale. Moreover, the vertical and horizontal components have been accentuated. The composition has thus acquired a somewhat schematic appearance—a feature of the Neo-Classical façade facing the courtyard, as well (Plate 32). The building was designed to house several families and contains several apartments, each with its richly-decorated salon. The other rooms, however, are most reticent in their decoration.

When Loyer addressed the Lyons Academy on the subject of modern interior-decoration, in January 1762 (see pages 257–60), he made it clear that he had already then designed and built at least three salons in various houses, all presumably in the new taste. The salon he describes in greatest detail has not been identified; it cannot have been that in the Hôtel de Varey but it must have possessed something of the same character. It had Doric, not Ionic, pilasters but the dimensions were much the same. See also Rogatien Le Nail, *Lyon, architecture et décoration aux 17e et 18e siècles*, Paris, n.d., pages 45–6.

Plate 35

SALON AT THE HÔTEL DE TOUROLLES. Executed about 1758–59, after designs by Etienne-Louis Boullée.

The mural-decorations of this room in the Tourolle family-house in the Rue d'Orléans (now Rue de Charlot No. 10), are normally said to date from the mid-1760s but are discussed in the issue of *L'Avant-coureur* of 21st January 1760.

The room was moved in the middle of the last century to a house in the Rue du Faubourg Saint-Honoré and is now in the possession of the *Cercle Interallié*. The present chimney-piece is of later date. The over-doors originally contained oval medallions with allegorical scenes representing the Four Seasons painted by Deshays who had also decorated the ceiling with a Triumph of Venus.

As far as is known, this is the earliest surviving Neo-Classical room in Paris but similar rooms must have existed at the time—for instance, at the Hôtel de Chavannes (Plate 31) and in the Hôtel de Persan which lay opposite (see page 59).

For further information about the Hôtel de Tourolles, see F. Contet, ed., *Les vieux hôtels de Paris*, série 20, pages 11–12, (text by Paul Jarry), 1930. See also page 48.

Plate 36

DESIGN FOR A TAPESTRY. Painted in 1758 by Maurice Jacques after a sketch by Jacques-Germain Soufflot. *Musée de la Manufacture des Gobelins.*

Novel features of this design are the wide border with its Classical ornaments and the regularity of the composition with its oval and rectangular panels linked by garlands. The panels contain representations of paintings by Boucher. This design offers alternative border-designs, at top and bottom, and two proposals for the training of the garlands.

Jacques, who was the Gobelins' accredited painter of ornament, also executed in 1762 a painted design showing a complete room hung with such tapestries and with a set of chairs and a *canapé* covered with the same material—all *en suite*. There was also a bed hung with the same material. As Eileen Harris has pointed out (*The Furniture of Robert Adam*, London, 1963, page 10) it is possible that the chairs, for which Soufflot presumably also made sketch-designs, had backs of oval shape to echo the medallions of the wall-hangings. A water-colour sketch for a similar wall-hanging has been discovered among the Earl of Jersey's papers at Osterley Park where a room is still hung with tapestries of this type woven at Les Gobelins in 1775. It is marked in *pieds* and was probably in the nature of a prospectus showing what the firm could offer. No chairs are shown in this sketch which confines itself to the rectangular hanging.

From 1764 onwards, a comparatively large number of sets of tapestry were woven after this general scheme which had the great advantage of being extremely flexible in that hangings of various sizes could be woven with the minimum of adjustment to the cartoons. The factory could thereby satisfy the individual requirements of its customers at no great extra cost. This was particularly important by this period when tapestries were usually fixed permanently to the wall and therefore needed to fit accurately the particular space available. See also pages 61 and 86.

Plate 37

DESIGN FOR THE FRONT OF A HOUSE. Drawn by J.-F. de Neufforge in or before 1758 and engraved by him for publication as Plate 87 in his *Recueil Elémentaire d'Architecture*, vol. II.

The second volume of the *Recueil*, which comprises seventy-two Plates (Nos. 73–144), was placed before the *Académie d'Architecture* on 20th November 1758. One may presume that the Plates for this volume were not engraved until those for the first volume (Nos. 1–72) had been finished—that is to say, not before

5th September 1757, when the first volume was published, or thereabouts. One cannot say when the original drawings for the engravings were executed; perhaps they were made already in 1756 (see Note to Plates 28 and 29). See also page 47.

Plate 38

MONUMENT TO MADAME LALIVE DE JULLY IN THE CHURCH OF SAINT-ROCH, PARIS. Executed in 1754 by Etienne-Maurice Falconet. Drawing by Carl Wilhelm Carlberg. *Röhsska Museum, Gothenburg.*

This monument to Lalive's first wife, who died in 1752, was erected in a special chapel in the church. Opposite was an altar with a painting by L.-J. Le Lorrain showing St. Catherine. The epitaph was removed from the church during the Revolution but the portrait medallion was later returned and re-erected in the church but in a different position—where it may still be seen. The monument has hitherto only been known from an anonymous and unfinished drawing in the Musée Carnavalet (see L. Reau, *Falconet*, Plate XXXIV). The present drawing, made by a Swedish architect who was in Paris in 1778, is more detailed and quotes the inscription which gives the year of its completion—a fact not previously known.

After the monument had been set up, it was said that Lalive had designed it himself but Falconet denied this with some vehemence. All the same, the general style coincides very much with that in which Le Lorrain was to design the furniture for Lalive not long afterwards (see page 68) and this suggests that the style at least was that favoured by Lalive. See also pages 46 and 53.

Plate 39

DESIGN FOR A MONUMENT TO THE MARÉCHAL DE BELLE-ISLE. Drawn by Augustin Pajou in 1761. *Cooper Union Museum for the Arts of Decoration, New York.*

This allegorical composition shows the Marshal, having entered the tomb, being greeted by his wife and son who had predeceased him. The Angel of Death is closing the door of the tomb—a reference to the fact that the Marshal was the last of his line. The monument was never executed.

The figures reveal the influence of Roman Baroque sculpture, notably that of Bernini. But the architectural features are entirely Neo-Classical in taste. This symmetrical composition is viewed from directly in front, and consists of several cuboidal elements of the utmost simplicity. The proportions are reminiscent of those embodied in Lalive de Jully's furniture (cf. Plates 85 to 89).

Plates 40 and 41

TWO DESIGNS FOR SEPULCHURAL MONUMENTS. Drawn and engraved by Raux; dated 1758.

Raux was established as a private teacher of architecture and, otherwise, is only known for having published various sets of designs for fountains, monuments and so forth (see Gallet, *Demeures*, pages 27 and 198).

Plates 42 and 43

CATAFALQUE FOR THE KING AND QUEEN OF SPAIN. (Plate 43 shows the decoration of the ceiling.) Erected for the memorial service held on 15th January 1760 in Notre-Dame. Designed by Michel-Ange Slodtz. Engraved by A. Martinet.

The decorations erected in the church on this occasion were elaborate and were couched in the new style. The *Mercure de France* (February 1760, page 215) informed its reader that 'Toute cette décoration étoit dans le goût antique' ('The entire scheme is couched in the Antique taste'). The Gothic arches of the choir were entirely masked by an arcade of Ionic pilasters of scagliola with gilded details. Between the pilasters were draped hangings 'rayés d'hermine' ('striped with ermine'). An altar of white scagliola stood in a niche, and the catafalque was placed at the entrance to the choir. Its decoration echoed that of the mural-ornaments; the Ionic columns were of green scagliola with gilded bases and capitals, while the remainder was of yellow scagliola with gilded ornaments. The pyramid above was of imitation *brêche violette* on a pedestal of white scagliola. This catafalque formed a surround for the porphyry-like sarcophagus on which lay a pall embroidered in gold.

A description of this catafalque appeared in *L'Année Littéraire* (1760, I s.325–329). The author was most enthusiastic about Slodtz's creation and bemoaned the fact that the monument could not be preserved. He furthermore says that 'Dans toute cette décoration, on n'a vû aucun de ces ornemens mesquins qu'on prodigue d'ordinaire pour masquer par une richesse apparente une pauvreté réelle, aucune de ces petites imaginations que quelques modernes avoient mises en vogue, aucun de ces colifichets qui dégradent la majesté de l'Architecture Greque & Romaine, aucune de ces formes tortueuses si long-temps regardées comme les efforts du génie: tout étoit grand, simple, noble & vraiment riche.' ('In this whole scheme of decoration one sees none of those mean ornaments that are generally allowed to proliferate in order to hide the poverty of invention with apparent richness. Nor are there any of those silly inventions that certain modern artists have brought into fashion, none of those gewgaws that so degrade the majesty of Greek and Roman architecture, none of those contorted shapes that have for so long been regarded as the products of true genius. Everything in this scheme is majestic, simple, noble and veritably rich'.) See also page 34.

Plate 44

STUCCO CEILING IN PIERRE DE MONLONG'S VILLA NEAR LYONS. Executed in 1760–61 after a design by the painter François Boucher.

My attention has been drawn by Madame Roches-Jauneau, Director of the Musée des Beaux-Arts at Lyons, to some papers in private hands that have not yet been published in which it is made clear that the *échevin*, Pierre de Monlong, ordered a set of designs for the mural and ceiling decorations of a dining-room at his villa outside Lyons. The drawings apparently survive. The work was carried out by a local painter and has now been transferred to the Musée des Beaux-Arts in that city. The present photograph was taken before the room was moved. This Classical ornament bears witness to Boucher's versatility as an artist and reminds us that he did much excellent work devising scenery for the theatre, in addition to all his other activities. See also page 60.

Plate 45

DETAIL OF PAINTED DECORATION IN A CHAPEL IN THE CHURCH OF SAINTE-MARGUERITE, PARIS. Executed about 1763–64 by Gaetano Brunetti after designs by Victor Louis.

This little chapel was dedicated to the Souls of True Believers and the intention was to make it resemble a proper church. The illusory plan was that of an Early Christian basilica with central nave flanked by rows of columns (in this case—of the Ionic Order with fluted shafts) and aisles. The vaulted, coffered ceiling, on the other hand, seems to derive from the Renaissance style of Alberti. Above the columns run friezes with simulated bas-reliefs depicting the Death of Jacob on one side and his body being taken up to Cana. Between the columns are representations of white marble statues symbolising the Stages of Life and the transient nature of Man's Mortality. In front of the archivolt is depicted, on each side of the nave a sarcophagus surmounted by an urn, all supported by a pair of columns. The altar takes the form of an Early Christian sarcophagus and on it stood a pair of *lampadaires* in the Antique taste.

If considered as the design for a full-scale church, this scheme is quite revolutionary, even if it must be admitted that several young French architects were by this time thinking along similar lines; none of their work had so far been executed, however. Another early essay was to be Louis-François Trouard's Saint-Symphorien at Versailles (1770). The doctrinaire modernist, Le Père Laugier, praised this chapel exceedingly. He claimed that 'cette Chapelle fait beaucoup d'effet par la simplicité de l'ordonnance & par la grande manière qui régne dans tous les ornemens. Ce n'est qu'une Architecture feinte. Que seroit-ce si elle étoit exécuté en réalité? Telle qu'elle est, c'est un des plus beaux desseins d'Architecture que nous ayons à Paris' ('This chapel makes its great impact through the simplicity of its disposition and the grand manner which pervades all its ornaments. It is nothing more than a make-believe structure. What would it be like if it had been erected in earnest? Even in its present guise, it is one of the most beautiful architectural compositions that we have here in Paris'; *Observations sur l'architecture*, 1765, page 115). See also p. 53.

Plate 46

DESIGN FOR A VILLA. Designed about 1760 by J.-F. de Neufforge, and engraved by him for publication in his *Recueil Elémentaire d'Architecture*. Plate 237 in the fourth volume.

This volume was laid before the Académie Royale d'Architecture on 7th December 1761. Since the author himself did the engraving of all the numerous plates in this ambitious work, one may presume that the drawings for this and the subject of the next illustration existed a year or two before that date.

This building is completely square with four equal façades, each with a flight of steps leading up to an entrance flanked by two columns. Palladio's Villa Rotunda appears to have been a source of inspiration.

Plate 47

DESIGN FOR A VILLA. Plate 253 in Volume IV of Neufforge's *Recueil Elémentaire* (see Plate 46).

This and Plate 46, as well as the design reproduced here as Plate 37, display elements that derive from Palladio and were also incorporated by Gabriel in his Petit Trianon (see Plates 50 and 51).

Plate 48

THE VILLA OF MADAME LEPRÊTRE DE NEUBOURG, PARIS. Built in 1762 after designs by Marie-Joseph Peyre. Engraving by Michel Loyer.

When Peyre was not more than thirty-five years old, he published a book under the not exactly modest title of *Oeuvres d'Architecture de Marie-Joseph Peyre* (1765) which he dedicated to the Marquis de Marigny describing it as the 'fruit de mes Etudes en Italie' ('fruit of his studies in Italy'). He said of this design that 'J'ai orné la Façade de Colomnes formant le Pérystile, comme le sont la plûpart des Cazins Italiens, afin de lui donner le jeu & le mouvement qui rendent en général l'effet de ces sortes de Bâtimens très-agréable; on en voit un très-grand nombre d'exemples dans Palladio.' ('I have decorated the façade with columns that form a peri-style like those to be seen on most Italian casinos. This lends it a playfulness, a rhythm, that tend to produce an exceedingly pleasing effect in that type of building—one sees many examples in the work of Palladio'.)

The house lay on the southern outskirts of Paris in the area then known as the Clos Payen, between the present Boulevard Auguste Blanqui (No. 68) and the Rue Corvisart (No. 54). It was demolished in 1909. See also page 60.

Plate 49

ENTRANCE TO THE HÔTEL DE GAMACHES. Built before October 1762, architect unknown. *Archives Nationales*, $Z^2$2459.

The drawing is dated October 1762, and the inscription informs us that the entrance to the house lay in the Rue Saint-Lazare. The contractor's name was Pierre Gillet Habert but there is no reason to suppose that he designed the house as well (see Gallet, *Demeures*, page 63). See also page 60.

Plates 50 to 53

THE PETIT TRIANON. Built about 1763–67 after designs by Ange-Jacques Gabriel.

The building is square in plan. Each façade is divided into five equal intervals. The three principal façades have projecting centre-sections, two of which are decorated with Corinthian pilasters and the third with Ionic. On account of the different levels on the site, only two of the three storeys can be seen on the north and west fronts. The south front opens into a *cour d'honneur*.

The Petit Trianon is comparatively small and is not therefore built in the imposing style which would have been adopted for any larger royal edifice—or, indeed, for any large public building, like the two palais which Gabriel built on the Place de la Concorde (Plate 19). If this point is borne in mind, it will be appreciated that the Petit Trianon does not represent any radical change in Gabriel's style although he has obviously been seeking to establish a purer Classical idiom. It is particularly in the handling of the actual wall-surfaces that one senses the development; these have acquired greater significance, and the cuboidal aspect of the building is further stressed by the fact that there are no ornaments on the balustrade which runs round the edge of the roof.

Fiske Kimball (*Creation*, figs. 270–1), published two preliminary elevations which reveal that Gabriel originally intended to divide each façade into three sections decorated with columns and pilasters that would have produced a less restful effect. The rhythm would have been counter-pointed by a central window with a segmental pediment. When compared with the final design, this would have produced an old-fashioned, almost Baroque effect and would have represented a step backwards rather than forwards in Gabriel's stylistic development. A similar uncertainty is to be seen in the various projects Gabriel put forward for the new Opera-hall at Versailles (Plates 61 and 74). Who was hesitant—the King or Gabriel? It can hardly have been the latter.

In Neufforge's *Recueil* are included some projects (Plates 37, 46 and 47) which are reminiscent of the final appearance of the Petit Trianon. Neufforge's designs are earlier than Gabriel's first proposals for the house but it is inconceivable that this sixty-five year-old royal architect should have required the assistance of a dry pendant like Neufforge; he must have been at least as able to draw on Palladio for inspiration as the next man, even though he had never himself been to Italy.

See Plates 66 and 67 for illustrations of the interior. See also page 61.

Plate 54

PROPOSAL FOR A CHIMNEY-PIECE. Designed about 1760–64 by Louis-Félix de la Rue. Engraved and published by Ph. L. Parizeau in 1771.

De la Rue died in 1764 so this and his related designs cannot have been made later. How much earlier than that it was executed, it is difficult to say. Parizeau published several hundred designs in this same style in the 1770s. They cannot all have been drawn in the last months before de la Rue's death. If one recalls that many of Neufforge's Neo-Classical engravings (see Plates 28 and 29) were available for sale by 1756, it seems fair to conclude that de la Rue's compositions were being produced four or five years before 1764.

Plate 55

DRAWING OF CHIMNEY-PIECE IN MADAME DE POMPADOUR'S BED-CHAMBER AT SAINT-HUBERT. Executed between 1756 and 1765, presumably under the supervision of Gabriel. Drawing by an unknown hand. *Archives Nationales*, o^1 1886.

This entirely Classical chimney-piece is of mottled red marble and has been re-erected in the Petit Trianon, in the so-called *Cabinet de retraite du Roi* which later came to be known as the *Chambre de Marie-Antoinette*. It was probably set up there in the 1760s when that building was under construction. The drawing is inscribed 'Brocatelle, Elle avoit Ettée faite pour La chambre a Coucher de Mdme. de pompadour a St. hubert' ('Brocatelle marble; this has been made for the bed-chamber of Mme. de Pompadour at St. Hubert') and the chimney-piece must therefore have been made before her death in April 1764, but how long before is uncertain. It may have existed by 1762 when an inventory of the contents of Saint-Hubert was made (Archives Nationales o^1 3438), and possibly even as early as 1758 when Lazare Duvaux supplied furniture for Madame de Pompadour's bed-chamber at the house—including a pair of fire-dogs which would suggest that a fireplace already existed (Livre-Journal, No. 3128). Our knowledge about this little hunting-lodge is all too slender but much indicates that it was decorated in a rather progressive manner (cf. Plate 203 and pages 58 and 62).

The chimney-piece is discussed by Verlet in his book on *Versailles* (page 590).

Plates 56 to 58

PROPOSALS FOR MURAL-DECORATION. Drawn by François-Dominique Barreau de Chefdeville between 1760 and 1765. *Archives Nationales, N III Gironde* 37.

The drawings were first discussed in F. G. Pariset's article on Barreau de Chefdeville (*Bulletin de la Société de l'Histoire de l'Art Français*, 1962–63, pages 77–99) who executed them for Charles-Robert Boutin, *intendant* at Bordeaux, when the decoration of his official residence in that city was under consideration. These sober, Neo-Classical schemes of decoration probably give a good idea of the style Barreau used at this same time (about 1761) when decorating the *Cabinet Flamand* in Lalive de Jully's Parisian apartment in the Rue de Menars, where the furniture designed by Le Lorrain about 1756 was to stand (see Plates 85 to 89). The bed shown in Plate 58 has pine-cone finials very like those of Lalive's chair (Plate 322) and *cartonnier* (Plate 89). See also pages 61 and 142.

Plate 59

THE CHURCH OF SAINT-NICOLAS AT NÉRAC (LOT-ET-GARONNE). Building started in 1762. Designed by Barreau de Chefdeville and Oudot de Maclaurin.

According to Pariset, who has investigated the history of this interesting building, the façade had reached a height of some twenty-four feet when Barreau died in 1765 and about thirty-two feet (just above the top niches) by February of the following year. This suggests that the simplicity and clarity of this composition was due to Barreau. The towers were designed by Maclaurin, Barreau's close friend, who probably respected the latter's intentions. Work was discontinued several times and the church was not in fact completed until the 1850s. See also pages 32 and 53.

Plate 60

THE FONTAINE DES HAUDRIETTES. Built in 1764 after a design by Pierre-Louis Moreau-Desproux.

The City of Paris acquired a site at the corner of the Rue des Vieilles-Haudriettes and what is now the Rue des Archives, in May 1763. This fountain was presumably designed in that year, when Moreau was also appointed *maître des bâtiments de la Ville de Paris.* The markedly sculptural form of this structure seems to owe something to typical Italian Baroque pedestals or plinths—which Moreau would of course have seen during his student-years in Rome. This edifice must have struck Parisians as a bold reply to Bouchardon's sensuous Fontaine des Innocents.

Plate 61

DESIGN FOR THE OPERA-HALL AT VERSAILLES. Original drawing by Ange-Jacques Gabriel, dated February 1763. *Archives Nationales*, o[1] 1786.

Gabriel produced a number of designs for his new opera-hall which was to be built in the Palace at Versailles. The space for it had already been allocated by Louis XIV. Gabriel's earliest proposals were in the Rococo style. Building was started and continued fitfully until halted by the Seven Years' War. When the war ended in 1763, the work was taken up again and the present design belongs to this phase. (It was first published by Pierre Verlet in *Le Jardin des Arts*, July 1957.) The design was not carried out but, like the Petit Trianon, it shows to what degree Gabriel—and the King, Louis XV—had adopted a classicising style by this date. The style is simpler and less over-powering than that used in French palace-interiors during the seventeenth century; but it had not yet been refined to the degree that was to be attained subsequently. A later project for this room, where a bold row of tall Ionic columns is introduced, is shown in Plate 74. See also pages 54 and 122.

Plate 62

THE HÔTEL D'UZÈS. Modernised about 1764–67 by C.-N. Ledoux. Old photograph taken before 1870 (reproduced by Marcel Raval, *Claude-Nicolas Ledoux*, fig. 13).

This house lay in the northern part of the Marais quarter near the Boulevard Poissonnière where the present Rue d'Uzès lies. It was pulled down in 1870. Ledoux's task was to modernise completely a seventeenth century house; he seems to have had to retain the original outer walls and the regular articulation of the façades. However, he managed to alter the exterior of the old building in many ways to bring it into line with Neo-Classical ideals. For example, he simplified the decoration, he provided windows and doorways with severely rectangular or semi-circular openings, and added gigantic Classical columns and pilasters. The house was not really suited to such treatment and the result was not particularly felicitous. All the same, Ledoux's exercise was of considerable significance and novelty; it was noticed and praised by, amongst others, J.-F. Blondel who was by that time an old man. When Ledoux published drawings of this house, many years later in his *De l'architecture considérée sous le rapport de l'art, des moeurs et de la législation*, I–II, 1804–47, he 'improved' its appearance in various ways so as to give it an even more modern look than it actually had at the time he carried out the work (see W. Hermann, 'The Problem of Chronology in Claude-Nicolas Ledoux's Engraved Works', *The Art Bulletin*, September 1960, and J. Langner, 'Ledoux' Redaktion der eigenen Werke für die Veröffentlichung', *Zeitschrift für Kunstgeschichte* 1960, pages 136–66). Designs for the interior are reproduced in Plates 64 and 65. See also page 62.

Plate 63

DESIGN FOR MURAL-DECORATION IN A DINING-ROOM. Drawn before 1765 by G.-P.-M. Dumont, engraved by J.-B. Richard.

According to the Bibliothèque Nationale, Département des Estampes, *Inventaire du fonds français, graveurs du dix-huitième siècle*, Marcel Roux (vol. 2, page 483, No. 40), this engraving was published in

1765. Dumont published a list of his works on 24th January 1765 (see The University of Michigan Museum of Art, *Architectural and Ornament Drawings*, 1965, No. 32) and it seems reasonable to assume that the original drawing was in existence at least a year earlier. Dumont's designs bear some resemblance to Neufforge's. Since the latter engraved some of Dumont's other architectural drawings, it is likely that these two architects knew each other.

Stoves like that depicted in the niche came into favour during the eighteenth century in France, replacing open fire-places. They might be made of terracotta, faïence, or stucco and were serviced from a room behind. These prominent fixtures offered considerable scope to decorators and architects. During the Neo-Classical period, many such stoves were given a monumental character, as in this instance. Lalive de Jully had a stove in his apartment in the Rue de Menars, to which he moved in 1762; it is known to have had a body in the form of a Classical column. It was probably not unlike the one illustrated here although it was surmounted by a terracotta figure of Iphigenia modelled by Michel-Ange Slodtz (see *Catalogue historique du cabinet de peinture et sculpture françoise de M. de Lalive*, 1764, page 17). See also page 61.

Plate 64

DESIGN FOR MURAL-DECORATION AT THE HÔTEL D'UZÈS. Probably drawn by Pierre-Noël Rousset in 1765. *Archives Nationales, N III Seine, 1265.*

This and the next illustration belong to a group of drawings which have been attributed to C. N. Ledoux. However, Michel Gallet, who has undertaken a study of the history of the building of this house, has kindly informed the present author that documentary evidence has now come to light indicating that the drawings are *not* by Ledoux. They must therefore be by Rousset and Cherpitel, who were paid a fee by the Duc d'Uzès in 1765 for putting forward designs for the house. Gallet believes this drawing to be by Rousset and the design shown in Plate 65 to be by Cherpitel (see Michel Gallet, 'Le salon de l'Hôtel d'Uzès', *Bulletin du Musée Carnavalet*, 22e année, 1969, No. 2 (1971)). See also Plates 396 to 398.

This is the earliest known example of the revival in France of the arabesque for mural-decoration (see the two panels). These present ornaments seem to derive from both Ducerceau and from Raphael's famous grotesques in the Vatican. Some of Ducerceau's engravings and seventeenth-century engravings of Raphael's compositions were republished in 1765 by Jombert in a work entitled *Répertoire des Artistes*, vol. 2 [see page 40]. See also page 63.

Plate 65

DESIGN FOR MURAL-DECORATION FOR HÔTEL D'UZÈS. Probably drawn by Mathurin Cherpitel in 1765. *Archives Nationales, N III Seine, 1265.*

See the previous entry and also Plates 396 to 398.

Plate 66

THE SALON DE COMPAGNIE AT THE PETIT TRIANON. Decorated in 1767–68 with panelling carved in Honoré Guibert's workshops, probably on the basis of general designs by Gabriel.

The walls were originally painted white and had no gilding. The chimney-piece is of mottled red marble. None of the furniture now in the room is original to it.

Quentin-Claude Pitoin provided a pair of gilt bronze fire-dogs which the accounts indicate must have been in the Neo-Classical taste. They consisted of small fluted pedestals of square section, on which were draped lion's skins, surmounted by Classical vases festooned with garlands of oak-leaves. There must also have been sconces in the room, at least flanking the chimney-glass, but their form is not known. The window-curtains were of 'damas de Gênes cramoisy' and the same material was used for upholstering the forty-four chairs, the folding screen and the fire-screen, as well as a *portière* for one of the doors. All this furniture was provided by the upholsterer (*maître et marchand-tapissier*) Claude-François Capin but the chair-frames were made for him by Nicolas-Quinibert Foliot and their carved decoration was executed by Toussaint Foliot, Nicolas' brother. The carved ornament was Classical in style echoing that on the walls. The chairs, however, had legs of cabriole form. These were described as being 'à rouleaux' (i.e. with scrolled toes). None of these chairs have been identified to date but they probably resembled those shown in Plates 160 to 163 or 179 and 180. See also pages 62, 122 and 126.

Plate 67

DETAIL OF A CARVED PANEL IN THE ROOM JUST DISCUSSED. Carved about 1767–68.

Plates 68 and 69

PROPOSALS FOR MURAL-DECORATION AT THE HÔTEL MÉLUSINE. Drawn by Henri Piètre in 1766. *Archives Nationales.*

The Hôtel Mélusine (now No. 6, Rue des Valois) was once part of the Palais Royal complex, and Henri Piètre must have drawn these designs in his capacity of Assistant Chief Architect to the Duc d'Orléans. The Duc's mistress, Madame de Montesson, was subsequently installed in these apartments but it is not known whether these proposed decorations were executed beforehand. In any case, these designs are of interest on account of their unmistakable and somewhat uncompromising Neo-Classical character. Attention was first drawn to them by Michel Gallet (see *Bulletin du Musée Carnavalet*, June 1960). See also Plates 399 and 400 and page 63.

Plate 70

PROPOSAL FOR THE DECORATION OF A BOUDOIR IN THE ROYAL PALACE AT WARSAW. Dated 'Paris, 1766'. Attributed to Victor Louis. *University Library, Warsaw.*

Victor Louis and Jean-Louis Prieur's Neo-Classical redecoration of the Warsaw Palace were largely destroyed already in the eighteenth century and are today only known through a series of designs deposited in the Library of Warsaw University which were shown in an exhibition that visited both Bordeaux and Paris in 1958 and 1959, largely due to the initiative of Stanislas Lorentz and François-Georges Pariset who had made a far-reaching study of the material (see their articles listed in the biography of Victor Louis, page 203). Other designs connected with this enterprise are reproduced in Plates 205 to 207 and 402 to 423.

The present drawing is not signed but Lorentz and Pariset ascribe it to Victor Louis who was placed in charge of the extensive programme of redecoration which was carried out in the second half of the 1760s in the Palace (see page 63). It is not easy to decide which designs were provided by Louis and which by Prieur but the detail-drawing for the *casolettes* (perfuming pans) above the niches (Plate 412) and for the sofa (Plate 411) have been attributed to the latter. Whatever the case, Victor Louis must have had the final say in all the questions of design. It is known that the Marquis de Marigny was shown the designs for the Palace and declared himself highly satisfied with them. (See page 188.)

The designs were executed in Paris during 1765 and 1766; the panelling, furniture, bronzes, upholstery etc. was then prepared in Paris between 1766 and 1768. It took many years before these splendid creations reached Poland, however.

The panelling, incidentally, was made by a *menuisier* named Jadot and we happen to have a view of his workshops in an engraving by Chenu, taken from a drawing by J. F. Amand which was shown at the *Salon* of 1767—the very time when work for the Polish Court must have been on Jadot's benches. Indeed, a journeyman is shown working on a door with panels decorated in the Neo-Classical style and it is not impossible that this was part of the commission intended for Warsaw. (See Seznec and Adhémar, *Diderot Salons*, vol. III, fig. 61.)

Plate 71

DESIGN FOR A PAIR OF CHIMNEY-PIECES TO BE INSTALLED IN THE 'CHAMBRE DES PORTRAITS' IN THE WARSAW PALACE. Dated 'Paris 1766'. Ascribed to Jean-Louis Prieur. *The University Library*, *Warsaw*.

The two identical chimney-pieces were made of grey marble by a statuary named Adam and had gilt bronze mounts provided by Philippe Caffieri. It is interesting that the chimney-opening is provided with a pair of bronze doors which are treated as an integral part of the design. It had long been the practice to fit a 'chimney-board' into the opening of fire-places in summer or when the fire was not in use, especially in bed-chambers. These were usually humble structures of wood or of painted canvas, and have therefore usually been lost. Hinged metal doors like those illustrated were a great refinement.

An estimate of costs incurred by August 1768 in the great Warsaw undertaking (Archives Nationales, Z^{1J} 921) show that these chimney-pieces were not then quite finished and that several changes had been made to the design since this drawing was made in 1766. For instance the ponderous garlands on the bronze doors had been replaced by four rosettes placed at the corners.

The mounts and the pair of doors cost no less than 7,000 livres per chimney-piece and each unit was only 1.13 metres high!

For a discussion of the authorship of the drawing, see the previous Note.

Plate 72

THE HÔTEL D'HALLWYL, COUR D'HONNEUR. Designed about 1766 by C.-N. Ledoux.

The drawings for the renovation of this house were sent to the Paris planning authorities for approval on 14th June 1766, so Ledoux's work was presumably done during the early months of that year (see Gallet, *Demeures*, page 188). The front of the house, facing on to the narrow Rue Michel Le Comte is difficult to photograph satisfactorily but is in the same style as the courtyard front shown here.

The dominant character of the flat wall-surfaces stresses the block-like structure. The illustration published years later by Ledoux in his *De l'architecture considérée sons le rapport de l'art, des moeurs et de la législation* (1804–47) is not correct, as in the case of the front of the Hôtel d'Uzès (see Note to Plate 62). See also page 64.

Plate 73

DESIGN FOR A BATH-NICHE. According to the inscription, this drawing was executed for a Mr. Charton in April 1767. It is signed 'Loyer'. *École des Beaux-Arts*, *Paris* (*Collection Masson*).

Comparison of this signature with those of Toussaint Loyer in the Archives de l'Hôtel Dieu at Lyons seem to confirm that this drawing is actually the work of the Lyonnais architect who, amongst other things, built the Hôtel de Varey in that city (see Plates 32 to 34). 'Mr. Charton' may be identical with Jean Charton who was *conseiller du Roi en la Chancellerie près la Cour des Monnoies de Lyon* and was, like Loyer, attached to the La Charité hospital at Lyons.

Plate 74

DESIGN FOR THE OPERA-HALL WITHIN THE PALACE AT VERSAILLES. Pen and ink drawing by Pajou (?), about 1765–68. *Archives Nationales*, o[1] 1787.

As pointed out in the note to Plate 61, this theatre had been planned already under Louis XIV and Gabriel had put forward several proposals for it. In 1765, however, it seems to have been decided that the second floor should be decorated with a dominant colonnade and that the royal box should no longer be accentuated as it had so definitely been in Gabriel's earlier design. The present drawing may have been made to show the disposition of the various groups of sculpture which were to be executed in Pajou's workshops. The three groups of cherubs were dropped, as were the trophies flanking the central entrance. Decorative vases were placed in front of the bases of the columns instead. On 18th March 1768, Louis XV ordered his architects to have the hall completed so it could be inaugurated to celebrate the wedding of the Dauphin with Marie-Antionette which was to take place on 16th May 1770—twenty-two months later. See also pages 54 and 122.

Plate 75

THE SALON OF THE PAVILLON DE LA BOISSIÈRE. Decorated during the Spring of 1769 after designs provided by Guillaume-Martin Couture. Detail of an engraving by Le Rouge.

The wall-decoration of this small, circular room—known as the *Salon Apollon* or the *Salon de stuc*—was executed in scagliola by his stuccador Louis Mansiaux (Archives de la Seine, 5B[6]—2738 fol. 37 *verso*). The six female figures offering the fruits of the various climates to the Sun God were likewise of scagliola, partly gilded. The cornice was of imitation white marble. According to Mansiaux's account-book, there were medallions on the frieze and garlands on the six pedestals but these are not shown on this small illustration which is reproduced four times its actual size.

This pavilion was demolished early in the last century. It stood on Montmartre on what is now the Square Vintimille. It was built between 1751 and 1754 to the designs of Le Carpentier for Charles-François Gaillard de la Boissière, a *fermier-général.* It was one of the most famous of all the *petits maisons* in the Paris environs during the eighteenth century. Presumably the original decoration was in the Rococo style and it is known that two of the rooms retained their Rococo panelling until the house was pulled down. This little house was altered inside several times during the course of only a few years. Le Carpentier's pupil, Couture, carried out significant changes during the second half of the 1760s. The decoration illustrated here replaced a scheme which Mansiaux had installed only three years before, and which may have been somewhat like this; at any rate, it also included six female figures bearing baskets—a motif that was to become very popular—but the plan of the room was then oval. See also pages 55–6.

Plate 76

THE MARQUIS DE MARIGNY'S HOUSE AT ROULE. Built between 1768 and 1771 after designs by J.-G. Soufflot. Drawing by Sir William Chambers. *Royal Institute of British Architects.*

Marigny had already in 1759 bought a site at Roule, a suburb now swallowed up by the city of Paris; this lay at the junction of the present Rue du Faubourg Saint-Honoré and the Rue de Monceau. His chief residence was of course in the city and Roule only served as a summer retreat. During 1768, Soufflot prepared designs for the new house in consultation with Marigny. The foundations were laid and the walls were going up by the end of that year. The house was finally completed in 1771 and was demolished during the last century.

Chambers' drawing of the house, presumably executed in 1774, probably gives a more trustworthy impression than other better-known views. For example, we learn from it that the house had a hipped roof which was visible from the ground, and that it had banded rustication like buildings then being erected by Ledoux. (This drawing was first published by John Harris, 'Sir William Chambers and his Parisian Album', *Architectural History*, 6, 1963, fig. 15.)

Thiéry wrote in 1795 (*Paris*, vol. 1, page 64) that Soufflot had wanted to 'introduire le genre vénitien' ('to introduce the Venetian style') in the house. Indeed, it may well be that the building embodies recollections of Soufflot and Marigny's famous journey to Italy which began in 1749. The fenestration certainly has Italianate features.

At the entrance from the road Marigny planned to erect a pair of small pavilions similar in style to the main building. He wrote to Soufflot on 18th December 1768 that these were to be linked to the latter 'par une balustrade au-dessous de laquelle serait une porte mâle et carrée à la Michel-Ange' ('by a balustrade below which there will be a doorway of masculine and rigidly rectilinear character in Michel-Angelo's manner'; see Monval, *Soufflot*, page 400). As for the interior decoration, Marigny entrusted this building to Soufflot. On 12th June he wrote that 'Quant à la décoration je m'en raporte entierement à vous; je vous la demande d'aussi bon goût que la façade que vous m'avez donné' ('As for the decoration of the interior, I trust you entirely; I would like you to provide something in as good taste as the exterior you have already created'; Monval, op. cit., page 398). Clearly he expected the interior and furnishing to be in the Classical style. See also pages 36 and 64.

Plate 77

THE HOUSE OF MADEMOISELLE GUIMARD. Built between 1770 and 1773 after designs by C.-N. Ledoux. Drawing by Sir William Chambers. *Royal Institute of British Architects.*

The house lay on the Rue de la Chaussée d'Antin on the way up to Montmartre. It was built for Marie-Madeleine Guimard, a twenty-seven-year-old dancer at the *Opéra de Paris*, and paid for by the Maréchal de Soubise. According to Michel Gallet (*Demeures*, page 188), the design for it received approval in June 1770 and the building was completed in 1773. As is so often the case with those buildings by Ledoux which have disappeared, it is difficult to gain a proper impression of the appearance of this house (see Note to Plate 62), but the drawing reproduced here is probably a fair representation of it, and is anyway likely to be more faithful than the view shown in Ledoux's *Architecture* from which one gets the impression that the house had banded rustication overall and that the building was far more massive and block-like. See also page 66.

Plate 78

THE PAVILLON CARRÉ DE BEAUDOUIN. Built in 1770 and the following years, after designs by P.-L. Moreau-Desproux.

The house was erected for a man named Nicolas Carré de Beaudouin on the heights at Ménilmontant (it is now No. 121, Rue de Ménilmontant), with a fine view over Paris. Michel Gallet (*Demeures*, page 74) has been able to date it securely and to show that it was built by Moreau-Desproux, who had designed the Hôtel de Chavannes in 1758 and the Fontaine des Haudriettes in 1763–4 (Plates 31 and 60). Gallet has moreover pointed out the resemblance between this building and Palladio's now demolished Villa Ragona at Ghizzoda. See also page 66.

Plate 79

MADAME DU BARRY'S PAVILLON AT LOUVECIENNES. Designed by C.-N. Ledoux in 1770, erected in 1771. Drawing by Sir William Chambers. *Royal Institute of British Architects.*

An inscription on a drawing of the house by Moreau *le jeune* tells us that the house was first used on 2nd September 1771. Chambers illustrates the façade at the rear, facing the Seine. The structure has been sadly disfigured in more recent times by the addition of a superstructure. See also page 66.

Plate 80

THE DINING-ROOM AT THE PAVILLON DE LOUVECIENNES. Designed in 1770 by C.-N. Ledoux and built in 1771.

This is the little dining-room one sees in Moreau *le jeune*'s famous water-colour (Colour Plate B; a detail is shown here as Plate 474), which is dated 2nd September 1771. The room in fact served as a vestibule since it lay immediately beyond the apsoidal entrance and one passed through it to reach the main salon (through the door on the left).

The drawing shows that there were originally *portières* in front of all the doors, and festooned curtains hung above the balcony-boxes where spectators and musicians could sit.

The walls were decorated with sixteen Corinthian pilasters of grey scagliola which once had gilt bronze bases and capitals made in Gouthière's workshops—as were the door-handles and mirror-frames. There are looking-glasses between the pilasters and each one had a small semi-circular girandole suspended by a ribbon in front of it so that it appeared to be circular, due to the reflection. Above the mirror are reliefs with *putti*, trophies and Madame du Barry's coat-of-arms. See also page 66.

Plate 81

PARQUET IN THE DUC DE CHOISEUL'S HOUSE IN PARIS. Enlarged detail of a miniature by Louis-Nicolas van Blarenberghe, painted about 1770 and mounted on a gold snuff-box made by Louis Roucel bearing the date-mark for 1770–71. *French private collection.*

See the Note to Plate 463. The miniature shows the Duc's *Premier Cabinet*. This detail has been enlarged about ten times and the illustration is consequently rather indistinct. Yet it serves to show that the parquet had a Greek key-fret pattern round the edge. The other floors in the house were apparently just as advanced in taste, as far as we can judge from other miniatures on this box (see F. J. B. Watson, *The Choiseul Box* (1963), where the present miniature is shown in full as fig. 2). It has not yet been possible to establish exactly when these floors were laid. See also page 67.

Plate 82

THE SALON AT THE HÔTEL GRIMOD DE LA REYNIÈRE. Decorated between about 1772 and 1775 after designs by Charles-Louis Clérisseau. Part of a drawing by J. C. Kamsetzera executed in 1782. *The University Library, Cracow.*

This Hotel lay on the Rue Boissy d'Anglas (formerly the Rue Bonne Morue) near the Place de la Concorde. It was built during the late 1760s to the designs of Nicolas Barré. Eight panels painted on canvas with decorations that seem to be exactly like those shown are in the Victoria and Albert Museum in London, and are presumed to be the identical set although it is not known how they came to England. (See also Plates 83, 218 and 483.)

Various authorities have proposed dates for these mural-decorations, ranging from 1769 to 1782 (see E. Croft-Murray, 'The Hôtel Grimod de la Reynière: the Salon Decorations', *Apollo*, November 1963). However, the salon is first mentioned in the *Almanach historique et raisonné des architectes, peintres, sculpteurs, graveurs et cizeleurs* for 1777 (pages 84–6 and 188). In fact the censor's permission to print the work, which is printed at the end of the book in the normal way (page 248), is dated 23rd November 1776.

On the same and the next two pages is printed the wording of the royal *brevet* which empowered the author, L'Abbé Le Brun, to publish the work, 'qu'il desireroit faire imprimer & donner au Public' ('which he wished to have printed and published'). This is dated 29th November 1775. From this we can deduce that the manuscript for the almanac was at any rate ready by November 1776, and possibly by November 1775. It therefore seems that the salon at the Hôtel Grimod was finished by November 1776 and quite possibly some time before that. The manuscript may well have been prepared by the time the work received royal approbation, in which case the references to the salon must have been written some time beforehand. If one allows time for the work to be carried out as well, it is possible that Clérisseau's designs for this decoration were executed not later than 1774. Comparison with the projected decoration at the Hôtel d'Uzès (Plates 64 and 65) suggests, in fact, that the designs could date from as early as 1769—the year Clérisseau was elected a member of the Académie de la Peinture. However, the *Almanach* tells us that this salon had been 'nouvellement décoré' ('recently decorated'), so it would be safest to place it in the early 1770s until more definite information comes to light.

Confusion about the date of these mural-decorations is not diminished by the statement that it was Etienne de Lavallée Poussin who executed 'les peintures d'histoire' of the salon and the fact that this artist did not return to Paris from his stay in Italy until 1777! However, this information comes from Thiéry's *Guide des Amateurs* which only appeared in 1787; perhaps Thiéry was misinformed, or perhaps Lavallée painted the ceiling—or something quite different. See also page 66.

Plate 83

THE CARPET IN THE SALON OF THE HÔTEL GRIMOD DE LA REYNIÈRE. About 1772–75? Drawing by J. C. Kamsetzera. *The University Library, Cracow.*

(See Note to Plate 82.)

It is likely but not certain that this carpet was also designed by Clérisseau, probably about 1772–75. If one compares it with the Duc de Choiseul's parquet of about 1770 or just before (Plate 81), such a date is quite possible. There is a not dissimilar carpet in the front drawing-room at Syon House, made at Moorfields in 1769. See also page 67.

Plate 84

THE AMPHITHEATRE AT THE ÉCOLE DE CHIRURGIE. Designed and built by Jacques Gondoin between 1769 and 1786. Engraving by C. R. G. Poulleau, published as Plate XXIX in *Description des Écoles de Chirurgie . . . par M. Gondoin*, Paris, 1780.

The building was not entirely completed until 1786 but work went ahead quickly at first, as can be seen from a painting by Hubert Robert of 1773, a gouache by Demachy of 1774, and a water-colour by Gabriel de Saint-Aubin of the same year. (See Leon Binet and Pierre Vallery-Radot, *La Faculté de Médecine de Paris*, 1952.) Many of the large buildings of this extensive complex were erected by that time and the semi-dome depicted here was certainly completed. In September and October 1775, the chair-maker Louis Delanois delivered a consignment of furniture to the college, which rather suggests that some of the rooms were by then in service. See also page 143.

Plate 85

WRITING-TABLE AND FILING-CABINET. Designed by Louis-Joseph Le Lorrain; made for Ange-Laurent de Lalive de Jully, about 1756–7. Bronze mounts by Philippe Caffieri. *Musée Condé, Chantilly.* (See also Plates 86 to 89 and Colour Plate A.)

The mark of the *ébéniste* J.-F. Leleu is stamped underneath the table but the filing-cabinet is unmarked.

Presumably Leleu, who only became a *maître* in 1764, had the table in his workshops at some point for repairs. The actual construction of these two pieces seems to have been supervised by Caffieri and the name of the cabinet-maker who executed the woodwork is not yet known. (See pages 68–9, and the present author's article on 'Lalive de Jully's Furniture "à la grecque"' in the *Burlington Magazine*, August 1961, concerning the identification and dating of these pieces of furniture.) A corner of the table and a chair, made *en suite* but not yet discovered, are to be seen in Greuze's portrait of Lalive (Plate 322) which was shown at the *Salon* in 1759.

This furniture is veneered with ebony and sports elaborate bronze mounts. The inlaid stringing and the flutes on the legs are of ungilded brass or bronze. The same combination of materials is of course also characteristic of much so-called 'Boulle' furniture from the time of Louis XIV and, indeed, Mariette actually says that these pieces were 'dans le goût de ceux de Boulle' ('in the taste of those made by Boulle in former times'; *Abécédario*; article on Le Lorrain) although he later makes it clear that he is referring to the technique used and not the style. 'Il y a bien de la distance de ses ornements à ceux de Boulle', he writes ('There is a considerable difference between these decorative pieces and those made by Boulle'). When Lalive's furniture was sold in 1770, it was described in the sale-catalogue as being an 'ensemble de la plus grande conséquence à l'imitation du fameux Boule' ('an ensemble of the greatest importance made in imitation of work by the famous cabinet-maker, Boulle').

According to several contemporary sources, it was this suite of furniture—which includes the above-mentioned chair, an inkstand (Plate 86) and a clock (Plate 187)—that was the direct source of inspiration for the first phase of what we today call the Neo-Classical style in France and which then went by the name of 'le goût grec'. Lalive himself confirms this (see page 49). Cochin stated that it was largely because the Comte de Caylus had praised this group of furniture with so much enthusiasm that it came to enjoy such renown (see page 269).

Plate 86

INKSTAND. Gilt bronze. *Bibliothèque Communale, Versailles.*

We have a description of the inkstand belonging with Lalive de Jully's writing-table (Plate 85) in the catalogue of the sale of his effects in 1769, and it is depicted in Saint-Aubin's engraving of a portrait of him by Greuze (illustrated in the article by the present author referred to in the previous Note). It must have somewhat resembled that shown here, even though the quality of the chasing on Lalive's inkstand was probably much finer. The workmanship of the clock which belongs to this set is of a much higher standard (Plate 187).

A similar inkstand is in the Musée Nissim de Camondo (Cat. No. 370).

Plates 87 and 88

THE WRITING-TABLE also shown in Plate 85.

Plate 89

THE FILING-CABINET also shown in Plate 85.

A full-size photograph of the clock (or one identical to it) which once stood on the cabinet has been placed on top. Since this photograph was taken, the clock (Plate 187) has been bought by the Musée Condé and placed in the correct position (see Colour Plate A).

Plates 90 to 93

CYLINDER-TOP DESK, KNOWN AS 'LE BUREAU DU ROI LOUIS XV'. Started in 1760 by J.-F. Oeben; completed and delivered in May 1769 by J.-H. Riesener. *Château de Versailles.*

The complete documentation of this famous piece of furniture is given by Verlet in his *Mobilier Royal*, II (pages 65–75). The desk was ordered for the *Cabinet Intérieur du Roi* at Versailles. Already in that room were Gaudreaux's commode-like medal-cabinet, made in 1738, and the pair of corner-cupboards provided by Joubert in 1755 to accompany it. The red lacquer *bureau plât*, made in 1759 and now in the Metropolitan Museum, also stood there. These pieces, and the carved *boiseries* which are still in the room, were in a moderate version of the Rococo style with features that one might call almost Classical. The King himself must certainly have sanctioned their appearance, so the furniture in this room must to a large extent reflect his tastes. The desk was made specially to stand in the centre of the room.

One does not know who designed the desk. It is possible that Michel-Ange Slodtz made the preliminary sketches; in 1758, he had been appointed *dessinateur des Menus-Plaisirs*. Moreover his brothers—or one of them—had provided designs for the above-mentioned medal-cabinet. In style, the desk is in fact not unlike the altar made by Slodtz for the Cathedral at Vienne (Plate 12). The subtle mechanism operating the cylinder-top, with its pair of springs, can only have been the invention of Oeben who was a skilful engineer. The carcass and much of the marquetry was of course also produced in his workshops and his assistant, Wynant Stylen, is known to have worked on the marquetry. One of the Duplessis, the father or the son, produced the models for the mounts, some of which were ready by the time Oeben died in January 1763 (amongst other items 'quatre Termes, figures dans le goût grec' ('four terminal figures in the Grecian style') were finished; these were probably those to be seen in Plate 92). The bronzes were cast by Etienne Forestier and chased by Louis-Barthelemy Hervieu. It is difficult to ascertain how much of the work remained outstanding when Riesener took over the workshops after Oeben's death. On stylistic grounds it seems possible that he designed and had executed the marquetry-panels on the cylinder-top and on the back of the superstructure, and he must have had to co-ordinate the work of the sub-contractors—for example, that of Jean-Antoine Lepine who had to provide the double-faced clock that was to be set into the superstructure. This presented great difficulties because it was essential that it should remain unaffected by the operation of the heavy cylinder-top immediately below. At any rate, Riesener signed the piece.

In its serpentine conformation, this piece of furniture belongs stylistically to the fashion that had prevailed for many years by 1760, but much of the decoration is unmistakably Classical. There are heavy garlands of bay-leaves hanging from rosettes and tied with waving ribbons. The gallery is faced with a regular, Classical border-pattern. Below it is a moulding resembling *fasces*. The interior is decorated with a mosaic pattern and the small terminal figures already mentioned—providing an almost pure Classical aspect. No contemporary opinions about this desk are known to us but there can be no doubt that someone like Blondel would have approved of it. It is a supreme expression of the Golden Mean between the exuberance of the Rococo and the ponderous Classicism of the Age of Louis XIV, which Blondel advocated when discussing Contant d'Ivry's work at the Palais Royal (see Plates 22 and 23 and page 42). We would call it an example of the moderate form of early Neo-Classicism in France, in contrast to Lalive de Jully's furniture (Plates 85 to 89) which exemplifies the extreme version of the new taste.

It should be added that the oval porcelain plaques with the three graces are of later date; they replace the King's monogram which was executed in marquetry. See also pages 73–4, 121 and 127.

Plate 94

FALL-FRONT SECRETAIRE. One of a pair stamped 'J. F. Oeben', about 1760–62. *Musée du Louvre* (Dreyfus, *Louvre Catalogue Mobilier*, No. 64).

When Oeben died in January 1763, there were at least six completed or nearly finished secretaires in his workshops which, judging by the descriptions, seem to have been of the type shown here. (See J. J. Guiffrey, *Inventaire de Jean-François Oeben.*) Quite a few examples of this type of early Neo-Classical secretaire are known; they all have much the same mounts. Especially characteristic are the feet, with their angular scroll which may derive from an engraving by Berain showing a commode with similar feet that was probably made by Boulle late in the seventeenth century. Feet of similar shape are to be seen on the desk here attributed to G. Haupt in the Museum at Tours (Plate 115). The Haupt desk and this pair of secretaires are supposed to have belonged to the Duc de Choiseul. Secretaires similar to this are to be seen in the views of Choiseul's house reproduced in Plate 464.

When the stock from Oeben's workshops were sold after his death, it was stated that all the furniture was 'd'un goût nouveau'. Sixteen commodes belonging to Madame de Pompadour, which presumably also came from his workshops, were described as being 'à la grecque'. Since she died in 1764, most of these pieces must have been made some while before he died (see pages 71–2 and 76).

Plate 95

COMMODE. Stamped 'J. F. Oeben', about 1760–62. *The Bensimon Collection, Paris.*

Among the items of furniture in Oeben's workshops after his death in 1763 (see the previous Note) was a large commode which must have been very like the one illustrated here. Judging from the description the same ram's-head corner mounts are found on a table bearing his stamp and on the table to be seen in the portrait of Madame de Pompadour, which must date from before 1764 when she died and is presumably an example of Oeben's work (Plate 372).

The Classical key-fret in the frieze and the general shape, which is very different from that of the typical Rococo commode of the 1750s, cause one to speculate whether this might not be one of the sixteen commodes 'à la grecque' which belonged to Madame de Pompadour and which were probably supplied by Oeben. The ring-handles are noteworthy; a *chiffonière* in Oeben's stock listed after his death had 'anneaux a rosette' ('rings with rosettes') which were probably like these. Baskets of flowers were favourite subjects for execution in marquetry by Oeben; compositions similar to that on the front of this commode appear on several of his works. In the very room in which he died, there were four oil-paintings on canvas set into the panelling which represented 'des corbeilles de fleurs'.

See Watson, *Louis XVI Furniture*, Plate 25. See also page 72.

Plate 96

CORNER-CUPBOARD, one of a pair. Stamped 'J. F. Oeben', about 1760–62. *Victoria and Albert Museum (Jones Collection, No. 36).*

The marble slab and brass band are additions.

This pair of *encoignures* has much in common with the commode shown in Plate 95 and has legs reminiscent of those on the secretaire shown in Plate 94. What is more, the handles are similar to those on the commode, which were discussed in the previous Note. The *encoignure* stamped by P. Garnier, shown in Plate 98, is almost identical in shape and decoration although the colouring and woods used are different.

The marquetry panel is edged with the double fillet found on much of Oeben's work and is framed by a border with indented, concave corners, similar to that to be seen on the Sèvres tray illustrated in Plate 268, dated 1757. See also pages 71–2.

Plate 97

COMMODE, one of a pair. Stamped 'P. Garnier' and 'B. Durand', about 1762–65. *Gripsholm Palace, Sweden.*

It is difficult to explain the presence of two cabinet-makers' stamps on this piece. Stylistically it has much in common with other furniture known to be by Garnier, and it is tempting to assume that he designed this commode and its pair. The characteristic handles are found on other Garnier pieces (e.g. the table shown in Plate 99) and are not recorded on the work of other cabinet-makers. We know from a letter written by the Marquis de Marigny that Garnier designed bronze-mounts (see page 127).

Durand only became a master in 1761 and his role may have been confined to making the commodes to designs provided by Garnier, or he may merely have sold them for Garnier.

These commodes are here given an early date on account of their archaic design and because we know that Garnier was one of the very first Parisian cabinet-makers to produce furniture in the Neo-Classical taste (see page 71).

The commode and the stamped marks were published by Åke Setterwall in his article 'Signed French Furniture in the Swedish Royal Collection', *Opuscula in Honorem C. Hernmarck*, Stockholm, 1966, page 244.

Plate 98

CORNER-CUPBOARD, one of a pair. Stamped 'P. Garnier', about 1760–65. *Present whereabouts unknown; sold at Messrs. Christie, Manson and Woods, 21st November 1963 (lot 108).*

This closely resembles the piece by Oeben illustrated in Plate 96, but we do not know that Garnier ever collaborated with Oeben. There were several pairs of corner-cupboards among the pieces of furniture sold from Oeben's workshops after his death in 1763. Perhaps Garnier bought one or more pairs and completed them. At any rate, they must be fairly early examples of Neo-Classicism in French furniture, since both Oeben and Garnier produced furniture in the new taste at an early stage (see pages 69–74).

Plate 99

WRITING-DESK. Stamped 'P. Garnier', about 1762–65. *The Huntington Collection, San Marino, California.*

The date here suggested for this table is based on the fact that Garnier was producing furniture in a Classical style by 1761 (see page 71) and that similar tables are depicted in drawings by Carmontelle (Plates 349 and 350) which are thought to date from these years. (See also the Note that follows.)

Tables by Garnier with the same characteristic mounts are to be seen at Longleat, in Somerset, and in the Gulbenkian Collection in Lisbon, while a third was once at Schloss Sagan in Germany.

See R. Wark, *The Huntington Collection*, No. 55. See also page 77.

Plate 100

WRITING-DESK. Stamped 'I. Dubois', about 1760–65. *Present whereabouts unknown; in the hands of a London dealer.*

When Jacques Dubois died in 1763, his widow carried on the business and his son, René, apparently ran the workshops and would have been responsible for the production of this table.

On 12th March 1765, the Parisian *marchand-mercier*, Poirier, forwarded to the Earl of Coventry 'un Bureau à la grec' which was fitted with 'deux tablettes qui se tirent sur les côtés' ('two writing-leaves which pull out at the sides'; see page 134). A table which could be the one so described is to be seen on an old photograph of the Tapestry Room at Croome Court, taken sometime before 1880 (see the *Bulletin* of The Metropolitan Museum of Art, November 1959, page 93); it appears to have a 'tablette qui se tire'. Tables of this kind are to be seen in illustrations by Carmontelle that are presumed to date from the first half of the 1760s (e.g. Plates 349 and 360). The author is grateful to Mrs. Eileen Harris for having drawn his attention to Poirier's account and to Mr. Geoffrey Beard for having provided photographs of it from the Croome Court Archives.

A pair of very similar tables still stand in the Library at Osterley Park, for which they were made about 1772. A pedestal library-table, of the typical English conformation, is *en suite* and the set is undoubtedly English. All the same, the form of this pair of tables must derive from that of a French table very similar to the one illustrated here; perhaps Lord Coventry's table was the source of inspiration. See also page 77.

Plates 101 to 103

WRITING-DESK, FILING-CABINET AND INKSTAND. Sometimes called 'The Tilsit Table'. Stamped 'I. Dubois', about 1765. *The Wallace Collection.*

The provenance of this table has been discussed by Francis Watson (*Burlington Magazine* XCII, pages 165–7 and *Wallace Collection Catalogue* F. 178, 287 and 330). It is presumed to date from the mid-1760s because the later Tsar Paul I (born 1754) is said to have used it as a child. The monumental format also suggests an early date, as do various details which are to be found on more securely dated pieces of furniture. The double-tailed sirens on the table and on the inkstand occur also on a design for a table by De Wailly (Plate 329) of 1760, and on a cartel-clock which is represented in a painting by Hallé of 1765 (Plate 376). The heavy garlands on the filing-cabinet are reminiscent of those on Lalive de Jully's furniture of about 1757 (Plate 85) and on various early Neo-Classical buildings. Lion-masks, like those on the lower section of the filing-cabinet, were to be seen in Rousset's design for a console-table (Plate 396) which should date from about 1765, while the spiral fluting on the legs occurs on Cherpitel's console-table of the same date (Plate 397). See also page 71.

Plates 104 and 105

FALL-FRONT SECRETAIRE. Stamped 'I. Dubois' once, and 'J. Goyer' twice, 1765–70. *The National Trust, Waddesdon Manor.*

It is not easy to determine the position of this curious and huge piece of furniture (it is over four metres high) in the development of early Neo-Classicism. All one can possibly say about it is that it must at one point have been in the hands of Dubois (René, rather than Jacques who died in 1763; see the Note to Plate 100) and in those of Jean Goyer who specialised in providing cases for clocks. From what we know of the Dubois firm, it is possible that Dubois sub-contracted this commission—it must have been a special order—to Goyer who executed the cabinet-work, or most of it. Dubois may have supplied the design, however. On the other hand, Goyer had started his career as a bronze-founder and in 1765 he was accused of having illegally engaged some other bronze-founders in his cabinet-making workshops (see page 188). It may therefore be that Goyer had some influence on the appearance of this strange piece of furniture which is so richly furnished with bronze mounts (cf. Goyer's clock shown in Plate 107).

As far as its date is concerned, several features point to a date in the late 1760s. For instance, delicate punching and chasing of the mounts occurs on many bronzes in the 1770s but is rare in the 1760s. On the other hand, the serpentine form of the case points to an earlier date and one would not be at all surprised if it turned out that the piece was made quite early in the second half of the 1760s. This secretaire may have been made for some foreign potentate. This would explain its somewhat incongruous appearance and our difficulty in deciding its date, since it does not fit into the mainstream of the development in strictly Parisian terms. Perhaps it was made for a Russian or Polish nobleman. At any rate, whoever ordered it must have been well-to-do as it would have cost a great deal—50,000 livres, perhaps.

The author is much indebted to Miss Rosamund Griffin and Mr. Geoffrey de Bellaigue for information about the stamps on this piece. Had one not had this evidence, one might well have concluded that it was not made in France at all! See page 75.

Plate 106

FALL-FRONT SECRETAIRE. Stamped 'I. Dubois', about 1765–70. *Private Collection.*

Several details seem to indicate a comparatively early date for this piece, notably the prominent key-fret, the old-fashioned corner-mounts, and the slightly splayed legs. Since Jacques Dubois died in 1763, it was probably made by his son, René (see page 173). This desk was first published by Francis Watson (*Louis XVI Furniture*, Plate 88).

Plate 107

MINIATURE REGULATOR CLOCK. The case is stamped 'J. Goyer', about 1765–70. *Formerly Dr. James Hasson Collection.*

This clock is only 68.5 cm. high (27 in.). It has been illustrated in a number of publications, including the catalogue of the sale in which it was sold in 1969 (Christie's, March 20th 1969, lot 43); in every case it has been stated that the case was stamped F. Goyer, for François Goyer (Jean Goyer's father, who died in 1763, not in 1768, as is often claimed) or his widow who kept the workshop going until 1768. If this had been so, we should have had a secure *terminus ante quem* for this clock. As it is, the clock may well date from the early 1760s. (See also Plates 104 and 105.)

The movement is signed 'Riderau a Paris'.

Plate 108

COMMODE. Stamped 'I. Dubois', about 1765–70. *The Wallace Collection.*

Like the furniture shown in Plates 100 to 106, this piece was probably also made by Jacques Dubois' son, René (see Note to Plate 100). The sirens are almost identical to those on the table shown in Plate 101.

See Francis Watson, *Wallace Collection Catalogue*, F. 425.

Plate 109

FALL-FRONT SECRETAIRE. Stamped 'L. Boudin', about 1765–75. *The Cleveland Museum of Art, Bequest of John L. Severance.*

This small writing-desk cannot be dated at all closely on the slender evidence available. The rather heavy corner-mounts with a key-fret above—reminiscent of certain mounts used by Joubert (cf. e.g. Plate 120)—and the marks suggest a date around 1770, and it could have been made as late as the mid-1770s. On the other hand, the shaped marble slab could have been produced nearer the middle of the century. Whatever the case, this piece—with its serpentine form and its sprinkling of Classical ornaments—represents very well the transitional phase between the Rococo and Neo-Classicism.

See the *Catalogue of the John L. Severance Collection*, Cleveland, 1942, No. 84.

Plate 110

A GUERIDON-TABLE. Unsigned about 1765–70. *The Wallace Collection.*

It is reasonable to suppose that this piece was made in the workshops of Riesener or Leleu, since they were virtually the only Parisian cabinet-makers of the period who took the trouble to use coupled stringing of light and dark woods to outline the various compartments of the veneering—a feature clearly to be seen on the present little stand. The drawing of the basket of flowers is most like that of Leleu. Moreover, unlike Riesener (and his master, Oeben, before him), Leleu was not too conscientious about disguising the screw-heads used to fix the mounts on his pieces; the screw-heads securing the feet of this table are quite obvious and could easily have been positioned so as to be invisible.

The squared-scroll feet, the veneering of the legs, and the pierced galleries of the trays are features that call to mind the little table to be seen in the portrait of Madame de Pompadour, painted in 1763–64 (Plate 372).

See Watson, *Wallace Collection Furniture*, F.313.

Plate 111

SMALL WRITING-DESK. Stamped 'M. Carlin'. The Sèvres plaques bear date-marks for the year 1766. *Musée Nissim de Camondo* (Jean Messelet, *Musée Nissim de Camondo*, 1960, No. 126).

Several tables of this model exist. The present example and one like it at Waddesdon Manor are the earliest, according to the marks on Sèvres plaques with which they are all decorated.

As Pierre Verlet has shown, it must have been the Parisian *marchand-mercier*, Simon-Philippe Poirier, who first commissioned furniture to be made that was set with porcelain plaques. We do not know whether Poirier could draw but he must have had designers working to his instructions (see pages 133–5).

Carlin became a *maître-ébéniste* on 30th July 1766, and the ledgers of the Sèvres factory show that Poirier did not purchase any porcelain plaques during the first half of that year, while no less than 112 plaques of varying size were delivered to him during the later part of the year. From this we may conclude that this little table was not completed much before the end of 1766 or early in 1767. On the other hand, designs for the desk as a whole and for its many components (it has sixteen plaques of nine different sizes and shapes, for instance) must have been prepared no later than early that year and quite possibly in 1765.

Plate 112

COMBINED WRITING-DESK AND WORK-TABLE. Unsigned, about 1765–70. *The Charles B. Wrightsman Collection, New York.*

The corner-mounts and shoes seem to be identical to those on the desk by Carlin, shown in the previous illustration, which dates from about 1766. It seems safe to ascribe the present table to him as well. Francis Watson (*Wrightsman Collection*, page 268) has suggested that it was made by a cabinet-maker like Leleu who had worked as a journeyman under Oeben. Carlin may have been trained by Oeben; he anyway married one of Oeben's sisters.

Plate 113

FALL-FRONT SECRETAIRE. Stamped 'J. F. Oeben', about 1765–67. *Collection of Major-General Sir Harold Wernher, Bart.*

Oeben died in 1763 but the presence of his stamp on a piece of furniture in such an advanced style must indicate that the piece was made during the years that his widow was continuing in business, aided by Oeben's foreman, J.-H. Riesener. The latter married widow Oeben on 6th August 1767 and himself became a master in January 1768, whereupon he presumably acquired his own stamp. The present piece of furniture—and one rather like it in Lord Rosebery's collection—is therefore likely to have been made before Riesener formally took over and used his own stamp, although it is difficult to say how long before. Several motifs in the marquetry and on the mounts are found in works that Riesener produced throughout the 1770s; a desk he made for Versailles as late as 1780 has identical mounts at the centre and on the corners, and the same marquetry trophy with cock as well (see Watson, *Louis XVI Furniture*, Plate 75). See also page 76.

Plate 114

WRITING-TABLE. Signed by Georg Haupt and dated 1767. *Institut Géographique National, Paris.*

During restoration in the 1960s, the inscription 'George Haupt Suedois a fait cet [sic] bureau a Chanteloup 1767' ('Georg Haupt, the Swede, made this desk at Chanteloup 1767') was discovered under the top, together with the inventory mark of Chanteloup castle, the country-residence of the Duc de Choiseul. This has been published by Marshall Lagerquist and Madame Madeleine Jarry in *Revue de l'Art Français*, 1953, pages 239–40. It is of solid mahogany, a timber not much used in France until a decade or so later. This fact and the simple form would normally suggest a substantially later date for this table than the inscription actually indicates. The craftsmanship is not of the highest order, especially in the carved parts. It will be noticed that the top has a broken outline with rectangular protrusions at the corners. The same feature is to be seen on the desk illustrated in Van Blarenbergh's view of the Duc de Choiseul's house in Paris (Plate 464). The table shown in Plate 144 also has this feature. See also pages 77 and 118.

Plate 115

WRITING-DESK AND FILING-CABINET. About 1766–67. *Musée des Beaux-Arts, Tours.*

The inventory-marks of the castle of Chanteloup are to be found on the back of the cabinet, and one can therefore assume this set was made for the Duc de Choiseul. It has been attributed to Oeben on stylistic grounds, but it seems inconceivable that it came from his establishment because the quality of the workmanship throughout is noticeably inferior to that which one normally finds bearing Oeben's *estampille*. The shoes are admittedly almost identical to those found on Oeben pieces like the secretaire shown in Plate 94 which also came from Choiseul's collection. Possibly Choiseul wanted the desk made *en suite* with the secretaire.

This desk and cabinet may have been made by Haupt who was working at Chanteloup in 1766 and 1767 (see the previous Note). It has the same 'broken' corners as the table shown in Plate 114.

The shape of this desk, with its pedestals of drawers, seems to reflect English influence although the placing of a filing-cabinet at one end is a typically French feature. Presumably the design of the desk was approved by Choiseul but one cannot help wondering whether Haupt did not already then have some connection with England which he was to visit in 1768–69. His use of mahogany for the table discussed in the foregoing entry could also be due to some contact with England. See also pages 77 and 144.

Plate 116

REGULATOR CLOCK AND BAROMETER. The mounts signed by Philippe Caffieri and dated 1767. The case is unsigned. The movement is by Ferdinand Berthoud. *The Frick Collection, New York.*

A similar clock with a Berthoud movement and a case bearing the stamp of B. Lieutaud, is at Versailles; its mounts are not signed, however. Several versions exist with different surmounting ornament (see Watson, *Wallace Collection Catalogue*, pages 133–4). It is not known who designed this group of clocks. See also page 77.

Plate 117

ORNAMENTAL CUPBOARD. Stamped 'B.V.R.B.', about 1765–75. *The Samuel H. Kress Collection at the Metropolitan Museum of Art.*

This was probably made by Bernard III Vanrisamburgh rather than his father, who used the same *estampille* (see page 224). The heavy classicising bronzes suggest quite an early date—in the 1760s—but the splayed feet are reminiscent of those on the commode by Riesener shown in Plate 147 which dates from 1774.

See *Decorative Art from the Samuel H. Kress Collection at the Metropolitan Museum*, 1964, No. 10. See also page 78.

Plate 118

CYLINDER-TOP DESK. Stamped 'J. F. Leleu', about 1767. *The Huntington Collection, San Marino, California.*

This is set with no less than twenty-four Sèvres plaques bearing the date-letter for 1767. The author does not know of any other examples of exactly this type of table, with its dozen fancily-shaped plaques. These must have been specially designed for the table and vice versa, so the designs for the ensemble must have been executed in 1767 or before. Since we know that the *marchand-mercier* Poirier was the only person buying plaques of this kind from the Sèvres factory at this stage (see note to Plate 111 and page 75), one must presume that the desk was designed by his draughtsmen and that he then placed the order for its construction with Leleu (see Robert R. Wark, *French Decorative Art in the Huntington Collection*, page 87).

Plate 119

COMMODE. Stamped 'R.V.L.C.', delivered to the *Garde-Meuble de la Couronne* by Gilles Joubert on 5th July 1769. *The Frick Collection, New York.*

This commode was identified by Verlet (*French Royal Furniture*, pages 109–10) as being the one ordered on 16th February 1769 for Madame Victoire's rooms at Compiègne. Joubert charged 4,260 livres for it, and the marble slab cost a further 350 livres.

The four initials with which this commode is stamped stand for Roger Vandercruse La croix who must therefore at least have had some part in its creation. We also know that Vandercruse worked for Joubert because Joubert owed him 2,150 livres in March 1771 (see page 193). Joubert also owed the marble-contractor Jouniaux the sum of 4,443 livres for marble slabs which the latter had provided in 1769. It is very probable that the slab for this commode was one of these. The bronze mounts probably came from Forestier (see page 193).

In 1769, Joubert was an old man of about eighty and his workshop was not very extensive. It is therefore to be presumed that many of the pieces of furniture he provided for the Court in these later years were sub-contracted, as was the case with the commode illustrated here. All the same, Joubert must have retained complete control of each commission and probably provided the requisite designs—although we have no evidence of this.

The commode is an excellent example of the Transitional style; it has an old-fashioned shape but most of the ornaments are Classical in taste, with the exception of the apron-mount which, in a late eighteenth century inventory (see Verlet, op. cit.) is described as a 'rinceaux de rocaille'. The vases depicted in marquetry on the end-panels are taken from an engraving by Maurice Jacques which is reproduced here as Plate 392.

This was not Joubert's earliest commode of this type: on 11th May the year before, he delivered one that must have been rather similar, judging by the description given in the Journal of the *Garde-Meuble de la Couronne*, although the veneering was probably more like that shown in Plate 120. The mounts were decidedly Classical in spirit, however (see Archives Nationales, o^1 3318 fol. 193). See also pages 77–8.

Plate 120

COMMODE. Delivered to the *Garde-Meuble de la Couronne* by Gilles Joubert on 28th August 1769. *The J. Paul Getty Museum, Malibu, California.*

The identity of this commode was established by Pierre Verlet (*French Royal Furniture*, pages 111–12). It is not known whether the piece is stamped because the slab is now fixed rigidly. (See the previous Note concerning Joubert's practice of sub-contracting.) It was ordered for Madame Louise's apartment at Versailles and Joubert charged 4,680 livres for it; its marble slab cost a further 350 livres. The straight legs lend this piece a rather more modern air than the commode shown in Plate 119.

Madame Louise received a second commode like this but that had a slab of a different kind of marble. The year before (on 31st December 1768) she accepted a somewhat similar commode which had no side-cupboards, and was probably furnished with less elaborate mounts. On the other hand, its marquetry decoration seems to have been similar to that on the commode made for her sister—that illustrated in Plate 119. It is described as having 'au milieu un cartouche des attributs des arts liberaux et sur les cotez des colonnes d'architecture accompagnés de bouquets et guirlandes de fleurs' ('in the centre, a cartouche with the attributes of the Liberal Arts and, at the sides, columns with bouquets and garlands of flowers'; cf. Archives Nationales, o^1 3318, fol. 225). See also pages 77–8 and 82.

Plate 121

JEWEL-CASKET ON STAND. About 1770. *The Metropolitan Museum of Art, Gift of the Samuel H. Kress Foundation.*

One of the twelve Sèvres plaques bears the date-letter for 1768, seven of them that for 1770, and a single one that for 1775. If the last is considered to be a replacement, we may conclude that the designs and models for this piece were being prepared no later than 1768, and that its final shape was decided on by 1770.

As has been explained (see page 75), it was the *marchand-mercier*, Poirier, who launched the fashion for mounting furniture with Sèvres plaques and it seems that he had the monopoly in this field, judging by the Sèvres factory records. Most of the plaques on this piece are dated 1770 and Poirier purchased a total of 104 plaques of different sizes from Sèvres in that year. The descriptions in the Sèvres ledgers are too brief to enable one to associate them with particular plaques on this piece, however, but there can be little doubt this is one of Poirier's confections. It was presumably constructed for him by Martin Carlin.

A casket of this kind is mentioned in a bill rendered by Poirier on 13th December 1770 to Madame du Barry. Like the present example, hers had plaques with a green ground. It cost 1,800 livres.

This piece hardly represents a big step forward, stylistically—especially when compared with the table shown in Plate 111, made in 1766, presumably for Poirier as well. Yet the bronzes are considerably more elaborate and delicately chased, and this was to become a characteristic feature of the best French furniture during the next phase. All the ornaments, including the chased, gilt mouldings which secure the plaques, are Classical in taste.

See *Decorative Art from the Samuel H. Kress Collection at the Metropolitan Museum of Art*, 1964, No. 20. See also pages 75, 81 and 134.

Plate 122

WORK-TABLE. Stamped 'M. Carlin', 1771. *The Charles B. Wrightsman Collection, New York.*

The three shaped Sèvres plaques, forming a band round the body of this table, have date-marks for the year 1771. As Verlet has pointed out (*Les meubles français du XVIIIe siècle, II, ébénisterie*, page 125) these were called 'quarts de cercles' at the factory and it was in 1771 that Poirier (see page 73) acquired three plaques of this class from the factory for the first time. They cost 15 livres each. In 1771–76, the factory sold just under seventy such plaques—sufficient for about twenty-two tables like this—to Poirier and his successor, Daguerre. Several similar tables are known; some have a circular plaque in the top and on the tray between the legs. Since Poirier only purchased three 'quarts de cercles' in 1771, this table must presumably be the prototype for the whole series. Madame du Barry bought a table from Poirier for 840 livres on 30th December 1773; the description suggests it was of just this type (see G. Wildenstein, 'Simon-Philippe Poirier, fournisseur de Madame du Barry', *Gaz.des B.-A.*, vol. 60, 1962, page 377). See also pages 81 and 134.

Plate 123

WRITING-DESK. Delivered by J. H. Riesener on 21st September 1771 to Pierre-Elizabeth de Fontanieu, *Intendant général des Meubles de la Couronne. Petit Trianon.*

Verlet says (*Mobilier Royal*, vol. 1, page 18) it is quite likely that Fontanieu had a hand in the design of this table which was one of the very first pieces of furniture to be supplied to the *Garde-Meuble de la Couronne* with straight legs. Fontanieu was something of an artist himself, as one can see from the *Collection de vases* which he had published in 1768 (see Plates 449 to 52). He clearly had progressive tastes. On 23rd December 1771, two months after the present table was delivered, he acquired a fall-front secretaire for his own use which must have been something in the nature of a cross between that illustrated in Plate 113 and that shown in Plate 145, judging by the description (see Archives Nationales, o^1 3319, fol. 76). See also pages 79 and 81.

Plate 124

WRITING-DESK AND FILING-CABINET. Stamped 'Montigny', about 1765–70. *From the Woburn Abbey Collection; by kind permission of His Grace the Duke of Bedford.*

This was first published by Francis Watson (*Apollo*, December 1965, fig. 3). Philippe-Claude Montigny was made a *maître-ébéniste* on 29th January 1766. His stamp is found on many tables veneered with ebony or, as in this case, with imitations made of stained pearwood and the like. It is also found on some tables very like that stamped 'I. Dubois' shown in Plate 100, which ought to date from 1760–65. The pine-cone finials on the filing-cabinet are reminiscent of those on Lalive's famous piece (see Plate 89) while the guilloches with rosettes in the frame resemble those on, for example, Joubert's commode of 1769 shown in Plate 119, and the table shown in a portrait of 1771 here reproduced as Plate 471. The latter also seems to be veneered in a very dark wood.

Plate 125

COMMODE. Probably identical with the one Simon-Philippe Poirier delivered to Madame du Barry in 1772. *Private Collection.*

This is mounted with five very large plaques of Sèvres porcelain decorated with scenes copied from paintings by Watteau and Carle Van Loo. On account of these exceptional ornaments, there can be little doubt that this commode is the one which stood in Madame du Barry's bed-chamber at Versailles (see

Verlet, *Versailles*, page 569) which Poirier sent down there on 21st August 1772 and for which he charged the very high price of 9,750 livres (Wildenstein, 'Simon-Philippe Poirier', *Gaz.d.B.-A.*, vol. LX, 1962, page 376). The commode is unsigned but was probably made by Martin Carlin who was at this time Poirier's regular contractor for furniture mounted with porcelain plaques. Moreover, the same apron-mount with a lion's head is to be seen on a commode in the Huntington Collection bearing Carlin's stamp (Robert Wark, *French Decorative Art in the Huntington Collection*, 1961, No. 66). Curiously enough there seems to be no mention of these five plaques in the Sèvres factory-records.

With its cabriole legs and its shaped sides, this must have been one of the least advanced pieces of furniture in Madame du Barry's luxuriously-appointed bed-chamber, in spite of the Classical character of its mounts and in spite of the fact that it was not delivered until two years after the rest. The bed, for instance, had four posts fluted like Classical columns, and its feet had spiral fluting; it was covered in rich carving in the Antique taste. The thirteen gilded chairs in the room were in the same advanced style, with straight legs with spiral fluting (see Plate 172). According to Verlet (loc. cit.), there was a clock on the chimney-piece like that shown in Plate 198 and, in front of the fire, was a screen with carved ornaments like that of the chairs. See also pages 78–9.

Plate 126

WRITING-DESK. Stamped 'J. F. Leleu', about 1772. *Private Collection.*

This is similar in style to the expensive furniture Leleu produced for the Prince de Condé's Palais Bourbon in 1772 (Plates 127 to 130). From an architectural point of view, it is slightly awkward, notably in the way a circular capital has been introduced between a leg of square section and the severely rectangular frame above. But the workmanship is of the same high order as that found on the Palais Bourbon furniture and, while no table like this is listed in the bills Leleu rendered to the Prince, it is probably not far wrong to assume it is contemporary with the Bourbon pieces.

In the nineteenth century, the table belonged to the Comtesse de Flahaut, a lady of Scottish birth who married Auguste-Charles-Joseph Comte de Flahaut in 1817. His father was a brother of the Comte d'Angivillier, who succeeded the Marquis de Marigny as *directeur général des bâtiments du Roi* and whose mother was Marigny's sister. It is not, however, known whether the Comtesse purchased the table herself or inherited it. See also pages 79 and 81.

Plate 127

CYLINDER-TOP DESK. Probably made in 1772 by J. F. Leleu. *Formerly in the collection of Comte Boni de Castellane in Paris; present whereabouts unknown.*

The present author only knows this desk from the illustration reproduced here which is taken from Emile Molinier's *Le mobilier au XVIe et au XVIIIe siècle* (*Histoire générale des arts appliqués à l'industrie*, vol. II, 1898, page 165). Presumably the desk bears no stamp and Molinier very reasonably attributed it to Riesener on stylistic grounds. However, there can be little doubt that this is the desk Leleu provided for the Prince de Condé, on 9th November 1772, to stand in the *Salon Roze* at the Palais Bourbon. It seems to agree in every detail with the description given in Leleu's bill, still preserved in the Archives Condé, which runs as follows:—

'Du 9 Novembre. Salon roze de S.A.Sme. Avoir fourni un bureau à Cylindre de 2 pieds 6 pouces de long, 18 pouces de profondeur, 3 pieds 3 pouces de haut (i.e. 0.81 × 0.48 × 1.05 m). Le corps d'en haut est composé de Six tiroirs en bois Satiné, massif, plaqué en Mosaique, et la tablette ferrée d'une machine faisant jouer l'abbattant qui est garni d'un velours vert. Le corps d'en bas est composé de cinq tiroirs en bois d'Acajou massif, dont un ovale ou est posée la serrure, faisant fermeture de toute la pièce par d'autres machines. Le dit Secrétaire est à pieds quarrés et angles renfoncés. du dessus ce sont des consoles en bois d'Amarante, massif, cannlées en cuivre lisse, les pieds plaqués en bois d'Amarante et rose, filets noirs et blancs, les panneaux et L'Abbattant en Mosaique nuancée, deux clefs, une à L'Angloise, l'autre cizelée et armoirée. Le corps dudit Sécrétaire est orné de 4 Sabots à boules, et feüilles d'eau dans les angles des pieds, quatorze bouts de guirlandes à feuilles de chesne; au dessus huit doubles feuilles d'eau, les carrés à graine de Chapelet, a douze testes de Lyon, une moulure unie pour le pilastre dix huit baguettes et fleurons à Laurier, Six feuilles d'ornemens, dix fleurons a rouleaux. Sur les côtés et devant sont cinq cadres à Laurier dont un ovale, dans le milieu un Soleil; pour le carderon est une moulure à feuilles d'Acanthe. Le corps d'en haut, les côtés ornés de deux demi cercles de double poste à jour. La partie cintrée de devant, et la frize du même ornement. Audessus est une moulure unie faisant cadre du marbre, le tout bien fini et doré d'or moulu pour ce 4760 livres.'

('9th November. For His Highness's Pink Salon

To one cylinder-top desk, two feet six inches long, eighteen inches deep, three feet three inches high. The top section fitted with six drawers of solid satinwood, veneered with a lattice-pattern, and with a writing-leaf, faced with green velvet, that is linked to a mechanism which causes the cylinder-top to close over it. The lower section contains five drawers of solid mahogany, of which one is oval and incorporates the lock that enables the whole piece to be secured by means of linked locking mechanisms. The said desk has legs of square section with indented corners; above them are brackets of solid purple wood with flutes lined with polished bronze, while the feet are veneered with purple and tulip wood and with black and white stringing. The panels of the carcass are veneered with a shaded lattice-pattern. Two keys, one of the English type, the other chisled and bearing a coat-of-arms. The wooden body of this desk is furnished with [the following bronzes]—four small bun-feet, husk-mouldings on the chamfered edges of the legs, fourteen garlands of oak-leaves; above are eight double-tongue mouldings, cappings with pearl-decoration, twelve lion's heads, a plain moulding on the pilasters, eighteen ornaments of bay-leaves for the flutes, six pieces of ornamental foliage, and ten floral scrolls. On the flanks and front face are five frames of bay-leaves, one being oval; in the centre is a sun-burst. The moulding at the base of the top section consists of acanthus leaves. The top section has, on its sides, semicircles composed of a double vitruvian scroll in openwork; the same ornament is on the curved front and on the frieze. On top is a moulding forming a frame for the marble slab. The whole neatly finished and the bronzes gilded . . . 4,760 livres.')

Leleu's price was, as usual abated by about a fifth, so he was finally only paid 3,940 livres. Even so, this was by far the most expensive piece of veneered furniture made for this splendid house. The high cost was probably to some extent due to the complicated mechanisms for the closing of the cylinder-top and the drawers with which it was fitted.

The lion's masks on the outer faces of the blocks from which the legs spring—mentioned in the description—are unusual features (at this period) and the sun-burst within an oval is noteworthy.

This desk was ordered specially for the *Salon roze*, a room described in an inventory of 1779 as the Prince's 'Cabinet donnant sur la térasse' (see Verlet, *La maison*, pages 270–84). The room had pink and white striped hangings, curtains and chair-covers. The desk was the only piece of veneered furniture in the room; this may explain why it had such a different appearance from the rest of the furniture ordered for the Palais Bourbon which include the items illustrated in Plates 128 to 130. (See also the bronzes, Plates 453 to 461.) The commode shown in Plate 129 was in fact delivered on the same day as this desk. See also pages 79–81 and 119.

Plate 128

COMMODE. Stamped 'J. F. Leleu', 1772. *The Wallace Collection.*

As Verlet has explained, this commode originally had a highly ornamental panel of marquetry in front, somewhat like that on the front of the commode shown in Plate 130, but with the Prince de Condé's cypher and fleurs-de-lis instead. (See 'Two pieces of furniture by Leleu', *Burlington Magazine*, 1949, page 110.) It was dispatched by Leleu to the Prince de Condé on 28th December 1772. Leleu charged 10,715 livres for it but was only paid 8,970 (see the previous Note).

It was placed in the bed-chamber of the Duchesse de Bourbon, the Prince's daughter-in-law, in the recently modernised Palais Bourbon (see the previous two Notes). The commode shown in Plate 130, and its pair, were placed in the same room four months later. The Duchesse's bed, which does not seem to have survived, was also richly decorated in the Classical taste. The woodwork alone, executed by Charles Lachenait, cost 13,046 livres and the upholstery was correspondingly expensive. It is to be presumed that all this furniture was made after designs—either in the form of preliminary sketches or as finished drawings—by Le Carpentier or Bellisard, architects to the Prince de Condé. Noteworthy are the Ionic capitals surmounting the legs. This is probably the earliest surviving example of the use of capitals to surmount columnar legs although the feature is portrayed in the design for a console-table of 1765 ascribed to Cherpitel (Plate 397), in Prieur's design of 1766 shown in Plate 408, and in the engraving by Baudouin of 1767 where a chair can be seen with such a detail. A pair of *canapés* in the *Salon chinois* of the Palais de Bourbon also had Ionic capitals used in this way.

See Watson, *Wallace Collection Furniture*, F. 246. See also pages 79–80 and 119.

Plate 129

COMMODE. Stamped 'J. F. Leleu', 1772. *Musée du Louvre.*

Delivered by Leleu on 9th November 1772 for use in the Prince de Condé's bed-chamber in the Palais Bourbon (see Verlet, *La Revue des Arts*, 1954, pages 47–8). This was the only piece of veneered furniture in the room. It cost 2,400 livres.

The carver Charles Lachenait provided the bed for this room which was to stand in an alcove. He also provided a *canapé*, two *bergères*, and six chairs without arms. The whole set had straight, fluted legs and was upholstered with blue silk damask, which material was also used for the curtains of the four windows. (See Lachenait's account in the Archives Condé, and Verlet, *La Maison*, page 272.) See also pages 79–80.

Plate 130

COMMODE, one of a pair. Stamped 'J. F. Leleu', 1773. *Petit Trianon.*

Delivered on 1st May 1773 by Leleu for use in the Duchesse de Bourbon's bed-chamber where the commode shown in Plate 128 was already standing (see the relevant Note, above). Like that piece, these both had intricate marquetry-work in the now plain lozenge-shaped panel. See also pages 79–81.

Plate 131

COMMODE. Stamped 'A. Foullet' and 'L. Boudin', about 1770–75. *Nationalmuseum, Stockholm.*

It was Francis Watson who discovered that this piece was not stamped by Pierre-Antoine Foullet but by his father Antoine, who died in 1775 (see *Louis XVI Furniture*, page 106). Thus we have a firm *terminus ante quem* for this piece. Presumably the presence of two stamps indicates that Foullet made the piece and that Boudin sold it from his shop. It has been stated that Boudin did not set up shop as a dealer in furniture until 1777 but, in fact, he was already calling himself *marchand-ébéniste* in 1775 (see page 156) by which time he could have been engaged in this trade for some while.

Antoine Foullet is best known for his clock-cases in the Rococo taste. As a cabinet-maker, he was unusual in that he had his own large stock of models for bronze mounts. The mounts on this piece, notably the triglyphs, the 'broken' framing of the panels, and the apron-mount in the form of a smoking incense-burner, are all found on furniture bearing his son's stamp (e.g. see Plates 132 and 152) but were probably all produced under the father's direction. His regular bronze-founder was Claude-Bernard Hében. See also page 78.

Plate 132

COMMODE. Stamped 'P. A. Foullet', about 1770–75. *Frederiksborg Castle, Denmark.*

This is very similar to the previous commode which bore P. A. Foullet's father's stamp (see the Note above). The vase rendered in marquetry is taken from an engraving by Maurice Jacques (Plate 394). Several commodes like this exist; most of them bear P.-A. Foullet's stamp. See also page 78.

Plate 133

COMMODE. Stamped 'P. Roussel', about 1770–75. *Musée Jacquemart-André, Paris.*

The corner-mounts and the shoes on this piece are reminiscent of those on the commode shown in Plate 119 although they are not of the same high quality. The marquetry panel has much in common with those on pieces by Charles Topino, both in the subject-matter and the somewhat coarse execution (cf. Plate 138). Possibly Topino provided Roussel with this marquetry panel in the form of a veneer ready-made for application to the front of the piece. This commode is related to the upright secretaire shown in Plate 135, which also bears Roussel's stamp.

See Watson, *Louis XVI Furniture*, Plate 29. See also page 78.

Plate 134

CASE FOR A TEA-SET. Unmarked, about 1770–75. *The Antique Company of New York.*

The tea-set is of Sèvres porcelain bearing the date-letter 'Q' for 1769. The marquetry is reminiscent of that produced by Topino (cf. Plate 138).

Marquetry with somewhat similar motifs was apparently to be seen on a small secretaire delivered by Joubert on 1st June 1774 for the use of the Comte d'Artois. According to the Journal of the *Garde-Meuble*, it was decorated with 'des paniers de fleurs, fruits, Theyeres, Tasses facon de la chine, Le tout en marqueterie' ('baskets of flowers, fruit, tea-pots, and cups of Chinese form, all executed in marquetry'; cf. Archives Nationales, o[1] 3319 fol. 133 *verso*). No doubt the marquetry on the Artois desk was of higher quality than that on the present box.

Plate 135

FALL-FRONT SECRETAIRE. Stamped 'P. Roussel', about 1770–75. *Metropolitan Museum of Art, gift of the Samuel H. Kress Foundation.*

This presumably dates from the same years as the commode shown in Plate 133 which is likewise stamped by Roussel, and has several mounts similar to those seen here. The three marquetry panels on the front are renderings of engravings by J. F. Blondel (see James Parker, *Decorative Art from the Samuel H. Kress Collection at The Metropolitan Museum of Art*, page 90). On the sides (not visible) are renderings of vases illustrated in engravings by Maurice Jacques—one of which is again used on the commode shown in Plate 119 of 1769 and on the sides of the secretaire shown in Plate 153. The mounts in the form of a vase with a garland, fitted to the 'feet', seem to have been inspired by part of the apron-mount on Riesener's commode of 1775, shown in Plate 149.

Plate 136

FALL-FRONT SECRETAIRE, ON A STAND. Stamped 'M. Carlin', about 1773. *The Metropolitan Museum of Art, gift of the Samuel H. Kress Foundation.*

The Sèvres plaques bear the date-letter for 1773. This piece was no doubt made for the *marchand-mercier*, Poirier, who had a virtual monopoly in the field of furniture decorated in this way (see Note to Plate 111). Several desks of this kind are known; the present specimen is the earliest example known. At Waddesdon Manor, Buckinghamshire, is another with the date-letter for 1777 on its plaques.

This piece was published by James Parker and Carl C. Dauterman (see *Metropolitan Museum of Art Bulletin*, May 1960, pages 281–2). See also pages 81 and 135.

Plate 137

LADY'S DESK. Stamped 'R.V.L.C.' (for Roger Vandercruse, called Lacroix), about 1770–75. *From the Woburn Abbey Collection, by kind permission of His Grace the Duke of Bedford.*

The curvilinear form of this desk seems old-fashioned but the entirely regular mosaic marquetry can hardly be earlier than 1770. This was first published by Francis Watson (*Apollo*, December 1965, fig. 7).

The tray has apparently been reversed. See also page 75.

Plate 138

LADY'S DESK. Stamped 'C. Topino' and 'L. Boudin', about 1770–75. *Nationalmuseum, Stockholm.*

The shape of this table is not unlike that of the one shown in Plate 111 which dates from 1766. It was probably made by Topino for sale at Boudin's shop (see Note to Plate 131). In fact, there are entries in Topino's account-book showing that he sold goods to Boudin between 1772 and 1775 (Salverte, *Les ébénistes*, article on Topino). Topino specialised in marquetry but most of his work lacks sophistication; the drawing of the motifs is simple as can be seen on the present example. He seems to have copied motifs depicted on Oriental lacquer, and liked to combine them with ornament of a Classical nature—again, somewhat crudely drawn, like the Vitruvian scroll seen on the drawer-front. In spite of these deficiencies, however, his marquetry often lent considerable charm to the furniture decorated therewith.

In 1771, Topino sent some unmounted panels of marquetry to his brother in Marseilles, which were described as comprising '40 poteries ombréz de diferentes nature' ('forty pottery vessels of different kinds, shaded') while, in 1776 the Parisian *ébéniste* Denizot received from him a circular table with 'poteries chinoise' ('Chinese pots') (see Geoffrey de Bellaigue, 'Engravings and the French Eighteenth-century Marqueteur', *Burlington Magazine*, July 1965, pages 358–9). On the table-top and tray of the present little desk there are likewise representations of tea-pots, cups, vases and bottles which could well be described as 'poteries de diferentes natures'.

Topino sold ten 'tables à gradin' (i.e. with a superstructure at the back) to Boudin between 21st October 1772 and 11th February 1775, at a cost of 110 livres the piece (Archives de la Seine, D^5 B^6 395 fol. 1–2). These were 'avec des sujets chinois' ('with Chinese subjects'). In view of the fact that both their names are on this desk, it seems likely that it was one of the ten. A very similar table, stamped N.-A. Lapie (died in 1775) was once in the collection of the Duke of Leeds (see *The Illustrated London News*, 23rd June 1934). See also page 75.

Plate 139

COMBINED DRESSING-TABLE AND DESK. Stamped 'M. B. Evald', about 1770–74. *Formerly in the Coty Collection, Paris;* now *Walters Art Gallery, Baltimore.*

Evald is believed to have left Paris in August 1774, as a result of financial difficulties, and that provides a *terminus ante quem* for this table. It is not easy to say how much before that date it could have been made, however. In its general shape, and in the scale-decoration on the legs, it is reminiscent of the table shown in Besse's drawing of 1776, illustrated in Plate 499.

Evald's furniture is not common; it is usually decorated with marquetry of considerable delicacy. His stamp is often given as 'Evalde' but this point has been checked and there can be no doubt that it has no final 'e'. See also page 81.

Plate 140

FALL-FRONT SECRETAIRE. Stamped 'M. B. Evald', about 1770–74. *The National Trust, Saltram, Devon.*

As explained in the previous note, furniture bearing the mark of this master cannot have been made later than 1774. The inlaid representation of a gallery with turned brass balusters suggests that the piece cannot be much earlier than 1770 even if the intricate frontal marquetry seems to possess much of the spirit of engraving like that by Lucotte shown in Plate 390, which dates from 1765. The two vases of flowers below are after engravings by Maurice Jacques (see Plate 392).

Several motifs executed in marquetry occur also on a secretaire and a cupboard, both stamped 'L. Boudin', sold in Paris in 1969 (Palais Galliéra, 21st March 1969, lots 112 & 113). Presumably Evald worked for Boudin, like Topino and Foullet are believed to have done (see Plates 131 and 138).

This piece was published by Geoffrey Wills (see *The Connoisseur Year Book*, 1958, page 7). See also pages 81–2.

Plate 141

CYLINDER-TOP DESK. Stamped 'J. H. Riesener', 1773. *The Calouste Gulbenkian Museum, Lisbon.*

As Verlet has demonstrated, this desk was made for the Comtesse de Provence (see *French Royal Furniture*, page 117). It bears the inventory mark of the Palace of Versailles and the serial-number 2729 which shows it was delivered on 30th December 1773 by Joubert, even though it is stamped by Riesener (Archives Nationales, o[1] 3319, fol. 125). In its general form, this is a scaled-down version of the famous *Bureau du Roi* (Plates 90 to 93) but there is a greater delicacy about some of the mounts.

Three months later, the Comte de Provence acquired the much more up-to-date desk shown in Plate 143. Why was the Princesse's desk so old-fashioned? She had been brought up in Turin and she may possibly have been less advanced in her tastes than her husband. One can at least not believe that either Joubert or Riesener had much say in the matter. Perhaps Madame du Barry's taste is reflected here; the Comtesse was trying to curry favour with her at the time. We know that Joubert had the carcass of a cylinder-top desk standing in his workshops in 1771 (see page 193). Could it be that Joubert sent this round to Riesener's to be faced with suitable marquetry and that it was then sent out to Versailles for the use of the Comtesse?

Plate 142

CORNER-CUPBOARD, one of a pair. Unstamped, 1773. *The Wallace Collection.*

Verlet has shown that this pair of *encoignures* was delivered to the *Garde-Meuble de la Couronne* by Gilles Joubert on 30th November 1773 (see *French Royal Furniture*, and also Watson, *Wallace Collection Catalogue*, F. 273). Like the commode *en suite* with these *encoignures*, delivered by Joubert three weeks earlier (8th November), they were designed to stand in the bed-chamber of the sixteen-year-old and newly-married Comte d'Artois at Versailles, in the apartment then being furnished for him at the King's expense. Originally, there was a bronze-trophy, comprising a lion's-skin and a quiver, within the oval frame, as

Verlet has explained. Watson drew attention to certain similarities (notably in the representations of armour and bay-leaves) between the mounts on this piece and those on the secretaire here illustrated in Plate 152, which cannot have been made earlier than 1776; there is, however, no evidence that these pieces of furniture were ever associated with each other in the eighteenth century.

See also the fire-dogs illustrated in Plate 227 which were made for the same apartment. See also page 81.

Plate 143

CYLINDER-TOP DESK. Unstamped, 1774. *The National Trust, Waddesdon Manor, Buckinghamshire.*

J.-H. Riesener delivered this desk to the *Garde-Meuble de la Couronne* on 28th March 1774 for the use of the Comte de Provence, only three months after the desk shown in Plate 141 had been provided for his wife. The documentation for this has been published by Verlet (*Burlington Magazine*, April 1937, page 188). The stylistic differences between the two-desks are striking. That made for the Comtesse has an old-fashioned serpentine conformation while her husband's is composed of regular forms with many straight lines—apart from the wildly curving candelabra which seem to have been cast from the same model as those on the earlier desk.

This was not the earliest piece with straight legs delivered to the couple, however. Already on 27th May 1771, they had received from Joubert 'un Bureau le pied en guaîne' which went into their rooms at the Château de Marly (Archives Nationales, o[1] 3319, fol. 57). See also page 81.

Plate 144

WRITING-DESK. Stamped 'S. Oeben', about 1774. *Victoria and Albert Museum, Jones Collection.*

Simon Oeben was the brother of the more famous Jean-François Oeben who died in 1763. The two brothers married two sisters and Simon's sister-in-law, Jean-François' widow, later married Riesener (see page 219). Since Simon Oeben and Riesener came to be closely linked by marriage, it is not surprising that one finds similarities in their work. The bronze mounts on the legs of the table are almost identical to those on Riesener's desk made for the Comte de Provence, delivered in 1774 and shown in the previous illustration. If they did not actually borrow each others models when having mounts made, there would at least have been nothing to prevent their copying each other's productions.

Simon Oeben must have taken up the new style at a comparatively early date or he would not have become the regular contractor of veneered furniture to both the Marquis de Marigny and the Duc de Choiseul. Haupt also worked for Simon Oeben and for the Duc de Choiseul, as is explained in the Note to Plates 114 and 115. A table in the Duc's rooms, depicted in the miniature illustrated in Plate 464, seems to have the same bold mounts on the legs as those on this and the desk shown in Plate 143.

Plate 145

FALL-FRONT SECRETAIRE. Unstamped, 1774. *Victoria and Albert Museum.*

Robert Cecil published this piece (*Burlington Magazine*, January 1960, pages 35–6) and deciphered the almost illegible inventory-number 2768 on the back. This enabled Verlet to prove that it had been delivered to the *Garde-Meuble de la Couronne* on 30th June 1774 by Gilles Joubert. The records do not indicate for which member of the royal household this piece was provided; they only reveal that it was intended 'pour servir au besoin dans les Maisons Royales' ('to serve where needed in the royal palaces'), and it has not so far been possible to establish where it was first installed (see Verlet, *French Royal Furniture*, page 122).

The main lineaments of this secretaire are decidedly Neo-Classical but some of the mounts have a strangely old-fashioned appearance—notably that on the apron and the key-hole escutcheons which would not have looked at all out of place on a piece of Rococo furniture a quarter of a century earlier. There is a similar secretaire in the J. Paul Getty Museum in California (see Sotheby's sale-catalogue, 21st April 1939, lot. 104) which has rather more cleanly Classical mounts relating it closely to the commode shown in the next illustration. It is stamped 'R.V.L.C.' (for Roger Vandercruse, called Lacroix) but Joubert was presumably also responsible for its creation, because it is so closely related to pieces securely documented as having been provided by him.

Verlet (op. cit. page 120) mentions that a commode stood in Marie Antoinette's bed-chamber at Fontainebleau already in 1770 which had bronze terminal-figure mounts in the form of children. From Joubert's account rendered for furniture delivered to the *Garde-Meuble* in that year (Archives Nationales o^{1} 3622, fol. 4) it is apparent that this piece was ordered on 26th July and was delivered already on 29th September, and that this was the first occasion on which mounts of this kind had been used, for they are described as being 'deux nouveaux Models d'Enfants à demi corps' ('two of the new model with half-length figures of children'). Considering the comparatively short period taken to fulfil this order, it would seem that the models for these mounts already existed when the order was given that July and that Joubert had caused them to be made on his own account in the hope that they might eventually appeal to royal tastes. On 30th September 1771, he delivered for use in the Comtesse de Provence's rooms at Fontainebleau (see Archives Nationales o^{1} 3319, fol. 69 *verso*) a commode with mounts of the same sort—in the form of 'enfans tenans des fleurs et oyseaux terminés en queu de poisson' ('children holding flowers and birds, their bodies ending in fishes' tails'). Several other pieces of furniture with these mounts were delivered during the next few years. The children are, as may be seen, rather large in proportion to the piece of furniture to which they are attached and tend to make it look rather top-heavy. In 1771, however, Joubert produced some furniture for Marie Antoinette's appartment at Versailles (see Verlet, loc. cit.) with some new corner-mounts (cf. 'tous models nouveaux'; Archives Nationales o^{1} 3623, fol. 6 *verso*) in the form of human figures of considerably more elegant proportions and in a style that one imagines would have suited the Queen's taste for lightness and elegance far better. Of this series, only one commode in a private collection is now known.

Plate 146

COMMODE. Unstamped, 1774. *Victoria and Albert Museum.*

This was delivered to the *Garde-Meuble de la Couronne* on 22nd June 1774 by J.-H. Riesener (see Verlet, *Burlington Magazine*, April 1937, page 188 or *French Royal Furniture*, pages 120–1).

Verlet mentions (*French Royal Furniture*, page 120) that Joubert provided a commode for the Dauphine's apartment at Versailles on 30th September 1771 which had a mount in the form of 'un bas relief d'une figure de femme couchée accompagné de deux amours' ('a bas relief consisting of the figure of a reclining woman accompanied by two cupids'). Presumably this mount was taken from the same model as that on the apron of the present piece. The Comte d'Artois also had a commode with a mount in the form of a pictorial relief, in this case, depicting Bacchus with two *amorini* (Archives Nationales, o^{1} 3319, fol. 119). It was delivered by Joubert on 8th November 1773.

As it is Riesener's name that is recorded in the Journal of the *Garde-Meuble*, we must presume that the commode came from his workshop. However, stylistically the commode is so closely related to furniture known to have been manufactured by, or for, Gilles Joubert (notably the secretaire Plate 145) that it seems reasonable to say that Riesener executed this commode to designs delivered by Joubert. As mentioned in the Note to Plate 119, Joubert was by this time a very old man, now about eight-five years old, his workshops were comparatively small, and he was assisted by various cabinet-makers to fulfil the orders of his royal master. Riesener and Joubert seem to have had many dealings with each other during these years; in 1773 Riesener worked for the venerable master-cabinet maker on the desk shown in Plate 141 and in October 1774 we find him taking over some partly-finished furniture standing in Joubert's establishment awaiting completion and dispatch to the *Garde-Meuble de la Couronne*. He may have performed a like service in the present case. See also pages 78 and 81–2.

Plate 147

COMMODE. 1774. *H.M. The Queen, Windsor Castle.*

Verlet has demonstrated that this was handed over to the *Garde-Meuble de la Couronne* by Riesener on 22nd August 1774 (*French Royal Furniture*, pages 123–6). Furthermore, he explains how the order for it was placed after the death of Louis XV on 10th May of that year, and that the intention was to stand it in the late King's private bed-chamber to replace the now exceedingly old-fashioned Rococo commode made for the room by Gaudreaux and J. Caffieri in 1739 (*Wallace Collection Catalogue*, F. 86). However, it was moved already during the next year and finally was placed in the *Cabinet intérieur* where Oeben and Riesener's *Bureau de Roi* (Plates 90 to 93) as well as Joubert's corner-cupboards of 1756 and Gaudreaux's medal-cabinet of 1738 already stood (see page 73). This commode originally had a white marble top; the present red top was fitted to make it match the marble of the chimney-piece in the *Cabinet intérieur*.

Apart from the marquetry picture, which is entirely in Riesener's style, the commode is very much 'à la Joubert', as Verlet pointed out. For instance, the corner-mounts, with their female-heads, are very like those on Joubert's commode of 1769 shown in Plate 120. The Hercules mask in the frieze, on the other hand, is closely similar to one on the secretaire by Riesener illustrated in Plate 113. It is quite possible that this commode was something of a rush-order, required to have the late King's apartments refurnished before the Court returned to Versailles on 1st September. It would hardly have been easy to get a commode with this degree of elaboration constructed and decorated in only four months! Perhaps Riesener had a carcass standing ready which could be adapted in a hurry and decorated suitably. Maybe there was not sufficient time to produce new models for all the mounts, and old ones had to be used—perhaps some were borrowed from Joubert's stock. Whatever the case, Riesener rendered an account claiming that the mounts had all been modelled in wax and then carved in wood 'pour faire les models'. See also page 78.

Plate 148

COMMODE. Stamped 'B. Durand', about 1772–75. *M. le Marquis de Contades, Château de Montgeoffroy.*

The Maréchal de Contades caused his family seat near Angers to be entirely rebuilt and modernised between 1772 and 1775. He seems to have placed large orders for complete sets of furnishings of which much still survives in the house today. Verlet has published the inventory made in 1775 when the work was completed (*La Maison*, pages 260–9). This has enabled the present owner to retain many of the individual pieces of furniture in their original rooms.

Among the surviving pieces are several commodes similar to the one illustrated here, some of which are stamped 'B. Durand', others 'P. Garnier'. In a private collection in Paris are two more commodes from the same Château; one bears both stamps.

The chairs at Montgeoffroy are in the Rococo taste and the veneered furniture—like this commode—is in the transitional style. However, the panelling is in the purest Neo-Classical taste and this style is embodied in several console-tables (see Verlet, *La Maison*, page 123, fig. 78) and in certain fittings like sconces and fire-dogs (Plates 215, 216, and 233).

See M. Binney, 'The Château de Montgeoffroy', *Country Life*, 24th June and 1st July 1971. See also pages 78 and 83.

Plate 149

COMMODE. 1775. *Musée National de Céramique, Sèvres.*

This commode was identified by Verlet (*Mobilier Royal Français*, vol. II, pages 80–1) as being the piece delivered by Riesener on 7th April 1775 to the *Garde-Meuble de la Couronne*, having been commissioned only a month earlier (on 9th March). It cost 410 livres and was intended for Louis XVI's apartment in the old building occupied by the Royal Porcelain factory at Sèvres. It is of solid mahogany. In spite of its serpentine legs, and the fancy shape of the apron, this piece must have seemed ultra-modern in its day on account of the timber used. Mahogany was still very rarely used for furniture in France at this stage, and then chiefly as a veneer or for marquetry details. Madame Adelaïde is known to have had an eight-leaf screen, the frame of which was of solid mahogany (Archives Nationales, o[1] 3319, fol. 75 *verso*). It was provided by Joubert on 21st December 1771 but the wooden component of such a screen is less noticeable than its textile covering, and it is anyway sensible to make the frame of a dense wood. In the case of a commode, on the other hand, it represents something of a luxury. See also page 78.

Plate 150

COMMODE. Stamped 'N. A. Lapie', about 1773–74. *Juelsberg, Denmark.*

In the Juelsberg archives (now in the Landsarkiv in Odense) are bills showing that this commode and the pair of corner-cupboards stamped Mewesen illustrated in the following Plate were acquired in 1774. The corner-mounts with the lion's masks appear to be like those on Riesener's commode of 1775 shown in Plate 149. The ring-handles formed like wreaths, with Roman portraits on their back-plates, must have been something of a novelty at the time. See also pages 78 and 81.

Plate 151

CORNER-CUPBOARD, one of a pair. Stamped 'P. H. Mewesen', about 1773–74. *Juelsberg, Denmark.*

Bought in 1774 for Juelsberg with the commode shown in the previous illustration (see the Note above). See also pages 78 and 81.

Plate 152

FALL-FRONT SECRETAIRE. Unstamped, the main marquetry panel signed 'foulet', about 1776–77. *The Wallace Collection.*

This secretaire has a great deal in common with the corner-cupboards made by Joubert for the Comte d'Artois in 1773 (Plate 142) and one might well conclude that they are all *en suite*. However, this piece cannot have been produced earlier than 1776 for the following rather involved reason.

Geoffrey de Bellaigue has shown that the left-hand section of the marquetry on the fall-front has been copied from the title-page of J. C. Delafosse's *Quatrième livre de trophées contenant divers attributs pastorals* (*Apollo*, January 1963, pages 20–1). This series of engravings is undated but bears the serial letters 'OO' and can thus not have been published before 1776 and probably not before 1777. In his *L'Art du peintre, doreur*, editions of which appeared in 1773, 1776 and 1785, J. F. Watin included a list of those engravings by Delafosse that had so far been issued, and 'OO' is not in either the 1773 or the 1776 editions. The 1776 list ends with 'GG' but a note makes clear that the engraving of further plates was then actively being pursued. The series 'HH' and 'KK' are in fact dated 1776 but one cannot say how many more were engraved that year; all one knows is that the whole work had long been published by the time Watin's third edition of 1785 came out: the list in that edition ends with series 'UU'.

At any rate, the scene on the fall-front cannot be earlier than 1776 or 1777. The writing of the signature 'foulet' (reproduced by Watson, *Wallace Collection Catalogue*, page 147) seems very like that of the *ébéniste* Pierre-Antoine Foullet as it appears in various documents, including the inventory made on the death of his father, Antoine Foullet, in 1775 (Archives Nationales, Minutier Central, XXVIII–452, 30th September 1775).

It is difficult to decide whether Foullet was responsible for the entire production of this elaborate piece of furniture. The marquetry on the sides (not visible here), and some of the bronze framings, are in the style used by both the elder and the younger Foullet (cf. Plates 131 and 132) and the basket of flowers executed in marquetry occurs on the secretaire shown in the next illustration which can also be attributed to the Foullets. P. A. Foullet's affairs were in a poor state at this time and it seems unlikely that he would have been able to undertake the risk of producing such a complicated piece of work on his own account. Perhaps some other *ébéniste* subcontracted this commission to him. The bronze on the apron seems to be identical to some found on works by Riesener (cf. Plate 113 of 1766, and a secretaire of 1770 illustrated by Verlet, *French Royal Furniture*, fig. 18a). It is also found on a commode bearing Garnier's stamp (see Verlet, *Les meubles du XVIIIe siècle*, II, ébénisterie, Plate XXI, 1). See also pages 81–2.

Plate 153

FALL-FRONT SECRETAIRE. Unsigned, about 1770–75. *Nationalmuseum, Stockholm.*

Probably executed by Pierre-Antoine Foullet (rather than by Antoine Foullet, his father—see Note to Plate 131). The triglyph-like mount is to be seen on the commode attributed to Antoine Foullet shown in Plate 131. On the other hand, the frieze is decorated with two entwined ribbons and rosettes, and this is a feature that only seems to be found on pieces bearing the son's mark (e.g. on a commode sold at Christie's on 12th May 1955, lot 109, illustrated in the catalogue). The basket of flowers and garlands executed in marquetry on the doors occurs also on the secretaire of 1776 shown in the previous illustration which can be attributed to Pierre-Antoine Foullet with reasonable certainty. The oval bronze medallion-frames are likewise identical. The vases rendered in marquetry on the sides of this piece are copied from engravings by Maurice Jacques, including that illustrated on Plate 392—the same motif having been used on Joubert's commode of 1769 shown in Plate 119 and on Evald's secretaire shown in Plate 140.

Plate 154

COMBINED WRITING-DESK AND DRESSING-TABLE. Unstamped, about 1776–77. *Victoria and Albert Museum (Jones Collection*, No. 48).

As far as its shape is concerned, this piece could date from as early as 1760 or so; even the gallery, with its Classical pattern, could be of that date (cf. the gallery on the *Bureau du Roi*, Plates 90 and 93). The two heads of huntsmen flanking the gallery and cylinder-top might even have come from a piece of furniture dating from about 1750. On the other hand, most of the other mounts point to a date around 1770. The various amorous symbols on this piece suggests it was made for a lady while the presence of a lion's mask and trophy of arms leads one to suppose it was the gift of some gentleman.

The double interlaced border forming a heart-shaped panel for the central marquetry picture is very similar to that found on an unsigned table at Waddesdon Manor (see Geoffrey de Bellaigue, 'Eighteenth century French Furniture and its Debt to the Engraver', *Apollo*, January 1963, fig. 8). One of the trophies is copied from an engraving by Delafosse which belongs to series 'RR' (see Note to Plate 152) which must date from about 1776–77. The military trophy on the right-hand side of the cylinder is partially taken from Delafosse—from series 'OO' which belongs to the same years. For these reasons, the desk can presumably be dated about 1777; it is difficult to conceive that it could have been made much later.

It is decorated with marquetry on all four sides, indicating that it was designed to stand in the middle of the room—or, at least—not against a wall. In fact, being a dressing-table, it was probably placed near a window where the light would have been good. For furniture like this, which was to be free-standing, it seems to have been the convention to retain a serpentine conformation for far longer than in other classes. Moreover, it may well have been accepted that one avoided any severe form of Classicism—any hint of 'le goût mâle'—in furniture intended expressly for feminine use. This might well account for the great stylistic differences between the two desks made respectively for the Comte and the Comtesse de Provence in 1773 and 1774 (Plates 141 and 143).

Plate 155

WRITING-CHAIR. Stamped 'E. Michard', about 1765. *Musée Nissim de Camondo.*

While the outlines of this chair are curvilinear, the carved ornament is clearly Classical in inspiration. Note particularly the interlaced pattern on the seat-rail and the angular scroll at the base of the arm-support, the rosette within a rectangle at the top of the leg, and the garland looped round the back.

Dating this chair is not easy. A *terminus post quem* is the year 1757 during which Claude-Etienne Michard became a *maître-menuisier*. Chairs with features similar to those of this chair are to be seen in three portraits dating from 1761 to 1763 by the Swedish artist Alexander Roslin who became a fashionable portrait-painter in the French capital during these years (see Plates 353, 355 and 371). The small sunken, rectangular panel with a rosette within, on the other hand, points to a date towards the later 1760s—as far as French chairs are concerned. A rosette so placed is to be seen on a chair illustrated in an engraving by P. A. Baudouin which is dated 1765 (Plate 389) and on a chair designed by Prieur in 1766 for the Polish Court (Plates 411 to 414). We, furthermore, know that the Marquis de Marigny, who sat for one of the portraits just mentioned (Plate 353), had bought, already in July 1763, twenty-eight chairs and three sofas which are described as having legs 'à gaines avec des plinthes caré' ('straight legs with squared blocks') in the tapissier Antoine Godefroy's account (see the present author's 'Marigny and Le Goût Grec', *Burlington Magazine*, March 1962, page 98). Perhaps the sunken rectangular panels with rosettes on the chair here illustrated could also be described as 'plinthes caré' although the legs are of course not 'à gaines'.

See Jean Messelet, *Musée Nissim de Camondo*, 1960, No. 199. See also page 84.

Plate 156

ARMCHAIR. Stamped 'L. Delanois', about 1765. *Valentine Abdy Collection, Newton Ferrers, Cornwall.*

This chair was first published by Verlet (*La Maison*, Plate 94) where, however, it is stated by mistake that the chair is stamped by Nicolas Heurtaut and that there are two of them. It is in fact a single chair and is not stamped by Heurtaut but by Delanois. No other example is known.

Although this piece has a serpentine form, the unusually rich carving, which is mostly of Antique inspiration, bears witness to a very positive Neo-Classical inclination. This chair corresponds stylistically to the *Bureau du Roi* produced by Oeben and Riesener between 1760 and 1769 (see Plates 90 to 93).

It cannot be earlier than 1761 when Delanois became a master. In style, it somewhat resembles a chair to be seen in Roslin's portrait of the Marquis de Marigny, painted in 1761 (Plate 353) while the curious flutes on the seat-rails occur on a chair depicted by the same painter in the portrait of Count Czernichev, executed a year later (Plate 355). On the other hand, there is absolutely no mention of a chair of this description in Delanois' accounts before 1768. However, his account-book only covers furniture bought by customers who were given credit. Maybe he was paid cash for it.

Customers sometimes asked for a specimen chair to be made when considering the placing of an order for a set of seat-furniture and this piece may well be such a 'pattern chair' (these sometimes had alternative treatments on the arms and on the legs, so the customer could select one form of ornament or the other). It might also have been made by Delanois as a workshop model, in which case it would certainly not have figured in the accounts. See also pages 84–5.

Plate 157

ARMCHAIR. Stamped 'I. P. Letelier', about 1765. *M. Bernard Dillée, Paris.*

From a set of six, said to come from the Château de Menars, the Marquis de Marigny's country-house in the Loire Valley (see pages 84–5).

Plate 158

ARMCHAIR. Unsigned, about 1765. *Messrs. Alexander & Berendt Ltd., London.*

This bears the same inventory-mark as the table shown in Plate 115, here attributed to Haupt, and must presumably also come from Chanteloup, the Duc de Choiseul's country-house near Tours. See also pages 84–5.

Plate 159

ARMCHAIR. Stamped 'I. Pothier', about 1765. *Metropolitan Museum of Art, gift of J. Pierpont Morgan.*

The general shape of this chair is in the traditional Rococo taste but it has certain Neo-Classical features. The crest-rail rises to a point in the centre (cf. Plate 156) and this suggests an early date—perhaps in the early 1760s. But the strictly horizontal lines of the seat-rails can hardly be earlier than 1765 (cf. the chairs illustrated in Baudouin's engraving of that year, shown in Plate 389). The 'à la grecque' border must of course also have been a very advanced feature on a chair in 1765—remembering that chair-makers tended to be much more conservative than cabinet-makers.

Jean-Jacques Pothier became a master chair-maker in 1750 but is not known to have been a man of particularly progressive ideas. On the other hand, he lived next door to Delanois in the Rue de Bourbon Villeneuve, and we do know that the latter was one of the very first Parisian chair-makers to adopt the new taste. See also pages 84–5.

Plate 160

ARMCHAIR. Not stamped, about 1765–70. *Musée des Arts Décoratifs, Paris.*

This chair, and the one shown in the next illustration, both have a basically Rococo form but the decoration is mainly Classical and the seat-rails are essentially horizontal. The bold carving suggests an early date. They are probably not unlike the chairs ordered from Nicolas-Quinibert Foliot for the Petit Trianon in 1767 although the latter were no doubt richer in their decoration. None of the chairs from the Petit Trianon have so far been identified but we know a good deal about them from the accounts of Nicolas Foliot and those of his brother, Toussaint, who executed the carving (both are preserved in the Archives Nationales, o[1] 3619[1]). Toussaint's bill shows how his carving was consonant in style with that of the *boiseries* carved by Honoré Guibert.

One item reads as follows: 'Grande Salle à Manger. Vingt quatre chaises composé dans les Cadres de plusieurs Corps de architecture dont le Superieur est taillé d'un ornement en Entrelas enrichi de Treffles avec des rosasses dans le milieu, et sur les coins des revers de feuilles et Cartels, dans les bas des pieds sont des bouquets de jasmin noués avec des rubans et dans les traverses des ornements à l'antique dans le goût de l'apartement . . .' ('The Large Dining-room. Twenty-four chairs, the framing of which are composed of several architectural ornaments, the crest-rail carved with an interlaced ornament enriched with trefoils and rosettes at the centre. At the corners of the top are leaves and cartouches; at the root of the legs are bunches of jasmine tied with ribbons, and on the seat-rail are ornaments in the Antique taste consonant with the *décor* of the room'.) The chairs in the Small Dining-room were similar; the gilder Bardou specifically states that they were 'sculptées à la Grecque' ('carved *à la Grecque*'). See also page 85.

Plate 161

ARMCHAIR. Not stamped, about 1765–70. *Musée des Arts Décoratifs, Paris.*

See the previous Note.

Plate 162

CHAIR, one of a pair. Stamped 'L. Delanois', about 1765–70. *Formerly in the Collection of Clive Howe Ltd., New York.*

The regular curve of the crest-rail virtually precludes a date before 1765 for this chair. The presence of Classical ornament carved with great deliberation speaks of a date anywhere between 1765 and 1770. Such ornament is often described as being with *entrelacs* and *rubans tournants* in Delanois' account-book but it has not been possible to trace an entry which undoubtedly corresponds with these actual chairs. See also pages 84–5.

Plate 163

ARMCHAIR, one of a set of six. Stamped 'M. Gourdin', about 1765–70. *The Wallace Collection.*

What has been said about the Delanois chair shown in Plate 156 also applies to the present example. The model is undoubtedly from the second half of the 1760s although this actual set may have been produced as late as 1777 or even after that, because there is a fleur-de-lis stamped alongside Gourdin's mark and this may indicate that they were not made until he had become Chair-maker to the French Court in 1777 (see Watson, *Wallace Collection Furniture*, page 100). See also pages 84–5.

Plate 164

ARMCHAIR. Stamped 'L. Delanois', about 1765–70. *Formerly with André Carlhian's Collection, Paris.*

The owner of this imposing chair had it upholstered in something like the original manner, although the festoons would probably have been trimmed with fringe as well. A drawing of 1765 showing a chair upholstered in this way is shown in Plate 398. In fact, it is not easy to date this chair. Like the chair made for Lalive de Jully about 1758 (Plate 322), this piece would seem to have been designed by an architect. It has something of the spirit of Neufforge's designs for chairs which appeared in 1768 (Plates 434 to 436) but probably dates from a few years before that.

Mention of chairs with rectilinear configurations first occurs in Delanois' accounts on 28th June 1768, on which day he delivered a 'fauteuil carré les pieds tourné a lantique' to a *marchand-tapissier* named Caumont. A tall armchair with a square back like that on this example is depicted in an engraving entitled *Le Dédomagement de l'Absence* which was executed by Géraud Vidal in 1770 after a drawing by J. E. Schenau (Plate 467).

The Marquis de Marigny, who was known for his progressive leanings, acquired a chair from the *marchand-tapissier* Godefroy on 12th January 1768. The relevant entry in Godefroy's account reads 'pour Servir dans la chambre de Monsieur fait un grand fauteüil, comode, tout caré par devant et sur tous sens les bras de toute la profondeur les pieds sculptés a moulures avec une baguette au pourtour du fond, peint en blanc adoucy et garni de crin' ('to stand in his Lordship's bed-chamber, a large armchair, quite square in front and in each direction, the arms running the whole length, the legs carved with mouldings and a fillet round the seat-rail, painted off-white, covered with horse-hair cloth'; Bibliothèque Historique de la Ville de Paris, nouv. acq., MS. 106 bis, fol. 421). The present chair can, however, hardly be identical with that made for Marigny since neither the Marquis nor Godefroy were numbered among Delanois' customers.

See Pierre Devinoy and Madeleine Jarry, *Le Siège en France du moyen âge à nos Jours*, Paris, 1948, Plate 220. See also page 92.

Plate 165

ARMCHAIR. Stamped 'L.Delanois', about 1768–70. *Comte Jean-Louis de Maigret, Paris.*

Although this richly carved and no doubt very expensive chair has several characteristics which should make it easily identifiable, it has not been possible to equate it with a specific entry in Delanois' account-book. Chairs with oval backs and straight legs are first mentioned in his ledger on 28th June 1768 where a large consignment was dispatched to Count Grimod d'Orsay (see the present author's *Delanois*, pages 32 and 52). Prieur was designing chairs with these features already in 1766 for the Palace at Warsaw (Plates 412 and 414) and several chairs embodying them were included in Volume VIII of Neufforge's *Recueil d'Architecture* which appeared in 1768 (Plates 434 to 436). By 1769, several chairs of this sort are mentioned in Delanois' account. Moreau's famous view of the party at the Pavillon de Louveciennes, showing such chairs, was executed in 1771 (Plate 474) and Roubo illustrates some in that section of his *L'Art du menuisier* which appeared in 1772 (Plates 476 and 477). An almost oval chair-back may be discerned in a gouache by Baudouin of 1765 which was subsequently engraved by Jean Massard (Plate 389).

This chair has various archaic features which suggest it is an early essay in Neo-Classicism, like the fore-going square-backed chair. Both are massive in their proportions and in their members. Note particularly the heavy garland of bay leaves surrounding the back and the obtrusive consoles supporting the arms. The back is connected to the seat-rail by a large squared volute similar to those forming the feet on Oeben's secretaire shown in Plate 94, which should date from about 1760 or so. A similar volute can just be seen in Prieur's design for a chair of 1766 shown in Plate 412. The joint between the strictly horizontal arm-rest and the oval back is rather unsatisfactory and betrays the experimental nature of this design. This awkward junction is slightly more successfully handled on a somewhat similar chair by Delanois in the Metropolitan Museum of Art (see Eriksen, *Delanois*, Plate XXXV). See also page 92.

Plates 166 and 167

SOFA AND ARMCHAIR, from a set originally comprising two sofas (*canapés*) and twelve chairs. Stamped 'N. Heurtaut', about 1768–69. *Musée du Louvre.*

Monsieur Pierre Verlet has kindly drawn my attention to the fact that these splendid examples of French seat-furniture, which are now in the Louvre, came from the Château de la Roche-Guyon. One can see an illustration of them in what is presumably their original setting in *Les anciens châteaux de France* (6e série, *L'Ile-de-France*, Plates 9 to 11, edited by F. Contet). They are there seen in a large Neo-Classical drawing-room which is said (by Paul Jarry, who wrote the text) to have been completed in 1769. This date agrees with what we know about the four large tapestries with scenes from the Story of Esther which the Gobelin's factory was producing for the room. According to Maurice Fenaille (*Etat général des tapisseries de la*

Manufacture des Gobelins, vol. IV, pages 36 and 396) these were manufactured during 1768 and 1769 together with covers for two *canapés* and twelve armchairs. It seems reasonable to assume that the wooden frames for this set were designed, assembled, carved and gilded at about the same time.

The shape of the backs and the form of the arms retain elements of the Rococo tradition, but the straight legs with their fluting and the carved decoration are Classical in inspiration, and this set of furniture must have seemed extraordinarily advanced in taste when it was new. The backs of this set are upright and one can assume it was designed to stand firmly against the wall. One might therefore expect that the curious profile of the backs—repeated thrice on the sofas—was intended to correspond with the profiles of the *boiseries* against which these pieces stood, but this is not the case. This strange shape must therefore be the result of trying to make a traditional Rococo chair-back agree with a new, and still not fully formulated, notion of how a chair in the Classical taste ought to look. See also pages 85 and 90.

Plates 168 and 169

SOFA AND ARMCHAIR, one of a set comprising two sofas and twelve chairs. Not stamped, about 1768–70. *The Wallace Collection.*

Although this set was believed to have been acquired shortly before 1778 by the 14th Earl of Shrewsbury for his house, Heythrop Hall (see Watson, *Wallace Collection Furniture*, pages 106–7, F.219–232) it seems probable, on stylistic grounds, that they were made about a decade earlier. The shape of the chair-backs suggest a date about, or shortly before 1770. Boldly carved floral ornament and garlands in full relief, such as is to be seen on this set, occur in the designs for seat-furniture composed by Prieur in 1766 for the Warsaw Palace (see page 88 and Plates 411 to 414). Indeed, this sofa is particularly reminiscent of the one Prieur designed for that important commission. We know from the gilder Cagny's detailed accounts that Madame du Barry also had a set of furniture made for her apartment in 1769–70 which had carving of a similar accentuated character.

The rosettes carved on the shoulders are a curious feature. The same motif is to be seen on Heurtaut's furniture of 1768–69 which was the subject of the two previous illustrations.

Incidentally, Mrs. Lybbe Powys, writing in 1778 after visiting Heythrop Hall, where this set of furniture once stood, speaks of 'two sofas ninety guineas each, each chair thirty. They are of tent stitch—work[ed] at Paris, the carved frames made there and gilt in England' (*Wallace Collection Catalogue*, loc. cit.). Her statements may well refer to this actual set.

Plate 170

ARMCHAIR, one of a set of four. Stamped 'N. Heurtaut', about 1768–70. *Charles B. Wrightsman Collection, New York.*

Originally part of a larger set formerly in the collection of Madame Jacques Balsan; a sofa from the set is illustrated by Charles Packer (*Paris Furniture by the Master Ebénistes*, fig. 106) but its present whereabouts are not known. The sofa has a back rather like that of the sofa by Carpentier shown in Plate 174, which dates from about 1770. The arms of the present chair are virtually identical to those on the set illustrated in the two previous Plates which were made about 1768–70. These chairs must be of about the same date.

See Watson, *Wrightsman Collection*, No. 10. See also page 88.

Plate 171

ARMCHAIR. One of a set comprising sofa, six armchairs and two *bergères*. Stamped 'L. Carpentier' (two additionally stamped 'C.J.Y.M.'), about 1768–69. *Present whereabouts unknown.*

These were sold at Christie's on 19th May 1966 (lots 110 and 111).

A chair of this type is to be seen in Alexander Roslin's portrait of Bertin, the Minister of Finance, painted in 1769 (Plate 447). What seems to be the Bertin chair, also stamped by Carpentier, is preserved in a Parisian collection which, however, is not illustrated here because it is at present covered with a material that has an anachronistic pattern which tends to confuse the matter (it is illustrated by Verlet, *La Maison*, fig. 37). This chair must have been in existence at any rate by 1769 and probably a year or so earlier, since it naturally took time not only to paint the portrait but to make the chair beforehand.

The present chair differs only slightly from the Bertin chair and, since it is by the same maker, must presumably date from about the same period.

The stamp 'C.J.Y.M.' is found not unfrequently alongside the stamp of a chair-maker. It may be the mark of a carver. See also page 90.

Plate 172

CHAIR. Stamped 'L. Delanois', 1769–70. *Madame Arturo Lopez-Willshaw, Neuilly.*

As Salverte originally pointed out, this chair is without doubt one of the large set provided for Madame du Barry's Pavillon de Louveciennes (*Les ébénistes*, article on Delanois). Delanois completed the frames on 1st December 1769 after which they were carved by Joseph-Nicolas Guichard and then gilded by Jean-Baptiste Cagny. It is not known who designed these chairs, however. Ledoux, the architect of the Pavillon, can hardly have done so, since the chairs are not mentioned in his apparently very carefully itemised accounts for the work. Perhaps they were designed by Gondoin who had been attached to the *Garde-meuble de la Couronne* since 1767 and who, in 1769, became its designer of furniture. This suggestion cannot be substantiated, however, by any evidence whatsoever, at present. At any rate, Delanois' part in this matter was entirely subordinate; there is no reason to believe he had a hand in designing these chairs or even in producing a model.

The delicacy of the carving on this chair is noteworthy. It is of a quality reminiscent of goldsmith's work. In this respect they are quite different from other French chairs of the 1760s (cf. Plates 158 to 161). Minute elaboration in the carving was to become a characteristic feature of really luxurious seat-furniture made in the next decade, on the other hand. See also page 91.

Plate 173

CHAIR. Stamped 'L. Delanois', 1769–70. *Madame Arturo Lopez-Willshaw, Neuilly.*

Although there is no proof, stylistic features make it probable that this chair, like the previous example, was made for the Pavillon de Louveciennes. It has carved ornament of the same delicacy (see Note to Plate 172).

Plate 174

SOFA, from a set consisting of two sofas, four *bergères*, eight armchairs and four backstools. Stamped 'L. Carpentier', about 1770. *Formerly in the collection of Baron L. d'Ivry, Paris; present whereabouts unknown.*

This sofa and its companion pieces were sold at the Baron d'Ivry Sale held in the Galerie Georges Petit on 7th–9th May 1884 (lot 307); only one sofa was illustrated in the catalogue and this hazy photograph is reproduced here. According to the catalogue, the whole set was upholstered in Gobelins tapestry which had multi-coloured flowers with dark blue stalks and leaves on a lighter blue ground. The legs had spiral fluting and there were *entrelacs* carved on the seat-rails. The back was carved with *feuilles d'eau*. From this, one can see that the ornaments were entirely Neo-Classical in style.

In a report on the forthcoming sale of 1884, Paul Eudel wrote (*L'Hôtel Drouot et la curiosité en 1883–84*, pages 329–30) that this set came from the Château d'Hénonville which, in the eighteenth century, had belonged to a Baron d'Ivry, the grand-father of the Baron who was selling the furniture. This man had been a *fermier-général* and he had had the house modernised by the architect Barré who had already built the Hôtel Grimod de la Reynière in Paris, and who later designed the Château de Marais and altered the Château de Montgeoffroy. Paul Eudel, whose statement can scarcely be pure invention, adds that he has before him as he writes the accounts of those who collaborated over the renovations at the Château d'Hénonville, from which it became clear to him that the Baron had spent no less than 418,601 livres on the task between 1765 and 1771. Eudel quotes from some of the bills but gives no precise dates. All the same, he mentions that the sum of 3,300 livres was paid to Sieur Carpentier *menuisier de meubles* (sic) and 7,200 to MM. des Gobelins.

It is to be presumed that Baron d'Ivry did not give much thought to the furniture he would require until the alterations he was making were well under way. Thus orders are not likely to have been placed for this set much before 1770. In May of that year, Lachenait began to execute the carved decoration on the chairs intended for the Prince de Condé's Palais de Bourbon, for which Carpentier also provided the frames. Lachenait's very precise accounts (Chantilly, Archives Condé, ledger 76, fol. 3) show that the Palais Bourbon furniture was richer but in other respects it must have been very similar to this set.

Even from this poor illustration, one can see that the Gobelins tapestry is not exactly like that on the La Roche-Guyon set (see Plates 166 and 167) but is identical in pattern to that made between 1765 and 1769 for a set of seat-furniture intended for Moor Park, the seat of Sir Laurence Dundas. The frames for this set were produced in London by the firm of Turton and Fell and not by that of Samuel Norman, as has previously been asserted (see E. Harris, *The Furniture of Robert Adam*, 1963, fig. 105—a window stool; also C. Musgrave's book, in the present series, on *Adam and Hepplewhite . . . Furniture*, 1966, figs. 61 and 82—a chair and a sofa. The set is now in the Philadelphia Museum of Art). Fenaille does not mention the Ivry set in his *Etat général des tapisseries de la Manufacture des Gobelins*.

The cover on the La Roche sofa corresponds with that on the set of seat-furniture made in 1769 for Lord Coventry and formerly at Croome Court where they were associated with Gobelins tapestries on the walls. The whole set is now at the Metropolitan Museum, New York (see Musgrave, op. cit., figs. 63 and 102). See also page 80.

Plates 175 and 176

TWO ARMCHAIRS, part of a set of six. Two stamped 'L. Delanois' and two 'G. Jacob', about 1770. *Present whereabouts unknown.*

These chairs were seen publicly when they were sold at an auction in Paris in 1968 (Palais Galliéra, 22nd October 1968, lot 143). The fact that they bear the stamps of two different chairmakers may indicate that the set was commissioned by a *marchand-tapissier* and that it was a rush order that could only be met by spreading the task over two workshops. Actually, Delanois and Georges Jacob were acquainted—they may even have been good friends—and it is not surprising to find them collaborating.

These chairs cannot be definitely associated with any single entry in Delanois' accounts but one comes across several descriptions of chairs produced by him around 1770 which had features similar to those of these chairs. For example, the *marchand-tapissier*, Mallet, received from Delanois on 8th March 1771 some chairs with 'dossiers ovals' and 'pieds à gaine', as well as 'consolles torces'—that is, with oval backs, straight legs and snaking arm-supports. See also page 83.

Plates 177 and 178

SOFA AND ARMCHAIR, from a set comprising two sofas and eight chairs. Stamped 'L. C. Carpentier', about 1770. *Formerly in Viscount Astor's Collection, Cliveden.*

Comparison with Carpentier's sofa of about 1770 (Plate 174) and his chair of slightly earlier date (Plate 171), suggests that the present set must date from about 1770 or shortly after. The still serpentine form of the chair-back can hardly be later than 1775. The tapestry covers may be original. They belong to the series entitled *Les quatre parties du Monde* which was first woven in 1748 (see Fenaille, *Etat général des tapisseries de la Manufacture des Gobelins*). The nearly horizontal top to the back of the sofa was perhaps designed to fit under a rectangular panel of the *boiseries* in its original setting (cf. the *canapé* in the view of the salon at the Hôtel Grimod de la Reynière; Plate 82). See also page 90.

Plate 179

ARMCHAIR. Stamped 'N. Q. Foliot', about 1772–73. *Musée du Louvre.*

This is part of the set sometimes called *Le Mobilier des Dieux* after the Gods depicted on the tapestry covers which, incidentally, are reproductions. The set comprises an armchair and four backstools, all made in the eighteenth century, and three more backstools plus two sofas which are all copies produced in the last century (see Verlet, *Mobilier Royal*, I, pages 61–5). Verlet's studies have also shown that, in 1786, there were in store two armchairs and four backstools, and that this group was then supplemented by a pair of *bergères* and a stool (*tabouret*) specially designed to go *en suite*. The whole set was then re-upholstered and placed in Marie-Antoinette's rooms at the Château de Choisy.

So far, it has not been possible to discover whence the set of chairs that were in store in 1786 originally came. They must by that time have been of some age, since their gilding was then stated to have been in need of cleaning and restoration. In fact, it seems probable that they date from about 1772 or 1773—years from which there are regrettable gaps in the Garde-Meuble's craftsmen's accounts in the Archives Nationales. For example, none of Foliot's or Gondoin's accounts from this period seem to survive. One cannot place them back in the 1760s on stylistic grounds; we have plenty of contemporary evidence to show that chairs like those made for the Petit Trianon (cf. Plate 160) had boldly carved ornament of an architectural nature, and this is not a feature of this chair and its companion-pieces. Indeed, the sole 'architectural' ornament consists of small-scale border patterns (pearl-motifs and *rais-de-coeur*). It is the floral decoration that is dominant and, in this respect, the set has more in common with furniture like that shown in the next illustration, which dates from 1775. However, the seat-rail still has a marked serpentine form that betokens an earlier date. For these reasons, a date between 1767, when the Petit Trianon set was made, and 1775 is proposed; 1772–73 would seem about right.

Plate 180

CHAIR. Stamped 'F. Foliot', 1775. *Château de Versailles.*

As Pierre Verlet has shown, this is part of a large set on which work was started in August 1774—four months after the death of Louis XV. The chairs were designed by Gondoin and the frames made by François II Foliot, after which his brother Toussaint Foliot did the carving. They then of course had first to be gilded and then upholstered in the atelier of Capin, the *maître-tapissier*. Capin's accounts show that they were 'à carreaux' (fitted with cushions) and covered with crimson silk damask; the present upholstery probably gives a reasonably faithful idea of their original appearance (see Verlet, *Mobilier Royal*, II, pages 121–25).

When new, the set consisted of twenty-five chairs and two screens—one with six leaves and one with four. They were to go in the *Cabinet des Jeux*, also known as the *Cabinet de la Pendule*, at Versailles. This room was faced with *boiseries* carved in the full Rococo style by Verberckt, executed some twenty-five years earlier. In the centre of the room stood the imposing pendulum clock by Passement, with its exceedingly elaborate Rococo case by Jacques Caffieri. It is hardly conceivable that Gondoin, in designing this set, did not take the character of these existing furnishings into account. This may be why he did not give the chairs straight legs or square backs—why he played down the Classical element. All the same, they are notably less serpentine in their general conformation than, for example, chairs like that shown in the preceding illustration which is here dated about 1772–73. The top edge of the seat-rail, for example, is now strictly horizontal, and the lower edge runs parallel to it except where it curves down into the legs. The carved decoration consists of a mixture of Classical and floral motifs.

By the beginning of 1774, before this set was ordered and while Louis XV was still alive, there were still no chairs with straight legs at Versailles except in Madame du Barry's apartment, where several sets of chairs entirely Neo-Classical in character and richly carved, were already installed (see Plates 168 and 169). By the end of that year, with the King dead, his mistress dethroned, and all her possessions removed from the Palace, one could probably not find a single straight-legged chair or sofa in the place! It was not until 16th October 1775 that orders were given for some seat-furniture that was to be as advanced in design as the sets Madame du Barry had had in her rooms. The order was for four round stools with straight legs; it was placed with Nicolas-Quinibert Foliot (see Foliot's account in the Archives Nationales, o[1] 3624). All the other chairs Foliot provided for the Court, even at this late date, still had serpentine legs. The next year, however, several chairs in the new style were ordered but chairs continued to be purchased with the old serpentine forms right into the 1780s (e.g. Madame Adelaïde's seat-furniture of 1785; see Verlet, *Mobilier Royal*, II, Plates XXXVI–XXXVII).

Plate 181

CHAIR, one of a set of six. Stamped 'L. Delanois', about 1770–75. *Pavlovsk Palace, U.S.S.R.*

From 1768 onwards, many chairs figure in Delanois' account that must have resembled this, judging from the descriptions. One sees chairs of this kind in Moreau's famous picture of the party given in the Pavillon du Louveciennes in 1771 (Plate 474), and Roubo illustrates something like it in his *L'Art du menuisier* of 1772 (see Plates 476 and 477, here). It will be noted that the legs are highly tapered. This may be an archaic feature and therefore the set may have been made nearer 1770 than 1775. The nailing is now too widely-spaced. See also page 92.

Plate 182

ARMCHAIR, from a set of four. Stamped 'N. Heurtaut', about 1770–75. *Present whereabouts unknown.*

These were sold at Sotheby's on 22nd November 1963 (lot 41). The upholstery may possibly be the original. A similar chair with a tapestry cover of what appears to be the same pattern is illustrated in Duclos' engraving of 1774 (Plate 486). All the same, this chair could be slightly earlier in date—like the chair shown in the preceding plate. Certain details suggest an early date (e.g. the fact that the blocks at the top of the front legs are not square but rectangular, which seems a 'primitive' feature).

Plates 183 and 184

A PAIR OF CARVED FRAMES containing Sèvres plaques. 1768. *Rosenborg Castle, Copenhagen.*

The two porcelain plaques were among presents given to the King of Denmark (Christian VII) when he visited France in November 1768. The plaque shown in Plate 183 bears the date-letter 'O' for 1767; the other bears a 'P' for 1768, and is signed by the decorator Dodin who also added the date. On the reverse of each frame are pasted strips of paper which partly cover the plaques as well. These strips are waste paper from the Sèvres factory's offices; they have been cut from large manuscript cash-books like those still preserved at the factory in which the wages paid to workmen were recorded. There can therefore be no reason to doubt that these frames have been associated with these porcelain plaques from the very beginning.

While these are the earliest known dateable Neo-Classical frames in existence, we know that one could see frames of similar character in the workshops of Honoré Guibert about 1760–61 (Plates 345 to 348).

Plate 185

THE STRONG-BOX OF THE STRASBOURG JOINERS' COMPANY. By François de Paule-Joseph Kaeshammer, 1770–71. *Musée de la Ville de Strasbourg.*

This is inscribed 'Boëte de la Communauté des Maîtres Menuisiers Français de la Ville de Strasbourg. Agrée par Mrs les XV. Fait pour chef-d'oeuvre et donné pour présent à ladite Maîtrise par François de Paule-Joseph Kaeshammer, l'an MDCCLXXI' ('Strong-box of the Guild of French Master-Joiners in the City of Strasbourg. Accepted by the Honourable Fifteen [members of the Court of Assistants]. Made by François de Paule-Joseph Kaeshammer in the year 1771 as his masterpiece and subsequently presented to the Guild'; quoted from Salverte, *Les Ebénistes*, pages 171–2). Kaeshammer became a master-joiner on 3rd January 1771. Since this was offered as his master-piece, it must have been made before that date—during 1770.

This box exemplifies the 'archaic' style of early Neo-Classicism as construed by 'primitives' like Delafosse.

Plate 186

TRIPOD. About 1773. *Charles B. Wrightsman Collection, New York.*

This may well be one of the original *Athéniennes* (see page 138). The form was devised by J.-H. Eberts and advertised for the first time in September 1773 (see Plate 484). Both Madame du Barry and the Duc de Chartres owned *Athéniennes* (see Watson, *Wrightsman Collection*, vol. 1, pages 103–4).

Plate 187

URN-SHAPED CLOCK. Gilt bronze. Probably designed by L.-J. Le Lorrain. Movement by J. Le Roy, about 1756–57. *Musée Condé, Chantilly.*

This is very likely the clock designed to stand on Lalive de Jully's filing-cabinet, illustrated in Plate 89. If so, we may assume that the gilt bronze case was designed by Louis-Joseph Le Lorrain who designed the filing-cabinet and its accompanying table. Moreover, the bronze-work was probably executed by Philippe Caffieri (see the Note to Plate 85). The movement is signed by Julien Le Roy.

A clock which seems to be similar in all details was in the Marcel Boulanger sale held at the Hôtel Drouot on 14th November 1929 (lot 166, illustrated). According to the catalogue, this case was signed 'Osmond', which may stand for Robert Osmond, a bronze-founder of considerable standing in his day. Osmond seems to have been a friend of Caffieri's; both were among the founders who signed the articles governing the copying of designs on 21st April 1766. The presence of his name on an identical case is, at any rate, unlikely to mean that he had been guilty of plagiarising Caffieri's design; it is more probable that Caffieri lent or transferred the model to Osmond for some reason.

It is as well to know that Parisian bronze-founder Alfred Beurdeley, who was active in the second half of the last century, seems to have made some clock-cases of this type. When his stock was sold at the Galerie Georges Petit between 6th and 8th May 1895, lot 86 consisted of a 'Pendule de style Louis XVI, en bronze ciselé et doré, ayant la forme d'un vase-urne, à anses de mufles de lion, anneaux mouvants, couvercle surmonté d'une pomme de pin, piédouche creusé de canaux en spirale; socle quadrangulaire à gorge et guirlandes de chêne' ('Clock in the *Louis Seize* style, of gilt and chased bronze, in the form of an urn with lion's masks holding swinging ring-handles; the cover surmounted by a pine cone. The stand decorated with spiral fluting and supported by a square plinth with orifices from which hang garlands of oak leaves'.) It is interesting to note that the pattern was described as 'Modèle d'Osmont'!

Plate 188

MANTEL CLOCK. Gilt and patinated; wooden base, stamped 'Joseph' (Baumhauer). Movement by Ferdinand Berthoud, about 1758–65. *The Wallace Collection.*

During the winter of 1758, Lazare Duvaux sold two clocks that might well have been of this type; the descriptions, which are almost identical in their wording, run as follows 'Une pendule à sonner de J. Le Roy, composée d'une figure couchée représentant l'Etude en bronze doré d'or moulu' ('A striking clock by J. Le Roy, with a recumbent figure emblematic of study executed in gilt-bronze'; *Livre-Journal*, No. 3240 and 3260). The first was paid for by Louis XV and presented to the young Duc de Bourgogne; it cost 1,200 livres. The other cost only 950 livres and was bought by the Comte du Luc.

It is not known who designed this case, nor do we know who produced the bronze case, but the base, which is of oak veneered with mahogany, is stamped by the cabinet-maker Joseph Baumhauer who died in 1772. Francis Watson (*Wallace Collection Catalogue*, F. 267) mentions five other examples of this model including one that originally stood in Horace Walpole's villa at Strawberry Hill and which Geoffrey de Bellaigue believes is the one now at Waddesdon Manor. There are further examples at Schloss Wilhelmshöhe near Kassel and at the Château de Rambouillet. On none of the known examples is there a bronze-founder's signature.

The bold Vitruvian scroll is a characteristic 'archaic' Neo-Classical feature, as we have noted. See also page 99.

Plate 189

MUSICAL CLOCK. Gilt and patinated bronze. Model by Augustin Pajou, 1765–67. *The Danish Royal Collection, Amalienborg Palace, Copenhagen.*

The model for this very large clock (it is four feet high) was produced by the sculptor Augustin Pajou and was exhibited at the Paris *Salon* held in the autumn of 1765. The casting and chasing of the case was carried out by the founder Jean-Joseph de Saint-Germain during 1766 and 1767. The clock was commissioned by the King of Denmark, Frederik V, and cost 6,000 livres (see Mario Krohn, *Frankrigs og Danmarks kunstnersiske Forbindelse i det 18. Aarhundrede*, Copenhagen, 1922, Vol. II, pages 205–6).

The patinated figures are emblematic of Agriculture, Commerce, Seafaring, Art and Science.

The movement is Danish and a replacement. See also page 100.

Plate 190

MANTEL CLOCK. Gilt bronze. About 1766. *Formerly in the Royal Palace at Warsaw; present whereabouts unknown.*

According to Stanislas Iskierski (*Les bronzes du château royal et du palais de Lazienki*, 1929, page 22) the movement of this clock was inscribed 'Le Paute de Belle Fontaine à Paris'. There were several clockmakers by the name of Le Paute. Nothing is said of any bronze-founder's signature, however, but we can be fairly sure that the clock-case was among the numerous items of furniture executed in Paris about 1766. The model was presumably by J.-F. Prieur who may also have supervised the casting (see Plate 406).

Until the outbreak of the Second World War, this clock was still in the Warsaw Palace. This building was certainly destroyed by the Germans but it is quite conceivable that the clock was preserved and still survives. Whether one should seek it East or West of Warsaw, on the other hand, is not certain! See also page 100.

Plate 191

MANTEL CLOCK. Gilt bronze. About 1766–70. *Present whereabouts unknown.*

This case is not signed but it may tentatively be attributed to Jean-Louis Prieur who signed the clock shown in the next illustration. There are also close similarities between this clock and that shown in the drawing of 1766 illustrated in Plate 408. This clock was included in the Albert von Goldschmidt-Rothschild's auction, held in Berlin on 14th March 1933 (lot 38, illustrated). See also page 100.

Plate 192

MANTEL CLOCK. Gilt and patinated bronze. Signed 'Prieur Sculpteur Paris', about 1766–70. *Present whereabouts unknown.*

The Prieur who signed this clock-case is without doubt identical with Jean-Louis Prieur who was both a *maître-sculpteur* and a *maître-fondeur*. He is best known for the work he did in connection with the large orders for furnishings for the Palace at Warsaw that were placed with a number of first-rate Parisian craftsmen in the second half of the 1760s, working to the designs of Prieur and Victor Louis (see page 63). Among Prieur's designs of 1766 are two for clocks (see Plates 406 and 408) in a style similar to that of the clock shown here.

The clock was sold in the same sale as the previous example, as lot 36. See also page 100.

Plate 193

MANTEL CLOCK. Gilt bronze. The base signed 'Lepaute à Paris', about 1770. *Present whereabouts unknown.*

An identical clock was in an anonymous sale at the Galérie Charpentier in Paris on 12th March 1937 (lot 20, illustrated in the catalogue); it was, however, signed 'Osmond' while the movement was by Montjoie. As explained in the note to Plate 187, Robert Osmond was a prominent Parisian bronze-founder and the presence of his name on the clock-case suggests that it was he and not the clockmaker who retained the copyright of this particular model.

In a portrait of the Abbé Chanlatte dated 1771, a rather similar clock is depicted (Plate 466). On the front it is apparently inscribed 'Le Paute horloger du Roi'.

This present clock was sold at Sotheby's on 22nd November 1963 (lot 24). A similar clock, also signed by Lepaute, formed lot 529 in the Hamilton Palace sale in 1882; it is illustrated in the catalogue of that astonishing sale. See also page 100.

Plate 194

CARTEL CLOCK. Gilt bronze. About 1765–70. *The Royal Palace, Stockholm.*

The idea of providing a clock with a lyre-shaped case goes back at least to 1758 because one is depicted in a portrait of Madame de Pompadour of that date (Plate 309). Paris de Monmartel, the Court Banker who died in 1766, had a clock in his bed-chamber which is described as being 'Une petite pendule . . . dans sa boîte en forme de lyre de bronze doré en or moulu' ('A small clock . . . in its case in the form of a lyre, of gilt bronze'; R. Dubois-Corneau, *Paris de Monmartel*, 1917, page 243) while a clock of this form is illustrated in an engraving by Baudouin (Plate 444) that cannot be later than 1769. According to the inventory of Philippe Caffieri's stock made in December 1770 (page 377), this craftsman was then actually preparing a model for the case of a lyre-shaped cartel clock (item 47 in the inventory reproduced on page 379). One can therefore reasonably claim that the model for the present clock-case came into being at some time during the second half of the 1760s.

In the 1760s, in fact, there was a growing interest in the lyre as a musical instrument which may have sprung from the fact that it had also gained ground among the ornamental motifs favoured by designers. A musician named Favier and a *luthier* named Michelot announced in 1764 that they could offer customers a lyre 'en forme des anciens' ('of the type used in Ancient times'; *Mercure de France*, March and November 1764, and *Annonces, Affiches, Avis Divers*, 21st March 1764). Both advertisers pointed out that not only was the lyre a delightful instrument but that it made a particularly suitable attribute for ladies to hold when they were having their portraits painted! A drawing of 1767 by Moreau *le jeune* representing a piece of festival architecture had a huge lyre as its principal motif (see *Gaz. de B.-A.*, February 1968, page 69, fig. 260). A pair of fire-dogs in the Louvre, which should date from the early 1770s, also feature the lyre as their dominant ornamental device (see Verlet, *La Maison*, fig. 19), while Drouais depicted Madame du Barry with a lyre, in his portrait of her dated 1771, in order to remind the viewer that she was interested in music. (See Seznec and Adhemar, *Diderot Salon*, vol. IV, fig. 76). One could cite many other instances of the lyre being used as a decorative motif at this period. As Verlet mentions (*Versailles*, page 522), Louis XV had a clock in his bed-chamber that was in the form of a lyre but it is uncertain when he acquired it. On the King's death in 1774, the clock was inherited by the Duc d'Aumont, by way of a perquisite, as is made clear by notes Saint-Aubin made in his personal copy of the catalogue of the Duc's sale which lies in the *Bibliothèque d'Art de d'Archeologie* in Paris. The clock, which may well still survive, is described in the catalogue in the following terms: '335 Une Pendule, mouvement par M. Digue . . . Cette Pendule est renfermée dans une boîte forme de lyre, ornée de branchages de laurier, surmontée d'une renommée tenant une couronne, & placée sur un nuage; sa terrasse a larges rinceaux supporte sur la droite deux figures, l'une assise représentant la France, & l'autre Minerve debout, protégeant les arts qui sur la gauche sont caracterisés par trois enfants: haute 38 pouces, largeur 31 pouces' ('335. Clock, movement by M. Dique . . . this clock is enclosed in a case in the form of a lyre decorated with branches of bay-leaves, and is surmounted by the figure of Fame holding a crown; it stands on a cloud. Its boldly scrolled base has on it two figures on the right, one seated representing France, and Minerva standing, protecting the Arts which are to be seen on her left in the form of three children; height 38 inches, width 31 inches').

A few months before his death, the King also ordered, through the Duc d'Aumont, some designs from Belanger for two clocks that were to be placed in the *Salle du Conseil* and one of these was lyre-shaped. In Belanger's account, we read of these 'Deux desseins de Pendulle pour le feu Roi destinées a être mises dans la Salle du Conseil, l'une représentante le Jour et la nuit apuié sur une lire dont la partie inferieure Contient le Cadran . . .' ('Two designs for clocks for the late King which he had intended should be placed in the Salle du Conseil, one emblematic of Day and Night leaning on a lyre, the lower part of which contained the dial . . .'; Stern, *Belanger*, vol. I, page 48, Archives Nationales, o[1] 3044, pièce 362, année 1774.) See also page 100.

Plate 195

CARTEL CLOCK. Gilt bronze. The movement by Bourgeois, Paris. About 1765–70. *The Bowes Museum, Barnard Castle, County Durham.*

This must resemble the clock with a movement by the same maker which was supplied on 31st December 1770 by a certain Sieur Henry—possibly a *marchand-mercier* to the *Garde-Meuble de la Couronne* which is described in the records of that organisation as 'Une Pendule faite par Bourgeois horloger a Paris, allant 15 jours et sonnant les heures et les demy heures, le cadran d'Email et Les aiguilles de cuivre doré dans une boëte formée par un cartel d'architecture antique de bronze cizelé et doré d'or moulu ayant sur les cotez deux pilastres accompagnéz d'une guirlande de feuilles de Laurier qui regne autour du corps et se joint par le bas et surmonté d'un bouquet, sur le haut un vaze orné de draperie soutenu par des anses et terminé par une pomme de pin, Le bas accompagné de quatre pommes de pin terminé par un fleuron renversé. La ditte boëte ayant 14. pouces de large sur 2. pieds 1/2 de haut' ('Clock made by Bourgeois, clock-maker of Paris, with a fifteen-day movement that strikes on the hour and half-hourly, the dial of enamel and the hands of gilt copper. The case of gilt bronze of Classical architectural form, having pilasters on each side with garlands of bay-leaves which fall down the sides of the body of the case and join at the bottom, there being a bouquet of flowers at the top, surmounted by a vase with drapery fixed to a pair of handles and with a pine cone finial. The base is decorated with a floral scroll and has four pine cones. The case is 14 inches wide and 2½ feet high'; Archives Nationales o[1] 3319, fol. 42 *verso*). See also page 100.

Plate 196

CARTEL CLOCK. Gilt bronze. The case signed 'Osmond'; the movement by Julien le Roy. About 1765–70. *Nationalmuseum, Stockholm.*

Several clock-cases of this form are known, many of them bearing the signature of Robert Osmond; there are examples in the Musée Nissim de Camondo and in the Archives Nationales in Paris, in the Musée des Arts Décoratifs at Nantes, at Gunnebo near Göteborg in Sweden and in several private collections. A clock with a case that would seem to have been of this type was delivered by the clock-maker Jean-Antoine Lepine on 19th December 1767 to the *Garde-Meuble de la Couronne* for placing in the bed-chamber of Madame Victoire at Versailles. The description reads as follows: 'Une Pendule . . . La boëte en cartel de bronze doré d'or moulu orné par le haut d'une tête de femme surmonté d'un vaze à l'antique terminé d'une flame liée par un ruban qui perce des deux cotez et par le bas d'une guirlande de feuilles de Laurier. Le pied terminé par une graîne, ayant 17 pouces de large sur 32 pouces de haut' ('A clock . . . the case to hang on the wall, of gilt bronze, decorated at the top with a female head surmounted by a Classical vase from which rises a flame. The vase is tied with a ribbon which passes through its two sides and there is a garland of bay-leaves below. The base ends in a husk. It is 17 inches wide and 32 inches high'; Archives Nationales o[1] 3318, fol. 179 *verso*). Another clock which may possibly have had a similar case was that provided by the same Lepine on 12th May 1770 for use in the Dauphin's apartment at Versailles. He describes it as 'Une pendule . . . dans une boëte en cartel formé par des Palmes et guirlandes de Laurier ornée sur Les cotés d'un ruban passant dans des anneaux et surmonté par une tete couronnée d'un vaze. Le tout de bronze cizelé et doré d'or moulu ayant environ 16 pouces de large sur 34 de haut' ('A clock . . . in a case to hang on the wall, in the form of palm leaves and garlands of bay-leaves, decorated at the sides with a ribbon passing through rings, the whole being surmounted by a head above which is a vase. All of chased and gilt bronze, being about 16 inches wide and 34 high'; Archives Nationales o[1] 3319, fol. 24 *verso*). See also page 100.

Plate 197

MANTEL CLOCK. Gilt bronze set with Sèvres plaques with a dark blue ground. About 1768. *Private collection.*

The *marchand-mercier* Poirier provided Madame du Barry with a clock of this type at a cost of 912 livres on 18th November 1768. His description of it ran as follows: 'Une pendule à vase et serpent, en bronze doré d'or moulu, le cadran tournant, le pied d'estal garni de trois morceaux de porcelaine de france, fond bleu, avec des enfants en miniature, le dard du serpent fait en marcassite' ('A clock in the shape of a vase with a serpent, of gilt bronze, the dial rotating, the pedestal-base decorated with three plaques of Sèvres porcelain with a blue ground and [painted with] children in miniature, the serpent's tongue being made of marcasite'). The description fits this clock so exactly that one is tempted to conclude that this is actually the piece owned by Madame du Barry. See also page 100.

Plate 198

MANTEL CLOCK. Gilt bronze. The case signed 'Vion' and 'Lepaute à Paris'. About 1768–69. *Musée du Louvre.*

The Vion of the signature was presumably François Vion, the bronze-founder who became a *maître-fondeur* on 17th January 1764 (Archives Nationales, Y 9328). Lepaute must have been one of the members of the well-known family of Parisian clockmakers.

Madame du Barry appears to have owned a clock like this. Poirier (see the previous Note) provided her with 'Une pendule dorée d'or de Germain, elle représente les trois grâces qui supportent un vase dans lequel est un cadran tournant et dessus est un amour qui avec sa flèche indique l'heure: le tout élevé sur un pied d'estal très bien cizelé et doré comme le reste, 2,400 livres' ('A gilded clock by Germain, representing the Three Graces who support an urn on which is the dial, above which is a cupid who indicates the hour with an arrow; the whole stands on an exceedingly well chased pedestal, gilt like the rest, 2,400 livres'). The Germain mentioned here is perhaps identical with the famous goldsmith F.-T. Germain who is known also to have worked in bronze. However, it may also be that the man in question was the bronze-founder Saint-Germain. From what we know of the regulations governing the copyright of designs for bronzes (see page 271), the rights pertaining to this model belonged to Poirier, or to Germain, or to Lepaute. Vion perhaps acquired the rights subsequently. It is not known who actually made the model from which the bronze was taken. The name of Falconet has been put forward but he was in Russia from 1768 to 1778 so it cannot have been he.

Several clocks of this sort survive—for example, in the Musée des Arts Décoratifs in Paris, in the Metropolitan Museum of Art and in the Huntington Collection, San Marino, California. Another was sold at Sotheby's on 2nd May 1969 (lot 15); this was signed 'Vion' and 'Lepaute le fils' and the movement was likewise signed 'Lepaute le fils'. See also page 100.

Plate 199

BAROMETER AND THERMOMETER. Gilt bronze set with Sèvres porcelain plaques. The barometer signed by Siméon Passemant. 1769. *The Metropolitan Museum of Art, Kress Collection.*

Several cases of this type survive. Some contain a clock-movement instead of a barometer. The example shown here can be dated 1769 by the Sèvres plaques which bear the date-letter for that year; other versions of this model have plaques with later code-letters. The accompanying thermometer-and-clock has plaques with date-latters for 1763 or 1764 but they are clearly nineteenth-century replacements (see *Kress Collection catalogue*, Fig. 220).

As Carl Dauterman and James Parker have pointed out, Poirier sold Madame du Barry a barometer-cum-thermometer on 20th December 1769, which he described as 'Un Baromètre et Thermomètre, de Passemant, montés très richement en bronzes dorés d'or moulu et ornés de trois plaques de procelaine de france à enfants en miniature' ('A Barometer and thermometer by Passemant with exceedingly rich gilt bronze mounts decorated with three plaques of Sèvres porcelain displaying miniature children'). It cost

1,056 livres. Barometers of this class seem to have been in production over a period of at least six years; Poirier, and his successor Daguerre, bought a 'Garniture de Plaques pour Baromette' from the Sèvres factory for 168 livres in 1776 (see Archives de la Manufacture de Sèvres, Registre des ventes, 1776; Poirier and Daguerre's full account of purchases for the first six months of that year). See also page 100.

Plate 200

BAROMETER AND THERMOMETER. Gilt bronze. The movement by Lange de Bourbon. About 1770. *The Metropolitan Museum of Art, Kress Collection.*

Note the Classical form of the pointer and the key-fret; both have a certain archaic appearance indicative of a comparatively early date. See also page 100.

Plate 201

URN-SHAPED CLOCK. Marble and gilt bronze. The plinth is dated 1774 and inscribed 'Doublet inv. Julia fec.' *The National Trust, Waddesdon Manor, Buckinghamshire.*

The Doublet whose name is on the plinth was perhaps identical with a painter named Simon-Hubert Doublet, and Julia may be the name of a sculptor known to have been working for Pajou.

The clock has an accompanying piece which serves as a calendar; the *putti* and the relief on the plinth are different but otherwise the two pieces form a pair. See also page 100.

Plate 202

SCONCE, one of a set of four. Gilt bronze. By François-Thomas Germain, 1756. *Formerly in the collection of the Earl of Rosebery, Mentmore.*

These were sold at Sotheby's on 17th April 1964 (lot 18). Although the catalogue does not record the fact, two of the sconces are inscribed 'Fait par F. T. Germain Sculp^r^. Orf^re^. du Roy. Aux Galleries du Louvre. A Paris, 1756' ('Made by F. T. Germain, sculptor, silversmith to the King. The Louvre Galleries, Paris, 1756'), and all four bore a punched inventory mark—the letters 'CP' surmounted by a closed crown and 'No. 28'. The catalogue does, however, state that two are also marked '1051 Lux I' and the other two '1051 Lux II'. The CP mark stands for the Château de Compiègne and dates from the eighteenth century, while the 'Lux' mark seems to date from the nineteenth century and presumably refers to the Palais du Luxembourg.

In spite of these very precise references, it has not yet proved possible to associate these sconces with any particular entry in the French royal archives from 1756 onwards; they do not seem to be recorded in the Journal of the *Garde-meuble*, nor are they in the inventory of Compiègne, made in 1764 (Archives Nationales, o^1 3386). As was pointed out in *Connaissance des Arts* (September 1968, page 76), these sconces resemble those shown in a view of the salon at the Palais Royal (Plate 23) which was being redecorated to the designs of Contant d'Ivry at that very time—1756. Germain is known to have provided a chimney-piece for the room (see Plate 27) and it is conceivable that these sconces were in fact also produced by him for the Palais Royal in the first place, and subsequently came into the hands of the *Garde-Meuble*. But we do not know, and there are many other possibilities.

One must admit that there are no Classical details in this composition yet they reflect a definite step away from the Rococo taste towards a Classical ideal. Each sconce consists of a naturalistic representation of three small branches of bay-leaves with berries, all tied with a large bow. The bow is the only 'frivole' feature of the composition. Blondel, who so heartily approved of Contant d'Ivry's work at the Palais Royal (see page 42), would presumably also have been pleased to accept these sconces as excellent examples of the same good taste, on account of their faithful naturalism. It was items such as these, with their controlled serpentine forms, that Blondel wanted to see forming 'contrasts' in interiors couched in the Classical taste. See also page 92.

Plate 203

SCONCE, one of a set of six. Gilt and partly patinated bronze. The model attributed to Philippe Caffieri; it was probably executed about 1758. *Her Grace The Duchess of Roxburghe, Floors Castle.*

These sconces are 93 cm. high, and take the form of a hunting trophy. Each consists of three symmetrically placed hunting-horns backed by branches of oak leaves, and they are suspended by means of a large ribbon tied with a bow. The one shown here has the head and hide of a roe-buck; others have the head and hide of a fox, wolf or wild-boar.

Certain technical features indicate that the sconces at Floors Castle are unlikely to have been cast in the eighteenth century; they probably date from the last century but it seems that they reproduce very faithfully a model which Caffieri first produced in about 1758 for Louis XV's hunting-lodge, Saint-Hubert, which lay in the Yvelines Forest. In an article dated 27th October 1771, which appeared in the December issue of the *Journal de l'Agriculture, du Commerce, des Arts et des Finances*, mention is first made of some fire-dogs installed in a *salon de chasse*; it then continues 'Les bras assortissans pour ce salon sont des têtes de daim accompagnées de cors de chasse et de branches de chêne. L'invention nouvelle en a été exécutée pour la première fois pour le Roi à Saint-Hubert. S.M. en fut si contente qu'elle eut la bonté d'en faire compliment à M. Caffiéri. Plusieurs ouvriers ont travaillé depuis à l'imiter, mais ils n'ont pas réussi' ('The sconces made for this salon have heads of fallow-deer and hunting-horns with branches of oak. This new design has been executed for the first time for the King's hunting lodge at Saint-Hubert. His Majesty is so pleased with them that he has been so gracious as to compliment M. Caffieri on them. Several craftsmen have since tried to imitate this design but without success'; see Guiffrey, *Les Caffieri*, pages 489–92). The article in fact seems to be a piece of publicity on behalf of Caffieri; maybe he even wrote it himself.

Caffieri's works made for Saint-Hubert must date from the late 1750s, when this little building was being renovated. He received a payment of 3,000 livres for work done for the place in 1758 (Archives Nationales, o^1 2258, fol. 103) but there is no description of the items concerned. They are mentioned in *L'Avantcoureur* of 7th July 1760 (see the Note that follows) but, again, no description is vouchsafed.

Although the quotation just given seems to show that all the original Saint-Hubert sconces were decorated with the heads of fallow deer, Caffieri also had models for sconces with wolf or fox-heads—like some of those now at Floors. This is proved by the inventory of his stock, made in 1770 (see page 377), where model No. 2 in the list is for 'Un bras a cor de chasse formant trois branches avec une tête de loup' ('A sconce, hunting-horn form, making three branches with a wolf's head'). There can be little doubt that this is the same model that was still No. 2 when a fresh inventory was made after Caffieri's death in 1774 (Archives Nationales, Minutier Central, XXXIV–697, 14th October 1774). This reads: 'Un bras a Cor de Chasse formant trois branches avec une tête de renard' ('A sconce, hunting-horn form, making three branches with a fox's head'). The wolf's head has been mistaken for that of a fox, but that is an error it would be easy to make. Sconces with foxes' heads were seen at a sale in Paris on 8th April 1783, in which lot 229 was described as being 'Une paire de Bras, par Caffieri, à trois branches, composées de cors-de-chasse dorés, avec rubans & peau de renard de bronze en couleur' ('A pair of sconces by Caffieri, with three branches in the form of gilt hunting-horns, with ribbons and the hide of a fox of patinated bronze').

Like the previous example, this sconce has no essentially Classical features, but the total naturalism and the strict symmetry of the composition betoken an unmistakable reaction against the indiscipline and incongruity so characteristic of the Rococo style. See also pages 58, 97, 121, 124 and 126.

Plate 204

CANDELABRUM, one of a set of six. Produced by Philippe Caffieri in 1770, the model made in 1760. *Bayeux Cathedral.*

This Neo-Classical candelabrum was executed in 1770–71 by Caffieri from the model he had made in 1760 for the now lost candelabra he supplied for use in Notre-Dame, Paris. With this set, Caffieri also provided a crucifix, having agreed with the Bayeux authorities that the whole ensemble should be executed 'sur le modèle et tout semblables dans leurs ornemens, sculptures et cizelures à ceux de Notre-Dame de Paris' ('After the model made for Notre-Dame in Paris, similar in all its ornament and chasing'; Rene Dubosq, 'Les richesses de la Cathédrale de Bayeux: l'oeuvre de Philippe Caffieri', *Revue Illustrée du Calvados*, 1911, Nos. 4 and 5).

The form of this candelabrum seems to show that Caffieri had entirely gone over to Neo-Classicism by 1760. Earlier that year he had provided some nine-branched candelabra for Notre-Dame; these must also have been in the Neo-Classical idiom, for a reporter in *L'Avantcoureur* (7th July 1760, page 397) was most enthusiastic about them and drew attention to their style which he could see owed much to that prevailing before the Rococo had engulfed 'Good Taste'. His exact words were: 'On voit à Notre-Dame sur les deux piedestaux de la balustrade du sanctuaire deux torchères de bronze, de trois pieds & demi de haut, à neuf lumières chacune, terminées par deux cassolettes à l'antique. Ces morceaux, qui sont d'un très-bon goût, sont de la main du sieur Caffieri, artiste connu par de très-beaux ouvrages de ce genre qu'il a faits pour Saint-Hubert. L'étude assidue que le sieur Caffieri a faite en Italie des bonnes formes de l'antique, donne lieu d'espérer que l'on verra reparoître dans les six chandeliers & la croix, qu'il fait actuellement, le vrai goût des ornemens, auquel avoit succédé, en dépit de la nature, un goût baroque, dont les productions irrégulières ne ressemblent à rien' ('One may see, on two pedestals of the sanctuary-rail at Notre-Dame, a pair of bronze torchères, three and a half feet high, with seven nozzles each, the body in the form of Classical incense-burners. These are in the very best taste and are the work of M. Caffieri, an artist who is known for his exceptionally beautiful work in this field which he executed for Saint-Hubert. The studies of Classical forms which M. Caffieri has made in Italy permit one to hope that, in the six candlesticks and the cross which he is making at the moment, one will see the reappearance of good taste in the decorative arts, which—contrary to what is natural—had given way to a bizarre fashion, the irregular products of which looked like nothing on earth').

The claim that Caffieri had visited Italy, incidentally, is corroborated by an entry in Madame Caffieri's inventory of chattels (Arch. Nat., Minutier Central, XCVIII, 589, p. 36) in which it is said that two marble busts representing 'Alexandre' and 'Olimpia' were executed 'à Rome par Mr. Caffieri L[é]'. It is however difficult to say when his sojourn there may have taken place.

In the inventory of Caffieri's stock, made in 1770 (see page 279), item No. 53 concerns the model for a candelabrum 'dans le goût grec'; possibly this was the original model for these pieces. The two sets of candelabra, those at Notre-Dame and at Bayeux, were mentioned in an article which appeared in the December 1771 issue of the *Journal de l'Agriculture, du Commerce, des Arts et des Finances* (which is dated 27th October) and to which reference was also made in the previous entry. The two sets are much praised and we are informed that Caffieri's pattern has since been much copied by others. 'En examinant les croix et chandeliers qui décorent les autels de la plupart des églises, à Paris notamment, on est frappé de l'analogie de leur forme et de leurs ornements avec les chandeliers et la croix de Bayeux. Ce sont les mêmes guirlandes autour du pied triangulaire, accompagnant un médaillon central avec figure de Vierge ou de sainte, suivant le patron de l'autel. Le modèle inventé par Caffieri pour Notre-Dame de Paris et pour Bayeux se trouve aujourd'hui reproduit à l'infini dans presque toutes les églises, et ceux qui ne l'imitent pas exactement s'en rapprochent plus ou moins' ('After inspecting the crosses and candlesticks which adorn the altars of most churches, especially those in Paris, one is struck by the similarity of their form and decoration with those of the candlesticks and cross at Bayeux. They have the same garlands round the triangular base, accompanied by a central medallion bearing the head of the Virgin or a saint, according to whom the altar is dedicated. The models composed by Caffieri for Notre-Dame in Paris and for Bayeux have since been copied *ad infinitum* in almost every church, and those which are not actual copies resemble them to a lesser or greater extent'; see Guiffrey, *Les Caffieri*, page 489). See also page 98.

Plate 205

CANDELABRUM, one of a pair. Gilt bronze. After a model by Jean-Louis Prieur, 1765 or 1766. *Lazienki Palace, Warsaw.*

The inscription on Prieur's drawing, reproduced in Plate 405, shows that six such candelabra were produced; while that reproduced in Plate 408, which is dated 1766, reveals that they were to be placed in the King of Poland's own bed-chamber in the Palace at Warsaw. The modernisation and re-decoration of the Palace is discussed on pages 63–4. Since no such candelabra appear in the list of Philippe Caffieris deliveries to the Polish Court (Archives Nationales, Z^{1J} 921), it must be assumed that they were produced by Prieur himself since he was not only a designer but also a bronze-founder.

See S. Iskierski, *Les bronzes du Château Royal et du Palais de Lazienki à Varsovie*, 1929, page 22, No. 7.

Plate 206

CANDELABRUM, one of a set of six. Gilt bronze. Made by Philippe Caffieri, 1766–68. *Lazienki Palace, Warsaw.*

Like the piece illustrated alongside, this was also made for the Warsaw Palace. All six are signed by Caffieri; one is dated 1766, another 1767, and two 1768 (two are undated). In the estimate of Caffieri's work for the Polish Court, it is stated that the set was to be silvered (Archives Nationales, Z^{1J} 921). Indeed this is how they were first treated but they were later gilded. Caffieri charges 4,000 livres each for the six. Considering their size (96 cm. high), this does not seem an exorbitant charge.

It is interesting to compare this model with the similar form of tripod candelabrum (or pastille-burner) being designed by Neo-Classical artists in England at this time. One is represented in James 'Athenian' Stuart's proposals for the mural-decoration at Kedleston, executed about 1757, and for the Painted Room at Spencer House of 1759, as well as in Robert Adam's design for the sideboard in the dining-room at Kedleston which is dated 1762 (see Eileen Harris, *The Furniture of Robert Adam*, 1963, figs. 1–3). A pastille-burner based on these designs (E. Harris, fig. 6) has a triangular plinth which is not dissimilar to that of the Warsaw pieces. No special conclusion need be drawn from this comparison, however. All the designers concerned must have been familiar with the Classical prototype for such stands. Even so, it is instructive to note the different ways in which the theme could be adapted.

See Stanislas Iskierski, *Les bronzes du Château Royal et du Palais de Lazienki à Varsovie*, 1929, page 21, No. 1. See also page 100.

Plate 207

SCONCE, one of a set of eight. Gilt bronze. Designed by J.-L. Prieur, 1766–8. *Musée Nissim de Camondo, Paris.*

Monsieur F. G. Pariset pointed out that these lamps may have come from the Palace at Warsaw (see Pariset, 'Note sur Victor Louis et Varsovie', *Biuletyn Historii Sztuki*, XXIV, 1962, page 155). They were designed by J.-L. Prieur (see Plate 404) and were probably made in his workshops (see the Note to Plate 205). No mention is made of such sconces in the list of work done for the Palace by Caffieri, so he cannot have been responsible (Archives Nationales, Z^{1J} 921). According to Pariset, eight more such sconces are in a private collection, and there are also two copies still in Warsaw (see Stanislas Iskierski, *Les Bronzes du Château Royal et du Palais de Lazienki à Varsovie*, 1929, page 21, No. 3, fig. 3).

Plate 208

CANDELABRUM, one of a pair. Gilt bronze. About 1765–70. *The Wallace Collection.*

The dating proposed here is based on a comparison with the silver candelabra made between 1766 and 1768 by Robert-Joseph Auguste, shown in Plates 261 and 262. Moreover, the manner in which the arms end in scrolls is to be seen again in the drawing by Caffieri reproduced in Plate 425 which dates from 1766–67.

The French term *girandole* was normally used in reference to a candelabrum like this (the word derives from the Italian word for a rotating firework like a 'Catherine wheel' known as a *girandola*) and it may be pertinent to note that the dealer, Poirier, sold Lord Coventry 'Une paire de Girandoles de Bronze doré d'or moulu avec Enfants de bronze de couleur antique' for 720 livres on 23rd June 1768 ('A pair of candelabra of gilt bronze with children of antiqued bronze'; Croome Court Archives, Worcestershire, No. 53).

See Watson, *Wallace Collection Furniture*, F. 128. See also page 100.

Plate 209

SCONCE, one of a pair. Gilt bronze. About 1765–70. *Musée du Louvre.*

Each arm is in the form of a cornucopia, while the back-plate is like a caduceus entwined round branches of bay-leaves, tied with a ribbon. In many ways this resembles the sconce illustrated in a drawing reproduced here in Plate 441 which cannot be later than 1767. A version with only two arms was sold at the Josse sale in Paris on 28th May 1894 (lot 147, illustrated in the catalogue).

Cornucopia-arms were a feature of some sconces that Madame du Barry bought from Poirier on 10th October 1770. In Poirier's account, they are described as 'Une paire de bras à deux branches en bronze doré d'or moulu, model à figures et cornes d'abondance' ('A pair of sconces with two branches [each] of gilt bronze, with figures and cornucopiae'; see G. Wildenstein, 'Simon-Philippe Poirier, *fournisseur* de Madame du Barry', *Gaz. d. B.-A.*, 1962, page 375. They cost 200 livres each.

See E. Dumonthier, *Les bronzes du Mobilier National, bronzes d'éclairage et de chauffage*, Paris, n.d., Plate 5, fig. 7. See also page 100.

Plate 210

SCONCE, one of a set of four. Gilt bronze. About 1765–69. *Juelsberg, Denmark.*

A sconce of this not uncommon type is to be seen in the portrait of the Marquis de Marigny shown in Plate 442, a painting exhibited at the *Salon* of 1769. If one compares it with the candelabra made for the Polish Court (Plates 205 to 207) and Prieur's and Caffieri's drawings (Plates 403 to 405, and 422 to 425) all of which were made about 1766, there is no reason why the present model should not have been in existence before 1769. On 4th October 1768, Claude de la Roüe sent over to the *Garde-Meuble de la Couronne* 'quatre paires de bras a 2 branches assorties par deux paires en cuivre cizelé et doré d'or moulu à vazes et guirlandes de fleurs' ('four pairs of sconces with two branches [each] of gilt and chased copper [i.e. bronze], with vases and garlands of flowers'; Archives Nationales, o^1 3318, fol. 214 *verso*). These were presumably richer than the one illustrated here but could well have been of much the same type. See also pages 100 and 102.

Plate 211

SCONCE. Gilt bronze. About 1770–75. *Château de Fontainebleau.*

The first occasion on which Pitoin, the accredited Court bronze-founder, records delivering sconces suspended from a bow formed in bronze was on 14th October 1773 (Archives Nationales, o[1] 3319, fol. 118 *verso*) but the feature seems to have occurred regularly on his productions for the *Garde-meuble de la Couronne* after that. The idea was of course not new. Caffieri had used the motif for the Saint-Hubert sconces in the late 1750s and, in the inventory of his stock, made in December 1770 (see page 277), several sconces with this feature are mentioned. No. 11 in the list, for instance, is 'Une paire de bras à deux branches attachées par un ruban formant le neud au haut de la plaque avec un vase, et une guirlande de lauriers, dans le gout antique' ('A pair of sconces with two branches attached to each other by a ribbon forming a bow at the top of the plate with a vase and a garland of bay-leaves in the Antique taste'). The sconces described as items 67 and 70, moreover, were all surmounted by a bunch of flowers with a poppy (*pavot*) in the centre—symbolising sleep.

The presence of the poppy suggests that Caffieri may have made the sconce shown here. Furthermore, there are various similarities in its composition and in that of the sconce depicted by Caffieri in the drawing shown in Plate 453, notably in lower part where the inward-turned volutes form an unusual feature in both cases.

See E. Dumonthier, *Les bronzes du Mobilier National, bronzes d'éclairage et de chauffage*, Paris, n.d., Plate 3, fig. 6. See also pages 100–1.

Plate 212

SCONCE, one of a pair. Gilt bronze. About 1770. *Musée des Arts Décoratifs, Paris.*

Neither the name of the designer nor of the maker is known but it can be dated with reasonable accuracy on stylistic and typological evidence. Pitoin, the official Court bronze-founder, is known to have made sconces with goat's heads in 1771 and thereafter (see the Note to Plate 214), and Caffieri had a model with such a feature among his stock when the inventory was drawn up in December 1770 (see page 277). At Thurebyholm, a country-house in Denmark, there is a set of sconces with goat's heads that are thought to have been bought in Paris in March 1769 and are in much the same style as the one shown here. (I am much indebted to Dr. V. Thorlacius-Ussing for transcribing for me the relevant document from the archives of the Moltke family which seems to confirm the date of the Thurebyholm sconces.) See also page 100.

Plate 213

SCONCE, one of a set of six. Gilt and patinated bronze. About 1768–70. *Lazienki Palace, Warsaw.*

Although sconces like this are not mentioned in the estimate of work done by Caffieri for the Warsaw Palace, it seems probable that the model was produced by him. In the inventory of his stock (see page 281), item No. 94 was 'Une paire de grands bras à trois branches en couleur avec des grandes Guirlandes de laurier agraphées dans les rouleaux des branches et nouées d'une draperie en noir de fumée avec un Vase dont le corps est aussi en noir de fumée' ('A pair of large sconces [each] with three branches in colour [i.e. in this case, gilt bronze] with large garlands of laurel attached to the scrolls of the branches and knotted by a drapery of smoke-black colour with a vase whose body is also smoke-black'). It was valued at 650 livres. The unusual features, black drapery and a black vase, are also to be seen on this sconce, and there is a marked similarity between the arms of this piece and those shown in Caffieri's drawing for a sconce for Notre-Dame (Plate 425).

See Stanislas Iskierski, *Les bronzes du Château Royal et du Palais de Lazienki à Varsovie*, 1929, page 23, No. 11. See also page 100.

Plate 214

SCONCE, one of a set of four. Gilt bronze. About 1770–75. *Musée Nissim de Camondo, Paris.*

Apart from the goat's heads, which do not seem to have been favoured as ornaments on sconces made for use in the French royal palaces, this piece agrees with the descriptions of sconces provided by the accredited Court Bronze-founder, Quentin-Claude Pitoin, about 1770. Twice, however, pairs of sconces with this feature were provided for some of the younger Princes of the Blood. On 24th June 1771, for instance, Pitoin delivered 'Deux Paires de bras a 3 branches dorez d'or moulu de forme antique a tête de bellier' for the Comte de Provence's apartment in the Château de Compiègne ('Two pairs of sconces of gilt bronze, with three branches [each], in the antique taste, with ram's heads'; Archives Nationales, o^1 3319, fol. 61), and on 22nd May 1772 'Deux Paires de bras antique à 3 branches de bronze doré d'or moulu la plaque en forme de guaîne cannelé décoré par le haut d'une tete de bellier' for installation in the Comte d'Artois' rooms in the same palace ('Two pairs of gilt bronze sconces in the Antique style, [each] with three branches, the backplate in the form of a fluted term topped by a ram's head; Archives Nationales, o^1 3319, fol. 87 *verso*).

See Jean Messelet, *Musée Nissim de Camondo*, 1960, No. 246. See also pages 100 and 103.

Plates 215 and 216

TWO SCONCES. Each one of a pair. Gilt bronze. About 1772–74. *M. le Marquis de Contades, Château de Montgeoffroy.*

Like the commode shown in Plate 148 and the fire-dogs shown in Plate 233, these two sconces were among the new furniture acquired by the Maréchal de Contades when he modernised the Château de Montgeoffroy, the family's country-house near Angers, between 1772 and 1774. The sconce shown in Plate 215 is the most elaborate in the house and today hangs, with its pair, on the chimney-breast in the *Grand Salon* where it may always have hung. At any rate, in the inventory of the house drawn up in August 1775, there were '2 paires de bras à trois branches dorés d'or moulu' ('two pairs of sconces with three branches [each] of gilt bronze'; see Verlet, *La Maison*, page 261 and Plate 188).

Plate 217

PRICKET CANDLESTICK. Gilt bronze. Made by Philippe Caffieri, 1771. *Clermont-Ferrand Cathedral.*

This very tall candle-stand (it is 180 cm. high) serves as the Cathedral's 'chandelier pascal' ('Easter candlestick'). It is inscribed 'Inventé Et Exécuté par P. Caffierj Lainé à Paris En Lanné 1771' ('Designed and made by P. Caffieri the Elder, in Paris, in the year 1771') but in spite of its enormous size, it seems to have been created in less than twelve or thirteen months for, when the inventory of Caffieri's stock was taken on 3rd December 1770, no mention was made of such a gigantic piece (see page 279; Nos. 53–56 are all smaller). The article dated 27th October 1771, describing various works by Caffieri (see Note to Plate 204) makes it clear that this candlestick was not completed by that date.

The candlestick was first published by Louis Réau in his article 'Le chandelier pascal de Philippe Caffieri à la cathédrale de Clermont-Ferrand', *B.S.H.A.F.*, 1927, pages 12–15. See also page 101.

Plate 218

SIX-BRANCH CANDLESTICKS, one of a pair. Gilt and patinated bronze. Probably executed about 1775 by Jean-Claude-Thomas Duplessis after a model designed by himself or C. L. Clérisseau. *Private collection.*

Close study will show that these apparently resemble in every detail the candlesticks shown in the drawing of the salon at the Hôtel Grimod de la Reynière. (Plate 82: see the enlargement reproduced as Plate 483.)

The candlestick shown in the drawing was one of four executed by Duplessis for that salon which was being re-decorated for the financier, Grimod de la Reynière, about 1772–75 after designs by Clérisseau. As explained in the Note to Plate 82, the salon (including its candlesticks) was described in an article that appeared in the *Almanach des artistes* for 1777. The article informs us that 'Ces candelabres, dont le travail est très-soigné, ont été exécutés par M. Duplessis, fameux Ciseleur de Paris' (page 85) and that Duplessis 'travaille d'après ses dessins' while 'c'est lui qui a cizelé les beaux Candelabres qu'on voit sur les encoignures du beau Sallon de M. de la Reiniere dont nous avons parlé plus haut' ('These candelabra, of which the craftsmanship is of the most delicate quality, were executed by M. Duplessis, the famous Parisian bronze-chaser . . . they were made by him after his own designs . . . he himself carried out the chasing of these beautiful candelabra which may be seen on the corner fittings of M. de la Reinière's salon, of which we have already spoken'). From this we gather that Duplessis habitually worked to his own designs but it does not state that he had designed those intended for this room. It is, in fact, rather more likely that Clérisseau designed them—at least, in their essentials—since he was apparently responsible for the decoration of the room as a whole. Duplessis, who was proud to call himself *sculpteur-ciseleur* (see page 175) probably worked up the model from Clérisseau's designs (he may have produced finished drawings himself, of course, based on sketches supplied by Clérisseau) and then proceeded to cast the bronzes and to chase them etc.

A similar pair, perhaps the missing two from the original set of four, was acquired at Christie's on 24th June 1971 (lot 30) by the Detroit Museum of Art. This pair had formerly been in the Demidoff Collection, and was entirely gilt at the time of the sale. See also page 105.

Plate 219

A LAMP, one of a pair. Gilt bronze; glass bowl. About 1770–75. *The Charles B. Wrightsman Collection, New York.*

The heavy garlands and the bold Vitruvian scroll suggest an early date, while the pearl-ornament points to a date closer to 1775.

See Watson, *Wrightsman Collection*, No. 176.

Plate 220

TABLE-LAMP. Gilt bronze; the shade of metal, painted green. About 1770–75. *Formerly in Madame Jules Fribourg's collection.*

Such a lamp (*lampe bouillotte*) is to be seen in Ingouf's engraving, reproduced in Plate 494, which is dated 1774.

On 10th March 1774, Fontanieu, the director of the *Garde-Meuble de la Couronne* received, from the goldsmith Roëttiers, a lamp which must have been very like this although it was of silver. It was described in the Journal of the *Garde-Meuble* as 'Un flambeau à Gardevue a double branche, le pied rond, la tige formée par une colonne cannelée dont le chapiteau enrichi de deux têtes de beliers et d'une guirlande de fleurs porte une Cassolette avec anneaux mobiles, La branche d'acier terminée par en haut d'une pomme de pin, Le gardevue de fer blanc . . .' ('A lamp with a shade and two branches, a circular foot, the upright in the form of a fluted column, with a capital embellished with a pair of ram's heads and a garland of flowers, on top of which stands an incense-burner with two ring-handles. The steel rod has a pine cone finial; the shade is of tin'; Archives Nationales, o[1] 3318 fol. 129 *verso*). See also page 105.

Plate 221

PAIR OF FIRE-DOGS. Gilt bronze. About 1760–65. *Musée Lyonnon's des Arts Décoratifs.*

The date proposed here is entirely hypothetical. The stump of a Classical column would seem to be evidence of a new spirit and suggests a date early in the 1760s (cf. Plates 236, 244, 247, 323 and 324, all dating from between 1756 and 1765). On the other hand, the scrolls, with their Rococo accent, are not likely to have been used much after 1765 or so.

There is a similar pair of fire-dogs in the collection of Mr. and Mrs. Charles B. Wrightsman (Watson, *Wrightsman Catalogue*, No. 196).

Plate 222

FIRE-DOG, one of a pair. Gilt bronze. About 1765–70. *Musée des Arts Décoratifs, Paris.*

The date suggested for this piece is based on the similarity of the surmounting urn with dated designs for vases (e.g. Plates 310 to 318) and on comparison with some of the bronzes made for the Polish Court about 1766 (see Plates 402 to 409). It is not impossible that the piece is rather earlier, however—perhaps from the early 1760s; it has features in common with the plinth Caffieri made in 1761 which is shown in Plate 236.

Plate 223

PAIR OF FIRE-DOGS. Gilt bronze. About 1765–70. *Formerly in the Marquis de Biron's collection; present whereabouts unknown.*

The form of the plinths is closely similar to that shown in the drawing by Prieur shown in Plate 402 which should date from 1766. The dog and the cat may well have been taken from a much older model. The bronze-founder Jacques Caffieri, the father of Philippe Caffieri, had models for a pair of cat-and-dog fire-dogs in stock when an inventory of his workshop was taken in 1755. Philippe also had the models for 'Un feu à chien et à chat' ('A [pair of] fire-dog[s] with a cat and a dog') in stock, according to the 1770 inventory (see page 278). Whether this set was identical with that which had been there in his father's time, it is not possible to say. Philippe Caffieri, incidentally, supplied a set featuring a cat and a dog to the Prince de Condé in 1773 and was paid 1,120 livres for it (Archives Condé, A.C. 7, Caffieri's bill, items 69 and 70).

In the catalogue of the Marquis de Biron sale (Paris, June 1914, lot 345), whence this illustration is taken it is claimed that this set is the work of a bronze-founder named Disnematin. A similar set was in the Viguier sale, held at the Palais Galliéra on 21st March 1968. See also pages 100–1.

Plate 224

FIRE-DOG, one of a pair. Gilt bronze. About 1765–70. *Musée Lyonnais des Arts Décoratifs.*

These correspond, in their general configuration, with two sets Pitoin, the official Court Bronze-Founder, delivered to the *Garde-Meuble de la Couronne* in 1767. One set was for Madame Victoire's bed-chamber at Saint-Hubert while the other was for the Palace of Compiègne. The former set cost 2200 livres and was sent across to the Royal Wardrobe on 12th May. The Journal of the *Garde-Meuble* describes one in detail: 'Une grille a 4 branches de fer poly ayant sur le devant un piedestal quarré à cannelures creuses sur lequel est attaché un peau de lyon dont les pattes pendent sur les cotez surmonté d'une vaze dont la face est ornée d'une guirlande de feuilles de chêne et terminé par une flame, Le tout de bronze cizelé et doré d'or moulu' ('A grille of four bars of polished steel with, in front, a square and fluted pedestal over which lies the hide of a lion, the paws of which hang down the sides. Above is an urn hung with a garland of oak-leaves, with flames at the top. The whole is made of chased and gilt bronze'; Archives Nationales, o[1] 3318, fol. 155.)

The model may well have been created some time earlier. Pitoin was, at any rate, providing fire-dogs in a Neo-Classical style already by 1765; some went to Fontanieu, the Director of the *Garde-Meuble*, others to the King and his daughters. Fire-dogs, being essentially part of the chimney-piece and its furnishings were of course more readily acceptable in a strictly architectural style than furnishings that were not directly related to the architectural elements of the room.

On 29th November 1773, Pitoin delivered a further pair of fire-dogs—this time, for the use of the Comte d'Artois at Versailles. The description runs as follows; 'Un autre feu à vaze terminés d'une flame avec Recouvrement sur lequel est posé deux vazes moins forts et a anses sur piedestaux a consolles ornés de masques de lyon avec leurs peaux et pattes pendantes' ('Another pair of fire-dogs with flaming urns and with a side-piece on which stand two smaller vases with handles with their bases decorated with lion's masks; the lion's skins and paws hang down'; Archives Nationales, o[1] 3319, fol. 120 *verso*). At the Château de Montgeoffroy is a pair of fire-dogs which were certainly acquired in the years around 1774 and appear to be contemporary copies of the model shown here (see Verlet, *La Maison*, fig. 188 showing a view of the salon at Montgeoffroy). See also pages 100 and 102.

Plate 225

FIRE-DOG, one of a pair. Gilt bronze. About 1765–70. *Musée des Arts Décoratifs, Paris.*

The *marchand-mercier*, Claude de la Roue provided the Dauphin with some fire-dogs on 21st September 1770, one of which was described in the Journal of the *Garde-Meuble*, as being 'Une tres forte grille à colonnes surmonté d'un vaze avec un lyon couché sur la Balustrade servant de recouvrement . . . Chambre de Mr Le Dauphin' ('A very substantial grille with column surmounted by an urn with a couchant lion on the balustrade that serves as a side-piece . . . for the Dauphin's Bed-chamber'; Archives Nationales, o[1] 3319, fol. 33 *verso*). They cost 1,000 livres (ibid., o[1] 3622, de la Roue's bill). The present piece seems to answer to this description and probably resembles de la Roue's bronzes fairly closely. A pair of somewhat inferior quality is to be seen at the Hôtel Dieu in Lyon. See also page 100.

Plate 226

PAIR OF FIRE-DOGS. Gilt bronze. About 1765–70. *The Wallace Collection.*

Molinier once attributed these to Philippe Caffieri (see Watson, *The Wallace Collection Catalogue*, Nos. 279–80) because of a certain affinity with the plinth illustrated in Plate 236 which is dated 1761. However, no fire-dogs quite like this are listed in the inventory of Caffieri's stock, made in 1770 (see page 277). Closest would seem to be those he delivered on 19th October 1771 to the Prince de Condé which he described in his account as being 'pour la chambre à coucher de Monseigneur au palais Bourbon petit appartement un feu representant deux enfans qui se chauffent; une petitte fille et un petit garçon de L'autre coté . . . 610 livres 10 sols' ('for the Bed-chamber of Monseigneur in the Palais Bourbon's private apartments, a pair of fire-dogs in the form of two children warming themselves; on one is the figure of a little girl, on the other a small boy . . . 610 livres 10 sols'; Archives Condé, A.C.7, item Yy). These must have been much smaller than those shown in Plate 459 which are known to have cost 3,879 livres. All the same, items 76 and 77 in the Caffieri inventory show that he did have a number of bronze children in stock and these may have been intended for the decoration of fire-dogs. Of course, Caffieri was not the only bronze-founder who made fire-dogs with figures of children on them. Prieur, for instance, also favoured children and lion's paws as decorative motifs for his bronzes (see Plates 190 to 192, 205 and 403). See also page 100.

Plate 227

PAIR OF FIRE-DOGS. Gilt bronze. About 1770–75. *Mobilier National, Paris.*

One of the pair is signed by a bronze-founder called Dambière and dated 'le 25 novembre 1775'. Apart from certain details, however, these seem to correspond with the description in the Journal of the *Garde-Meuble* concerning two pairs of fire-dogs which Pitoin sent over to that institution in 1771 and 1773—one set for the bed-chamber of the Comtesse de Provence at Versailles, the other for the Comtesse d'Artois' room at the same palace. The description of the former pair runs as follows: 'Un fort feu en vaze et Recouvrement de bronze doré d'or moulu de 20 pouces de profondeur, Le piedestal quarré orné sur la face d'un panneaux de mozaiques et au dessus un medaillon avec deux branches de laurier qui tombent perpendiculairement. Le vaze posé dessus; orné d'une tete de mascaron d'ou sort de la bouche deux guirlandes de feuilles de laurier qui passent de chaque coté des pieds Estaux en forme de guaine, orné de Cannelures sur les faces, de feuilles d'eau, et graines. Sur Les Pieds estaux sont posés deux vazes ornés de Cannelures creuses et gaudrons avec anses, Le Tout terminé par des pommes . . .' ('A pair of massive fire-dogs with urns and side-pieces of gilt bronze, 20 inches deep. The front of the square pedestal is decorated with a diaper-pattern; above is a medallion with two garlands of bay-leaves falling straight down the sides. The urn stands on top; it is decorated with a mask, from the mouth of which spring two garlands of bay-leaves that are connected on both sides with term-like, fluted pedestals which have rushes and ears of corn on their faces. On these pedestals are fluted and ribbed urns with handles and finials'; Archives Nationales, o[1] 3319, fol 54 *verso*).

See E. Dumonthier, *Les bronzes du Mobilier National, bronzes d'éclairage et de chauffage*, Paris, n.d., Plate 9, fig. 1. See also page 100.

Plate 228

PAIR OF FIRE-DOGS. Gilt bronze. Perhaps by Pitoin. About 1770–75. *Mobilier National.*

This set bears the inventory-mark of the palace of Fontainebleau and the number '48'. This makes it possible to show that they were standing in the *Pièce des Nobles* at Fontainebleau in 1787 (Archives Nationales, o[1] 3398, page 91). They may well be identical with one of the two pairs the Court Bronze-Founder, Pitoin, sent to the *Garde-Meuble de la Couronne*, respectively on 17th February 1772 and on 29th November 1773. Both were intended for Versailles, one pair for the *Garde-Meuble*'s director, Fontanieu, and the other for the Comte d'Artois. They are each described as consisting of 'Une grille a 4. branches de fer poly garnie sur le devant d'un Vaze dont le corps est orné de guirlandes de laurier attachées par un cloud et passant dans les anneaux, porté sur un piedestal a pans coupés orné de masques et feuilles de persil, Le recouvrement composé de feuilles de chêne liées de rubans ayant d'un coté un casque sur un faisceau d'armes et de l'autre coté une bombe qui eclatte sur un carquois Le dessus orné de branches de laurier Le tout de bronze cizelé et doré d'or moulu . . .' ('A grille of four rods of polished steel on the front of which is an urn, the body of which is decorated with garlands of bay-leaves secured with a stud and passing through the rings [forming handles]. It stands on a pedestal with masks on the four faces and acanthus leaves. The side-piece is in the form of oak-leaves tied with ribbon with, on one side, a helmet and bundle of arms, while on the other side a grenade explodes on a quiver. Above are branches. The whole is of chased and gilt bronze . . .'; Archives Nationales, o[1] 3319, fol. 82 *verso*). These fire-dogs seem to answer this description exactly.

A similar pair was included in the Jacques Doucet sale held in Paris in 1912 (lot 271) and subsequently as lot 105 in the Alfred Sussmann auction held at the Galerie Georges Petit in May 1922. A pair which seems to have been very like those illustrated were provided by Pitoin on 14th September 1775 for use in Madame Adelaïde's rooms at Versailles (Archives Nationales, o[1] 3319, fol. 168 *verso*).

See E. Dumonthier, *Les bronzes du Mobilier National, bronzes d'éclairage et de chauffage*, Paris, n.d., Plate 10, fig. 7. See also page 100.

Plates 229 and 230

PAIR OF FIRE-DOGS. Gilt bronze. Made by Pitoin, 1772. *Musée du Louvre.*

As Verlet has explained (*Burlington Magazine*, June 1950, page 155) these were made by Pitoin, accredited bronze-founder to the royal household, and not by Gouthière, as has been stated. They were made for Madame du Barry but not for her Pavillon de Louveciennes; in fact they were produced to go in her rooms at Fontainebleau. Pitoin dispatched them to the *Garde-Meuble* on 28th October 1772. The records of that establishment refer to them as follows; 'Pour servir dans le Sallon de Madame La Comtesse Dubarry au Chateau de fontainebleau. Une Grille de fer poly de 28. pouces de profondeur ornée par devant d'un Cerf et d'un Sanglier assis sur des rochers posés sur piedestaux enrichis de tetes de chiens avec frizes au pourtour remplis de branche de lierre, La face represente un bas relief composé de divers animaux, Le Recouvrement lié avec le pied est orné des attributs de la Chasse en trophée Le tout de bronze cizelé surdoré d'or moulu avec pelle, pincettes et tenailles a boutons de bronze aussy doré d'or moulu' ('For Madame du Barry's salon at Fontainebleau. A grille of polished steel 28 inches deep, on the front of which are the figures of a stag and a wild boar seated on rocks resting on pedestals, decorated with the heads of hounds and a frieze ornamented with ivy, on the front face of which is a bas relief with various animals. The side-piece is decorated with attributes of the Chase in a trophy. The whole is of chased and gilt bronze. *En suite* are a fire-shovel and tongs of two kinds with finials, also of gilt bronze'; Archives Nationales, o^1 3319, fol. 99 *recto.*)

There is a closely similar pair in the Wrightsman Collection, New York (Watson, *Wrightsman Catalogue*, No. 199). A shorter pair is to be seen in the Château de Compiègne, and these are like a set at the Rijksmuseum, Amsterdam, which are inscribed 'No. 9'.

Plate 231

FIRE-DOG, one of a pair. Gilt bronze. About 1770–75. *Mobilier National, Paris.*

Caffieri produced several fire-dogs decorated with tripod stands like this, as the inventory of his stock, made in 1770, shows (see page 279, e.g. Nos. 38, 40–42 and 80). Some of these also have lion's masks on the bowls of the vessel, like those on this example. None of the descriptions, however, is sufficiently long or explicit to allow one to associate it with this fire-dog and its pair. All one can say is that the type certainly existed by 1770. See also page 101.

Plate 232

FIRE-DOG, one of a pair. Gilt bronze. About 1770–75. *Musée des Arts Décoratifs, Paris.*

For the reasons given in the previous Note, one can say that this type, surmounted by a Classical tripod, was in existence by 1770. This model does not correspond with any item in the inventory of Caffieri's stock (see page 277). The notable delicacy of the ornaments on the side point to a date after 1770.

See E. Dumonthier, *Les Bronzes du Mobilier National, bronzes d'éclairage et de chauffage*, Paris, n.d., Plate 9, fig. 8.

Plate 233

PAIR OF FIRE-DOGS. Iron and chased bronze. About 1772–75. *M. le Marquis de Contades, Château de Montgeoffroy.*

Like the commode shown in Plate 148 and the sconces shown in Plates 215 and 216, these fire-dogs were acquired for the Château de Montgeoffroy between 1772 and 1775, when that country-house was being modified by the Maréchal de Contades.

Plate 234

FIRE-IRONS. The handles of gilt bronze. About 1772–75. *M. le Marquis de Contades, Château de Montgeoffroy.*

See the previous Note.

Plate 235

INKSTAND. Gilt bronze set with green Sèvres plaques. 1761. *The Wallace Collection.*

According to Francis Watson (*Wallace Collection Catalogue*, F. 286), the plaques bear the date-letter 'I' for 1761. However, there is no mention in the Sèvres accounts of the sale of any plaques specially made for inkstands until 1764 when Poirier, the well-known *marchand-mercier*, bought forty-two pieces. Perhaps this particular inkstand was a prototype, made on the factory's own account or, for some other reason, not recorded in the usual ledger. At any rate, the designs for this pattern of inkstand must have existed before the plaques were made at Sèvres.

Three similar pieces are at Waddesdon Manor, Buckinghamshire (*Waddesdon Sèvres Catalogue*, Nos. 64–66) and have plaques dated 1765. See also pages 98 and 134.

Plate 236

PLINTH FOR A VASE. Gilt bronze. Signed by Philippe Caffieri, dated '1761'. *Musée du Louvre.*

Monsieur Pierre Verlet has most kindly drawn my attention to the fact that the statement in the Louvre's old furniture catalogue that this piece is dated 1767 is inaccurate (see Carle Dreyfus, *Musée du Louvre, Mobilier du XVIIe et du XVIIIe siècle*, 1922, No. 394). The plinth may therefore be regarded as an example of the more extreme form of early Neo-Classicism, of which—for instance—Lalive de Jully's furniture (Plates 85 to 89) is another example, and both the furniture and this plinth remind us that Philippe Caffieri was an early exponent of the new style in its most uncompromising form. See also page 98.

Plate 237

VASE, one of a pair. Blue Chinese porcelain with gilt bronze mounts. About 1760–64. *Musée du Louvre.*

Carle Dreyfus informs us in his catalogue (*Musée du Louvre, Mobilier du XVIIe et du XVIIIe siècle*, 1922, No. 426) that this pair came from Jean de Jullienne's collection. Jullienne died on 20th March 1766 and his collection was sold during the following year. This pair, described in the catalogue (lot 1424) as being 'richement ornés de bronze, goût antique' ('with rich bronze mounts in the Antique taste'), fetched 3,600 livres. Jullienne owned a large number of valuable pieces of Oriental porcelain with mounts with bronze ornaments; about a dozen are described in the catalogue as having mounts 'dans le goût antique' (lots 1385, 1401, 1405, 1416, 1432, 1460–61, 1469, 1470, 1474 and 1486). It is to be presumed that Jullienne, a passionate collector all his life, at any rate acquired these vases before 25th May 1764, when he wrote his will; he was then eighty-three years old (see Emile Dacier and Albert Vuaflart, *Jean de Jullienne et les graveurs de Watteau au XVIIIe siècle*, vol. 1, *Notices et documents biographiques*, by Jacques Herold and Albert Vuaflart, 1929, page 219). It may be relevant to note in passing that he bought 'Un socle carré, à moulures, en bronze doré d'or moulu, pour un vase de porcelaine' ('A square plinth with mouldings of gilt bronze, for a vase of porcelain') for 96 livres from Lazare Duvaux on 28th July 1758. If one bears in mind the style of Lalive de Jully's furniture (Plates 85 to 89, 321 and 322) which must date from about 1757, it is by no means impossible that Jullienne's square plinth or pedestal was couched in the new taste, and that it was one of the pieces later described as being 'dans le goût antique'. See also page 98.

Plate 238

POT-POURRI VASE, one of a pair. Green Sèvres porcelain with gilt bronze mounts. About 1765–70. *The National Trust, Waddesdon Manor, Buckinghamshire.*

Several vases of this type are known; some are of green porcelain, others blue and some are aubergine-coloured, but all have virtually identical mounts.

The vases, in colour, texture and shape, are made to resemble Chinese porcelain and were probably intended to deceive, once they had been mounted in this way (see page 103 and *The James A. de Rothschild Collection at Waddesdon Manor, Sèvres Porcelain*, 1968, page 232). The earliest known examples of this type are to be found at The Vyne, Hampshire and, as Francis Watson has pointed out, must be two of the three blue vases that Horace Walpole bought in Paris in 1765–66 for his friend John Chute (Francis Watson, 'Walpole and the Taste for French Porcelain in Eighteenth-century England', in *Horace Walpole: Writer, Politician, and Connoisseur*, 1967, page 329). See also pages 104 and 135–6.

Plate 239

CANDELABRUM, one of a pair. Green Sèvres porcelain with gilt bronze mounts. About 1765–70. *The National Trust, Waddesdon Manor, Buckinghamshire.*

Like the vase embodied in the previous example, this porcelain is also a Sèvres imitation of the genuine Oriental article (see *The James A. de Rothschild Collection at Waddesdon Manor, Sèvres Porcelain*, 1968, page 235 where it is illustrated in colour). This piece would seem to be of the same date as the vase and ewer shown in Plates 238 and 240. See also pages 103–4 and 135.

Plate 240

EWER, one of a pair. Green Sèvres porcelain with gilt bronze. About 1767. *The National Trust, Waddesdon Manor, Buckinghamshire.*

The price is still to be seen written in ink on the base of each vase. It states that they cost 42 livres each. From this one can date them to 1767 with a fair degree of certainty (see *The James A. de Rothschild Collection at Waddesdon Manor, Sèvres Porcelain*, 1968, page 232).

Like the two previous examples such vases were sold by the Sèvres factory without mounts. They were bought by an un-named dealer and it was presumably he who furnished the mounts. Once again, the vases are an imitation of Oriental originals, and there is no mistaking the Neo-Classical style of the mounts. See also pages 103–4 and 135.

Plate 241

THREE DECORATIVE VASES. Imitation porphyry with gilt bronze mounts. About 1765–70. *Lazienki Palace, Warsaw.*

There seems to be no documentation for these vases but they are known to have stood in the Royal Palace at Warsaw (see Stanislas Iskierski, *Les bronzes du Château Royal et du Palais Lazienki à Varsovie*, 1929, page 27, Nos. 15–16) and presumably date from the second half of the 1760s when that residence was being modernised and a large quantity of Parisian furnishings were being provided for the new rooms (see page 100)'. The two vases at the sides closely resemble one engraved by Joseph Vien which is illustrated in Plate 323.

Plate 242

THREE POT-POURRI VASES. Sèvres porcelain with gilt bronze mounts. About 1769. *Formerly in the collection of Madam Jules Fribourg.*

The author does not know whether these are marked but an identical set was in the Erich von Goldschmidt-Rothschild sale, held in Berlin on 23rd March 1931 (lot 206), and they bore the Sèvres date-letter 'q' for 1769.

The roses painted in the reserved compartments derive from the Rococo tradition but the wreath-like framing of bay-leaves reflect the cautious approach to the new style that prevailed at the Sèvres factory. The mounts, on the other hand, are already in the full-blown Neo-Classical style. See also page 104.

Plate 243

PERFUME-BURNER. Red jasper and gilt bronze. Probably designed by F.-J. Belanger and executed by Pierre Gouthière, about 1772–75. *The Wallace Collection.*

Executed for the Duc d'Aumont. Bought at his sale in 1782 (lot 25) by Queen Marie-Antoinette for 12,000 livres (see Watson, *Wallace Collection Furniture*, page 144).

It is not easy to date this piece. It was not among the items Gouthière had under preparation when the Duc died in 1782, all of which were described with care during the subsequent valuation (*Rapports d'Experts*, col. 121–130). It must therefore have been made somewhat earlier. We know that Belanger executed a number of designs for the *Menus Plaisirs* on the Duc d'Aumont's orders in February and November 1772 which included some for tripod stands that must have been very like this example, judging by the description (Archives Nationales, o^1 3044, pièce 362; see also the passages from a similar document quoted by Robiquet in his *Gouthière*, pages 99–100). Apart from this, Belanger noted in a letter addressed to Aumont on 17th November 1774 that he had just visited Gouthière's workshop and seen 'tous les travaux qui se font pour vous . . . je les suis avec exactitude et je ne les perdrai point de vue qu'ils ne soient entièrement terminés' ('all the works he is carrying out for you . . . I am keeping an eye on what he is doing and will not cease to do so until every item is completely finished'; J. Stern, *Belanger*, page 46). It is worth bearing in mind that it was the Duc d'Aumont who had arranged that Belanger and Gouthière should be given appointments on the staff of the *Menus Plaisirs*. See also page 105.

Plate 244

TEA-KETTLE, STAND AND SPIRIT-LAMP, one of a pair. Silver. Paris hall-marks for 1756–63. Signed by F.-T. Germain. *Museu Nacional de Arte Antiga, Lisbon.*

The stand bears the mark 'q' for 1756/57; the triangular frame resting on the rams'-heads bears the mark 'Y' for 1762/63. The kettle is inscribed 'FAIT·PAR·F·T·GERMAIN·SCULP·ORF·DU·ROY·AUX·GALLERIES·DU·LOUVRE·A·PARIS·1762'.

These tea-kettles form part of the large set ordered for the Portuguese Court in 1756. Some pieces were ready in 1757 but the rest were only delivered during the course of the next few years. The difference in dates between the stand and the kettle is curious. Possibly it was not the original intention to have two such disparate components associated in this manner? The triangular frame would appear to be an addition that made it possible to use the kettle with this stand. The stand was made at about the same time as that famous early essay in Neo-Classicism, the furniture of Lalive de Jully (Plates 85 to 89, 321 and 322), and is in almost as extreme a form of the new style. A few moderating curves of the old tradition linger on however (note the root of the handle, for instance).

See the catalogue of the *Lisbon Exhibition*, 1934, No. 171. See also pages 106 and 125.

Plates 245 and 246

SOUP-TUREEN AND STAND. Silver. Paris hall-marks for 1762/63; maker's mark of Antoine-Jean de Villeclair. *Formerly in the Félix Doistau Collection; present whereabouts unknown.*

The general shape of the tureen is traditional but the rosettes and the border resembling *fasces* reflect a new spirit. These suit the entirely regular shape of the stand which is oval and not lobed, as would normally have been the case with such a piece if it were couched in the Rococo style.

Villeclair died in 1764. See also page 106.

Plate 247

CANDLESTICK, one of a pair. Silver-gilt. Paris hall-mark for 1762/63. Signed by François-Thomas Germain and dated 'Paris 1762'. *Musée Nissim de Camondo, Paris.*

The three heraldic castles on the nozzle resemble those which appear on the coat-of-arms of Madame de Pompadour, and it has therefore been suggested that these candlesticks are identical with some described in the inventory made after her death (see Jean Cordey, *Inventaire des biens de Madame de Pompadour*, 1939, No. 1872 and Jean Messelet, *Musée Nissim de Camondo*, 1960, No. 216). Certainly, they are in much the same style as the little work-table at which the Marquise is shown sitting in the portrait by Drouais, painted in 1763–64 (Plate 372). A somewhat similar candlestick by Germain, with the same heavy garlands is dated 1765 and was in the Cassel van Doorn sale, held at the Galerie Charpentier on 30th May 1956 (lot 64). The candlestick shown in Plate 257 has much in common with that illustrated here. See also page 106.

Plate 248

CRUET-STAND. Cut-glass and silver. Paris hall-mark for 1763/64; maker's mark of Jean-Charles Gordière. *Victoria and Albert Museum.*

The cut-glass cruets are of later date than the stand which is clearly Neo-Classical in taste. Drapery or a garland threaded through apertures at the top of the legs was a favourite motif among the early advocates of the new style (e.g. Plates 85, 100 and 124). See also page 106.

Plate 249

SNUFF-BOX. Gold. Paris hall-mark for 1762/63; maker's mark of Jean Frémin. *Musée du Louvre.*

Oval snuff-boxes did not come into fashion again until the middle of the eighteenth century. A few were produced early in the 1750s: one is in the Louvre and is dated 1753/54 (see Nocq and Dreyfus, *Tabatières*, No. 34) and another in the Rijksmuseum, Amsterdam bears the same date; both are by Noel Hardivilliers. The form became common in the 1760s but it was apparently not until then that they came to be decorated with Classical ornament.

It was actually in 1763 that Baron Grimm made the point (see page 264) that Classical ornament had climbed down from the buildings erected by architects and was now to be seen everywhere. The whole of Paris, he said, was now 'à la grecque' and men-about-town—'petits-maîtres' as he called them—would consider themselves totally 'déshonorés' if they were not found armed with a snuff-box that was in this style!

See Nocq and Dreyfus, *Tabatières*, No. 76. See also page 107.

Plate 250

SNUFF-BOX. Gold. Paris hall-mark for 1762/63; maker's mark of Jean George. *Musée du Louvre.*

Note the terms on the side which seem to be supporting the lid of this little box.

See the remarks made about the previous example and Nocq and Dreyfus, *Tabatières*, No. 40.

Plate 251

SNUFF-BOX. Red lacquer ground with gold. Paris hall-mark for 1762/63; maker's mark of Robert-Joseph Auguste. *Musée du Louvre.*

Auguste was making articles in the Neo-Classical taste already by 1761 when he produced some ornaments in bronze designed by the architect Charles De Wailly (see page 148).

See the remarks made about Plate 249 and Nocq and Dreyfus, *Tabatières*, No. 63.

Plate 252

SNUFF-BOX. Gold, with inset miniature paintings in enamel. Paris hall-mark for 1762/63; no maker's mark. *The National Trust, Waddesdon Manor, Buckinghamshire.*

Note the tightly-woven and rather heavy garland forming the bold borders: these are typical early Neo-Classical features.

The association of such formal elements with outright Rococo subjects like those of the miniatures is characteristic of this early phase in which the maker or the vendor could not be sure that the purchaser would be imbued with sufficiently advanced tastes to accept such trifles in a more thorough-going version of the new style. See also page 107.

Plate 253

SNUFF-BOX. Gold, set with miniature-paintings in enamel. Paris hall-mark for 1762/63; maker's mark of Jean Formey. *A La Vieille Russie, New York.*

While the miniature-paintings on the boxes illustrated in Plates 250 and 252 showed no traces of Classicism, this box is decorated with a scene showing Mars and Bellona on the lid. Note the key-fret and pendant swags. See also page 107.

Plate 254

SNUFF-BOX. Gold set with miniature-paintings on enamel. Paris hall-mark for 1762/63; maker's mark of J.-M. Tiron. *Musée du Louvre.*

Note the paired pilasters at the corners and the Vitruvian scroll at the base of this rectangular box, all lending a vaguely Classical air to this small box with its Rococo enamels.

See Nocq and Dreyfus, *Tabatières*, No. 58. See also page 107.

Plate 255

SNUFF-BOX. Gold, set with miniature-paintings in enamel. Paris hall-mark for 1763/64; unidentifiable maker's mark but also signed by Louis Roucel. *Victoria and Albert Museum* (*Jones Collection*, II, No. 330).

There can be no mistaking the Neo-Classical character of the paintings which seem to be inspired by the works of Joseph Vien. See also page 107.

Plate 256

SNUFF-BOX. Gold, with plaques of enamel. Paris hall-mark for 1766/67; signed by B. Barnabé Sageret. *Musée du Louvre.*

The arabesques painted in enamel by an unknown artist are without doubt inspired by the famous grotesques of Raphael at the Vatican. It may be no co-indicence that engravings of these sixteenth-century frescoes were again published in 1765, this time by Jombert in his *Répertoire des artistes*, vol. 2 (see also pages 40–1).

See Nocq and Dreyfus, *Tabatières*, No. 85.

Plate 257

TWO-BRANCH CANDLESTICK, one of a pair. Silver. Paris hall-mark for 1765/66; maker's mark of François-Thomas Germain. *Museu de Arte Antiga, Lisbon.*

This presumably belongs to a toilet-set which also includes the next two items. This candlestick closely resembles the one shown in Plate 247.

See catalogue of the *Lisbon Exhibition*, No. 179. See also page 108.

Plate 258

BOX (*carreau*), one of a pair. Silver. Paris hall-mark for 1764/65; maker's mark of François-Thomas Germain. *Museu de Arte Antiga, Lisbon.*

Part of the toilet-set to which also belongs the dressing-mirror shown in the next illustration and probably also the candlestick shown in the previous example. On the sides of the two boxes are the profile heads of Greek and mythological characters. Similar heads could of course be found on French silver of sixty or seventy years earlier and, even in its general shape, this box does not appear so advanced in taste as the mirror and the candlestick.

See catalogue of the *Lisbon Exhibition*, No. 179. See also page 108.

Plate 259

DRESSING-TABLE MIRROR. Silver frame. Signed by François-Thomas Germain and dated 'Paris 1766'. *Museu de Arte Antiga, Lisbon.*

The support at the back is decorated with engraved palmettes and with a Classical head like those to be seen on the two boxes (Plate 258). The irregular shape of the frame and the medallion set at an angle and upheld by a *putto* on the cresting lend this mirror a less rigorously Classical air than that of the mirror shown in Plate 260, which was also provided by Germain in the same year. On the other hand the heavy garland which forms the frame betokens a new style, while the feet hark back to metalwork and furniture of the *Louis Quatorze* period.

See the catalogue of the *Lisbon Exhibition*, No. 179. See also page 108.

Plate 260

TOILET-SET. Silver-gilt. Made in 1766 by François-Thomas Germain, *The Hermitage, Leningrad.*

The date is given by I. S. Davidson (*Francuzkoe serebro XVIII-načala XIX veka v sobranii Gosudarstvennogo Ermitaža*, Leningrad, 1963, page 24) and the set was illustrated by Germain Bapst (*Les Germain*, Paris, 1887, pages 107, 135 and 137) when it belonged to the Grand-Duke Alexis. It is not known for whom it was originally made. The mirror is couched in a rather severe form of the new taste but retains much of the traditional Baroque shape which is not totally disguised by the Classical trimmings. See also pages 108 and 125.

Plate 261

CANDLESTICKS, one of a pair. Silver. Paris hall-mark for 1766/67; maker's mark for Robert-Joseph Auguste. *From the Woburn Abbey Collection, by kind permission of His Grace the Duke of Bedford.*

These can be converted from two-branch into single-nozzle candlesticks in the usual way. Published by Arthur Grimwade (*Apollo*, December 1965, page 505). By a strange coincidence, the same issue of *Apollo* contained an advertisement for a set of four similar candlesticks by the London silversmiths John Peter and Edward Wakelin which bore the hall-marks for 1770.These were presumably copied from the Woburn pair or from another set which had been imported from France. See also page 108.

Plate 262

THREE-BRANCH CANDELABRUM, one of a pair. Silver. Paris hall-mark for 1767/68; maker's mark of Robert-Joseph Auguste. *Metropolitan Museum of Art, Bequest of Catherine D. Wentworth.*

A set of twelve identical candelsticks, but with branches of different form, are in the Swedish Royal Collection at Stockholm Palace. They are hall-marked 1775–76. (See Åke Setterwall and Stig Fogelmarck, *Stockholm Slott och dess konstskatter*, 1950, page 162.)

See also Faith Dennis, *Three Centuries of French Domestic Silver*, 1960, No. 14. And see also page 108.

Plate 263

SOUP-TUREEN AND STAND. Silver. Paris hall-mark for 1770/71; maker's mark of Jacques-Nicolas Roëttiers. *Metropolitan Museum of Art* (*Rogers Fund*).

This belongs to the large and entirely Neo-Classical dinner-service ordered by Catharine the Great and given by her to Prince Gregory Orloff (see also Plate 265). There were originally twenty-two tureens in all; some are still in Russia (in Leningrad and Moscow museums) while others are in numerous European and American collections. Yves Bottineau drew attention to the fact that Roëttiers made some very similar tureens, with only small variations, for Mesdames, the daughters of Louis XV, in 1775 (see *Musée du Louvre et Musée de Cluny, Catalogue de l'orfèvrerie*, 1958, page 127).

Note the garlands of bay-leaves which form the handles. The overlapping lobed plates (*piastres*) on the members forming the legs were a favourite motif among Neo-Classical designers (see e.g. Plates 99 and 178).

See Faith Dennis, *Three Centuries of French Domestic Silver*, 1960, No. 296. See also page 109.

Plate 264

SERVING FORK, now one of a pair. Silver. Paris hall-mark for 1770/71; maker's mark of Jacques-Nicolas Roëttiers. *Musée du Louvre* (*Donation Stavros S. Niarchos*).

The model for this large fork (it is 37 cm. long and weighs 625 grs.) goes back to 1766 when Roëttiers was commissioned to execute some tureens and forks for Louis XV. As Bottineau pointed out (see *Musée du Louvre et Musée de Cluny*, *Catalogue de l'orfèvrerie*, 1958, page 127), the description of the forks he then made corresponds closely to that of the fork illustrated here. They were 'ornées de mascarons michel-angesques et sur la poignée ornée de cartels dont partent des guirlandes de lauriers et sur la baguette enroulés de double rang de rubans . . .' ('decorated with masks in the style of Michel-Angelo, the butt of the handle embellished with a cartouche from which spring garlands of bay-leaves, the stem being entwined with two ribbons . . .').

Presumably such tureens and forks were for serving pâté. See also page 109.

Plate 265

WINE-COOLER. Silver. Paris hall-mark for 1770/71; maker's mark of Jacques-Nicolas Roëttiers. *Musée Nissim de Camondo, Paris.*

Part of the Orloff Service (see Plate 263). There are said to have been sixteen wine-coolers in the service; four are in the Musée Nissim de Camondo. This piece is 24 cm. high.

See Jean Messelet, *Musée Nissim de Camondo*, 1960, No. 225.

Plate 266

SOUP-TUREEN AND STAND. Silver. Paris hall-mark for 1771/72; maker's mark of Robert-Joseph Auguste. *Private Collection, Lisbon.*

The stand of this elegant piece reflects a totally fresh approach to the design of such a component, freed entirely of all Rococo undertones.

See the catalogue of the *Lisbon Exhibition*, No. 701. See also page 109.

Plate 267

MUSTARD-POT. Silver, and blue glass. Paris hall-mark for 1773/74; maker's mark of Vincent Bréant. *Victoria and Albert Museum* (*Fitzhenry Collection*).

Plate 268

SMALL TRAY. Sèvres porcelain bearing the date-letter 'E' for 1757. *Formerly in the Nicolier Collection, Paris.*

Rectangular and square trays were being turned out at the Royal French Porcelain Factory already while it was still at Vincennes. In 1757, a year after the factory moved over to Sèvres, they seem to have begun to provide such trays with rims formed of a pierced Vitruvian scroll. This is the earliest sign of a Classical revival on the Sèvres production. It is not known who was responsible for introducing this new feature but it is difficult to avoid putting forward the name of the sculptor Falconet, who in that very year, was appointed 'directeur des travaux de sculpture' and is known to have designed purely decorative objects like vases and urns (see Plate 270) as well as providing models for proper sculpture.

The tray shown here and one in the British Museum (Eckstein Bequest) are the only two known to the present writer that bear the date-letter for 1757; several made in the following years are known including that illustrated in the next Plate.

The ground-colour of this early example is green. This is bordered by a simple linear framing with indented corners that is at least as much a reflection of the new taste as the Vitruvian scroll of the rim. Such indented frames marked a clear reaction against the typical Rococo equivalent and, came to be much used on furniture of a slightly later date (cf. Oeben's corner-cupboard, shown in Plate 96, on which naturalisticly drawn flowers are also present). See also page 110.

Plate 269

SMALL TRAY. Sèvres porcelain bearing the date-letter 'F' for 1758. *The National Trust, Waddesdon Manor, Buckinghamshire.*

This shows the Vitruvian scroll framing the border. It was made the year after the tray shown in the previous illustration, the Note concerning which should be consulted for further information.

See the *Waddesdon Sèvres Catalogue*, No. 35.

Plate 270

ORNAMENTAL VASE. Dark blue Sèvres porcelain, bearing the date-letter 'I' for 1761. *Collection of H.M. The Queen, Buckingham Palace.*

As far as is known, this is the earliest example of a type of ornamental vase which was popular during the 1760s and early 1770s (a similar vase at Schloss Wilhelmshöhe in Germany bears the date-letter 'S' for 1771).

This model was the earliest of a whole sequence of not especially charming vase forms which are characterised by their simple, clearly-defined shapes and their sculptural ornaments that are mostly inspired by Antique Classical examples—either directly or indirectly. None of the vases seem to be direct copies of Classical originals, however; they seem rather to be original conceptions in their own right, produced by one or several designers working in a consciously modern or anti-Rococo spirit very like that which fired Le Lorrain to produce such determinedly novel designs for Lalive de Jully's furniture (Plates 85 to 89).

It is not known for certain who was responsible for this abrupt change in style at Sèvres but it is likely that Falconet had considerable influence in these matters (see Note to Plate 268). He was appointed to the staff of the factory in 1757 and *L'Avantcoureur* for January 1763 claims that it was he who had designed all the ornamental vases produced at Sèvres which had been exhibited at Versailles, the month before. Falconet had demonstrated already in 1754 that he could handle the Neo-Classical idiom in the decorative arts when he designed the monument for the late Madame Lalive de Jully (Plate 38). Vases like that illustrated here are naturally very different in character from the monument but there does seem to be a certain stylistic correspondence between them and the epitaph. It does in fact seem possible that Falconet was an important innovator in this field.

See Laking, *Sèvres*, No. 38. See also page 111.

Plate 271

POT-POURRI VASE. Sèvres porcelain having the date-letter 'I' for 1761. *The National Trust, Waddesdon Manor, Buckinghamshire.*

In the present context, the important feature of this vase is its essentially Neo-Classical foot which is in the same style as the gilt bronze plinth. The main part of the vase is a variant of a basic form, presumably designed by the elder Duplessis, that originally made its appearance in 1754. The development of this form is discussed at length in the catalogue of the collection of Sèvres porcelain at Waddesdon Manor (page 136); at first a soup-tureen, it finally came to be adopted for a sugar bowl. It may well have been Duplessis himself, or his son (who was also a designer at the factory), who modernised the foot, especially as the new foot required a bronze plinth and bronze-founding was the Duplessis' family business! Other versions of this basic shape have scrolling feet of Rococo form.

See the *Waddesdon Sèvres Catalogue*, No. 49. See also page 110.

Plate 272

ORNAMENTAL VASE. Sèvres porcelain bearing the date-letter 'K' for 1763. *From the Woburn Abbey Collection, by kind permission of His Grace the Duke of Bedford.*

The general shape of this vase may owe something to Oriental or Meissen porcelain but the 'à la grecque' border round the neck is obviously the result of an attempt to add a dash of modernity to the vase. It is not known who designed this model, but it can hardly have been Falconet, who was more thorough-going in his Neo-Classicism and who would have made a better job of it. In 1763, when this vase was made, John, the fourth Duke of Bedford, was sent as British Ambassador to Paris to handle the peace negotiations following the Seven Years' War; he may well have acquired this vase and its pair (now lost) on that occasion.

Plate 273

POT-POURRI VASE. Dark blue Sèvres porcelain bearing the date-letter 'K' for 1763. *The National Trust, Waddesdon Manor, Buckinghamshire.*

Only two examples of this large vase (it is 58 cm. high) are known, the other being in the Henry E. Huntington Collection at San Marino in California. The latter is said to bear the date-letter 'F' for 1758 but this is masked by a plinth which is now glued in place. This date is most surprising because the *roze marbré* decoration of the Huntington vase is not otherwise known until the early 1760s, and Pierre Verlet has shown that this form was probably not sold by the factory before May 1763 (see *The Art Quarterly*, 1954, page 234). Until further evidence comes to light, it would therefore seem safest to accept 1763 as the earliest production date of this model although it may well have been designed and in preparation a year or so earlier.

The form displays a curious mixture of Classical motifs which are handled in what in many ways seems to be a Baroque manner. The curious scrolls on the spine behind the goat's heads are reminiscent of the 'auricular' forms (what the Germans call the *Ohrmuschelstil*) and it is worth recording that Joseph Vien, who was essentially a Neo-Classical artist, flirted with this style and designed a series of vases decorated with such ornament while he was in Rome; the series was engraved by Watelet and published in 1749.

Although Falconet is known to have been designing ornamental vases for Sèvres at this stage, one feels that a design so lacking in clarity cannot be his work (see the previous Note and that for Plate 270). It is more likely to be the work of one of the Duplessis but there were other designers working at Sèvres—for example, Jacques François Deparis who was the elder Duplessis' assistant and acted as modeller.

See the *Waddesdon Sèvres Catalogue*, No. 57.

Plate 274

ORNAMENTAL VASE, Dark blue Sèvres porcelain bearing the date-letter 'K' for 1763. *H.M. The Queen, Buckingham Palace.*

According to Troude (*Choix de modèles*, Plate 104), the factory called this model the 'vase antique ferré, dit de Fontenoy'. The first part of this title is probably correct but the second is surely a piece of nineteenth-century romanticism. The vase shown here is the earliest known example of this model; one date-marked

1767 is in the Wallace Collection. The model seems to have remained in production until 1780 (see Verlet, *Sèvres*, note to Plate 60). The sales ledgers at Sèvres from the 1760s mention, but rarely describe, the vases sold by the factory and do very occasionally specify the model's name. The kiln-registers, on the other hand, often do (the registers of the early period are in the library of the Institut de France; MS. 5675). From this source we learn that '11 vazes antiques' were removed from a kiln on 30th December 1764 and that three of the same description were taken out on 31st December the following year.

See Laking, *Sèvres*, No. 49. See also page 112.

Plate 275

ORNAMENTAL VASE. Dark blue Sèvres porcelain bearing the date-mark 'L' for 1764. *H.M. The Queen, Buckingham Palace.*

We do not know the original title given to this model at the factory. The example shown here is the earliest known but the model remained in production well into the 1770s. One may perhaps attribute the design to Falconet (see Notes to Plates 268 and 270). The curious strap-like handles are of a form which occurs in Neufforge's *Recueil d'architecture*, (e.g. Plate 312) which dates from about 1756–58 (see page 207).

See Laking, *Sèvres*, No. 51.

Plate 276

ORNAMENTAL VASE. Dark blue Sèvres porcelain bearing the date-letter 'O' for 1767. *The British Museum (Eckstein Bequest).*

This is so far the earliest known example of this thoroughly 'antique' model which was probably that known at the time as a 'vase cassolette à festons' (see Troude, *Choix de modèles*, Plate 112). A vase with the same decoration, which may be its pair, is at Waddesdon Manor (see the catalogue of the collection of Sèvres porcelain at Waddesdon, No. 78). The model was still being produced in the 1790s (see Verlet, *Sèvres*, note to fig. 93). See also page 112.

Plate 277

VASE, one of a pair. Dark blue Sèvres porcelain bearing the date-letter 'M' for 1765. *The Wallace Collection.*

The simulated slots round the neck are reminiscent of pastille-burners and it would not be surprising if the factory's name for this model had therefore included the word 'cassolette'. However, the plaster model for this vase, which is preserved at the factory, has a label with a nineteenth-century inscription describing it as a 'vase allemand uni'. All the same, it may be relevant to note that the factory's kiln-book for 1760–71 (Institut de France, MS. 5675 . . .) shows that two vases actually described as 'cassolettes' were removed from a kiln on 30th December 1764 and two more at some date in 1765 (the precise day is not given). This vase and its pair, as well as a pair at Goodwood House (The Duke of Richmond and Gordon's Collection) may possibly be the actual four concerned.

Plate 278

ORNAMENTAL VASE. Dark blue Sèvres porcelain; undated but about 1766–70. *H.M. The Queen, Buckingham Palace.*

The portrait-medallion on the side of this vase shows a profile of Louis XV while on the reverse is one with the profile of the Empress Maria Theresa. The plaster model of this vase, preserved at the Sèvres factory, is inscribed 'vase ovale Mercure' (Troude, *Choix de modèles*, Plate 110) and the oval form of the body explains this title although it is difficult to understand how Mercury comes into it; perhaps the original vase had medallions displaying a figure of this God.

The kiln-books (Institut de France, MS. 5675) show that a 'vaze ovale' was removed from a kiln at some date between 1st July 1766 and New Year 1767, while a 'vaze Mercure' came out at some point during the same period in 1767. The vases would have come out furnished only with their ground colour: they then had to be gilded. On 9th March 1769, the factory delivered a 'Vaze Ovale Bleu Nouveau Et or' ('an oval vase with the new blue and gilded') to the Messrs. Bouffet and Dangirard bankers, and this may very well have been one of the two mentioned above.

The presence of Maria Theresa's portrait on this vase alongside that of Louis XV have been occasioned by the betrothal of her daughter, Marie-Antoinette, to the Dauphin (later Louis XVI) in 1768 or by the subsequent wedding which took place in 1770.

See Laking, *Sèvres*, No. 98.

Plate 279

VASE. Dark blue Sèvres porcelain, undated but about 1765–66. *His Grace The Duke of Richmond and Gordon, Goodwood House.*

Most of the Sèvres in the collection at Goodwood bears the date-letters for 1765 and 1766 and one may presume that it was all acquired by the then Duke and Duchess of Richmond when they spent the winter of 1765 in Paris. The dinner-service they acquired is mentioned in the diary of the Rev. William Cole (12th November 1765, *Journal of my Journey to Paris*, 1931, page 234).

Troude tells us that this model was known as the 'vase flacon à mouchoir' (*Choix de modèles*, Plate 95). The kiln-book of the Sèvres factory (Institut de France, MS. 5675) reveals that two 'vazes flaccons' were taken out of a kiln on 1st January 1768; possibly these are the two now in the Wallace Collection. A larger type of vase, also known as a 'flacon', was apparently in production a couple of years later, for we know that the decorator Cuvillier was paid 24 livres for having painted the ground of two 'Grands flaccons' blue (see Sèvres Archives, F. 10, travaux extraordinaires).

Plate 280

EWER, one of a pair. Dark blue Sèvres porcelain, undated but made about 1765–67. *Musée du Louvre.*

Ewers of this type were known as 'vazes en burettes' at Sèvres. A ewer datable to 1767 was once in the Pierpont-Morgan Collection (Chavagnac, No. 126) and two vases 'en Burettes' were removed from a kiln at the factory already on 31st December 1765 (Institut de France, MS. 5675), by which time they had received their ground-colour but still needed painting and gilding, and then re-firing in the *petit feu*. Possibly the ewer shown here was one of the two concerned.

Formerly in the collection of the Earl of Harewood; sold at Christie's, 1st July 1965, lot 33.

Plate 281

ORNAMENTAL VASE. Sèvres porcelain. Undated, about 1765–68. *H.M. The Queen, Buckingham Palace.*

Blue ground with a portrait medallion of Louis XV. The original designation of this form is not known to us. It may have been the 'vaze à couronne' to which references occur in factory's sales ledgers during 1765; it might also have been known as the 'vaze à medaillon du Roy', a term that is found among the entries for 1768.

See Laking, *Sèvres*, No. 42.

Plate 282

PAIR OF VASES. Dark blue and gilt Sèvres porcelain. Undated, about 1769. *Victoria and Albert Museum (Jones Collection, No.* 149).

This must be the form known as the 'vaze à pied de globe' in the factory's records. The term is found several times in connection with payments to certain decorators who must have executed the painted ornament (Sèvres Archives, F. 11, travaux extraordinaires, Sieur Genest). Two vases of this type at the Wallace Collection are dated 1769 and are probably identical with those with '2 medallions en Sacrifice 2 têtes Et ornemens' mentioned in the accounts.

The regular masonry-like pattern executed in gold on the ground is presumably that known as 'à briques d'or'—a term which crops up in the sales ledgers for 1769. In the Duke of Bedford's collection at Woburn Abbey there is a cup and saucer of this description dated 1770 (Plate 289). Medallions imitating marble were also a new feature in 1769 (see Plates 283 to 286).

Plate 283

ORNAMENTAL VASE. Grey-blue Sèvres porcelain. Undated, about 1768–69. *Major-General Sir Harold Wernher, Bart., Luton Hoo, Bedfordshire.*

This form was presumably that referred to as the 'vaze à col cylindrique' in the factory's records. Its unusual ground-colour, directly onto which the garlands of flowers are painted (i.e. they are not in reserved panels), enables one to date this piece, since the firm's accounts show that this type of decoration was only done in 1768 and 1769 (see Sèvres Archives, travaux extraordinaires, F. 10, Sieur Bertrand, and F. 11, Sieur Genest).

Plate 284

ORNAMENTAL VASE. Blue Sèvres porcelain, 1769. *The National Trust, Waddesdon Manor, Buckinghamshire.*

Such a vase went by the name of 'vaze à palmes' at the factory in its day. The decoration of flowers painted directly on the blue ground-colour was discussed in the previous entry. This vase belongs in a set with the next item.

See the *Waddesdon Sèvres Catalogue*, No. 86.

Plate 285

ORNAMENTAL VASE. Sèvres porcelain, 1769. *The National Trust, Waddesdon Manor, Buckinghamshire.*

This type of vase was entitled the 'vase en console' or 'vase console'. This is part of a *garniture* of five vases which includes two like the foregoing item. It is illustrated in colour in the catalogue of the Sèvres porcelain at Waddesdon Manor (No. 86) where its date is also discussed (but see the Note for Plate 283, here).

Plate 286

ORNAMENTAL VASE, one of a pair. Sèvres porcelain. Undated, about 1768–69. *The National Trust, Waddesdon Manor, Buckinghamshire.*

For some reason, this form was called the 'Vase Carrache' at Sèvres. The date of this pair of vases is discussed in the catalogue of the Waddesdon collection of Sèvres porcelain (No. 252). Amongst other things, the dating rests on the presence of the simulated marble medallion-portraits which were first introduced in 1768 and only used for a year or two.

Plate 287

ORNAMENTAL VASE, one of a pair. Dark blue Sèvres porcelain. Bearing the date-letter 'R' for 1770. *H.M. The Queen, Buckingham Palace.*

Troude informs us that the form was described as the 'vase grec à ornements' in the factory records and, while there is no evidence for an earlier dating, one cannot help feeling that the ponderous Neo-Classical ornament must belong to the Archaic phase of that movement. It may therefore be relevant to point out that a 'Vase Grec à Médaillons' was sold to Monsieur De Machault in December 1766. Making the design and the model for such a piece would take perhaps a year or so; the original conception might therefore well have taken place during the first half of the 1760s—a date which would suit this type far better.

See Laking, *Sèvres*, No. 101.

Plate 288

ORNAMENTAL VASE, one of a pair. Dark blue Sèvres porcelain. Undated, about 1772–76. *Schloss Wilhelmshöhe, Kassel, Germany.*

This is based on one of the designs executed by Pierre-Elisabeth de Fontanieu, the director of the *Garde-Meuble de la Couronne*, which were published in 1770 under the title *Collection de vases.* At Wilhelmshöhe, the pair flank a third which is of the same shape as that shown in Plate 270 and bears the date-letter 'T' for 1772. The three may well have formed a *garniture* together.

The factory records show that nine 'vazes fontanieux' were sold in December 1772—three of them to Marie-Antoinette, two to Madame Sophie and four to Madame Adelaïde. On 1st August 1775, Baron de Buchevale bought two more such vases. The Mesdames de France followed up their earlier purchases with the acquisition of two 'Vases fontanieux' on 3rd July 1776. The piece shown here is probably one of the items referred to. See also page 129.

Plate 289

CUP AND SAUCER. White and gilt Sèvres porcelain. Bearing the date-letter 'R' for 1770. *From the Woburn Abbey Collection, by kind permission of His Grace the Duke of Bedford.*

The simple shape of this set existed as far back as 1752 (see the Waddesdon Sèvres catalogue, page 132) and responsibility for it cannot therefore be laid at the door of Neo-Classicism.

However, the handle has been modernised: the break at the bottom of the scroll has been ironed out. The gilt diaper-pattern 'en briques d'or' was apparently introduced in 1769 (see the Note to Plate 282). See also page 110.

Plate 290

WINE-GLASS COOLER. White Sèvres porcelain. Bearing the date-letter 'S' for 1771. *The National Trust, Waddesdon Manor, Buckinghamshire.*

This formed part of a large set originally entitled the 'Service avec Petits Vazes Et Guirlandes' which was delivered to Madame du Barry on 29th August 1771 (see Verlet, *Sèvres*, page 215). It bears her initials. The form of this cooler goes back to the 1750s but the painted decoration, with its Classical oil-lamps and garlands of flowers of a new type, marks a fresh departure, that, according to Verlet (loc. cit.), may be due to the initiative of Augustin de Saint-Aubin.

See the *Waddesdon Sèvres Catalogue*, No. 93. See also page 113.

Plates 291 to 293

THREE ORNAMENTAL VASES. Drawn and engraved by Jacques-François-Joseph Saly in 1746 while in Rome.

From a series of thirty etchings, each showing a vase or urn; published during the very year in which Saly left Rome after having spent eight years there. We know he was an admirer of the work of Bernini and his vase-compositions do in fact possess a certain picturesque Baroque character. They also betray a markedly romantic attitude towards Classical Antiquity, an attitude shared by many of the other young French artists who were attending the French Academy in Rome at that time. It will be noted that many of the details in these compositions are somewhat indistinct, as if covered in moss or corroded in some way. No doubt he wished to convey the impression that these objects had recently been excavated from the very soil of Ancient Rome! On the other hand, the actual shapes of the vases are clearly defined and they are Classical in conception. The applied figures—the sirens and the masks—are typical of the period. One finds similar features in the work of many contemporary artists; they appear, for instance, on much porcelain including some vases designed by Duplessis *père* who, incidentally, owned a set of Saly's vase-compositions. Lalive de Jully was also interested in these designs; he is known to have copied three of the compositions in the year 1754 (see page 196). Jardin, Saly's friend from their student days in Rome, chose one of these compositions for execution to form the carved ornaments constituting the focal points of the buffets at each end of the early Neo-Classical dining-room in the house of Count Moltke in Copenhagen, constructed in 1757 (Plate 30). These designs for vases were so popular that they were later republished in Paris by the print-seller, Basan. See also page 33.

Plate 294

A ROMAN TRIPOD. Drawn in Rome between 1740 and 1748 by Jacques-François-Joseph Saly and published as Plate III in Volume II of the Comte de Caylus *Recueil d'Antiquités* of 1756.

This is of course not an original design but shows a true relic of Antiquity. All the same, it gives an idea of the kind of thing that interested Saly—and no doubt also many of the other young French artists in Rome at the time. It is worth noting that Le Lorrain, who was to design for Lalive de Jully the radically new suite of furniture illustrated in Plates 85 to 89, was also resident at the French Academy while Saly was there and that he too provided drawings for Caylus' archaeological works. Caylus actually devoted six pages of text in his *Recueil* (figs. 161 to 168) to a discussion of the Classical tripod. Of the piece shown here he writes that 'Les études que Sali [sic], Sculpteur du Roi, a faites à Rome, m'ont fourni le Trépied que je présente ici' ('The studies which Saly, the Royal Sculptor, made in Rome have furnished me with [the drawing for] the tripod illustrated here'), and adds that it was found in the ruins of Hadrian's villa. It is now in the Louvre.

Plate 295

TITLE-PAGE OF THE 'MASCARADE TURQUE'. Drawn and engraved in 1748 by Joseph Vien.

This is one of a series of thirty etchings, the full title of which was the *Caravanne du Sultan à la Meque. Mascarade Turque donnée à Rome par Messieurs les Pensionnaires de l'Académie de France et leurs Amis au Carnaval de l'Année 1748*. This title, and a letter of 27th March 1748 written by De Troy, the Director of the French Academy at Rome (*Corr. des Dir.*, No. 4629), show that all the costumes and other properties needed for this masquerade were designed and produced by the stipendiaries attending the courses at this establishment. It follows that costumes and vases shown in Vien's illustration are likely to have been designed by several of the young artists. The Classical vases may thus have been the work of Vien himself, or of Le Lorrain, or of one of the Challe brothers—all of whom are known to have designed vases at some point. In any case, all of the students must have been well aware of these activities and must have studied such compositions with some interest.

Plate 296

A FOUNTAIN. Detail of a pen and ink drawing entitled *Le Printemps* signed by Joseph Vien and dated 1753. *Musée Atger, Faculté de Médecine de Montpellier.*

This and several other drawings in the same style at Montpellier (see Plates 299 and 300) seem to be projects for decorative panels. It is not known whether they were ever executed. In many ways they are reminiscent of the work of Rococo artists like Boucher but free use is made of Classical motifs while the compositions are essentially symmetrical. It seems as if the artist has consciously been seeking to conjure up a sense of monumentality by reference to Classical principles. It is not impossible that Vien was to some extent influenced by the work of Poussin at this stage.

Plates 297 and 298

TWO VASES. Drawn by Louis-Joseph Le Lorrain in 1752 or earlier. *Musée des Arts Décoratifs, Paris.*

These drawings have been attributed to L.-F. de la Rue but they were published, with other drawings of vases by Le Lorrain, in 1752 in the form of etchings by Claude-Henri Watelet who dedicated the series to Madame Geoffrin. The series was entitled *Raccolta Di Vasi Dedicata All. Ill. Signora Geoffrin Delle Arti Amante riamata.* It is not known when Le Lorrain actually executed the drawings; they need not have been fresh when Watelet etched the compositions. Comparison with Saly and Vien's compositions for similar subjects (see Plates 291 to 295) suggests that Le Lorrain may well have designed these while in Rome where he attended the French Academy from 1740 until 1748. The fact that Watelet subsequently published the designs under an Italian title may be relevant. The Musée des Arts Décoratifs owns a further sixteen designs for vases by him and there are six more in the Académie des Beaux-Arts (Collection Masson).

According to the accounts of the Royal Porcelain Factory (then still at Vincennes), a certain 'S. Lorain' was paid 48 livres on 6th March 1754 for 'plusieurs Traits de vases antiques' ('several designs for vases in the Antique taste'; Sèvres, Archives of the Manufacture Nationale de Porcelaine, F. 2, liasse 2, Compte pour 1754). It seems likely that the reference is to our Le Lorrain and that the designs for Antique vases were of the type illustrated here. See also page 33.

Plates 299 and 300

TWO FOUNTAINS. Pen and ink drawings by Joseph Vien, dated 1753. *Musée Atger, Faculté de Médecine de Montpellier.* (See Note to Plate 296.)

From a set of four similar compositions for wall-decoration, the two shown here being emblematic of Autumn and Spring.

Plates 301 and 302

FURNITURE AND MURAL-DECORATION IN THE DUCHESSE D'ORLÉANS' ROOMS AT THE PALAIS ROYAL. Engraved by Le Canu after drawings executed about 1755–57 by Contant d'Ivry. Illustrations which accompany J.-F. Blondel's chapter on 'Architecture et parties qui en dependent' that is included in Diderot's and Alembert's *Dictionnaire des Sciences*, published in 1762. The two Plates shown here are in fact part of the same plate which is folded down the centre.

As was explained in the Note to Plates 22 and 23, J.-F. Blondel regarded Contant d'Ivry's re-decoration of the Duchesse d'Orléans' apartment as a highly satisfactory expression of the Golden Mean between the turbulent Rococo and the over-powering Classicism of seventeenth-century French decoration. Blondel's comments on the present furnishings are quoted in full on pages 253-4. To our eyes, there is no very startling difference between the style of the objects illustrated here and much other work in the Rococo style, but one must concede that these compositions are imbued with a strong sense of symmetry. This must have struck contemporary observers as something quite new, and was to become a salient feature of future developments. One should therefore take Blondel's statement seriously and reserve for the new decorations at the Palais Royal an important position in the history of taste at this period.

Verlet has published three console-tables (see *Mobilier Royal*, I, Nos. 20, 21 and 22) which were made in 1737, 1739 and 1757 respectively. These also show very clearly the development in the Rococo taste. Stylistic indiscipline was at its most rampant during the 1740s; by the second half of the 1750s, however, the Rococo had become noticeably tamed. See also pages 42 and 124.

Plate 303

VIGNETTE. Drawn in 1752 by Charles-Nicolas Cochin, and engraved by C. C. Gallimard. This appeared on the title-page of the second volume of Jombert's edition of Blondel's *Architecture Française*.

The vignette is a *trompe l'oeil* representation of an Antique relief that seems to betray signs of age. The heavy garland along the top is a form that was to become much loved by many early Neo-Classical artists in France. Le Lorrain used the motif prominently in the decoration of Lalive de Jully's furniture of about 1757 (see notes to Plates 85 to 89). Cochin was later to deride this excessive use of 'guirlandes en forme de corde à puits', as he called them ('garlands like well-ropes'). See also pages 40 and 56.

Plate 304

VIGNETTE. Drawn by Charles Eisen and engraved in 1756 by N. Le Mire. Used for the title-page of volume II of the *Recueil d'estampes d'après les plus célèbres tableaux de la Galerie Royale de Dresde*, which was published in Dresden in 1757.

Note the strings of husks, the Vitruvian scroll, the triglyphs, and other Classical features.

Plates 305 to 307

LALIVE DE JULLY'S COAT OF ARMS, as represented on three different etchings dating from 1751 to 1759.

305. Etching dedicated to Lalive de Jully by J.-P. Le Bas of a painting by Joseph Vernet entitled *Port de Mer d'Italie* that belonged to Soufflot. The etching was discussed in the *Mercure de France* in October 1751. See also pages 46 and 115.
306. A. Le Canu's etching of L.-J. Le Lorrain's *Projet d'une Place pour le Roy*, dedicated to Lalive de Jully and dated 1756.
307. Etching, dated 1759, by P. Martenasie of Greuze's painting *La Lecture de la Bible* which belonged to Lalive de Jully.

No evidence has so far come to light to show that Lalive concerned himself in any way with the appearance of the coats of arms on these three etchings—or anywhere else, for that matter—but it seems most unlikely that the three artists concerned should not have consulted him on such a personal matter, especially as Lalive was himself something of artist and was known as an *amateur* of the Arts. At any rate, the three examples shown here are very different in character. That by Le Bas of 1751 is still couched in the purest Rococo taste, with the escutcheon set obliquely. Le Canu's is markedly more controlled; the shield is set strictly upright and is in itself symmetrical. It is threaded through with a heavy garland of bay-leaves. Presumably this reflects Lalive's taste by 1756; it was at just about this time that he was having his famous set of furniture made after designs by Le Lorrain (see Plates 85 to 89). By the time Martenasie's engraving of Greuze's painting was executed (in 1759), the Neo-Classical spirit had become even more positive (note the key-fret, for instance). This was produced in the same year as Greuze's portrait of Lalive which shows him amid his ultra-modern furniture (see Plates 321 and 322).

Plate 308

A CABINET. Detail of a portrait executed in 1757 by Alexander Roslin and engraved by J. Daullé in 1761.

The painting was executed in Paris. Until recently, it was only known through the engraving but the original appeared in a sale held on 25th November 1970 at Sotheby's (illustrated in the catalogue). It shows the Countess Anastasie of Hesse-Homburg, née Princess Troubetskoi. It is illustrated in its entirety in Gunnar W. Lundberg's biography of Roslin where it is discussed at length (Cat. No. 95).

The cabinet shown in the background seems to be decorated with boulle-work (i.e. veneered with ebony, inlaid with fillets of metal, and furnished with ormolu mounts). It is surmounted by a clock, presumably of gilt bronze, supported by a female figure and a cherub. In the centre of the main panel is an oval medallion which probably sported a relief. In general style, this cabinet has much in common with Boulle-type furniture of the late seventeenth century but the inlay is rather less elaborate and the heavy, tightly bound, garlands are of a type unknown in the seventeenth century but which appear on French furniture not infrequently after Lalive de Jully's furniture (Plates 85 to 89) had been constructed. In the present case, one can say that, if the cabinet is not a figment of Roslin's imagination (which seems highly unlikely), it must, in 1757, have been one of the earliest pieces displaying this motif. Moreover, it was no doubt quite a new piece of furniture when the portrait was painted. A cabinet-maker like Dubois, who made the pieces of furniture shown in Plates 101 to 103 might well have produced this cabinet. The Princess is resting her arm on a table which is probably also of boulle-work and somewhat resembles one in the Victoria and Albert Museum bearing the mark of another member of the Dubois family (Jones Collection, No. 5). See also page 69.

Plate 309

BOOK-CASE. Detail of a portrait of Madame de Pompadour painted in 1758 by François Boucher. *Private collection.*

In this famous portrait of the King's mistress, we see her seated in front of a mirror (part of the garland-entwined palm-stem forming the frame may be seen in this detail) in which is reflected a book-case surmounted by a lyre-shaped clock flanked by cherubs and decorated with olive branches. The books are protected by a glass-fronted door, above which is a frieze with an heraldic tower (her crest) flanked by ornament that vaguely recalls a Vitruvian scroll. The portrait is reproduced by Pierre de Nolhac's biography of Boucher (1935, Plate facing page 120). In the foreground of the painting, there is a small Rococo table.

It has not been possible to prove that such a definitely Neo-Classical book-case ever belonged to the Marquise; no such piece is listed in the inventory of her belongings, nor does there seem to be any reference to anything of this sort in the journals of the *Garde-Meuble de la Couronne*. It is possible that it was an entirely imaginary object, thought up by Boucher who was in fact far more sympathetic to the Neo-Classical ideals than is generally realised (see, for example, the ceiling he designed about 1760–61, Plate 44). He was also conversant with the most up-to-date developments in design at the Gobelins, with which he was associated and where Soufflot was director. Madame de Pompadour must anyway have approved of the representation of such a book-case in her portrait and we know that she owned, at the time of her death in 1764, several commodes described as being 'à la grecque' (see Note to Plate 94). Moreover, in Drouais' portrait of her, painted in 1763–64, a small work-table is depicted which might well have been described in the same way (Plate 372). See also pages 69 and 116–17.

Plates 310 to 318

NINE ORNAMENTAL VASES. Details from architectural compositions designed by J.-F. de Neufforge and published in the first two volumes of the *Recueil Elémentaire d'Architecture* (1757–58).

The drawings for these plates may well have been in existence already in 1755–56 or even earlier (see Note to Plate 37). See also page 33.

Plates 319 and 320

TWO VIGNETTES. Designed by Jean-Baptiste-Marie Pierre and engraved by Claude-Henri Watelet for the latter's *L'Art de peindre, poëme* which appeared in 1760.

Pierre drew the frontispiece and all the vignettes used in this work. Watelet was an *amateur* who had long been a friend of Pierre's. He had engraved Pierre's designs for *Sei Vazes* already in 1749.

Diderot did not admire Watelet's text, but greatly praised Pierre's vignettes. 'Si le poëme m'appartenait', he wrote 'je couperais toutes les vignettes, je les mettrais sous des glaces, et je jetterais le reste au feu' ('If this poem had belonged to me, I would have cut out all the vignettes and put them behind glass—and I would have thrown the rest in the fire!'; see Maurice Henriet 'L'Académicien Watelet', *Gaz. d. B.-A.*, 1922, II, page 179).

Plates 321 *and* 322

TABLE AND CHAIR, designed by L.-J. Le Lorrain about 1756 and executed for Ange-Laurent de Lalive de Jully. Details from the portrait of Lalive de Jully painted by Jean-Baptiste Greuze in 1759. *National Gallery of Art, Washington, D.C.* (*Kress Collection*).

The late Fiske Kimball was the first to recognise that the furniture depicted in this portrait was no new expression of Greuze's imagination but must be part of the set Lalive had caused to be made about 1756–57 for his *Cabinet Flamand* and which were already noted at the time as being the earliest essays in the style which came to be termed 'à la grecque' (see 'The Beginnings of the Style Pompadour 1751–59', *Gaz.d.B.-A.*, 6th series, XLIV, 1954, pages 57–64). The table and its *cartonnier* (Plates 85 and 87 to 89) have since been located in the Musée Condé at Chantilly which recently acquired a vase-shaped clock (Plate 187) that presumably belongs to the same set of furniture. The chair has so far not been recognised; it was separated from the rest already after the sale of Lalive's belongings in 1770. It was in fact of a quality somewhat inferior to that of the other items; the wood was imitation ebony and not the real thing, while the ornaments were not of bronze but of carved and gilt wood (see the present author's 'Lalive de Jully's Furniture "à la grecque" ', *Burlington Magazine*, August 1961, pages 340–7).

Apart from the rectilinear form of this curious chair, and its Classical ornaments, it has highly unusual arms or side-pieces. One can just see (in the complete painting, which is illustrated in the articles already mentioned) that the forward ends are decorated with a sunken quarter circle—a motif to be seen on certain ancient Roman thrones including one now in the Louvre (see Gisela M. A. Richter, *Ancient Furniture* etc., 1926, fig. 275). See also pages 46, 68 and 85.

Plate 323

TITLE-PAGE, to the *Suite de Vases composée dans le goût de l'Antique* designed by Joseph-Marie Vien and engraved by his wife in 1760.

The set comprises twelve engravings, each with a vase or urn in the same style as those shown here. The series was advertised in *L'Avantcoureur* on 2nd June 1760. See also page 33.

Plates 324 to 330

DRAWINGS OF VASES AND TABLES. Designed and engraved by Charles De Wailly, published in 1760. *Bibliothèque des Arts Décoratifs, Paris.*

One can date this series of etchings because it was advertised in *L'Avantcoureur* on 30th June 1760. The set from which the present illustrations are taken may be the only one to survive; that which was once in the Berlin Print Room was destroyed during the last war.

This set is of especial importance because we know that a table and a vase designed by De Wailly were shown at the *Salon* of 1761 (see page 70). Nothing is known about these objects except that they were very different from anything anyone had seen before and must have been ultra-modern. It is not unreasonable to suppose they were in the same style as those shown here.

De Wailly had been a pupil of Le Geay's and certain details—notably a predilection for grotesque beasts of a rather spooky kind—recall the debt to his master. The shapes of the two vases shown in Plates 325 and 326, with their chunky geometrical shapes, are clearly inspired by the work of Sir William Chambers who was a close friend of De Wailly's. Compare, for instance, these two vases with the objects illustrated on Plates IV, IX and XII of Chambers' *Designs of Chinese Buildings, Furniture, Dresses, Machines and Utensils* (1757).

The table was presumably intended to be executed in some kind of boulle-work. De Wailly's conception of the legs on the second table shows an astonishing originality and suggests he was thinking in terms of a metalwork structure. See also pages 33, 71 and 128.

Plate 331

TRADE-CARD OF DANGIS DE BELLEGARDE, engineer. Designed and engraved by B.-L. Prevost in 1760. *Waddesdon Manor Library, Buckinghamshire.*

Plate 332

TRADE-CARD OF L. G. TARAVAL, architect, designed and engraved by Taraval himself in 1760. *Waddesdon Manor Library, Buckinghamshire.*

Plates 333 to 338

DESIGNS FOR TABLES, CHAIRS, AND VASES. Designed by Louis-Félix de la Rue, about 1760–64; engraved and published some time after 1771 by Ph.-L. Parizeau.

As explained in the Note to Plate 54, De la Rue died in 1764 and, since Parizeau published at least eleven series of etchings after De la Rue's drawings, many of these must have been executed some while before his death. The various series comprised several hundred motifs and included ornamental vases, urns, ewers, tripods, tables, chairs, chimney-pieces, candelabra, etc., most of the series being 'dans le goût antique', as their titles state. One set was discussed in the *Mercure de France* in June 1775 (page 186) and the writer indicated that 'Cette suite de gravures ne peut donc manquer d'intéresser, par la variété des objets qu'elle présente, les Amateurs & les Artistes, & tous ceux qui dirigent les Manufactures de porcelaines, ou qui sont dans le cas de commander des ouvrages aux Sculpteurs, Orfèvres, Ciseleurs, &c.' ('This set of engravings cannot but be of interest, on account of the variety of objects that are depicted, to *amateurs* and artists, to all those who are in control of porcelain factories or those who are in a position to place orders for carving, goldsmith's work, or bronzes etc.'). See also page 86.

Plates 339 to 341

THREE VASES. Designed and engraved by Jacques Beauvais in 1760.

Beauvais issued three series of designs for vases or urns in the same highly geometrical style as those reproduced here.

Plate 342

CANDELABRUM. Part of the decorations designed by Michel-Ange Slodtz and erected in connection with the memorial service for the King and Queen of Spain, held at Notre-Dame in Paris on 1st January 1760. Engraving by A. Martinet. (See Note to Plates 42 and 43.) See also page 98.

Plate 343

DOORS OF THE CHANCEL-RAIL, SAINT-ROCH. Executed in wrought-iron in 1760 by Germain Doré. Engraving by N.-B. Richard after a drawing by J.-F. Blondel and published in the latter's *Cours d'Architecture* (1777, vol. V, Plate XXXIV).

The date of this very early Neo-Classical artefact, which no longer exists, can be established from contemporary references (see page 53). One such statement (*Affiches, Annonces, Avis Divers*, 4th February 1761, page 19) carries the implication that Doré had designed the railing himself but one cannot exclude the possibility that one of the other Neo-Classical artists working at Saint-Roch at the same time might have supplied the design. Falconet was among them and his early essays in this style have already been discussed (see pages 53 and 112).

Plate 344

DOORS OF THE CHANCEL-RAIL IN THE CHURCH OF SAINT-GERMAIN L'AUXERROIS, in wrought iron executed by Pierre Deumier between 1763 and 1767. Engraving by Ransonnette published in Blondel's *Cours d'Architecture*, 1777, vol. V.

These doors survive. They must have been the first Neo-Classical feature to be introduced into this fine Gothic building and must surely have been somewhat startling in those surroundings when new and gleaming—the iron polished and partly gilded.

It has been said that these doors were designed by J.-F. Forty but one may wonder who first thought of putting up such a modern structure in the old church. It may well have been the Comte de Caylus who was not only a man of great influence who enjoyed throwing his weight about, but was also a resident in this very parish and incidentally hoped to have his memorial set up in this church—a monument which was to be surmounted by an urn of porphyry (see page 163). On the other hand the no less influential Marquis de Marigny may also have been responsible. He lived in the same parish and it is recorded that Deumier invited him to call and inspect the railing when it was ready (see page 172).

Plates 345 to 348

FIVE PICTURE-FRAMES. Designed and carved in 1760 and 1761. Sketches by Gabriel de Saint-Aubin in this artist's copy of the Catalogue to the Exhibition at the *Salon* of 1761. *Bibliothèque Nationale, Paris.*

345. Frame round L.-M. Van Loo's portrait of Louis XV. The frame was designed and carved by Honoré Guibert; it was about 15 ft. 9 ins. high and carved with exceedingly rich ornament. It cost 2,098 livres before gilding.
346. Frame round Alexander Roslin's portrait of the Marquis de Marigny, designed and carved by

Honoré Guibert. This frame was only 6 ft. 6 ins. high and was far less elaborate than that furnished for the King's portrait (Plate 345) but was ordered from Guibert at the same time. It cost 368 livres. A detail of the actual painting is reproduced as Plate 353 showing the armchair which was in an almost equally advanced style. This portrait was to hang at the Académie d'Architecture and must have attracted much attention.

347. Frame of Greuze's portrait of the Dauphin, designed and carved by Honoré Guibert. This frame was 3 ft. 10 ins. high and cost 136 livres.

348. Two oval frames round Roslin's twin portraits of François Boucher and his wife. It is not known who carved this pair of frames but it may well have been Guibert.

The date of these frames and their authorship is discussed in the present writer's article 'Marigny and "le goût grec"' (*Burlington Magazine*, March 1962, pages 96–101). Guibert's frames are mentioned in *L'Avantcoureur* for 7th September 1761 (pages 570–1) after a report on a carved shop-front made for a silk-mercer's premises in the Rue Saint-Denis which must have been an object of no less a Neo-Classical aspect than the frames. The report states that 'On a moins remarqué au sallon du Louvre les autres productions de cet artiste, parce que le tableau s'attirant d'abord les regards, ne permet guère à l'oeil de s'arrêter sur le cadre; cependant il en est qui méritent d'être considérés, & ceux de M. Guibert sont de ce nombre. Celui qui entoure le portrait du roi de M. Michel Vanloo, est un chef-d'oeuvre en ce genre; les trophées de guerre, les palmes, les lauriers dont il est enrichi, distribués sagement & sans confusion, font l'honneur au goût de l'artiste. Les cadres des portraits de M. le dauphin, de M. le marquis de Marigny, & plusieurs autres bordures ornées de fleurs d'un bon choix, se font également distinguer' ('One has paid less attention to the other works by this artist in the *Salon* at the Louvre, for the simple reason that one tends to look principally at a picture and not at the frame. However, there are [frames] which deserve attention, especially those of M. Guibert. That which surrounds the portrait of His Majesty by M. Michel Vanloo is a masterpiece of its kind. The trophies of arms, the palm- and bay-leaves with which it is decorated are disposed in an orderly fashion and are a great credit to this artist. The frames [he has made] for the portraits of the Dauphin, the Marquis de Marigny, and several others, decorated with flowers of various kinds selected with discrimination, also stand out'). It is not improbable that Guibert himself composed this passage which may well be a disguised advertisement for his establishment. Similar reports on his work appeared in the same journal on 16th April 1764 and on 4th March 1765. Saint-Aubin did not sketch a single Rococo frame in his catalogue. He drew most of the paintings without bothering to illustrate their frames. The conclusion would therefore seem warranted that Saint-Aubin drew the Neo-Classical frames because they struck him as something entirely new and strange. See also page 126.

Plate 349

WRITING-DESK. Detail of a portrait of Ange-Laurent de Lalive de Jully, drawn by Louis Carrogis, called Carmontelle in 1760 (?). *The Charles B. Wrightsman Collection, New York.*

An identical drawing in the Musée Condé at Chantilly bears the date 1760. While this date is not in Carmontelle's hand-writing, it would seem to be correct. We know that Lalive became mentally deranged towards the end of the 1760s when he cannot have been in a fit state to pay calls at the Château de Saint-Cloud (where this drawing was made), the residence of the Duc d'Orléans. Lalive was born in 1725 so he would have been about thirty-five in 1760 but Carmontelle makes him look rather younger.

This or similar desks (e.g. that shown in Plate 350 which dates from 1761) are often illustrated in drawings by Carmontelle made at Saint-Cloud. There may well have been several tables of this sort in the Duc d'Orléans' collection. They have much in common with a number of tables which bear the *ébéniste* Pierre Garnier's mark (see Plate 99). What is more we know that Garnier produced a table of advanced form which was exhibited at the *Salon* of 1761 (see page 69).

Plate 350

WRITING-DESK. Detail of a portrait of Daniel Charles Trudaine drawn in 1761 (?) by Louis Carrogis, called Carmontelle, and etched by an unknown artist, possibly Jean Baptiste Delafosse.

One cannot say whether the date repoduces one inscribed on the original drawing by Carmontelle himself. Trudaine was born in 1703 and should then have been fifty-eight when this drawing was made—which seems quite reasonable. Like the portrait of Lalive de Jully (Plate 349), this was also executed at Saint-Cloud, the Duc d'Orléans' house. See also page 71.

Plate 351

TABLE-LEGS. Detail of a painting entitled *Une jeune Grecque, qui orne un vase de bronze, avec une guirlande de fleurs* executed in 1761 by Joseph Marie Vien. Engraved by J. J. Flipart and published in 1765 by J.-H. Eberts under the title of *La jeune Corinthienne.*

Also depicted in this painting is the chair shown in Plate 354. The painting was shown at the 1761 *Salon* and was discussed by the Abbé de la Porte in the *Observateur littéraire*. His observations were repeated in the *Mercure de France* (October 1761, pages 151–2). He says that 'Le caractère gracieux, mais noble & simple de la tête, le goût sage des draperies, la forme du vase, tout dans ce tableau est tellement dans la manière grecque, que sans la fraîcheur du coloris, il pourroit paroître un monument précieux, conservé à Athènes par une sorte de miracle . . .' ('The noble, straight-forward character of this graceful head, the sober good taste with which the drapery is depicted, the shape of the vase, everything in this painting is so imbued with the spirit of Ancient Greece that, were it not for the freshness of its colours, one might think it a precious monument preserved in Athens by some miracle . . .'). The above-mentioned Eberts bought the original; he was the creator of the *Athénienne*—that fashionable piece of furniture based on the Classical tripod (see Notes to Plates 186 and 484).

A *Louis Seize* console-table in the Musée du Cinquantenaire in Brussels, which does not appear to be French, seems to have been inspired by the table in Vien's picture.

Plate 352

WRITING-DESK. Detail of a portrait of Prince Dmitri Galitzin painted in 1762 by F.-H. Drouais. Engraved by J. Tardieu in 1769.

The original is in the Pushkin Museum, Moscow. It is dated 1762 and this date also appears on Tardieu's engraving which was shown at the *Salon* of 1769. This table of course resembles that made for Lalive de Jully a few years earlier (see Plate 85). One cannot say whether the table belonged to the Prince or to Drouais, or whether it was a figment of the latter's imagination but based on a knowledge of Lalive's desk. See also page 68.

Plate 353

ARMCHAIR. Detail of the portrait of Marquis de Marigny painted in 1761 by Alexander Roslin. *Château de Versailles.*

The chair is in the transitional style and must have belonged to Roslin as it appears in other paintings of his from 1761 (see G. W. Lundberg, *Roslin*, Plates 41 and 42). Moreover, we happen to know that this portrait was painted in Roslin's atelier and not at Marigny's house. The artist later acquired a new and much more modern sitter's chair (see Plate 447).

The table at which Marigny is seated, as well as a pedestal supporting the porphyry urn and the picture-frame on the wall, are all in the Neo-Classical taste. The same applies to the carved frame into which the portrait was finally put: this was carved by Honoré Guibert. Gabriel de Saint-Aubin sketched the picture and its frame in his copy of the catalogue of the 1761 *Salon* (see Plate 346) where the portrait was first shown. It was intended finally to hang at the *Académie d'Architecture*.

While the furniture shown in this portrait may not have belonged to Marigny, we cannot doubt that he approved of it and that it therefore to some extent reflects his own tastes. However, not until 3rd July 1763 have we documentary proof that Marigny acquired furniture for his own use that must have been appreciably different from ordinary Rococo furniture. For on that day he bought a complete set of seat-furniture described as having legs 'à gaines avec des plintes caré' (i.e. straight and tapering) (see page 86 and the present writer's article 'Marigny and "le goût grec"', *Burlington Magazine*, March 1962, pages 96–101). See also page 84.

Plate 354

CHAIR. Detail of J.-M. Vien's painting of 1761 discussed in the Note to Plate 351.

Plate 355

CORNER OF A CHAIR. Detail of a portrait of Count Peter Gregorievitz Czernichew, painted in 1762 by Alexander Roslin and engraved in 1765 by N. Dupuis.

This picture was shown at the *Salon* in 1762; it is illustrated in its entirety by G. W. Lundberg (*Roslin*, Plate 48). This shows that this is not the same chair as Roslin was using in his atelier for his sitters when he painted the portrait of Marigny in 1761 (Plate 353). Note how the seat-rail is bowed but is decorated with channelling. The table at which the Count sits is shown in Plate 356.

Plate 356

WRITING-TABLE. Detail of a portrait of Count Peter Gregorievitz Czernichew by Alexander Roslin, painted in 1762 and engraved by N. Dupuis in 1765.

Part of a chair shown in this painting is reproduced in Plate 355. The table is presumably imaginary; Roslin depicted it with numerous small variations in various other paintings (see G. W. Lundberg, *Roslin*, Plates 38, 96, 100 and 117).

Plates 357 to 364

EIGHT DESIGNS FOR CARNIVAL COSTUME 'à la grecque'. Anonymous artist, about 1763. *The Museum of Decorative Art, Copenhagen.*

On 1st May 1763, Baron Grimm wrote in his *Correspondance littéraire* that the artist Carmontelle had as a joke composed two small illustrations of a man and a woman wearing fancy dress consisting of ornaments taken from Classical architecture. Grimm says that Carmontelle was poking fun at the current 'fureur du goût grec' ('rage for the Greek taste'). Grimm adds that this absurdity was quickly imitated and a 'suite d'habillement à la grecque' ('set of dresses in the Greek manner'), was soon published which, according to Grimm, was 'sans esprit et d'un goût détestable' ('without wit and in a detestable taste'; see page 264 for the full text).

It has not so far been possible to locate copies of Carmontelle's drawings, which were engraved, but the compositions shown here may well be the plagiarisms to which Grimm referred. At least, the latter must have been very like them. As is well known, Petitot issued a similar series in 1771. See also page 51.

Plate 365

SURROUND OF AN ENGRAVING. Portrait of the poet Jean-Baptiste Rousseau, father of the more famous Jean-Jacques Rousseau, painted by Jacques-André-Joseph Aved in 1736. Engraved by Etienne Ficquet in 1763.

It is not known who designed the frames for this and the next item. The respective engravers may have been responsible but they were both specialists in portrait-engravings and it is possible that they turned to other artists for ideas when they needed a truly modern framing like those depicted here. Whatever the case, these two surrounds, with their monumental character and motifs culled from the Antique, must have struck contemporary observers as ultra-modern in 1763.

Plate 366

SURROUND OF AN ENGRAVING. Portrait of J.-J. Rousseau by Maurice-Quentin De La Tour. Engraved by C. A. Littret de Montigny in 1763.

See the previous entry.

Plate 367

WRITING-DESK AND INKSTAND. Detail of a portrait of the Duc de Choiseul painted in 1763 by L.-M. Van Loo and engraved in 1769–70 by Etienne Fessard.

The original painting seems to have disappeared but various copies exist (e.g. one at the Château de Versailles). The whole engraving is shown here as Plate 462.

It is not certain whether this table ever existed, either in Choiseul's or the painter's possession. However, we know that Choiseul came to favour the Neo-Classical taste at quite an early date (see page 118 and Plates 462 to 464). The table is of course a variant of Lalive's famous piece (Plate 85). See also page 68.

Plates 368 and 369

DESIGNS FOR A TABLE AND A MIRROR. Designed by J.-F. de Neufforge and published in 1763 in the fifth volume of his *Recueil Elémentaire d'Architecture*, Plates 310 and 348.

In style, these two objects differ in no way from those illustrated in earlier volumes of Neufforge's *Recueil* and it is quite probable that they were designed some time before 1763 when they were published (see the Note to Plate 37 and Neufforge's biography, page 207). See also page 47.

Plate 370

TRIPOD. Detail of an engraving by J. J. Flipart, published in 1765 under the title of *La Vertueuse Athénienne* which was taken from a painting executed in 1763 by Joseph-Marie Vien originally entitled *Une Prêtresse qui brûle de l'encens sur un trépied.*

The painting was shown at the *Salon* of 1763 and was executed as a pendant to the picture entitled *Une Jeune Grecque, qui orne un vase de bronze, avec une guirlande de fleurs* which is here reproduced as Plate 351. Diderot praised Vien's two pictures in his review of the exhibition and commented that 'Comme tout cela sent la manière antique' ('They are the absolute embodiment of the Antique taste'; see Seznec and Adhemar, *Diderot Salons*, vol. 1, page 209).

Both Madame Geoffrin and J.-H. Eberts (who published the engraving) owned versions of the painting (see also Note to Plate 351). A decade later Eberts produced the small tripod table on stand which he named the *Athénienne* after the tripod shown here (see Plate 484).

Plate 371

BACK OF AN ARMCHAIR. Detail of a portrait of Comtesse d'Egmont Pignatelli painted by Alexander Roslin in 1763. *Château de Dampierre.*

Although the chair has serpentine contours in the Rococo taste, the carved ornament is Classical in style (here, one can see a garland of bay-leaves and pearl-chain ornament; on the arms there is money-moulding, then known as *piastres*). The model rests her arm on a table like that shown in Plate 356 which is probably imaginary although based on current forms of an advanced nature. The chair is not apparently one of Roslin's sitter's chairs (see Plates 353 and 447) so it presumably belonged to the Comtesse. The painting is illustrated by G. W. Lundberg (*Roslin*, No. 171). See also page 84.

Plate 372

WORK-TABLE. Detail of the famous portrait of Madame de Pompadour by François-Hubert Drouais, 1763–64. *The Earl of Rosebery's Collection, Mentmore, Buckinghamshire.*

Madame de Pompadour is shown seated with her embroidery. The complicated little work-table standing by her appears to have a swivelling turret fitted with drawers labelled with the names of various colours—presumably those of the spools of silk thread kept in the little drawers. The gilt bronze loop-handles above must be for turning the turret to present the desired drawer. The table is veneered with woods of various kinds and set with elaborate ormolu mounts. This piece of furniture must have seemed very advanced in style when the portrait was painted in 1763–64 on account of its ornaments, which are all of Classical derivation, and of its tripod-like form which would certainly have conjured up images of Antiquity in the mind of any educated beholder at the time.

The small panels of marquetry are bordered by stringing composed of a dark and a light fillet, running parallel. J.-F. Oeben was one of the few *ébénistes* who took the trouble to provide his furniture with the extra refinement of a double fillet like this. Oeben was a specialist in mechanical fittings and the turret surmounting this table is quite likely to have been his invention. The presence of this feature and the double fillet, coupled with the fact that he was Madame de Pompadour's favourite cabinet-maker allows one to attribute this little table to him with a fair degree of certainty. The unusual appearance of the table as a whole precludes it having been a figment of the painter's imagination.

The table does not seem to be listed in the inventory of Madame de Pompadour's possessions, drawn up after her death in 1764; nor has any mention of it been traced in the records of the *Garde-meuble de la Couronne*. See also pages 74 and 117.

Plate 373

CHAIR. Detail of a painted altar-piece with a scene from the life of St. Ambrose. Painted in 1764 by Louis-Jean-François Lagrenée. *Église de Sainte-Marie, Paris.*

The artist's signature and the date are painted on the chair. The picture was shown at the *Salon* the following year. Since it represents an imaginary scene, there is no reason to suppose that a real chair like this existed in Lagrenée's atelier in 1764. It is a piece of artistic licence very typical of its time, embodying a conscious attempt to reproduce an Antique chair. The decorative motifs, while certainly borrowed from Classical Antiquity, are those so beloved by the early Neo-Classical designers in Paris during what may be called the Archaic phase of the new style. However, in the autumn of 1762, Corneille's *Cinna* was put on in the theatre at Versailles. Papillon de la Ferté, who was responsible for the costumes and properties, wrote in his diary that 'J'ai fait faire, pour la pièce de Cinna, des sièges à l'antique, et pour Auguste, Cinna et Maxime, des toges de satin blanc . . .' ('For this production of *Cinna*, I have had some chairs in the Antique taste made, along with togas of white satin for Augustus, Cinna and Maximus . . .'; *Journal de Papillon de la Ferté*, 4th November 1762, ed. 1887, pages 90–1). So it is possible that reconstructions of Antique furniture were to be seen on the stage and some of it may have been in the same 'style' as the chair shown here.

The chair is, incidentally, painted in such a way as to cause one to envisage it as made of marble or porphyry. The complete painting is reproduced by Seznec and Adhémar in their *Diderot Salons*, vol. II, 1765, Plate 23. See also page 87.

Plate 374

DETAIL OF 'LA MARCHANDE À LA TOILETTE'. Painted in 1763 by Joseph Vien. *Palais de Fontainebleau.*

This well-known painting was inspired by a Classical painting discovered in 1759 at Gragnano and reproduced in the third volume of *Antichità di Ercolano*. The furnishings, however, are entirely Vien's own invention. They are in a ponderous Neo-Classical style reminiscent of that of Neufforge. See also page 87.

Plate 375

TITLE-PAGE OF THIBAUD'S 'BALLADE'. Drawn by H. Gravelot; engraved in 1764 by N. Le Mire.

As has been explained on page 87, the table and chairs illustrated here were presumably meant to be reconstructions of seventeenth-century furniture consonant with the style of the costume. However, the forms and slender proportions seem to point the way to the coming *Louis Seize* style. Gravelot had enjoyed great success both in London and Paris as an illustrator in the Rococo style and had shown an interest in furniture-design already in the 1730s (see page 88). In London, he was associated with Hogarth who illustrated several scenes from the life of Henry VIII in which furniture vaguely of the period made its appearance. While in England, he had also become conversant with the Neo-Palladian version of Classicism as expressed in the work of William Kent and his multifarious followers. So he must have been well equipped to flirt with old styles in the field of furniture *and* to handle fresh combinations of Classical motifs with understanding.

Already in 1764, the same year that this title-page was engraved, Gravelot had published an *Almanach Iconologique* in which the illustrations were in a pure Neo-Classical style: as one might almost have guessed, it was dedicated to the Marquis de Marigny. In a notice in the *Mercure de France* of December 1763, probably inserted by Gravelot himself, we are told most emphatically and with great modesty that any new ideas which may be found in these compositions can in no way detract from 'la noble simplicité, dont l'antiquité nous donne l'éxemple' ('that noble simplicity, for which Classical Antiquity set the example . . .'). See the Note to Plate 373.

Plate 376

INTERIOR WITH TABLE AND CHAIR. Detail of a painting entitled *L'Education des riches* by Noël Hallé, dated 1764. *Private Collection, Paris.*

This detail shows the left-hand section of a painting exhibited at the *Salon* of 1765. The date 1764 may be seen on the plan of some fortification that leans against the table-leg. The whole picture is reproduced by Seznec and Adhémar in their *Diderot Salons*, vol. II, Plate 21.

If one bears in mind the determinedly Neo-Classical aspect of the rooms at the Hôtel de Varey, in Lyons, of about 1760 (Plate 34) and some of Neufforge's and Barreau de Chefdeville's projects of the time (e.g. Plates 28, 29, 56 to 58), one must face the possibility that this view shows an actual room that existed in Paris in 1764. One finds it difficult, however, to believe that furniture quite like this really existed even if some of Neufforge's projects come perilously close to being as awkwardly and clumsily designed. See also page 86.

Plate 377

A KEY-FRET BORDER. Drawn in 1764 by a member of the Saint-Aubin family. *Waddesdon Manor Library, Buckinghamshire.*

This Grecian border enframes a cryptogram which has nothing whatever to do with Neo-Classicism! Under the title of *Avanture à la Grecque*, and with the telling postscript 'mode de 1764', there is a little anecdote which Sir Anthony Blunt has kindly interpreted for me as follows:

J'ai hérité mille écus. J'ai été
au pays. J'ai eu une abbaye. J'ai
aimé Hébé. Elle a chassé deux
héros et deux abbés. Elle a été
émue, agitée. Elle a aimé.
Elle a cédé, et j'ai vaincu. Hier
Elle a cassé une écuelle à chat.

(I inherited a thousand écus.
I went to the country.
I obtained an abbey.
I fell in love with Hebe.
She dismissed two heroes [military men] and two abbés.
She was stirred, agitated.
She was moved to love.
She yielded, and I conquered.
Yesterday, she broke the cat's bowl!)

Plate 378

BORDER OF AN ENGRAVED ILLUSTRATION in the first volume of Le Président Hénault's *Nouvel Abrégé chronologique de l'Histoire de France* of 1768. Drawn by Charles-Nicolas Cochin *le jeune* in 1765 and engraved by Jacques Aliamet.

Plates 379 to 387

DESIGNS FOR SNUFF-BOXES, JEWELLERY, CANE-HEADS, FOBS AND SIGNETS. Drawn by Nicolas-Joseph Maria, engraved by Pierre-Edme Babel. Published in 1765.

These are among the illustrations in Maria's *Premier Livre de desseins de jouaillerie et bijouterie* of 1765. This work comprises 34 Plates with 254 drawings of jewellery etc., all in the Neo-Classical style.

Plate 388

A BED AND A POT-POURRI JAR. Detail of an engraving by N. Delaunay after a gouache by P.-A. Baudouin painted in 1765.

The original was shown at the *Salon* of 1765 under the title of *La fille éconduite* but Delaunay's engraving bears the title of *Le carquois épuisé.*

The furnishings are entirely Neo-Classical in taste. This not only applies to the bed and the jar shown in this detail, but to the chimney-piece, a cartel clock in the form of a sun-burst, and a chair. Baudouin was one of the first artists to introduce furniture in the new taste into his illustrations. Why he should have been prompted to do so is unknown to us but it could well be that he was influenced by his brother-in-law, the son of François Boucher, who was to become well known as a designer of furniture. See also page 153.

Plate 389

ARMCHAIR. Detail of an engraving by Jean Massard after a gouache by P.-A. Baudouin executed in 1765.

The gouache was exhibited at the 1765 *Salon* and was entitled *Une jeune femme à qui on passe sa chemise, ou Le lever* (see the previous entry). This is the earliest illustration of a chair with an oval back known to this author. Note the rather massive proportions and the sturdy members. See also page 86.

Plate 390

DESIGN FOR A FALL-FRONT SECRETAIRE. Drawn by J.-R. Lucotte and published in 1765 in the volume of Plates accompanying Diderot and Alembert's *Encyclopédie.*

See also pages 76 and 82.

Plate 391

TITLE-PAGE. Drawn by Maurice Jacques about 1765.

For a book of designs for vases or urns (see Plates 392 to 395). A *terminus ante quem* for this series of engravings is provided by two dated gold snuff-boxes decorated with vases taken from this source. One is by J. M. Tiron and bears the Paris date-letter for 1765/66 (sold at Sotheby's, 3rd December 1962, lot 157), and one with Jacques Roëttiers' mark and his date-letter for 1766/67 (National Museum, Stockholm).

Plates 392 to 395

FOUR VASES. Drawn by Maurice Jacques about 1765.

See the previous entry for a note concerning the date of these compositions. Jacques' vases were a source of inspiration to many designers, not only in France. These compositions were copied in media of all kinds, not least as marquetry-decoration on furniture.

The vase reproduced in Plate 393 is the one copied on the Roëttiers snuff-box while that shown in Plate 395 appears in miniature on the Tiron box (see the previous entry). See also page 78.

Plate 396

DESIGN FOR A CONSOLE-TABLE. Probably designed by Pierre-Noël Rousset in 1765 as a proposal for the furnishings of the Hôtel d'Uzès. Enlarged detail of a drawing associated with the design reproduced as Plate 64 (see the relevant Note, above).

Note the plinth connecting the legs. See also pages 63 and 128.

Plate 397

DESIGN FOR A CONSOLE-TABLE. Enlarged detail of a proposal for the Hôtel d'Uzès presumably designed in 1765 by Mathurin Cherpitel. This drawing accompanied the drawing shown in Plate 65; see the Note concerned. See also pages 63 and 128.

Plate 398

DESIGN FOR A SOFA. Probably drawn by Pierre-Noël Rousset in 1765 as part of the proposals for the Hôtel d'Uzès. Enlarged detail of the drawing shown in Plate 63; see the relevant entry. See also page 88.

Plates 399 and 400

DESIGN FOR A SOFA AND A CONSOLE-TABLE. Designed by Henri Piètre in 1766 for the Hôtel Mélusine. Enlarged details of the drawing shown in Plate 68; see the Note concerned.

Plate 401

FIRE-DOG. Enlarged detail of a trade-card engraved by Gabriel de Saint-Aubin, dated 1767.

This etching shows the interior of an ironmonger's shop, in which one sees this Neo-Classical fire-dog and an old-fashioned balustrade for a balcony. The card bears the address 'A LA TESTE NOIRE PERIER M[D] QUAY DE LA MEGISSERIE'. See also page 99.

Plate 402

FIRE-DOG FOR THE ROYAL PALACE, WARSAW. Drawing presumably executed in Paris by Jean-Louis Prieur in 1766. *The University Library, Warsaw.*

Inscribed 'Grande Salle' and 'feux de Cheminé éxécutés à Paris' ('fire-dog, executed in Paris'). No fire-dogs are mentioned in the list of bronzes being furnished by Philippe Caffieri for Warsaw; they were therefore presumably produced by Prieur (see page 100). They do not seem to have survived.

Plate 403

CANDLE-STAND. Presumably to be made of gilt bronze. Produced in Paris in 1766 for the Royal Palace in Warsaw. Drawing probably by Jean-Louis Prieur. *The University Library, Warsaw.*

The drawing is inscribed 'Dessein d'un gueridon pour la chambre du Dais' and 'env de Paris en 1766' ('Design for a candle-stand for the Daïs [Alcove] Bed-chamber . . . despatched from Paris in 1766'). The gueridon, which has long since disappeared, is not listed among the goods executed by Philippe Caffieri for the Polish Court, so one may presume it was made by Prieur whose work was never listed in the same way (see page 100 and also the previous entry).

Plate 404

SCONCE, for the Royal Palace at Warsaw. Drawing by Jean-Louis Prieur, who probably also made the sconces. They must have been executed in Paris about 1766. *The University Library, Warsaw.*

The drawing is inscribed 'Grande Salle' and 'Dessein de Bras exécuté à Paris' ('Design for a sconce, made in Paris'). One of the sconces made to this design is illustrated in Plate 207. See also page 100.

Plate 405

CANDELABRUM, for the Royal Palace at Warsaw. Drawing by Jean-Louis Prieur in about 1766. *University Library, Warsaw.*

One of the six candelabra executed after this design, probably by Prieur himself, is illustrated in Plate 205. The drawing is inscribed '6 jirondols en Bronze prete a reçevoir la Dorur' ('Six bronze candelabra, ready to be gilded'). The drawing shown in Plate 408 shows two of them in place on a console-table in the King's Bed-chamber.

Like the items shown in Plates 402 and 403, these candelabra do not appear in the list of items made by Caffieri for this great enterprise and they must therefore presumably be the work of Prieur. See also page 100.

Plate 406

MANTEL CLOCK, for the Royal Palace at Warsaw. Drawing presumed to be by Jean-Louis Prieur, about 1766. The clock-case was of gilt bronze and was executed in Paris. *University Library, Warsaw.*

The drawing is inscribed 'Pendul pour metre sur la ditte Table, Table toute fondue et en Grande partie Sisélée et prete a finire' ('Clock to stand on the aforesaid table, cast and largely chased, ready for finishing'). The table with this clock was to stand in the King's Bed-Chamber. The ensemble is shown in Plate 408. The finished article, with its gilt-bronze case, is shown in Plate 190. It will be seen that the clocks shown in the two drawings differ from each other. Plate 408 must be an earlier proposal: the inscription proves that the present illustration was executed when the clock was almost finished—presumably to show His Majesty what he would one day receive! See also page 100.

Plate 407

CONSOLE-TABLE, for the Royal Palace at Warsaw. Dated 1766. Probably by Victor Louis. *University Library, Warsaw.*

Inscribed 'Dessein de la table de la Chambre Numero 13. Envoyé de Paris en 1766' ('Design for the table to go in Bed-chamber No. 13. Despatched from Paris in 1766'). Someone has added the words 'de Louis'. This attribution may have been based on accurate information and is quite probably justified.

The table is of polished steel and gilt bronze, and was made in Paris, perhaps by the locksmith Pierre Deumier who had made a table of this type already in 1763 (see page 171). Several similar tables like this and the one shown in Plate 409 are known; there is a pair in the Musée Nissim de Camondo in Paris (Cat. No. 190) and in various French and English private collections.

It is interesting to compare these accomplished designs with Robert Adam's early essay in the same vein—the table he designed in 1765 for Sir Laurance Dundas (see E. Harris, *The Furniture of Robert Adam*, London, 1963, fig. 8. The design for this is reproduced by Clifford Musgrave in his book in the present series, *Adam and Hepplewhite Furniture*, London, 1966, fig. 21). The largely parallel course taken by Neo-Classicism in England and France at this date suggest that there was a higher degree of cross-fertilisation in the field of design than is generally realised (see Chapter III, 4, page 139).

Plate 408

CONSOLE-TABLE, CLOCK AND CANDELABRA, for the Royal Palace at Warsaw. 1766. Drawing attributed to Jean-Louis Prieur or to Victor Louis. *University Library, Warsaw.*

This is probably a proposed design. It is inscribed 'Table de la chambre à coucher en face du lit avec l'Esquisse de la Pendule qu'elle doit porter. Paris 1766' ('Table for the bed-chamber, to go opposite the bed. With a sketch of the clock that it is to have standing on it. Paris 1766'). It is not known whether the table was ever made but one of the candelabra may be seen in Plate 205. The drawing shown in Plate 405 is probably a sketch executed when it and its five companion pieces were ready for dispatch just as the drawing of a clock shown in Plate 406 was clearly also executed shortly before it was completed. Although both that drawing (Plate 406) and the present design are concerned with objects for a 'chambre à coucher' (presumably the King's own Bed-chamber), there are notable differences between the two clock-cases. Possibly Prieur had more than one model of this type in stock or perhaps the design was altered after the present drawing was made. See also page 100.

Plate 409

CONSOLE-TABLE, for the Royal Palace at Warsaw, 1766. Probably designed by Victor Louis. *University Library, Warsaw.*

Executed in Paris; of polished steel and gilt bronze. The drawing is inscribed 'Dessein en grand de la table en fer poli N° C. Sur le petit plan' ('Design for the large table of polished steel, No. C. On the small plan'). It was to go 'Sous le trumeau entre les fenetres de la pièce N° 13. Envoyé de Paris en 1766' ('Under the pier-glass between the windows in room N°. 13. Despatched from Paris in 1766'). From these facts, it is apparent that this drawing is meant to show the same table as the drawing reproduced in Plate 407. The small variations could be due to the drawings having been executed by different hands or after the table had been dispatched.

Plate 410

FALL-FRONT SECRETAIRE, CLOCK AND CANDELABRA, for the Royal Palace at Warsaw. 1766. Attributed to Jean-Louis Prieur or Victor Louis. *University Library, Warsaw.*

Inscribed 'Secrétaire du Cabinet du Boudoir N° 15. Paris 1766' (this presumably implies that the desk was for serious use in Boudoir No. 15. It was no lady's desk for writing casual notes). This may only be a proposal since none of these items are recorded as having been made. See also page 88.

Plates 411 to 416

DESIGNS FOR FURNITURE, for the Royal Palace at Warsaw. Drawn in 1765–66 by Jean-Louis Prieur. *University Library, Warsaw.*

None of the pieces executed after these drawings seem to have survived but most of them were made by Louis Delanois, the joiner and chair-maker, and carved by Denis Coulonjon. The sofa and armchair shown in Plate 412 were to go in the boudoir, part of which is illustrated in Plate 407 (one can there see a corner of the sofa and two of the chairs).

It is interesting to note that the inscriptions on the drawings of the bed and two of the chairs (Plates 413 to 415) inform us that models of each of the items had been made. In the case of the bed, they actually took the trouble to gild the model ('le Model qui est fait et doré'). This suggests a complete, full-scale mock-up was made (see page 92). The model of the chair shown in Plate 414 was executed in wax ('le Model est tout fait en Sire') and perhaps a full-scale model was then made although the inscription says that the wax model, which would have been quite small, was 'pour executer d'apres' ('to be copied when executing the chair'). See also page 88.

Plates 417 to 421

DESIGNS FOR CANDLESTICKS, preparations for a series of engravings. About 1765–66. Drawn by Jean-Louis Prieur. *University Library, Warsaw.*

The series comprises eight such designs, gathered under the title 'Dessins de diferents flambeaux Composé et dessiné Par Jean Louis Prieur Scupteur' ('Designs for various candlesticks composed and drawn by J. L. Prieur, Sculptor'). See also page 217.

Plates 422 and 423

DESIGNS FOR CHANDELIERS, to hang in the Royal Palace at Warsaw. Drawn in 1765–66 by Jean-Louis Prieur. *University Library, Warsaw.*

One of the drawings is inscribed 'Lanterne du Boudoir N^{O} 15, Paris 1766' (lit: 'Lantern for Boudoir No. 15, Paris 1766'), the other 'Lustre de bronze pour la chambre des Seigneurs. Envoyé de Paris en 1766' ('Chandelier of bronze for the Chambre des Seigneurs. Despatched from Paris in 1766'). These items are not on the list of bronzes provided for the Polish Court by Philippe Caffieri, so one must presume they were executed by Prieur who made these drawings (see the Notes to Plates 402, 403 and 405). See also page 100.

Plates 424 and 425

DESIGNS FOR SCONCES OR GIRANDOLES, for Notre-Dame in Paris. About 1765–66. Drawn by Philippe Caffieri in about 1766–67. *Archives Nationales.*

The drawings were mentioned by Jules Guiffrey (*Les Caffieri*, 1877, pages 126–8; he gave the ref. L.511 in the Archives Nationales but this has now been changed to L.534). The drawings are undated but are accompanied by a bill, sanctioned for payment on 20th March 1767, for various projects and models that Caffieri had supplied since January 1766; they probably belong to the group concerned. These are the earliest known drawings by Caffieri but he had been producing candelabra etc. in much the same style since 1760 (e.g. Plates 203 and 204).

Plates 426 and 427

ARMCHAIR AND BED. Enlarged details of J.-M. Moreau *le jeune's* etching of the gouache by P.-A. Baudouin of 1767 entitled *Le couché de la mariée.*

This was exhibited at the *Salon* of 1767. The scene shows an interior decorated entirely in the Neo-Classical style, with the exception of the small night-table and the chair. The chair has a back in the Rococo taste but its legs are straight, tapering, and fluted while an Ionic capital may just be discerned at the top. The bed is couched in the same ponderous version of the new style as Lalive de Jully's furniture of a decade earlier. See also page 89.

Plate 428

SCARF WITH AN 'A LA GRECQUE' DESIGN. Detail of a portrait by Alexander Roslin of an unknown lady, dated 1766. *Private collection, Stockholm.*

The complete portrait is illustrated by G. W. Lundberg (*Roslin*, Plate 72). The scarf is almost certainly of silk gauze with a woven pattern. This material enjoyed great popularity during the middle decades of the century for collars, fichus, scarves, and *engageantes* (the frilly cuffs attached to the short sleeves of ladies' dresses at that time). The present example has a pattern that seems to be a reflection of the new craze for Classical ornaments. The pattern may be compared with that carved on the chair shown in Plate 389 which dates from 1765.

Plate 429

EMBROIDERED UNIFORM. Detail of an equestrian portrait of Louis XV drawn by Louis Durameau and engraved by A.-J. de Fehrt. Presumed to have been executed between 1764 and 1769.

Note the Vitruvian scroll and the *baton rompu* embroidered as borders on the coat; these are of course both ornaments of Classical derivation. This portrait must have been executed before 1769 when Fehrt went to Denmark. Durameau was in Italy between 1760 and 1764; he is unlikely to have drawn the portrait before his departure but probably did so soon after his return.

Plate 430

DESIGN FOR A CARRIAGE FOR THE MARQUIS DE MARIGNY. Anonymous drawing, attributed to J.-F. Chopard, dated 20th November 1767. *The Robert Dumas-Hermès Collection, Paris.*

Dr. Rudolf Wackernagel, who first published this drawing, has kindly provided the photograph for this illustration. He attributes the drawing to Chopard in his informative work *Der französische Krönungswagen von 1696–1825*, Berlin, 1966 (page 213). The drawing bears the Marquis de Marigny's signature as a sign of approbation. The simple lines of the carriage are scarcely relieved by ornament at all. There is a cresting in the form of a Vitruvian scroll and the painted ornament is reminiscent of compositions by Delafosse. Marigny seems not to have approved of the latter and directs that 'aulieu du cartel du millieu', he wanted his cipher. See also page 118.

Plates 431 to 433

DESIGNS FOR CANDLESTICKS. Drawn and engraved about 1765–68 by J.-F. Forty; published in the third volume of Forty's *Oeuvres d'orfèvrerie.*

On the title-page of each volume, which bears no date, Forty gives his address as 'Rue de Bourbon proche celle du Petit Carreau chez Mr delanois . . .'. Delanois must be the famous chair-maker who moved from that address in 1768 (see the present author's book *Louis Delanois, Menuisier en sièges*, 1968, page 34). Forty must therefore have produced these designs before that date. See also page 129.

Plates 434 to 436

SOFA AND TWO CHAIRS. Designed by J.-F. de Neufforge and published in Volume VIII of the *Recueil d'architecture*, 1768, as Plates 578 and 584.

See page 207 for a discussion of the dates of the illustrations in the various volumes of this extensive work. See also pages 47, 86, 89 and 128.

Plates 437 and 438

TWO PICTURE-FRAMES. Drawn by Jean-Charles Delafosse in 1767 or earlier, published in his *Nouvelle Iconologie Historique* of 1768 as Plates 75 and 76.

As is explained on page 170, Delafosse's *Iconologie* was ready for the press in July 1767 except for the notes to the Plates; much of the material had been ready for 'some years'. See also page 128.

Plates 439 and 440

TWO CONSOLE-TABLES. Drawn by Jean-Charles Delafosse in 1767 or earlier, and published in his *Nouvelle Iconologie Historique* as Plates 29 and 30.

See the previous entry.

Plate 441

WALL-SCONCE IN THE FORM OF A CADUCEUS. Sketch by Gabriel de Saint-Aubin, 1769. This sketch is to be seen in Saint-Aubin's copy of the catalogue to the Gaignat sale held in Paris in 1769.

Louis-Jean Gaignat, a former *secrétaire du Roi*, died on 11th April 1768 aged seventy-one. An auction-sale of his belongings was held in 1769 and Saint-Aubin sketched this sconce in his personal copy of the sale-catalogue. The sconce must at any rate have been in existence before Gaignat died in 1768. Such forms could well have been produced well before 1768; they are not so very dissimilar from the sconces Caffieri made for the Saint-Hubert hunting-lodge—with their candle-branches shaped like hunting-horns (Plate 203). The general format is the same; both are symmetrical compositions of naturalistic forms.

We do not know who made this pair. Gaignat patronised Poirier, the *marchand-mercier* and they may have been acquired through him (see page 215). See also page 100.

Plate 442

TWO-BRANCHED SCONCE. Detail of a portrait of the Marquis and Marquise de Marigny, painted in 1769 by L.-M. Van Loo. *Private Collection.*

This painting was exhibited at the *Salon* of 1769; it is reproduced by Seznec and Adhémar, *Diderot Salons*, vol. IV, Plate 3. Marigny stands beside his young wife who is sitting on a Louis XV chair alongside a flounced toilet-table on which stands a fine Louis XV silver toilet-set. The sconce is the only Neo-Classical feature in the whole scene. This intimate portrait was clearly made as a personal record; it was in no way an official commission like the portraits reproduced in Plates 346 and 353. See also page 100.

Plate 443

STOOL. Detail of a gouache by P.-A. Baudouin executed in 1769 or earlier, and engraved by N.-J. Voyez under the title *Le Chemin de la Fortune*.

The *terminus ante quem* for this picture is 1769 when Baudouin died. The scene is set in a Neo-Classical interior; only an armchair on the right is still in the Rococo taste.

Plate 444

LYRE-SHAPED CARTEL CLOCK. Detail of a gouache by P.-A. Baudouin executed in 1769 or earlier; engraved by N. Ponce in 1771 with the title *La Toilette*.

See the previous Note concerning date. The whole scene is reproduced by Pierre Verlet in *La Maison du XVIIIe siècle en France*, page 222. (See the Note to Plate 194 concerning the lyre as a fashionable instrument and as decorative motif.) See also page 100.

Plate 445

ARMCHAIR AND FIRE-SCREEN. Detail of a gouache by P.-A. Baudouin executed in 1769; engraved by J.-M. Moreau *le jeune* under the title *Le Modèle Honnête*.

The gouache was shown at the *Salon* of 1769; it is reproduced by Seznec and Adhémar, *Diderot Salons*, vol. IV, Plate 17. The scene is of an artist's studio: all the furniture except the artist's own chair is in the Neo-Classical taste.

Plate 446

TABLE. Detail of a painting by J.-E. Schenau, engraved in 1769 by J. Chevillet, entitled *La bonne amitié*.

Plate 447

ARMCHAIR. Detail of a portrait of the Minister of Finance, Henri Léonard Jean Baptiste Bertin, painted by Alexander Roslin in 1769 and engraved by René Gaillard.

The complete picture is reproduced by G. W. Lundberg in his *Roslin*, Plate 96. Next to the chair stands a table of a type seen in several other portraits by Roslin (e.g. Plate 356). It is possible that Roslin had such a chair in his studio even though it does not occur in other portraits by him. Certainly chairs like this existed; one bearing the mark of the chair-maker Carpentier is shown in Plate 171. See also page 90.

Plate 448

DESIGN FOR A JEWEL-CABINET. Drawn in 1769 by François-Joseph Belanger. *Bibliothèque Nationale, Cabinet des Estampes, Paris.*

The actual cabinet has disappeared but it was designed to hold Marie-Antoinette's wedding-present. The design received official approbation on 24th August 1769 or shortly before; it bears the inscription 'approuvé pour etre executé' ('design approved and ready to be carried out') and the signature of the Duc d'Aumont, one of the directors of the *Menus Plaisirs*, the organisation that supplied ceremonial properties of this kind and to which Belanger was attached as designer—as the inscription at the top proves.

The cabinet-making was executed by the *ébéniste* M.-B. Evald; the carved stand was the work of a certain sculptor named Augustin Bocciardi. The stand had subsequently to be gilded. Jacques-Philippe Houdon, brother of the famous sculptor, provided the model for the head of Apollo which Gouthière then executed in bronze. The interior fittings were lined with expensive silken materials—crimson velvet and blue satin. The cabinet was delivered on 4th May 1770, the day before Marie-Antoinette's wedding to the Dauphin (note, incidentally, the dolphin-symbolism in the decoration). It cost 22,786 livres—something over a third of the cost of the *Bureau du Roi* (Plates 90 to 93). See also pages 79 and 81.

Plates 449 to 452

FOUR DESIGNS FOR VASES. Drawn by Pierre-Elisabeth de Fontanieu and published in 1770 under the title *Collection de vases.*

Fontanieu was *contrôleur général des meubles de la Couronne.* He had various hobbies which he took up during his spare time. One of them was executing turnery-work on a lathe. All his designs for vases were intended for production in this technique, and each pattern is therefore represented by two drawings, one of the finished vase with all its ornaments, and one of the unadorned body shown as if taken straight from the lathe.

Several of his designs were soon reproduced at Sèvres in porcelain. At Wilhelmshöhe there is a Sèvres vase (Plate 288; *c.* 1772) which is taken from the design shown here in Plate 452; a vase of 1773 at Buckingham Palace (Laking, Plate 49) derives from the same source. See also page 129.

Plates 453 to 461

NINE DRAWINGS OF GILT BRONZES, executed by Philippe Caffieri between 1770 and 1772 for the Prince de Condé's Palais de Bourbon. Marginal drawings in Caffieri's account (*now in the Archives Condé, Château de Chantilly*, carton A.C. 7).

This is the first time these drawings have been published. They were first discovered by Pierre Verlet who has most generously waived his rights and given the author permission to introduce them here. The relevant red-ink drawings are executed in the margin of the account alongside the description of the item concerned. Unfortunately it has not yet been possible to locate any of these superb *bronzes d'ameublement.*

The bill is headed 'Mémoire des ouvrages que S.A.S. Monseigneur Le Prince de Condé a lui même ordonné Le 1er Mars 1770 pour Son palais Bourbon d'après les Modelles et esquisses composés allégoriquement aux différentes pièces sous La conduite de M[r] Le Carpentier architecte du roy et Sous Le controlle de Mr Bellisard architecte éxécuté par moy Philipe Caffieri L'ainé Sculpteur Cizeleur du Roy' ('List of items for which His Highness the Prince de Condé himself placed orders on 1st March 1770 for his Palais Bourbon after having had submitted to him models and sketches composed according to the allegorical scheme of the various rooms under the direction of M. Le Carpentier, Architect to His Majesty, and under the supervision of M. Bellisard, his architect, by me, Philippe Caffieri the Elder, Sculptor and Chaser of Bronzes to His Majesty'). See also pages 104 and 119.

*

Plate 453

FIVE-BRANCH SCONCE, one of a set of four. Made by Philippe Caffieri for the *Salon chinois* in the Duchesse de Bourbon's apartment at the Palais de Bourbon.

Caffieri's description is as follows: 'Pour Le même Salon chinois deux paires de bras à cinq branches; L'une pour la cheminée, L'autre pour Le trumau de glace qui fait vis avis a La cheminée ces bras dans le goût chinois ornés de fleurs et fruits du païs et Surmontés d'une figure chinoise homme et femme pour pendant, Le tout etant dun travail tres considérable et doré d'or moulû a raison de 2,600 livres La paire Les deux font 5,200 livres' ('For the same Chinese Saloon, two pairs of sconces with five branches each—one pair for the chimney-piece, the other to flank the pier-glass opposite the fireplace. They are in the Chinese taste, decorated with exotic flowers and fruit, and the sconces comprising each pair are respectively surmounted by figures of a Chinaman and woman. The whole has involved much work. Gilt bronze, 2,600 livres the pair. Total 5,200 livres'). The charge was reduced to 3,828 livres in the final analysis. The model alone cost 150 livres. Only one of the four sconces was completed by December 1770 when an inventory of Caffieri's workshops was taken (see page 280, item 69).

The *Salon chinois* was also called the *Salon de Compagnie*. In the inventory of the Palais de Bourbon published by Verlet (*La Maison*, pages 276–7), the room went under the latter name and the sconces are item No. 105. In the fire-place stood a pair of fire-dogs, of which one is shown in Plate 461. There were also eighteen chairs, twelve armchairs, and two sofas (*canapés*). The sofas were richly carved by Charles Lachenait; they had legs with Ionic capitals and were embellished with Chinese figures (see Lachenait's detailed bill which is also in the Archives Condé).

Plate 454

FOUR-BRANCHED SCONCE, one of a pair. Made in 1770–71 by Philippe Caffieri for the *Salle des Gentilshommes* in the Duchesse de Bourbon's apartments at the Palais de Bourbon.

Caffieri's account describes this as 'Une paire de bras a quatre branches pour la cheminée, très ornées de guirlandes de fleurs, et dans Le milieu un Bouquet de fleurs a Soleil le tout attaché par un rubans et doré dor moulu du prix de 2,400 livres' ('A pair of sconces, each with four branches, for the chimney-piece. Highly decorated with garlands of flowers. In the centre, a bouquet of flowers tied with a ribbon. Gilt bronze. The price, 2,400 livres'). The price was later abated to 1,783 livres. The model for these sconces cost 150 livres. One of them seems to be identical with an item in the inventory of Caffieri's work-shops made in 1771 (see page 280, No. 66).

Plate 455

THREE-BRANCHED SCONCE, one of a set of eight. Made in 1770–72 for the *Grande Gallerie* in the Palais de Bourbon, by Philippe Caffieri.

As Caffieri's bill shows, these sconces were originally made to have five branches: '8 grands bras a cinq branches ornés d'une couronne de Laurier et de trompettes indiquant La Victoire, bien finie et doré d'or moulû Mais il faut observer sur ces bras, qu'étant finis faits et montés tout prets à dorer Le 11 9bre 1772, il m'a été ordonné d'en Suprimer deux branches; ce qui m'a obligé de scier les parties qui Les contenoient de faire refondre d'autres morceaux pour reparer et écarter Les autres branches restantes Opérations tres couteuses vû Le peu de tems Sur tout, c'est pourquoy ils doivent être passés au même prix qu'avant Le changement c'est a raison de 1,000 livres piece Les 8 feront cy 8,000 livres' ('Eight large sconces, each with five branches, decorated with a coronet of bay-leaves and with trumpets emblematic of Victory, of finely chased and gilded bronze. It should be noted that, after they were completed, and ready for gilding on 11th November, 1772, I was ordered to remove two branches. This involved sawing off the pieces concerned and casting new sections to restore the sconces and separate the remaining branches—a costly operation, especially in the short time given. For this reason the price must remain the same as before the change was made, namely 1,000 livres each. The total for all eight being 8,000 livres'). In spite of his remarks, Caffieri was forced to reduce his bill slightly—to 7,064 livres. The model for this set cost 130 livres.

The symbols of Victory echoed the rest of the *décor* in this Gallery which was designed to remind the visitor of the military exploits of the Grand Condé—the grandfather of the current Prince; the room was hung with huge paintings of the great Marshal's victories at Rocroi, Fribourg etc. Even the fire-dogs were decorated with martial symbols.

The Gallery was also furnished with four large sofas (each ten feet long), eight armchairs and twenty-four ordinary chairs. All had straight fluted legs; they were embellished with exceedingly rich carving in a Classical vein. This is all revealed by the carver Lachenait's bills in the Archives Condé.

Plate 456

HANDLES FOR FIRE-IRONS, made by Philippe Caffieri for the same chimney-piece as the fire-dogs shown in the next two illustrations.

See the next Note.

Plates 457 and 458

PAIR OF FIRE-DOGS. Provided for the *Grande Gallerie* at the Palais de Bourbon, by Philippe Caffieri.

Caffieri describes this in his account as 'un feu representant d'un coté Mars qui ordonne a Bellone placé de l'autre coté de porter la fureur et le carnage parmi les Combattans, ces deux figures sont assises sur des trophées de guerre, comme casques, cuirasses canons &c. Ces dites figures assises portant 21 pouces de haut; les Etudes en ont été faite d'après nature Le fer très fort a 3 Barreaux de chaque coté, est orné dans toute la façade de bronze tant d'une tête de Lion avec sa peau et ses pattes, que de deux bombes enflamées servant de pommes, Les pelles pincettes et tenailles qui en dependent sont garnis de leurs Boutons et de deux Croissants doubles a L'antique réprésentant deux Serpents qui s'entrelassent Le tout très bien finis et doré d'or moulu du prix de 6,000 livres' ('a pair of fire-dogs with figures representing, on one side, Mars who orders Bellona, on the other, to carry Fury and Carnage among the Combatants. The two figures are seated on trophies of arms—helmets, breast-plates, cannon etc. They are 21 inches high. The studies for them were made from Nature. The iron grille, consisting of three strong bars on each side, is decorated along its whole face with bronze—with a lion's mask, skin and paws, as well as flaming grenades which serve as finials. The fire-shovels and tongs *en suite* are decorated with finials. Two sets of pincers in the form of entwined serpents.

The whole of bronze, neatly finished and gilt. Price 6,000 livres'). The price was reduced to 4,590 livres in the end. The models for the pair cost 500 livres.

Work on these fire-dogs seems to have been under way in 1770, for the inventory made of Caffieri's workshops in October of that year refers to a figure of Bellona (see page 279, No. 60) which may have been the model for one of the fire-dogs forming this pair. At any rate, the two models were ready by 27th October 1771 when the writer of an anonymous article in the *Journal d'Agriculture* saw them (see Guiffrey, *Les Caffieri*, page 491).

The martial character of the Gallery was discussed in the Note to Plate 455.

Plate 459

FIRE-DOG, one of a pair. Made by Philippe Caffieri for the Duchesse de Bourbon's bed-chamber in 1771–72.

This fire-dog is described in Caffieri's account as '. . . un grand feu représentant quatre enfans deux de chaque côté qui se groupent et se chauffent vers Le feu de La cheminée assis sur un socle dans le goût antique sur le quel est étendûe une peau de Lion Le dit feu Garni de son fer très fort pelles pincettes tenailles et Croissants Le tout doré d'or moulû du prix de 5,500 livres' ('a pair of fire-dogs with four children, two on each side, huddled warming themselves at the fire in the fireplace, seated on plinths of Antique aspect over which are spread lion-skins. Fitted with a strong polished steel grille, with tongs and pincers. All of gilt bronze. Total price 5,500 livres'). The price was subsequently abated to 3,879 livres. The model for it cost 350 livres.

These fire-dogs do not seem to be mentioned in the inventory of Caffieri's workshop taken in December 1770 (see page 277) so they had presumably not been started by then. They are, on the other hand, mentioned in the article of 27th October 1771 to which reference was made in the previous Note.

To flank the chimney-piece and the pier-glass opposite, Caffieri provided two pairs of sconces which are described in his accounts as 'deux paires de bras à quatre branches . . . ornés de guirlandes de fleurs de pavots allégoriques au Sommeil melés de roses et dorées dor moulu' ('two pairs of sconces, each with four branches . . . decorated with garlands of poppies, symbolising sleep, mixed with roses. Of gilt bronze'). These do, on the other hand, appear in the inventory of 1770 (see page 280, No. 67).

It was for this room that Leleu provided the commodes shown in Plates 128 and 130 (one of a pair). See the relevant Notes above.

Plate 460

FIRE-DOG, one of a pair. Made by Philippe Caffieri in 1771–72 for the Prince de Condé's *Grand Cabinet*.

In Caffieri's accounts, this is described as 'un feu representant deux globes l'un celeste l'autre terrestre posé sur un pied d'estal qui est ornée de guirlandes et La partie de La draperie Servant de voile aux globes qui en est détachés est jettée artistement Sur Le feu pour L'orner en Le couvrant . . .' ('a pair of fire-dogs with two globes, one terrestrial, the other celestial, resting on pedestals decorated with garlands. The drapery that serves to cover the globes has been cast aside and falls artistically over the fire-dogs and thus decorates them . . .'). For this pair of fire-dogs and their attendant fire-irons, Caffieri charges 3,500 livres but was only paid 1,294 livres. The wax models for this pair cost 180 livres.

In the inventory of the house made in 1779, these fire-dogs seem to have been moved into the Duchesse de Bourbon's *Salon de musique* (see Verlet, *La Maison*, page 280, No. 139).

Plate 461

FIRE-DOG, one of a pair. Made in 1771–72 by Philippe Caffieri for the *Salon chinois* at the Palais de Bourbon.

Described in Caffieri's bill as 'un grand feu de 4 figures chinoise représentant d'un coté un mandarin à qui une jeune chinoise présente Le caffé, Le dit mandarin assis sur des coussins posés Sur un terrein et un rocher chinois, sur Le quel est un vases qui contient une plante chinoise; de L'autre côté une chinoise pareillement assise sur des cousins qui sont posés de La même maniere sur un terrein et rocher chinois; est réprésentée prenant d'une main des fruits qui Lui sont présentés par un esclave dans une jatte; ce feu garni d'un fer très fort pelles, pincettes, tenailles, et Croisants Le tout doré d'or moulu du prix de cy 6,000 livres' ('a large pair of fire-dogs with four Chinese figures—on the one hand, a mandarin being handed coffee by a young Chinese girl amid a Chinese setting of rocks where stand urns containing Chinese shrubs; on the other, is a Chinese woman seated on cushions in a rocky Chinese setting. With one hand, she takes some fruit offered to her in a bowl by a slave. The grille consists of robust steel bars. Accompanied with tongs. All of gilt bronze. Price 6,000 livres'). The price was subsequently reduced to 2,938 livres. The models cost 400 livres. These items are not mentioned in the list of goods in Caffieri's workshop, made in December 1770, so they were presumably made after that.

The sconces for this room are illustrated in Plate 453 and discussed in the Note concerned.

*

Plate 462

BORDER OF A PORTRAIT OF THE DUC DE CHOISEUL. Engraved in 1770 by Etienne Fessard, after a painting by L.-M. Van Loo of 1763.

It is possible but not certain that Fessard himself designed this framing for the portrait. Whatever the case, the Duc must have approved of its style. The Van Loo portrait is discussed in the Note to Plate 367 which reproduces a corner of the painting showing the table.

Plate 463

INTERIOR OF THE DUC DE CHOISEUL'S PARIS RESIDENCE. Enlarged detail of a miniature painted by Louis-Nicolas van Blarenberghe about 1770 and mounted in a gold snuff-box made by Louis Roucel which bears the date-mark for 1770–71. *Private Collection.*

The *terminus post quem* for this painting and the other miniatures adorning the box (see Watson, *The Choiseul Box*, 1963) is given by Greuze's painting *L'Offrande à l'Amour* which may be seen on the wall to the right. This was exhibited at the *Salon* of 1769, so the scene must have been painted after that.

The miniature shows the Duc's bed-chamber. Note the pair of Neo-Classical fall-front secretaires which seem very like that shown in Plate 94 and may perhaps be attributed to Oeben's workshops. The picture-frames are also Classical in taste. On the other hand, the chairs, fire-screen and commode are in the Rococo style, and so is the bed which may here be seen reflected in the chimney-glass but more of which is shown in the complete picture. A parquet floor with a Neo-Classical pattern in one of the other rooms is illustrated in Plate 81. See also pages 65, 85 and 118.

Plate 464

INTERIOR OF THE DUC DE CHOISEUL'S PARIS RESIDENCE. Enlarged detail of a miniature painted about 1770 by L.-N. van Blarenberghe.

See previous Note.

This shows the *Cabinet à la Lanterne* which had a glass dome. This detail shows a *bureau plât* with *cartonnier* and a clock of the type known as *La Liseuse* (see Plate 188). The protruding angular corners of the table are to be seen on a table made by Georg Haupt in 1767 (see Plate 114), a cabinet-maker who is known to have worked for Choiseul at Chanteloup, the Duc's country-seat. On the other hand, Choiseul's principal cabinet-maker was Simon Oeben, and the form of the legs of this desk is reminiscent of that found on certain pieces of furniture attributed to him (e.g. Plate 144).

Everything in the room, with the exception of some picture-frames, is in the Neo-Classical taste. See also pages 65, 85, 89, 100 and 118.

Plate 465

VASE. Detail of an engraving of *Le Dédomagement de l'Absence* made in 1770 by Géraud Vidal of a painting by J.-E. Schenau.

The engraving is dated 1770 and was advertised on 9th April of that year in *L'Avantcoureur*. Presumably the picture was painted a year or so earlier. The whole scene shows a woman seated in a square-backed chair (see Plate 467) in front of her dressing-table on which stand two vases of which one is shown here. The room itself is couched in the Neo-Classical style as are the visible furnishings which include a chimney-piece, fire-dogs and a stool.

Plate 466

URN-SHAPED CLOCK. Detail of a portrait of the Abbé Nicolas Chanlatte painted in 1771 by Guillaume Voirot. *Present whereabouts unknown.*

This picture was sold as lot 115 at an anonymous auction held at the Galérie Charpentier on 12th June 1936 (illustrated in the sale-catalogue). According to the catalogue, the clock bore an inscription reading 'Le Pautre horloger du Roi'. The Abbé is seated at a table of Neo-Classical aspect in a chair of Rococo form. See Plate 471 for a detail of the table.

Plate 467

CHAIR-BACK. Detail of an engraving entitled *Le Dédomagement de l'Absence*, executed in 1770 by Géraud Vidal after a painting by J.-E. Schenau.

See Plate 465 concerning this picture.

The legs of the chair cannot be seen in the picture but alongside it stands a stool with straight fluted legs, and one may presume the chair was *en suite* with this stool.

Plates 468 to 470

DESIGNS FOR POCKET-WATCHES. Drawn by L. Van der Cruycen and published in 1770 in his *Livre de desseins.*

Plate 471

WRITING-DESK. Detail of a portrait of the Abbé Nicolas Chanlatte, painted in 1771 by Guillaume Voirot. *Present whereabouts unknown.*

See also Note 466.

Plate 472

LEG OF A SOFA, detail of a portrait of Madame du Barry, painted in 1771 by F.-H. Drouais. *Chambre de Commerce, Versailles.*

This was exhibited at the *Salon* of 1771 and is illustrated as a whole by Seznec and Adhémar, *Diderot Salons*, vol. IV, Plate 76.

Plate 473

SOFA. Detail of an engraving entitled *Le miroir cassé*, engraved by J. Chevillet about 1770 after a painting by J.-E. Schenau.

The engraving was advertised on 3rd December 1770 in *L'Avantcoureur.*

Plate 474

CHAIRS IN THE DINING-ROOM AT THE PAVILLON DE LOUVECIENNES. Detail of a drawing by J.-M. Moreau *le jeune*, executed in 1771. *Louvre, Cabinet des dessins.*

This well-known drawing represents the party given on 2nd September 1771 by Madame du Barry for Louis XV at her newly built pavilion at Louveciennes. The complete picture is illustrated in Colour Plate B. The room itself is shown in Plate 80.

Most of the chairs that furnished this little building were supplied by Louis Delanois (Plates 172 and 173) but these particular chairs do not seem to be from his workshop, judging by the description of the pieces he provided which are given in his accounts. See also page 91.

Plate 475

SOFA. Detail of a drawing of the *Salon* of the Comte de Lauraguais' Hôtel de Brancas. About 1771. *Musée des Arts Décoratifs.*

This house was redecorated in 1771 after designs by François-Joseph Belanger. See also page 129.

Plates 476 to 478

TWO CHAIRS AND A DAY-BED. Drawn by André-Jacques Roubo and published as Plates 235 and 237 in his *L'Art du menuisier* of 1772.

See also page 132.

Plates 479 and 480

TWO CHAIRS. Drawn by Jean-Charles Delafosse in 1773 or earlier.

These chairs are described as being 'dans le gout antique' and appear on Plate 3 in the first set (Série A) of Delafosse's engravings of designs for furniture. The *terminus ante quem* for these engravings is provided by notes supplied by J.-F. Watin (see page 128). It appears that thirty of Delafosse's *Séries*, comprising 120 sheets, were ready in 1773. One may therefore assume that the earliest series must have been completed several years earlier.

Watin, who not only sold engraved designs but also dealt in furniture, informed his customers that they could have pieces made after the designs he had for sale. He added that 'Nous observons aux amateurs, qu'ils ne doivent pas se flatter que l'exécution répondra toujours aux idées quelquefois compliquées de la gravure. Le célebre M. de Lafosse, par exemple, qui a tracé la forme de tous les ameublements les plus à la mode & les plus somptueux, se livre quelquefois trop à la fougue de sa riche imagination . . . Si on vouloit en rendre tous les détails, l'exécution seroit sûrement trop chere pour la fortune des plus riches particuliers' ('We would draw the attention of *amateurs* to the fact that the objects made after these designs will not necessarily correspond in every detail. The celebrated M. Delafosse, for example, who set down the lineaments of all the most fashionable and sumptuous furnishings, sometimes allowed his fertile inspiration to run away with him . . . If one should seek to follow his designs in all their intricate detail, the cost of doing so would surely be too high for even the most wealthy private person').

Plates 481 and 482

TWO FIRE-SCREENS. Drawn by Jean-Charles Delafosse in 1773 or earlier.

See the previous entry. These two designs come from series 'E' so they should be of slightly later date than the compositions included in earlier series (e.g. the chairs shown in Plates 479 and 480).

Plate 483

FURNITURE IN THE SALON OF THE HÔTEL GRIMOD DE LA REYNIÈRE. Enlarged detail of a drawing by J. C. Kamsetzera. *University Library, Cracow.*

The date of this room is discussed in the Note to Plate 82. It is not unreasonable to suppose that seat-furniture, like the room itself, was designed by C.-L. Clérisseau. The four large torchères placed in the corners of the room (one is shown here) were made by Duplessis *fils* (see Plate 218) who may possibly have designed them as well. See also page 67.

Plate 484

TRIPOD STAND. Engraving advertising the original *Athénienne*, by J.-H. Eberts, about 1773. *University Library, Warsaw.*

Below the illustration, the caption informs us that an *Athénienne* was a 'Nouveau Meuble/Servant/de Console/de Casolette/de Rechaud/de Pot de Fleurs/de Terrasse/de Reservoir/Inventé et Gravé par I.H.E.' This small piece of furniture is in fact shown serving two of these purposes in a highly improbable combination—as a perfume-burner (*cassolette*) and as a flower-vase!

The engraving is not dated but the *L'Avantcoureur* of 27th September 1773 carried an advertisement for Eberts' little tripod. On page 353 of J. F. Watin's *L'Art du peintre, doreur* etc. (1776), the *Athénienne* is stated to be of wood and to cost between 300 and 750 livres—according to the quality of the gilding and carving.

Eberts was the owner of the painting by Joseph Vien which, when engraved by Flipart, acquired the title of *La vertueuse Athénienne* (Plate 370). In this will be seen a Classical tripod which presumably inspired Eberts to give his invention its curious title.

A tripod which may be one of the original *Athéniennes* is shown in Plate 186. The history of this piece of furniture has been given by Emile Dacier in his 'L'Athénienne et son inventeur' (*Gaz. d. B–A.*, 1932, pages 112–22), and by Svend Eriksen and F. J. B. Watson 'The Athénienne and the revival of the Classical Tripod' (*Burlington Magazine*, March, 1963, pages 108–12). See also page 138.

Plate 485

FIREPLACE WITH FIRE-SCREEN. Detail of an etching entitled *Le Coucher* by A.-J. Duclos after a composition by J.-H. Eberts and S. Freudeberg, published in 1774.

This forms Plate 12 in their *Suite d'estampes pour servir à l'histoire des moeurs et du costume des François.* See also Plates 490 and 492.

Plate 486

ARMCHAIR. Detail of the same etching as the previous item. Dated 1774.

Incidentally, the fire-screen (Plate 485) seems to have been supplied *en suite* with this chair—and presumably the other chairs that were in this room; both are covered with a material (embroidery, tapestry ?) decorated with the same pattern—a quiver-like basket of flowers suspended by a ribbon from a floral surround. It was of course the convention to have a large measure of uniformity in the furnishing of a fashionable room during the eighteenth century. This remained the case even during the Rococo phase but the convention acquired renewed sanction in the Neo-Classical interior where regularity and a formal effect were demanded—however abandoned may have been the life which was sometimes led in such rooms! Freudeberg, like Baudouin (see Plates 388, 389, 426, 427, 443 to 445), often shows Neo-Classical interiors in active use and in considerable disarray.

Plate 487

DRUM-SHAPED OCCASIONAL-TABLE. Detail of an etching entitled *Le Boudoir* engraved in 1774 by Pierre Maleuvre after a composition by J.-H. Eberts and S. Freudeberg.

Plate 1 in their *Suite d'estampes pour servir à l'histoire des moeurs et du costume des François.*

Note the cabriole legs of this little table, a reminder that free-standing pieces of furniture (especially those intended for use in a lady's apartment) frequently retained the less obtrusive forms of the Rococo, long after Neo-Classicism had won the day.

Plate 488

SOFA. Drawn in 1774–75 by François Boucher *le jeune*; engraved by P.-G. Berthault.

Published as Plate 1 in the eleventh series (*Série K*) of Boucher's projects for furniture and interior decoration. The date is provided by Jean-Félix Watin in the third edition of his *L'Art du peintre, doreur . . .*, edition of 1776, page 339.

Plate 489

CHANDELIER. Designed about 1772 by Charles De Wailly for the *Salon Spinola* in the Palazzo Serra in Genoa.

Detail of an engraving showing the whole room, published in 1777 in the volume of Plates accompanying Diderot and d'Alembert's *Encyclopédie.*

Plate 490

SCONCE. Detail of an etching by A.-J. Duclos after a composition by J.-H. Eberts and S. Freudeberg, published under the title of *Le Coucher* and dated 1774.

See also the details reproduced in Plates 485, 486 and 492.

Plate 491

MANTLE CLOCKS. Detail from an etching entitled *La soirée d'hyver* engraved in 1774 by F.-R. Ingouf after a composition by J.-H. Eberts and S. Freudeberg, issued as Plate 10 in their *Suite d'estampes pour servir à l'histoire des moeurs et du costume des François.*

There can be little doubt that this is an accurate rendering of a domestic scene, judging by the faithful representation of the bulb-flasks with their hyacinths about to bloom on the mantlepiece.

Plate 492

MANTLE CLOCK. Detail of the same etching as that mentioned in the previous Note.

Plates 493 and 494

FIRE-DOG AND A READING-LAMP. Ibid.

Plates 495 and 496

CHAIRS MADE FOR THE MARQUIS DE MARIGNY IN 1775. Marginal drawings in a bill rendered by the firm of Charpentier and Thibault, japanners. *Bibliothèque historique de la Ville de Paris, MSS. nouv. acq. 102, fol. 350 verso.*

The bill is headed 'Mémoire des ouvrages de Dorure et Peinture d'Impression faites pour Monsieur Le Marquis de Marigny en son hotel a Paris les d. ouvrages faites suivant les ordres de Monsieur Soufflot . . . en 1775 par Charpentier Et Thibault Entrepreneurs des Batimens du Roy' ('List of the gilding and japanning carried out for the Marquis de Marigny at his house in Paris, carried out on the instructions of M. Soufflot . . . in 1775 by Charpentier and Thibault, contractors to the Royal Office of Works').

Plate 497

DESIGN FOR A CHAIR. Drawn in 1774–75 by François Boucher *le jeune*; engraved by J.-V. Dupin.

Detail of Plate 13 in the third series of Boucher's designs for furniture and interior decoration. The date is given by Watin (see Note to Plate 488). This curious three-legged chair is designated a 'Duchesse à la Romaine'.

Plate 498

SOFA. Detail of a portrait of the Duc de Chartres and his family painted by C. Le Peintre about 1775–76. Engraved in 1779 by A. de Saint-Aubin and H. Helmann.

This shows a room that was very probably in the Duc's residence. If so, the sofa may be one of a pair provided by the chair-maker Louis Delanois on 6th November 1771. Delanois' accounts reveal that he supplied the Duc de Chartres with an entire set of seat-furniture which his descriptions show must have been at least as Classical in taste as this sofa (see the author's *Louis Delanois*, 1968, page 58). On the left of the picture, which is reproduced as a whole by Verlet in *La Maison* (page 234), stands an *Athénienne* very like that illustrated in Plate 484. See also page 92.

Plate 499

PROJECT FOR A TABLE. Drawn by A. Besse, dated 1776. *Bibliothèque d'Art et d'Archéologie, Paris.*

Inscribed 'Table à gradin à La greque', the 'gradin' being the superstructure at the back. See also page 81.

INDEX

All places named are in France unless otherwise indicated and, except for châteaux, are in Paris unless noted. Entries in **bold** type are the main references to the Select Biographies (pages 147–225), which may contain information also referred to in the index sub-headings following the person's name. Plate numbers are in *italics*.

ARCHITECTURAL WORKS

1. SERVANDONI. Design for St. Sulpice, Paris, about 1732

2. Le Geay, about 1740?

3–6. Le Geay, about 1740?

7. CONTANT D'IVRY. Design for St. Eustache. Paris, 1744

8. Le Lorrain. Chinea Festival set-piece, Rome, 1745

9. Le Lorrain. Chinea Festival set-piece, Rome, 1746

10. G.-P.-M. DUMONT. Projected Temple of the Arts, Rome, 1746

11. N.-H. JARDIN. Project, Rome, 1747 or 1748

12. M.-A. SLODTZ. High altar, Vienne Cathedral, 1744–47

13. E.-A. PETITOT. Chinea Festival set-piece, Rome, 1749

14. GAETANO BRUNETTI. Mural-decoration, Hôtel de Luynes, Paris, about 1748

15. LE LORRAIN. Design for the dining-room at Åkerö, 1754

16. SERVANDONI. Triumphal arch, Paris, 1754

17. SOUFFLOT. The theatre at Lyons, 1754–56

18. BOULLÉE. Proposal for the Paris Mint, before June 1756

19. GABRIEL. Building on the Place Louis XV, Paris, 1755

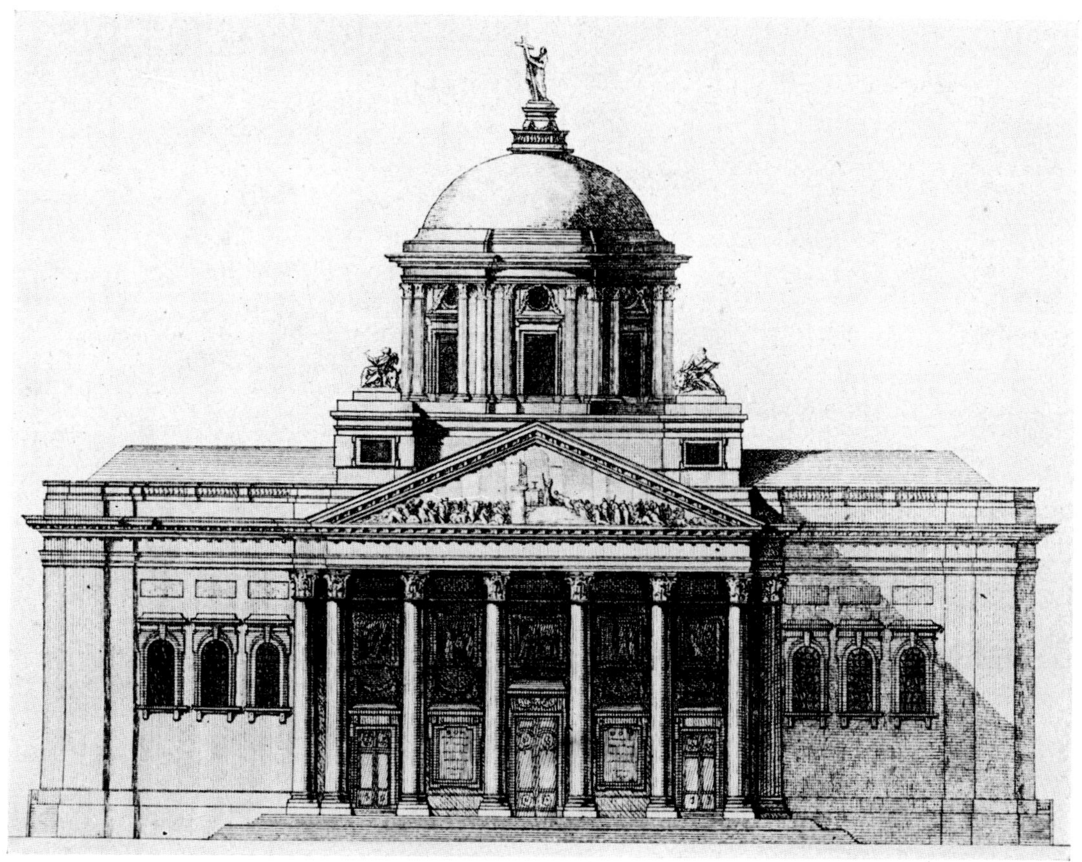

20. SOUFFLOT. Design for Ste. Geneviève, Paris, 1757

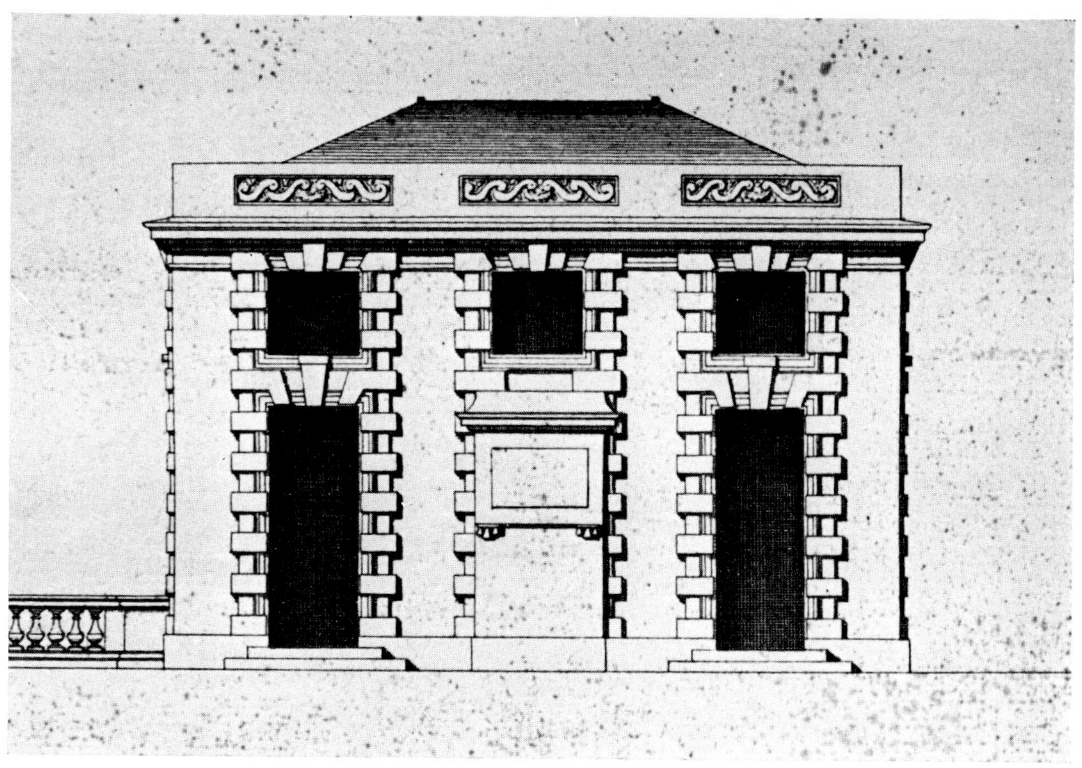

21. GABRIEL. Guard-house on the Place Louis XV, Paris, 1755–57

22, 23. CONTANT D'IVRY. Decoration in the Duchesse d'Orléans' salon at the Palais Royal, Paris, about 1755–57

24. Mirror-frame at Count Bernstorff's house, Copenhagen. Probably designed by CONTANT D'IVRY. 1755–57

25a, b. Pier-glass and console-table at Count Bernstorff's house (see Plate 24)

26. Console-table at Count Bernstorff's house (see Plate 24)

27. Chimney-piece at Count Bernstorff's house (see Plate 24)

28–29. NEUFFORGE. Proposals for mural-decorations, about 1755

30. JARDIN. Count Moltke's dining-room, Copenhagen, 1757

31. Moreau-Desproux. Hôtel de Chavannes, Paris, 1758–60

32, 33. Loyer. Hôtel de Varey, Lyons, 1758–60

34. LOYER. Salon at the Hôtel de Varey, Lyons, about 1760

35. BOULLÉE. Salon at the Hôtel de Tourolles, Paris, about 1758–59

36. SOUFFLOT and JACQUES. Design for a tapestry, 1758

37. NEUFFORGE. Design for a façade, before 1758

38. FALCONET. Monument to Madame Lalive de Jully in Saint-Roch, Paris, 1754

39. PAJOU. Projected monument for the Maréchal de Belle-Isle, 1761

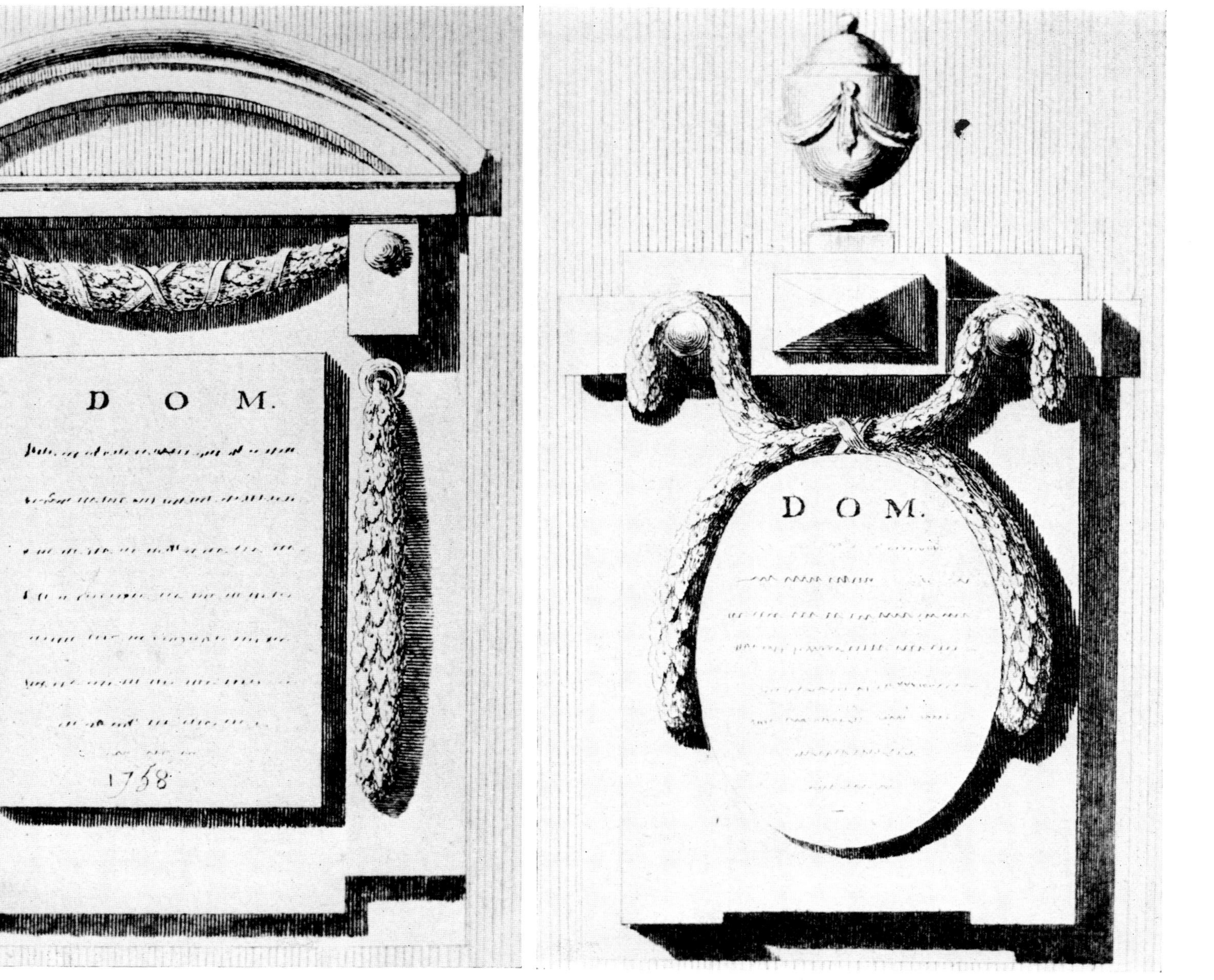

40, 41. RAUX. Designs for sepulchral monuments, 1758

42, 43. M.-A. SLODTZ. Catafalque erected in Notre-Dame, Paris, 1760

44. F. BOUCHER. Ceiling in Pierre de Monlong's villa, near Lyons, 1760–61

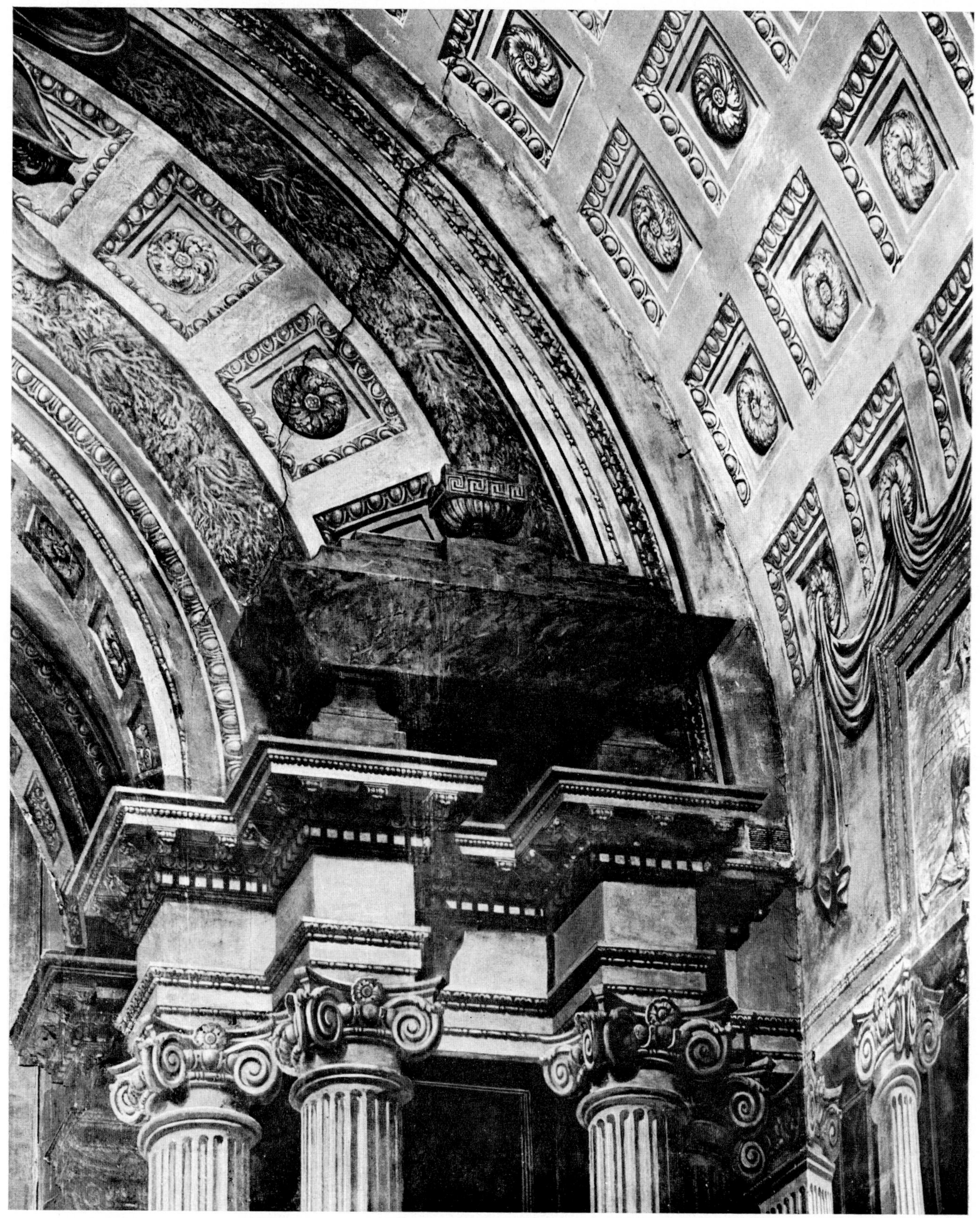

45. Victor Louis and Gaetano Brunetti. Decoration in Ste. Marguerite, Paris, about 1763–64.

46, 47. NEUFFORGE. Designs for villas, about 1760

48. PEYRE. The villa of Madame Leprêtre de Neubourg, Paris, 1762

49. ANONYMOUS. Entrance to the Hôtel de Gamaches, Paris, about 1762

50. GABRIEL. South front of the Petit Trianon, Versailles, about 1763–67

51. GABRIEL. North front of the Petit Trianon.

52. GABRIEL. Detail of the south front of the Petit Trianon

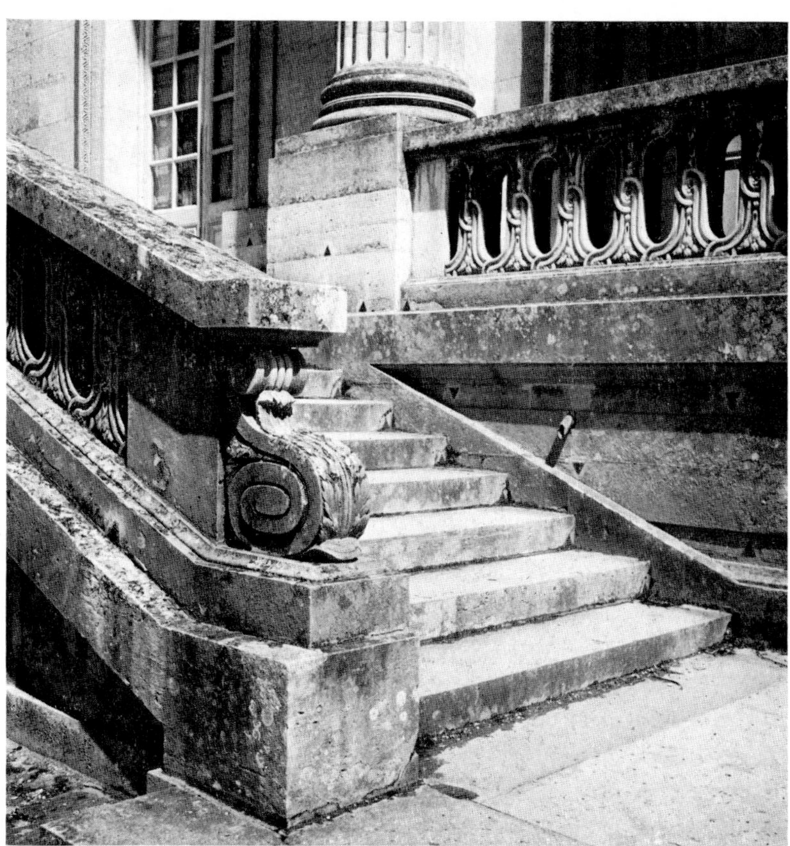

53. GABRIEL. Detail of the west front of the Petit Trianon

54. De la Rue. Design for a chimney-piece, about 1760–64

55. Attributed to Gabriel. Chimney-piece for the Saint-Hubert hunting-lodge, about 1756–64

56, 57, 58. Barreau de Chefdeville. Designs for the Intendant's Residence at Bordeaux, 1760–65

ARCHIVES

59. Barreau de Chefdeville. St. Nicolas at Nérac, begun in 1762

60. Moreau-Desproux. The Fontaine des Haudriettes, Paris, 1764

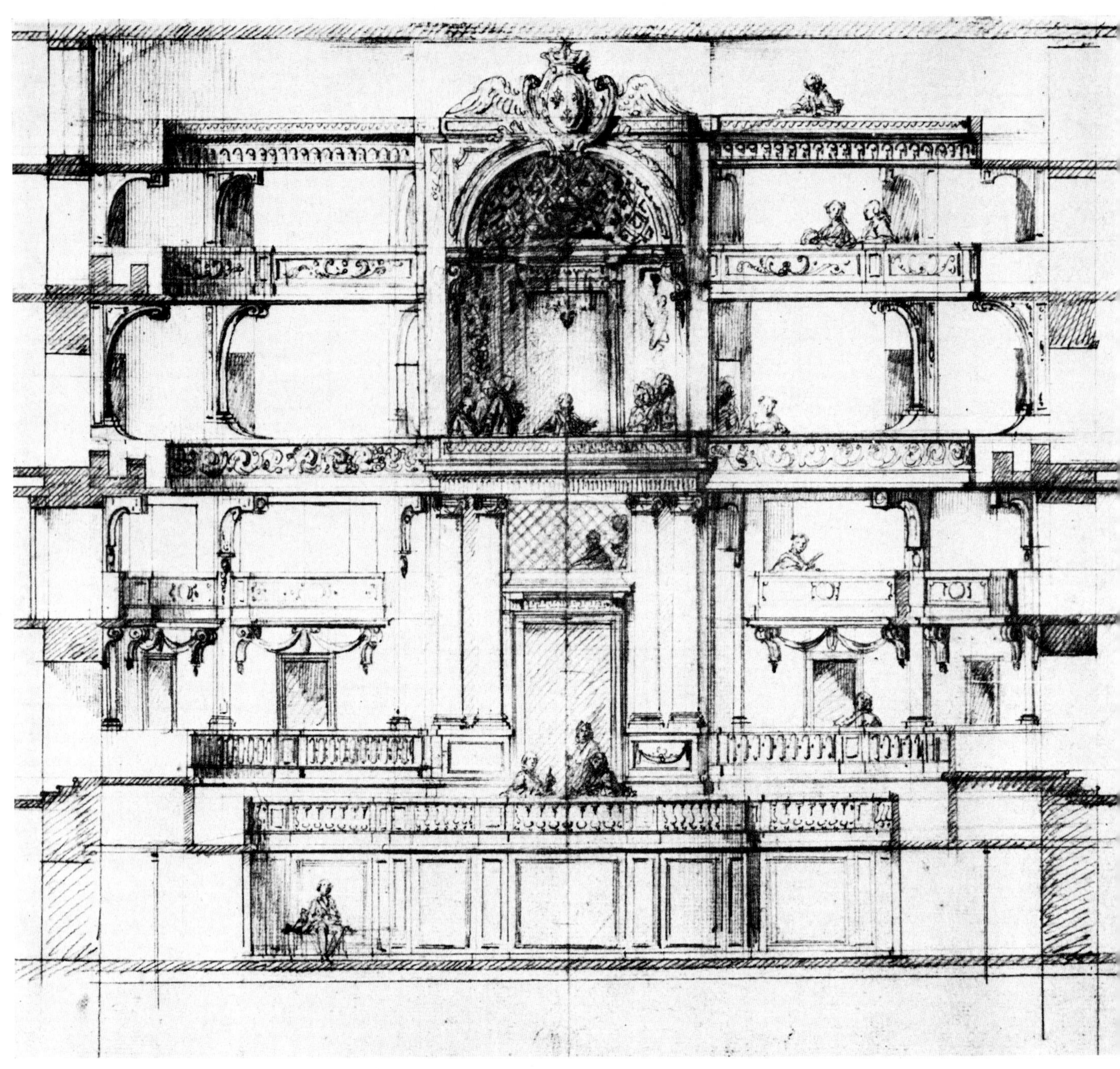

61. Gabriel. Proposal for the Opera-hall in the Palace at Versailles, 1763

63 (opposite). Dumont. Design for a dining-room, before 1765

62. LEDOUX. The Hôtel d'Uzès, Paris, about 1764–67

64. Ascribed to Rousset. Design for the salon at the Hôtel d'Uzès, Paris, 1765?

65. Ascribed to Cherpitel. Design for mural-decoration in the Hôtel d'Uzès, Paris, 1765?

66. Gabriel and Guibert. The Salon de Compagnie at the Petit Trianon, 1767–68

67. Guibert. Detail of the panelling shown in Plate 66

68, 69. PIÈTRE. Designs for the Hôtel Mélusine, Paris, 1766

70. Ascribed to VICTOR LOUIS. Design for a room in the Palace at Warsaw, 1766

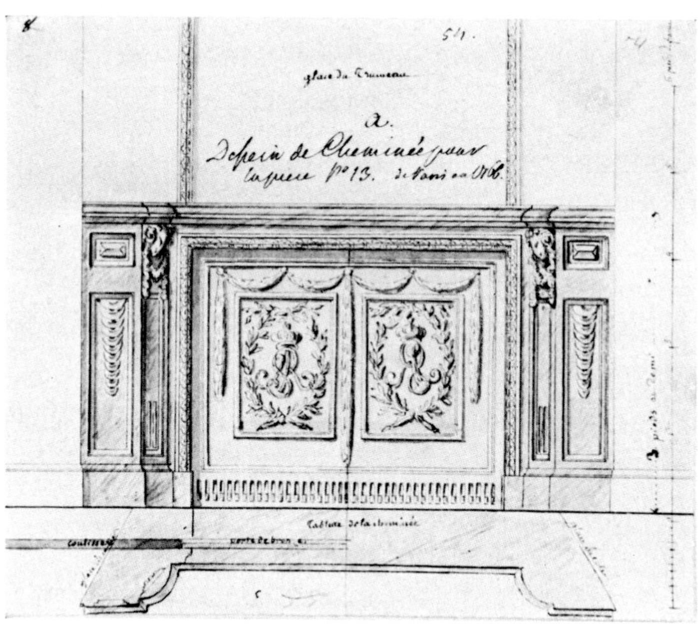

71. Ascribed to PRIEUR. Design for a chimney-piece in the Palace at Warsaw, 1766

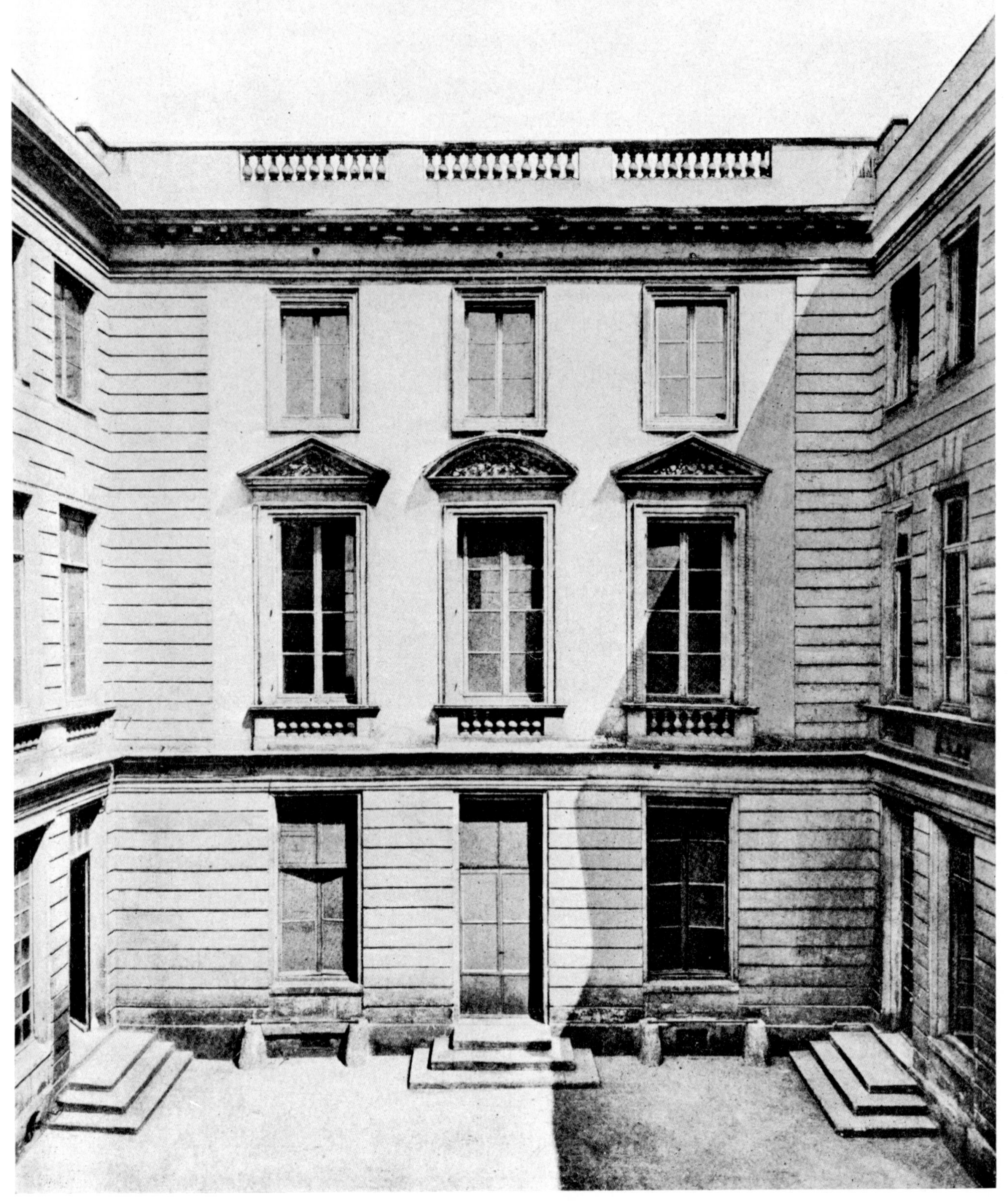

72. LEDOUX. Hôtel d'Hallwyl, Paris, about 1766

73. LOYER. Design for a bath-niche, 1767

74. Gabriel or Pajou (?). Proposed decoration for the Opera-hall in the Palace at Versailles, about 1765–68

75. COUTURE. The salon at the Pavillon de la Boissière, Paris, 1769

76. SOUFFLOT. Marigny's house at Roule, 1768–69

77. LEDOUX. Mademoiselle Guimard's house in Paris, 1770–73

78. Moreau-Desproux. The Pavillon Carré de Beaudouin, Paris, started in 1770

79. Ledoux. The Pavillon de Louveciennes, 1770–71

80. LEDOUX. Dining-room in the Pavillon de Louveciennes, 1770–71

81. ANONYMOUS. Parquet in the Hôtel de Choiseul, Paris, about 1770

82. Clérisseau. Salon in the Hôtel Grimod de la Reynière, about 1772–75

83. Clérisseau (?). Carpet in the salon at the Hôtel Grimod, about 1772–75

84. GONDOIN. Amphitheatre in the École de Chirurgie, Paris, started in 1769

VENEERED FURNITURE

85. LE LORRAIN. Furniture made for Lalive de Jully, about 1756–57

86. Inkstand resembling that made for Lalive de Jully, about 1760

87, 88. Details of table shown in Plate 85

89. Filing-cabinet (see Plate 85) with mock-up of clock (see Plate 187)

90, 91, 92, 93. J.-F. OEBEN, RIESENER, DUPLESSIS and others. The *Bureau du Roi*, 1760–69

94. J.-F. Oeben, about 1760–62

95, 96. J.-F. Oeben, about 1760–62

97. GARNIER and DURAND, about 1762–65

98. GARNIER, about 1760–65

99. Garnier, about 1762–65

100. Dubois, about 1760–65

101, 102, 103. DUBOIS, about 1765

104, 105. DUBOIS and GOYER, about 1765–70

106. DUBOIS, about 1765–70

107. GOYER, about 1765–70

108. DUBOIS, about 1765–70

109. Boudin, about 1765–75

110. ANONYMOUS (perhaps LELEU), about 1765–70

111. Carlin and Poirier, 1766

112. Attributed to CARLIN, about 1765–70

113. Attributed to RIESENER, about 1765–67

114. HAUPT, 1767

115. Attributed to HAUPT, about 1766–67

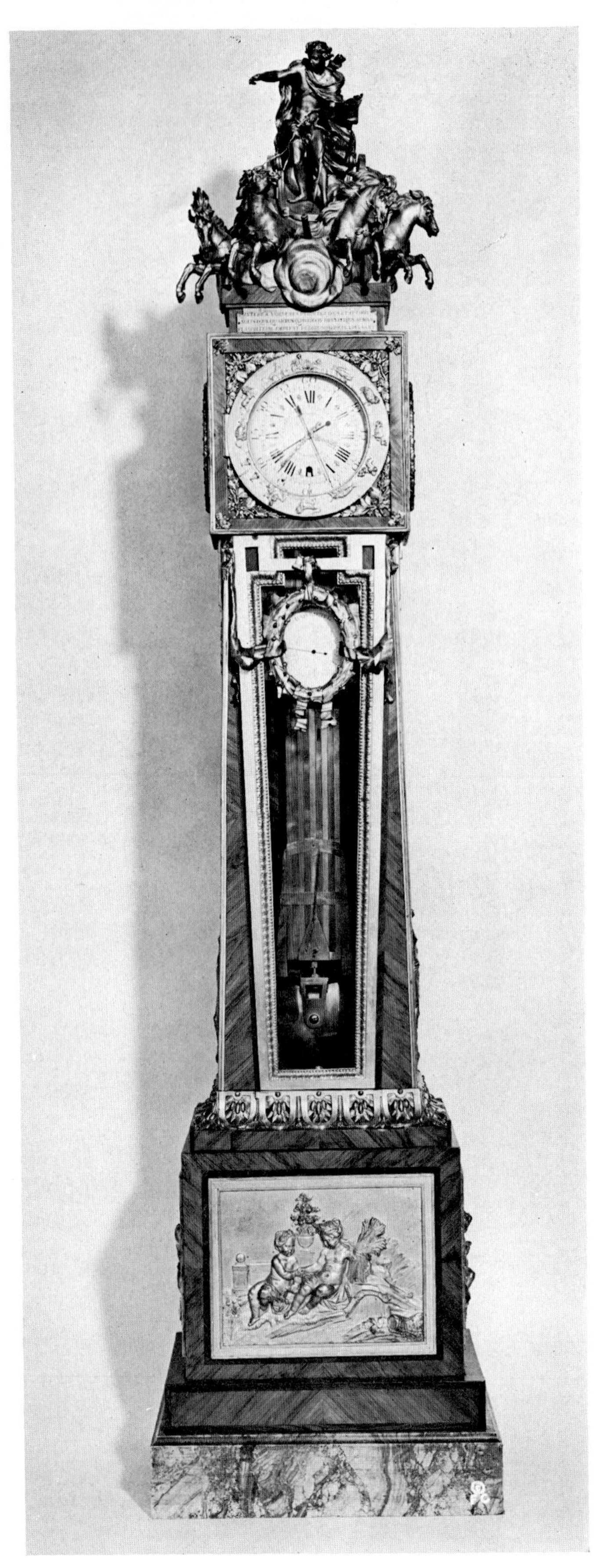

116. Lieutaud (?) and Caffieri, 1767

117. B.V.R.B., about 1765–75

118. POIRIER (?) and LELEU, about 1767

119. Joubert and Lacroix, 1769

120. JOUBERT, 1769

121. Poirier and Carlin (?), about 1770

122. Poirier and Carlin, 1771

123. Riesener, 1771

124. Montigny, about 1765–70

125. POIRIER and CARLIN (?), 1772

126. LELEU, about 1772

127, 128. Leleu, 1772

129. Leleu, 1772

130. Leleu, 1773

131. FOULLET and BOUDIN, about 1770–75

132. P.-A. FOULLET, about 1770–75

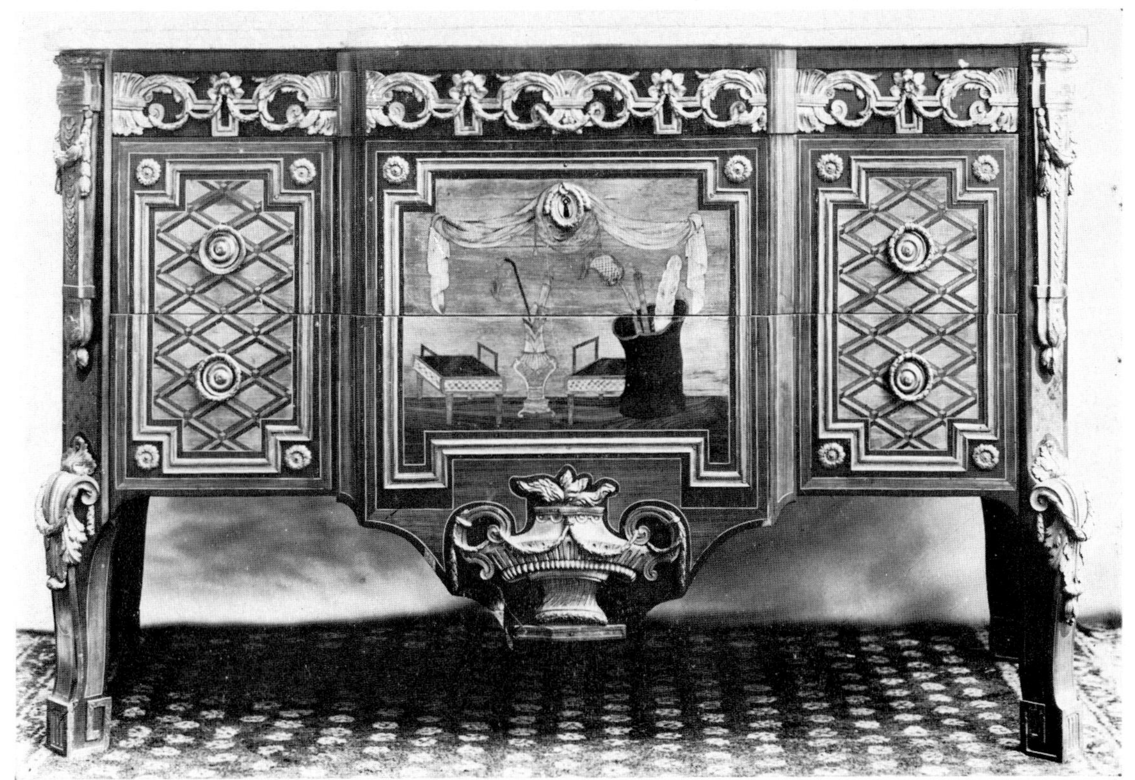

133. ROUSSEL, about 1770–75

134. ANONYMOUS, about 1770–75

135. ROUSSEL, about 1770–75

136. Carlin, about 1773

137. Lacroix, about 1770–75

138. TOPINO and BOUDIN, about 1770–75

139. Evald, about 1770–74

140. EVALD, about 1770–74

141. Riesener, 1773

142. Joubert, 1773

143. Riesener, 1774

144. Simon Oeben, about 1774

145. Joubert, 1774

146. JOUBERT and RIESENER, 1774

147. RIESENER, 1774

148. DURAND or GARNIER, about 1772–75

149. RIESENER, 1775

150. LAPIE, about 1773–74

151. MEWESEN, about 1773–74

152. P. A. Foullet (?), about 1776–77

153. P. A. FOULLET (?), about 1770–75

154. ANONYMOUS, about 1776–77

CARVED FURNITURE

155. MICHARD, about 1765

156. Delanois, about 1765

157. Letelier, about 1765

158. ANONYMOUS, about 1765

159. Pothier, about 1765

160. Anonymous, about 1765–70

161. ANONYMOUS, about 1765–70

162. Delanois, about 1765–70

163. GOURDIN, about 1765–70

164. Delanois, about 1765–70

165. DELANOIS, about 1768–70

166, 167. HEURTAUT, about 1768–69

168, 169. ANONYMOUS, about 1768–70

170. HEURTAUT, about 1768–70

171. Carpentier, about 1768–69

172. Delanois, 1769–70

173. Delanois, 1769–70

174. CARPENTIER, about 1770

175, 176. DELANOIS and JACOB, about 1770

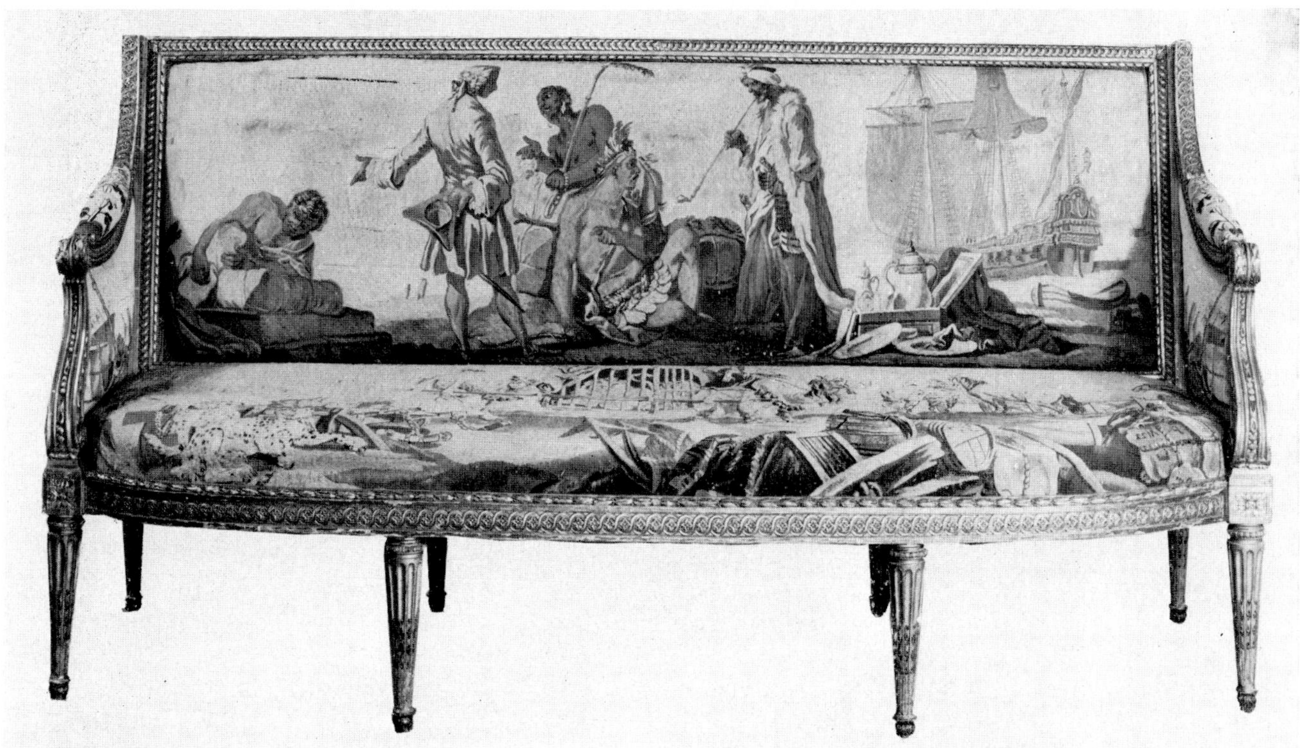

177, 178. Carpentier, about 1770

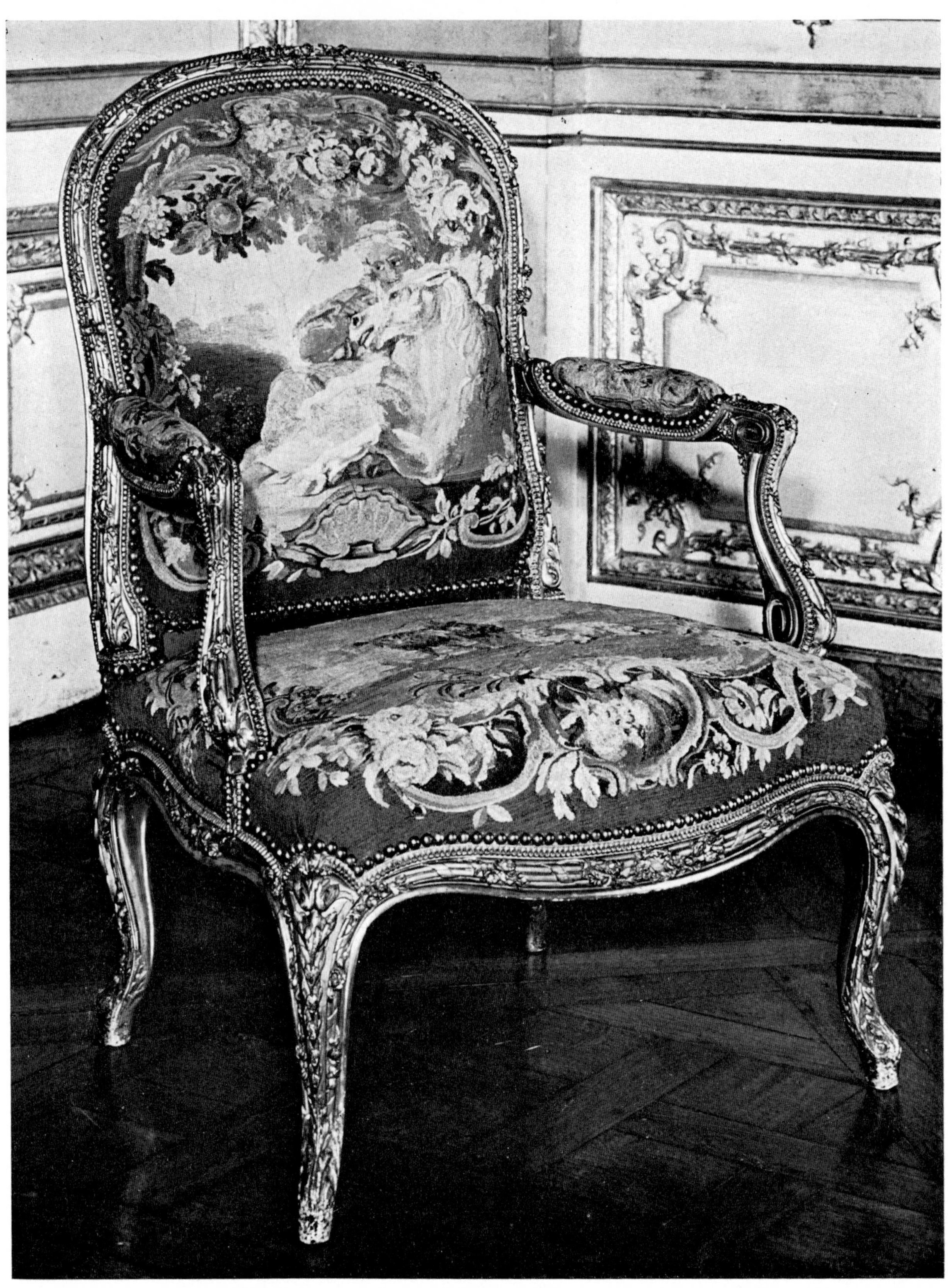

179. GONDOIN and FOLIOT, 1772–73

180. GONDOIN and FOLIOT, 1775

181. Delanois, about 1770–75

182. Heurtaut, about 1770–75

183, 184. ANONYMOUS, 1768

185. KAESHAMMER, 1770–71

186. ANONYMOUS, about 1773

BRONZES

187. Attributed to LE LORRAIN and CAFFIERI, about 1756–57

188. ANONYMOUS, about 1758–65

189. PAJOU and SAINT-GERMAIN, 1765-67

190. Attributed to PRIEUR, about 1766

191. Attributed to PRIEUR, about 1766–70

192. PRIEUR, about 1766–70

193. Anonymous, about 1770

194. Anonymous, about 1765–70

195. ANONYMOUS, about 1765–70

196. OSMOND, about 1765–70

197. Attributed to POIRIER and another, about 1768

198. GERMAIN? SAINT-GERMAIN? POIRIER? VION? About 1768–69

199. Poirier, 1769

200. ANONYMOUS, about 1770

201. DOUBLET and JULIA, 1774

202. Germain, 1756

203. Attributed to CAFFIERI, about 1758

204. CAFFIERI, 1760

205. Attributed to PRIEUR, about 1765–66

206. Caffieri, 1766–68

207. Attributed to PRIEUR, 1766–68

208. ANONYMOUS, about 1765–70

209. ANONYMOUS, about 1765–70

210. ANONYMOUS, about 1765–69

211. ANONYMOUS, about 1770–75

212. ANONYMOUS, about 1770

213. Attributed to CAFFIERI, about 1768–70

214. ANONYMOUS, about 1770–75

215, 216. ANONYMOUS, about 1772–74

217. Caffieri, 1771

218. Attributed to DUPLESSIS, about 1775–76

219. ANONYMOUS, about 1770–75

220. ANONYMOUS, about 1770–75

221. ANONYMOUS, about 1760–65

222. ANONYMOUS, about 1765–70

223. Attributed to CAFFIERI, about 1765–70

224. ANONYMOUS, about 1765–70

225, 226. ANONYMOUS, about 1765–70

227. DAMBIÈRE, about 1770–75

228. Attributed to PITOIN, about 1770–75

229, 230. PITOIN, 1772

231, 232. Anonymous, about 1770–75

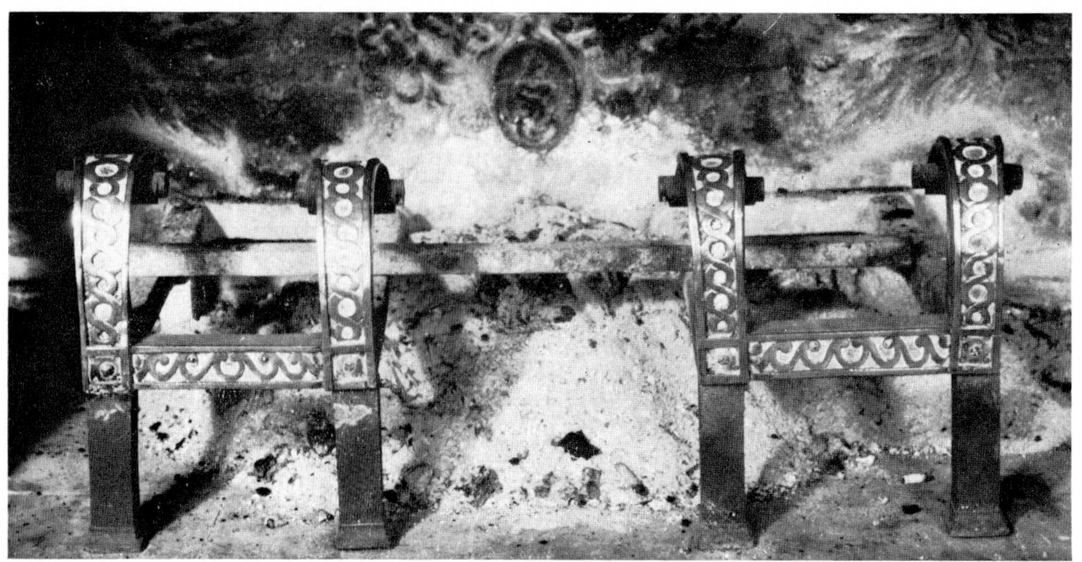

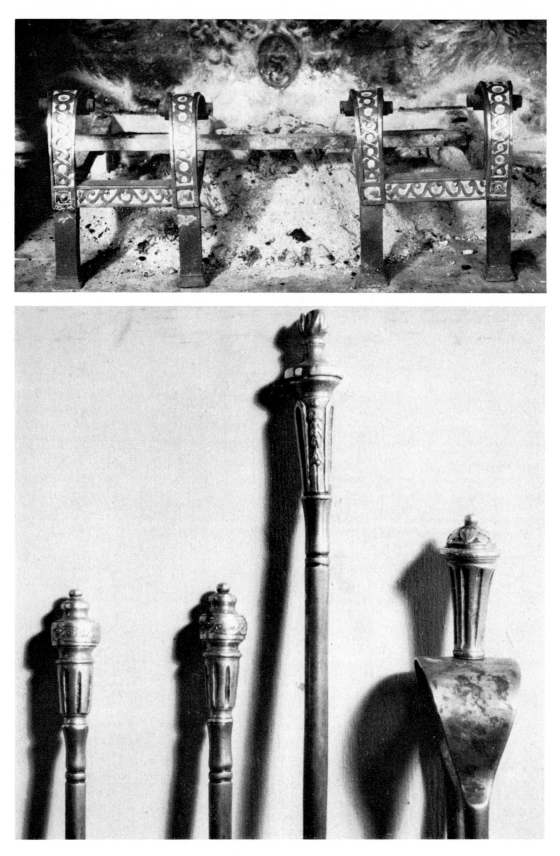

233, 234. ANONYMOUS, about 1772–75

235. Attributed to POIRIER, 1761

236. CAFFIERI, 1761

237. ANONYMOUS, about 1760–64

238. Anonymous, 1765–70

239. ANONYMOUS, about 1765–70

240. Anonymous, about 1767

241. ANONYMOUS, about 1765–70

242. Anonymous, about 1769

243. BELANGER (?) and GOUTHIÈRE, about 1772–75

GOLD AND SILVER

244. Germain, 1756–63

245, 246. VILLECLAIR, 1762–63

247. GERMAIN, 1762

248. GORDIÈRE, 1763–64

249. Frémin, 1762–63

250. George, 1762–63

251. AUGUSTE, 1762–63

252. ANONYMOUS, Paris, 1762–63

253. Formey, 1762–63

254. Tiron, 1762–63

255. ROUCEL, 1763–64

256. SAGERET, 1766–67

257. GERMAIN, 1765–66

258. GERMAIN, 1764–65

259, 260. GERMAIN, 1766

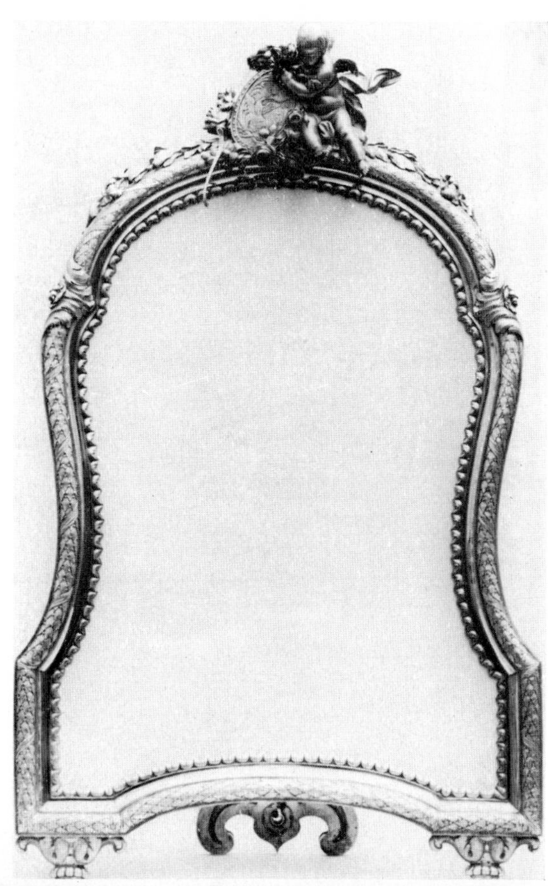

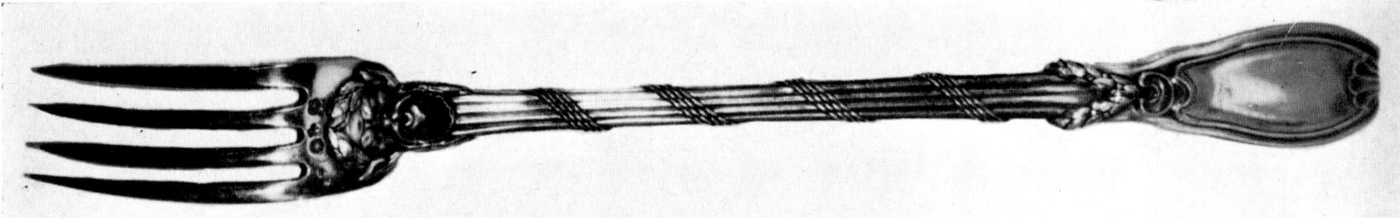

263, 264. Roëttiers, 1770–71

265. Roëttiers, 1770–71

266. Auguste, 1771–72

267. Bréant, 1773–74

PORCELAIN

268. Sèvres, 1757

269. Sèvres, 1758

270. Sèvres, 1761

271. Sèvres, 1761

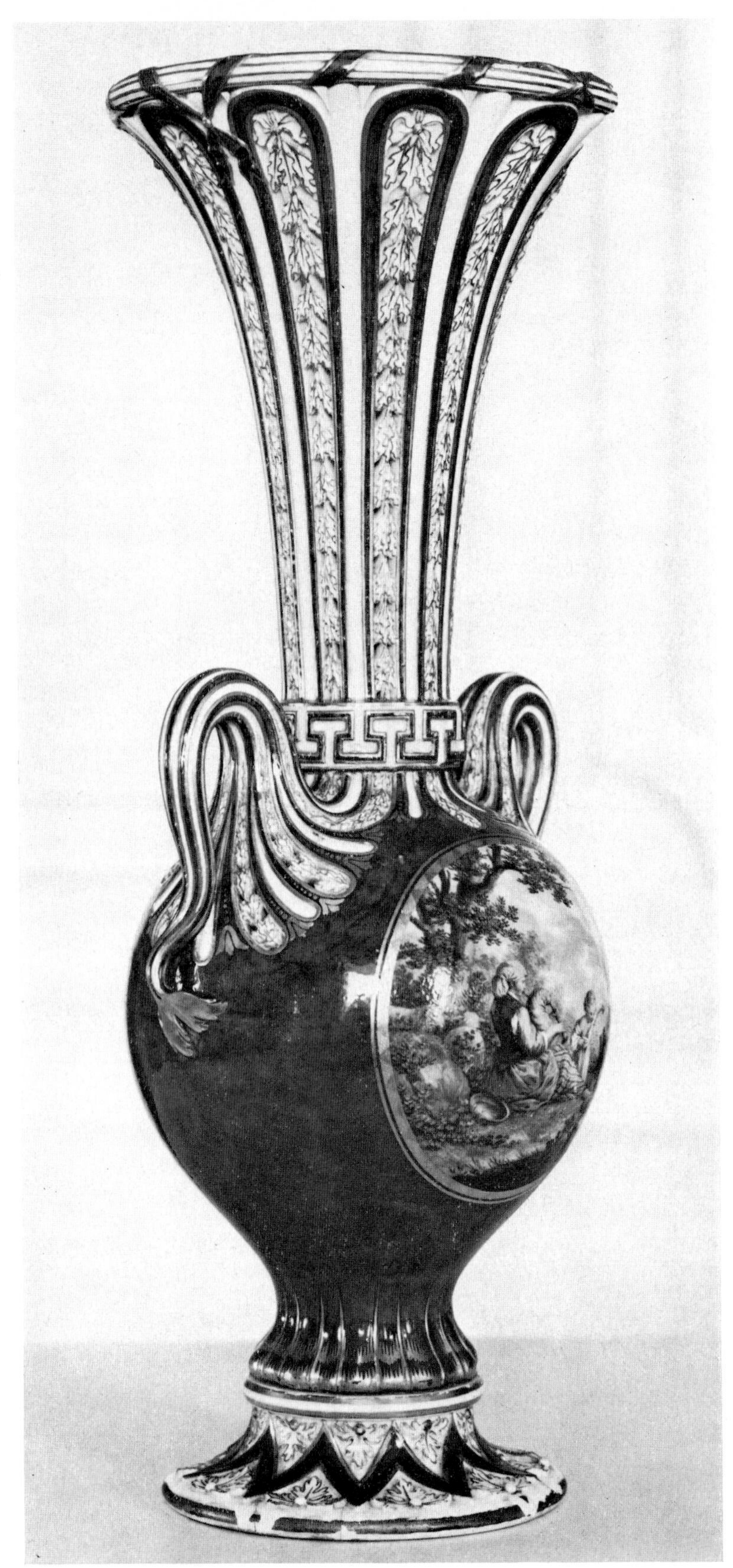

272. Sèvres, 1763

273. Sèvres, 1763

274. Sèvres, 1763

275. Sèvres, 1764

276. Sèvres, 1767

277. Sèvres, 1765

278. SÈVRES, about 1766–70

279. SÈVRES, about 1765–66

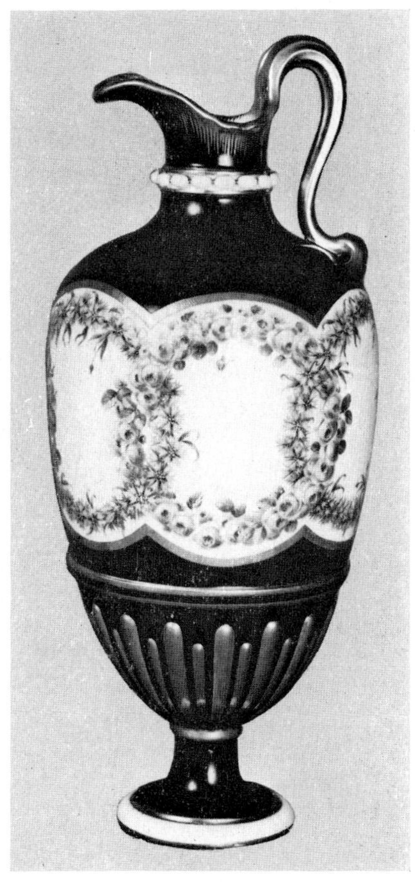

280. SÈVRES, about 1765–67

281. SÈVRES, about 1765–68

282. SÈVRES, about 1769

283. SÈVRES, about 1768–69

284. Sèvres, 1769

285. Sèvres, 1769

286. Sèvres, about 1768–69

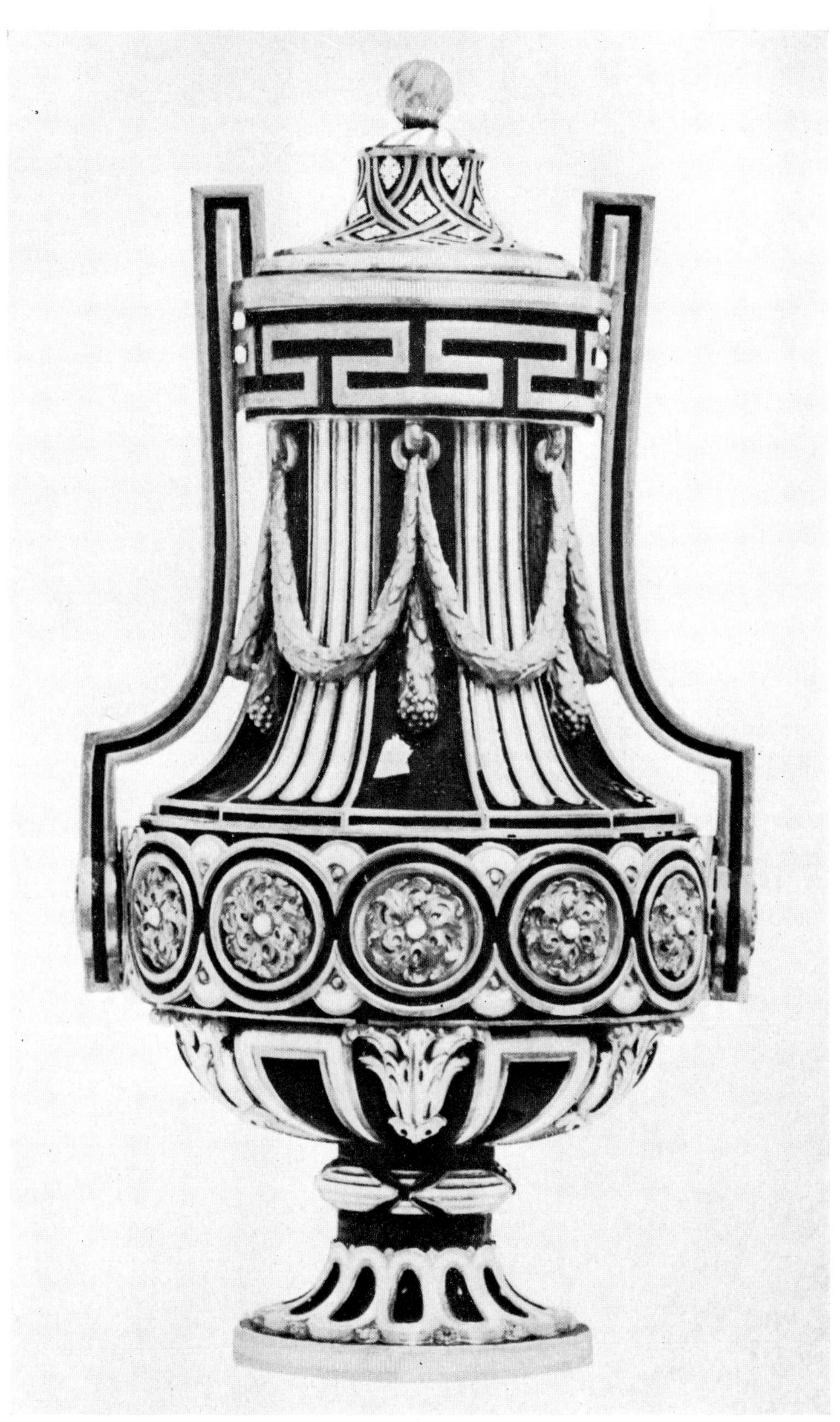

287. Sèvres, 1770

288. Sèvres, about 1772–76

289. SÈVRES, 1770

290. SÈVRES, 1771

DOCUMENTARY PRINTS, ETC.

291, 292. Saly, 1746

293. Saly, 1746

294. Saly, 1740–48

295. VIEN, 1748

296. VIEN, 1753

297, 298. LE LORRAIN, 1752 or earlier

299, 300. VIEN, 1753

301, 302. CONTANT D'IVRY, about 1755–57

Dessus de porte de la Chambre de Parade 2.
Table de marbre et Girandole placée en face de la Cheminée du Sallon.

303. Cochin, 1752

304. Eisen, 1756

305. Le Bas, 1751 or earlier

306. Le Canu, 1756

307. Martenasie, 1759

308. Roslin, 1757

309. Boucher, 1758

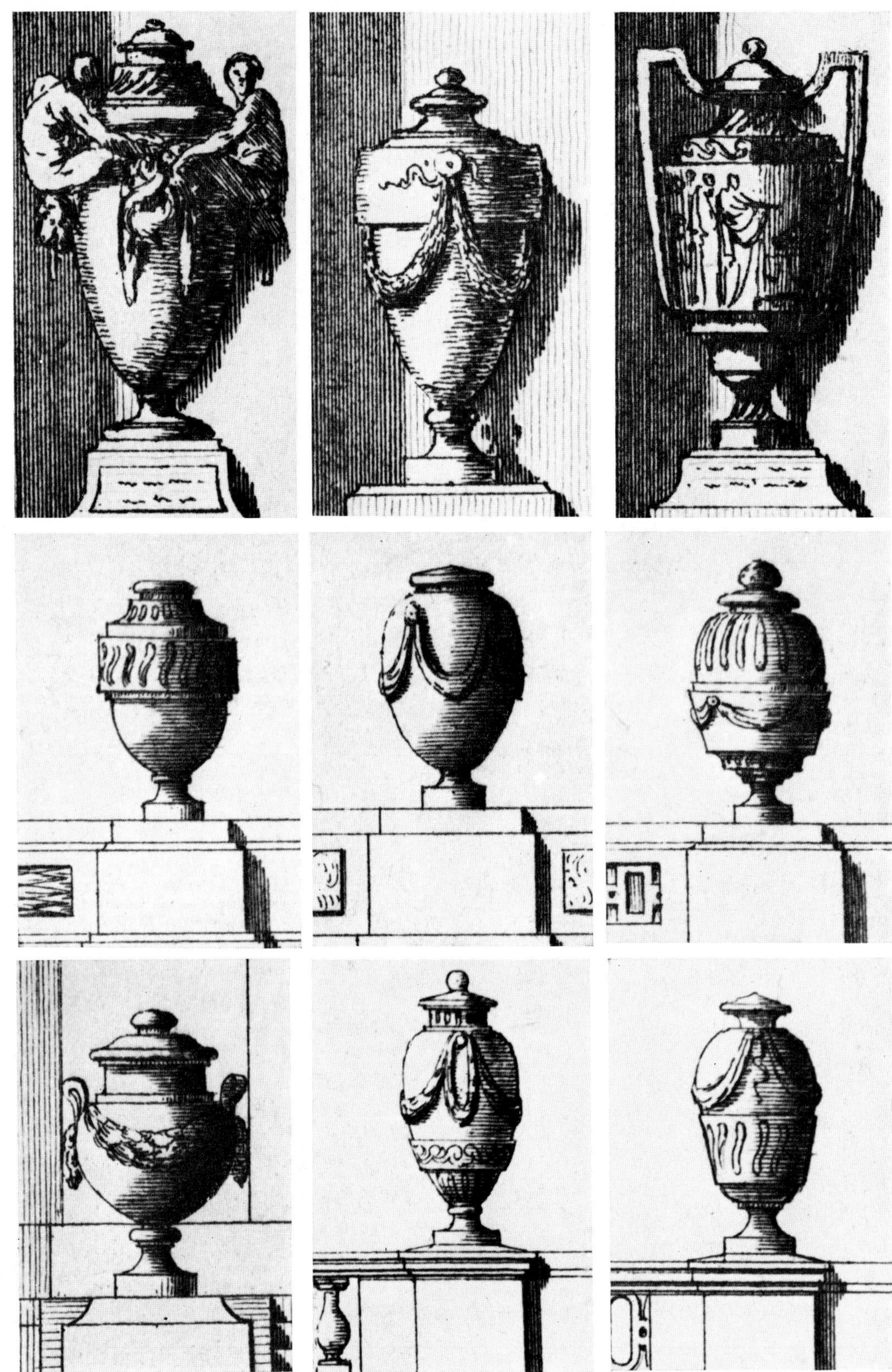

310–318. NEUFFORGE, about 1755–56

319, 320. PIERRE, about 1759

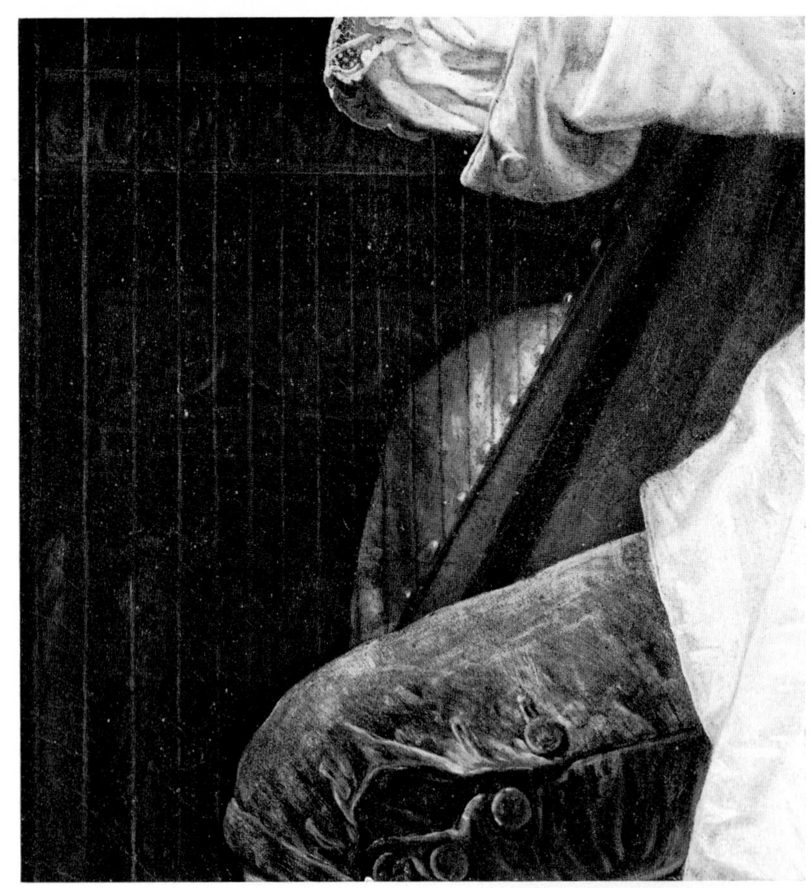

321, 322. GREUZE, 1759

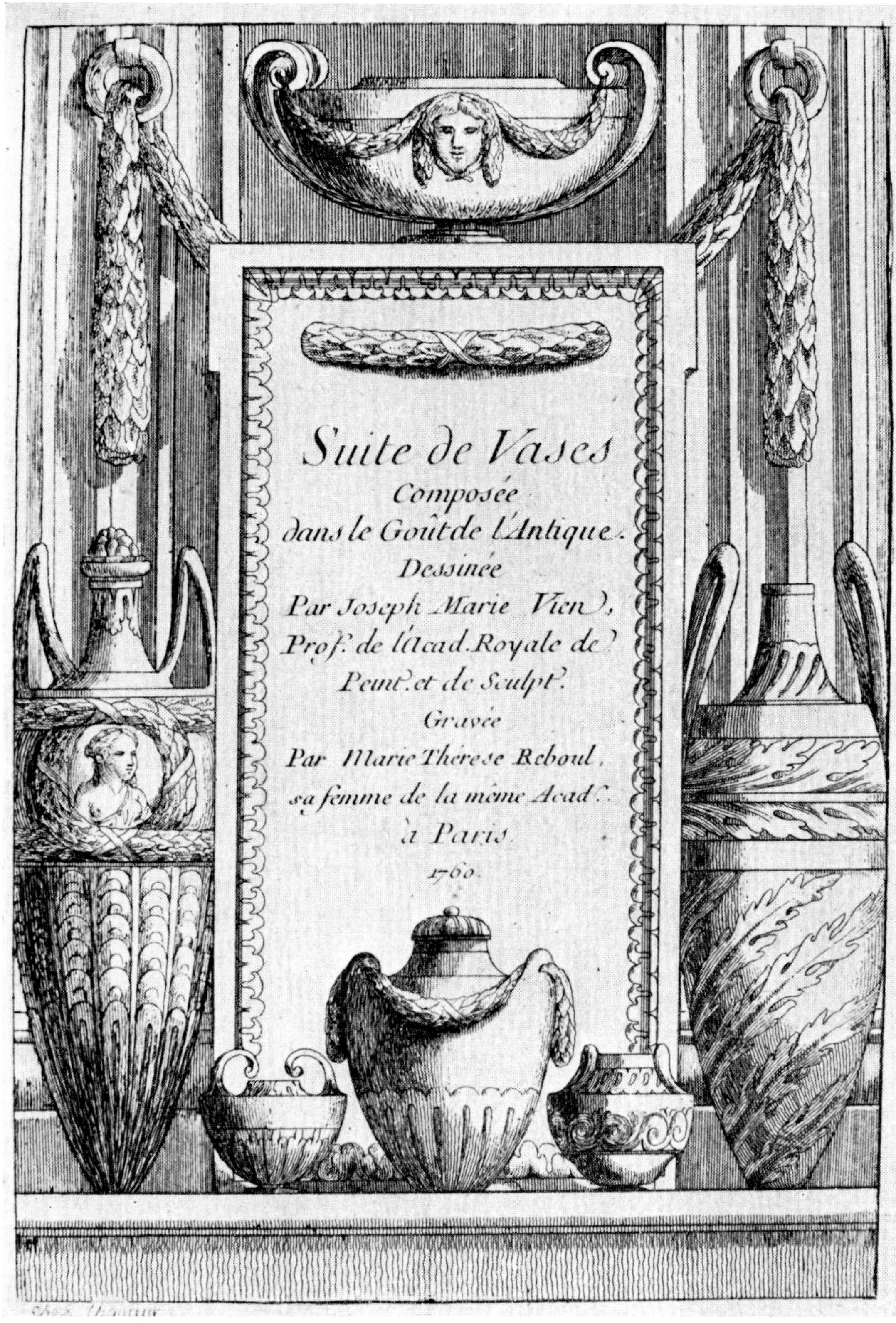
Suite de Vases
Composée
dans le Goût de l'Antique.
Dessinée
Par Joseph Marie Vien,
Prof. de l'Acad. Royale de
Peint. et de Sculpt.
Gravée
Par Marie Thérese Reboul,
sa femme de la même Acad.
à Paris
1760.

323. VIEN, 1760

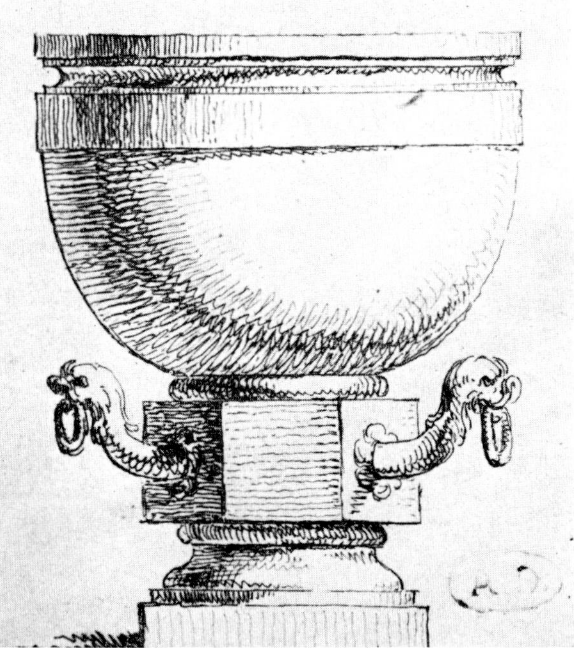

324, 325, 326. De Wailly, 1760

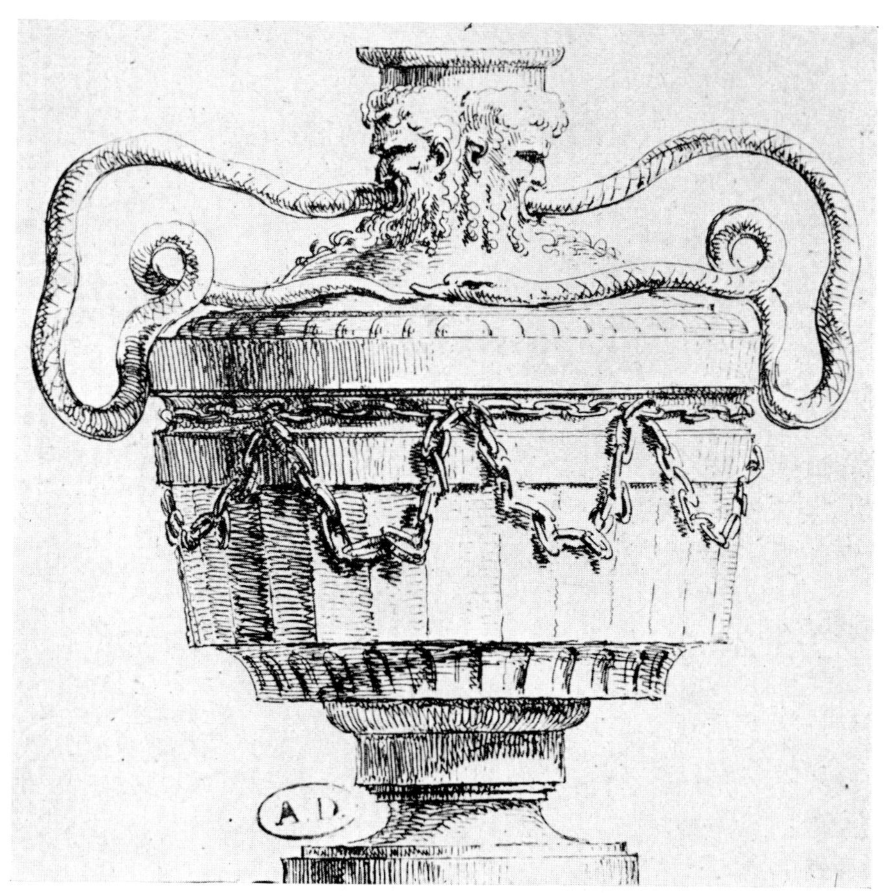

327, 328. De Wailly, 1760

329, 330. De Wailly, 1760

331. PREVOST, 1760

332. TARAVAL, 1760

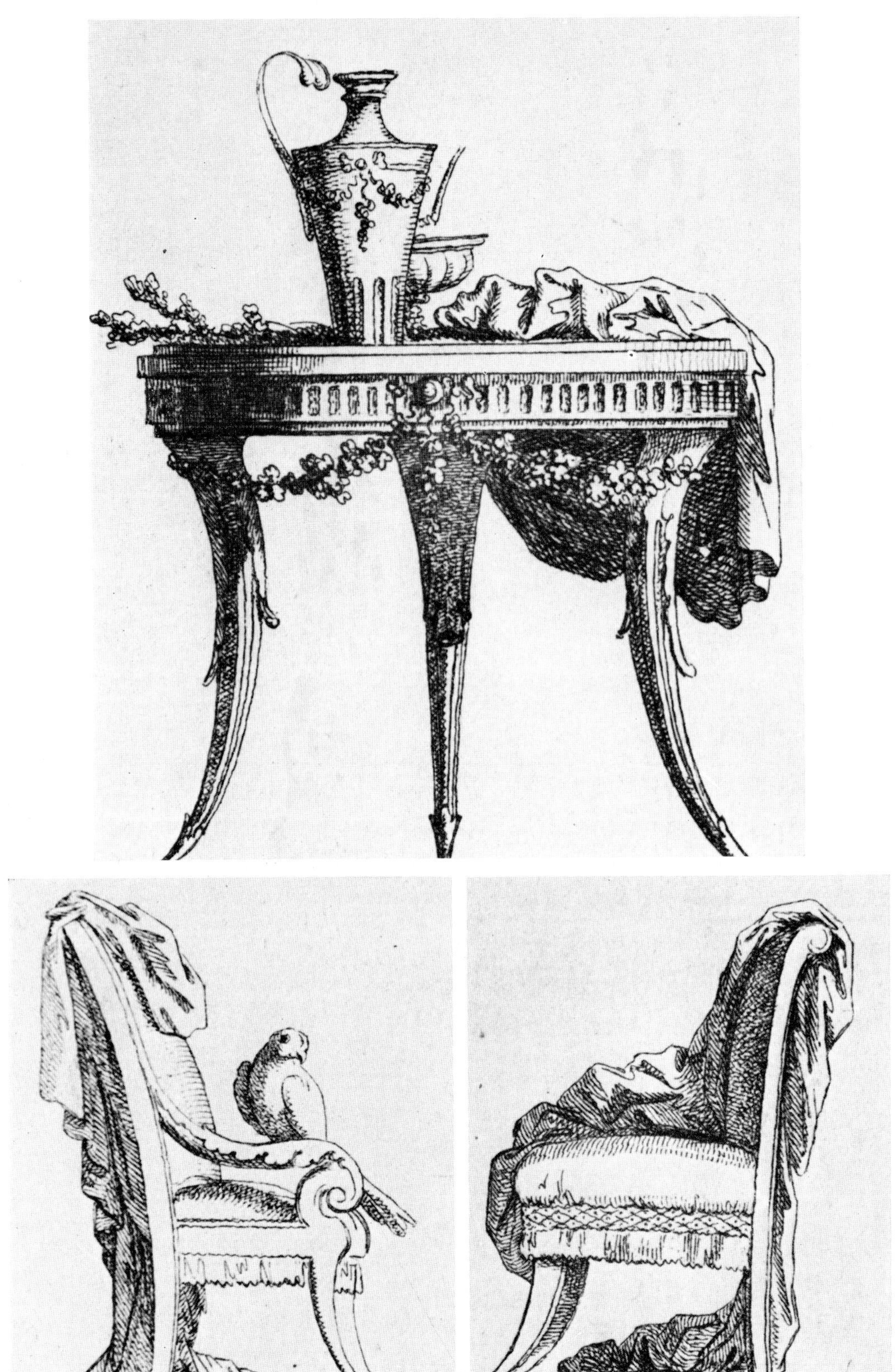

333, 334, 335. De la Rue, about 1760–64

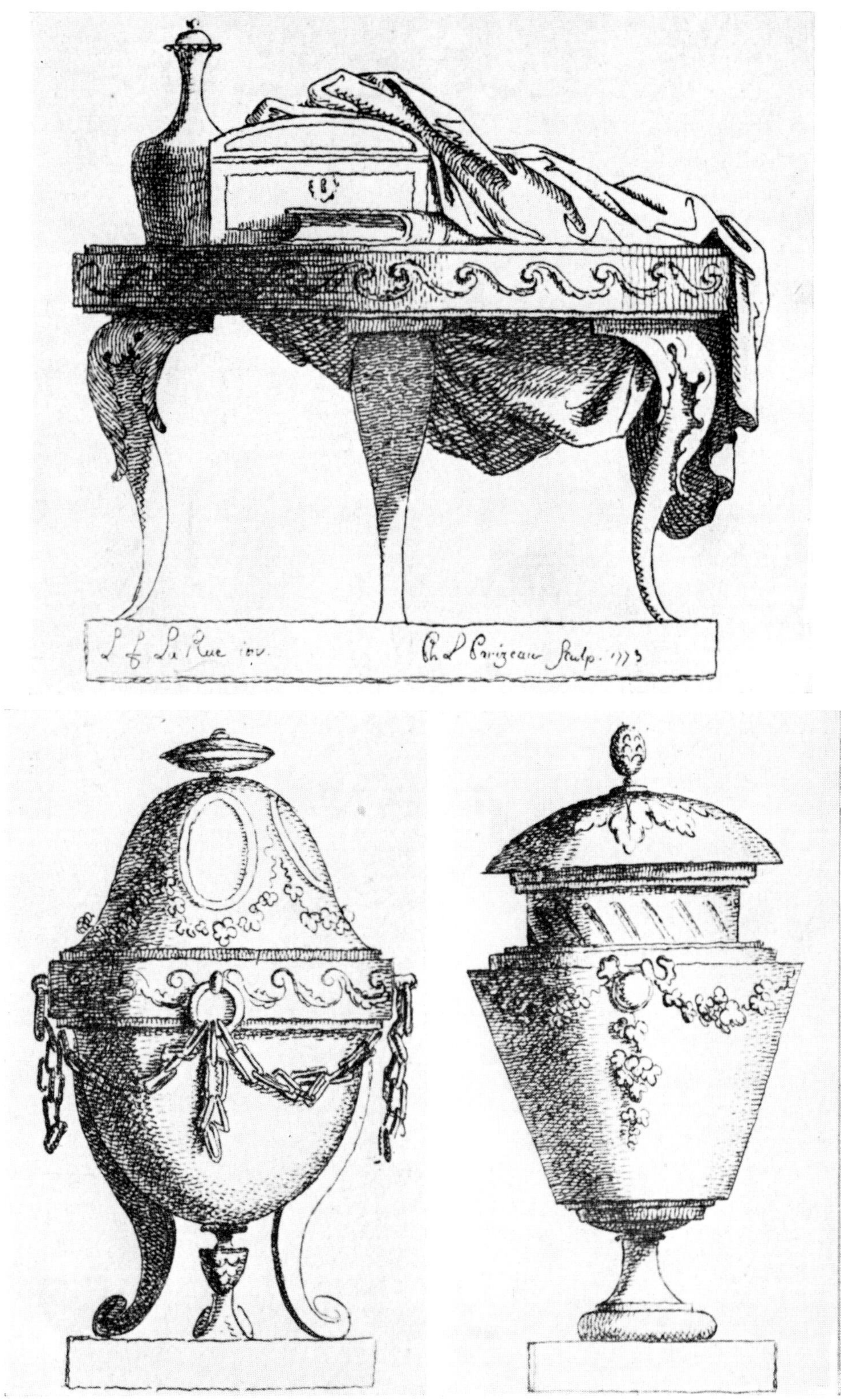

336, 337, 338. DE LA RUE, about 1760–64

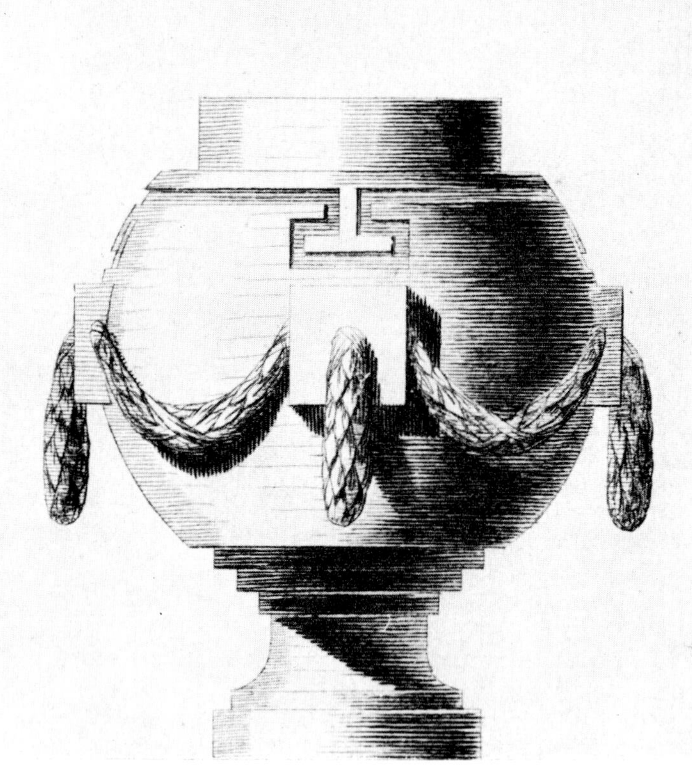

339, 340. Beauvais, 1760

IIIE. SUITE
DE VASES
DEDIÉE,
A M. CHALLE
Peintre du Roi.
Par Son très hum-
ble et tres Obeissant
Serviteur Beauvais.

341. Beauvais, 1760

342. Slodtz, 1760

343. Doré, 1760

344. Deumier, 1763–67

345–348. Guibert, 1760–61

349. CARMONTELLE, 1760?

350. CARMONTELLE, 1761?

352. DROUAIS, 1762

351. VIEN, 1761

353. ROSLIN, 1761

354. VIEN, 1761

355. ROSLIN, 1762

356. ROSLIN, 1762

357–360. ANONYMOUS, about 1763

361–364. Anonymous, about 1763

365. Ficquet, 1763

366. Littret, 1763

367. Van Loo, 1763

368, 369. NEUFFORGE, 1763 or earlier

370. VIEN, 1763

371. Roslin, 1763

372. Drouais, 1763–64

373. Lagrenée, 1764

374. VIEN, 1763

375. GRAVELOT, 1764

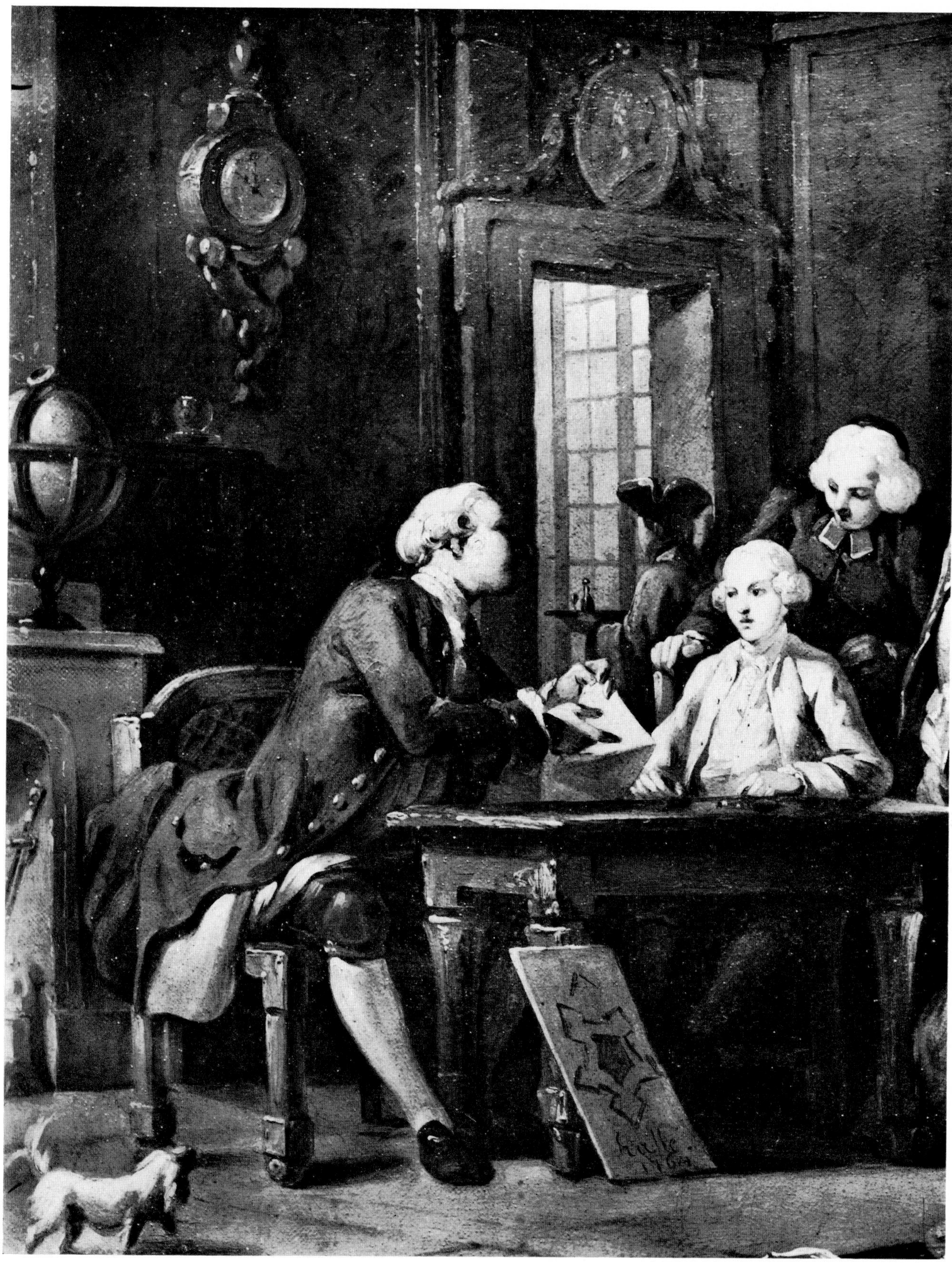

376. Hallé, 1764

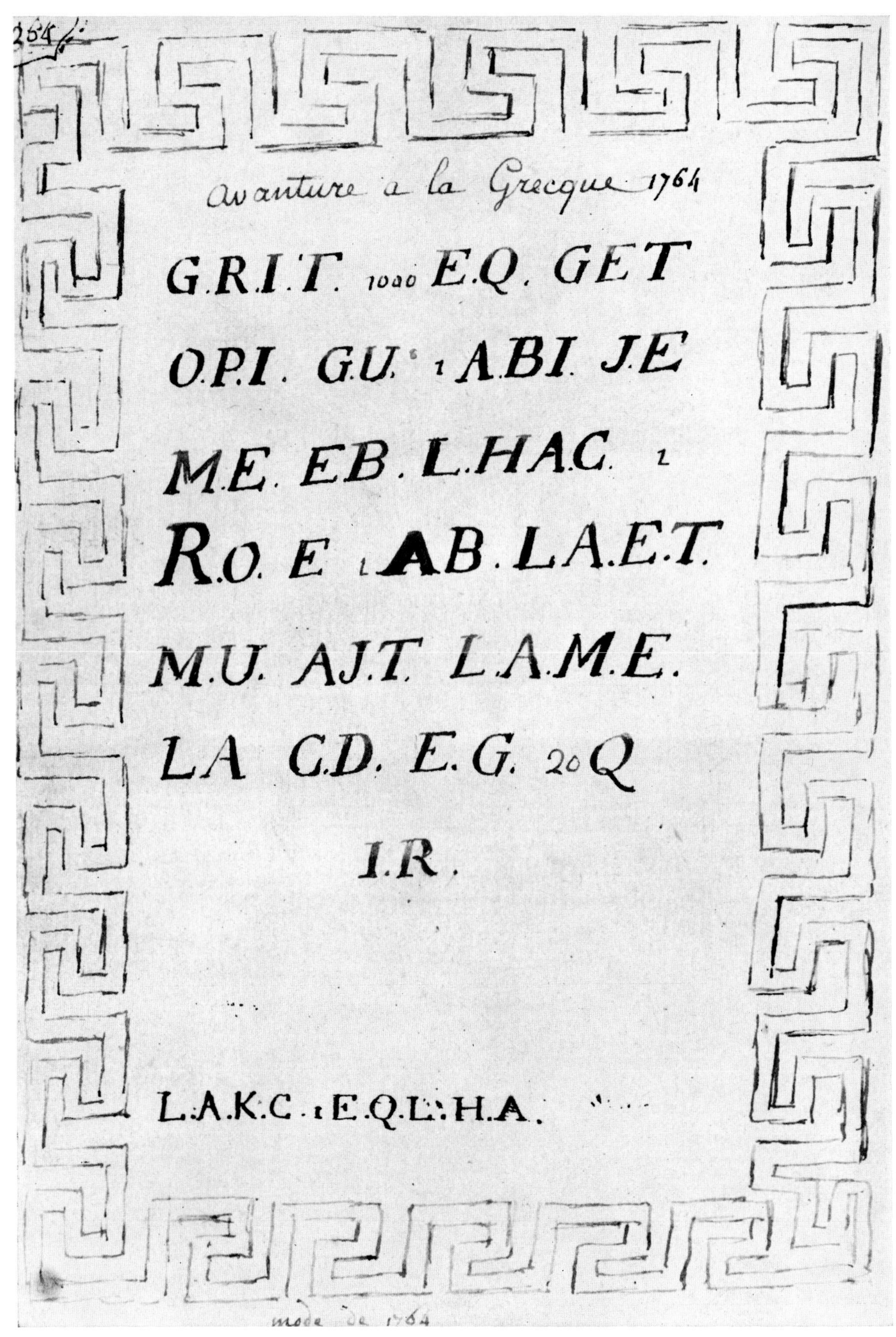

377. Saint-Aubin, 1764

Tom. I.
Pag. 128.
PHILIPPE I. ROY DE FRANCE.
PHILIPPE I.
Roy en 1060. Mort en 1108. Agé de 57 ans
PHILIPPE enseveli dans l'obscurité entre les bras de la volupté et entouré de vices, tandis que la gloire éleve l'Etendard de la Croix et que le zéle poussé une foule de guerriers à la délivrance de la Croix chargée de fers.
C.N. Cochin filius del. 1765.
A.P.D.R.
J. Aliamet Sculp.

378. Cochin, 1765

379, 380. Maria, 1765

381, 382. Maria, 1765

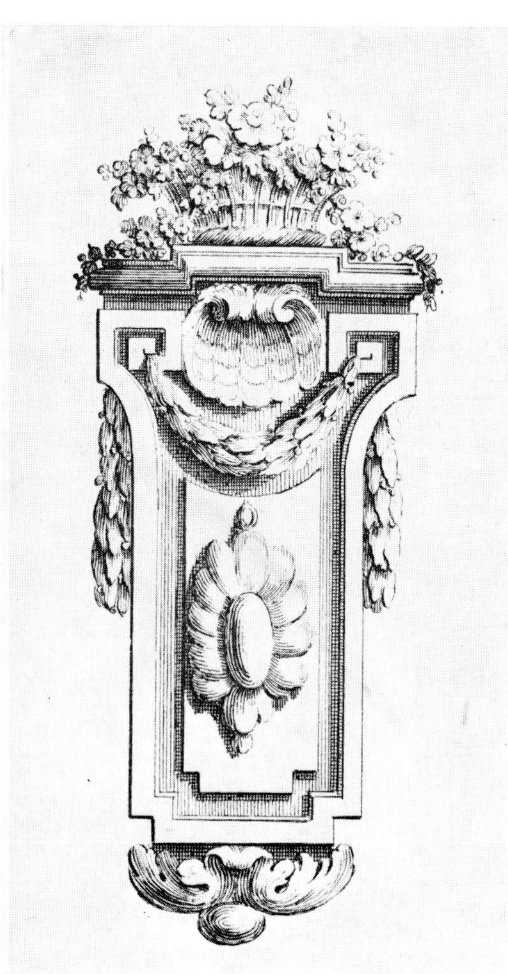

383–387. MARIA, 1765

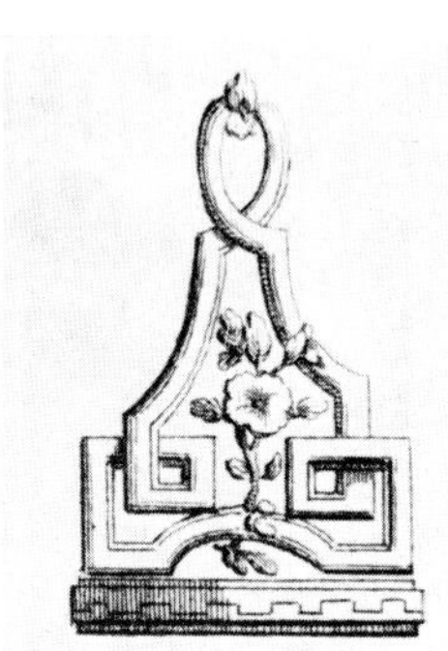

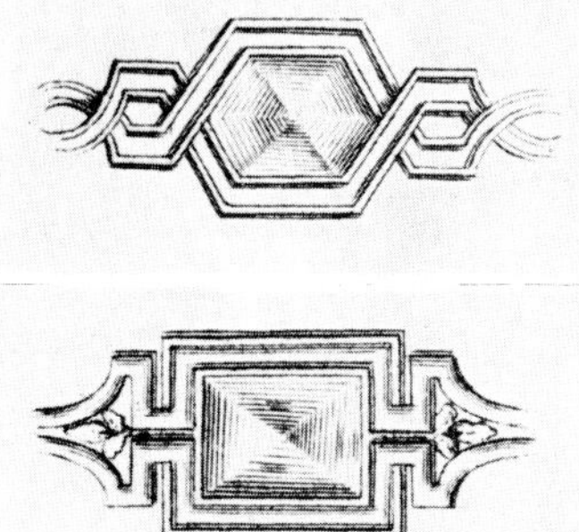

388, 389. Baudouin, 1765

390. Lucotte, 1765

391. Jacques, 1765 or earlier

392–395. JACQUES, 1765 or earlier

396. Attributed to ROUSSET, about 1765

397. Attributed to CHERPITEL, about 1765

398. Attributed to ROUSSET, about 1765

399, 400. Piètre, 1766

401. Saint-Aubin, 1767

402. Attributed to Prieur, 1766

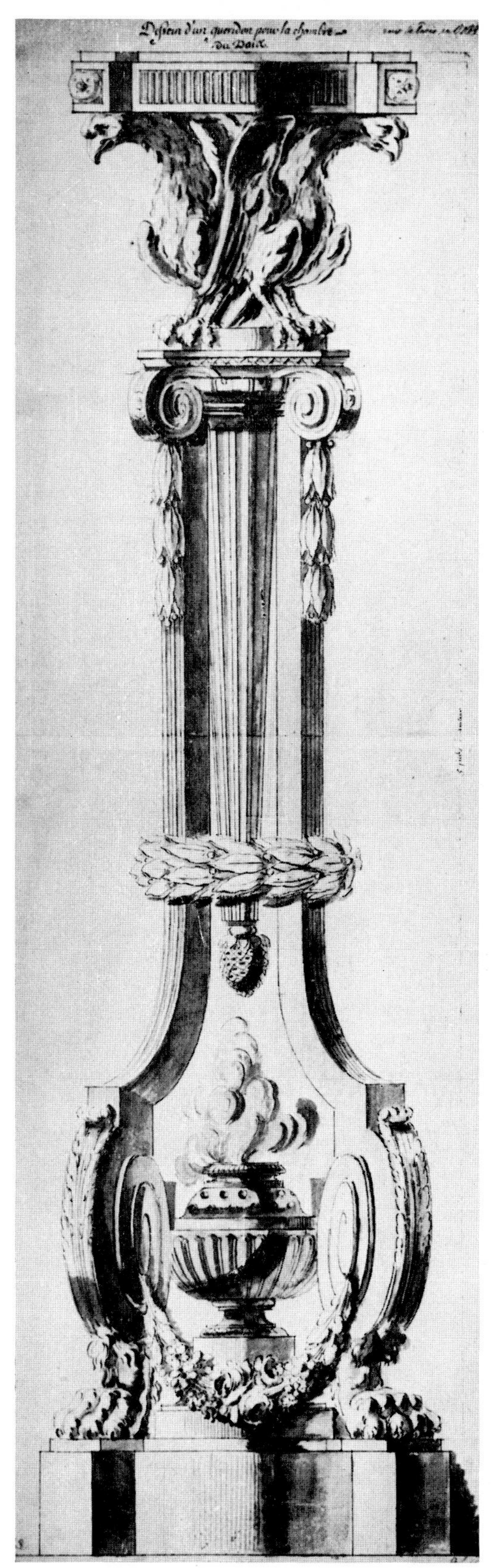

403, 404, 405. Attributed to PRIEUR, 1766.

406. Attributed to PRIEUR, about 1766

407. Attributed to LOUIS, 1766

408. PRIEUR or LOUIS, 1766

409. Attributed to PRIEUR, 1766

410. Prieur or Louis, 1766

411, 412. Prieur, 1765–66

413, 414. Prieur, 1765–66

415, 416. Prieur, 1765–66

417–421. Prieur, about 1765–66

422, 423. Prieur, 1765–66

424, 425. Caffieri, about 1765–66

426, 427. BAUDOUIN, 1767

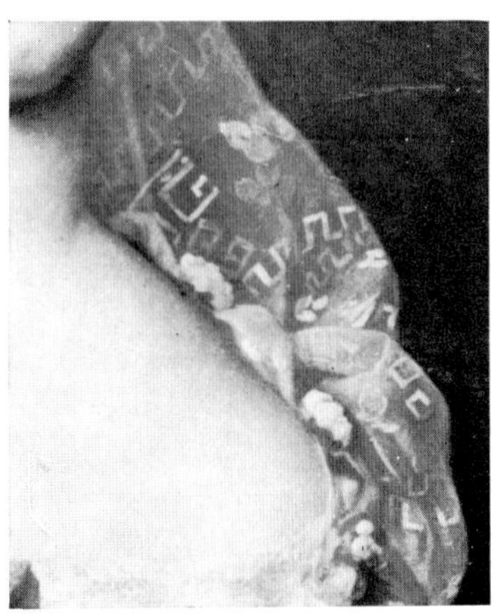

428. ROSLIN, 1766

429. DURAMEAU, about 1764–69

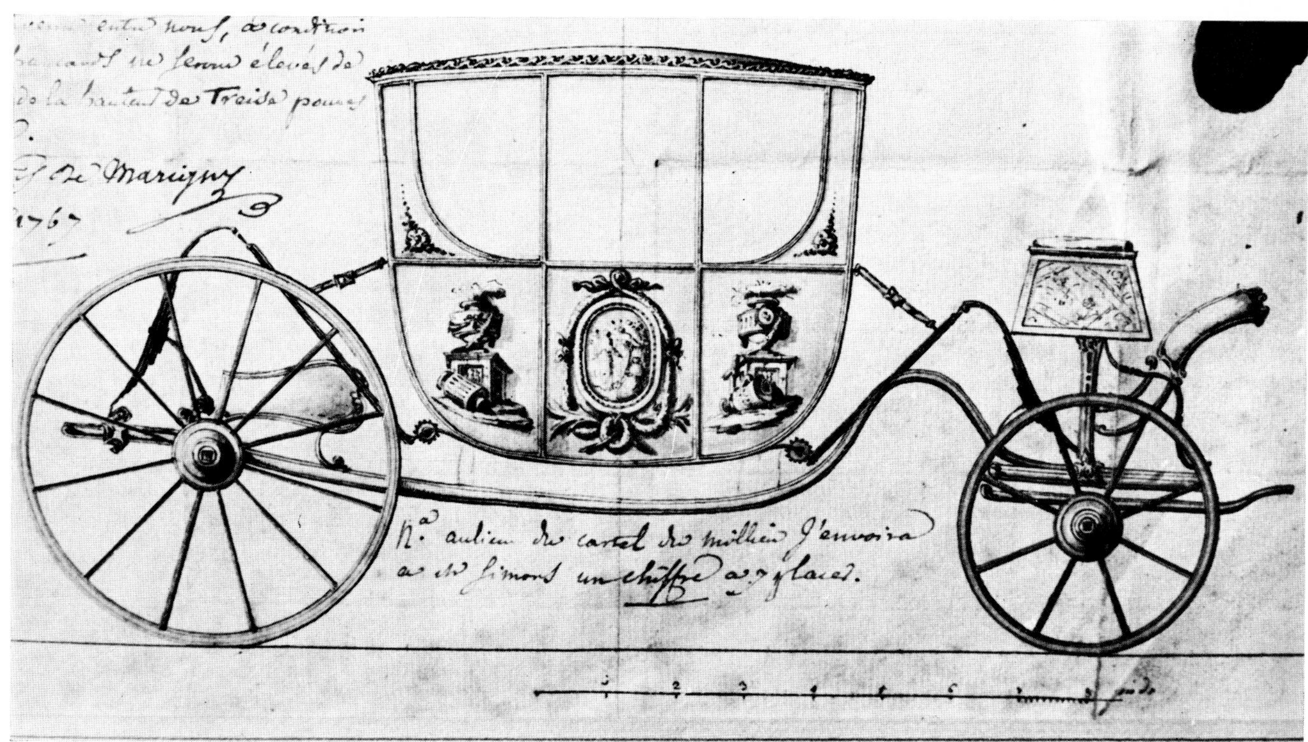

430. Attributed to CHOPARD, 1667

431, 432, 433. FORTY, about 1765–68

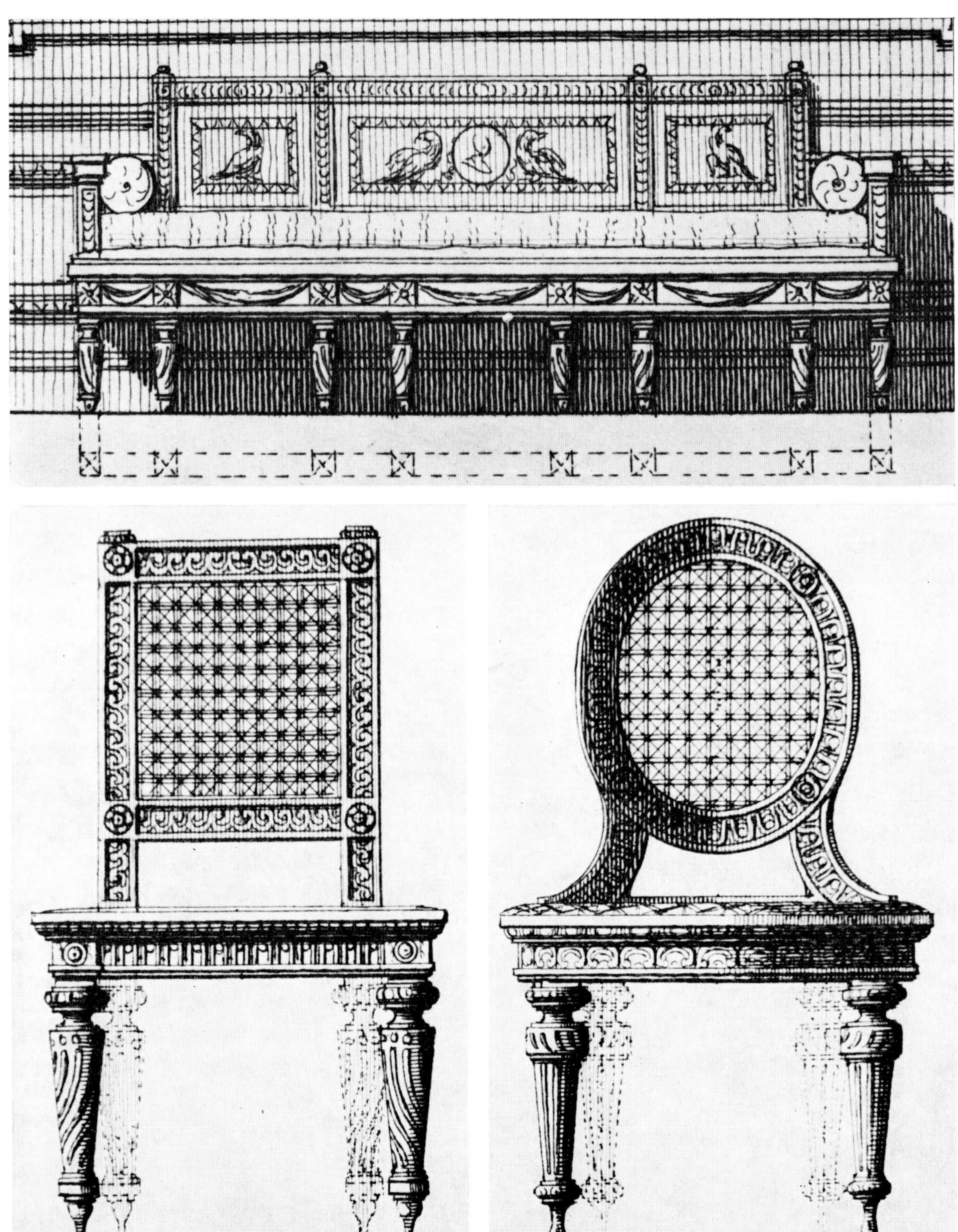

434, 435, 436. NEUFFORGE, 1768 or earlier

437–440. DELAFOSSE, 1767 or earlier

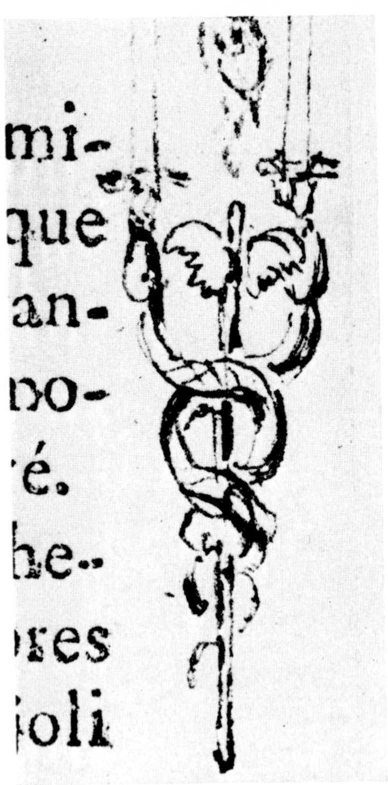

441. Saint-Aubin, 1769

442. Van Loo, 1769

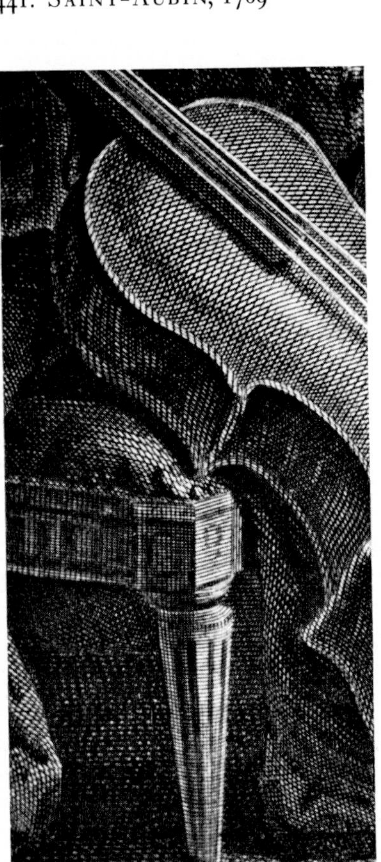

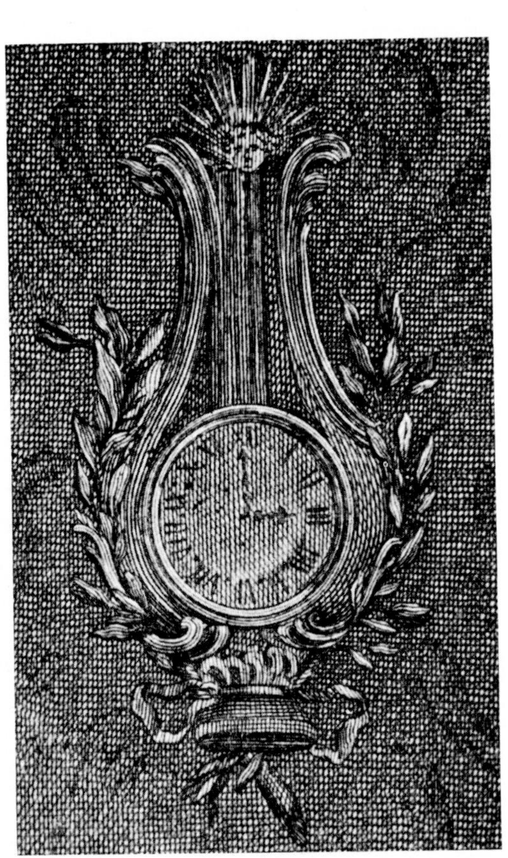

443, 444. Baudouin, 1769 or earlier

445. Baudouin, 1769

446. Schenau, 1769 or earlier

447. Roslin, 1769

448. BELANGER, 1769

449–452. Fontanieu, 1770

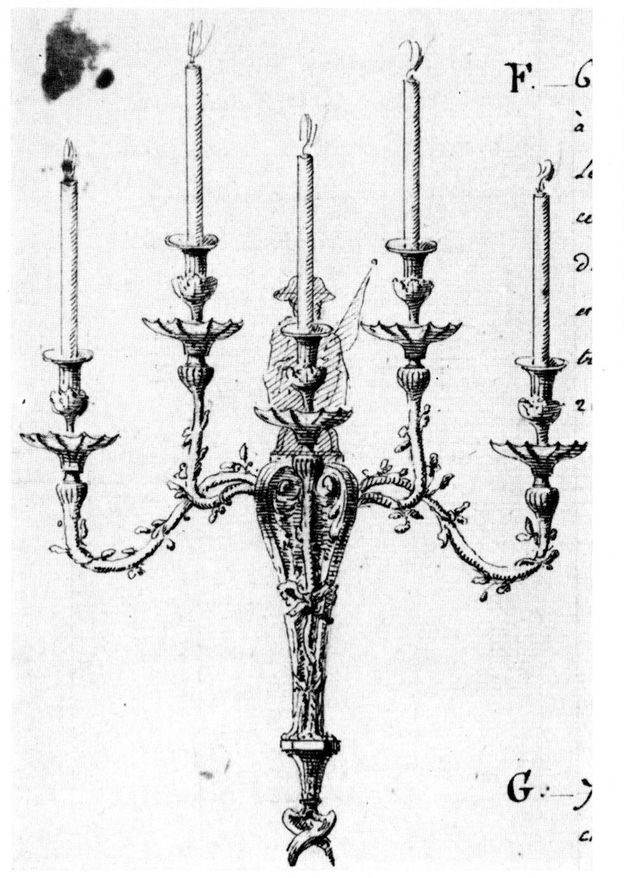

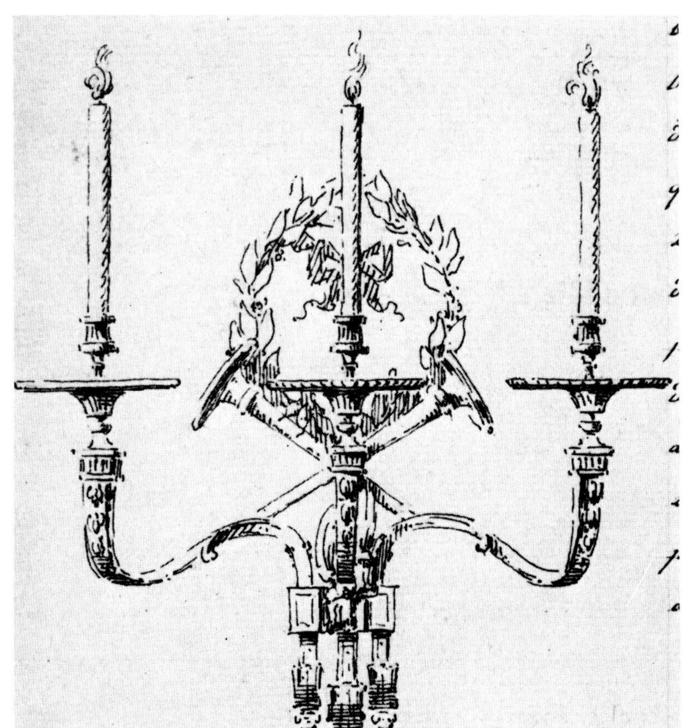

453–456. Caffieri, 1770–72

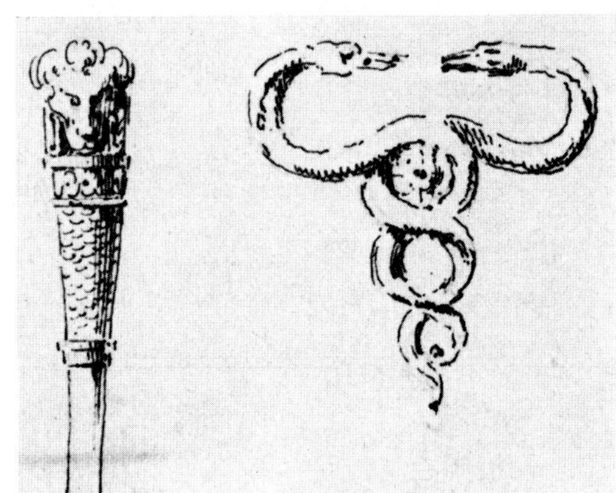

457–461. Caffieri, 1770–72

462. Fessard, 1770

463. VAN BLARENBERGHE, about 1770

464. VAN BLARENBERGHE, about 1770

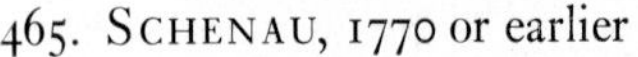

465. SCHENAU, 1770 or earlier

466. VOIROT, 1771

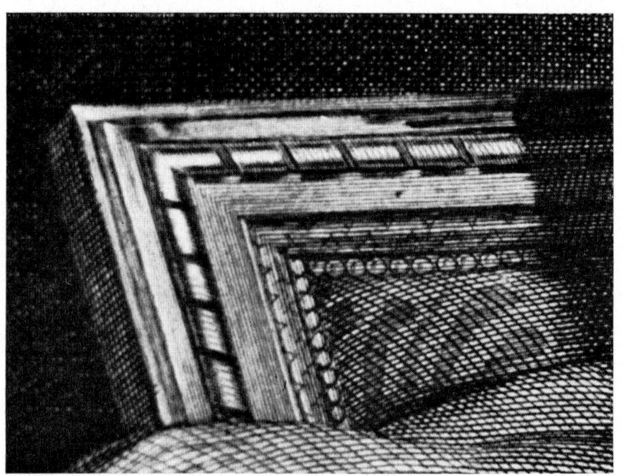

467. SCHENAU, 1770 or earlier

468, 469, 470. VAN DER CRUYCEN, 1770

471. VOIROT, 1771

472. DROUAIS, 1771

473. SCHENAU, about 1770

474. MOREAU *le jeune*, 1771

475. BELANGER, about 1771

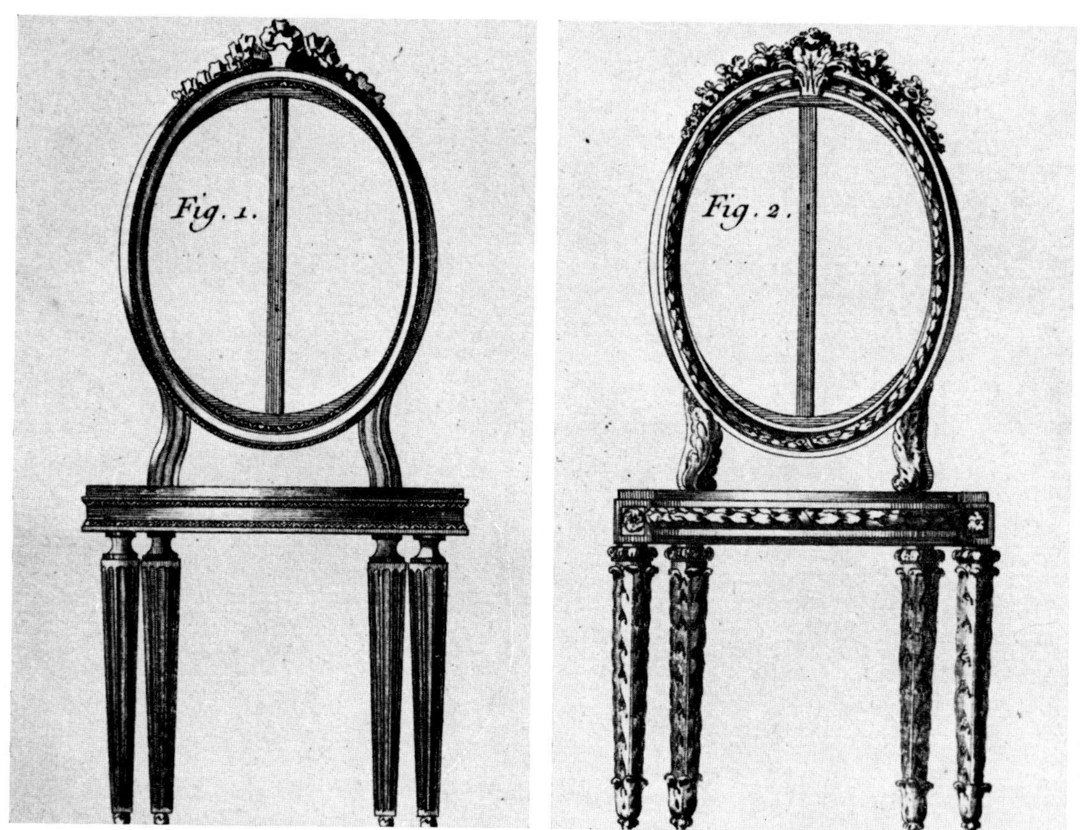

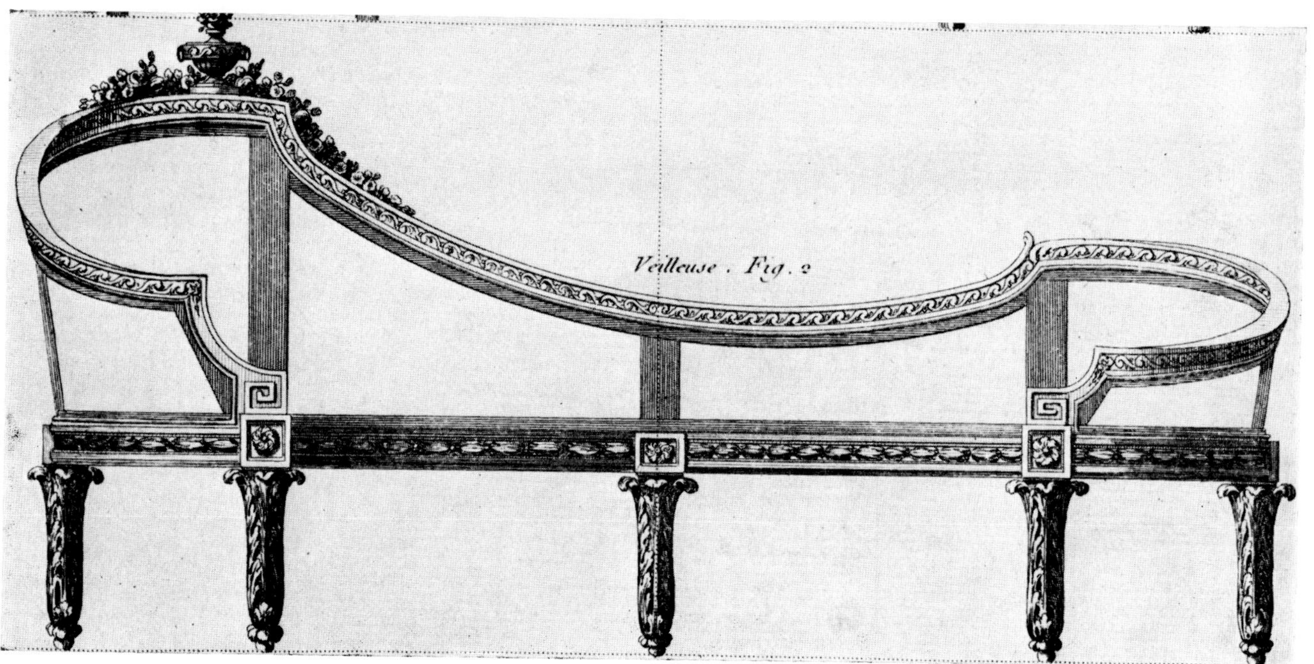

476, 477, 478. Roubo, 1772

479–482. DELAFOSSE, 1773 or earlier

483. CLÉRISSEAU, about 1772–75

484. EBERTS, about 1773

485. EBERTS and FREUDEBERG, 1774

486, 487. EBERTS and FREUDEBERG, 1774

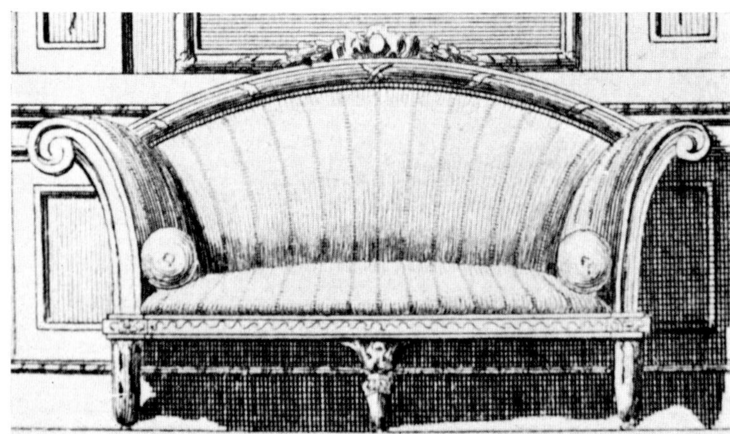

488. BOUCHER *le jeune*, 1774–75

489. De Wailly, about 1772

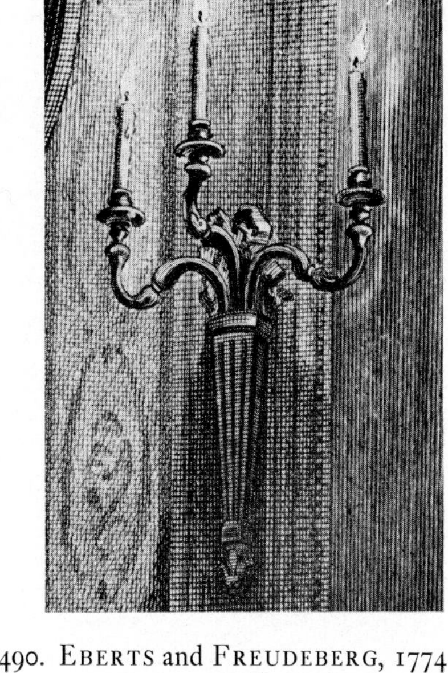

490. Eberts and Freudeberg, 1774

491, 492. Eberts and Freudeberg, 1774

493, 494. Eberts and Freudeberg, 1774

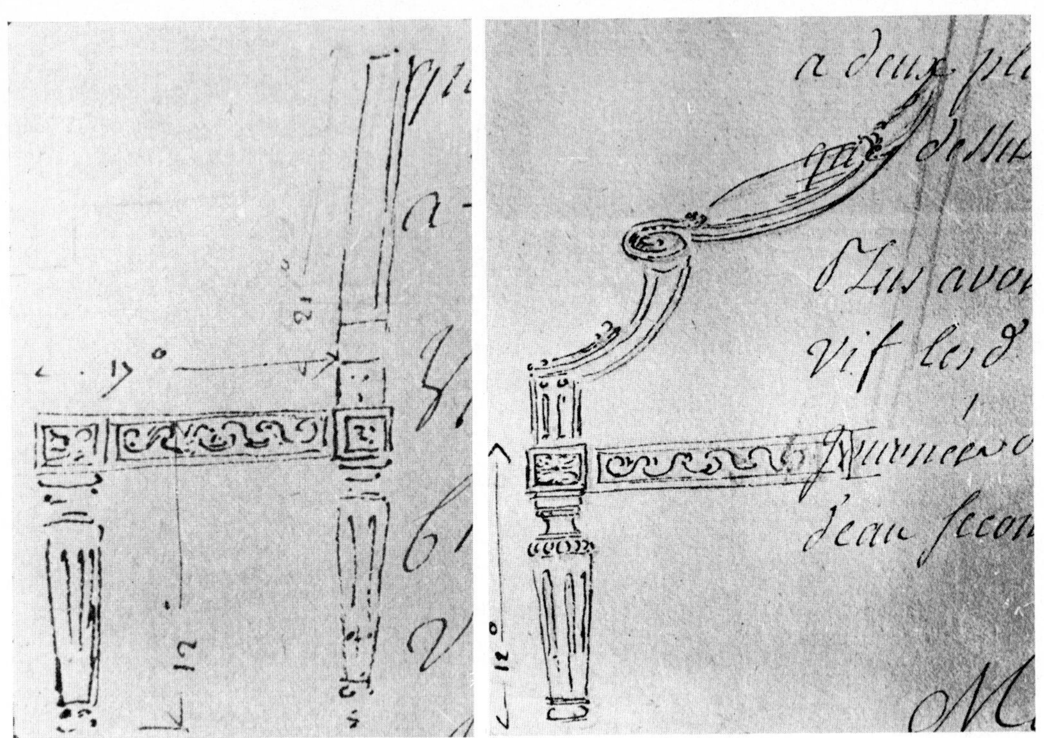

495, 496. ANONYMOUS, 1775

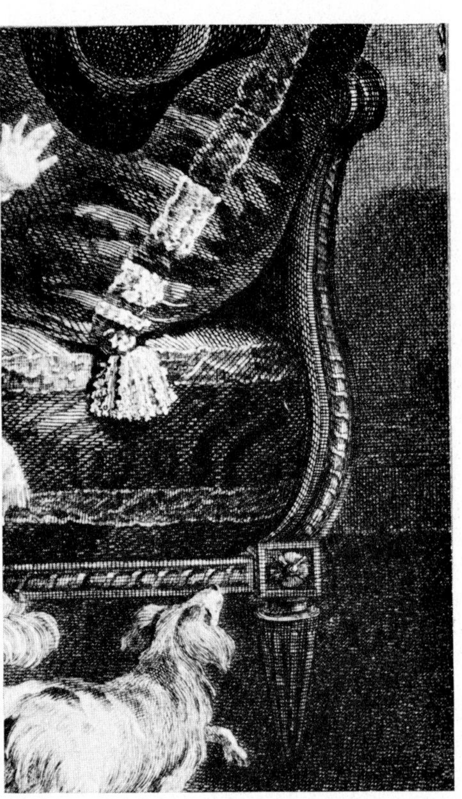

498. LE PEINTRE, about 1775–76

497. BOUCHER *le jeune*, 1774–75

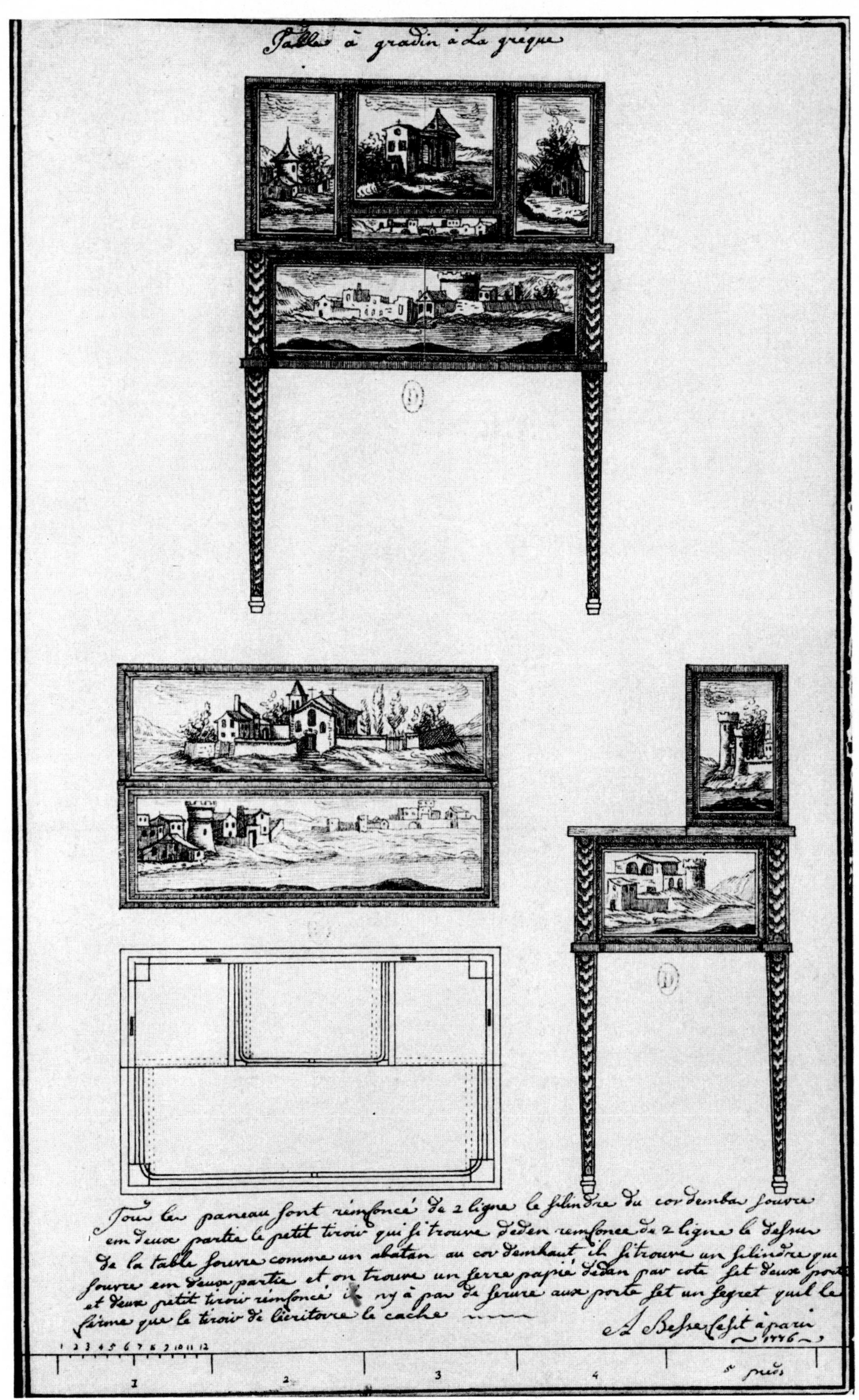

499. BESSE, 1776